Fodor's

TOKYO

Fodor's Features

MAPS

Contents

Welcome to Tokyo

Lights, sushi, manga! Sprawling, frenetic, and endlessly fascinating, Japan's capital offers pockets of calm between famously crowded streets. Mom-and-pop noodle houses share street space with Western chains and exquisite fine dining. Shopping yields lovely folk arts as well as the newest electronics. And nightlife kicks off with karaoke or sake and continues with techno clubs and more. Whether you seek the traditional or the cutting edge, Tokyo will provide it. As you plan your upcoming travels to Tokyo, please confirm that places are still open and let us know when we need to make updates by writing to us at editors@fodors.com.

TOP REASONS TO GO

★ **Ultimate cityscape:** A skyline of neon-lit streets and vast high-rises awes the senses.

★ **Incredible eats:** From humble ramen to sumptuous sushi, Tokyo is foodie heaven.

★ **Green havens:** Pristine gardens and lush city-center parks soften the urban scene.

★ **Fashion-forward shops:** From Muji to Miyake, Tokyo is a playground for shopaholics.

★ **Contemporary art:** The Mori Art Museum caps a stunningly diverse scene.

★ **Sacred spaces:** Senso-ji Complex and the Meiji Shrine offer spiritual retreats.

Chapter 1

EXPERIENCE TOKYO

23 ULTIMATE EXPERIENCES

Tokyo offers terrific experiences that should be on every traveler's list. Here are Fodor's top picks for a memorable trip.

1 Shinjuku Gyoen National Garden

Tokyo's many parks and gardens offer an essential contrast to the city's skyscrapers and neon. Shinjuku Gyoen National Garden is especially beautiful in cherry blossom season but its gardens and central lawn are a peaceful retreat year-round. (Ch. 9)

2 Explore Tokyo's Neighborhoods

Odaiba has arcades and quirky museums. Ryogoku has Sumo. Shimokitazawa has vintage goods. Harajuku is a pop culture hub. Ginza is a ritzy shopping district.

3 Tour the Imperial Palace Gardens

While you can't tour the Imperial Palace itself, the Imperial Palace East Gardens are open to the public, free, and boast charming moats and gates as well as orchards and Japanese gardens. (Ch. 4)

4 Visit Tokyo Skytree

One of the tallest towers in the world, Tokyo Skytree boasts a restaurant, café, the highest walkway in the world, shopping, and two observation decks offering the best views in the city. (Ch. 13)

5 Visit Mt. Takao

You can hike on Mt. Takao in Meiji Memorial Forest Park or take one of the cable cars to its peak; it's a popular day trip, roughly an hour by train from central Tokyo. (Ch. 15)

6 Experience Kabuki

Kabuki is a traditional Japanese form of theater that is characterized by elaborate staging and makeup, and exaggerated acting, singing, and dancing. Kabuki-za Theater is its most famous venue. (Ch. 5)

7 Stay at a Ryokan

A stay in a ryokan, a traditional Japanese guesthouse, typically includes minimalist rooms with tatami mats, *yukata* robes and slippers, a multicourse kaiseki dinner, and a traditional Japanese breakfast. (Ch. 12)

8 Top Temples and Shrines

Tokyo's shrines and temples are some of the most interesting sights in the city to visit. Highlights include Senso-ji, the Meiji Shrine, Zojoji Temple, and Nezu Shrine. (Ch. 12)

9 Anime Adventures

Anime fans flock to Tokyo's "electric town," the Akihabara neighborhood, an area jam-packed with cosplay and maid cafés, anime shops, and arcades. (Ch. 11)

10 Get Crafty

Make your own souvenirs at Tokyo stores offering workshops like Chochin paper lantern painting or *washi*-paper–making classes. (Ch. 4, 13)

11 Explore Yokocho Alleys

Drink with locals in narrow lantern-lit Yokocho or alleyways like Golden Gai, lined with tiny izakayas and bars, offering cheap drinks and small dishes. (Ch. 9)

12 Take Tea

A full tea ceremony is long and tedious, but you can also just have a feel of one at Nakajima no Ochaya in Hama-rikyu Gardens and the tea house at Shinjuku Gyoen National Garden. (Ch 6, 9)

13 Shibuya Scramble Crossing

Nothing quite captures the essence of Tokyo quite like the busiest intersection in the world. Brave the crossing or find a good angle to photograph the thousands of pedestrians crossing. (Ch. 7)

14 Try a Love Hotel

Love hotels are escapes from normality. Tokyo has a huge variety of themed hotels you and your partner might enjoy for a night, from the lavish to outlandish. (Ch. 9)

15 Soak in an Onsen

Don't miss the opportunity to slide into a steamy natural hot spring; the best place is to try this is on an excursion in Hakone, a popular stop on the way to Mt. Fuji. (Ch. 15)

16 Sample Sumo

Tokyo's Ryogoku district is the epicenter of Japan's national sport. Book a tour to visit a sumo stable to watch morning practice or watch a match at the top sumo sports stadium, Ryogoku Kokugikan. (Ch. 13)

17 Visit a Karaoke Bar

Karaoke culture is next-level in this part of the world; check out the popular Pasela chain, either in Shibuya or Roppongi. (Ch. 7, 8)

18 Visit Odaiba

This man-made island, accessible via the Rainbow Bridge, is home to an amusement park where you can sample the latest high-tech entertainment and a stroll along a lively waterfront area. (Ch. 6)

19 Ghibli Museum

Fans of the Studio Ghibli and artist Hayao Miyazaki will want to visit this whimsical multistory museum offering life-size re-creations of his film settings and adored characters. (Ch. 14)

20 Fish Markets

Tokyo's top fish market is now now at Toyosu, having moved from its historic Tsukiji—which still hosts "the outer market," a series of market-related shops and eateries. (Ch. 5, 6)

21 Shop 'til You Drop

Get your shopping fix on Omotesando, packed with high-end retail; Ginza Six, a luxury shopping mall; and Takeshita-dori, a hot spot for Harajuku teen fashion. (Ch. 5, 7)

22 Find Your Inner Samurai

After the Japanese Sword Museum in Ryogoku, stop by the Kanda Myojin Shrine in Akihabara to get a feel for a definitive era in Japanese history. (Ch. 11, 13)

23 Hit Top Tokyo Museums

Along with classics like the Tokyo Metropolitan Art Museum, see what's on at Mori Art Museum in Roppongi or the nearby 21_21 Design Sight. (Ch. 8)

WHAT'S WHERE

1 Marunouchi and Nihonbashi. The Imperial Palace stands at the center of Tokyo. Marunouchi is home to plush retail and office complexes; Nihonbashi is the city's financial center.

2 Ginza and Tsukiji. Ginza is where you'll find Tokyo's traditional high-end stores and equally ritzy restaurants. Nearby, Tsukiji (once home to the world's largest fish market) is still home to the "outer market" and seafood restaurants.

3 Shiodome and Odaiba. Shiodome is a massive development zone with plenty of shops, hotels, and restaurants. Odaiba is an island with shopping, restaurants, family-oriented amusement, and parks.

4 Aoyama and Shibuya. Aoyama (and nearby Harajuku) are chic neighborhoods saturated with shopping. Shibuya is packed with people and hip shops. Shimokitazawa is known for vintage clothing and antiques.

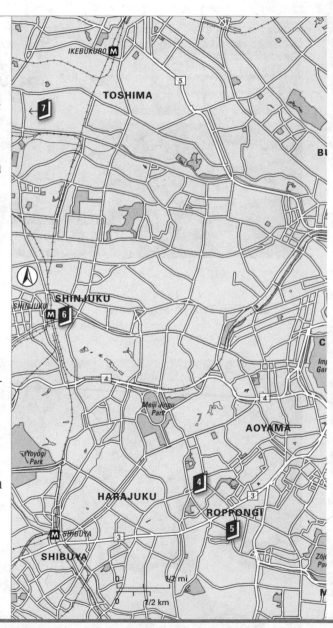

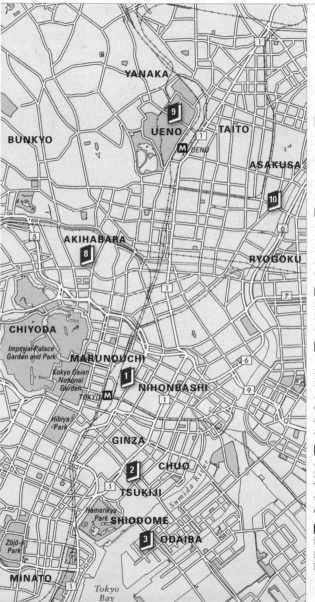

5 Roppongi. With a rich and sometimes sordid history of catering to foreign nightlife, Roppongi has gone more upscale with the massive Roppongi Hills and Tokyo Midtown developments.

6 Shinjuku. The train station here is supposedly the busiest in the world. And when the sun sets, the bars and clubs in the red-light area of Kabuki-cho come to life.

7 West Tokyo. Quieter and more residential, the neighborhoods west of Shinjuku such as Nakano and Tama have their own charms.

8 Akihabara. Akihabara is famed for its electronics stores, manga shops, and video arcades.

9 Ueno and Yanaka. Ueno Park is home to museums, a university of fine arts, and a zoo. Adjoining Yanaka is a charming area of temples and winding, narrow alleys.

10 Asakusa and Ryogoku. Asakusa has Tokyo Skytree and Senso-ji Temple, the city's oldest temple. Ryogoku is the city's Sumo center.

11 Greater Tokyo. Covering all of Tokyo plus large parts of its neighboring prefectures.

Tokyo Today

IT'S HUGE!

While it probably goes without saying, Tokyo is enormous (and that might even be an understatement). The Greater Tokyo area is home to 37 million people. And like most cities that have developed organically through history, storied neighborhoods with character are the norm. To further Tokyo's neighborhood identities, most places are centered around a train station (Tokyo, rather confusingly, has JR lines, private rail lines, and two metro systems, but it all works out). The larger stations in Tokyo are generally connected by the Yamanote JR Line, which is a loop linking these major nodes of activity, some of which are among the busiest train stations in the world. Perhaps unsurprisingly, then, these bustling station areas are probably what you picture when you think of Tokyo, but go a bit beyond the immediate station areas, and off onto some of the many back streets to appreciate the variety and the interconnected maze of paths that make up this remarkable city.

THE MANY FACES OF TOKYO

Cities are never-ending construction sites, ever-changing human landscapes that respond to our collective needs and desires, though rarely within any one person's lifetime. Tokyo's in particular is a story of constant rebirth. The city's layers of history have not only been periodically wiped clean in fires, earthquakes, and world wars, but continue to be created alongside a seemingly anything-goes attitude toward architecture.

DESTRUCTION AND REBIRTH

Fire, probably more than anything else, has shaped Tokyo. The two major resets for Tokyo in the 20th century were, first, the Great Kanto Earthquake of 1923, which experts estimate left more than 60% of the city homeless. The late morning timing of the quake exacerbated the situation since many fires were already burning in preparation for lunch. Tokyo's overwhelmingly large share of low, wooden structures packed together on narrow lanes allowed the fires to quickly ravage the city. And while Japan is known for its wooden architecture, a traditional wooden house in Tokyo is a rare find since they were banned as hazards after 1923. Most of the wooden buildings that survived the earthquake and subsequent fires were then destroyed during the city's next calamity, World War II.

Tokyo was heavily firebombed by the Americans during the war, and few places were spared. One area that did manage to survive is the Yanaka neighborhood, whose numerous temples and their associated cemeteries (Yanaka Cemetery is a beautiful place for cherry blossom viewing) acted as firebreaks after the earthquake and a deterrent to American bombs as the Americans were (with some notable failures) trying to avoid bombing religious sites.

That same neighborhood has seen its share of destruction since, but only in the name of progress. Many of the older homes that survived the war have been torn down and replaced with modern structures. These street scenes might feel incongruous at times, but they reflect Tokyo's story. The city does not as a rule hold a romantic view of history versus progress. It's been progress all the way, especially in the latter 20th and 21st centuries.

Today's Tokyo shows this story. The wide six- and sometimes eight-lane roads serve not to shuffle your taxi through town quickly, but as firebreaks. And while Tokyo might not have an answer to

London's Hyde Park or New York's Central Park, parks are scattered throughout the capital in every neighborhood (and are home to emergency supplies). And since street width determines building height in Tokyo, these large firebreak roads are generally lined with tall buildings; behind those towers, you'll often find a much quieter respite from all the rushing around and a slower slice of Tokyo that is on a much more human scale.

THE NEW AND THE MODERN

A premium is placed on newness all over Japan, not only in Tokyo, even as a reverence for lost and near-lost styles of architecture (typically embodied in shrine and temple complexes) gives people the impression that Japan preserves its historical buildings. And while there is a movement to retrofit and use older structures, it is definitely worth appreciating that the preservation done at temples and shrines, in particular, is the preservation of the carpentry *techniques* and not the buildings themselves.

Traditional carpentry is as much a system of assembly as it is architecture. And if something can be assembled, it can be disassembled. Wood, even with weathering protections, doesn't last long in a climate like Japan's, so being able to disassemble and reassemble structures is an important part of the preservation of the buildings themselves. This means that while a temple might have a history dating back hundreds of years, the structures you see have been built and rebuilt, which blurs the lines of both historic conservation and what counts as old.

After the calamities of the 20th century, however, and the loss of some neighborhood charm here and there in the name of progress, Tokyoites have finally come around to the idea of adaptive reuse. This has produced another layer to Tokyo's history—a place one can go, often to enjoy a meal or a drink in a retro atmosphere reflecting one of Tokyo's many eras. And yet standing just next to an old house-turned-restaurant is a concrete and glass office building reflecting the current era.

Many might consider the "real" Tokyo to be the tiny back streets and wooden buildings, while others think of Tokyo as a flashy jumble of futuristic neon and glass. In a metropolis as eclectic as Tokyo, isn't it all "real" in some way?

The challenge for any traveler with a limited time is learning to read this landscape. Let the draw of the tiny alley pull you in. Or explore any number of Tokyo's shopping streets that might very well lead you to a traditional crafts shop, a cute six-seater bar, or a Michelin-starred restaurant.

You don't even have to try hard to find good food here. The appreciation for quality food and the large population has created an environment with numerous so-called *B-kyu gurume* (B-grade gourmet) restaurants serving more down-home meals, or things such as ramen and okonomiyaki. They are more casual, but will still provide you with a delicious meal, just as most *izakaya,* which might be best described as gastropubs—where the food is good and the drinks creative. Or perhaps more familiar might be the craft beer establishments dotting the city.

Tokyo is frantic, but it's also home to moments of calm. Eateries and drinking establishments rarely disappoint and can give you a little break from the pace of Tokyo. And while that pace is part of its charm—Tokyo knows how to party—remember to slow down and look around. In a place this packed, sometimes the gems are hidden in plain sight. Give yourself some time because Tokyo is a journey and a destination all in one.

What to Eat and Drink in Japan

SUSHI

It goes without saying that you'd be remiss in visiting Japan without sampling sushi, the most well-known genre of Japanese cuisine. While the world's largest fish market has moved from Tsukiji to Toyosu, the Tsukiji neighborhood is still a great place to sample the best, and freshest, sushi in Tokyo.

JAPANESE WHISKEY

The big whiskey brands in Japan are Yamazaki, Hibiki, Hakushu, Fuji Gotemba, Chichibu, and White Oak. You can visit Fuji Gotemba's distillery at the foot of Mt. Fuji on a day trip from Tokyo. Top whiskey bars in Tokyo include Zoetrope in Shinjuku or Cask Strength in Roppongi.

SOBA

In addition to being delicious, soba noodles have the added benefit of having more nutritional value (they're more digestible and contain antioxidants) than wheat noodles.

TEPPANYAKI

Don't call it "hibachi" but do reserve a counter seat at Ginza Fujiya Miyako in Shibuya to watch a skilled chef at work as he prepares duck confit and beautifully marbled miyazaki beef.

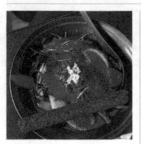

RAMEN

From the miso-based broth of Hokkaido to the milky-in-color pork bone broth of Fukuoka, each region of Japan has developed its own variation on the perennially popular soup. When in Tokyo, head to the Shin-Yokohama Ramen Museum, where you can sample a wide array of ramen from restaurants all over Japan.

OKONOMIYAKI

"Okonomi" means "whatever you like," and "yaki" means "grilled." *Okonomiyaki* are made with cabbage, flour, eggs, green onions, and usually some type of protein all mixed together and then shaped into a sort of veggie-based, savory pancake. Try all the variations and don't forget the toppings.

SAKE

Nihonshu (sake), also known as Japanese rice wine, is Japan's most famous variety of alcohol. It can be enjoyed hot or cold and paired to your meal. Head to the Japan Sake and Shochu Information Center for 100 varieties.

Chanko nabe

CHANKO NABE

Chanko nabe—a giant pot of soup made with chicken broth, plenty of good-for-you protein sources, bok choy, and lots of vegetables—is the signature meal of sumo wrestlers actively working on gaining weight as part of their training. It's probably best enjoyed after watching a sumo wrestling demonstration..

SHABU-SHABU

Shabu-shabu is similar to chanko nabe in the sense that it's a "hot pot"-style dish that can include myriad ingredients. But instead of eating your portion from a single bowl, shabu-shabu is cooked one piece at a time.

YAKITORI

The beauty of *yakitori* is in its simplicity. Skewered chicken is cooked over a charcoal grill and seasoned with a little salt and tare sauce. There's a reason it's a staple of late-night street food and izakayas. For a perfectly calibrated Michelin-starred yakitori experience, visit Birdland in Ginza.

10 Quirky Souvenir Stores in Tokyo

GEE!STORE GACHAPON MACHINES
Upstairs from Cospatio, Gee!STORE houses more than 450 gachapon machines—small vending machines where you insert a coin and a figurine pops out. There are literally thousands of types of prizes, which range from anime character toys to cats wearing kimonos to underpants for your smartphone.

COSPLAY AT COSPATIO
Dressing up is big business in Japan, and serious players come to Cospatio (also known as Cospa), a manufacturer and one of the biggest cosplay stores in Tokyo, for its comprehensive collection of merchandise.

CAN-CAN AT MR. KANSO
The ordinary becomes a novelty at this series of bars dotted around the city that they stock nothing but canned goods—from sardines to smoked liver. Even the drinks are canned at this quirky, distinctly Japanese hangout.

NAKANO BROADWAY
Just follow the covered shopping arcade north of Nakano Station to find four floors of shops selling everything from anime and manga figurines to vintage video games.

YAMASHIROYA TOY STORE
One minute's walk from Ueno station, Yamashiroya's seven floors of childhood heaven packed with toys, figurines, games, and comics is a bucket-list stop for any kid (or kid at heart). Look for a Pokémon chess set and an entire corner devoted to Totoro.

KNICKKNACKS AT TOKYU HANDS
From stationery to toilet-seat covers, reflexology slippers to bee-venom face masks, and novelty party supplies to board games, Tokyu Hands has everything you never knew you needed to buy for yourself and everyone on your list.

OTAKU AT AKIHABARA RADIO KAIKAN
The iconic Akihabara landmark is dedicated to Japanese pop culture, making it an *otaku* (anime, manga, video-game nerd) paradise with 10 floors of shops selling manga, anime, and collectibles such as models and figurines, fanzines, costumes, and accessories.

Don Quijote

EVERYTHING AT DON QUIJOTE

Open 24/7, Don Quijote is a jumble of tall, crowded shelves and sells everything from designer handbags and watches, clothing, and electronics to cheap cosmetics, costumes, and more. It's your one-stop shop for souvenirs including the famed flavored Kit Kats (yes, you *need* every variety).

WORK WEAR AT MANNEN-YA

This 50-year-old store specializing in Japanese-style construction clothes stocks everything from baggy pants to reinforced shirts to *jika-tabi* (split-toe work shoes). You can also find high-vis helmets, white *cho-cho zubon* (butterfly pants), split-toe socks, and even Hello Kitty merchandise.

MASKS AT OMOTE

Actors, mask makers, and headwear enthusiasts all frequent this boutique mask store whose selection ranges from noh masks to Venetian-style masks to *hyottoko* (Japanese-style clown masks), with prices starting at a few thousand yen and stretching to the hundreds of thousands.

Free (or Cheap) Things to Do in Toyko

PICNIC IN THE PARK

Grab a bento lunch box from the nearest supermarket or local bento shop and head to Yoyogi Park—a sanctuary of trees in the middle of Tokyo's urban buzz. The north side of the park in particular is a lush expanse of greenery where you can spread a picnic blanket and relax.

WORLD-FAMOUS FISH MARKET(S)

While you can reserve tours to see Tokyo's two renowned fish markets—Tsukiji (old) and Toyosu (new)—you can also easily visit on your own for free. The historic Tsukiji outer market is not really a fish market anymore, but still has clusters of eateries and stalls selling pickles, bamboo rolling mats, dried nori, and other items.

ULTRATRENDY SHOPPING

Since opening its doors in 1979, SHIBUYA 109 has been a fashion utopia for Tokyo's younger generations and a Shibuya landmark known for its 10 floors bursting with the latest trends in clothing, shoes, and accessories. One of the hippest hangouts in the city, each of the hundreds of stores is seemingly trying to outdo the others for the most unique concept.

TAKESHITA STREET

One of Japan's most popular youth subculture destinations, Harajuku's *kawaii* (cutesy) culture hub Takeshita Street is one of the city's prime people-watching destinations. On weekends, if you're lucky, you'll see young people from the region gather here, fully clad in cosplay, Lolita, and other outlandish garb. It's also where you'll find shops that sell some of that gear.

CONTEMPORARY ART CRAWL

Go see SCAI the Bathhouse, a contemporary art gallery with ever-changing exhibits. The refurbished building is fascinating on its own even if you don't care for the show. If you're looking to make a day of free exhibits, check Tokyo Art Beat (🌐 www.tokyoartbeat.com/en/events/condId/free) and see what is available during your trip.

FREE PANORAMIC VIEWS

If you're put off by Skytree entry prices, head for the twin towers of the Tokyo Metropolitan Government Building in Shinjuku. Both the south and north tower observatories provide far-reaching panoramic views of Tokyo—and even across to Mt. Fuji on a clear day.

NISSAN CROSSING

Take a gander at Nissan's latest supercar concept vehicles as well as rare classic models at its flagship showroom located in the flashy district of Ginza. Check out the rare models or the theater where you can be immersed in the sights and sounds of fast cars.

THE PARASITE MUSEUM

One of Tokyo's more peculiar museums, the Meguro Parasitological Museum is perhaps not the first thing to come to mind when planning a visit to the city, but in recent years it has become an oddly popular tourist attraction. Come here to see more than 300 creepy-crawly specimens for free.

SUMO STABLE

Japan's national sport is famously tough to get tickets for and competitions are held sporadically, making it difficult to be in the right place at the right time to catch the sumo. The next best thing is to head to a sumo stable to watch the wrestlers doing their morning practice. Arashio-beya stable is one location where visitors can usually watch the morning practice session through windows on the street.

THE AD MUSEUM TOKYO

One of the city's coolest free museums, the historic displays and immersive exhibits at the Advertising Museum Tokyo provide an intriguing visual history of commerce in Japan over the past century.

Top Temples and Shrines in Tokyo

TOYOKAWA INARI TOKYO BETSUIN

Toyokawa Inari Tokyo Betsuin celebrates a multitude of deities and is popular with celebrities and those praying for good fortune. One aesthetic draw here is the path lined with tall, narrow crimson flags that's flanked by dozens of carved stone foxes.

SENSO-JI TEMPLE AND ASAKUSA SHRINE

Navigate beyond the shopping arcade dating back to the 17th century and you'll find two of the most important religious sites in Tokyo, the Buddhist Senso-ji and Shinto Asakusa Shrine. This spot is always busy so visit in the evening or early morning if you're not into crowds.

NAMIYOKE INARI SHRINE

This beautiful site was originally built in the mid-1600s to house and honor a Shinto spirit that protected the neighborhood from the waves of Tokyo Bay. Walk through the tree-framed stone *torii* gate into the home of that spirit and you'll find carved stone statues dedicated to fish and other foods associated with nearby Tsukiji Fish Market.

NEZU SHRINE

This shrine near Ueno Park is home to what is likely the oldest building in Tokyo, having survived both the 1923 Great Kanto Earthquake as well as World War II. Due to its being constructed before Shinto and Buddhism were divided by edict, the building shows many design elements of a Buddhist temple and the grounds are home to a hillside of azaleas that bloom in late April or early May.

HIE SHRINE

Hie Shrine is a Shinto place of worship in Akasaka where Oyamakui-no-kami, the god of Mount Hie in Shiga prefecture, is enshrined. What draws in a great many travelers and photo-takers, though, is the tunnel of tightly packed crimson torii, which lead you up the hill to the shrine.

ZOJOJI TEMPLE

Founded in 1393 but relocated to its present site in 1598, Zojoji is the primary temple for the hugely influential Jodo-Buddhist sect, and one of the most important religious sites in Tokyo, and with its beautiful architecture and gorgeous interior art, it's one of Tokyo's most notable temples.

MEIJI SHRINE

One of Japan's most famous shrines, the Meiji Shrine is less flashy than other places of worship with its large, unpainted *torii* gates that frame the sky and forest. Meiji's inner garden features a spiritual "power spot" called Kiyomasa's Well.

KANDA MYOJIN SHRINE

First built in 730 and moved to this location in 1616, this two-tiered, intricately painted shrine is of great historical importance. Its proximity to Akihabara makes it popular with otaku and the tech-obsessed. Look for a charm to ward off IT problems.

SHIBA MARUYAMA KOFUN

Just a short walk from the iconic red-and-white Tokyo Tower, this ancient tomb is one of many pre-historic (and pre-Shinto) tomb sites found all along the archipelago. It is located inside Shiba Park and near a stone monument dedicated to Tadataka Ino, the creator of Japan's first modern map. Climb to the top of the hill and explore the area, which, of course includes a Shinto shrine.

SHINOBAZUNOIKE BENTENDO TEMPLE

At the center of Shinobazu Pond in Ueno Park lies Shinobazunoike Bentendo Temple, a two-story Buddhist temple with an octagonal roof dedicated to the goddess Benzaiten. Shinobazunoike is known as a place for good luck.

Traditional Crafts to Buy

EDO KIRIKO GLASSWARE

Edo Kiriko glassware is created by carving patterns into the surface of layered colored glass using a diamond-tipped grinder. Ryuichi Kumakura's kometsunagi, or rice-chain pattern, is particularly revered and achieved by subtly varying the size of the rice grain shapes he engraves.

FUROSHIKI WRAPPING CLOTHS

Harajuku may be mecca for the latest in youth fashion, but it's also home to some classic craft shops like Musubi, a charming boutique specializing in traditional *furoshiki* cloths. Used to wrap everything from gifts to bento lunch boxes, these beautifully decorated material squares are the perfect eco-friendly wrapping solution. Around 500 varieties line the shelves in traditional, seasonal, and modern designs made from a variety of fabrics including cotton, silk, and *chirimen* (silk crepe), and using various dying and weaving techniques.

FINE BAMBOO CRAFTS

Bamboo craft shop Midoriya, established in 1908, is located along the Yanaka Ginza traditional shopping street. Here, three generations of artists have honed their craft. The family-run shop and studio sells bamboo products ranging from the everyday to the exquisite. Traditional *mushikago* insect cages come in a range of shapes and sizes, as well as bamboo bugs and birds to put inside. You'll also find flower baskets, chopsticks, bookmarks, and lunch boxes. *Renkon* (lotus root) coasters are a cheap and trendy takeaway at ¥500.

VINTAGE FABRIC FASHION

Kukuli is a tiny textiles shop located in the crafty pocket of Kagurazaka, a former geisha hub renowned for its picturesque cobblestone streets. This delightful boutique recycles vintage fabrics and transforms them into trendy fashion pieces. You can buy cloths, tea towels, scarves, and bags made with woven fabric drawn from different regions of the country. These precious and sometimes century-old fabrics are then hand-dyed and redesigned into stylish new products. Alongside the classical motifs of cherry blossom and koi carp, expect to find simple but chic stripes, checks, and geometric patterns.

TENUGUI HAND TOWELS

Tenugui are long multipurpose traditional hand towels made from dyed cotton cloth. They are considered by many Japanese as a daily necessity and their multiple uses include drying hands after washing them, wiping sweat from your brow on humid summer days, or covering your lap as a napkin during a meal. They have also become a fashion item with people wearing them as headbands, head scarves, and neck scarves.

JAPANESE-STYLE CLOTHING AND TEXTILES

Opened in the 1990s in the peaceful backstreets of Daikanyama, Okura sells clothing and other textiles based on traditional Japanese designs and tailoring techniques. "Okura" in

Musubi

Japanese means a store-house full of old treasures and memories from childhood. The seashells, driftwood, shards of glass, and other materials that are embedded in the ceiling and floor were collected from the beach during the store's construction, and there is a weathered curtain over the entrance. You can find a wide range of items including *aizome* (a traditional Japanese indigo dyeing method) shirts, denims, jackets and sweaters, and the shop stocks men's and women's clothing under their own original brands, including the indigo brand BLUE BLUE JAPAN. The second floor stocks the women's range, where you'll find hairpins, purses, cloths, kimono-motif tops, and all kinds of other things.

FOLK TOYS AND SOUVENIRS

For traditional souvenirs with a trendy twist, toy shop Atelier Gangu stocks folkcraft toys directly bought from the crafts-men of various regions around Japan as well as the postcards made with papercut art. The postcards depict the folkcraft toys that are no longer available or difficult to find. On its shelves, you will see every-thing from papier-mâché animals to kites to hand-crafted *maneki-neko* (lucky cats) all made by veteran craftsmen.

JAPANESE KITCHEN KNIVES

The history of kitchen-supply store Kama-Asa extends all the way back to 1908 when the shop was first opened in Asakusa's Kappabashi (also known as Kitchen Town). The elegant store specializes in handcrafted kitchen knives (roughly 80 different kinds) and Nanbu Tekki iron pans, woks, and steamers. There is also a selection of knives for left-handed cooks and the friendly staff will engrave a knife for you in Japanese symbols or roman letters at no extra cost.

TRADITIONAL WASHI PAPER

Founded in 1806, Haibara specializes in making gorgeous letter sets, notebooks, *uchiwa* (round-shaped fans), and envelopes featuring *mizuhiki* knots from traditional *washi* paper. The elegant design of their products can be traced back to the Meiji and late Edo periods when Haibara's founders collaborated with the most renowned painters of that era. They are best known for *gampi* paper made from the outer bark fibers of gampi trees, giving it a smooth texture and silky surface. The shop exterior is a futuristic-looking gray cube just off of Chuo-dori in the Nihon-bashi district.

Best Tours in Tokyo

PERSONALIZED TOUR

Join a small group tour to hit all the highlights of Tokyo or to hire a private guide to take you to off-the-beaten-path Tokyo with InsideJapan Tours' team of experts and knowledgeable locals on the ground to help you make the most of your time. ⊕ *www.insidejapantours.com.*

HISTORY TOUR

Get a first-hand glimpse into the life of the *shogun* (military dictators), *daimyo* (feudal lords), and *samurai* (Japanese warrior class) on Walk Japan's two-day Tokyo tour, which gives an introduction to the establishment of Edo (Tokyo), how it came to be, and how it developed from a traditional samurai society to a modern-day glitzy metropolis. ⊕ *www.walkjapan.com/tour/tokyo-tour.*

FOOD TOUR

Sample delectable Japanese dishes on one of Arigato Japan's three-hour foodie tours of Tokyo. Drop into five Shibuya food stops or wander through Tokyo's traditional district of Yanaka while sampling dishes from around Japan and shopping the wares of creative artisans and craftspeople. ⊕ *arigatojapan.co.jp.*

TOKYO AFTER DARK

Get an education as you enjoy the food offerings hidden in the back haunts of Shibuya that most visitors would likely never stumble upon with Context Travel's Tokyo After Dark tour. You'll learn about the history of the *izakaya* and its role in both drinking and culinary culture of the area. ⊕ *www.contexttravel. com/cities/tokyo/tours/ tokyo-after-dark-night-food-tour.*

FISH MARKET TOUR

An early-morning trip to the giant Toyosu fish market is a bucket-list item for many visitors to Tokyo, but it can be overwhelming to navigate it on your own. There are several tour groups that will take you through. Several fish market tours (some for the new market and some for the old Tsukiji Market's surrounding neighborhood) are offered by Viator. ⊕ *Viator.com.*

CHERRY BLOSSOM TOUR

To experience Tokyo during the *sakura* (cherry blossom) season is to experience the city at its most exquisite. Make the most of it by joining a walking tour and taking advantage of a local guide's knowledge to suss out the best blooms in the city. A private guide will take you to the best viewing spots, and some tours will include a tea ceremony experience or a *hanami* experience where you can have a picnic under the blossoms. ⊕ *toursbylocals.com.*

CYCLE THROUGH TOWN

If you are looking for something a bit more active, try Tokyo Great Tours for cycling or even kayaking around town. The Tokyo Transformation (Route C), for example, will take you

Akihabara

from the east side of central Tokyo to the west to see the whole variety of modern architecture and historic locations. ⊕ *tokyogreat-tours.com*.

DISCOVER THE ANIME AND MANGA CULTURE OF AKIHABARA

Dive into the world of Japanese pop culture on Context Tours' Geek to Chic expedition, which explores the famed electronics town of Akihabara, Tokyo's *otaku* (anime and manga geek) hub. The tour also covers one of the more unconventional aspects of otaku culture—cosplay ("costume play")—by visiting a maid café. During your visit, you will experience the peculiar rituals and customs of these establishments. ⊕ *contexttravel. com/cities/tokyo/tours/ otaku-from-geek-to-chic*.

BAR-HOPPING TOUR

Tokyo is famous for its nightlife but it can be hard to know where to start. Magical Trip's Tokyo bar-hopping night tour is one of its most popular walking tours. They take you to the Harajuku and Shibuya districts, including the famous Shibuya Scramble, before heading over to Shinjuku to explore the areas of Kabukicho and Golden Gai. You'll pop into hidden bars that you'd never otherwise find, indulge in tasty street foods, and eat delicious Japanese dishes in traditional *izakaya* (Japanese pubs). ⊕ *magical-trip.com*.

GET TO KNOW THE CITY FOR FREE

If you're seeing the city on a budget, hit up Tokyo's SGG club (Systemized Goodwill Guide Club) for their free 90-minute and two-hour guided tours of popular

areas in Tokyo (departs once a day at 1 pm), but you'll need to make reservations in advance. Volunteer guides hold a two-hour walking tour of the Imperial Palace East Gardens every day except Monday and Friday. ⊕ *tokyo-sgg.jp/guide.html*.

SUMO STABLE TOUR

Wrestlers live in communal stables where all aspects of their daily lives are dictated by strict tradition. During a tour, guests learn about the historical roots of sumo wrestling, gain a deeper understanding of sumo rituals, and even get a photo with the sumo wrestlers after the session. Many sumo stables offer events aimed at tourists. To find activities, check ⊕ *sumoexperience.com*.

What to Read and Watch

TOKYO: A SPATIAL ANTHROPOLOGY

The perfect travel preparation book, particularly if you plan to wander the streets of Tokyo, Hidenobu Jinnai's book provides you with layers of context to the streets and buildings you'll see. The Japanese architectural historian uses this work of nonfiction to explore the roots of the city, using visuals to walk the reader through what went into forming the Tokyo of today from the centuries of architecture and natural disasters to wars and cultural influences.

SHOPLIFTERS

Director Hirokazu Koreeda's indie movie premiered in 2018 to much critical and popular acclaim, winning a Palme d'Or at Cannes Film Festival, an Oscar nomination, and the Japan Academy Prize for Picture of the Year. The film's Japanese title, *Manbiki Kazoku* (*The Shoplifting Family*), is perhaps more striking and tells the viewer that we will be learning more than just crime, but a touching story about the relationships between people on the margins of society and how all that can be upended when their secrets are exposed.

IN THE MISO SOUP

Economic decline in late 20th-century Japan, as an inflation bubble burst, inspired a wave of crime fiction full of political and social commentary. Ryu Murakami's is one of these works that have been translated into English. It is a violent thriller about a Japanese man who leads "sex tours" for tourists through the back alleys of Tokyo's Shinjuku District. It's a story of an American serial killer, but also of a young Japanese protagonist disillusioned with his hometown and its economic situation—and of Shinjuku's underbelly, and the violence that too often appears there.

TOKYO GODFATHERS

No list of Tokyo cinema would be complete without some anime (animated movies), a widely popular genre that has earned a cult international following, and focuses on colorfully drawn characters and their dramatic, often fantastical adventures. Directed by Satoshi Kon, this anime is a bit more rooted in reality, if not a tragic one, featuring a group of homeless residents, each with their own distinct story, and a lost baby. Heartfelt and entertaining, this is a great piece of anime and a fun exploration of the, albeit animated, scenes of Tokyo.

THE WIND-UP BIRD CHRONICLE

Haruki Murakami is an essential figure in Japanese contemporary literature, especially for an English-speaking audience since quality translations of his work are easy to find. His novels are typically set in Tokyo, often infused with illusory or futuristic elements that distort—or sometimes magnify—the city. Three Murakami novels are particularly good introductions to his work: alluring mystery and exploration in *The Wind-Up Bird Chronicle*; nostalgic longing in *Norwegian Wood*; or a single late-night out on the Tokyo streets in *After Dark*.

TAMPOPO

Juzo Itami wrote and directed this 1985 comedy that celebrates food and its influence on Japanese society. The offbeat and satirical humor in the story explores human nature, prescriptive habits of the Japanese, class, and feelings of obligation (an important background theme in much of Japanese storytelling), all within the backdrop of a ramen shop.

STRANGE WEATHER IN TOKYO

Hiromi Kawakami's story of a woman's unlikely relationship with an elderly former teacher lays out delicious morsels of daily Tokyo life, described in beauty and detail, from its cherry trees and markets, to bottles of sake and dishes of delicacies. It is Kawakami's quirky and fascinating characters that really bring her writing to life. *The Nakano Thrift Shop* is another of her funny explorations of human interactions and relationships.

GODZILLA (1954)

Now somewhat kitschy and distorted by its Americanized franchise and wider pop culture, the original 1950s *Godzilla*—about a lizardlike behemoth terrorizing Tokyo—is a classic film, with haunting undertones about a grieving country in the wake of World War II and specifically the use of atom bombs in Nagasaki and Hiroshima. The miniaturized sets of Tokyo used here are added entertainment; these early special effects set the stage for many action-packed Japanese movies to come.

THE CAT AND THE CITY

Following the story of a stray cat in Tokyo, author Nick Bradley ties together the cat's movement through human spaces and the connections to the people who also occupy the fast-changing city. The cat is the link between the different characters who are also struggling in the big city, and she slowly draws them together.

AN AUTUMN AFTERNOON

The Japanese title of this 1962 film, *Sanma no Aji* (*The Taste of Sanma* [a fish commonly eaten in the fall]) is a hint at the timing in the story of the patriarch of a family coming to realize the responsibilities expected of him. This was the final film by Yasujiro Ozu, who is known for filming as if sitting in *seiza* (the seating posture on one's knees, which is expected in polite situations).

OUT

In the first of Natsuo Kirino's popular books that have been translated in English (by Stephen Snyder), Kirino makes sharp social commentary as she takes on Japanese crime fiction with a feminist gaze. This novel is full of surprising, often dark and grotesque twists. What appears as a simple thriller, following a group of female factory workers involved in a murder, comes with layers of perspective on contemporary Tokyo and the societal challenges faced by women.

TO LIVE (IKIRU)

Akira Kurosawa is a giant of Japanese film. This 1952 film tells the story of a terminally ill bureaucrat in Tokyo trying to make his last days meaningful. While Kurosawa's films are widely celebrated and for good reason, this one is perhaps his most moving story.

Budget Travel Tips

Tokyo can be painfully expensive, but here are some tips that can help ease the strain on the travel budget.

LODGING

Big chain hotels can be expensive, but Japan also has "business hotels" that provide small, basic rooms at very reasonable prices that often include breakfast. Look for chains like Toyoko Inn, Dormy Inn, and Comfort Inn. You can sometimes get discounted rates by signing up for free membership cards, especially at Toyoko Inn.

Another saving option, if you or someone you know can read Japanese, is to book via one of Japan's discount travel companies, which usually give good rates that include extras like breakfast.

If there are four of you traveling together, youth hostels can be an attractive budget option—rooms are often set up for four people, so there will be no sharing with strangers. Hostels also tend to be very clean, usually offer meals at a good price, and are often in popular tourist areas.

TRANSPORTATION

If you are traveling around Japan, the JR Pass will save you a fortune in fares and allow you to use most Shinkansen services. It will also get you on JR sleeper trains, which can save on accommodation costs. If you are just planning a weekend out of Tokyo, stop by a major train station and ask about passes for the area. The Hakone Free Pass, which can be bought at Shinjuku Station, covers the train fare to and from Hakone on the Odakyu Line as well as unlimited use of otherwise expensive buses, sightseeing boats, cable cars, and local trains for two or three days in Hakone.

FOOD

Eating takeout from department store basement food halls is one way to save money. You will save even more if you wait until about an hour before closing, when many prepared foods are marked down 25%–50%. Ready-made lunches and dinners can be found at supermarkets like Summit and Ito Yokado (and many smaller local ones) and convenience stores like Lawson and 7-Eleven. They all sell bento and pasta dishes for under ¥500, as well as *onigiri* (rice balls) and sandwiches for under ¥500, and are actually good.

To save on higher-end dining, eat at lunchtime. Many expensive restaurants do smaller, but still extremely good, lunches at a fraction of the price of their evening courses.

SHOPPING

For deals on the (almost) latest Japanese cameras and accessories, try somewhere like Map Camera in Shinjuku. Many Japanese amateur photographers frequently upgrade to the newest models, so you will find plenty of very modern but well-priced used gear in great condition.

For more bargain-hunting, head to the Ameyoko Street Market by JR Ueno Station. You can find everything from the freshest seafood to a can of Spam, real Rolex watches to fake Gucci bags, and everything else in between, lots of it at fairly decent prices.

Flea markets can also be a good place to find great souvenirs at budget-friendly prices. There's a major antiques market usually held the first and third Sunday of the month at Tokyo International Forum in Yurakucho, weekend flea markets at Shinjuku Chuo Park, as well as many other flea markets set up at shrines, such as the Sunday market at Hanazono Jinja in Shinjuku.

ISOLATION AND ENGAGEMENT:
A HISTORY OF JAPAN By Robert Morel

A century and a half after opening its shores to outsiders, Japan is still a mystery to many Westerners. Often misunderstood, Japan's history is much deeper than the stereotypes of samurai and geisha, overworked businessmen, and anime. Its long tradition of retaining the old while embracing the new has captivated visitors for centuries.

Much of Japanese history has consisted of the ongoing tension between its seeming isolation from the rest of the world and a desire to be a part of it. During the Edo period, Japan was closed to foreigners for some 250 years. Yet while the country has always had a strong national identity, it has also had a rapacious appetite for all things foreign. Just 50 years after opening its borders, parts of Tokyo looked like London, and Japan had become a colonial power in Asia.

Much earlier, the Japanese imported Buddhism, tea, and their first writing system from China.

In the 19th century, the country incorporated Western architecture, technology, and government. More recently, the Japanese have absorbed Western fashion, music, and pop culture. Nevertheless, the country's history lives on in local traditions, festivals, temples, cities, music, and the arts.

Senso-ji Complex in Tokyo's Asakusa neighborhood

(Top) Horyu-ji Temple, (Bottom) Nihon Shoki, (Right) Large Buddha statue at Todai-ji Temple

Ancient Japan
10,000 BC–AD 622

The first people in Japan were the hunters and fishers of the Jomon period, known for their pottery. In the following Yayoi period, hunting and fishing gave way to agriculture, as well as the introduction of rice farming and metalworking. Around AD 500 the Yamato tribe consolidated power in what is now the Kansai plain, with Yamato leaders claiming descent from the sun goddess Amaretsu and taking the title of emperor. Prince Shotoku promoted the spread of Buddhism from China and commissioned Horyu-ji Temple in Nara in 607.

■ Horyu-ji Temple (Nara)
■ National Museum (Tokyo)

Nara Period
710–784

As Japan's first permanent capital and urban center, Nara is often considered the birthplace of Japanese culture. Under the Emperor Shomu, who commissioned the Great Buddha at Todai-ji Temple, Buddhism rose to prominence. The first Japanese written histories, the *Kojiki* and *Nihon Shoki*, were compiled during this period, as was the *Manyoshu*, Japan's first collection of poetry. Since the country was the Eastern terminus of the Silk Road, Japan's royal family amassed an impressive collection of treasures from mainland Asia, many of which are still on display at Todai-ji Temple's Shoso-in.

■ The Great Buddha at Todai-ji Temple (Nara)

Heian Period
794–1160

Partly to escape intrigues and the rising power of the Nara's Buddhist Priests, in 794 the Emperor Kammu moved the capital to Heian-kyo (now Kyoto). *Heian* translates roughly as "peace and tranquility," and during this time the Imperial court expanded its power throughout Japan. Inside the court, however, life was far from calm. This was a period of great courtly intrigue, and struggles for power between aristocrats, the powerful Fujiwara clan (the most powerful of Japan's four great noble families), and the new military class known as *bushi*. Though some emperors managed to maintain control of the court, the Heian

794–1160: The capital is moved from Nara to Heian-kyo (now Kyoto)

1467–77: The Onin Wars initiate a 100-year period of civil war

| 1100 | 1250 | 1400 | 1550 |

(Right) Zen Garden at the Ryoan-ji Temple, (Top) Noh masks, (Bottom) Kyoto Imperial Palace's wooden orange gates.

period saw the slow rise of the military class, leading to a series of wars that established them as the ruling class until well into the 19th century. Considered Japan's great classical period, this was a time when courtly arts flourished. The new Japanese kana script gave rise to a boom in literature. Compiled in 990, Sei Shonagon's Pillow Book gave a window into courtly life, and Shibuki Murasaki's Tale of Genji is often regarded as the world's first classic novel. Japanese *waka* poetry experienced a revival, breeding the new forms of poetry such as tanka that are still in use today.

■ The Imperial Palace (Kyoto)

Kamakura Period
1185–1335

As the Imperial Court lost control, the Genpei War (1180–1185) resulted in the defeat of clans loyal to the emperor in Kyoto and the rise of a new government in Kamakura. Yoritomo Minamoto named himself Sei-i Tai Shogun and established the Kamakura bakufu, a spartan military government. During this time, Japan repelled two Mongol invasions, thanks to timely typhoons that were later dubbed "kamikaze", or "divine wind." In this militaristic climate, Zen Buddhism, with its focus on self-reliance and discipline, exploded in popularity.

■ Eihiji Temple (Fukushima)
■ Hachimangu Shrine and the Great Buddha (Kamakura)

Muromachi (Ashikaga) Period
1336–1568

The heyday of the samurai, the Muromachi period was one of near constant civil war. Feudal lords known as *daimyo* consolidated their power in local fiefdoms. Peasant rebellions and piracy were common. Nevertheless, trade flourished. The movement of armies required daimyo to build roads, while improved communications gave birth to many merchant and artisan guilds. Trade with China grew, and in 1543 Portugal began trading with Japan, introducing firearms and Christianity. Noh theater and the tea ceremony were founded, and Kyoto's most famous temples were built in this period.

■ Kinkaku-ji Temple (Kyoto)
■ Ryoan-ji Temple (Kyoto)

(Left) Matsumoto Castle, (Top) three wise monkeys at Toshogu shrine, (Bottom) woodcut of Kabuki actor by Utagawa Toyokuni

National Unification (Momoyama Period)

1568–1600

In 1568 Oda Nobunaga, a lord from Owari in central Japan, marched on Kyoto and took the title of Shogun. He controlled the surrounding territories until his death in 1582, when his successor, Toyotomi Hideyoshi, became the new Shogun. After unifying much of central and western Japan, he attempted unsuccessful invasions of Korea before his death in 1598. In 1600 Tokugawa Ieyasu, a top general, defeated Hideyoshi's successor in the battle of Sekihagara.

- Osaka Castle (Osaka)
- Matsumoto Castle (Matsumoto)

Edo (Tokugawa) Period

1600–1867

The Edo period ushered in 250 years of relative stability and central control. After becoming Shogun, Ieyasu Tokugawa moved the capital to Edo (present-day Tokyo). A system of *daimyo*, lords beholden to the Shogun, was established along with a rigid class system and legal code of conduct. Although Japan cut off trade with the outside world, cities flourished. By the mid-18th century, Edo's population had grown to more than 1 million, and urban centers like Osaka and Kyoto had become densely populated. Despite such rapid growth, urban life in the Edo period was highly organized, with districts managed by neighborhood associations that have persisted (in a modified way) to the present day. Popular entertainment and arts arose to satisfy the thriving merchant and artisan classes. Kabuki, flashy and sensational, overtook Noh theater in popularity, and Japan's famed "floating world" (*ukio*), with its theaters, drinking houses, and geishas emerged. Sumo, long a Shinto tradition, became a professional sport. Much of what both Japanese and foreigners consider "Japanese culture" dates to this period. But by 1853, the Shogun's hold on power was growing tenuous.

- Toshogu (Nikko)
- Katsura Imperial Villa (Kyoto) Muhammad Ali Mosque

1800	1853: U.S. Commodore Matthew Perry reopens Japan to foreign trade	1850	1868: Meiji Restoration begins	1900	1941: Japan attacks Pearl Harbor	1950

(Top) Tokyo University, (Left) wedding in Meiji Shrine, (Bottom) A6M5 fighter plane at Yusyukan museum.

Meiji Period

1868–1912

The Tokugawa Shogunate's rigid class system and legal code proved to be its undoing. After U.S. Commodore Matthew Perry opened Japan to trade in March 1854, the following years were turbulent. In 1868, the last Shogun, Tokugawa Yoshinobu, ceded power to Emperor Meiji, and Japan began to modernize after 250 years of isolation. Adopting a weak parliamentary system from Germany, rulers moved quickly to develop national industry and universities. Victories over China and Russia also emboldened Japan.

- Tokyo University (Tokyo)
- Heian Shrine (Kyoto)
- Nara National Museum (Nara)

Taisho Period

1912–1925

In the early 20th century, urban Japan was beginning to look a lot like Europe and North America.

Fashion ranged from traditional *yukata* and kimono to zoot suits and bobbed hair. In 1923 the Great Kanto Earthquake and its resulting fires destroyed Yokohama and much of Tokyo. Although city planners saw this as an opportunity to modernize Tokyo's maze of streets, residents were quick to rebuild, ensuring that many neighborhood maps look much the same today as they did a century ago.

- Asakusa (Tokyo)
- The Shitamachi Museum (Tokyo)
- Meiji Shrine (Tokyo)

Wartime Japan

1926–1945

Although Japan was was increasingly liberal throughout the 1920s, the economic shocks of the 1930s helped the military gain greater control, resulting in crackdowns on left-leaning groups, the press, and dissidents. In 1931 Japan invaded Manchuria; in 1937 Japan captured Nanking, killing many civilians. Joining the Axis powers in 1936, Japan continued its expansion in Asia and in 1941 attacked Pearl Harbor. After the atomic bombings of Hiroshima and Nagasaki, the Emperor announced Japan's surrender on August 15, 1945.

- Hiroshima Peace Memorial Park (Hiroshima)
- Yasukuni Shrine Museum (Tokyo)

TIMELINE

| 1964: Tokyo hosts the Summer Olympic games | 1989: Emperor Hirohito dies | 2006: Shinzo Abe elected as the country's youngest prime minister | 2009: Liberal Democratic Party loses power | 2019: Emperor Akihito abdicates. Reiwa period begins. |

1970   1990   2010   2030

(Top) 1964 Summer Olympics, Tokyo, (Bottom) manga comic books, (Right) Shinjuku, Tokyo

Postwar Japan and the Economic Miracle

1945–1989

The initial postwar years were hard on Japan. More than half of Japan's total urban area was in ruins, its industry in shambles, and food shortages common. Kyoto was the only major metropolitan area in the country that escaped widespread damage. Thanks to an educated, dedicated population and smart planning, however, Japan was soon on the road to recovery. A new democratic government was formed and universal suffrage extended to all adult men and women. Japan's famous "Peace Constitution" forbade the country from engaging in warfare. With cooperation from the government, old companies like Matsushita (Panasonic), Mitsubishi, and Toyota began exporting Japanese goods en masse, while upstarts like Honda pushed their way to the top. In 1964 Japan joined the Organization for Economic Cooperation and Development's group of "rich nations" and hosted the Tokyo Olympics. At the same time, anime began gaining popularity at the box office and on TV, with Osamu Tezuka's classic *Tetsuwan Atom* (*Astro Boy*) making a splash when it aired in 1963. In the 1970s and '80s Japan became as well known for its electronics as its cars, with Nintendo, Sony, and Panasonic becoming household names abroad.

- Showa-Kan (Takayama)
- National Stadium (Yoyogi Park)

From Goods to Culture

1990–PRESENT

Unfortunately, much of Japan's rapid growth in the 1980s was unsustainable. By 1991 the bubble had burst, leading to 20 years of limited economic expansion. Japan avoided an economic crisis, and most people continued to lead comfortable, if somewhat simpler, lives. After decades of exporting goods, Japan has—particularly since 2000—become an exporter of culture in the form of animation, video games, and cuisine. Japan, famous for importing ideas, has begun to send its own culture to the world.

- Shinjuku, Harajuku, and Shibuya, (Tokyo)
- Akihabara (Tokyo)
- Manga Museum (Kyoto)

TRAVEL SMART

2

Updated by
Jay Farris

★ **CAPITAL:**
Tokyo

👥 **POPULATION:**
9.66 million in central Tokyo;
37 million in the Greater
Tokyo region

💬 **LANGUAGE:**
Japanese

$ **CURRENCY:**
Japanese yen; pronounced
"en" in Japanese

☎ **COUNTRY CODE:**
+81

⚠ **EMERGENCIES:**
Police service 110;
ambulance and fire services
119

🚗 **DRIVING:**
On the left

⚡ **ELECTRICITY:**
110v/50 cycles; plugs have
two flat prongs

🕐 **TIME:**
Japan Standard Time
(GMT+9)

🌐 **WEB RESOURCES:**
www.gotokyo.org
www.japan.travel/en

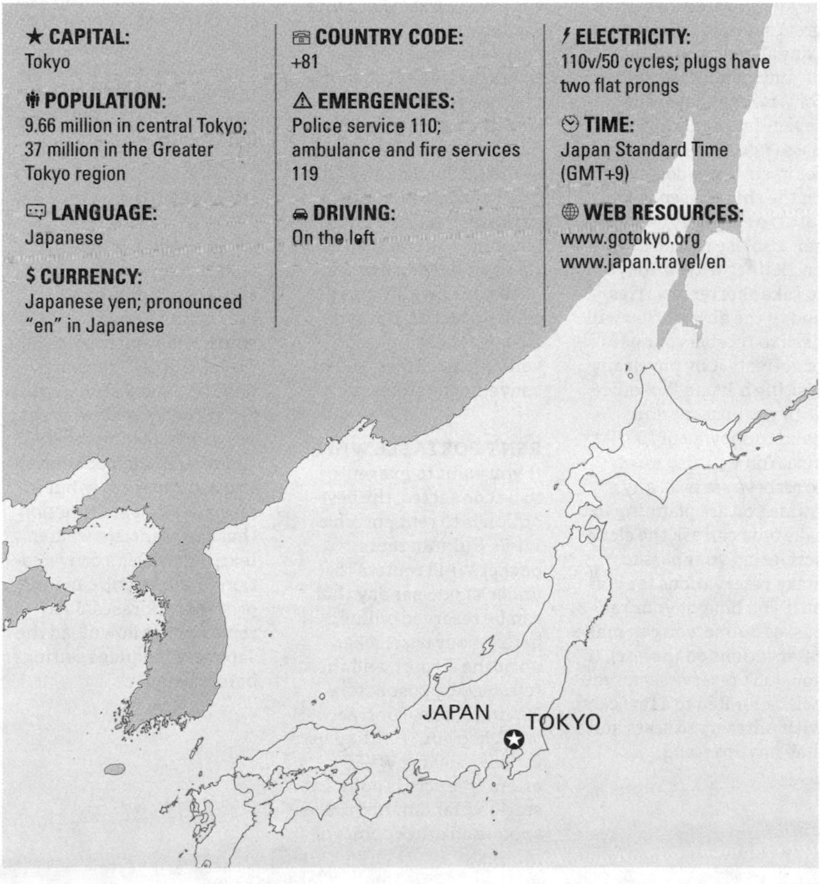

JAPAN   TOKYO

Know Before You Go

Should you tip? Is the water okay to drink? Can you trust that your luggage will arrive safely if you send it ahead to your next hotel? And what's this about not opening or closing the taxi doors?

GET A RAIL PASS

If you are visiting other parts of Japan, consider a JR Rail Pass. This should be purchased before coming to Japan (within three months of your visit) and offers great savings on unlimited trips all over the country on almost all JR services for 7, 14, or 21 days. The seven-day standard class pass (¥33,610) almost pays for itself if you do a side trip on the shinkansen to Kyoto (¥14,170 each way), and you can also use it for travel on JR lines within Tokyo, to take shorter day trips, and to the airport. You will need to receive your pass or activate it by physically visiting a Japan Rail office with your passport in hand to show your tourist visa. You will also want to reserve seats on any trains you are planning to take (you can ask the clerk activating your pass to make reservations for you or, if you bought your rail passes online, you can make reservations on the site). If you don't reserve seats, you will be limited to a few cars with unreserved seats and may have to stand.

TAKE PUBLIC TRANSPORT

Tokyo's train and subway network serves every part of the city you could wish to visit. To make using it easy, buy a Pasmo or Suica rechargeable IC card. They cost ¥500 from station ticket machines (a deposit you can get back minus a small processing fee if you hand in the card at a station to reclaim any money left on it) and can be charged at ticket machines at all stations. You can then tap them on ticket gates and have your fare automatically deducted. You can also use them on buses, at vending machines, and in convenience stores.

RENT PORTABLE WI-FI

If you want to guarantee to be connected, the best option is to rent portable Wi-Fi. PuPuRu rents pocket Wi-Fi routers for under ¥1,000 per day that can be reserved online before your trip, picked up at the airport, and then returned by post before leaving Japan. For free Wi-Fi, look out for the Japan Connected Free Wi-Fi. It offers free access points at stations, landmarks, tourist spots, and other points of interest.

THERE'S (ALMOST) NO NEED TO TIP

Generally speaking, there is no tipping in Japan, regardless of how much you appreciate the service and staff. It is not expected. There is some flexibility to this rule: if you hire a private guide or a private driver who are used to tourists, feel free to tip them, but it's best to always hand money to people in an envelope and ideally with both hands. Tipping is also acceptable at a ryokan where meals are served in your room. Tip ¥1,000–¥2,000 per person per day at a ryokan where you have an attendant. You should be handing the tip over *during check-in* and in an envelope. If you mess this up, don't worry. Everyone is forgiving about these kinds of things.

DOWNLOAD A TRANSLATION APP

While English is understood, it is not widely spoken in Japan, so you may want to download a translation app before you travel. Google Translate handles Japanese to English consistently well (with the occasional incomprehensible translation of menus). You can type into it, but it also has a camera function that can translate written text, and with its conversation function you can interpret short phrases. Just remember to download the Japanese language settings before using it.

LEARN A FEW WORDS

You will get by just fine in Tokyo without speaking a word of Japanese, but learning and using a few key phrases is appreciated by locals. Try *konnichiwa* (a more formal hello), *arigato* (thank you), and the multipurpose *domo* (casual hello or thank you). And don't forget *sumimasen* (excuse me) and *gomen nasai* (sorry).

NOW, SHUSH!

The trains may be crowded but you will quickly notice that they are also—remarkably—silent. Out of respect for fellow passengers, keep your phone on silent mode when you travel on public transport. While you're at it, keep your voice low, too, and you'll fit right in.

DO NOT EAT ON THE GO

While it is common to see commuters snacking and drinking Starbucks on the go in most major cities, this is seen as kind of crude in Japan. It's considered bad manners to eat inside trains, the exception being on the Shinkansen or other long-distance express trains. And you will see signs at markets to eat at the stall rather than to wander with food. Your manners will be rewarded with a clean city and public transportation system and an increased appreciation for your food at mealtimes. (You'll also rarely see a trash can on the street, so you have to carry all your trash.)

KNOW HOW TO TAKE A TAXI

Taxis are a good (albeit costly if traveling alone) way to get around Tokyo. Taxis can be found on busy corners and can be hailed on the street. Drivers are for the most part courteous, though not necessarily chatty. Unless you're going to a well-known destination such as a major hotel, it's advisable to have your destination written out in Japanese (your hotel concierge can do this for you). Drivers speak varying levels of English so it's best if they can use their car navigation system. Also, don't open or close the doors yourself; the driver does that using a lever by his seat. They expect cash, but do accept credit cards. Remember, there is no need to tip.

SHIP YOUR LUGGAGE BETWEEN HOTELS

Avoid hauling luggage (and your accumulating souvenirs) around with you on crowded public transport as you travel between hotels by taking advantage of Takkyubin luggage delivery services, a convenient service for sending parcels, luggage, and various other types of goods from door to door nationwide. Delivery can usually be arranged at your hotel and is often same-day (within the same city) or the next day, and costs are moderate. This is a common thing to do since trains don't have a lot of storage space. Plus, nothing beats arriving at your hotel to find your bags waiting for you. You can even ship your bags from Narita Airport to your hotel on your day of arrival).

KNOW WHEN TO SMOKE

Despite tougher laws enacted in 2018, smokers can still light up in many restaurants and bars. Establishments that allow smoking will have a small green smoking sign near the door. Non-smoking establishments are becoming more common as the smoking rates decline. Smoking on the street is also prohibited in many places, but there are designated smoking areas throughout the city.

BE PREPARED FOR A QUAKE

It's not a fun thing to think about when planning a trip, but it's important to remember that Japan (Tokyo included) experiences frequent earthquakes. Make a note of emergency contact numbers for your embassy. It's also worth taking a minute to check the evacuation route from your hotel room (usually on the door) and reading up on what to do in an earthquake (stay away from windows, get under something sturdy to protect your head, and hold on). There is also an early warning system, which sends warnings to phones ahead of a quake. If you hear lots of alarms all at once, that's probably what it is, so prepare. Luckily, Japan has strict building codes. Download the NHK World app on your smartphone so that you are updated with any emergency alerts in English. You can also visit ⊕ www3.nhk.or.jp/nhkworld for updates in English.

Getting Here and Around

Air

Flying time to Japan is 14 hours from New York, 13 hours from Chicago, and 10 hours from Los Angeles. The trip east, because of tailwinds, can be even an hour shorter, and the trip west that much longer because of headwinds.

Most major U.S. airports offer multiple direct flights to Tokyo each day.

Flights to Osaka or Nagoya usually involve a transfer, though some west coast hubs like San Francisco and Los Angeles run direct flights. Because of the distance, fares to Japan tend to be expensive, usually around $1,600 for a seat in coach.

Both of Japan's major carriers have reduced prices for flights within the country. JAL offers the Japan Explorer Pass; ANA has similar special fares. These are real cost-savers if your trip includes destinations such as Kyushu or Hokkaido, though there are restrictions on use in peak times, and often must be booked well in advance, so be sure to check these before your arrival. All domestic flights in Japan are no-smoking.

■ TIP➜ **Visit a tourist information center to find out about local transportation packages that include tickets to major museum exhibits or other special events.**

FLIGHTS

Japan Airlines (JAL), United Airlines, American Airlines, Delta Airlines, and All Nippon Airways (ANA) link North American cities with Tokyo's Haneda and Narita airports. Most of these airlines also fly in and out of Japan's two other international airports, Kansai International Airport, located south of Osaka and Centrair, near Nagoya.

Travel Times from Tokyo

To	By air	By car or bus	By train
Osaka	1¼ hours	7–8 hours	2½ hours
Hiroshima	1½ hours	10 hours	4 hours
Kyoto	1¼ hours	7 hours	2 hours
Fukuoka	2 hours	14 hours	5 hours
Sapporo	1½ hours	15 hours	8 hours

AIRPORTS

The major gateway to Japan is Tokyo's Narita Airport (NRT), 80 km (50 miles) northeast of the city. The Haneda Airport International Terminal also has flights to major international cities and is only 20 km (12 miles) south of central Tokyo.

Most domestic flights to and from Tokyo are out of Haneda Airport.

There are three terminals at Narita Airport. Terminals 1 and 2 are for international flights, while the newer Terminal 3 is for flights on domestic and international low-cost carriers. Terminal 1 has two adjoining wings, north and south. When you arrive, convert some money into yen or withdraw yen from an ATM; you may need it for transportation into Tokyo. In both wings, ATMs and money-exchange counters are in the wall between the customs inspection area and the arrival lobby. All three terminals have a Japan National Tourism Organization information center, where you can get free maps, brochures, and other visitor information. Ticket counters for airport limousine buses and express trains to Tokyo are directly across from the customs-area exits at Terminals 1 and 2.

If you have time to kill at Narita, take a local Keisei Line train into Narita (the town) 15 minutes away, where a traditional shopping street and the beautiful

Narita-san Shinsho Temple are a peaceful escape from airport noise.

Flying into Haneda provides visitors with quicker access to central Tokyo, which is a short monorail or Keikyu Line ride away. Stop by the currency exchange and Tourist Information Desk in the second-floor arrival lobby before taking a train into the city. There are also numerous concierge staff on hand to help passengers with any questions.

GROUND TRANSPORTATION

Known as "The Gateway to Japan," Narita is at least 90 minutes—depending on traffic—by taxi or bus from central Tokyo. The Keisei Skyliner and Japan Railways N'EX are the easiest and fastest ways to get into the city.

Directly across from the customs-area exits at both terminals are the ticket counters for buses to Tokyo. Buses leave from platforms just outside terminal exits, exactly on schedule; the departure time is on the ticket. The Airport Limousine has shuttle-bus service from Narita to Tokyo starting at ¥2,900. Cheaper options include Airport Bus TYO-NRT (¥1,300).

Japan Railways trains stop at Narita Airport Terminals 1 and 2. The most comfortable is the Narita Limited Express (N'EX), which serves more central stations (and beyond). Trains from the airport go directly to the central Tokyo Station in just about an hour, then continue toward Yokohama, but other routes stop at Shibuya and Shinjuku. Daily departures begin at 7:43 am; the last train is at 9:44 pm. In addition to regular seats, there is a first-class Green Car. All seats are reserved.

The Keisei Skyliner train runs every 20–30 minutes between the airport terminals and Keisei-Ueno Station. The trip takes around 40 minutes. The first Skyliner leaves Narita for Ueno at 7:28 am, the last at 10:30 pm. From Keisei-Ueno to

Narita, the first Skyliner is at 5:40 am, the last at 8:20 pm. Keisei's slightly slower Access Express service also runs between Narita and Keisei-Ueno. If you are arriving with a Japan Rail Pass and staying in Tokyo for a few days, it might be best to pay for the transfer into the city and wait to activate the rail pass for travel beyond Tokyo.

TRANSFERS BETWEEN AIRPORTS

Transfer between Narita and Haneda airports is easiest by the Airport Limousine Bus, which should take 65-85 minutes and costs ¥3,200. The Keisei Access Express also runs between the two airports but some routes require a transfer at Aoto Station. While Haneda has some international flights now, it's the main domestic airport for Tokyo.

 ## Bus

Japan Railways (JR) has a number of long-distance buses that are comfortable and inexpensive and also runs short-distance buses in some areas that have limited rail service. You can use Japan Rail Passes on some, but not all, of these buses. Japan Rail Passes, however, are not accepted by private bus companies.

Bus routes and schedules are constantly changing, but tourist information offices have up-to-date details. It's now possible to travel from Osaka to Tokyo for less than ¥5,000 one way. Buses are generally modern and very comfortable, even some of the overnight buses. Daytime highway buses are often an excellent way to get to many interesting out-of-the-way destinations.

City buses, especially outside of Tokyo, are quite convenient, but be sure of your route and destination, because the bus driver probably won't speak English. Buses in the city usually have a set cost,

Getting Here and Around

Travel Times into Tokyo

FROM NARITA	TO	FARES	TIMES	NOTES
Airport Limousine (buses)	Various hotels in Tokyo and JR Tokyo and Shinjuku train stations	¥3,200	Roughly hourly until 8 or 9 pm	70–90 mins, can be longer in traffic
Airport Limousine (buses)	Tokyo City Air Terminal (TCAT)	¥2,800	At least one bus per hour, 7 am–10:55 pm	
Airport Bus TYO-NRT	Tokyo and Ginza Stations	¥1,300	Every 20-30 mins, 7 am–11 pm	
Narita Limited Express (N'EX)	Central Tokyo Station, then continue to Yokohama or Shinjuku	One-way fare ¥3,070 (return ¥4,070); Green Car from ¥5,340	Daily departures begin at 7:37 am; last train is at 9:44 pm	All seats are reserved.
Keisei Skyliner train	Keisei-Ueno Station	¥2,470	Every 20–30 mins, 7:23 am–11 pm	All seats are reserved.
Keisei Access Express	Keisei-Ueno Station	¥1,240	Every 20–30 mins, 5:46 am–10:34 pm	No seats are reserved.
Taxi	Central Tokyo	¥30,000 or more		
FROM HANEDA	**TO**	**FARES**	**TIMES**	**NOTES**
Tokyo Monorail	Central Tokyo	¥500	Every 20 mins, 5:18 am–midnight	Trip takes 25–30 mins. Connect to other major stations via the Yamanote Line at Hamamatsucho Station (18 mins from Haneda).
Taxi	Central Tokyo	¥5,000–¥6,000		

anywhere from ¥100 to ¥210, which you pay as you board at the front of the bus. Outside Tokyo, depending on the route and municipality, you typically board at the back, take a ticket or tap your card and the cost is determined by the distance you travel. You then put the ticket and the fare in the box as you get off the bus, or tap your card to pay. Bus schedules can be hard to fathom if you don't read Japanese, however, so it's best to ask for help at a tourist information office. The Nihon Bus Association has information about routes and which companies have English Web information.

Car

You must have an international driving permit (IDP) to drive in Japan. IDPs are available from the American Automobile Association and are valid only in conjunction with your regular driver's license (they are really nothing more than a multilingual translation of the information on your driver's license). Drivers must be 18 years of age. Driving is on the left.

Major roads in Japan are sufficiently marked in English, and on country roads there's usually someone to ask for help. However, it's a good idea to have a detailed map with town names written in *kanji* (Japanese characters) and *romaji* (romanized Japanese).

Car travel along the Tokyo–Kyoto–Hiroshima corridor and in other built-up areas of Japan is not as convenient as the trains. Roads are congested, gas is expensive, and highway tolls are exorbitant (tolls alone between Tokyo and Kyoto would cost you around ¥10,550).

Car-rental rates in Tokyo begin at around ¥5,500 a day, and some companies offer a roughly ¥35,000 weekly package, including tax, for an economy car with

unlimited mileage. You should return the car with a full tank of gas, or pay their rate per kilometer traveled.

PARKING
There is little on-street parking in Japan. In busy areas, parking is usually in automated or staffed parking lots or in parking towers within buildings. Expect to pay upward of ¥300 per hour. On busy streets, parking regulations are strictly enforced, and illegally parked vehicles are towed away. Recovery fees start at ¥30,000 and increase hourly. If you're looking to park, look for a large "P" that is typically used to indicate parking.

ROAD CONDITIONS
Roads in Japan are often narrower than those in the United States, but they're well maintained in general. Driving in cities can be troublesome, as there are many narrow, one-way streets and little in the way of English road signs except on major arteries. Japanese drivers tend to stick to the speed limit (except on the expressways), but widely ignore bans on mobile phone use and dashboard televisions.

Motorcycle

Japan is a pleasure to explore via motorcycle provided you are an experienced rider. There are many bikers in Japan, so highways, rest stops, and campgrounds are all equipped to handle whatever bike you choose to tour with. Japan Bike Rentals allows you to do all the paperwork in English—and online. All riders need a passport, a valid unrestricted motorcycle license from their own country, and an International Driving Permit. Japan Bike Rentals is open seven days a week, but you need to make your booking online first, whether to rent a bike, rent a GPS for a self-guided tour, or join a

Getting Here and Around

guided tour. Rental819 has a number of branches in Tokyo featuring Harley-Davidson, Ducati, and Triumph motorcycles.

Ⓜ Public Transport

Tokyo Metro and Toei operate separate subway lines in Tokyo, with Tokyo Metro operating the majority of them. The companies charge separate fares—that is, a ticket from one company is not valid on a train operated by the other, so you want to complete a journey on lines operated by one company rather than switching. Some especially useful lines for visitors are the Ginza Line, which moves between Asakusa and Shibuya, and the Oedo and Marunouchi lines, which loop around the city center.

PURCHASING TICKETS

Basic train and subway fares within Tokyo are between ¥130 and ¥310, depending on how far you travel. If you need to purchase tickets, you'll find machines that take coins or cash near the gates. Maps above each machine—usually in Japanese and English in central Tokyo—list destinations and fares.

■ TIP➜ Sometimes the station map will be written only in Japanese. In that case, buy the lowest-price ticket and adjust the fare upon arrival.

PREPAID CARDS AND PASSES

Suica is a rechargeable debit card that can be used on JR and non-JR trains (see Train Travel below) and also subways. It's also accepted for payment at convenience stores and some vending machines. PASMO, another rechargeable prepaid card, operates the same way. You

need to pay a ¥500 deposit to be issued a Suica or PASMO card, but it's worth it to avoid buying tickets and worrying about fares and have the flexibility to flit between all of Tokyo's transportation networks. The Tokyo 1-Day Ticket (Tokyo Furii Kippu) is a one-day pass for unlimited travel on JR lines, subways, and buses within Tokyo's 23 wards; it costs ¥1,600 and is available at subway stations and JR ticket offices.

Taxi

Taxis are expensive in Japan. In central Tokyo, for instance, the first 1 km costs ¥420 and it's ¥80 for every additional 233 meters (250 yards). Between 10 pm and 5 am there is a 20% service charge on top of that. If possible, avoid using taxis during rush hours (7:30 am–9:30 am and 5 pm–7 pm). The trains will be faster.

In general, it's easy to hail a cab: do not shout or wave wildly—simply raise your hand if you need a taxi. Japanese taxis have automatic door-opening systems, so do not try to open the taxi door. Stand back when the cab comes to a stop—if you are too close, the door may slam into you. When you leave the cab, do not try to close the door; the driver will do it. Only the curbside rear door opens. A red light on the dashboard (visible through the front window) indicates an available taxi (and more and more indicate that in English as well as Japanese), and a green light indicates an occupied one.

Train

Riding Japanese trains is one of the pleasures of travel in the country. Efficient and convenient, trains run frequently and on schedule. The Shinkansen (bullet train), one of the fastest trains in the world, connects major cities north and south of Tokyo. It is only slightly less expensive than flying, but is in many ways more convenient because train stations are more centrally located than airports.

Other trains, though not as fast as the Shinkansen, are just as convenient and substantially cheaper. There are three types of train services: *futsu* (local service), *tokkyu* (limited express service), and *kyuko* (express service). Many tokkyu and kyuko trains have a first-class compartment known as the Green Car.

■TIP➔ **Because there are no porters or carts at train stations, it's a good idea to travel light when getting around by train. You can ship your larger bags to your next destination and bring only a carry-on.**

If you plan to travel by rail, get a Japan Rail Pass, which provides unlimited travel on Japan Railways (JR) trains (covering most destinations in Japan) but not on lines owned by other companies. For the Sanyo, Tokaido, and Kyushu Shinkansen lines, the pass is valid on any trains except the Nozomi and Mizuho, which stop infrequently. However, it is valid on all trains on the Yamagata, Tohoku, Joetsu, Akita, and Hokuriku Shinkansen lines.

The JR Pass is also valid on some local buses operated by Japan Railways, though not on the long-distance JR highway buses. You can make seat reservations without paying a fee on all trains that have reserved-seat coaches, usually long-distance trains. The Japan Rail Pass does not cover the cost of sleeping compartments on overnight trains.

You can purchase one-, two-, or three-week passes. A one-week pass is about as expensive as a regular round-trip ticket from Tokyo to Kyoto on the Shinkansen. You must obtain a rail pass voucher prior to arrival in Japan (you cannot buy them in Japan), and the pass must be used within three months of purchase. The pass is available only to people with tourist visas. Buy it from a travel agent, or reserve it directly online before your trip.

■TIP➔ **When you arrive in Japan, you can exchange your voucher for the Japan Rail Pass. You can do this at the Japan Railways desk in the arrivals hall at Narita Airport or at JR stations in major cities. When you make this exchange, you determine the day that you want the rail pass to begin, and, accordingly, when it ends. You do not have to begin travel on the day you make the exchange.**

Japan Rail Passes are available in coach class and first class (Green Car), and as the difference in price between the two is relatively small, it's worth the splurge for first-class luxury, especially on the Shinkansen. A one-week pass costs ¥33,610 ordinary class, ¥44,810 first class; a two-week pass costs ¥52,690 ordinary class, ¥72,310 first class; and a three-week pass costs ¥66,200 ordinary class, ¥91,670 first class. The one-week pass pays for itself after one Tokyo–Kyoto round-trip Shinkansen ride.

Rail pass holders must still reserve their train seats in advance. Free reservations can made up to two weeks in advance or just minutes before the train departs. If you fail to make a train, there's no penalty, and you can get on the next one.

Transportation Planner

GETTING AROUND BY TRAIN

Japan (and Tokyo in particular) has one of the world's best train and subway systems: trains are nearly always on time, have clean facilities, and provide a safe environment.

Shinkansen: The JR Shinkansen "bullet" trains travel up and down Honshu and into Kyushu. Tokyo Station is Tokyo's main hub, with lines heading north, south, and west. Other Shinkansen lines run to Nagano and Kanazawa, Niigata, Yamagata, and other areas of Tohoku.

Regional trains: About 70% of Japan's railways are owned by Japan Railways (JR Group), the other 30% are owned by private companies. Non-JR lines include Tokyu's Toyoko Line between Tokyo's Shibuya and Yokohama to the south. The main line of the Odakyu Company and Keio Inokashira Line use Shinjuku and Shibuya, respectively, as hubs to serve the west of Tokyo. For service to Saitama Prefecture, Tobu offers the Tojo Line, which leaves Tokyo from Ikebukuro Station. The most important JR-owned regional line in Tokyo is the Yamanote Line, which loops around the city, while its Sobu and Chuo lines cross that circle east to west; JR trains also travel to Tokyo Disneyland.

Subways: The easiest way to explore Tokyo is via subway. There are two subway companies: Tokyo Metro and Toei. Because these are separate entities, they have separate fares, and it's cheaper to stay with one company. At the outer edges of the subway networks, private companies operate the line. If you're going far afield, be prepared to pay an additional fare.

Tokyo monorail: Beginning at Hamamatsu-cho Station, the monorail provides the simplest access to Haneda Airport.

PURCHASING TICKETS

In Tokyo and other major cities basic fares (train or subway) are between ¥120 and ¥330. Tickets can be purchased from machines that take coins or cash near the gates. Maps above the machines—usually in Japanese and English—give destinations and corresponding fares.

■TIP→ **Get a rechargeable train card to make train travel much smoother as you don't have to figure out the ticket price for every trip. These cards can be used for most trains (and some buses) throughout Japan regardless of the city where you buy it.**

The cards have different names depending on the city: in Tokyo, it's **Suica** (from JR machines) or **PASMO** (from subway machines); in Hokkaido, **Kitaca**; in much of the JR West service area, **ICOCA** cards. Tokyo has some one-day passes including the **Tokunai Pass** for unlimited use of JR lines and the **Tokyo Free Kippu,** which covers subways and buses. Purchase tickets for Shinkansen lines and other long-distance regional lines that require a seat reservation at a ticket window.

JR PASS

The Japan Rail Pass can be used on all JR trains including the Shinkansen bullet trains—except for the fastest Nozomi trains on the Tokaido and Sanyo lines and Mizuho trains on the Kyushu Shinkansen. Hikari or Kodama trains and Sakura or Tsubame trains, however, serve these same respective routes and are included. The pass is also valid on local JR buses and on the JR ferry to Miyajima. Passes must be purchased at an authorized JR outlet outside of Japan before your trip and are available for 7-, 14-, or 21-day periods. Activate them on arrival at a major rail station or Narita Airport. A first-class version allows access to the Shinkansen Lines' special Green Cars.

HOW TO USE A TICKET MACHINE

Use the map above the ticket machine to determine how much money to put on your ticket. The numbers next to each stop indicate the price from your current station.

⚠ You'll need your ticket to enter the train's boarding area as well as to exit the station.

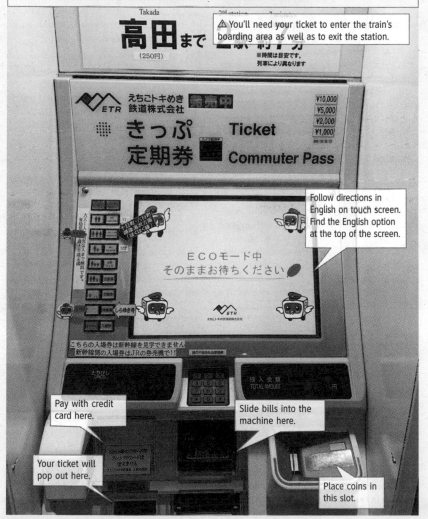

Follow directions in English on touch screen. Find the English option at the top of the screen.

Pay with credit card here.

Slide bills into the machine here.

Your ticket will pop out here.

Place coins in this slot.

Essentials

🧭 Addresses

The simplest way to decipher a Japanese address is to break it into parts. For example: 6-chome 8–19, Chuo-ku, Fukuoka-shi, Fukuoka-ken. In this address the "chome" indicates a precise area (a block, for example), and the numbers following chome indicate the building within the area. In most cases, 6-chome 8-19 will be written just as 6-8-19 in English. Note that buildings aren't always numbered sequentially; numbers are often assigned as buildings are erected. Only local police officers and mail carriers in Japan seem to be familiar with the area defined by the chome. Sometimes, instead of chome, "machi" or "cho" (town) is used. Written addresses in Japan also have the opposite order of those in the West, with the city coming before the street. "Ku" refers to a ward (a district) of a city, "shi" refers to a city name, and "ken" indicates a prefecture, which is roughly equivalent to a state in the United States. It's not unusual for the prefecture and the city to have the same name, as in the above address. There are a few geographic areas in Japan that are not called ken. One is Tokyo, which is called Tokyo-to. Other exceptions are Kyoto and Osaka, which are followed by the suffix "-fu"—Kyoto-fu, Osaka-fu. Hokkaido, Japan's northernmost island, is also not considered a ken. Not all addresses conform exactly to the above format. Rural addresses, for example, might use "gun" (county) where city addresses have "ku" (ward). Even Japanese people cannot find a building based on the address alone, but map apps usually can.

■ TIP➜ If you get in a taxi with a written address, do not assume the driver will be able to find your destination. It's always good to know the location of your destination in relation to a major building or department store.

🍴 Dining

Tokyo is undoubtedly one of the most exciting dining cities in the world. Seasonal ingredients reign supreme here, and there's an emphasis on freshness—not surprising given raw seafood is the cornerstone of sushi. And though Tokyoites still stubbornly resist foreign concepts in many fields, the locals have embraced outside culinary styles with gusto.

While newer restaurants targeting younger diners strive for authenticity in everything from New York–style bagels to Neapolitan pizza, it is still not uncommon to see menus serving East-meets-West concoctions such as spaghetti topped with cod roe and shredded seaweed. That said, the city's best French and Italian establishments can hold their own on a global scale. Naturally, there's also excellent Japanese cuisine available throughout the city, ranging from the traditional to nouveau, which can be shockingly expensive.

That is not to imply that every meal in the city will drain your finances—the popular *B-kyu gurume* (B-class gourmet), restaurants that fill the gap between nationwide chains and fine cuisine, serve tasty Japanese and Asian food without the extra frills of tablecloths and lacquerware. All department stores and many office buildings have at least one floor of restaurants that are accessible, affordable, and reputable.

DRESS
Dining out in Tokyo does not ordinarily demand a great deal in the way of formal attire. If you are attending a business meal with Japanese hosts or guests, dress conservatively: for men, a suit and tie; for women, a dress or suit in a basic color and minimal jewelry. Minimal should also apply to cologne and

perfume. On your own, follow the unspoken dress codes you'd observe at home.

For Japanese-style dining on tatami floors, keep two things in mind: wear shoes that slip on and off easily and presentable socks, and choose clothing you'll be comfortable in for a few hours with your legs gathered under you.

MENUS

Many less-expensive restaurants have picture menus or plastic replicas of the dishes they serve, displayed in their front windows, so you can always point to what you want to eat if the language barrier is insurmountable.

RESERVATIONS

Reservations are always a good idea: we mention them only when they're essential or not accepted. Book as far ahead as you can, and reconfirm as soon as you arrive.

PRICES

Eating at hotels and famous restaurants is costly; however, you can eat well and reasonably at standard restaurants that may not have signs in English.

Many less-expensive restaurants display in their front windows plastic replicas of the dishes they serve, so you can always point to what you want if the language barrier is insurmountable. You will also often find picture menus in cheaper restaurants. Many Japanese restaurants offer *omakase* (chef's choice of a set of dishes), which is a convenient way to order; locals frequently order this way, although it is often the most expensive option.

Good places to look for moderately priced dining spots are in the restaurant concourses of department stores and larger office buildings, usually on the basement levels and the top floors.

All restaurants charge 10% tax, and the price on the menu should include the tax. *Izakaya* (Japanese pubs) often charge a flat table fee (around ¥500 per person), which includes the tiny appetizer that's served to all guests. More expensive restaurants typically add a service charge of 10%, as do some other restaurants when serving large parties. This is usually indicated at the bottom of menus.

Japanese-style restaurants often serve set meals called *teishoku,* which may include rice; soup, and pickled vegetables in addition to the main course—this often costs only slightly more than the main dish itself, which at some restaurants will also be available without the full set.

Prices in the reviews are the average cost of a main course at dinner or, if dinner is not served, at lunch.

What It Costs in Yen			
$	$$	$$$	$$$$
AT DINNER			
Under ¥1,500	¥1,500–¥3,000	¥3,001–¥5,000	over ¥5,000

✚ Health

Japan is a safe, clean country for travelers, with good drinking water and no major water- or insect-borne diseases. Drugs and medications are widely available at drugstores, although the brand names and instructions are in Japanese, so if you're on regular medication, take along enough supplies to cover the trip. As with any international travel, be sure to bring your prescription or a doctor's note just in case. Condoms are sold widely, but they may not have the brands you're used to. Speak with your physician and/or check the CDC or World Health

Essentials

Organization websites for health alerts, particularly if you're pregnant or traveling with children or have a chronic illness.

COVID-19

COVID-19 has disrupted travel since March 2020, and travelers should expect sporadic ongoing issues well into 2023. Always travel with a mask in case it's required, and keep up to date on the most recent testing and vaccination guidelines for Japan.

SPECIFIC ISSUES IN JAPAN

There is always a chance of being caught up in an earthquake in Japan. Information on earthquakes is broadcast (in Japanese) as news flashes on television within minutes, and during major disasters national broadcaster N.H.K. broadcasts information in English on radio and television. Minor tremors occur nearly every month, and sometimes train services are temporarily halted. Check emergency routes at hotels and higher ground if staying near coastal areas.

Mosquitoes can be a minor irritation during the rainy season, and while there is no risk of malaria there have been cases of Japanese encephalitis in recent years. If you are staying for a prolonged period, and spending time in rural Japan, the Japanese encephalitis vaccine is recommended.

OVER-THE-COUNTER REMEDIES

In Japan, medication can be bought only at pharmacies, but every neighborhood seems to have at least one. Ask for the *yakyoku*. Pharmacists in Japan are usually able to manage at least a few words of English and certainly able to read some, so have a pen and paper ready, just in case. In Japanese, aspirin is *asupirin* and Tylenol is *tairenoru*. Following national regulations, Japanese drugs contain less potent ingredients than foreign brands,

so the effects can be disappointing; check advised dosages carefully.

 ## Internet

Except for some traditional ryokan and minshiku, nearly all hotels have Wi-Fi. There are some free services that allow tourists to access a number of hotspots around the country. The most useful way to find free public Wi-Fi service in Japan is to check ⊕ *japanfreewifi.com*.

It's also possible to rent a pocket Wi-Fi router so you can use Google Maps to navigate your way around or to use an online translation app, both of which can be very helpful when you are out and about.

Japan Wireless has plans from ¥4,319 for 10 days though it is more expensive per day the shorter the rental. Ninja WiFi has unlimited data rental plans from ¥990 per day regardless of the rental length. For both, it is best to order online before your trip. You can pick up the portable wi-fi device at a number of airports or have it sent directly to your hotel.

 ## Lodging

Japan may have experienced more than two decades of stagnation following the collapse of the asset-inflated "bubble" economy of the late '90s, but one wouldn't know it from the steadily increasing number of high-end hotels throughout the metropolis. As land prices subsequently fell, Tokyo's developers seized the chance to construct centrally located skyscrapers. Often, hotels from international brands were installed on the upper floors of these glimmering towers. This boom has complemented the spare-no-expense approach taken by many of the domestic hoteliers a decade earlier, when soaring atriums, elaborate concierge floors, and oceans of marble were all the rage. The result: Tokyo's present luxury accommodations rival those of any big city in the world.

Are there bargains to be had? Absolutely, but you'll have to do your homework. Lower-profile business hotels are decent bets for singles or couples who do not need a lot of space, and, in addition to hostels, exchanges, and rentals, the budget-conscious traveler can utilize plenty of Japanese accommodations: ryokan, minshuku, "capsule" hotels, homes, and temples.

A number of boutique hotels—typified by small rooms, utilitarian concepts, and quirky, stylish elements—have popped up in Tokyo. Modern room furnishings of neutral hues are prevalent, but so are such Japanese touches as paper lanterns and tatami flooring. Reception areas are simple spaces bathed in dim lights and surrounded by earth-tone wall panels. Given that these accommodations often contain only a few floors, their locations are likely not easy to find. But when priced at around ¥20,000 a night, they can offer some of the best bargains in a city known for being incredibly expensive.

PRICES
Deluxe hotels charge a premium for good-size rooms, lots of perks, great service, and central locations. More affordable hotels aren't always in the most convenient places and have disproportionately small rooms, as well as fewer amenities. That said, a less-than-ideal location should be the least of your concerns. Many moderately priced accommodations are still within the central hubs; some have an old-fashioned charm and a personal touch the upscale places can't provide. However, wherever

you're staying, Tokyo's subway and train system—comfortable (except in rush hours), efficient, inexpensive, and safe—gets you back and forth.

Prices in the reviews are the lowest cost of a standard double room in high season.

What It Costs in Yen			
$	$$	$$$	$$$$
HOTELS			
under ¥15,000	¥15,000–¥30,000	¥30,001–¥45,000	over ¥45,000

TIMING
It is essential to make your Tokyo hotel reservations before you arrive, especially if traveling during Japan's peak holiday periods—late April to early May, August, and the New Year period.

WESTERN-STYLE LODGING OPTIONS
If culture shock has taken its toll, or you're simply looking for the standard amenities you associate with a hotel stay, try booking one of these options.

INTERNATIONAL HOTELS
Japan's international hotels resemble their counterparts the world over—expect Western-style quarters, English-speaking staff, and high room rates—and they are among the most expensive, tending to fall into the higher price categories.

Most major Western hotel chains, including Hilton, Hyatt, and Sheraton, have built hotels across Japan. Virtually all these properties have Western and Japanese restaurants, room service, Wi-Fi, minibars, *yukata* (cotton robes), concierge services, porters, and business and fitness centers. A few also have swimming pools. And a handful offer Japanese-style rooms—with tatami mats and futons—but these are more expensive.

Essentials

Where Should I Stay?

	NEIGHBORHOOD VIBE	PROS	CONS
Ueno	Entertainment area with rail hub	Large park in area; convenient access to Narita Airport	Some areas are a bit rough for Tokyo.
Asakusa	Historic temple area with quaint shops and restaurants	Plenty of shops selling souvenirs; historic area	Not exactly central
Shiodome	Bayside district of office towers	Numerous hotel options; nearby park	Access for pedestrians can be confusing
Ginza	High-end area with shopping and restaurants	Numerous gallery, restaurant, and shopping options	Can be expensive; a bit sterile
Nihombashi	Historic district that has grown into a trendy dining and shopping spot	Traditional area with numerous restaurant choices	Quiet on weekends
Marunouchi	Business area with numerous shopping and restaurant options	Convenient access to transportation; plenty of shops and restaurants	Business area with a businesslike feel
Akasaka	Business area with lively nightlife scene	Located in central Tokyo; many restaurant and bar choices	Can be noisy and crowded
Shibuya	Shopping and dining playground for young people	Fashionable; many shops, bars, and restaurants	Can be noisy and crowded; Ebisu section can be pricey
Roppongi	Entertainment and business district	Plenty of bars and restaurants; central location	Often noisy; some questionable nightlife
Shinjuku	Large business and entertainment area	Lively entertainment; many hotel choices; convenient access to transportation	Can be overwhelmingly crowded
Mejiro	Residential area	Pleasant, often overlooked area of Tokyo	Surrounding neighborhood might offer little of interest
Odaiba	Man-made island popular with tourists	Amusement parks in area; views of Tokyo Bay	Not located in a central location; touristy

BUSINESS HOTELS

Business hotels are for travelers who need only a place to leave luggage, sleep, and change. Rooms are small, and tend to have a phone, desk, TV (rarely with English-language channels), slippers, yukata or PJs, and bath with a pre-fabricated plastic tub, shower, and sink. These bathrooms are usually clean, but if you're basketball-player size, you might have trouble standing up in them. Other than those facilities, you'll probably only find a restaurant and perhaps a 24-hour receptionist, who probably doesn't speak much English. Business hotels are generally near railway stations. Most fall into the more moderate price categories.

JAPANESE-STYLE LODGING OPTIONS

Looking for someplace to rest your head that echoes the Japanese experience? There are numerous options: ryokan, capsule hotels, home visits, or a stay in a traditional temple.

RYOKAN

There are two kinds of ryokan. One is an expensive traditional inn, where you're served dinner and breakfast in your room and given lots of personal attention. Rates at such places can be exorbitant—at least ¥20,000 per person per night with two meals, but frequently much higher. The other type is an inexpensive hostelry, whose rooms come with futon beds, tatami floor mats, a scroll or a flower arrangement in its rightful place, and, occasionally, meal service.

Tokyo ryokan fall in the latter category. They're often family-run, and service is less a matter of professionalism than of goodwill. Many have rooms either with or without baths (where tubs are likely to be plastic rather than cedarwood) as well as street, rather than garden, views. Because they have few rooms and the owners are usually on hand to answer questions, these small ryokan are as hospitable as they are affordable (from ¥5,000 for a single room to ¥7,000 for a double). Younger travelers love them.

■ TIP→ Many modern hotels with Japanese-style rooms are now referring to themselves as ryokan, and though meals may be served in the guests' rooms, they are a far cry from the traditional ryokan.

CAPSULE HOTELS

Capsule hotels consist of plastic cubicles stacked one atop another. "Rooms" are a mere 3½ feet wide, 3½ feet high, and 7¼ feet long, and they're usually occupied by junior business travelers, backpackers, late-night revelers, or commuters who have missed the last train home. Each capsule has a bed, an intercom, an alarm clock, and a TV. Washing and toilet facilities are shared. You may like the novelty of sleeping in a capsule, but you'll likely limit yourself to one night. Be aware that some capsule hotels do not allow women.

TEMPLES

Accommodations in Buddhist temples provide a taste of traditional Japan. Some have instruction in meditation or allow you to observe their religious practices, while others simply provide a room. The Japanese-style rooms are very simple and range from beautiful, quiet havens to not-so-comfortable, basic cubicles. JNTO has lists of temples that accept guests. A stay generally costs ¥5,000–¥9,000 per night, which includes two meals.

RESERVATIONS

The JNTO's website can link you to booking sites with thousands of reasonably priced accommodations in Tokyo and throughout Japan. These properties welcome foreign tourists, and include business hotels, ryokan, and minshuku. There are roughly 2,500 listings that charge less than ¥8,000 per night.

Essentials

The JTB operates Japanican.com, which allows you to reserve and confirm hotel rooms all over the country, not just in Tokyo.

Nippon Travel Agency is a full-service agency for making all manner of Japan travel arrangements, including lodging reservations.

Rakuten allows you to make all manner of hotel reservations around Japan.

Item	Average Cost
Cup of coffee	¥250–¥600
Glass of wine	¥600–¥1,000
Glass of beer	¥500–¥800
Sandwich (convenience store)	¥300
1-mile taxi ride in capital city	¥700
Museum admission	¥1,000

💲 Money

The unit of currency in Japan is the yen (¥). There are bills of ¥10,000, ¥5,000, ¥2,000, and ¥1,000. Coins are ¥500, ¥100, ¥50, ¥10, ¥5, and ¥1. Japanese currency floats on the international monetary exchange, so changes can be dramatic.

Japan can be expensive, but there are ways to cut costs. This requires, to some extent, an adventurous spirit and the courage to stray from the standard tourist paths. One good way to hold down expenses is to avoid taxis and try the inexpensive, efficient subway and bus systems; instead of going to a restaurant with menus in English and Western-style food, go to places where you can rely on your good old index finger to point to the dish you want, and try food that the Japanese eat.

ATMS AND BANKS

It can be difficult to exchange foreign currency in Japan. The easiest way to obtain yen is at convenience-store ATMs; 7-Eleven stores and Seven Bank ATMs accept most internationally branded cards. Post offices also have ATMs that accept Visa, MasterCard, American Express, Diners Club, and Cirrus cards. However, ATMs at most regular Japanese banks *do not* accept foreign-issue ATM or credit cards.

UFJ and Shinsei banks are members of the Plus network. In more rural areas, it can be difficult to find suitable ATMs, so it is best to get cash before venturing into the countryside. PINs in Japan are made up of four digits. Most machines also have English on-screen instructions.

▼ Nightlife

The sheer diversity of nightlife in Tokyo is breathtaking. Rickety street stands sit yards away from luxury hotels, and wallet-crunching hostess clubs can be found next to cheap and raucous rock bars. Whatever your style, you'll find yourself in good company if you venture out after dark.

Most bars and clubs in the main entertainment districts have printed price lists, often in English. Drinks generally cost ¥800–¥1,200, although some small exclusive bars and clubs can set you back a lot more. Be wary of establishments without visible price lists. Hostess clubs and small backstreet bars known as "snacks" or "pubs" can be particularly treacherous territory for the unprepared. That drink you've just ordered could set you back a reasonable ¥1,000; you might, on the other hand, have wandered unknowingly into a place that charges you ¥30,000 up front for a whole bottle—and slaps a

¥20,000 cover charge on top. If the bar has hostesses, it's often unclear what the companionship of one will cost you, but you can bet a lot. Ignore the persuasive shills on the streets of Roppongi and Kabuki-cho, who will try to hook you into their establishment. There is, of course, plenty of safe ground: in hotel lounges, jazz clubs, craft beer pubs, sake bars, and sedate retreats where the social lubricant flows past millions of tonsils nightly.

Major nightlife districts in Tokyo include Aoyama, Ginza, Roppongi, Shibuya, Shinbashi, and Shinjuku. Each has a unique atmosphere, clientele, and price level.

◻ Packing

Pack light, because porters can be hard to find and storage space in hotel rooms may be tiny. What you pack depends more on the time of year than on any dress code. Pack for Tokyo as you would for any American or European city. At the most exclusive restaurants and bars men may need to wear a jacket and tie, although dress codes for most places are generally far more casual. Jeans are as popular in Japan as they are in the United States, and are perfectly acceptable for informal dining and sightseeing.

Although there are no strict dress codes for visiting temples and shrines, you will be out of place in immodest outfits. For sightseeing leave sandals and open-toe shoes behind; you'll need sturdy walking shoes for the gravel pathways that surround temples and fill parks. Make sure to bring comfortable clothing that isn't too tight to wear in traditional Japanese restaurants, where you may need to sit on tatami-matted floors.

Japanese people do not wear shoes in private homes or in any temples or traditional inns. Having shoes you can quickly slip in and out of is a decided advantage. Take wool socks to help you through those shoeless occasions in winter.

Lodgings generally provide a thermos of hot water or electric kettle and bags of green tea in every room. Western-style accommodations may also have in-room instant coffee or free coffee in the lobby. If not, you can buy very sweet coffee in a can from a vending machine or purchase packets of instant coffee at local convenience stores for your room. If you're staying in a Japanese inn, there's a chance that coffee will not be included with your breakfast.

Many hotels provide toiletries, toothbrushes, slippers, and even pajamas.

Take along small gift items, such as scarves or perfume sachets, to thank hosts (on both business and pleasure trips), whether you've been invited to their home or out to a restaurant.

◻ Performing Arts

Tokyo's rich cultural history entwines itself with an influx of foreign influences, so Tokyoites get the best of both worlds. An astonishing variety of dance and music, both classical and popular and much of it Western, can be found in Tokyo, alongside the must-see traditional Japanese arts of Kabuki and Noh.

The city is a proving ground for local talent and a magnet for orchestras and concert soloists from all over the world. Tokyo also has modern theater—in somewhat limited choices, to be sure, unless you can follow dialogue in Japanese,

Essentials

but Western repertory companies can always find receptive audiences here for plays in English. And it doesn't take long for a hit show from New York or London to open. Musicals such as *Mamma Mia!* have found enormous popularity here—although the protagonists speak Japanese.

Among about 10 professional dance troupes in Japan, the best known are the New National Ballet, which usually performs at the New National Theater, and the K-Ballet Company and the Tokyo Ballet, both of which stage performances at the Bunka Kaikan in Ueno and Orchard Hall of the Bunkamura complex in Shibuya. Tokyo has plenty of venues for opera, and few groups to perform in them, so touring companies like the Metropolitan, the Bolshoi, Sadler's Wells, and the Bayerische Staatsoper find Tokyo a very compelling venue—as well they might when even seats at ¥30,000 or more sell out far in advance.

Tokyo movie theaters screen a broad range of films—everything from big Asian hits to American blockbusters and Oscar nominees. The diversity brought by smaller distributors and an increased appetite for Korean, Middle Eastern, South American, and Aussie cinema have helped develop vibrant small theaters that cater to art-house fans. New multiplexes have also brought new screens to the capital, providing a more comfortable film-going experience than some of the older Japanese theaters.

Metropolis, a free English-language weekly magazine, has up-to-date listings of what's going on in the city; its available at hotels, book and music stores,

some restaurants and cafés, and other locations. The online magazine Time Out Tokyo also has up-to-date event, bar, and restaurant listings.

◉ Restrooms

The most hygienic restrooms are found in hotels and department stores, and are usually clearly marked with international symbols. You may encounter Japanese-style toilets, with bowls recessed into the floor, over which you squat facing the top of the tank. This may take some getting used to, but it's completely sanitary, as you don't come into direct contact with the facility. If you want to avoid squatting, check out the last cubicle in the row, because it may be a Western-style toilet.

In many homes and Japanese-style public places, there will be a pair of slippers at the entrance to the restroom. Change into these before entering the room, and change back when you exit.

Toilets in some train stations don't have toilet paper, though there are dispensers where packets can be purchased for ¥50 or so. Many locals accept the free tissue packets that are handed out as advertisements in the center of town for this reason. Similarly, paper towel dispensers and hand dryers are not always installed, so bring a small handkerchief or washcloth with you, as well as some hand sanitizer.

$ Taxes

A 10% national consumption tax is added to all hotel bills. There is also a local Tokyo tax of ¥100 per night for bills between ¥10,000 and ¥14,999 and ¥200 for bills over ¥15,000.

At first-class, full-service, and luxury hotels, a 10% service charge is added to the bill in place of individual tipping. At more expensive ryokans, where individualized maid service is provided, the service charge is usually 15%. At business hotels, minshuku, youth hostels, and economy inns, no service charge is added to the bill.

There's an across-the-board, nonrefundable 10% consumption tax levied on all sales. Authorized tax-free shops knock the tax off purchases over ¥10,000 if you show your passport and a valid tourist visa. A large sign is displayed at such shops. A 10% tax is also added to all restaurant bills. At more expensive restaurants a 10%–15% service charge can be added to the bill. Tipping is not customary.

$ Tipping

Tipping is not common in Japan. It's not necessary to tip taxi drivers, or at hair salons, barbershops, bars, or nightclubs. A chauffeur for a hired car usually receives a tip of ¥500 for a half-day excursion and ¥1,000 for a full-day trip. It's not customary to tip employees of hotels, even porters or cleaning staff, unless a special service has been rendered. You can tip servers in a traditional ryokan as meals are served in your room. Plan to tip ¥1,000 per day's stay.

⊙ Visitor Information

The Japan National Tourism Organization (JNTO) has offices in Japan, the United States, and other countries. The JNTO and Japan Tourism Agency have also certified more than 1,000 tourist information counters/offices nationwide. Look for the sign showing a red question mark and the word "information" at train stations and city centers.

⊞ When to Go

Spring and fall are the best times to visit. *Sakura* (cherry blossoms) begin blooming in Tokyo by early April, while fall has clear blue skies, albeit punctuated by the occasional typhoon. The short *tsuyu* (rainy season) in June brings humidity and rain that can linger into early July. July and August bring heat, mostly blue skies, and stifling humidity. Winter can be gray and chilly some days, mild and sunny others, with Tokyo and other areas along the coast receiving very little snow. Japanese vacation during three holiday periods: the few days before and after New Year's; Golden Week in early May; and the mid-August week for Obon. Travel's not advised during these times, as plane and train tickets book up fast.

Helpful Japanese Phrases

BASICS

Hello/Good day	こんにちは。	kon-ni-chi-wa
Yes/no	はい / いいえ	hai / ii-e
Please	お願いします	o-ne-gai shi-ma-su
Thank you (very much)	ありがとう (ございます)	a-ri-ga-tō (go-zai-ma-su)
You're welcome	どういたしまして。	dō i-ta-shi-mashi-te
I'm sorry (apology)	ごめんなさい。	go-men na-sai
Sorry (Excuse me)	すみません。	su-mi-ma-sen
Good morning	おはようございます	o-ha-yō go-zai-ma-su
Good evening	こんばんは。	kom-ban-wa
Goodbye	さようなら。	sa-yō-na-ra
Pleased to meet you	はじめまして。	haji-me-mashi-te
How are you?	おげんき ですか。	o-gen-ki desu-ka

NUMBERS

half	半分	han-bun
one	一 / 一つ	i-chi / hi-to-tsu
two	二 / 二つ	ni / fu-ta-tsu
three	三 / 三つ	san / mit-tsu
four	四 / 四つ	yon (shi) / yot-tsu
five	五 / 五つ	go / i-tsu-tsu
six	六 / 六つ	ro-ku / mut-tsu
seven	七 / 七つ	na-na (shi-chi) / na-na-tsu
eight	八 / 八つ	ha-chi / yat-tsu
nine	九 / 九つ	kyū / ko-ko-no-tsu
ten	十 / とう	jū / tō
eleven	十一	jū i-chi
twelve	十二	jū ni
thirteen	十三	jū san
fourteen	十四	jū yon
fifteen	十五	jū go
sixteen	十六	jū ro-ku
seventeen	十七	jū na-na
eighteen	十八	jū ha-chi
nineteen	十九	jū-kyū
twenty	二十	ni-jū
twenty-one	二十一	ni-jū i-chi
thirty	三十	san jū
forty	四十	yon jū
fifty	五十	go jū
sixty	六十	ro-ku jū
seventy	七十	na-na jū
eighty	八十	ha-chi jū
ninety	九十	kyū jū
one hundred	百	hyaku
one thousand	千 / 一千	sen / is-sen
ten thousand	一万	i-chi man
one hundred thousand	十万	jū man
one million	百万	hya-ku man

COLORS

black	黒	ku-ro
blue	青	ao
brown	茶色	cha-iro
green	緑	mi-do-ri
orange	オレンジ	o-ren-ji
purple	紫	mu-ra-sa-ki
red	赤	a-ka
white	白	shi-ro
yellow	黄色	ki-iro

DAYS OF THE WEEK

Sunday	日曜日	ni-chi yō-bi
Monday	月曜日	ge-tsu yō-bi
Tuesday	火曜日	ka yō-bi
Wednesday	水曜日	su-i yō-bi
Thursday	木曜日	mo-ku yō-bi
Friday	金曜日	kin yō-bi
Saturday	土曜日	dō yō-bi

MONTHS

January	一月	i-chi ga-tsu
February	二月	ni ga-tsu
March	三月	san ga-tsu
April	四月	shi ga-tsu
May	五月	go ga-tsu
June	六月	ro-ku ga-tsu
July	七月	shi-chi ga-tsu
August	八月	ha-chi ga-tsu
September	九月	ku ga-tsu
October	十月	jū ga-tsu
November	十一月	jū-i-chi ga-tsu
December	十二月	jū-ni ga-tsu

USEFUL WORDS AND PHRASES

Do you understand English?	英語がわかりますか。	ei-go ga wa-ka-ri-ma-su ka
I don't understand Japanese	日本語がわかりません。	ni-hon-go ga wa-ka-ri-ma-sen
I don't understand	わかりません。	wa-ka-ri-ma-sen
I don't know	知りません。	shi-ri-ma-sen
I understand	わかりました。	wa-ka-ri-ma-shi-ta
I'm American	私はアメリカ人です。	wa-ta-shi wa a-me-ri-ka jin de-su
I'm British	私はイギリス人です。	wa-ta-shi wa i-gi-ri-su jin de-su
I'm Australian	私はオーストラリア人です。	wa-ta-shi wa ō-su-to-ra-ri-a jin de-su
What's your name	お名前はなんですか。	o- na-ma-e wa nan de-su ka
My name is	[name] と申します。	[name] to-mō-shi-ma-su
What time is it?	今何時ですか。	i-ma nan-ji de-su ka
How?	どうやって ですか。	dō-yat-te de-su ka
When?	いつ ですか。	i-tsu de-su ka

Yesterday	昨日	ki-nō
Today	今日	kyō
Tomorrow	明日	ashi-ta
This morning	けさ	ke-sa
This afternoon	今日の午後	kyō no go-go
Tonight	今晩	kom-ban
What?	何ですか。	nan de-su ka
What is this / that?	これ / それ は何ですか。	ko-re / so-re wa nan de-su ka
Why?	どうしてですか。	dō-shi-te de-su ka
Who?	どなたですか。	do-na-ta de-su ka
Where is [place / thing]?	[place / thing] はどこですか。	[place / thing] wa do-ko de-su ka
station	駅	e-ki
subway station	地下鉄の駅	chi-ka-te-tsu no e-ki
bus stop	バス乗り場	ba-su no-ri-ba
airport	空港	kū-kō
post office	郵便局	yū-bin-kyo-ku
bank	銀行	gin-kō
hotel	ホテル	ho-te-ru
museum	博物館	ha-ku-bu-tsu-kan
art museum / art gallery	美術館	bi-ju-tsu-kan
hospital	病院	byō-in
elevator	エレベーター	e-re-bē-tā
Where is the restroom?	トイレはどこですか。	to-i-re wa do-ko de-su ka
Here / there / over there	ここ / そこ / あそこ	ko-ko / so-ko / a-so-ko
Left / right	左 / 右	hi-da-ri / mi-gi
Is it near / far?	近い / 遠い ですか。	chi-ka-i / tō-i de-su ka
Do you have	[item] が ありますか。	[item] ga a-ri-ma-su-ka
a room	部屋	he-ya
a city map	市内地図	shi-nai chi-zu
a road map	ロードマップ	rō-do map-pu
a notebook	ノート	nō-to
a notepad	メモ用紙	me-mo-yō-shi
a magazine in English	英語の 雑誌	ei-go no zas-shi
a postcard	はがき	ha-ga-ki
a stamp	切手	kit-te
a ticket	切符	kip-pu
envelopes	封筒	fū-tō
How much is it?	いくらですか。	i-ku-ra de-su ka
It's expensive / cheap	高い / 安い です。	ta-ka-i / ya-su-i de-su
A little / a lot	少し / たくさん	su-ko-shi / ta-ku-san
More / less	もっと多く / 少なく	mot-to ō-ku/ su-ku-na-ku
Enough / too many	十分 / 多すぎる	jū-bun / ō-su-gi-ru
I feel sick	体調が悪い。	tai-chō ga wa-ru-i
Call a doctor / ambulance	医者 / 救急車 を呼んでください。	i-sha / kyū-kyū-sha o yon-de ku-da-sai

Help!	助けて!	ta-su-ke-te
Stop!	やめて!	ya-me-te

DINING OUT

A bottle of / a cup of	一本 / 一杯	ip-pon / ip-pai
Two bottles of / two cups of	二本 / 二杯	ni-hon / ni-hai
Aperitif	食前酒	sho-ku-zen shu
Beer	ビール	bii-ru
Bill / check, please	お勘定 お願いします。	o- kan-jō o-ne-ga-i-shi-ma-su
Bread	パン	pan
Breakfast	朝食 / 朝ごはん	chō-sho-ku / a-sa go-han
Butter	バター	ba-tā
Cocktail	カクテル	ka-ku-te-ru
Coffee	コーヒー	kō-hī
Dinner	夕食 / 晩ごはん	yū-sho-ku / ban go-han
Fork	フォーク	fō-ku
I am a vegetarian	私は 菜食主義者 / ベジタリアンです。	wa-ta-shi wa saisho-ku shu-gi-sha / be-ji-ta-ri-an de-su
I cannot eat [item]	[item] は食べられません。	[item] wa ta-be-ra-re-ma-sen
I'm ready to order	注文 お願いします。	chū-mon o-ne-ga-i-shi-ma-su
I'm hungry	お腹が空いています。	o-na-ka ga su-i-te i-ma-su
I'm thirsty	喉が渇いています。	no-do ga ka-wai-te i-ma-su
It's delicious	美味しい です。	oi-shī de-su
It doesn't taste good	美味しくない です。	oi-shi ku-nai de-su
It's hot (Be careful, please)	暑いです。(気を付けてください。)	a-tsu-i de-su (ki-o-tsu-ke-te ku-da-sai)
Knife	ナイフ	nai-fu
Lunch	昼食 / 昼ごはん	chū-sho-ku / hi-ru go-han
Menu	メニュー	me-nyū
Napkin	ナプキン	na-pu-kin
Pepper	こしょう	ko-shō
Plate	皿	sa-ra
Please give me [item]	[item] をください。	[item] o ku-da-sai
Salt	塩	shi-o
Spoon	スプーン	su-pūn
Tea (Japanese teas)	お茶	o-cha
Tea (other teas)	紅茶	kō-cha
Water	水	mi-zu
Rice wine (sake)	日本酒	ni-hon-shu

Great Itineraries

Tokyo in 3 Days

Tokyo is a metropolis that confounds with its complexity: 37 million people occupy a greater metropolitan area that includes soaring towers of glass and steel, rolling expressways, numerous temples, parks, and mile after mile of concrete housing blocks. Since the end of World War II, the city has constantly reinvented itself. Few things have remained static other than Tokyo's preeminence as Japan's economic center.

DAY 1: GINZA AND SHIODOME

Start with a morning stroll through **Ginza** to explore its fabled shops and *depato* (department stores). Then hit a chic restaurant or café for lunch (more reasonably priced ones are found on the upper floors of most department stores). The skyscrapers of **Shiodome** are just down the street, in the direction of **Shimbashi**. Take a peek on the first floor of the **Shiodome Media Tower**; aerial photographs show Ginza as it was roughly 100 years ago—a network of canals. In the skyscrapers' shadows are the charming Hama Rikyu Teien Gardens, whose pathways and ponds are ideal for a stroll. In the evening, head back up toward Ginza and enjoy *yakitori* (grilled chicken) at one of the many small restaurants under the elevated railway lines in **Yurakucho.**

DAY 2: ASAKUSA AND UENO

Spend the morning at **Senso-ji** and adjacent **Asakusa Jinja** in Asakusa. If you're looking for souvenir gifts—sacred or secular—allow time and tote space for the abundant selection the local vendors along **Nakamise-dori** or any of the covered shopping streets have to offer. A 15-minute walk west is **Kappabashi**, a street dedicated to outfitting restaurants and bars with dishes, cups, chopsticks, and even plastic food models. From there go to **Ueno** for an afternoon of museums, markets, vistas, and historic sites, and take a break at **Ueno Park.** Keep in mind that in the evening the crowds in Asakusa are not as intrusive as during the day, and many of the major attractions, including the five-tier pagoda of Senso-ji, are brightly lighted. It's worth it to loop back to get a different view of the area and end the evening with dinner at one of Asakusa's *izakaya* (think of them as drinking dens with lots of food).

DAY 3: SHIBUYA AND SHINJUKU

Start off at Shibuya's **Hachiko Square** and the famous Shibuya Crossing intersection and hit nearby stores like **Shibuya 109,** which is crammed with teen fashion boutiques. Inside the station building is the once-lost masterpiece by avant-garde artist **Taro Okamoto** *Myth of Tomorrow,* while towering over the east side of the station is the 34-story **Shibuya Hikarie building,** one of the many recent redevelopments filled with shops, restaurants, and businesses to hit Tokyo. In the afternoon see the Shinto **Meiji Shrine,** and walk through the nearby Harajuku and **Omotesando** fashion districts. Spend the rest of the afternoon on the west side of **Shinjuku,** Tokyo's 21st-century model city, and savor the view from the observation deck of architect Kenzo Tange's monumental **Tokyo Metropolitan Government Building**; cap off the late afternoon by visiting **Shinjuku Gyo-en National Garden.** For those seeking a bit of excitement, the red-light district of **Kabuki-cho,** just to the east of **JR Shinjuku Station,** comes alive once the sun goes down; Kabuki-cho and neighboring Golden Gai are full of good places to eat and drink.

Tokyo in 5 Days

Add these two days onto the three-day itinerary.

DAY 4: AKIHABARA AND IMPERIAL PALACE

Spend the morning browsing in **Akihabara,** Tokyo's electronics quarter, and see the nearby Shinto shrine **Kanda Myojin.** In the afternoon, tour the **Imperial Palace** and the grounds surrounding it. The **Chidorigafuchi Moat** is surrounded by a wonderful park and has a boat-rental facility—both great for unwinding. If the **Yomiuri Giants** are in town, catch a game at **Tokyo Dome** in the evening. If not, try a traditional hot spring bath at LaQua or ride the roller coaster at adjacent Tokyo Dome City.

DAY 5: GET OUT OF TOWN TO KAMAKURA

For a different perspective of Japan, spend a day out of Tokyo. Easily accessible by train is **Kamakura,** the 13th-century military capital of the country. The **Great Buddha** (Daibutsu) of **Kotoku-in Temple** and nearby **Hase Temple** are but just some of the many treasures of art and architecture in and around Kamakura. An early start will allow you to see most of the important sights in a full day and make it back to Tokyo by late evening. As Kamakura is one of the most popular of excursions from Tokyo, avoid the worst of the crowds by going on a weekday, but time it to avoid rush-hour commuting that peaks roughly at 8 am and just after 6 pm.

IF YOU HAVE MORE TIME

With a week or more, you can make Tokyo your base for more side trips. An easy day trip is to take a train to **Yokohama,** with its scenic port and Chinatown. Farther off, but again an easy train trip, is **Nikko,** where the founder of the Tokugawa Shogun dynasty is enshrined. The decadently designed **Tosho-gu** shrine complex is a monument unlike any other in Japan, and the picturesque **Lake Chuzenji** is in forests nearby. Two full days, with an overnight stay, would allow you an ideal, leisurely exploration of both. Another option would be a trip to **Hakone,** where you can soak in a traditional onsen or climb to the summit of Fuji-san (Mt. Fuji). You could also putter around Tokyo some more to fill in the missing pieces: see the Buddhist temple, **Sengaku-ji,** in Shinagawa; the remarkable **Edo-Tokyo Museum** in Ryogoku; a tea ceremony; a Kabuki play; or a sumo tournament, if one is in town. Or head to Odaiba in Tokyo Bay for attractions that include the **National Museum of Emerging Science and Innovation** (simply known as the **Miraikan), Palette Town's** malls and Ferris wheel, and the **Oedo Monogatari Onsen** baths.

A Walk through Everyday Tokyo

Tokyo's soul is found in its *shitamachi*, the neighborhoods that define much of the city's east side. Spend a few hours walking here to discover old neighborhoods, ancient temples, and cultural riches.

YANAKA

The central shopping street **Yanaka Ginza** is crammed with mom-and-pop stores and small eateries, some having a feel as if they've remained unchanged since the Meiji era of the late 1860s through the early 1910s. Leave behind Yanaka's main street and you will soon be lost in a captivating maze of back alleys that lead past quiet temples and shrines, many eventually skirting the sprawling **Yanaka Cemetery,** a beautiful spot in cherry blossom season. The last of the Tokugawa shoguns is buried here, as are many other colorful characters in Tokyo's history.

UENO

Walking southeast from Yanaka, it's a fairly short walk to **Ueno Park** (or you can walk to JR Nippori Station and take the Yamanote Line to Ueno). Here you'll find the city's most well-known zoo, an ancient temple, and plenty of green spaces, but the main reason the park stands out is the museums that dot the grounds. On the north end, **Tokyo National Museum** holds an unparalleled collection of Japanese and Asian artifacts, dating from as far back as the Jomon period. Moving south, the **National Science Museum** is a great hands-on stop for kids, while at the southern end of the park the **Shitamachi Museum** does a wonderful job of revealing the history and development of Tokyo's working-class areas. Across the road from the park's southeast end, the vendors of the bustling **Ameyoko** street market sell everything from knock-off designer clothing to fine teas.

HIGHLIGHTS
The old, narrow streets of Yanaka, the museums and street market of Ueno, the culinary-ware stores of Kappabashi, historic Senso-ji, and the historic Asakusa district.

WHERE TO START
Start at the Yanaka Ginza shopping street, a couple of minutes' walk from the west exit of Nippori Station on the JR Yamanote Line.

TIME/LENGTH
6 km (4 miles); duration about three hours without food stops.

WHERE TO END
At Asakusa Station on the Ginza Line.

BEST TIME TO GO
Weekdays are best to avoid the worst crowds.

WORST TIME TO GO
Mid-July to mid-September, when the summer heat and humidity can make being outside for too long very unpleasant.

GETTING AROUND
The walk is best done entirely on foot, but an alternative is to take the Ginza subway line from Ueno Station to Kappabashi (Tawaramachi Station) and from there to Asakusa Station.

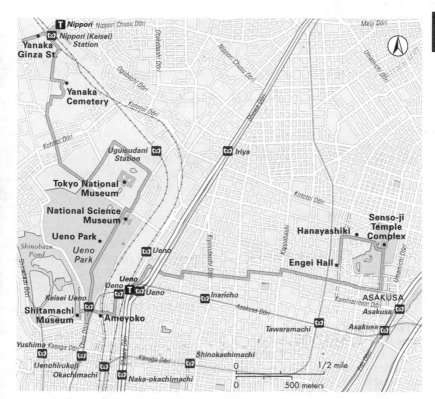

KAPPABASHI

Leaving Ueno and walking east, the next highlight is Kappabashi. In the early 1900s, merchants selling culinary wares began to converge on this half-mile-long street, and it is now where Tokyo's restaurant trade goes to stock up on everything from disposable chopsticks to hanging lanterns. Among the 170 shops here are several that specialize in the plastic replicas of food that many restaurants display in their windows.

ASAKUSA

East of Kappabashi's southern end is Asakusa. At the heart of this district is the mighty **Senso-ji Temple complex**, with its grand five-story pagoda, giant gateways, and colorful street stalls. A several-minute walk west of Senso's main temple building is **Hanayashiki,** a tiny amusement park that's home to Japan's oldest roller coaster. In the streets south of Hanayashiki are historic theaters like **Engei Hall,** which, like Hanayashiki, serve as reminders of Asakusa's prewar days as Tokyo's main entertainment district. The *yakitori-ya* that spill out on the street around here are great places to grab some grilled chicken and a beer and rest your feet.

On the Calendar

January

JANUARY BASHO
This tournament at Kokugikan Sumo Hall sees the sport's best get in their first licks of the year. Two 15-day tournaments take place in the same venue in May and September.

February

SETSUBUN
Celebrating the end of winter in the lunar calendar on February 3 or 4, people throw around dry soybeans to drive away evil at major temples and at home (you can buy devil masks and beans at convenience stores).

March

CHERRY BLOSSOMS
In late March and early April, Tokyoites celebrate the annual arrival of pink cherry blossoms by heading out in huge numbers to eat and drink at sakura spots all over the city.

OPENING DAY
Japan's 12 baseball teams kick off their season at the end of March. Tokyo teams include the Yakult Swallows and Yomiuri Giants, while the Chiba Lotte Marines, Seibu Lions, and Yokohama DeNA Baystars are based in neighboring prefectures within the region.

April

KANAMARA MATSURI
On the first Sunday in April, the Kanamara fertility festival in Kawasaki sees parades of giant pink phalluses and some of Japan's most interestingly shaped street food.

May

SANJA FESTIVAL
Asakusa's streets see dozens of portable shrines hoisted through huge crowds for three days in May.

June

SANNO MATSURI
One of Tokyo's biggest traditional events has parades of portable shrines accompanied by priests, musicians, and dancers.

July

SUMIDA RIVER FIREWORKS
The skies of eastern Tokyo burst with color on the last Saturday of July.

SHITAMACHI TANABATA FESTIVAL
Also known as the Star Festival, this early July traditional event celebrates the legend of two separated stars who can only meet once a year in the Milky Way. It is marked with parades, performances, and a custom where attendees write their wishes on paper and tie it to the bamboo branches that line the streets.

August

ASAKUSA SAMBA
On the last weekend of the month, dozens of samba troupes transform Asakusa at this high-energy, sun-baked annual event.

ASAKUSA TORO NAGASHI
Participants decorate lanterns, then set them afloat along the Sumida River at dusk as they make a wish. Lanterns are available to buy at the venue the day of, but expect long lines.

AWA-ODORI

In mid-August the streets of Koenji are packed with dancers and musicians for the Tokyo version of Tokushima's historic and frenzied dance festival.

HARAJUKU OMOTESANDO SUPER YOSAKOI FESTIVAL

This is one of Tokyo's most spectacular dance festivals, in which over 100 regional teams wear original costumes influenced by their local culture and inspired by modern trends as they parade, perform, and compete around the streets and stages of Omotesando and Harajuku.

September

REITAISAI

In the middle of the month, Tsurugaoka Hachimangu Shrine's early-autumn festival includes a spectacular display of horseback archery (*yabusame*). The same happens at the spring festival in AprIl.

TOKYO GAME SHOW

Fans of video games crowd the Makuhari Messe convention center in September to check out the hottest releases.

October

TOKYO INTERNATIONAL FILM FESTIVAL

Over 10 days in late October, films from around the world are screened at the theaters in the Roppongi Hills complex.

TOKYO DESIGN WEEK

The latest in art, fashion, design, and music gets showcased in late October and early November.

November

ILLUMINATIONS

As Christmas approaches, major complexes like Tokyo Midtown and districts like Marunouchi turn on spectacular street illuminations for a festive (and romantic) mood.

SHICHI-GO-SAN

In early November, tradition meets super-cute. Meaning "seven, five, three," children of those ages visit shrines in fine kimono to pray for a good future.

ASAKUSA TORINOICHI FAIR

Tori-no-ichi is an annual festival that has been celebrated at shrines and temples across Japan since the Edo period. In the Asakusa area of Tokyo, these festivities take place at two adjoining venues: Chokokuji Temple and Otori Shrine. The surrounding area buzzes until late at night with merchants selling beautiful gold- and silver-decorated kumade, ornamental rakes believed to bring their owners good fortune and prosperity. After making a purchase, the entire shop's staff will clap their hands rhythmically to show their appreciation and to bless you with good health, luck, and business.

TOKYO COMIC CON

This convention is a must if you are a fan or just want to experience the manga and anime culture in Japan.

December

COMIKET

The second installment (the first is August) of this semiannual comic and manga event draws hundreds of thousands of people to Tokyo Big Sight in December for the biggest convention of its kind in the world.

70

Contacts

Air

AIRPORTS Haneda Airport (HND). ☎ 03/5757–8111 ⊕ www.tokyo-airport-bldg.co.jp/en. **Narita Airport (NRT).** ☎ 0476/34–8000 ⊕ www.narita-airport.jp.

AIRPORT TRANSPORTATION Japan Railways. ☎ 050/2016–1603 for JR East InfoLine ⊕ www.jreast.co.jp/e. **Keisei Railway.** ☎ 0476/34–6261 ⊕ www.keisei.co.jp/keisei/tetudou/skyliner/us. **Tokyo Shuttle.** ⊕ www.keiseibus.co.jp/inbound/tokyoshuttle/en.

AIRLINE CONTACTS All Nippon Airways. ☎ 800/235–9262 in U.S., 03/6741–1120 in Japan ⊕ www.ana.co.jp. **American Airlines.** ☎ 800/433–7300 in U.S., 03/3298–7677 in Japan ⊕ www.aa.com. **Delta Airlines.** ☎ 800/241–4141 in U.S., 0570/077–733 in Japan ⊕ www.delta.com. **Japan Airlines.** ☎ 800/525–3663 in U.S., 03/6733–3062 in Japan ⊕ www.jal.co.jp/en. **United Airlines.** ☎ 800/864–8331 in U.S., 03/6732–5011 in Japan ⊕ www.united.com.

AIR PASSES ANA Experience Japan Fare. ☎ 800/235–9262 All Nippon Airways in U.S. ⊕ www.ana.co.jp. **Japan Explorer Pass.** ☎ 800/525–3663 Japan Airlines ⊕ www.jal.co.jp.

Bus

BUS INFORMATION Nihon Bus Association. ⊕ www.bus.or.jp/en. **Willer Express.** ☎ 050/5805–0383 ⊕ willerexpress.com/en.

Embassy

U.S. Embassy and Consulate. ✉ 1–10–5 Akasaka, Minato-ku, Tokyo ☎ 03/3224–5000 ⊕ japan.usembassy.gov Ⓜ Namboku Line, Tameike-Sanno Station (Exit 13).

Internet

WI-FI RENTAL Japan Connected-Free Wi-Fi. ⊕ www.ntt-bp.net/jcfw/en.html. **PuPuRu Mobile Phone Rental.** ☎ 03/3560–9566 ⊕ pupuruwifi.com.

Lodging

CONTACTS JNTO Hotel and Ryokan Search. ✉ Tokyo ⊕ www.jnto.go.jp/ja-search/eng/index.php. **Rakuten Travel.** ⊕ travel.rakuten.com. **Japanican.** ✉ Tokyo ⊕ www.japanican.com.

Motorcycle

CONTACTS Japan Bike Rentals. ☎ 03/4578–2086 ⊕ japanbikerentals.com. **Rental819.** ☎ 050/6861–5819 ⊕ www.rental819.com/english.

Public Transport

CONTACTS Toei. ⊕ www.kotsu.metro.tokyo.jp/eng. **Tokyo Metro.** ⊕ www.tokyometro.jp/en.

PREPAID CARDS AND PASSES PASMO. ⊕ www.pasmo.co.jp/en. **Suica.** ⊕ www.jreast.co.jp/e/pass/suica.html. **Tokyo 1-Day Ticket.** ⊕ www.jreast.co.jp/e/pass/tokyo_free.html.

Train

CONTACTS East Japan Railway Company. ☎ 050/2016–1603 ⊕ www.jreast.co.jp/e. **Jorudan Train Route Finder.** ⊕ world.jorudan.co.jp/mln/en.

BUYING A PASS Japan Rail Pass. ⊕ www.japanrailpass.net.

Chapter 3

A JAPANESE CULTURE PRIMER

3

Updated by
Jay Farris

Something about Japan led you to pick up this book and contemplate a trip. Perhaps it was a meal at your favorite sushi bar back home, the warm tones of an exquisite piece of Japanese pottery, or a Japanese novel or film. Whatever it was that sparked your interest, it's a good bet that something you find in this chapter will make your trip unforgettable.

There is a display of horsemanship called *yabusame* (now to be seen mainly at shrine festivals) in which a mounted archer, in medieval costume, challenges a narrow roped-off course lined at 260-foot intervals with small wooden targets on bamboo posts: the rider has to come down the course at full gallop, drop the reins, nock an arrow, aim and release, and take the reins again—with only seconds to set up again for the next target. Few archers manage a perfect score—but "merely hitting the target is secondary," explains a yabusame official.

Therein lies the key to understanding the fundamentals of Japanese identity as well as its various regional cultures: the passionate attention to form and process. The results are also important, of course; otherwise the forms would be empty gestures. But equally important—perhaps more important— is how you get there. Not for nothing are so many of these disciplines, from the tea ceremony to calligraphy to the martial arts, presented to us as Ways; excellence in any one of them depends on doing it the way it's supposed to be done according to traditions that may be centuries old. Philosophically, this is all about how rules can liberate: spend enough time and effort on the mastery of forms, and one day they leave the realm of conscious thought and become part of you. You are to lose yourself in the Way. Not for nothing, either, are so many elements of Japanese culture rooted in the teachings of Zen Buddhism, about breaking free from the limits of the rational self.

A TASTE OF JAPAN

By Aidan O'Connor

Get ready for an unparalleled eating adventure: from humble bowls of ramen to elaborate kaiseki feasts, a vast culinary universe awaits visitors to food-obsessed Japan.

Japan's food offerings are united by a few key philosophies. Presentation is paramount—a dedication to visual appeal means that colors and shapes are just as important as aromas, textures, and flavors. Details count—food is prepared with pride and care, and everything from a bowl's shape to a dish's finishing garnish carries meaning. Natural flavors shine through—seasonal ingredients star in minimally processed preparations, with condiments used to enhance flavors rather than mask them.

You'll find these culinary philosophies at all levels, from tiny noodle shops to lively robatayaki grills to elegant sushi restaurants. Here's what you need to know to make the most of your meals. As they say in Japan, *itadakimasho* (let's eat)!

Pressed sushi (*oshizushi*) and Japanese-style fried rice

THE JAPANESE MEAL

Breakfast (*asa-gohan*, literally "the morning rice") is typically eaten at home and features rice, fried fish, and miso soup. Lunch (*hiru-gohan*), mostly eaten out of the home at school or work, involves a bento lunch box of rice, grilled fish, vegetables, and pickles. The evening meal (*ban-gohan*) has the broadest range, from restaurant meals of sushi to traditional meals cooked at home.

For home-prepared meals, the basic formula consists of one soup and three dishes—a main dish of fish or meat and two vegetable side dishes. These are served together with rice, which is part of every meal. When entertaining guests, more dishes will be served. Classical

Japanese cooking follows the principle of "fives." An ideal meal is thought to use five cooking methods—boiling, grilling, frying, steaming, and serving raw; incorporate five colors—black or purple, white, red or orange, yellow, and green; and feature five tastes—sweet, sour, salty, bitter, and *umami* (the Japanese are credited with discovering umami, or savoriness). Ingredient quality is key, as cooking techniques are intended to coax out an ingredient's maximum natural flavor.

Staple ingredients include seafood, which plays a leading role in Japanese cuisine, with dozens of species available, from familiar choices like *maguro*

DINING ETIQUETTE

Here are a few tips to help you fit in at the Japanese table:

■ Don't point or gesture with chopsticks.

■ Avoid lingering over communal dishes with your chopsticks while you decide what to take. Do not use the end you have been eating with to remove food from the dish—use the serving chopsticks provided or the thick end of your own chopsticks.

■ When not in use, place your chopsticks on the chopstick rest.

■ Never pass food from your chopsticks to someone else's or leave chopsticks standing in your rice bowl (it resembles incense sticks at a funeral).

■ There is no taboo against slurping your noodle soup, though women are generally less boisterous about it than men.

■ Pick up the soup bowl and drink directly from it. Take the fish or vegetables from it with your chopsticks. Return the lid to the soup bowl when you are finished eating. The rice bowl, too, is to be held in your free hand while you eat from it.

■ When drinking with a friend don't pour your own. Pour for the other person first. He will in turn pour yours.

■ Japanese don't pour sauce on their rice. Sauces are intended for dipping foods into it lightly.

■ It is still considered tacky to eat as you walk along a public street.

Pouring sake into a traditional Japanese cup

(tuna) and *ebi* (shrimp) to more exotic selections like *anago* (conger eel) and *fugu* (blowfish). Meat options include chicken, pork, beef, and—in rural areas—venison and wild boar. Then there is a huge variety of vegetables and fungi (both wild and cultivated) such as *renkon* (lotus root), *daikon* (white radish), and matsutake mushrooms. Finally there is the soy bean, eaten whole as edamame, or fermented in tofu or miso.

Condiments range from tangy *shiso* (a member of the mint family) to spicy wasabi and savory soy sauce.

SUSHI

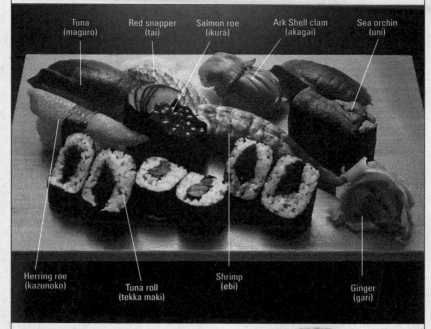

Tuna (maguro) • Red snapper (tai) • Salmon roe (ikura) • Ark Shell clam (akagai) • Sea orchin (uni)

Herring roe (kazunoko) • Tuna roll (tekka maki) • Shrimp (ebi) • Ginger (gari)

■ Sushi actually refers to anything, seafood or otherwise, served on or in vinegared rice. It is not raw fish. *Nigiri-zushi* (the sushi best known overseas) is actually a fairly recent development from Tokyo.

■ *Makizushi* is a sushi roll. These can be fat, elaborate rolls or simple sticks.

■ Other types of sushi include *chirashi-zushi* with fish and vegetables scattered artfully into the rice and, in Kyoto and Osaka, *oshizushi* in which preserved mackerel, among other fish, is pressed onto the rice. This is served in slices.

■ *Funazushi*, from around Lake Biwa near Kyoto, is perhaps the oldest type. The fish and rice are buried for six months. The rice is thrown away and the fish is eaten. This technique was historically used as a means of preserving protein. It is an acquired taste.

■ *Kaitenzushi* (conveyor belt sushi) outlets abound and are cheap. However, for the

Hand-rolled sushi

real experience, nothing matches a traditional sushi-ya.

■ Using your hands is acceptable. Dip the fish, not the rice, lightly in the soy.

■ The *beni-shoga* (pickled ginger) is a palate freshener. Nibble sparingly.

■ *Wasabi* may not be served with your sushi, as the chef often dabs a bit on the rice when making your sushi. If you want extra wasabi, ask for it.

■ Customers will often request *omakase* (tasting menu). The chef will then choose and serve the best fish, in the order he deems appropriate.

RAMEN

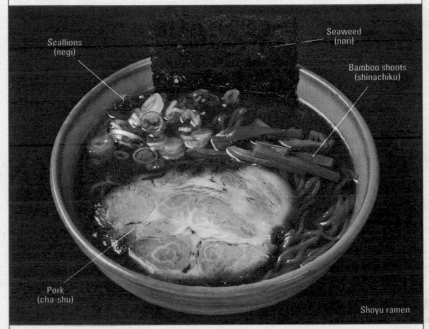

Scallions (negi)

Seaweed (nori)

Bamboo shoots (shinachiku)

Pork (cha-shu)

Shoyu ramen

■ Ramen is practically Japan's national dish. A ramen restaurant is never far away.

■ There are four main types: from the chilly north island of Hokkaido, there is *shio* **ramen** (salt ramen) and **miso ramen** (ramen in a miso broth). *Shoyu* **ramen** made with soy sauce is from Tokyo, while *tonkotsu* **ramen** (ramen in a white pork broth) is from Kyoto. Note that most ramen stocks contain meat or fish.

■ Each area has its own variation—corn and butter ramen in Sapporo; a stock made from pork and dried anchovies in northern Honshu; or Fukuoka's famed *Hakata* **ramen** with its milky tonkotsu broth and thin noodles with myriad toppings.

■ The reputation of a ramen restaurant depends on its stock, often a closely guarded secret.

■ Ramen is meant to be eaten with gusto. Slurping is normal.

■ Typical toppings include sliced roast pork, bean sprouts, boiled egg, *shi-nachiku* (fermented bamboo shoots), spring onion, *nori* (dried seaweed) and *kamaboko* (a fishcake made from white fish).

■ Beyond ramen, udon shops and soba shops also offer noodle dishes worth trying.

Miso ramen

Shio ramen

ROBATAYAKI

Grilled fish (tsukeba)

■ *Robata* means fireside, and the style of cooking is reminiscent of old-fashioned Japanese farmhouse meals cooked over a charcoal fire in an open hearth.

■ Robatayaki restaurants and izakaya taverns serving grilled foods can be found near any busy station.

■ It's easy to order at a robatayaki, because the selection of food to be grilled is lined up at the counter. Fish, meat, vegetables, tofu—take your pick.

■ Some popular choices are *yaki-zakana* (grilled fish), particularly *karei-shio-yaki* (salted and grilled flounder) and *asari saka-mushi* (clams simmered in sake).

■ Try the grilled Japanese *shiitake* (mushrooms), *ao-to* (green peppers), and the *hiyayakko* (chilled tofu sprinkled with bonito flakes, diced green onions, and soy sauce).

Matsutake mushroom

■ *O-tsukuri* (sashimi) and *katsuono tataki* (seared bonito) are very popular. The fish will vary according to the season.

■ Dipping sauces are concocted using soy, *dashi* (soup stock), and a hint of citrus such as yuzu.

■ Many robatayaki pride themselves on their wide selection of sake and shochu.

■ Most Japanese people will finish their meal with a rice dish.

TEMPURA

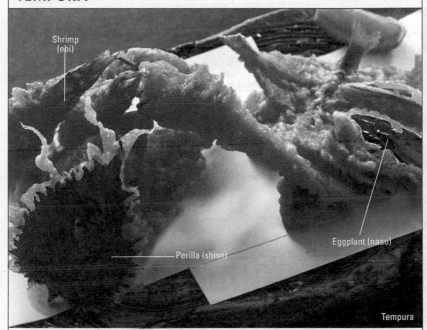

Shrimp (ebi)

Perilla (shiso)

Eggplant (nasu)

Tempura

■ Though tempura features in many busy eateries as part of a meal, it bears little resemblance to the exquisite morsels produced over the course of a full tempura meal at an intimate specialty restaurant.

■ The secret of good tempura lies in the quality of the ingredients, the freshness and temperature of the oil, and the lightness of the batter.

■ Good tempura is light and crispy, not crunchy like fried chicken.

■ Tempura is most often fried in soybean oil, but cottonseed or sesame oil also may be used.

■ Because only the freshest of ingredients will do, the menu changes with the season. Baby corn, green peppers, sweet potato, lotus root, shiitake mushrooms, and shiso leaves are the most common vegetables. In spring expect **sansai** (wild vegetables) picked that morning.

Shrimp Tempura with sweet potatoes

■ Prawns and white fish are also popular tempura items.

■ *Tsuyu* (dipping sauce) is made from dashi seasoned with soy and **mirin** (sweet rice wine). You may see a white mound of grated daikon on your plate. Add that to the tsuyu for a punch of flavor.

■ Alternatively, mixtures of salt and powdered green tea or salt and yuzu may be sprinkled on the tempura.

BENTO

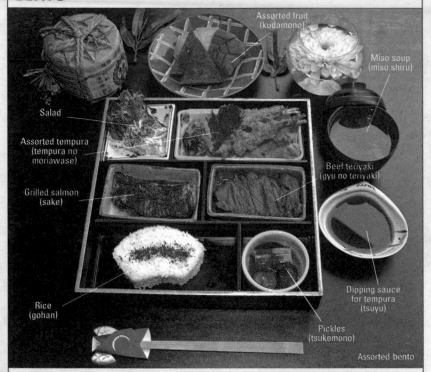

- Assorted fruit (kudamono)
- Miso soup (miso shiru)
- Salad
- Assorted tempura (tempura no moriawase)
- Grilled salmon (sake)
- Beef teriyaki (gyu no teriyaki)
- Dipping sauce for tempura (tsuyu)
- Rice (gohan)
- Pickles (tsukemono)

Assorted bento

■ Bento boxes, the traditional Japanese box lunch, can be bought everywhere from the basement level of a luxurious department store to a convenience store.

■ A typical bento will contain rice, grilled fish, a selection of vegetable dishes, some pickles, and perhaps a wedge of orange or other fruit.

■ Every region has its *meibutsu,* or speciality dish. These are often showcased in lunch boxes available at stations or local stores.

■ Though the humble bento is usually relatively inexpensive, more ornate and intricate boxes featuring kaiseki dishes or sushi are often bought for special occasions.

Bento lunch box

■ The bento exists in an almost limitless number of variations according to the region and the season.

■ A bento is designed to be taken out and eaten on the move. They are perfect on long-distance train rides or for a picnic in the park.

BEVERAGES

Sake

■ There are more than 2,000 different brands of sake produced throughout Japan. It is often called rice wine but is actually made by a fermenting process that is more akin to beer-making. The result is a fantastically complex drink with an alcoholic content just above wine (15–17% alcohol). It is the drink of choice with sashimi and traditional Japanese food.

■ There are four main types of sake: *daiginjo, ginjo, junmai,* and *honjozo*. The first two are the most expensive and made from highly polished rice. The latter two, however, also pack flavor and character.

■ Like wine, sake can be sweet (*amakuchi*) or dry (*karakuchi*). Workaday sake may be drunk warm (*atsukan*) while the higher grades will be served chilled. Sake is the only drink that can be served at any temperature.

■ Another variety is *nama-zake.* This is unpasteurized sake and is prized for its fresh, zingy taste.

■ *Shochu* is a distilled spirit that is often 25% alcohol or more. Like vodka, it can be made from potato, sweet potato, wheat, millet, or rice. It is drunk straight, on the rocks, with water, or in cocktails.

■ Any good izakaya or robatayaki will stock a diverse selection of both sake and shochu, and staff will make recommendations.

■ Beer is, perhaps, the lubricant of choice for most social situations. Japanese beer is of a high standard and tends to be lager. It has a relatively high alcohol content at 5% or more. Recently there has been a boom in microbreweries.

JAPANESE FINE ARTS

Japanese lacquerware

What raises Japanese handicrafts to the level of fine arts? It is, one could argue, the standards set by the nation's *Ningen kokuho*: its Living National Treasures, who hand down these traditional skills from generation to generation.

Legally speaking, these people are "Holders of Important Intangible Cultural Properties." A law, enacted in 1950, establishes two broad categories of Intangible Property. One comprises the performing arts: Kabuki, Noh, Bunraku puppet theater, and traditional music and dance. The other embraces a wide range of handicrafts, most of them in the various forms and styles of textiles, pottery, lacquerware, papermaking, wood carving, and metalworking—from all over the country. The tiny cohort of individuals and groups who exemplify these traditions at the highest levels receive an annual stipend; the money is intended not so much to support the title holders (Living National Treasures command very healthy sums for their work) as to help them attract and train apprentices, and thus keep the traditions alive.

CARRYING ON

Official sponsorship has proven itself a necessity in more than a few craft traditions. The weaving of *bashofu*, for example, a fabric from Okinawa, is on its way to becoming a lost art—unless the present Living National Treasure can encourage enough people to carry on with the craft. Papermaking, a cottage industry that once supported some 28,500 households nationwide, now supports only a few hundred.

LACQUERWARE

Japanese lacquerware has its origins in the Jomon period (10,000–300 BC), and by the Nara period (710–794) most of the techniques we recognize today, such as *maki-e* (literally, "sprinkled picture")—the use of gold or silver powder to underlay the lacquer—had been developed. The Edo period (1603–1868) saw the uses of lacquer extended to vessels and utensils for the newly prosperous merchant class.

Traditional Japanese papermaking

The production of lacquerware starts with refining sap from the Japanese sumac (*urushi*). The lacquer is layered on basketry, wood, bamboo, metal, and even paper. The polished black and red surfaces may have inlays of mother-of-pearl or precious metals, creating ⁣s and designs of exquisite beauty ⁣delicacy. Many regions in Japan are ⁣amous for their distinct lacquerware styles, among them Kyoto, Wajima, and Tsugaru. ■TIP➔ **Tableware with lacquer over plastic bases, rather than wood, are no less beautiful, but far less expensive.**

PAPERMAKING

Washi, Japanese paper, can have a soft translucent quality that seems to belie its amazing strength and durability. It makes a splendid material for calligraphy and brush painting, and it can be fashioned into a wide variety of traditional decorative objects. The basic ingredient is the inner bark of the paper mulberry, but leaves, fiber threads, and even gold flake can be added in later stages for a dramatic effect. The raw mulberry branches are first steamed, then bleached in cold water or snow. The fibers are boiled with ash lye, rinsed, beaten into pulp, and soaked in a tank of starchy taro solution. A screen is dipped into the tank, pulled up, and rocked to drain the solution and crosshatch the fibers. The wet sheets of paper are stacked to press out the excess liquid, then dried in the sun.

CALLIGRAPHY

Calligraphy arrived in Japan around the middle of the 6th century AD with the sacred texts of Buddhism, written in *kanji* (Chinese ideograms). By 800 the *kana* syllabic alphabets of the Japanese language had also developed, and the writing of both kanji and kana with a brush, in india ink, had become an art form—a wedding of meaning and emotion that was (and still is) regarded as a revelation of the writer's individual character. The flow of the line from top to bottom, the balance of shapes and sizes, the thickness of the strokes, the amount of ink on the brush: all contribute to the composition of the work. There are five main styles of calligraphy in Japan. Two are based on

A calligrapher at work

About 30 different styles of porcelain are made in Japan.

the Chinese: *tensho,* typically used for seal carving; and *reisho,* for the copying of sutras. Three are solely Japanese: *kaisho,* the block style often seen in wood carving; and the flowing *sosho* (cursive) and *gyosho* styles. *Sosho* is especially impressive—an expression of freedom and spontaneity that takes years of discipline to achieve; retouching and erasing is impossible.

CERAMICS

There are some 30 traditional styles of pottery in Japan, from unglazed stoneware to painted porcelain. Since the late 1600s, when Imari and Kakiemon porcelain were exported to Europe, the achievements of Japanese potters have delighted collectors.

Although people have been making pottery in the Japanese archipelago for some 12,000 years, the styles we know today were developed from techniques introduced from the Korean Peninsula and mainland Asia to Japan starting in the 5th century. Some craftspeople discovered deposits of fine kaolin clay in northern Kyushu, and founded the tradition in that region of porcelains like

Arita-yaki, with brilliantly colored enamel decoration over cobalt blue underglaze. Other porcelain wares include Tobe-yaki from Ehime Prefecture, Kutani-yaki from Ishikawa Prefecture, and Kiyomizu-yaki from Kyoto.

These apart, most Japanese pottery is stoneware—which has an earthier appeal, befitting the rougher texture of the clay. Stoneware from Mashiko, where celebrated potter Hamada Shoji (1894–1978) worked, is admired for its rustic brown, black, and white glazes, often applied in abstract patterns. Many regional potters use glazes on stoneware for coloristic effects, like the mottled, crusty Tokoname-yaki, with its red-iron clay. Other styles, among them the rough-surfaced Shigaraki-yaki made near Kyoto; the white or blue-white Hagi-yaki; and Bizen-yaki from Okayama Prefecture, are unglazed: their warm tones and textures are accidents of nature, achieved when the pieces take their colors from the firing process, in sloped, wood-burning through-draft kilns called *anagama* or *nobori-gama,* built on hillsides. The effects depend on the choice of the wood the potter uses, where he places a particular piece in the kiln, and how he manipulates the heat, but the results are never predictable.

Main pottery towns include Hagi, Bizen, and Arita, but you can always find their products in Kyoto and Tokyo. If you do go on a pilgrimage, call ahead to local kilns and tourist organizations to verify that what you want to see will be open and to ask about sales.

Recommended reading: *Inside Japanese Ceramics* by Richard L. Wilson.

TEXTILES

Run your fingers over a Japanese textile, and you touch the fabric of Japanese social history. As the caste system took shape under Buddhist and Confucian influences, it created separate populations of samurai, farmers, artisans, and merchants (in descending order). Rules and conventions emerged—enforced in the Edo period by strict sumptuary laws—about who could wear what and on what occasions. Appearances identified people. One glance at a kimono, and you knew the wearer was a woman of middle age, the wife of a prosperous tradesman, on her way to the wedding of a family connection. Order was maintained. You were what you wore. Courtesans and actors, of course, could dress over-the-top; their roles gave them the license. And little by little, the merchants also found ways around the laws, to dress as befit their growing wealth and power. Evolving styles and techniques of making fabrics gave weavers and dyers and designers new opportunities to show their skills.

Western clothing follows the body line in a sculptural way; the kimono is meant as a one-size-fits-all garment in which gender matters, but size and shape are largely unimportant. Whatever the wearer's height or weight, a kimono is made from one bolt of cloth cut and stitched into panels that provide ample surface for decoration.

Regional styles proliferate. Kyoto's *Nishijin-ori* silk brocade is as sumptuous as a Japanese textile can be. Okinawa produces a variety of stunning fabrics; one, called *bashofu*, is made of plantain-fiber threads, dyed and woven in intricate motifs, and feels like linen. Kyoto's and Tokyo's stencil dyeing techniques yield subtle, elegant geometric patterns and motifs from nature. Kanazawa's *Kaga yuzen* paste-resist dyeing on silk is famous for its flower and bird motifs, in elegant rainbow colors.

The used kimonos you often see in Kyoto or Tokyo flea markets can be bargains. Also look for lighter-weight *yukata* (robes), *obi* (sashes), or handkerchiefs from Arimatsu, near Nagoya, for example. Good introductions to these craft traditions can be seen at Kyoto's Fuzoku Hakubutsukan (Costume Museum) and Nishijin Orimono (Textile Center), and the Edo-period dress collection in Tokyo's National Museum.

Kaga yuzen textiles from Kanazawa exhibit a traditional flower motif.

PERFORMING ARTS

A highly stylized Noh theater performance

Gorgeous costumes, sword fights and tearful reunions, acrobatics and magical transformations, spectacular makeup and masks, singing and dancing, ghosts and goblins, and star-crossed lovers: traditional Japanese arts are not short on showmanship.

The performing arts all have roots in the trade and exchange with continental Asia. Kabuki makeup as well as *gagaku* ceremonial court music and dance are Chinese-inspired; the four-string *biwa* shares a Silk Road ancestry with the Persian *oud*. Collectively the theater traditions generate work for artisans—weavers and dyers, instrument makers, wood-carvers, and more—who make a special contribution of their own. Common features aside, the differences among them are astonishing. Kabuki is great showbiz, translatable and appreciable pretty much anywhere in the world. Most of an audience that will sit riveted by the graceful, suggestive movements of *buyo* (traditional dance) will fall asleep at a dance-recitation of Noh.

MASTER PERFORMERS

The performing arts also have National Treasures, but filling the 70 allotted slots is easier than in the fine arts. The worlds of Japanese theater are mainly in the grip of small oligarchies ("schools") where traditions are passed down from father to son. Some of these master performers are 9th- and even 22nd-generation holders of hereditary family stage names and specializations.

3

A Japanese Culture Primer PERFORMING ARTS

KABUKI

Tradition has it that Kabuki was created around 1600 by an Izumo shrine maiden named Okuni; it was then performed by troupes of women, who were often available as well for prostitution (the authorities soon banned women from the stage as a threat to public order). Eventually Kabuki cleaned up its act and developed a professional role for female impersonators, who train for years to project a seductive, dazzling femininity. By the latter half of the 18th century it had become Everyman's theater par excellence—especially among the townspeople of bustling, hustling Edo. Kabuki had spectacle; it had pathos and tragedy; it had romance and social satire. It had legions of fans, who spent all day at the theater, shouting out the names of their favorite actors at the stirring moments in their favorite plays.

Kabuki flowered especially in the "floating world" of Edo's red-light entertainment district. The theater was a place to see and be seen, to catch the latest trends in music and fashion, where people of all classes came together under one roof—something that happened nearly nowhere else in the city. Strict censorship laws were put in place and just as quickly circumvented by clever playwrights; Kabuki

A Kabuki mannequin from the Edo-Tokyo Museum

audiences could watch a *jidai-mono* (historical piece) set in the distant past, where the events and characters made thinly veiled reference to troublesome contemporary events.

The Genroku era (1673–1841) was Kabuki's golden age, when the classic plays of Chikamatsu Monzaemon and Tsuruya Namboku were written, and most of the theatrical conventions and stage techniques we see today were honed to perfection. The *mie*, for example, is a dramatic pose the actor strikes at a certain moment in the play, to establish his character. The use of *kumadori* makeup, derived from Chinese opera and used to symbolize the essential elements of a character's nature, also dates to this period. The exaggerated facial lines of the kumadori, in vivid reds and blues and greens over a white rice-powder base, tell the audience at once that the wearer is a hero or villain, noble or arrogant, passionate or cold. To the Genroku also date revolving stages, trapdoors, and—most important—the *hanamichi*: a long, raised runway from the back of the theater, through the audience, to the main stage, where characters enter, exit, and strike their *mie* poses.

Kabuki traditions are passed down through generations in a small group

The Oshika Kabuki troupe

The principal character in a Noh play wears a carved, wooden mask.

of families; the roles and great stage names are hereditary. The repertoire does not really grow, but stars like Ichikawa Ennosuke and Bando Tamasaburo have developed unique performance styles that still draw audiences young and old. This ancient art now has a stylish home in the Kengo Kuma–designed Kabuki-za theater in Tokyo's Ginza district, which opened in 2013.

Recommended reading: *The Kabuki Guide* by Masakatsu Gunji.

NOH

Noh is a dramatic tradition far older than Kabuki; it reached a point of formal perfection in the 14th century and survives virtually unchanged from that period. Whereas Kabuki was everyman's theater, Noh developed for the most part under the patronage of the warrior class. It is dignified, ritualized, and symbolic. Many of the plays in the repertoire are drawn from classical literature or tales of the supernatural. The texts are richly poetic, and even the Japanese find them difficult to understand. (Don't despair: the major Noh theaters usually provide synopses of the plays in English.) The action—such as it is—develops at nearly glacial pace.

The principal character in a Noh play wears a carved wooden mask. Such is the skill of the actor, and the mysterious effect of the play, that the mask itself may appear expressionless until the actor "brings it to life," at which point the mask can express a considerable range of emotions. As in Kabuki, the various roles of the Noh repertoire all have specific costumes—robes of silk brocade with intricate patterns that are works of art in themselves. Noh is not a very "accessible" kind of theater: its language is archaic; its conventions are obscure; and its measured, stately pace can put many audiences to sleep.

More accessible is the *kyogen,* a short comic interlude traditionally performed between two Noh plays in a program. The pace is quicker, the costumes (based on actual dress of the medieval period) are simpler, and most *kyogen* do not use masks; the comedy depends on the satiric premise—a clever servant who gets the best of his master, for example—and the lively facial expressions of the actors.

Like Kabuki, Noh has a number of schools, the traditions of which developed as the exclusive property of hereditary families. The major schools have their own theaters in Tokyo and Kyoto, with regular schedules of performances—but if you happen to be in Kyoto on June 1–2, don't miss the Takigi Noh: an outdoor performance given at night, by torchlight, in the precincts of the Heian Shrine. There are other torchlight performances as well in Tokyo, at the Meiji Shrine (early November) and Zojoji Temple (late September), and in Nara at the Kasuga Shrine (May).

BUNRAKU

The third major form of traditional Japanese drama is Bunraku puppet theater. Itinerant puppeteers were plying their trade in Japan as early as the 10th century; sometime in the late 16th century, a form of narrative ballad called *joruri*, performed to the accompaniment of a three-string banjolike instrument called the *shamisen*, was grafted onto their art, and Bunraku was born. The golden age of Bunraku came some 200 years later, when most of the great plays were written and the puppets themselves evolved to their present form, so expressive and intricate in their movements that they require three people acting in unison to manipulate them.

The puppets are about two-thirds human size and elaborately dressed in period costume; each one is made up of interchangeable parts—a head, shoulder piece, trunk, legs, and arms. The puppeteer called the *omozukai* controls the expression on the puppet's face and its right arm and hand. The *hidarizukai* controls the puppet's left arm and hand along with any props that it is carrying. The *ashizukai* moves the puppet's legs. The most difficult task belongs to the omozukai—a role

it commonly takes some 30 years to master.

Creating the puppet heads is an art in itself, and today there are only a handful of carvers still working. As a rule, the heads are shaped and painted for specific figures—characters of different sex, age, and personality—and fitted with elaborate wigs of human hair in various styles to indicate the puppet's social standing. Able to roll their eyes and lift their eyebrows, the puppets can achieve an amazing range of facial expressions.

The chanters, who provide both the narration of the play and the voices of the puppets, deliver their lines in a kind of high-pitched croak from deep in the throat. The texts they recite are considered to be among the classics of Japanese dramatic literature; the great playwright Chikamatsu Monzaemon (1653–1725) wrote for both Bunraku and Kabuki, and the two dramatic forms often adapted works from each other.

The most important Bunraku troupe is the government-supported National Bunraku Theatre in Osaka, but there are amateur and semiprofessional companies throughout the country.

Bunraku puppets are about two-thirds human size.

ONSEN AND BATHING

A lakeside rotenburo made from natural rocks

A chain of volcanic islands on the fiery Pacific Rim, Japan has developed a splendid subculture around one of the more manageable manifestations of this powerful resource: the onsen thermal spa.

The benchmark Japanese weekend excursion—be it family outing, company retreat, or romantic getaway—is the hot spring resort. Fissured from end to end with volcanic cracks and crannies, the country positively wheezes with geothermal springs. Hot water gushes and sprays almost everywhere—but most especially in the mountains; there are hot springs in every prefecture, on every offshore island—even in cities often built above the very fault lines themselves.

YUDEDAKO

The Japanese have a special term for that blissful state of total immersion—*yudedako* (literally, "boiled octopus")—and Japanese people of all ages will journey for miles to attain it. Soaking in hot springs is a step on the road to sound health, good digestion, clear skin, marital harmony—to whatever it is that gives you a general sense of being at one with the universe.

THE ONSEN EXPERIENCE

An onsen can refer to a particular region or subregion, like Yufuin in Oita Prefecture, Kinugawa in Tochigi, or Hakone in Kanagawa: a resort destination especially well endowed with thermal springs. Or it can mean more specifically a public bathhouse with a spring-fed pool, where you pay an admission fee and soak at your leisure. (At last count, there were some 6,700 of these nationwide.) Or it could mean a lodging—one of two basic varieties—with a spring of its own. One type is the *kanko* hotel: a mega-onsen with multiple baths, in grand pharaonic styles with mosaics and waterfalls, and banquet halls and dinner shows, as well as tatami-floored guest rooms that sleep six—and, inevitably, discos and karaoke bars and souvenir shops. The other type is the onsen of everyone's dreams: the picture-perfect traditional inn, a ryokan of half a dozen rooms, nestled up somewhere in the mountains all by itself, with a spectacular view and a *rotenburo*—an outdoor bath—to enjoy it from.

THE ROTENBURO

At smaller onsen you can sometimes book a rotenburo, an exquisitely crafted bath with stepping-stones, lanterns, and bamboo screens for a private soak: an hour or so of the purest luxury,

A spa in Shirahama Onsen

especially by moonlight. The rotenburo is a year-round indulgence; the view from the bath might be of a mountainside, white with cherry blossoms in spring; a lakefront doused in the red and gold of maples in autumn; or a winter panorama, with the snow piled high on the pines and hedges that frame the landscape. Whatever the season, you'll need to make reservations well in advance for the best onsen accommodations. Japan has more than 3,000 registered spas; collectively they draw nearly 140 million visitors a year, and hotel space is in high demand.

WHAT IS AN ONSEN?

By law, an onsen is only an onsen if the water comes out of the ground at a specified minimum temperature, and contains at least one of 19 designated minerals and chemical compounds—which makes for a wide range of choices. There are iron springs with red water; there are silky-smooth alkaline springs; there are springs with radon and sulphur sodium bicarbonate; there are springs with water at a comfortable 100°F (37.8°C), and springs so hot they have bath masters to make sure you stay only for three minutes and not a fatal second longer.

Gakenoyu Onsen in Nagano

Most onsen have single-sex bathing; a few have mixed bathing.

One reason many Westerners are reluctant to go bathing in Japan: Japanese communal bathing is done in the buff—but that shouldn't deter you from the experience. The bath is a great equalizer: in a sense the bath *is* Japan, in its unalloyed egalitarianism. Each bather offers the other an equal degree of respect and regard; people generally do not behave in a way that might spoil the enjoyment of any other bather; nor is anyone embarrassed. It is freeing and you can relax right into it.

ONSEN ETIQUETTE

Another reason you might have for your reluctance is the worrisome conviction that bathing with a bunch of strangers comes with a raft of rules—rules all those strangers are taught from childhood, but at least one of which you're bound to break, to your everlasting horror and shame. "What if I drop the something into the bath?" is a common fear.

But the pitfalls are not so bad. There certainly are protocols to follow, but it's a short list.

■ While there are still a few spas that keep alive the old custom of *konyoku* (mixed bathing), all of them have separate entrances for men and women, each labeled with Japanese characters.

■ A word of warning: body tattoos, in Japan, are indelibly associated with the yakuza—organized crime families and their minions—and spas commonly refuse entry to tattooed visitors to avoid upsetting their regular clientele. The rule is strictly enforced. Even foreign tourists, who are clearly not involved in Japanese organized crime, can be turned away for their tattoos. If your tattoo is small enough, put a bandage over it. Another option is to only bathe in *kashikiri-buro*, or private baths, which are available at larger onsen and many ryokan. This may also be an appealing option for those who'd rather not bare all in front of multiple strangers.

■ The first room you come to inside is the dressing room. It's often tatami-floored: take your shoes or slippers off in the entryway. The dressing room will have lockers for your keys and valuables, and rows of wicker or plastic baskets on shelves; pick one, and put your clothes in it. If you're staying overnight at an inn with a spa of its own, you'll find a cotton kimono called a *nemaki* in your room—you sleep in it, in lieu of pajamas—and a light quilted jacket called a *hanten*. Night or day, this is standard gear to wear from your room to the spa, anywhere else around the inn, and even for a stroll out of doors. Leave them in the basket.

■ Bring two towels: leave the bigger one in the basket to dry off with, and take the smaller one with you next door to the baths. (You will likely see that this towel to preserve your modesty is the accepted way of moving around in the spa.)

■ The bath area will have rows of washing stations along the walls: countertops with supplies of soap and shampoo, taps, a mirror, shower-head, stool, and bucket. Here's where you get clean—and that means *really* clean. Soap up, shower, scrub off every particle of the day's wear and tear. Leave no trace of soap.

■ You can take the towel with you to the bath, but don't put it in the water. Most people leave theirs on the side or set them folded on top of their heads. (Another item of protocol: spas don't insist on bathing caps, but they do want you to keep your head above water.)

■ Find a pleasant spot; soak in blissful silence if you prefer (but not too long if you're not used to it), or feel free to strike up a conversation with a fellow soaker: *atsui desu ne*—the local equivalent of "It's hot, isn't it?"—is a good start. The Japanese call their friendliest, most relaxing acquaintances *hadaka no o-tsukiai*: naked encounters.

Staying at a mega-onsen? Conviviality reigns in the baths of these establishments, with all sorts of amenities to help it along. At some inns, you can order a small floating table for yourself and your fellow boilers, just big enough for a ceramic flask of sake or two and a suitable number of cups. You get to warm your insides and outsides at the same time.

When you've soaked to your heart's content, dry yourself off with your smaller towel and head back to the dressing room. Depending on the onsen's water, you might want to rinse off before drying off. Grab your larger towel from the basket, wrap it around yourself, and rest a bit until your body temperature drops back to normal. Get dressed and head out to the post-bath rest area to have a cold glass of water and lounge on the tatami mats before heading back out into the world.

You clean yourself thoroughly before setting foot in the onsen.

THE RYOKAN

A traditional tatami-mat room in a ryokan

You're likely to find Japanese hospitality polished, warm, and professional pretty much anywhere you stay—but nowhere more so than in a ryokan: a traditional inn.

Ryokans are typically one- or two-story wooden buildings where the guest rooms have tatami floors; the bedding—stowed by day in a closet—is rolled out at night. The rooms have hardly any furniture—perhaps one low dining table and cushions on the floor, a chest of drawers with a mirror, and a scroll painting or a flower arrangement in the *tokonoma* (alcove)—but every room in a proper ryokan will have windows with sliding paper screens looking out on an exquisite interior garden or scenery. Rates are per person and include the cost of breakfast and dinner. Some top-of-the-line ryokans might expect first-time guests to have introductions from a known and respected client.

COSTS

Ryokans of august lineage and exemplary service are expensive: expect to pay ¥40,000 or even ¥60,000 per person per night with two meals. There are plenty of lower-priced ryokan in Japan, which start from ¥10,000 per person, including breakfast and dinner, though these may not have garden views. The Japan National Tourism Organization has a listing of some of the latter.

RYOKAN ETIQUETTE

Remove your shoes as you step up from the entryway of your ryokan, and change into slippers. An attendant will escort you to your room. (It might take you two or three tries thereafter to find it on your own. Ryokans pride themselves on quiet and privacy, and the rooms are typically laid out in a labyrinth of corridors, where you're seldom aware of the presence of other guests.) Slippers come off at the door; on tatami, only socks/stockings or bare feet are acceptable. Relax first with a cup of green tea, and then head for the bath. In ryokans with thermal pools—not all have them—you can take to the waters at nearly any time and you'll be told of any time restrictions upon checking in. Be mindful of the bathing rules; wash and rinse off thoroughly before you get in the tub for a long hot soak. After your bath, change into a nemaki, the simple cotton kimono you'll find in your room, that doubles as sleepwear—or as standard garb for an informal stroll. These days, ryokans often have private baths, but especially in more venerable establishments (even those with astronomical rates), all facilities may be shared.

Ryokans don't have legions of staff, and will appreciate if you observe their routines and schedules. Guests are

Bedding for a ryokan, which is laid out nightly

expected to arrive in the late afternoon and eat around six. The front doors are sometimes locked at 10, so plan for early evenings. Breakfast is served around eight, and checkout is typically at 10. It might feel rather regimented, but just remember that your only task is to relax.

FOOD

Not every inn that calls itself a ryokan offers meals. Some offer only breakfast; some have no meals at all. Seek out those that do; it's an important part of the experience. And while some ryokans will allow you to pay a lesser rate and skip dinner, it's worth paying extra for the feast of local specialties in beautiful dishes of all shapes and sizes (sometimes served in your room). When you're finished, your attendant will clear the table and lay out your futon bedding: a mattress filled with cotton wadding and (in winter) a heavy, thick comforter (this often happens when you've stepped out of your room, so don't be surprised). In summer the comforter is replaced with a thinner quilt. In the morning the attendant will clear away the futon and bring in your Japanese-style breakfast: grilled fish, miso soup, pickled vegetables, and rice. If you prefer, the staff will usually be able to come up with coffee and toast, not to mention a fried egg.

A ryokan meal served in myriad little dishes

JAPANESE POP CULTURE

Pikachu performs at the Pokémon Café

Step onto the streets of Shibuya—or brave the crowds of preening high-school fashionistas populating Harujuku's Takeshita-dori—and you'll get a crash course on Japanese pop culture that extends way beyond familiar exports like Hello Kitty and Godzilla. Japanese pop culture has long been a source of fascination—and sometimes bewilderment—for foreign visitors. New fashion styles, technology, and popular media evolve quickly here, and in something of a vacuum.

That leads to a constant turnover of unique, sometimes wacky trends you won't find anywhere outside Japan. Immerse yourself in the latest fads by walking through neighborhoods like Shibuya, Shimo-Kitazawa, Harujuku, and Akihabara.

DID YOU KNOW?

There are more than 4 million vending machines in Japan, making it the densest population of machines per capita anywhere in the world. Here automated machines sell everything from hot drinks to live lobsters. Some use facial recognition to verify age for tobacco and beer and even offer indecisive customers age-appropriate drink recommendations.

KAWAII

Kawaii, or "cute," is an aww-inducing aesthetic you'll see all over Tokyo; major airlines plaster depictions of adorable animation characters like Pikachu across the sides of their planes, and even at local police stations it's not unusual for a fluffy, stuffed-animal mascot to be on display. Duck into an arcade photo booth to take *purikura*—pictures that let you choose your own kawaii background—or head to Sanrio Puroland, an entire theme park dedicated to cuteness.

Matriarch of Japanese kawaii, Hello Kitty

J-POP IDOLS

The age of the pop group is not over in Japan. "Idol" groups are still popular. Over-the-top outfits, sugar-sweet synthesized beats, and love-professing lyrics (with the occasional English word thrown in) dominate the Japanese pop charts. AKB48, one of Tokyo's hottest groups of idols, has hundreds of members, but with a core group of around 48. The AKB in the name refers to Akihabara, which has become a center of pop. AKB48's own theater complex in Akihabara hosts performances or other events regularly. Beloved pop groups like all-male SMAP have been succeeded by younger male groups like Hey! Say! Jump.

ANIME AND MANGA

Animation (anime) and comic books (manga) are extremely popular with readers both young and old. Comic book addicts, known as *otaku,* claim Tokyo's Akihabara as their home base. Though *otaku* can be translated as "nerd" or "obsessive," the term has been embraced by some. Former prime minister Taro Aso declared himself an otaku and confessed to reading 10 to 20 manga a week.

VIDEO GAMES

Japan is the cradle of the video game industry, and ever since the early 1970s it's been a dominant force in the gaming market. As companies like Namco gave way to Sega, Nintendo, and Sony, the gaming systems also continued to evolve and become more sophisticated. Like manga and anime, games enjoy a mainstream following. If you're a gamer, you'll be happy to find games that are unreleased in the United States alongside rebooted classics like *The Legend of Zelda* and *Super Mario Bros.*

Distinctive manga style

BASEBALL IN JAPAN

Mazda Zoom-Zoom Stadium in Hiroshima

Sumo may be the most visible spectator event, but without question, the most popular sport in Japan is baseball. It was first introduced in 1872 by Horace Wilson and has been popular ever since.

Each October two major-league teams in the United States (or one major-league team from the United States and one major-league team from Canada) play the best of seven games to decide the World Series. But judging from the results of the World Baseball Classic (WBC) that Japan has won twice, any true world series of baseball would have to include Japan. Although the Japanese professional-league season is shorter than its American counterpart (around 140 games versus 162 games), the major-league season's brevity is more than made up for by the company-league season, the university circuit, and the spring and summer high school tournaments. In addition there are junior high school and elementary school leagues. Many municipalities and towns even have senior leagues for people over 60 years old. The game is played everywhere: from the southern islands of Okinawa to the northern tip of Hokkaido.

CATCHING A GAME

Even if you're not a baseball fan, you should try to take in a game on any level for the spectacle. Like the players, the fans come prepared. From team colors and fan paraphernalia to songs and boxed lunches, the Japanese fans have it down. The cheering starts with the first pitch and doesn't end until the last out. Wherever you go to see a game, you will be made to feel welcome and your interest or curiosity will be rewarded.

BASEBALL-DO

Martial arts in Japan (judo, kendo, kyudo) and many other activities including the tea ceremony (*chado*) and calligraphy (*shodo*) end in the suffix *do* (pronounced "doe," as in the female deer, and meaning "way"). In Japan baseball is also a *do,* an art rather than a sport. Of course, the Japanese watch baseball as they watch any sport, but in terms of their preparation and mental approach to the game, it is a do.

All of Japan's active arts require years of practice to achieve the level of intense concentration and mindlessness that mastery requires. The idea is that if you practice something long enough and hard enough, it will become pure reflex. Then you won't have to think about what to do or when to do it. You will just do it. Major players like Sakamoto, Suzuki, and Nakajima play with a fluidity and grace that is beyond athleticism, exhibiting true mastery of the sport, and the result can be breathtaking.

SPRING AND SUMMER HIGH SCHOOL TOURNAMENTS

If you're fortunate enough to be in Japan in either March or August, you can attend the high school baseball tournament held annually at Koshien Stadium in Nishinomiya (near Osaka), the mecca of Japanese baseball.

Players from the Japanese Little League

In what regard is high school baseball held? Well, the pro team that normally plays at Koshien (the Hanshin Tigers) has to hit the road for two weeks in August to make way for the summer tournament. Both high school tournaments last about two weeks. Many of the star high school players go on to be standout players in both Japan and the United States.

TICKET PRICES

Tickets for a professional baseball game (the season runs from late March to October) are a relatively good buy. At Koshien, home of the Hanshin Tigers, prices range from ¥1,600 for a seat in the outfield to ¥5,000 for a reserved seat on a lower level. When box seats are offered for sale, you can expect to pay around ¥6,000. Prices are similar at Tokyo Dome, where the Yomiuri Giants play.

Tickets for the high school baseball tournaments are even more affordable. Prices range from ¥500 for upper-reserved to ¥1,200 for lower-reserved to ¥1,600 for box seats. Seats in the bleachers are free throughout the tournaments.

Yokohama's baseball stadium, home to the DeNa BayStars

JAPANESE MARTIAL ARTS

A practice kendo session

Take all that chop-socky stuff in the movies with a grain of salt: the Japanese martial arts are primarily about balance—mental, spiritual, and physical—and only incidentally about attack and self-defense.

Judo and karate are now as much icons of Japan as anime or consumer electronics, and just as enthusiastically embraced abroad. Judo, karate, and aikido, all essentially 20th-century developments, have gone global; it would be hard to name a country anywhere without a network of *dojos* (martial arts academies or training halls) and local organizations, affiliates of the governing bodies in Japan, certifying students and holding competitions. Judo has been an Olympic sport for men since the 1964 games in Tokyo, and for women since 1988. An estimated 50 million people worldwide practice karate, in one or another of the eight different forms recognized by the World Union of Karate-do Federations. Aikido was first introduced abroad in the 1950s; the International Aikido Federation now has affiliates in 44 member nations. Korea and Taiwan have instruction programs in kendo (fencing) that begin at the secondary school level.

LEVELS

Levels of certification are as much a part of the martial arts as they are in other traditional disciplines—the difference being that marks of rank are clearly visible. Students progress from the 10th *kyu* level to the 1st, and then from 1st *dan* to 8th (or 10th, depending on the system or school). Beginners wear white belts, intermediates wear brown, dan holders wear black or black-and-red.

KYUDO: THE WAY OF THE BOW

Archery is the oldest of Japan's traditional martial arts, dating from the 12th century, when archers played an important role in the struggles for power among samurai clans. Today it is practiced as a sport and a spiritual discipline. The object is not just to hit the target (no mean feat), but to do so in proper form.

KENDO: THE WAY OF THE SWORD

Fencing was a mainstay of feudal Japan, but the roots of modern kendo date to the early 18th century, with the introduction of the *shinai*—a practice sword made of bamboo slats—and the distinctive armor (*bogu*) still in use to protect the specific target areas the fencer must strike to earn points in competition. Attacks must be executed with foot stamping and loud spirited shouts called *kiai*.

JUDO: THE GENTLE WAY

Dr. Kano Jigoro (1860–1938) was the proverbial 90-pound weakling as a teenager; to overcome his frailty, he immersed himself in the martial arts, and over a period of years developed a reformed version of *jujutsu* on "scientific principles," which he finally codified in 1884. The *ju* of judo means "softness" or "gentleness"—because you

Group of young students practicing *kyudo*

use your opponent's strength against them—but this really is a rough-and-tumble contact sport.

KARATE: THE EMPTY HAND

Odd as it may sound, *karate* (literally: "the empty hand") doesn't quite qualify as a traditional Japanese martial art. Its origins are Chinese, but it was largely developed in the Ryukyu Kingdom (Okinawa before it was annexed), and didn't come to Japan proper until 1922. It lays stress on self-defense, spiritual and mental balance, and *kata*—formal, almost ritual sequences of movement.

AIKIDO: THE WAY OF HARMONY

The youngest of the Japanese martial arts was developed in the 1920s by Ueshiba Morihei (1883–1969), incorporating elements of both jujutsu and kendo, with much bigger doses of philosophy and spirituality. Aikido techniques consist largely of throws; the first thing a student learns is how to fall safely. After a stylized strike or a punch; the.intended receiver counters by getting out of the way and pivoting into a throw or an arm/shoulder pin. The essential idea is to do no damage.

Competitors at a judo tournament

SUMO

Two wrestlers battle in the ring

This centuries-old national sport of Japan is not to be taken lightly—as anyone who has ever seen a sumo wrestler will testify.

Sheer mass, mind you, isn't necessarily the key to success—though it might seem that way. There are no weight limits or categories in sumo; contenders in the upper ranks average 350 pounds. But Chiyonofuji, one of the all-time great *yokozuna* (grand champions), who tipped the scales at a mere 280 pounds, regularly faced—and defeated—opponents who outweighed him by 200 pounds or more. That said, sumo wrestlers do spend a lot of their time just bulking up, consuming enormous quantities of a high-protein stew called *chanko nabe,* washed down with beer. Akebono, the first foreign-born yokozuna, weighed more than 500 pounds.

SUMO RULES

The official catalog of sumo techniques includes 82 different ways of pushing, pulling, tripping, tossing, or slapping down your opponent, but the basic rules are exquisitely simple: except for hitting below the belt (which is essentially all a sumo wrestler wears) and striking with a closed fist, almost anything goes. Touch the sand with anything but the soles of your feet, or get forced out of the ring, and you lose.

SUMO HISTORY

The earliest written references to sumo date back to the year 712; for many centuries it was not a sport, but a Shinto religious rite, associated with Imperial Court ceremonies. Its present form—with the raised clay *dohyo* (platform) and circle of rice straw bales to mark the ring, the ranking system, the referee and judges, the elaborate costumes and purification rituals—was largely developed in the 16th and early 17th centuries.

THE SUMO WORLD

Sumo is hierarchical and formal. To compete, you must belong to a *heya* (stable) run by a retired wrestler who has purchased that right from the association. The stable master, or *oyakata,* is responsible for bringing in as many new wrestlers as the heya can accommodate, for their training and schooling in the elaborate etiquette of sumo, and for every facet of their daily lives. Youngsters recruited into the sport live in the stable dormitory, doing all the community chores and waiting on their seniors while they learn. When they rise high enough in tournament rankings, they acquire servant-apprentices of their own.

All the stables in the association—now some 43 in number—are in or around

The ceremonial entrance of the tournament participants

Tokyo. Most are clustered on both sides of the Sumida River near the green-roofed Kokugikan (National Sumo Arena), in the areas called Asakusabashi and Ryogoku. Come early in the day, and you can peer through the windows of the heya to watch them practice, or ask your hotel concierge to find a way inside the heya. Some offer opportunities for people to watch the practice.

There are six official sumo tournaments throughout the year: three in Tokyo (January, May, and September); one each in Osaka (March), Nagoya (July), and Fukuoka (November). Wrestlers in the upper divisions fight 15 matches over 15 days. A few weeks before each tournament, a panel of judges and association *toshiyori* (elders) publish a table called a *banzuke,* which divides the 800-plus wrestlers into six ranks and two divisions, East and West, to determine who fights whom. Rankings are based on a wrestler's record in the previous tournament: win a majority of your matches and you go up in the next banzuke; lose a majority and you go down.

If you can't attend one of the Tokyo sumo tournaments, you may want to take a tour of a sumo stable to take in a practice session.

A wrestler in traditional dress outside the arena

THE GEISHA

A traditional geisha performance in Kanazawa

The geisha—with her white makeup and Cupid's-bow red lip rouge, her hair ornaments, the rich brocade of her kimono—is as much an icon of Japan, instantly recognizable the world over, as Mt. Fuji itself.

Gei stands for artistic accomplishment (*sha* simply means "person"), and a geisha must be a person of many talents. As a performer, she should have a lovely voice and a command of traditional dance, and play beautifully on an instrument like the *shamisen*. She must have a finely tuned aesthetic sense, and excel at the art of conversation. In short, she should be the ultimate party hostess and gracious companion. Geisha (or *geiko* in Kyoto dialect) begin their careers at a very young age, when they are accepted into an *okiya*, a sort of guildhall where they live and learn as *maiko* (apprentices). The okiya is a thoroughly matriarchal society; the owner-manager is called *o-kami-san*, who is addressed as *okaasan* (mother), to underscore the fact that the geishas have given up one family for another.

GEISHA LIFE

The okiya provides the apprentices with room and board, pays for their training and clothing (the latter a staggering expense), and oversees their daily lives. The maiko in turn do household chores; when they have become full-fledged geisha, they contribute a part of their income to the upkeep of the house and its all-female staff of teachers, dressers, and maids.

The world of the geisha reflects Japan's tendency toward mastery and apprenticeships. Sumo's system of heya also show hows traditions of old are not always in line with modern life, yet survive. In the past a young girl from a large family, for example, would likely join another family upon marriage (although boys also might join other households when they marry). An apprentice would join the house of the master for anything from knife-making to woodworking and geisha are no different. Traditionally, this is an opportunity for talented girls to have a job in a world that was much less fluid than modern Japan is today.

THE GEISHA BUSINESS

There are no free agents in the geisha world; to engage one for a party you need a referral. Geisha work almost exclusively at traditional inns (ryokan), restaurants (*ryotei*), and teahouses (*chaya*); the owners of one will contact an *okiya* with which they have a connection and make the engagement—providing, of course, that you've established yourself as a trustworthy client. That means you will understand and be prepared to pay the bill when it shows up sometime later. Fees for a geisha's or maiko's time are measured in "sticks"—generally, one hour: the time it would take a stick of incense to

Geishas on the streets of Kyoto

burn down—and the okiya can really stick it to you. Bills are based on the number of guests at the party and can run as high as ¥25,000 per person or more for a two-hour engagement.

There were as many as 80,000 geisha in the 1920s; today there may be 1,000 left, most of them living and working in the Gion district of Kyoto; in Kanazawa; and in the Shimbashi, Akasaka, and Ginza districts of Tokyo. Fewer and fewer young Japanese women are willing to make the total commitment this closed world demands (even a geisha who opts to live independently will remain affiliated with her okiya for the rest of her career); fewer and fewer Japanese men of means have the taste or inclination to entertain themselves or important guests in this elegant fashion. On the other hand, the profession—while it lasts—does provide considerable job security. A geisha is valued, not solely for her beauty, but for her artistic and social skills—and her absolute discretion (what she might see and hear, for example at a party hosted by a political bigwig for his important business connections, could topple empires).

Geishas in Kyoto

THE TEA CEREMONY

A woman in traditional dress prepares tea

The Way of Tea—in Japanese, *Cha-no-yu* or *sado*—is more than a mere ceremony: it is a profound spiritual and meditative ritual. Although you can view it rather inexpensively, the full experience of sado is the meditative experience of losing oneself in the known patterns of serving and drinking.

Tea came to Japan from China in the late 8th century, first as a medicinal plant; it was the Zen monks of the 12th century who started the practice of drinking tea for a refresher between meditation sessions. Rules and customs began to evolve, and they coalesced in the Muromachi period of the 14th and 15th centuries as the earliest form of the Cha-no-yu. The Way of Tea developed an aesthetic of its own, rooted in the Zen sense of discipline, restraint, and simplicity: an aesthetic in which the most valued tea bowls, vessels, and utensils were humble, unadorned—and even imperfect. The choreographed steps were devised to focus the appreciation—in Japanese, called *wabi*—for this subdued and quiet refinement.

THE TEA PAVILION

Contemplate a Japanese tea pavilion long enough, and you begin to see how much work and thought can go into the design of something so simple. A stone path through a garden, a thatched roof, a low doorway into a single room with a *tokonoma* (alcove) and tatami floor are barely big enough for the tea master and a few guests, and yet are a gateway to the infinite.

The poet-priest Sen no Rikyu (1522–91) is the most revered figure in the history of sado. Three traditional schools of the tea ceremony, the Ura Senke, the Omote Senke, and the Mushakoji Senke—with some variations among them—maintain the forms and aesthetic principles he developed.

A full-scale formal tea ceremony, called a *chaji,* is like a drama in two acts, involving a multicourse *kaiseki* meal, two different kinds of powdered green tea, and an intermission—and can take as long as four hours to perform. Most ceremonies are less formal, confined to the serving of *usucha* ("thin tea") and a confection for an intimate group; these are called *o-chakai.* Both forms demand a strictly determined, stately series of moves to be made by both guests and hosts.

Participants gather first in the *machiai,* a kind of waiting room or shelter in the garden, until they are invited to proceed to the teahouse. They remove their shoes, and enter the teahouse through a low doorway. It is customary to comment on the flower arrangement or scroll in the alcove. The guests sit in *seiza,* their legs tucked under them; the host enters from another small doorway, greets them, and carefully cleans the utensils: bowl, tea scoop,

An outdoor garden tea ceremony

caddy, ladle, whisk. No matter that they are spotless already; cleaning them is part of the ritual.

When the tea is prepared, it is served first to the principal guest, who turns the bowl in the palm of his hand, drains it in three deep, careful sips, and returns it to the host. The other participants are served in turn. The guests comment on the presentation, and the ceremony is over; when they leave the pavilion, the host bows to them from the door.

Should you be invited to a tea ceremony, you likely won't be expected to have the same mastery of the etiquette as an experienced guest, but the right frame of mind will get you through. Be prepared to sit in seiza for quite a long time. Make conversation that befits the serenity of the moment. (A well-known haiku poetess once said that what she learned most from sado was to think before she spoke.) Above all, pay close attention to the practiced movements of the host, and remember to praise the *wabi*—the understated beauty—of the utensils he or she has chosen.

Recommended reading: *The Book of Tea* by Okakura Kakuzo; *Cha-no-Yu: The Japanese Tea Ceremony* by A. L. Sadler.

A bowl of matcha green tea

JAPANESE GARDENS

The garden of Hogon-in, Kyoto

Oases of calm and contemplation—and philosophical statements in their own right—Japanese gardens are quite unlike the arrangements of flowers, shrubs, and trees you find in the West.

One key to understanding—and more fully enjoying—a Japanese garden is knowing that its design, like all traditional Japanese arts, emerged out of the country's unique mixture of religious and artistic ideas. From Shintoism comes the belief in the divinity or spirit that dwells in natural phenomena like mountains, trees, and stones. The influence of Taoism is reflected in the islands that serve as symbolic heavens for the souls of those who achieve perfect harmony. Buddhist gardens—especially Zen gardens, expressions of the "less is more" aesthetic of the warrior caste—evolved in medieval times as spaces for meditation and the path to enlightenment. The classic example from this period is the *karesansui* (dry landscape) style, a highly abstract composition of meticulously placed rocks and raked sand or gravel, sometimes with a single pruned tree, but with no water at all.

SHAKEI

Shakei (borrowed landscape) is a way of extending the boundaries of the visual space by integrating a nearby attractive view—like a mountain or a sweeping temple roofline, for example—framing and echoing it with plantings of similar shape or color inside the garden itself. A middle ground, usually a hedge or a wall, blocks off any unwanted view and draws the background into the composition.

GARDEN DESIGN

Historically, the first garden designers in Japan were temple priests; the design concepts themselves were originally Chinese. Later, from the 16th century on, the most remarkable Japanese gardens were created by tea masters, who established a genre of their own for settings meant to deepen and refine the tea ceremony experience. Hence the *roji*: a garden path of stepping-stones from the waiting room to the teahouse itself, a transition from the ordinary world outside that prepares participants emotionally and mentally for the ceremony. Gradually gardens moved out of the exclusive realm to which only nobles, wealthy merchants, and poets had access, and the increasingly affluent middle class began to demand professional designers. In the process the elements of the garden became more elaborate, complex, and symbolic.

The "hide-and-reveal" principle, for example, dictates that there should be no point from which all of a garden is visible, that there must always be mystery and incompleteness in its changing perspectives: the garden *unfolds* as you walk from one view to another along the winding path. References to celebrated natural wonders and literary allusions, too, are frequently

Koishikawa Korakuen Garden, Tokyo

used design techniques. Mt. Fuji might be represented by a truncated cone of stones; Ama-no-Hashidate, the famous pine-covered spit of land across Miyazu Bay, near Kyoto, might be rendered by a stone bridge; a lone tree might stand for a mighty forest. Abstract concepts and themes from myths and legends, familiar to many Japanese, are similarly part of the garden vocabulary. The use of boulders in a streambed, for example, can represent life's surmountable difficulties; a pine tree can stand for strength and endurance; islands in a pond can evoke a faraway paradise.

Seasonal change is a highlight of the Japanese garden. The designer in effect choreographs the different plants that come into their glory at different times of year: cherry and plum blossoms and wisteria in spring; hydrangeas, peonies, and water lilies in summer; the spectacular reds and orange of the Japanese maple leaves in autumn. Even in winter the snow clinging to the garden's bare bones makes an impressive sight. In change there is permanence; in permanence there is fluid movement—often represented in the garden with a water element: a pond or a flowing stream, or an abstraction of one in raked gravel or stone.

The gardens of Kinkaku-ji, Kyoto

RELIGION IN JAPAN

A Shinto shrine near Tokyo

Although both Buddhism and Shinto permeate Japanese society and life, most Japanese are blissfully unconcerned about the distinction between what is Shinto and what is Buddhist. A wedding is often a Shinto ceremony, while a funeral is a Buddhist rite. The religions were separated by edict in 1868.

There's a saying in Japan that you're Shinto at birth (marked with a Shinto ceremony) and Buddhist when you die (honored with a Buddhist funeral). The Japanese take a utilitarian view of religion and use each as suits the occasion. One prays for success in life at a shrine and for the repose of a deceased family member at a temple. There is no thought given to the whys for this—these things simply are. The neighborhood shrine's annual *matsuri* is a time of giving thanks for prosperity and for blessing homes and local businesses. *O-mikoshi,* portable shrines for the gods, are enthusiastically carried around the district by young locals. Shouting and much sake drinking are part of the celebration. But it's a celebration first and foremost.

RELIGION IN NUMBERS

Although roughly two-thirds of Japanese people identify themselves as Buddhist, most also practice and believe in Shinto, even if they don't identify themselves as Shinto followers per se. The two religions overlap and even complement each other, even though most Japanese people would not consider themselves "religious." The religions are just part of life.

SHINTO

Shinto (literally, "the way of the *kami* [god]") is a form of animism or nature worship based on myth and rooted to the geography and holy places of the land. It's an ancient belief system, dating back perhaps as far as 500 BC, and is indigenous to Japan. The name is derived from a Chinese word, *shin tao,* coined in the 8th century AD, when divine origins were first ascribed to the royal Yamato family. Fog-enshrouded mountains, pairs of rocks, primeval forests, and geothermal activity are all manifestations of the *kami-sama* (honorable gods). For many Japanese the Shinto aspect of their lives is simply the realm of the kami-sama and is not attached to a dogmatic religious framework as it would be in the West.

BUDDHISM

A Korean king gave a statue of Shaka—the first Buddha, Prince Gautama—to the Yamato Court in AD 538. The Soga clan adopted the foreign faith, using it as a vehicle to change the political order of the day. After battling for control of the country, they established themselves as political rulers, and Buddhism took permanent hold. Simultaneously Japan sent its first ambassadors to China, inaugurating the importation of writing and religion into Japan and the subsequent exchange of ideas in

The gates at Futura-san Jinja, Nikko

art, construction, language, and other aspects of society with mainland Asia. By the 8th century, Buddhism was well established.

Japanese Buddhism developed in three waves. In the Heian period (794–1185), Esoteric Buddhism was introduced primarily by two priests, both of whom studied in China: Saicho and Kukai. Saicho established a temple on Mt. Hie near Kyoto, making it the most revered mountain in Japan after Mt. Fuji. Kukai established the Shingon sect of Esoteric Buddhism on Mt. Koya, south of Nara. In Japanese temple architecture, Esoteric Buddhism introduced the separation of the temple into an interior for the initiated and an outer laypersons' area.

Amidism (Pure Land) was the second wave, introduced by the monk Honen (1133–1212), and it flourished in the late 12th century until the introduction of Zen in 1185. Its adherents saw the world emerging from a period of darkness during which Buddhism had been in decline, and asserted that salvation was offered only to the believers in Amida, a Nyorai (Buddha) or enlightened being. Amidism's promise of salvation and its subsequent versions of heaven and hell earned it the appellation "Devil's Christianity" from

A statue of Buddha at Todai-ji, Nara

The Senso-ji Complex is the heart and soul of the Asakusa District of Tokyo.

visiting Christian missionaries in the 16th century.

In the Post-Heian period (1185 to the present) the influences of Nichiren and Zen Buddhist philosophies pushed Japanese Buddhism in new directions. Nichiren (1222–82) was a monk who insisted on the primacy of the Lotus Sutra, the supposed last and greatest sutra of Shaka. Zen Buddhism was attractive to the samurai class's ideals of discipline and worldly detachment and thus spread throughout Japan in the 12th century. It was later embraced as a nonintellectual path to enlightenment by those in search of a direct experience of the sublime. More recently Zen has been adopted by a growing number of people in the West as a way to move beyond the subject-object duality that characterizes Western thought.

SHRINE AND STATE

Although the modern Japanese constitution expressly calls for a separation of church and state, it hasn't always been this way. In fact, twice over the last 150 years, Shinto was the favored religion and the government used all of its influence to support it.

During the Meiji Restoration (1868), the emperor was made sovereign leader of Japan, and power that had been spread out among the shoguns was consolidated in the Imperial House. Shinto was favored over Buddhism for two reasons. First, according to Shinto, the members of the Imperial Family were direct descendants of the kami who had formed Japan. The second reason was more practical: many of the Buddhist temples were regional power bases that relied upon the shoguns for patronage. Relegating Buddhism to a minor religion with no official support would have a weakening effect on the shoguns, while the government could use Shinto shrines to strengthen its power base.

Indeed, Buddhism was actively suppressed. Temples were closed, priests were harassed, and priceless art was either destroyed or sold. The collections of Japanese art at the Museum of Fine Arts, Boston and the Freer Gallery in

Washington, D.C., were just two of the indirect beneficiaries of this policy.

During the Pacific War (the Japanese term for World War II), Shinto was again used by the military (with the complicity of the Imperial House) to justify an aggressive stance in Asia. (It should be noted that Kokuchukai Buddhism was also used to sanction the invasion of other countries.) The emperor was a god and therefore infallible. Since the Japanese people were essentially one family with the emperor at the head, they were a superior race that was meant to rule the lesser peoples of Asia.

Once ancestor worship was allied with worship of the emperor, the state became something worth dying for. So potent was this mix that General Douglas MacArthur identified state Shinto as one of the first things that had to be dismantled upon the surrender of Japan. The emperor could stay, but shrine and state had to go.

RELIGIOUS FESTIVALS

Although there are religious festivals and holy days observed throughout the year, the two biggest events in the Japanese religious calendar are New Year's (Oshogatsu) and Obon. New Year's is celebrated from January 1 to 3. Many people visit temples or shrines the night of December 31 to ring in the New Year or in the coming weeks. Temple bells are struck 108 times to symbolize ridding oneself of the 108 human sins. This practice of visiting a temple or shrine for the new year is called *hatsumode*. Food stalls are set up close to the popular places, and the atmosphere is festive and joyous. Many draw fortune slips called *omikuji* to see what kind of a year the oracle has in store for them.

The other major religious event in the Japanese calendar is the Obon holiday,

traditionally held from August 13 to 15. Obon is the Japanese festival of the dead when the spirits come back to visit the living. Most people observe the ritual by returning to their hometown or the home of their grandparents. Graves are cleaned and respects are paid to one's ancestors. Family ties are strengthened and renewed.

VISITING A BUDDHIST TEMPLE

The first thing to do when visiting a temple is to stop at the gate (called *mon* in Japanese), put your hands together and bow. Once inside the gate, you should stop to wash your hands at the stone receptacle usually found immediately upon entering the grounds. Not all temples will have a place for hand washing, but shrines will. Fill one of the ladles with water using your right hand and wash your left hand first. Then refill the ladle with water using your left hand and wash your right hand, being careful to not let the water drip back into the receptacle (the water is considered impure once it touches your hands).

You might also want to light a candle in front of the main altar of the temple and place it inside the glass cabinet. Then put your hands together and bow. You can also light three sticks

Meiji Shrine in Tokyo

The massive *torii* (entrance gates) of the Meiji Shrine are more than 40 feet tall.

of incense (lighting them together is customary) and put them in the large stone or brass stand. This action is also followed with a prayer and a bow.

After praying at the main altar and/or sub-altar, you'll probably want to spend some time walking around the temple grounds. Many have gardens and sculpture worthy of a visit in their own right. Upon leaving many will stop at the gate, turn, put their hands together, and bow to give thanks.

VISITING A SHINTO SHRINE

Shrines, like temples, have gates, though they are called *torii* and are often painted a bright red-orange, but this varies regionally. There are stained wooden torii, stone, and even metal torii. In terms of their appearance, torii look much like the mathematical symbol for pi. As with the gates of temples, one enters and exits through the torii, bowing on the way in and again on the way out but without clasping the hands.

Inside the shrine grounds, wash your hands as you would at a temple (left hand and then right hand). Then proceed to the main entrance (usually a set of open doors at the top of some stairs), clap twice to alert the kami of your presence, and bow. If there is a bell to ring, that will also summon the kami, as will the sound of money tossed into the box at the shrine's entrance. At a larger shrine there may be special trees, stones, and other holy objects situated throughout the grounds where you can repeat the clapping and praying process. At the beginning of their prayers, people introduce themselves by name and address. Since gods in Japan are local, you are to identify yourself to the god that you are of this place or of some other place and visiting.

After you have finished visiting the shrine, you should turn around at the torii and bow upon leaving.

Chapter 4

MARUNOUCHI AND NIHONBASHI

4

Updated by
Alexandra Ziminski

👁 Sights   🍴 Restaurants   🛏 Hotels   🛍 Shopping   🍸 Nightlife

★★★★★   ★★★★☆   ★★★★☆   ★★★☆☆   ★★☆☆☆

MARUNOUCHI AND NIHONBASHI SNAPSHOT

TOP EXPERIENCES

■ **Enjoy a city oasis.** Located in the middle of Tokyo, the Imperial Palace East Gardens are a wonderful place to escape the hustle and bustle of the city.

■ **Visit a controversial shrine.** The Yasukuni Shrine (Shrine of Peace for the Nation), which represents Japan's militaristic past, has long been the source of political tension between Japan, Korea, and China.

■ **See some of Japan's finest art.** The finest collection of Japanese modern art is housed in the National Museum of Modern Art, while the Idemitsu Museum of Arts contains masterpieces of classic Japanese ceramics and ink painting as well as Chinese porcelain.

GETTING HERE

The Imperial Palace is located in the heart of central Tokyo, and the city's other neighborhoods branch out from here. Marunouchi lies between Tokyo Station and the Outer Garden of the Imperial Palace, extending south to Hibiya Park. Nihonbashi is situated on the other side of the station and is crowned by its namesake, the Nihonbashi Bridge.

For the Imperial Palace, take the Chiyoda Line to Nijubashimae Station (Exit 6) or the JR lines to Tokyo Station (Marunouchi Central Exit). There are three entrance gates—Ote-mon, Hirakawa-mon, and Kita-hane-bashi-mon.

PLANNING YOUR TIME

If going on your own, allow at least an hour for the East Gardens and Outer Garden. Visit Yasukuni Jinja after lunch and spend at least an hour there, taking a half-hour each for the small Yushukan (at Yasukuni Jinja) and Kogeikan museums. The modern art museum requires a more leisurely visit.

The best time to visit is in spring when the *sakura* (cherry blossoms) trees are in bloom between late March and early April. But avoid visiting the Imperial Palace on Monday, when the East Gardens and museums are closed; the East Gardens are also closed Friday.

PAUSE HERE

■ Marunouchi Naka-dori is the main street of Marunouchi and stretches from Otemachi to Yur-akucho. Take a stroll down the tree- and store-lined avenue, which is famous for its illuminations in the winter and alfresco dining in the warmer months. On weekdays from 11 to 3 and on weekends from 11 to 5, the road is closed, and outside chairs and tables replace cars. If you're lucky, you may be able to spot a market or event.

OFF THE BEATEN PATH

■ To the northwest of the Imperial Palace, past the Yasukuni Shrine, you'll discover a tranquil waterway that was once part of the 15th-century Edo Castle's outer moat. Starting at Yotsuya Station, this stretch of water also includes Sotobori Park, which is famous during spring for its picture-perfect views of cherry blossom trees along the railway.

■ Follow the water until it joins the Kanda River at Iidabashi Station. Here, you can take a casual lunch at Canal Cafe and enjoy a perfect photo spot with undisturbed views. If you'd like to venture further, then continue west towards Kagurazaka, a traditional yet classy spot, and visit the impressive Akagi Shrine.

The Imperial Palace district is the core of Japan's government. It is primarily comprised of the Nagata-cho (surrounding neighborhood), the Imperial Palace (Kokyo-gaien), the Diet (national parliament building), the prime minister's residence (Kantei), and the Supreme Court. The Imperial Palace and the National Diet Building are both important for visitors to see, but the Supreme Court is rather nondescript.

Marunouchi is one of Tokyo's main business districts, making it a good choice for dining and shopping. It is also home to a few notable sights such as Tokyo Station and the Idemitsu Museum of Arts. Its neighbor, Nihonbashi, is known for its shopping and has many time-honored stores where you can pick up a few unique souvenirs.

The Imperial Palace was built by the order of Ieyasu Tokugawa, who chose the site for his castle in 1590. The castle had 99 gates (36 in the outer wall), 21 watchtowers (of which three are still standing), and 28 armories. The outer defenses stretched from present-day Shimbashi Station to Kanda. Completed in 1640 (and later expanded), it was at the time the largest castle in the world.

The Japanese Imperial Family resides in heavily blockaded sections of the palace grounds. Tours are conducted by reservation only, and restricted to designated outdoor sections, namely, the palace grounds and the East Gardens.

While the East Gardens are open to visitors daily, the main grounds are open to the general public only twice a year, on January 2 and February 23 (the reigning emperor's birthday), when thousands of people assemble under the balcony to offer their good wishes to the Imperial Family. The prime minister's residence is only viewable from afar, hidden behind fortified walls and trees.

The Imperial Palace

Sights

Chidorigafuchi National Cemetery
(千鳥ヶ淵戦没者墓苑; *Chidorigafuchi Senbotsusha Boen*)
CEMETERY | High on the edge of the Imperial Palace moat, this cemetery holds the remains of thousands of unknown soldiers and is famous for its springtime cherry blossoms. The adjacent Chidorigafuchi Boathouse rents out rowboats and pedal boats. Only a small part of

Once the site of the Imperial Palace's innermost defense circles, the East Gardens now offer respite in a beautiful setting.

the palace's outer moat is accessible, but a walk here makes for a refreshing 30 minutes. The entrance to the garden is near Yasukuni Jinja. ⊠ *2 Sanban-cho, Chiyoda-ku, Imperial Palace* ☎ *03/3234–1948* 🎫 *Park free, boat rental from ¥800* ⊘ *Boathouse closed Dec.–Mar.* Ⓜ *Hanzomon and Shinjuku subway lines, Kudanshita Station (Exit 2).*

Hanzo Gate (半蔵門; *Hanzo-mon*)
MILITARY SIGHT | The house of Hattori Hanzo (1541–96) once sat at the foot of this small wooden gate. Hanzo was a legendary leader of Ieyasu Tokugawa's private corps of spies and infiltrators—and assassins, if need be. They were the menacing, black-clad ninja—perennial material for historical adventure films and television dramas. The gate is a minute's walk from the subway. ⊠ *Chiyoda-ku, Imperial Palace* Ⓜ *Hanzomon subway line, Hanzo-mon Station (Exit 3).*

Hirakawa Gate (平川門; *Hirakawa-mon*)
NOTABLE BUILDING | The approach to this gate crosses the only wooden bridge that spans the Imperial Palace moat. The gate and bridge are reconstructions, but Hirakawa-mon is especially beautiful, looking much as it must have when the shogun's wives and concubines used it on their rare excursions from the harem. ⊠ *Imperial Palace* Ⓜ *Tozai subway line, Takebashi Station (Exit 1A).*

★ **Imperial Palace East Gardens**
(皇居東御苑; *Kokyo Higashi Gyo-en*)
GARDEN | Formerly part of the grounds of Edo Castle, this garden was claimed for the imperial family after the 1868 Meiji Restoration. Though most of the old castle was torn down or lost to fire, the stone foundations hint at the scale of the country's former seat of power. In the East Gardens you'll find the National Police Agency *dojo* (martial arts hall) and the Ote Rest House; the Museum of the Imperial Collection is next door and features rotating exhibits of imperial household treasures. The Hundred-Man Guardhouse was once defended by four shifts of 100 soldiers each. Past it is the entrance to what was once the *ni-no-maru*, the "second circle" of the fortress. It's

now a grove and garden. At the far end is the Suwa Tea Pavilion, an early-19th-century building relocated here from another part of the castle grounds. The octagonal tower is the 1966 Tokagakudo Concert Hall. ✉ *1–1 Chiyoda, Chiyoda-ku, Imperial Palace* 📞 *03/3213–1111* 💴 *Free* 🕐 *Closed Mon. and Fri.* Ⓜ *Tozai, Marunouchi, and Chiyoda subway lines, Otemachi Station (Exit C13B).*

Imperial Palace Outer Garden
(皇居外苑; *Kokyo-Gaien*)
GARDEN | When the office buildings of the Meiji government were moved from this area in 1899, the whole expanse along the east side of the palace was turned into a public promenade and planted with 2,800 pine trees. The Outer Garden affords the best view of the castle walls and their Tokugawa-period fortifications: Ni-ju-bashi and the Sei-mon, the 17th-century Fujimi Yagura watchtower, and the Sakurada-mon gate. From 10 to 4 on Sunday, the road between the Outer Garden and Palace is closed to all vehicles except bicycles. ✉ *1–1 Kokyogaien, Chiyoda-ku, Imperial Palace* 💴 *Free* 🕐 *East Gardens closed Mon. and Fri.* Ⓜ *Chiyoda subway line, Nijubashimae Station (Exit 2).*

National Diet Building
(国会議事堂; *Kokkai-Gijido*)
GOVERNMENT BUILDING | The Japanese parliament occupies a perfect example of post–World War II Japanese architecture; on a gloomy day it seems as if it might have sprung from the screen of a German Expressionist movie. Started in 1920, construction took 17 years to complete. Guided tours are available most days, but it's best to call ahead to confirm times. The prime minister's residence, Kantei, is across the street; you can try and get a glimpse of it, but it's quite hidden by walls and trees. ✉ *1–7–1 Nagata-cho, Chiyoda-ku* 📞 *03/5521–7445* 🌐 *www.sangiin.go.jp* 💴 *Free* 🕐 *Closed weekends* Ⓜ *Marunouchi subway line, Kokkai-Gijidomae Station (Exit 2).*

The Grutto Pass

If you plan on visiting a lot of the city's sights, purchasing a **Grutto Pass** (🌐 *www.rekibun.or.jp/grutto*) is the way to go. The pass, which is only ¥2,500, gives visitors free or discounted admission to 101 sights throughout the city including museums, zoos, aquariums, and parks. Passes can be purchased at all participating sights, as well as the Tokyo Tourist Information Center. Keep in mind that passes expire two months after date of purchase.

National Museum of Modern Art, Tokyo
(国立近代美術館; *Tokyo Kokuritsu Kindai Bijutsukan*)
ART MUSEUM | Founded in 1952 and moved to its present site in 1969, this was Japan's first national art museum. Often referred to by its acronym, MOMAT, it features a range of 20th- and 21st-century Japanese and Western artworks. On the second to fourth floors, it houses a permanent collection, which includes paintings, prints, and sculptures by Rousseau, Picasso, Tsuguji Fujita, Ryuzaburo Umehara, and Taikan Yokoyama. ✉ *3–1 Kitanomaru-koen, Chiyoda-ku, Imperial Palace* 📞 *050/5777–8600* 🌐 *www.momat.go.jp/english/am* 💴 *¥500* 🕐 *Closed Mon.* Ⓜ *Tozai subway line, Takebashi Station (Exit 1B); Hanzo-mon and Shinjuku subway lines, Kudanshita Station (Exit 2).*

Ni-ju-bashi Bridge (二重橋)
BRIDGE | Making a graceful arch across the moat, this bridge is surely the most photogenic spot on the grounds of the former Edo Castle. Mere mortals may pass through only on February 23 (the reigning emperor's birthday) and January 2 to pay their respects to the imperial family. The guards in front of their small,

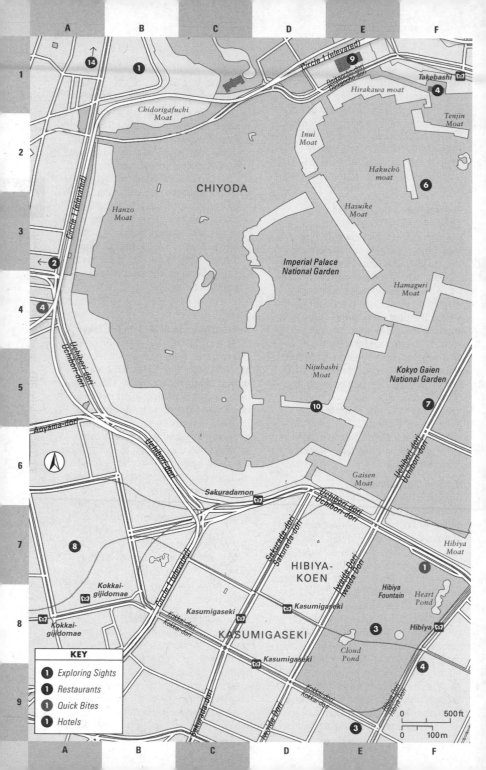

Imperial Palace District and Marunouchi

Sights ▼

1 Chidorigafuchi
  National Cemetery................ B1
2 Hanzo Gate......................... A3
3 Hibiya Park E8
4 Hirakawa Gate F1
5 Idemitsu Museum of Arts......... G7
6 Imperial Palace East Gardens F2
7 Imperial Palace Outer Garden F5
8 National Diet Building............. A7
9 National Museum of
  Modern Art, Tokyo................. E1
10 Ni-ju-bashi Bridge................ D5
11 Ote-mon Gate G3
12 Tokyo International Forum........ H7
13 Tokyo Station........................ I5
14 Yasukuni Shrine.................... A1

Restaurants ▼

1 Andy's Shin Hinomoto............. G8
2 Est H2
3 Heichinrou Hibiya.................. E9
4 Okonomiyaki Kiji I6
5 Robata Honten G8
6 T's Tantan Tokyo Station
  Keiyo Street I5
7 Trattoria Creatta H3

Quick Bites ▼

1 Hibiya Saroh........................ F7
2 Mihashi Tokyo Station............. J5
3 The Palace Lounge................ G3
4 Restaurant Patio.................... A4
5 Saza Coffee KITTE
  Marunouchi I6

Hotels ▼

1 Aman Tokyo I3
2 Four Seasons Hotel Tokyo at
  Marunouchi I6
3 Four Seasons Hotel Tokyo at
  Otemachi H2
4 Imperial Hotel, Tokyo.............. F9
5 Marunouchi Hotel I4
6 Palace Hotel Tokyo G3
7 The Peninsula Tokyo G8
8 Shangri-La Hotel, Tokyo........... J4
9 The Tokyo Station Hotel........... I5

octagonal, copper-roof sentry boxes change every hour on the hour—alas, with nothing like the pomp and ceremony at Buckingham Palace. ⊠ *1–7 Chiyoda, Chiyoda-ku* Ⓜ *Chiyoda subway line, Ni-ju-bashi-mae Station (Exit 2).*

Ote-mon Gate (大手門)

NOTABLE BUILDING | The main entrance to the Imperial Palace East Gardens was in former days the principal gate of Ieyasu Tokugawa's castle. Most of the gate was destroyed in 1945 but was rebuilt in 1967 based on the original plans. The outer part of the gate survived and offers an impressive entrance into the palace's East Gardens. ⊠ *1–1 Chiyoda, Chiyoda-ku* Ⓜ *Tozai, Marunouchi, and Chiyoda subway lines, Ote-machi Station (Exit C10).*

Yasukuni Shrine

(靖国神社; *Yasukuni Jinja*)
RELIGIOUS BUILDING | Founded in 1869, this shrine is dedicated to approximately 2½ million Japanese, Taiwanese, and Koreans who have died since then in war or military service. As the Japanese constitution expressly renounces both militarism and state sponsorship of religion, Yasukuni has been a center of stubborn political debate, particularly since 1978 when a shrine official added the names of several class-A war criminals to the list. Numerous prime ministers have visited the shrine since 1979, causing a political chill between Japan and its close neighbors, Korea and China, who suffered under Japanese colonialism. Despite all this, hundreds of thousands of Japanese come here every year, simply to pray for the repose of friends and relatives they have lost. These pilgrimages are most frenzied on August 15, the anniversary of the conclusion of World War II, when former soldiers and ultra-right-wing groups descend upon the shrine's grounds en masse.

The shrine is not one structure but a complex of buildings that include the Main Hall and the Hall of Worship—both built in the simple, unadorned style of the ancient Shinto shrines at Ise—and the Yushukan, a museum of documents and war memorabilia. Also here are a Noh theater and, in the far western corner, a sumo-wrestling ring. Sumo matches are held at Yasukuni in April, during the first of its three annual festivals. You can pick up a pamphlet and simplified map of the shrine, both in English, just inside the grounds.

Refurbished in 2002, the Yushukan presents Japan at its most ambivalent—if not unrepentant—about its more recent militaristic past. Critics charge that the newer exhibits glorify the nation's role in the Pacific War as a noble struggle for independence; certainly there's an agenda here that's hard to reconcile with Japan's firm postwar rejection of militarism as an instrument of national policy. Many Japanese visitors are moved by such displays as the last letters and photographs of young kamikaze pilots, while others find the Yushukan a cautionary, rather than uplifting, experience.

Although some of the exhibits have English labels and notes, the English is not very helpful; most objects, however, speak clearly enough for themselves. Rooms on the second floor house an especially fine collection of medieval swords and armor. Visiting on a Sunday offers a chance to forage at the flea market that runs from morning until sundown. ⊠ *3–1–1 Kudankita, Chiyoda-ku, Imperial Palace* ☎ *03/3261–8326* ⊕ *www.yasukuni.or.jp* ⊠ *Shrine free, Yushukan ¥1,000* Ⓜ *Hanzo-mon and Shinjuku subway lines, Kudanshita Station (Exit 1).*

☕ Coffee and Quick Bites

Restaurant Patio (レストラン パティオ)

$$ | EUROPEAN | Before exploring the Imperial Palace, enjoy breakfast at Patio, located inside the Grand Arc Hanzomon Hotel. On summer evenings, the restaurant also offers a relaxed beer garden with a reasonably priced set menu and all-you-can-drink options.

Known for: summer terrace; location opposite theater; reasonably priced breakfast. $ *Average main: ¥1,500* ⊠ *Hotel Grand Arc Hanzamon, 1–1 Hayabusa-cho, Chiyoda-ku, Imperial Palace* ☎ *03/3288–1636* ⊕ *www.grandarc.com* Ⓜ *Hanzomon Station.*

Marunouchi

👁 Sights

Hibiya Park (日比谷公園; *Hibiya Koen*)
CITY PARK | Hibiya Park opened in 1901 as the first Western-style park in Japan. Its nearly 40 acres of land contains beautiful seasonal flowers, a 500-year-old ginkgo tree, two ponds, and two open-air concert halls. It is the place to go for live music, festivals, and a leisurely stroll. ⊠ *1 Hibiya Park, Chiyoda-ku* ⊠ *Free* Ⓜ *Marunouchi subway line, Kasumigaseki Station (Exit B2); Hibiya, Chiyoda and Mita subway lines, Hibiya Station (Exits A10 and A14).*

★ Idemitsu Museum of Arts
(出光美術館; *Idemitsu Bijutsukan*)
ART MUSEUM | The strength of the collection in these four spacious, well-designed rooms lies in the Tang- and Song-dynasty Chinese porcelain and in the Japanese ceramics—including works by Nonomura Ninsei and Ogata Kenzan. On display are masterpieces of Old Seto, Oribe, Old Kutani, Karatsu, and Kakiemon ware. The museum also houses outstanding examples of Zen painting and calligraphy, wood-block prints, and genre paintings of the Edo period. Of special interest to scholars is the resource collection of shards from virtually every pottery-making culture of the ancient world. The museum is on the ninth floor of the Teikoku Gekijo building, which looks down upon the lavish Imperial Garden. Check ahead on the website to see if reservations are required when you plan to visit. ⊠ *Teigeki Bldg. 9F, 3–1–1 Marunouchi, Chiyoda-ku* ☎ *03/5777–8600* ⊕ *idemitsu-museum.or.jp/en* ⊠ *¥1,200* ⏱ *Closed Mon.* Ⓜ *Yurakucho subway line, Yurakucho Station (Exit B3); Yamanote Line, Yurakucho Station.*

Tokyo International Forum (東京国際フォーラム; *Tokyo Kokusai Foramu*)
PLAZA/SQUARE | This postmodern masterpiece, the work of Uruguay-born American architect Rafael Viñoly, is the first major convention and art center of its kind in Tokyo. Viñoly's design was selected in a 1989 competition that drew nearly 400 entries from 50 countries. The plaza of the Forum is that rarest of Tokyo rarities: civilized open space. There's a long central courtyard with comfortable benches shaded by trees, the setting for an antiques flea market the first and third Sunday of each month. The Forum itself is actually two buildings. Transit fans should take a stroll up the catwalks to the top, which concludes with a view of the Tokyo Station JR lines. ⊠ *3–5–1 Marunouchi, Chiyoda-ku* ☎ *03/5221–9000* ⊕ *www.t-i-forum.co.jp* Ⓜ *Yuraku-cho subway line, Yuraku-cho Station (Exit A-4B).*

Tokyo Station (東京駅; *Tokyo Eki*)
TRAIN/TRAIN STATION | This work of Kingo Tatsuno, one of Japan's first modern architects, was completed in 1914, with Tatsuno modeling his creation on the railway station of Amsterdam. The building lost its original top story in the air raids of 1945, but was promptly repaired. In the late 1990s, a plan to demolish the station was impeded by public outcry. The highlight is the historic and luxurious Tokyo Station Hotel, on the second and third floors. The area around the station is increasingly popular for dining, shopping, and entertainment. ⊠ *1–9–1 Marunouchi, Chiyoda-ku* Ⓜ *Marunouchi subway line and JR lines.*

🍴 Restaurants

After the working day is done, there must be somewhere for overworked office workers to grab a bite to eat. In fact, there are buildings and basements full of such places in Marunouchi.

★ Andy's Shin Hinomoto (新日の基)
$$ | **JAPANESE** | Also known as "Andy's," this izakaya is located directly under the tracks of the Yamanote Line, making the wooden interior shudder each time a train passes overhead. It's a favorite with local and foreign journalists and is actually run by a Brit, Andy, who travels to the seafood market every morning to buy seafood. **Known for:** favorite among Tokyo expats; expansive menu; cozy, lively atmosphere. [$] *Average main: ¥3,000* ✉ *2–4–4 Yurakucho, Chiyoda-ku* ☎ *03/3214–8021* 🌐 *shin-hinomoto.com* 💳 *No credit cards* 🕒 *Closed Sun. No lunch* [M] *JR Yurakucho Station (Hibiya Exit); Hibiya, Chiyoda, and Mita subway lines, Hibiya Station (Exits A2 and A6).*

Est (エスト)
$$$$ | **CONTEMPORARY** | On top of the Four Seasons Hotel Tokyo at Otemachi, there's a Michelin-starred restaurant serving contemporary French cuisine with a twist. Est presents eco-conscious, seasonal menus with 95% of ingredients locally sourced in Japan. **Known for:** a focus on sustainability; night view of Tokyo Skytree; seasonal outdoor terrace. [$] *Average main: ¥20,000* ✉ *Four Seasons Hotel Tokyo at Otemachi, 1–2–1 Otemachi, 39F, Chiyoda-ku* ☎ *03/6810–0655* 🌐 *www.est-tokyo.com* 🕒 *Closed Wed.* [M] *Marunouchi, Tozai, and Chiyoda subway lines, Otemachi Station (Exits C4 and C5).*

Heichinrou Hibiya (聘珍樓日比谷店)
$$$$ | **CHINESE** | A short walk from the Imperial Hotel, the Hibiya branch of one of Yokohama's oldest and best Chinese restaurants commands a spectacular view of the Imperial Palace grounds from 28 floors up. Call ahead to reserve a table by the window. **Known for:** kaisen ryori, a banquet of steamed seafood; lush, classic decor; a popular venue for power lunches. [$] *Average main: ¥13,000* ✉ *Fukoku Seimei Bldg., 2–2–2 Uchisaiwai-cho, 28th fl., Chiyoda-ku* ☎ *03/3508–0555* 🌐 *www.heichin.com* 🕒 *Closed Sun.* [M] *Mita Line, Uchisaiwai-cho Station (Exit A6).*

Okonomiyaki Kiji (お好み焼きじ)
$$ | **JAPANESE** | Sit down for a genuine taste of western Japan. The Kiji chain serves savory *okonomiyaki*, as well as other noodle dishes unique to its stores. **Known for:** okonomiyaki; no reservations and a line; smoky, fun ambience. [$] *Average main: ¥1,500* ✉ *Tokia Building, 2–7–3 Marunouchi, B1F, Chiyoda-ku* ☎ *03/3216–3123* 🌐 *www.o-kizi.jp* [M] *Marunouchi subway line, Tokyo Station (direct access); JR Yamanote Line, Tokyo Station (Marunouchi South Exit).*

★ Robata Honten (炉端本店)
$$$ | **JAPANESE** | Old, funky, and more than a little cramped, Robata is a bit daunting at first, but fourth-generation chef-owner Takao Inoue holds forth here with an inspired version of Japanese home cooking. He's also a connoisseur of pottery and serves his food on pieces acquired at famous kilns all over the country. **Known for:** country-style izakaya; no menu; dishes served on unique pottery collection. [$] *Average main: ¥5,000* ✉ *1–3–8 Yuraku-cho, Chiyoda-ku* ☎ *03/3591–1905* 💳 *No credit cards* 🕒 *Closed some Sun. each month. No lunch* [M] *JR Yuraku-cho Station (Hibiya Exit); Hibiya, Chiyoda, and Mita subway lines, Hibiya Station (Exit A4).*

T's Tantan Tokyo Station Keiyo Street (T'S たんたん 東京駅京葉ストリート店; *T's Tantan Tokyo Eki Keiyo Sutoriito Ten*)
$$ | **JAPANESE** | It can be hard to find a vegan restaurant in Tokyo, but T's thick and tasty, meat-free ramen satisfies that craving. Choose your soup base, from sesame to citrus flavors, and get a side of the vegetable dumplings—not to be missed. **Known for:** vegan ramen;

seasonal set meals; a lunch break between stations. $ *Average main: ¥1,500* ☒ *Tokyo Station Keiyo Street, 1–9–1 Marunouchi, 1F, Chiyoda-ku* ☎ *03/3218–8040* ⊕ *www.ts-restaurant.jp/ tantan/* Ⓜ *JR Tokyo Station.*

Trattoria Creatta (トラットリア クレアッタ)
$$$$ | ITALIAN | Sit down and savor a glass of carefully selected wine from Trattoria Creatta's impressive cellar. Sitting on the terrace beside Wadakura Moat on a warm summer's day, diners can choose from a modest, yet flavorful, selection of fresh pasta. **Known for:** reasonably priced prix-fixe courses; dining beneath cherry blossoms; free-flow Italian wine menu. $ *Average main: ¥5,500* ☒ *Nissay Marunouchi Gardentower, 1–1–3 Marunouchi, 1F, Chiyoda-ku* ☎ *03/3284–0020* ⊕ *www.creatta.tokyo* Ⓜ *Mita and Chiyoda subway lines, Otemachi Station (Exit D6).*

☕ Coffee and Quick Bites

Hibiya Saroh (日比谷サロー)
$ | EUROPEAN | After strolling through the flower gardens of Hibiya Park on a hot day, stop off for a cold pint of beer here; Hibiya Saroh is proud of the varieties on tap. There is no indoor seating, but with its view of Hibiya Park, you wouldn't want to be inside. **Known for:** simple, well-priced food; all-you-can-drink menu; auto rickshaw on the terrace. $ *Average main: ¥1,100* ☒ *1–1 Hibiya Park, Chiyoda-ku* ☎ *050/5304–4667* ⊙ *Closed Mon.* Ⓜ *Marunouchi subway line, Kasumigaseki Station (Exit B2); Hibiya, Chiyoda and Mita subway lines, Hibiya Station (Exits A10 and A14).*

Mihashi Tokyo Station (みはし東京駅一番街店; *Mihashi Tokyo Eki Ichibangai Ten*)
$ | JAPANESE | Mihashi offers traditional Japanese sweets in a comfortable environment. The staff is attentive and helpful, making it the perfect place to try desserts you may have never tried before. **Known for:** unlimited green tea refills;

Meiji-era anmitsu dessert; generous helping of fruit. $ *Average main: ¥1,000* ☒ *Tokyo Station, 1–9–1 Marunouchi, BF1, Chiyoda-ku* ⊹ *Next to Yaesu North Gate* ☎ *03/5220–0384* ⊕ *www.mihashi.co.jp* Ⓜ *JR Tokyo Station.*

The Palace Lounge (ザ パレス ラウンジ)
$$$ | EUROPEAN | In addition to its elegant decor, plush sofas, and outdoor patio, The Palace Lounge also offers one of Tokyo's best afternoon tea sets, which includes both Japanese and European sweets. The extensive tea menu also makes it a good place to try a variety of unique, high-end teas while taking a quiet break from the day's sightseeing. **Known for:** afternoon tea in a relaxed atmosphere; collection of teas; elaborate parfaits. $ *Average main: ¥4,000* ☒ *Palace Hotel Tokyo, 1–1–1 Marunouchi, Chiyoda-ku* ☎ *03/3211–5309* Ⓜ *Otemachi Station (Exit C13b).*

Saza Coffee KITTE Marunouchi (サザコーヒー)
$ | ETHIOPIAN | Serving aromatic coffee sourced from all over the world, this narrow, brick-lined café makes drinking an experience. The best seats are in front of the lab, where coffee bubbles in a siphon. **Known for:** not many seats; Ethiopian coffee beans; beautifully presented coffee. $ *Average main: ¥1,000* ☒ *Kitte Marunouchi, 2–7–2 Marunouchi, 1F, Chiyoda-ku* ☎ *03/6268–0720* ⊕ *www.saza.co.jp* Ⓜ *Marunouchi subway line, Tokyo Station (direct access); JR Tokyo Station (Marunouchi South Exit).*

🛏 Hotels

Some of the city's best hotels are located here in Marunouchi. You'll find a mix of top foreign and domestic brands.

★ Aman Tokyo (アマン東京)
$$$$ | HOTEL | Mixing modern design with Japanese aesthetics, the Aman Tokyo is more than a hotel; it is an experience in the center of the city. **Pros:** immaculate service; blend of Japanese aesthetics

and modernity; wonderful views. **Cons:** nearly double the price of other hotels in its class; immediate area is busy on weekdays, dead on weekends; Japanese aesthetic too minimalist for some tastes. [$] *Rooms from: ¥90,000* ✉ *The Otemachi Tower, 1–5–6 Otemachi, Chiyoda-ku* ☎ *03/5224–3333* 🌐 *www.amanresorts.com* 🛏 *84 rooms* 🍴 *No Meals* [M] *Hanzomon, Chiyoda, Tozai, and Marunouchi subway lines, Otemachi Station (Exits C11 and C8).*

★ Four Seasons Hotel Tokyo at Marunouchi (フォーシーズンズホテル丸の内東京)
$$$$ | **HOTEL** | A departure from the typical grand scale of most Four Seasons properties, the Marunouchi branch, set within the glistening Pacific Century Place, has the feel of a boutique hotel. **Pros:** convenient airport access; small number of rooms lends the hotel a boutique feel; helpful, English-speaking staff. **Cons:** high-priced; the only views are those of nearby Tokyo Station; trains are audible from some rooms. [$] *Rooms from: ¥66,000* ✉ *Pacific Century Pl., 1–11–1 Marunouchi, Chiyoda-ku* ☎ *03/5222–7222* 🌐 *www.fourseasons.com/marunouchi* 🛏 *57 rooms* 🍴 *No Meals* [M] *JR Tokyo Station (Yaesu South Exit).*

Four Seasons Hotel Tokyo at Otemachi (フォーシーズンズホテル東京大手町)
$$$$ | **HOTEL** | The latest Four Seasons Tokyo hotel was only unveiled at the end of 2020, but is already delighting guests with its unmatched hospitality and sweeping views of Tokyo landmarks and Mount Fuji. **Pros:** all rooms have views; incredible dining options; personable, friendly staff. **Cons:** far from nightlife; not easy to come and go; very high price tag. [$] *Rooms from: ¥66,000* ✉ *1–2–1 Otemachi, Chiyoda-ku* ☎ *03/6810–0600* 🌐 *www.fourseasons.com/otemachi* 🛏 *190 rooms* 🍴 *No Meals* [M] *Marunouchi, Tozai, and Chiyoda subway lines, Otemachi Station (Exits C4 and C5).*

Imperial Hotel, Tokyo
(帝国ホテル; *Teikoku Hoteru*)
$$$$ | **HOTEL** | Though not as fashionable or as spanking-new as its neighbor the Peninsula, the venerable Imperial can't be beat for traditional elegance. **Pros:** an old Japanese hotel with a long history; dining options are varied and superb; large rooms. **Cons:** layout can be confusing; some rooms have dated interiors; new tower building closest to trains can be noisy. [$] *Rooms from: ¥48,000* ✉ *1–1–1 Uchisaiwai-cho, Chiyoda-ku* ☎ *03/3504–1111* 🌐 *www.imperialhotel.co.jp* 🛏 *931 rooms* 🍴 *No Meals* [M] *Hibiya subway line, Hibiya Station (Exit 5).*

Marunouchi Hotel (丸ノ内ホテル)
$$ | **HOTEL** | Convenience is one reason to choose the Marunouchi Hotel, occupying the upper 11 floors of the Marunouchi Oazo Building and joining Tokyo Station via an underground walkway. **Pros:** convenient airport access; central location; helpful concierge. **Cons:** designed for business travelers; rooms are smallish; limited dining choices. [$] *Rooms from: ¥30,000* ✉ *1–6–3 Marunouchi, Chiyoda-ku* ☎ *03/3217–1111* 🌐 *www.marunouchi-hotel.co.jp* 🛏 *205 rooms* 🍴 *No Meals* [M] *JR Tokyo Station (Marunouchi North Exit).*

★ Palace Hotel Tokyo (パレスホテル東京)
$$$$ | **HOTEL** | This hotel has a handsome, refined look that sets the stage for a luxury experience. **Pros:** deluxe balcony rooms have excellent views; luxurious yet tasteful design; impeccable service. **Cons:** on the pricey side; business-traveler focus; regular deluxe rooms are overvalued. [$] *Rooms from: ¥66,000* ✉ *1–1–1 Marunouchi, Chiyoda-ku* ☎ *03/3211–5211* 🌐 *www.en.palacehoteltokyo.com* 🛏 *290 rooms* 🍴 *No Meals* [M] *Chiyoda, Tozai, Hanzomon subway lines, Otemachi Station (Exit C13).*

The Palace Hotel Tokyo is a historic hotel with a contemporary and spacious rooms.

The Peninsula Tokyo
(ザ・ペニンシュラ東京)
$$$$ | **HOTEL** | From the staff in caps and sharp suits, often assisting guests from a Rolls-Royce shuttling to and from Narita, to the shimmering gold glow emitting from the top floors, the 24-floor Peninsula Tokyo exudes elegance and grace. **Pros:** first-class room interiors; luxurious details; wonderful spa. **Cons:** crowded lobby and public areas can detract from the luxury feel; formal service can feel impersonal; high prices. [$] *Rooms from: ¥66,000* ✉ *1–8–1 Yurakucho, Chiyoda-ku* ☎ *03/6270–2888* 🌐 *www.peninsula.com* 🛏 *314 rooms* 🍴 *No Meals* [M] *JR Yamanote Line, Yuraku-cho Station (Hibiya-guchi/Hibiya Exit); Mita, Chiyoda, and Hibiya subway lines, Hibiya Station (Exits A6 and A7).*

Shangri-La Hotel Tokyo
(シャングリ・ラ ホテル 東京)
$$$$ | **HOTEL** | Boasting high-end luxury, lavish interiors, and superb views of Tokyo Bay and the cityscape from the top 11 floors of Marunouchi Trust Tower Main, Shangri-La Hotel Tokyo's 37-floor building is conveniently located near Tokyo Station. **Pros:** contemporary elegance with an Asian edge; some of Tokyo's most spacious guestrooms; atmospheric Tibetan-inspired Chi Spa. **Cons:** luxury does not come cheap; located in a business district; entrance might be hard to find. [$] *Rooms from: ¥68,000* ✉ *Marunouchi Trust Tower, 1–8–3 Marunouchi, Chiyoda-ku* ☎ *03/6739–7888* 🌐 *www.shangri-la.com* 🛏 *200 rooms* 🍴 *No Meals* [M] *JR Tokyo Station (Yaesu North Exit).*

The Tokyo Station Hotel
(東京ステーションホテル)
$$$$ | **HOTEL** | Convenience and nostalgia come together at this hotel, located inside the busy Tokyo train station, a grand building that recently refurbished its redbrick exterior. **Pros:** impeccable service; easy access to shopping; lovely, historic setting. **Cons:** rooms on the small side; views from some rooms limited; concierge service can be hit or miss. [$] *Rooms from: ¥55,000* ✉ *1–9–1 Marunouchi, Chiyoda-ku* ☎ *03/5220–1111*

All That Tokyo Jazz

The Tokyo jazz scene is one of the world's best, far surpassing that of Paris and New York with its number of venues playing traditional, swing, bossa nova, rhythm and blues, and free jazz. Though popular in Japan before World War II, jazz really took hold of the city after U.S. forces introduced Charlie Parker and Thelonius Monk in the late 1940s. The genre had been banned in wartime Japan as an American vice, but even at the height of the war, fans were able to listen to their favorite artists on Voice of America radio. In the 1960s Japan experienced a boom in all areas of the arts, and jazz was no exception. Since then, the Japanese scene has steadily bloomed, with several local stars—such as Sadao Watanabe in the 1960s and contemporary favorites Keiko Lee and Hiromi Uehara—gaining global attention.

Today there are more than 120 bars and clubs that host live music, plus hundreds that play recorded jazz. Shinjuku, Takadanobaba, and Kichijoji are the city's jazz enclaves. Famous international acts regularly appear at big-name clubs such as the Blue Note, but the smaller, lesser-known joints usually have more atmosphere. With such a large jazz scene, there's an incredible diversity to enjoy, from Louis Armstrong tribute acts to fully improvised free jazz—sometimes on successive nights at the same venue.

If you time your visit right, you can listen to great jazz at one of the city's more than 20 annual festivals dedicated to this adopted musical form. The festivals vary in size and coverage, but two to check out are the Tokyo Jazz Festival and the Asagaya Jazz Street Festival.

⊕ www.tokyostationhotel.jp ⇥ 150 rooms ⦿ No Meals Ⓜ JR Line, Tokyo Station (South Exit).

Nightlife

BARS

Marunouchi House (丸の内ハウス;)

BEER GARDENS | On the seventh floor of the Shin-Marunouchi Building, you'll find a 360-degree terrace that boasts a number of lively restaurants and bars. Take in the night views of the Tokyo Station building and Imperial Palace gardens and bar-hop 'til the early morning. On certain days, the venue hosts DJs and special events. ⊠ Shin-Marunouchi Building, 1–5–1 Marunouchi, 7F, Chiyoda-ku ☎ 03/5218–5100 ⊕ www.marunouchi-house.com Ⓜ Marunouchi subway line, Tokyo Station (Exit M7); JR Yamanote Line, Tokyo Station (Marunouchi South Exit).

Peter

BARS | Like most of Tokyo's high-end hotels, the Peninsula has a high-rise bar. But unlike many staid hotel bars, this 24th-floor spot with a forest of chrome trees, designed by Yabu Pushelberg, is lots of fun. ⊠ Peninsula Tokyo, 1–8–1 Yurakucho, 24th fl., Marunouchi ☎ 03/6270–2888 ⊕ www.peninsula.com Ⓜ Hibiya and Mita subway lines, Hibiya Station (Exit A6).

JAZZ CLUBS

Cotton Club (コットンクラブ)

LIVE MUSIC | In these intimate and luxurious surroundings you can listen to not only jazz but also a diverse range of music: soul, R&B, J-pop, and world music. The club has such an excellent sound system that musicians such as Ron Carter record here. Fine French cuisine lures music lovers for special nights out and important business entertaining.

Tokia Bldg., 2–7–3 Marunouchi, 2nd fl., Chiyoda-ku ☎ 03/3215–1555 ⊕ blue-notejapan.jp/en/brands/cottonclub Ⓜ JR and subway lines, Tokyo Station, directly connected to Tokia Bldg.

🎭 Performing Arts

MODERN THEATER
Takarazuka (宝塚)
THEATER | Japan's all-female theater troupe was founded in the Osaka suburb of Takarazuka in 1913 and has been going strong ever since. Today it has not one but five companies, one of which has a permanent home in Tokyo at the 2,069-seat Takarazuka Theater. Same-day tickets are sold at the box office at either 9:30 am or 10 am for later shows. Advance tickets are available through ticketing agencies and the theater's website. Any remaining tickets are sold at the theater box office. *⊠ 1–1–3 Yurakucho, Chiyoda-ku ☎ 03/5251–2001 ⊕ kageki.hankyu.co.jp/english/index.html ☚ From ¥3,500 Ⓜ JR Yamanote Line, Yuraku-cho Station (Hibiya Exit); Hibiya subway line, Hibiya Station (Exit A5); Chiyoda and Mita subway lines, Hibiya Station (Exit A13).*

TRADITIONAL THEATER
National Theater of Japan
(国立劇場; *Kokuritsu Gekijo*)
PERFORMANCE VENUE | Architect Hiroyuki Iwamoto's winning entry in the design competition for the National Theater building (1966) is a rendition in concrete of the ancient *azekura* (storehouse) style, invoking the 8th-century Shosoin Imperial Repository in Nara. The large hall seats 1,610 and presents primarily Kabuki theater, ancient court music, and dance. The small hall seats 590 and is used mainly for Bunraku puppet theater and traditional music. Performances are in Japanese, but English-translation headsets are available for many shows. Debut performances, called *kao-mise,* are worth watching to catch the stars of the next generation. Tickets can be reserved until the day of the performance by calling

the theater box office between 10 and 6. *⊠ 4–4–1 Hayabusa-cho, Chiyoda-ku ☎ 03/3265–7411 ⊕ www.ntj.jac.go.jp/en ☚ Varies depending on performance Ⓜ Hanzo-mon subway line, Hanzo-mon Station (Exit 1).*

🛍 Shopping

To the west of Tokyo Station, which for all intents and purposes is the entranceway to the city, is Marunouchi, a high-rise forest that is all about modernity. The arcades and shops attract sophisticated professionals who look for no-fuss quality. They also know how to let loose at the neighborhood's lounges and bars when the workday is done.

BOOKS
Maruzen (丸善書店; *Maruzen Shoten*)
BOOKS | FAMILY | In this flagship branch of the Maruzen chain in the Oazo building, there are English titles on the fourth floor as well as art books; the store also hosts occasional art exhibits. *⊠ 1–6–4 Marunouchi, Chiyoda-ku ☎ 03/5288–8881 Ⓜ JR Yamanote Line, Tokyo Station (North Exit); Tozai subway line, Otemachi Station (Exit B2C).*

HOUSEWARES
Nakagawa Masashichi Shoten
(中川政七商店)
CRAFTS | This Tokyo flagship of a homewares store established in Nara City in 1716 stocks a wide range of items and tools for your daily life, including the Hasami line of crockery made with Nagasaki porcelain. Look for hanafukin, a traditional cotton cloth originally used as mosquito netting, and the store's signature hanafukin tea towels, which are renowned for their soft texture and high absorbency. *⊠ Kitte, 2–7–2 Marunouchi, 4F, Chiyoda-ku ☎ 03/3217–2010 ⊕ www.nakagawa-masashichi.jp Ⓜ JR Tokyo Station.*

MALLS AND SHOPPING CENTERS

Kitte Marunouchi (キッテ丸の内)

DEPARTMENT STORE | The unique geometric shape of Kitte's interior, which was partly designed by renowned Japanese architect Kengo Kuma, sets this department store apart. It also has a notable free history museum (called Intermediatheque) and an expansive rooftop garden overlooking Tokyo Station on the sixth floor. The department store's name, Kitte, is a play on the Japanese words "stamp" and "come". It makes sense once you know that Japan Post was the building's developer. ⌧ *2–7–2 Marunouchi, Chiyo-da-ku* ☏ *03/3216–2811* ⊕ *marunouchi. jp-kitte.jp* Ⓜ *Marunouchi subway line, Tokyo Station (direct access); JR Tokyo Station (Marunouchi South Exit).* ()

Marunouchi Buildings (丸の内ビル)

SHOPPING CENTER | Bringing some much-needed retail dazzle to the area are these six shopping, office, and dining mega-complexes called Marunoucuhi, Shin-marunouchi, Oazo, Iiyo, Brick Square, and Tokia. Highlights include the fifth-floor open terrace on the Marunouchi building, with its view of Tokyo Station, and Bricksquare, which has its own oasislike European garden on the ground floor to rest in between bouts of shopping at the luxury and everyday boutiques. ⌧ *2–4–1 Marunouchi, Chiyoda-ku* ☏ *03/5218–5100* ⊕ *www. marunouchi.com* Ⓜ *Marunouchi subway line, Tokyo Station (Marunouchi Bldg. Exit); JR Yamanote Line, Tokyo Station (Marunouchi Minami-guchi/South Exit).*

Tokyo Midtown Hibiya
(東京ミッドタウン日比谷)

SHOPPING CENTER | Billed as a luxury entertainment-and-shopping complex, Midtown Hibiya's curvy glass-meets-greenery design is worth a visit for the architecture itself. The complex has six floors of shopping and dining, focusing on high-end and smaller brands. Two floors are devoted to Toho Cinema's premier theater. Outside, the grassy lawn of the sixth-floor garden often hosts events and is a great place to relax outside. ⌧ *1–1–2 Yurakucho, Chiyo-da-ku* ☏ *03/5157–1251* ⊕ *www.hibiya. tokyo-midtown.com* Ⓜ *Hibiya Station (Exit A11, A12); JR Yurakucho Station (South Exit).*

Nihonbashi

Sights

Artizon Museum (アーティゾン美術館; *Achizon bijutsukan*)

ART MUSEUM | Formerly the Bridgestone Museum of Art, the Artizon Museum is one of Japan's best private collections of French impressionist art and sculpture and of post-Meiji Japanese painting in Western styles by such artists as Shigeru Aoki and Tsuguji Fujita. The collection, assembled by Bridgestone Tire Company founder Shojiro Ishibashi, also includes works by Rembrandt, Picasso, Utrillo, and Modigliani. The museum also puts on exhibits featuring works from other private collections and museums abroad. ⌧ *1–7–2 Kyo-bashi, Chuo-ku* ☏ *03/5777–8600* ⊕ *www.artizon.museum* 💷 *From ¥1,200 depending on exhibition* ⊗ *Closed Mon.* Ⓜ *Ginza subway line, Kyo-bashi Station (Meijiya Exit) or Nihombashi Station (Takashimaya Exit).*

Bank of Japan Currency Museum
(日本銀行貨幣博物館; *Nihon Ginko Kahei Hakubutsukan*)

OTHER MUSEUM | The older part of the Bank of Japan complex is the work of Tatsuno Kingo, who also designed Tokyo Station. Completed in 1896, on the site of what had been the Edo-period gold mint, the bank is one of the few surviving Meiji-era Western-style buildings in the city. The annex building houses the Currency Museum, a historical collection of rare gold and silver coins from Japan and other East Asian countries. There's little English-language information here, but the setting of muted lighting and plush

The Nihonbashi neighborhood is named after its famous 17th-century canal bridge.

red carpets evokes the days when the only kind of money around was heavy, shiny, and made of precious metals. ⊠ 1–3–1 Nihonbashi-Hongokucho, Chuo-ku ☎ 03/3277–3037 ⊕ www.imes.boj. or.jp ⊠ Free ☺ Closed Mon. Ⓜ Ginza and Hanzomon subway lines, Mitsukoshi-mae Station (Exits B1 and A5).

Nihonbashi Bridge (日本橋)

BRIDGE | Originally built in 1603, this was the starting point of Edo Japan's five major highways and the point from which all highway distances were measured. Even today one sees signs noting the distance to Nihonbashi. Rebuilt in stone in 1911, the structure's graceful double arch, ornate lamps, and bronze Chinese lions and unicorns are unfortunately marred by an expressway running directly overhead. In the rush to relieve traffic congestion in preparation for the 1964 Olympics, city planners ignored the protestations of residents and preservation groups and pushed ahead with construction. Still, the sight of a modern highway running over the old stone bridge makes

for interesting photos and is worth a visit for history buffs. ⊠ 1–8 Nihonbashi-muromachi, Chuo-ku Ⓜ Tozai and Ginza subway lines, Nihonbashi Station (Exits B5 and B6); Ginza and Hanzomon subway lines, Mitsukoshi-mae Station (Exits B5 and B6).

Taimeiken Kite Museum (たいめいけん凧 の博物館; Tako no Hakubutsukan)

OTHER MUSEUM | FAMILY | Kite flying is an old tradition in Japan. The collection here includes examples of every shape and variety from all over the country, hand-painted in brilliant colors with figures of birds, geometric patterns, and motifs from Chinese and Japanese mythology. You can call ahead to arrange a kite-making workshop (in Japanese) for groups of children. ⊠ NS Bldg., 1–8–3 Nihonbashi, 2nd fl., Chuo-ku ☎ 03/3275–2704 ⊕ www.taimeiken.co.jp/museum. html ⊠ ¥210 Ⓜ Tozai subway line, Nihonbashi Station (Exit C5); JR Tokyo Station (Yaesu Exit).

Nihonbashi's quirky Kite Museum is jam-packed with hundreds of traditional paper and bamboo kites.

🍴 Restaurants

This historic district is all about legacy and tradition. It was home to the original seafood market in Tokyo before moving to Tsukiji and its current location in Toyosu. Some of the restaurants here have been passed down through generations. And Japan's oldest department store, Mitsukoshi, is also here; its basement *depachika* is filled with prepared foods for a quick bite.

Dhaba India (ダバ インディア)
$$ | INDIAN | With a focus on South India cuisine, Dhaba has built a reputation as having some of the best Indian flavors in town. A specialty here are the dosas, a kind of stuffed crepe, but the curries, whether the spicy coriander mutton or the fragrant lemon shrimp masala, are just as good. **Known for:** seafood curries like the Tamil fish pulsu; the best dosa in Tokyo; lunchtime lines can wrap around the corner. [$] *Average main: ¥2,300* ✉ *2–7–9 Yaesu, Chuo-ku* ☎ *03/3272–7160* 🌐 *dhabaindiatokyo.com* [M] *Ginza subway line, Kyobashi Station (Exit 5).*

★ **Nihonbashi Yukari** (日本橋ゆかり)
$$$$ | JAPANESE | Anyone looking to experience Japanese haute cuisine in a more relaxed atmosphere should look to this *kappo*-style restaurant, where diners order and eat at the counter. Third-generation chef—and 2002 Iron Chef champion—Kimio Nonaga displays his artistry in every element of Nihonbashi Yukari's menu. **Known for:** affordable for high-end kappo dining; excellent kappo-style lunch sets; chef Nonaga's creative take on Japanese cuisine. [$] *Average main: ¥15,000* ✉ *3–2–14 Nihonbashi, Chuo-ku* ☎ *03/3271–3436* 🕒 *Closed Sun.*

Signature (シグネチャー)
$$$$ | FRENCH | This elegant French restaurant on the 37th floor of the Mandarin Oriental Hotel has wonderful views of the Tokyo skyline as well an open kitchen, where diners can see the masterful chef Nicolas Boujéma and his staff at work. Boujéma has an impressive résumé, having worked in kitchens such

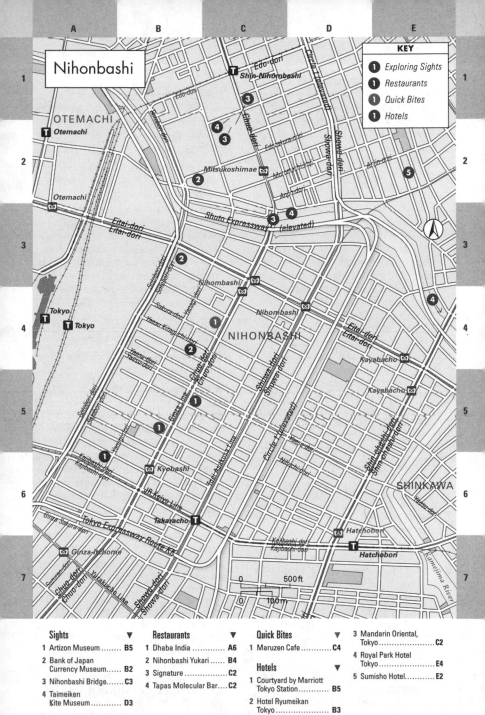

Nihonbashi

KEY

- **1** Exploring Sights
- **1** Restaurants
- **1** Quick Bites
- **1** Hotels

OTEMACHI

Otemachi

Otemachi

Edo-dori

Shin-Nihonbashi

Mitsukoshimae

Shuto Expressway (elevated)

Nihombashi

Nihombashi

NIHONBASHI

Eitai-dori

Kayabacho

Kayabacho

Tokyo

Tokyo

Kyobashi

SHINKAWA

Takaracho

Ginza-itchome

Tokyo Expressway Route KK

Hatchobori

Hatchobori

Kameijima River

500ft

100m

Sights ▼

1 Artizon Museum **B5**

2 Bank of Japan
Currency Museum...... **B2**

3 Nihonbashi Bridge....... **C3**

4 Taimeiken
Kite Museum **D3**

Restaurants ▼

1 Dhaba India **A6**

2 Nihonbashi Yukari **B4**

3 Signature **C2**

4 Tapas Molecular Bar.... **C2**

Quick Bites ▼

1 Maruzen Cafe **C4**

Hotels ▼

1 Courtyard by Marriott
Tokyo Station **B5**

2 Hotel Ryumeikan
Tokyo **B3**

3 Mandarin Oriental,
Tokyo **C2**

4 Royal Park Hotel
Tokyo **E4**

5 Sumisho Hotel............ **E2**

as La Tour d'Argent, Le Balzac, and most recently with Pierre Gagnaire. **Known for:** fine French cuisine with a Japanese flair; stunning views of the city below; luxurious, modern atmosphere. $ *Average main: ¥15,000* ✉ *Mandarin Oriental Tokyo, 2–1–1 Nihonbashi, Chuo-ku* ☎ *03/3270–8188* 🌐 *www.mandarinoriental.com/tokyo/dining/signature* [M] *Ginza subway line, Mitsukoshi-mae Station (Exit A7).*

Tapas Molecular Bar
(タパス モレキュラーバー)
$$$$ | **JAPANESE** | Occupying a mysterious place between traditional sushi counter, tapas bar, science lab, and magic show, this award-winning restaurant breaks new ground. In full view of diners, the team of chefs assemble a small parade of bite-size morsels in surprising texture and flavor combinations. **Known for:** a playful take on fine dining; exclusive, intimate atmosphere; watching the chefs is almost as good as the food itself. $ *Average main: ¥16,000* ✉ *Mandarin Oriental Tokyo, 2–1–1 Nihonbashi, Chuo-ku* ☎ *03/3270–8188* 🌐 *www.mandarinoriental.com/tokyo/dining/molecular* ⏲ *No lunch weekdays* [M] *Ginza subway line, Mitsukoshi-mae Station (Exit A7).*

Coffee and Quick Bites

Maruzen Cafe (丸善 カフェ)
$$ | **AMERICAN** | Known for its classic *hayashi* (hashed beef) rice, lemon herbal tea, and waffles with a side of fluffy ice cream, Maruzen Cafe is the perfect mid-afternoon stop. Its location on the third floor of Maruzen Bookstore and sleek, dark wooden furniture add to the homey atmosphere. **Known for:** an expansive menu and well-priced dishes; hayashi rice; attentive, polite staff. $ *Average main: ¥1,500* ✉ *Maruzen Nihonbashi, 2–3–10 Nihonbashi, 3F, Chuo-ku* ☎ *03/6202–0013* [M] *Ginza subway line, Nihonbashi Station (Exit B1).*

Hotels

A historic area to the east, Nihonbashi is primarily a stopover for business travelers. Some high-end accommodations are available, but you can also find good budget options.

Courtyard by Marriott Tokyo Station
(コートヤード・バイ・マリオット 東京ステーション)
$$ | **HOTEL** | Situated on the first four floors of the sleek Kyobashi Trust Tower, the Courtyard by Marriott is a convenient option for business travelers. **Pros:** convenient; many nearby dining options; attentive staff. **Cons:** small rooms; closet space limited; somewhat generic atmosphere. $ *Rooms from: ¥20,000* ✉ *2–1–3 Kyobashi, Chuo-ku* ☎ *03/3516-9600* 🌐 *www.cytokyo.com* 🛏 *150 rooms* 🍴 *No Meals* [M] *Ginza subway line, Kyobashi Station (Exit 1); JR lines, Tokyo Station (Yaesu Exit).*

★ **Hotel Ryumeikan Tokyo** (ホテル龍名館東京)
$$ | **HOTEL** | One of the most affordable hotels near Tokyo Station (a mere three-minute walk away), the Ryumeikan is a great option for the business traveler or those making side trips outside the city. **Pros:** great, convenient location; wonderful restaurant; English-speaking staff. **Cons:** busy area during the week; rooms can feel small; basic amenities. $ *Rooms from: ¥24,000* ✉ *1–3–22 Yaesu, Chuo-ku* ☎ *03/3271–0971* 🌐 *www.ryumeikan-tokyo.jp/english* 🛏 *135 rooms* 🍴 *No Meals* [M] *JR Tokyo Station (Yaesu North Exit).*

★ **Mandarin Oriental, Tokyo**
(マンダリン オリエンタル 東京)
$$$$ | **HOTEL** | Occupying the top nine floors of the glistening Nihonbashi Mitsui Tower, this hotel is a blend of harmony and outright modernity. **Pros:** wonderful spa and concierge service; nice city views; attractive room interiors. **Cons:** pricey; quiet area on the weekends; no pool. $ *Rooms from: ¥60,000* ✉ *2–1–1*

Nihonbashi Muromachi, Chiyoda-ku
☎ 03/3270–8800 ⊕ www.mandarinorien-
tal.com/tokyo ⇨ 178 rooms ⦿ No Meals
Ⓜ Ginza and Hanzomon subway lines,
Mitsukoshi-mae Station (Exit A7).

Royal Park Hotel Tokyo
(ロイヤルパークホテル)
$$ | HOTEL | A passageway connects
this hotel to the Tokyo City Air Terminal,
where you can easily catch a bus to
Narita Airport, making the Royal Park a
great one-night stopover option. **Pros:**
convenient airport access; nice lobby;
warm, friendly service. **Cons:** not located
near downtown; immediate area desert-
ed on weekends; beginning to show its
age. Ⓢ Rooms from: ¥28,000 ⊠ 2–1–1
Nihonbashi Kakigara-cho, Chuo-ku
☎ 03/3667–1111 ⊕ www.rph.co.jp ⇨ 407
rooms ⦿ No Meals Ⓜ Hanzo-mon sub-
way line, Suitengu-mae Station (Exit 4).

Sumisho Hotel (住庄ほてる)
$ | HOTEL | In a down-to-earth, friendly
neighborhood, this hotel is popular with
budget-minded foreign visitors who prefer
to stay near the small Japanese restau-
rants and bars of the Ningyo-cho area of
Nihonbashi. **Pros:** nicely priced; friendly
staff; neighborhood restaurants and pubs
have great food for a good price. **Cons:**
small rooms and baths; not particularly
stylish; quiet area on weekends. Ⓢ Rooms
from: ¥11,000 ⊠ 9–14 Nihonbashi-Kobu-
nacho, Chuo-ku ☎ 03/3661–4603 ⊕ sum-
isho-hotel.co.jp ⇨ 83 rooms ⦿ No Meals
Ⓜ Hibiya and Asakusa subway lines,
Ningyo-cho Station (Exit A5).

🎭 Performing Arts

TRADITIONAL THEATER
Suigian (水戯庵)
THEATER | The Suigian dinner theater
and lounge offers a taste of traditional
Japanese Noh and Kyogen plays and
geisha performances over a full-course
dinner, light meal, or drinks. While Noh
and Kyogen plays can often run hours
and be difficult to comprehend, the short

performances at Suigan focus on the
climactic scenes and give explanations of
the story and artistry of the performance.
Suigan has performances every evening
and during the day on weekends. Tickets
must be reserved in advance on the web-
site. ⊠ B1F, 2–5–10 Nihonbashimuroma-
chi, Chuo-ku ☎ 03/3527–9378 ⊕ suigian.
jp ⊠ Light meal plans from ¥4,400, full
dinner plans from ¥8,800 ⊗ Closed Mon.
Ⓜ Ginza and Hanzomon subway lines,
Mitsukoshi-mae Station.

🛍 Shopping

To the north of Tokyo Station is Nihon-
bashi, which sees historic department
stores facing off with 21st-century malls;
only a few mom-and-pop shops still
stand their ground.

BOOKS
Yaesu Book Center (八重洲ブックセンター)
BOOKS | English-language paperbacks,
art books, and calendars are available
on the seventh floor of this celebrated
bookstore. ⊠ 2–5–1 Yaesu, Chuo-ku
☎ 03/3281–1811 Ⓜ JR Yamanote Line,
Tokyo Station (Yaesu South Exit 5).

DEPARTMENT STORES
★ **Mitsukoshi Main Store**
(コレド日本橋; Mitsukoshi honten)
DEPARTMENT STORE | Founded in 1673 as
a dry-goods store, Mitsukoshi later played
one of the leading roles in introducing
Western merchandise to Japan. It has
retained its image of quality and excel-
lence, with a particularly strong representa-
tion of Western fashion designers. The
store also stocks fine traditional Japanese
goods—don't miss the art gallery and the
crafts area on the sixth floor. With its own
subway stop, bronze lions at the entrance,
and an atrium sculpture of the Japanese
goddess Magokoro, this flagship store
merits a visit even if you're not planning
on buying anything. ⊠ 1–4–1 Nihonbashi
Muromachi, Chuo-ku ☎ 03/3241–3311
Ⓜ Ginza and Hanzo-mon subway lines,
Mitsukoshi-mae Station (Exits A3 and A5).

FOOD
Yamamoto Seaweed (山本海苔店; *Yamamoto Noriten*)

FOOD | The Japanese are resourceful in their uses of products from the sea. Nori, the paper-thin dried seaweed used to wrap maki sushi and *onigiri* (rice balls), is the specialty here. If you plan to bring some home with you, buy unroasted nori and toast it yourself at home; the flavor will be far better than that of the preroasted sheets. ✉ *1–6–3 Nihonbashi Muromachi, Chuo-ku* ☎ *03/3241–0290* ⊕ *www.yamamoto-noriten.co.jp/english* Ⓜ *Hanzo-mon and Ginza subway lines, Mitsukoshi-mae Station (Exit A1).*

MALLS AND SHOPPING CENTERS
Coredo Nihonbashi (コレド日本橋)

MALL | Unlike other big stores in the Nihonbashi area, this sparkling mall feels contemporary thanks to an open layout and extensive use of glass. Neighboring it are three more new glittery towers: Coredo Muromachi 1, 2, and 3, which fuse traditional housewares stores with modern fashion boutiques. The in-house Nihonbashi Tourist Center runs workshops on everything from dressing like a Geisha to cooking food. ✉ *1–4–1 Nihonbashi, Chuo-ku* ☎ *03/3242–0010* ⊕ *mitsui-shopping-park.com/urban* Ⓜ *Ginza, Tozai, and Asakusa subway lines, Nihonbashi Station (Exit B12).*

PAPER
★ Haibara (榛原)

STATIONERY | Founded in 1806, this sleek, modern grey cube just off Chuo-dori in Nihonbashi, the elegant designs in the gorgeous notebooks, letter sets, fans, and traditional washi paper found here date to the Meiji and late Edo periods. Look for gampi paper, an artisinal paper made from the bark fibres of gampi trees. ✉ *Tokyo Nihonbashi Tower, 2–7–1 Nihonbashi, Chuo-ku* ☎ *03/3272–3801* ⊕ *www.haibara.co.jp/en* Ⓜ *Ginza line, Nihombashi Station.*

★ Ozu Washi (小津和紙)

STATIONERY | This shop, which was opened in the 17th century, has one of the largest *washi* showrooms in the city and its own gallery of antique papers. Best to check ahead of time, but they sometimes have classes for just ¥500 on how to make your own washi paper. ✉ *3–6–2 Nihonbashihoncho, Chuo-ku* ☎ *03/3662–1184* ⊕ *www.ozuwashi.net* ◷ *Closed Sun.* Ⓜ *Ginza and Hanzo-mon subway lines, Mitsukoshi-mae Station (Exit A4).*

SWORDS AND KNIVES
Kiya Blades (木屋本店; *Kiya Honten*)

OTHER SPECIALTY STORE | Workers shape and hone blades in one corner of this shop, which carries cutlery, pocketknives, saws, and more. Scissors with handles in the shape of Japanese cranes are among the many unique gift items sold here, and custom-made knives are available, too. Kiya is located in the Coredo Muromachi complex. ✉ *Coredo Muromachi, 2–2–1 Nihonbashi-Muromachi, Chuo-ku* ☎ *03/3241–0110* ⊕ *www.kiya-hamono.co.jp* Ⓜ *Ginza subway line, Mitsukoshi-mae Station (Exit A6).*

Chapter 5

GINZA AND TSUKIJI

Updated by
Rob Goss

👁 Sights	🍴 Restaurants	🛏 Hotels	🛍 Shopping	🍸 Nightlife
★★☆☆☆	★★★★☆	★★★★☆	★★★★★	★★★★☆

GINZA AND TSUKIJI SNAPSHOT

TOP EXPERIENCES

■ **Take a leisurely stroll.** On weekends, see the historic Wako department store, and explore the small side streets of this old shopping district without fear of traffic.

■ **Indulge in a feeding frenzy.** Check out the basement food halls in Mitsukoshi department store in Ginza, where you will find hundreds of delicious desserts and prepared foods.

■ **Experience traditional performance.** Take in a show of Kabuki, Noh, geisha dance, and other traditional arts at one of the area's famous theaters.

■ **Browse a lively market.** Visit several blocks of food stalls at the Tsukiji Outer Market, before grabbing a super-fresh sushi lunch.

GETTING HERE

Ginza is located on the other side of the Yamanote Line from the Marunouchi district and the Imperial Palace. It can be reached via the Yamanote's Yurakucho Station or more conveniently by Ginza Station on the Ginza, Hibiya, and Marunouchi subway lines. Tsukiji is a 15-minute walk southeast of central Ginza, and is directly served by Tsukiji-shijo Station on the Oedo Line and Tsukiji Station on the Hibiya Line.

PLANNING YOUR TIME

If you plan on visiting both Ginza and Tsukiji, start with the latter, as the Tsukiji Outer Market is best visited mid-morning. After that, you could visit Tsukiji Hongan-jk Temple, before heading into Ginza, where most stores will be open from 11 am until evening.

On weekend afternoons (October–March, Saturday 3–5 and Sunday noon–5; April–September, Saturday 2–6 and Sunday noon–6), Chuo-dori is closed to traffic from Shimbashi to Kyobashi and becomes a pedestrian mall with tables and chairs set out along the street. Note that some museums and other sights in the area close Sunday.

A VIEW OF NEW MEETS OLD

■ A short walk from Tsukiji Outer Market, Hama-rikyu Teien is one of Tokyo's classic landscaped gardens. Originally developed in the Edo era (1603-1868), it now provides a classic example of Tokyo old and new. Looking across its main pond toward the Nakajima-no-Chaya teahouse, you also see the shiny skyscrapers of the Shiodome business district towering above the garden. It makes a great photo.

PAUSE HERE

■ For a free-of-charge break from Ginza's busy shopping streets, head to the rooftop garden at the plush Ginza Six complex. Spread over 4,000 square meters (13,123 square feet), this green space has benches scattered between its lawns, trees, and bushes, while also providing a 360-degree view over Ginza. It's a lovely spot to take a coffee or bento.

Long known as Tokyo's ritzy shopping district, Ginza was originally the city's banking district, and the area owes its name to the business of moneymaking: in 1612 Ieyasu Tokugawa relocated a plant making silver coins to a patch of reclaimed land east of his castle. The area soon came to be known informally as Ginza (Silver Mint).

Today the neighborhood is still home to most of the country's major securities companies, but it's best known as the place where high-end shopping and Western styles first took root in Japan. That manifests itself in giant department stores and exclusive local and international boutiques, while the luxury also extends to Ginza's many Michelin-starred restaurants and refined bars.

Until 2018, Tsukiji, located a kilometer southeast of Ginza, was home to Japan's biggest wholesale seafood market, where the draw for many travelers was the early morning tuna auctions. That market has moved to a less interesting location in Toyosu, but many stalls still operate in Tsukiji's older outer market, making it a more than worthwhile destination, especially when combined with the traditionally landscaped Hama-rikyu Gardens nearby.

Ginza

 Sights

Kabuki-za Theater (歌舞伎座)
PERFORMANCE VENUE | Soon after the Meiji Restoration and its enforced exile in Asakusa, Kabuki began to reestablish itself in this part of the city. The first Kabuki-za was built in 1889, with a European facade. In 1912 the Kabuki-za was taken over by the Shochiku theatrical management company, which replaced the old theater building in 1925; it was damaged during World War II but restored soon thereafter. The most recent iteration of the building retains its classic architecture—until one notices the looming office building coming out of the middle. The interior has been vastly improved, though. Tickets are sold only at the theater's ticket booth. Reservations by phone are recommended. If you want to see what all of the hype is about, this is the place to see a Kabuki show. For a short 15- to 30-minute sampling, get a single-act ticket; the final act usually provides the best spectacle. English Earphone Guides are available for a small

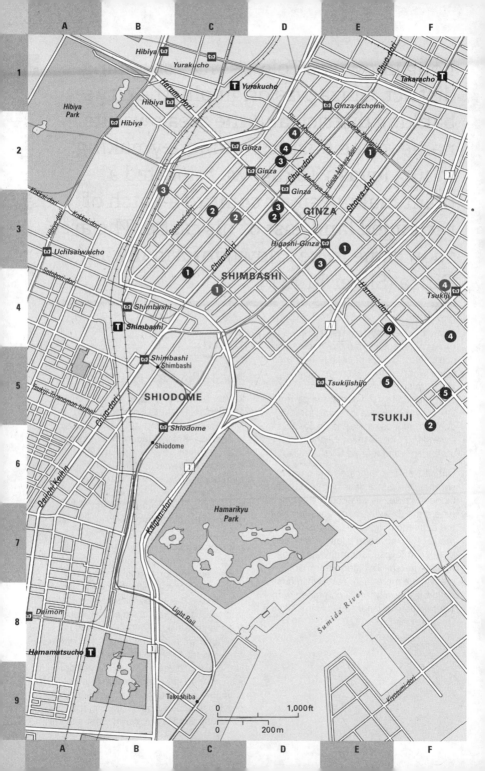

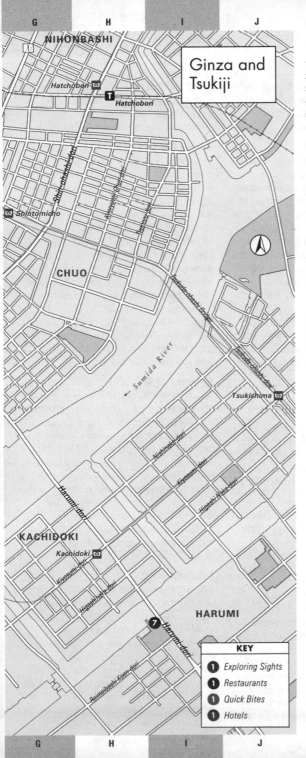

5

Sights ▼
1 Kabuki-za Theater E3
2 Namiyoke Shrine F5
3 Nissan Crossing D3
4 Tsukiji Hongan-ji Temple F4
5 Tsukiji Outer Market E5

Restaurants ▼
1 Kyubey C4
2 Oshima Ginza D3
3 Rangetsu D2
4 Sake no Ana D2
5 Takeno Shokudo F5
6 Tsukiji Edo-Gin E4

Quick Bites ▼
1 Cafe de l'ambre C4
2 Rose Bakery Ginza C3
3 Tachinomi Marugin B2
4 Turret Coffee F4

Hotels ▼
1 Hotel Monterey Ginza E2
2 Hyatt Centric Ginza Tokyo C3
3 Mitsui Garden Hotel Ginza
   Premier D3
4 Muji Hotel Ginza D2

fee and provide explanations and comments in English about the performance. ✉ *4–12–15 Ginza, Chuo-ku* ☎ *03/3545–6800* ⊕ *www.kabuki-za.co.jp* ✉ *From ¥3,000* Ⓜ *Hibiya or Asakusa subway line, Higashi-Ginza Station (Exit 3).*

Nissan Crossing

OTHER ATTRACTION | Located on one corner of the Ginza Crossing, across from Mitsukoshi and Wako, this incredibly slick two-floor showroom highlights Nissan's latest concept vehicles and technological innovations. The several cars on display change every few months or so, but as of writing include a GT-R, a Nissan Leaf Nismo rally car, and an e-4ORCE four-wheel drive. On the second floor, there's a boutique selling Nissan goods and model cars, as well as a café if you want to linger with a latte. ✉ *5-8-1 Ginza, Chuo-ku* ☎ *03/3573–0523* ⊕ *www.nissan.co.jp/crossing/en* ✉ *Free* Ⓜ *Ginza, Hibiya and Marunouchi subway lines, Ginza Station (Exits A3 to A5).*

🍴 Restaurants

At night neon lights fill the skies of Ginza with the names of eateries and bars. For a quick bite head into the basement of one of the department stores and select from the dizzying array of prepared foods.

Kyubey (久兵衛)

$$$$ | SUSHI | In contrast to the borderline solemn atmosphere at many top sushi restaurants, this world-famous spot proves that a high-end sushi restaurant does not have to be cold and unfriendly to be refined. In addition to their skill with a knife, many of the sushi chefs know English and are happy to chat with customers about the food and restaurant, making Kyubey a great choice for one's first high-end sushi experience. **Known for:** originator of the gunkan-maki style sushi rolls; a history of making excellent sushi dating back to 1935; easier to book than other high-end sushi restaurants (make reservations a couple

weeks in advance rather than months). ⓢ *Average main: ¥22,000* ✉ *8–7–6 Ginza, Chuo-ku* ☎ *03/3571–6523* ⊘ *Closed Sun. and Mon.* Ⓜ *Ginza and Hibiya subway lines, Ginza Station (Exit B3); JR Lines, Shinbashi Station (Ginza Exit).*

Oshima Ginza (大志満)

$$$$ | JAPANESE | The main draw at Oshima is sampling the *Kaga ryori* cooking of Kanazawa, a small city on the Sea of Japan known for its rich craft traditions. Waitresses dress the part in kimonos of Kanazawa's famous Yuzen dyed silk, and Kutani porcelain and Wajima lacquerware grace the exquisite table settings. **Known for:** jibuni (duck and potato stew); excellent seafood from the Sea of Japan; affordable introduction to kaiseki dining. ⓢ *Average main: ¥9,000* ✉ *Ginza Core Bldg., 5–8–20 Ginza, 9th fl., Chuo-ku* ☎ *03/3574–8080* ⊕ *www.oshima-site.com* Ⓜ *Ginza, Hibiya, and Marunouchi subway lines, Ginza Station (Exit A5).*

Rangetsu (銀座らん月)

$$$$ | JAPANESE | Japan enjoys a special reputation for its lovingly raised, tender, marbled domestic beef, and if your budget can bear the weight, Rangetsu serves excellent dishes with this beef as a star ingredient. Try the signature *shabu-shabu* or *sukiyaki* course for a primer. **Known for:** succulent snow crab; over 140 kinds of sake; semiprivate dining rooms. ⓢ *Average main: ¥10,000* ✉ *3–5–8 Ginza, Chuo-ku* ☎ *03/3567–1021* Ⓜ *Marunouchi and Ginza subway lines, Ginza Station (Exits A9 and A10).*

Sake no Ana (酒の穴)

$$$ | JAPANESE | With roughly 130 varieties of sake from all over Japan available by the carafe, Sake no Ana (literally, "the sake hole") has its own sake sommelier, Sakamoto-san, who can help diners make a selection. Though most sake-specialty restaurants are open only for dinner, Sake no Ana is also open for lunch. **Known for:** welcoming atmosphere, even for those new to sake; in-house sake sommelier; simple, hearty food.

The Power of Tea 🍴

Green tea is ubiquitous in Japan; it contains antioxidants twice as powerful as those in red wine that help reduce high blood pressure, lower blood sugar, and fight cancer. A heightened immune system and lower cholesterol are other benefits attributed to green tea.

In Japan pay attention to tea varietals, which are graded by the quality and parts of the plant used, because price and quality runs the spectrum within these categories. For the very best Japanese green tea, take a trip to the Uji region of Kyoto.

***Bancha* (common tea).** This second-harvest variety ripens between summer and fall, producing leaves larger than those of sencha and a weaker-tasting tea.

***Genmai* (brown rice tea).** This is a mixture, usually in equal parts, of green tea and roasted brown rice.

***Genmaicha* (popcorn tea).** This is a blend of bancha and genmai teas.

***Gyokuro* (jewel dew).** Derived from a grade of green tea called *tencha* (divine tea), the name comes from the light-green color the tea develops when brewed. Gyokuro is grown in the shade, an essential condition to develop just this type and grade.

***Hojicha* (panfried tea).** A panfried or oven-roasted green tea.

***Kabusecha* (covered tea).** Similar to gyokuro, kabusecha leaves are grown in the shade, though for a shorter period, giving it a refined flavor.

***Kukicha* (stalk tea).** A tea made from stalks by harvesting one bud and three leaves.

***Matcha* (rubbed tea).** Most often used in the tea ceremony, matcha is a high-quality, hard-to-find powdered green tea. It has a thick, paint-like consistency when mixed with hot water. It is also a popular flavor of ice cream and other sweets in Japan.

***Sencha* (roasted tea).** This is the green tea you are most likely to try at the local noodle or bento shop. Its leaves are grown under direct sunlight, giving it a different flavor from cousins like gyokuro.

[$] *Average main: ¥5,000* ✉ *3–5–8 Ginza, Chuo-ku* ☎ *03/3567–1133.*

☕ Coffee and Quick Bites

Cafe de l'ambre (カフェ・ド・ランブル)
$ | **CAFÉ** | In business since 1948, Cafe de l'ambre is a legendary haunt for Tokyo's coffee aficionados. The retro decor provides a snapshot of an older Tokyo, while the caffeine fix options include a dozen or so single-origin beans, including some that have been aged for years. **Known for:** doesn't open until noon; retro vibe; aged coffee beans. [$] *Average main: ¥700* ✉ *8-10-15 Ginza, Chuo-ku* ☎ *03/3571-1551* 🌐 *www.cafedelambre.com* 💳 *No credit cards* [M] *Ginza, Hibiya and Marunouchi subway lines, Ginza Station (Exit A3).*

Rose Bakery Ginza (ローズベーカリー)
$$ | **CAFÉ** | Satisfying the need for light, healthy food that is neither raw nor fried, this airy but rather nondescript bakery and café, which also has branches in Paris and London, serves up a tasty selection of salads, quiches, vegetables, and other deli-style dishes. Although the interior's rows of tables and blank white walls can feel a bit too much like a hip

reinterpretation of a school cafeteria, Rose Bakery is a good bet for a quick lunch or pastry while out wandering the Ginza area. **Known for:** lighter fare; flavorful sweets; crisp, fresh salads. $ *Average main: ¥2,000* ✉ *6–9–5 Ginza, Ginza Komatsu West Wing 7F, Ginza* ☎ *03/5537–5038* 🌐 *www.rose-bakery.jp* 💳 *No credit cards.*

Tachinomi Marugin (立呑みマルギン)
$$ | **JAPANESE** | This *yakitori* (grilled chicken) restaurant is an ideal place for a short stop inside Ginza. Skewered chicken breasts, small salads, and sausages are sure to put a smile on the face of even the weariest shopper. **Known for:** chargrilled chicken skewers (yakitori); opens daily from 5 pm to 6 am; cheap whiskey highballs. $ *Average main: ¥1,500* ✉ *7–2 Ginza, Chuo-ku* ☎ *03/3571–8989* 💳 *No credit cards* ⏲ *No lunch* [M] *Yamanote Line, Yurakucho Station.*

Hotels

The ritzy Ginza area is a blend of business and entertainment. For accommodation, domestic business hotel chains are a reasonably priced bet, although there are also luxury options on the area's outskirts.

Hotel Monterey Ginza
(ホテルモントレ銀座)
$ | **HOTEL** | Yes, the faux-stone exterior that attempts to replicate 20th-century Europe is a bit cheesy, but the Monterey remains a bargain in the middle of Ginza. **Pros:** multiple shopping choices in area; central location; reasonable prices considering the area. **Cons:** design lacks elegance; rooms are a tad small and a bit outdated; in-hotel dining options are limited. $ *Rooms from: ¥12,000* ✉ *2–10–2 Ginza, Chuo-ku* ☎ *03/3544–7111* 🌐 *www.hotelmonterey.co.jp/ginza* 🛏 *224 rooms* 🍴 *No Meals* [M] *Ginza subway line, Ginza Station (Exit A13).*

Hyatt Centric Ginza Tokyo
(ハイアット セントリック 銀座 東京;)
$$$ | **HOTEL** | The first Hyatt Centric in Japan when it launched in the heart of Ginza in 2018, this hotel offers an excellent location for shopping and nightlife, as well as being a very chic place to unwind after a busy day out and about. **Pros:** helpful English-speaking staff; spacious, well-designed rooms; excellent central location for shops and nightlife. **Cons:** gym is a little cramped; aimed more at 30s and 40s travelers rather than families; far better value breakfast options at cafes in Ginza. $ *Rooms from: ¥40,000* ✉ *6-6-7 GInza, Chuo-ku* ☎ *03/6837–1234* 🌐 *www.hyatt.com* 🛏 *164 rooms* 🍴 *No Meals* [M] *Ginza, Hibiya and Marunouchi subway lines, Ginza Station.*

Mitsui Garden Hotel Ginza Premier
(三井ガーデンホテル銀座プレミア)
$$ | **HOTEL** | A winning combination—chic and reasonable—this hotel occupies the top nine floors of the 24-story Ginza Mitsui Building in a convenient location at the edge of the bustling neighborhood. **Pros:** affordable; sharp design; plenty of nearby shopping. **Cons:** small rooms; in-hotel restaurant a tad pricey; geared toward business rather than leisure travelers. $ *Rooms from: ¥26,000* ✉ *8–13–1 Ginza, Chuo-ku* ☎ *03/3543–1131* 🌐 *www.gardenhotels.co.jp* 🛏 *361 rooms* 🍴 *No Meals* [M] *Ginza subway line, Ginza Station (Exit A3) or JR Shimbashi Station (Ginza Exit).*

Muji Hotel Ginza
$$ | **HOTEL** | Smack in the center of Ginza, this hotel was created in 2019 by budget Japanese retailer Muji, a company known for its natural toned, minimalist approach to interiors and fashion. **Pros:** superb central Ginza location; nice bakery for a budget breakfast; smart, fresh design. **Cons:** very small rooms, especially the "A" singles; no gym or business center for business travelers; slightly cheaper options available nearby. $ *Rooms from: ¥27,900* ✉ *3-3-5 Ginza, Chuo-ku* ☎ *03/3538–6101* 🌐 *hotel.muji.com* 🛏 *79*

In the spring, Noh performances can take place outdoors lighted by torchlight, just as they did in the 14th century.

rooms ⦿ No Meals Ⓜ JR Yamanote Line, Yurakucho subway line, Yurakucho Station (Central Exit); Ginza, Marunouchi, Hibiya subway lines, Ginza Station (Exit B4).

Nightlife

BARS

Ginza Lion (銀座ライオン)
PUBS | FAMILY | This bar, in business since 1899 and occupying the same stately Chuo-dori location since 1934, is remarkably inexpensive for one of Tokyo's toniest addresses. Ginza shoppers and office workers alike drop by for beer and ballast—anything from Japanese-style fried chicken to spaghetti. ✉ 7–9–20 Ginza, Chuo-ku ☎ 03/3571–2590, 0120/84–8136 for customer service center Ⓜ Ginza, Hibiya, and Marunouchi subway lines, Ginza Station (Exit A3).

Star Bar Ginza
BARS | It's often said that Ginza has all the best bars, and Star Bar may be the best of the lot. Owner and bartender Hisashi Kishi is the president of the Japan Bartenders Association, and his attention to detail in the narrow, dark, and calm room is staggering. ✉ 1–5–13 Ginza, B1 fl., Chuo-ku ☎ 03/3535–8005 ⊕ starbar. jp/english.shtml Ⓜ JR Yamanote Line, Yuraku-cho Station (Kyobashi Exit).

 Performing Arts

TRADITIONAL THEATER

Kanze Noh-gakudo (観世能楽堂)
THEATER | This is among the most important of the Noh family schools in Japan, and the current iemoto (head) of the school is the 26th in his line. In 2017 Kanze moved to a stylish new theater in Ginza. English-language summaries of the plots are available upon request. ✉ Ginza Six Bldg., 6–10–1 Ginza, B3 fl., Chuo-ku ☎ 03/6274–6579 ⊕ kanze.net 🎫 From ¥6,000 for reserved seats.

Shimbashi Enbujo (新橋演舞場)
THEATER | Dating to 1925, this theater was built for the geisha of the Shimbashi quarter to present their spring and autumn performances of traditional

music and dance. This is the top spot in Tokyo to see the nation's favorite traditional performing art. The theater is also the home of "Super Kabuki," a faster, jazzier modern version. Seats commonly run ¥3,000–¥16,500, and there's no gallery. ⊠ 6–18–2 Ginza, Chuo-ku ☎ 03/6745–0888 ⊕ www.shinbashi-enbujo.co.jp Ⓜ Hibiya and Asakusa subway lines, Higashi-Ginza Station (Exit 6).

⬤ Shopping

The exclusive shops in this area—including flagship stores for major jewelers like Tiffany & Co., Harry Winston, and Mikimoto—sell quality merchandise at high prices. Many affordable fashion and goods chains have also built towers in the area in recent years, creating a mix of high- and low-brow style that defines modern Tokyo's taste.

CLOTHING

★ Dover Street Market

MIXED CLOTHING | This multistory fashion playhouse is a shrine to exclusives, one-offs, and other hard-to-find pieces from luxury brands all over the world. Curated by Comme des Garçons, the selection may leave all but the most dedicated fashion fans scratching their heads, but the unique interior sculptures and rooftop shrine with Japanese garden alone warrant a visit. ⊠ 6–9–5 Ginza, Chuo-ku ☎ 03/6228–5080 ⊕ ginza.doverstreetmarket.com Ⓜ Ginza, Hibiya, and Marunouchi subway lines, Ginza Station (Exit A2).

Uniqlo (ユニクロ)

MIXED CLOTHING | FAMILY | Customers can wrap themselves in simple, low-priced clothing staples from the company's own brand. This 12-story location is the world's largest, and sells men's, women's, and children's clothing right on the main Ginza drag. ⊠ 6–9–5 Ginza, Chuo-ku ☎ 03/6252–5181 Ⓜ Ginza, Hibiya, and Marunouchi subway lines, Ginza Station (Exit A2).

DEPARTMENT STORES

Ginza Six

DEPARTMENT STORE | One of the biggest and swankiest commercial complexes in the city, Ginza Six opened with much fanfare in 2017 and didn't disappoint. Below the office spaces that occupy the upper floors, you'll find another six floors above and below ground home to outlets of brands like Celine, Fendi, and Jimmy Choo. There are also cosmetic stores, deli foods, restaurants, art installations, and even a basement Noh theater. It's immediately across the street from the 12-story flagship of budget fashion brand Uniqlo. ⊠ 6–10–1 Ginza, Chuo-ku ☎ 03/6891–3390 ⊕ ginza6.tokyo Ⓜ Ginza, Hibiya, and Marunouchi subway lines, Ginza Station (Exit A2).

★ Matsuya (松屋)

DEPARTMENT STORE | On the fourth floor, this gleaming department store houses an excellent selection of Japanese fashion, including Issey Miyake and Yohji Yamamoto. The European-designer boutiques on the second floor are particularly popular with Tokyo's brand-obsessed shoppers. The rooftop terrace is a welcome respite for the weary. ⊠ 3–6–1 Ginza, Chuo-ku ☎ 03/3567–1211 ⊕ www.matsuya.com Ⓜ Ginza, Marunouchi, and Hibiya subway lines, Ginza Station (Exit A12).

Mitsukoshi Ginza (三越銀座)

DEPARTMENT STORE | The Ginza branch of Japan's first department-store chain has been open since 1930 and remains the largest department store in the area, with a sprawling grass-covered terrace on the ninth floor that provides a respite from the shopping bustle. On the third floor is an area called "Le Place" that sells only local designer fashion, and the two basement floors have an impressive selection of delicacies. ⊠ 4–6–16 Ginza, Chuo-ku ☎ 03/3562–1111 ⊕ www.mitsukoshi.mistore.jp/ginza.html Ⓜ Ginza, Marunouchi, and Hibiya subway lines, Ginza Station (Exits A6, A7, and A8).

★ **Muji** (無印良品; *Mujirushi ryohin*)
DEPARTMENT STORE | FAMILY | The new
flagship store of this minimalist,
design-focused interiors and clothing
brand is home to a large selection
of furniture, appliances, bedding,
and clothes for the whole family. The
store also houses a café-bakery, diner,
children's play area, and hotel. ⊠ *3–3–5
Ginza, Chuo-ku* ☎ *03/3538–1311* Ⓜ *JR
Yamanote Line, Yurakucho subway line,
Yurakucho Station (Central Exit); Ginza,
Marunouchi, Hibiya subway lines Ginza
Station (Exit B4).*

Wako (和光)
DEPARTMENT STORE | This grand old depart-
ment store is well known for its high-end
watches, glassware, and jewelry, as well
as having some of the most sophisticated
window displays in town. The clock atop
the curved 1930s-era building is illuminated
at night, making it one of Ginza's more
recognized landmarks. ⊠ *4–5–11 Ginza,
Chuo-ku* ☎ *03/3562–2111* ⊕ *www.wako.co.
jp* Ⓜ *Ginza, Marunouchi, and Hibiya subway
lines, Ginza Station (Exits A9 and A10).*

ELECTRONICS
Sukiya Camera (スキヤカメラ)
CAMERAS & PHOTOGRAPHY | The cramped
Nikon House branch of this two-store
operation features so many Nikons—old
and new, digital and film—that it could
double as a museum to the brand. Plenty
of lenses and flashes are available as well.
⊠ *4–3–7 Ginza, Ginza* ☎ *03/3561–6000*
Ⓜ *JR Yamanote Line, Yurakucho Station
(Ginza Exit); Ginza, Hibiya, and Marunouchi
subway lines, Ginza Station (Exit B10).*

JEWELRY
Ginza Tanaka (銀座田中)
JEWELRY & WATCHES | One of the finest
jewelers in Japan was founded in 1892.
The store specializes in precious metals
and diamond jewelry. It also sells a wide
variety of art objects in gold, like those
found on Buddhist altars. ⊠ *1–7–7 Ginza,
Chuo-ku* ☎ *03/5561–0491* ⊕ *www.ginza-
tanaka.co.jp/en* Ⓜ *Yurakucho subway line,
Ginza 1-chome Station (Exit 7).*

★ **Mikimoto Ginza Main Store** (ミキモト銀
座本店; *Mikimoto Ginza honten*)
JEWELRY & WATCHES | Kokichi Mikimoto
created his technique for cultured pearls
in 1893. Since then his name has been
associated with the best quality in the
industry. Mikimoto's tower in Ginza is a
boutique devoted to nature's ready-made
gems; the building, like the pearls it
holds, dazzles visitors with a facade that
resembles Swiss cheese. ⊠ *4–5–5 Ginza,
Chuo-ku* ☎ *03/3535–4611* ⊕ *www.mikimo-
to.com* Ⓜ *Ginza, Hibiya, and Marunouchi
subway lines, Ginza Station (Exit C8).*

• **Tasaki Pearls Ginza Main Store**
(田崎銀座本店; *Tasaki Ginza honten*)
JEWELRY & WATCHES | Tasaki sells pearls at
slightly lower prices than Mikimoto. The
brand opened this glittery flagship tower in
Ginza that moved them from the old guard
into the contemporary big leagues. There's
a large collection of pearl and gem items,
from costume to bridal and fine jewelry. On
the fifth floor is an event space that holds
numerous art exhibits. ⊠ *5–7–5 Ginza,
Chuo-ku* ☎ *03/3289–1111* ⊕ *www.tasaki.co.
jp* Ⓜ *Ginza, Hibiya, and Marunouchi subway
lines, Ginza Station (Exit A2).*

KIMONOS
Tansu-ya (たんす屋)
OTHER SPECIALTY STORE | This small but
pleasant Ginza shop has attractive used
kimono, yukata, and other traditional
clothing in many fabrics, colors, and patterns. The helpful staff can acquaint you
with the somewhat complicated method
of putting on the garments. Tax-free
locations are scattered throughout the
city, including Shibuya, Asakusa, Aoyama,
and Shibuya. ⊠ *3–4–5 Ginza, Chuo-ku*
☎ *03/3561–8529* ⊕ *tansuya.jp* Ⓜ *Ginza,
Hibiya, and Marunouchi subway lines,
Ginza Station (Exit A13).*

PAPER
Itoya (伊東屋)
CRAFTS | Completely remodeled in 2015,
this huge paper emporium is brim-
ming with locally crafted and imported
stationery, much of which is designed to

translate traditional motifs onto contemporary office tools. ✉ *2–7–15 Ginza, Chuo-ku* ☎ *03/3561–8311* ⊕ *www.ito-ya.co.jp* Ⓜ *Ginza, Hibiya, and Marunouchi subway lines, Ginza Station (Exit A13).*

Kyukyodo (鳩居堂)
CRAFTS | Kyukyodo has been in business since 1663—and in this spacious Ginza location since 1880—selling wonderful handmade Japanese papers, paper products, incense, brushes, and other materials for calligraphy. ✉ *5–7–4 Ginza, Chuo-ku* ☎ *03/3571–4429* ⊕ *www.kyukyodo.co.jp* Ⓜ *Ginza, Hibiya, and Marunouchi subway lines, Ginza Station (Exit A2).*

SWORDS AND KNIVES
Token Shibata (刀剣柴田)
OTHER SPECIALTY STORE | This tiny, threadbare shop incongruously situated near Ginza's glittering department stores sells expensive well-worn antique swords. They can also sharpen your blade for you. ✉ *5–6–8 Ginza, Chuo-ku* ☎ *03/3573–2801* 🕐 *Closed Sun.* Ⓜ *Ginza, Hibiya, and Marunouchi subway lines, Ginza Station (Exit A1).*

Tsukiji

Sights

Namiyoke Shrine
(波除神社; *Namiyoke Jinja*)
RELIGIOUS BUILDING | Built in the mid-1600s to house and honor a Shinto spirit that calmed the waters of Tokyo Bay, this little shrine is worth a stop on your way to Tsukiji Outer Market. The name of the shrine literally means "protection from waves," and it is an unofficial guardian shrine for the marketplace and its workers. ✉ *6–20–37 Tsukiji, Chuo-ku* ☎ *03/3541–8451* ⊕ *www.namiyoke.or.jp* Ⓜ *Oedo subway line, Tsukiji-shijo Station (Exit A1); Hibiya subway line, Tsukiji Station (Exit 1).*

Tsukiji Hongan-ji Temple (築地本願寺)
TEMPLE | Disaster seemed to follow this temple, which is an outpost of Kyoto's Nishi Hongan-ji. Since it was first located here in 1657, it was destroyed at least five times, and reconstruction in wood was finally abandoned after the Great Kanto Earthquake of 1923. The present stone building dates from 1935. It was designed by Chuta Ito, a pupil of Tokyo Station architect Tatsuno Kingo. Ito's other credits include the Meiji Shrine in Harajuku; he also lobbied for Japan's first law for the preservation of historic buildings. Ito traveled extensively in Asia; the evocations of classical Hindu architecture in the temple's domes and ornaments were his homage to India as the cradle of Buddhism. But with stained-glass windows and a pipe organ as well, the building is nothing if not eclectic. Talks in English are held on the third Saturday of the month at 5:30. ✉ *3–15–1 Tsukiji, Chuo-ku* ☎ *03/3541–1131* ⊕ *www.tsukiji-hongwanji.jp* 🎫 *Free* ☞ *Daily services at 7 am and 4:30 pm* Ⓜ *Hibiya subway line, Tsukiji Station (Exit 1).*

★ Tsukiji Outer Market
(築地場外市場; *Tsukiji jyogai shijo*)
MARKET | Enjoying a sushi breakfast at this famous fish market is an integral part of any trip to Tokyo, even now that its famed inner market has been relocated to a nearby island in Tokyo Bay. If you have time for only one market, this is the one to see as the shopkeepers maintain the feeling of the original Tsukiji area. The three square blocks between the former site of Tokyo Central Wholesale Market and Harumi-dori have scores of fishmongers, plus shops and restaurants. Stores sell pickles, tea, crackers and snacks, cutlery (what better place to pick up a professional sushi knife?), baskets, and kitchenware. Hole-in-the-wall sushi bars here have set menus ranging from ¥1,000 to ¥2,500; look for the plastic models of food in glass cases out front. The area includes the row of little counter restaurants, barely more than

Locals making a purchase at Tsukiji Outer Market

street stalls, under the arcade along the east side of Shin-Ohashi-dori, each with its specialty. Come hungry and be sure to stop for *maguro donburi*—a bowl of fresh raw tuna slices served over rice and garnished with bits of dried seaweed. ✉ *Tsukiji 4-chome, Chuo-ku* ⊕ *www. tsukiji.or.jp/english* Ⓜ *Toei Oedo subway line, Tsukiji-shijo Station (Exit A1); Hibiya subway line, Tsukiji Station (Exit 1).*

🍽 Restaurants

The world's largest wholesale seafood market is no longer here, having moved just over 2 km (1½ miles) away in late 2018, but a visit to the remaining outer market is still a must for anyone interested in food. Browse the small restaurants and stalls serving sushi, ramen, and other quick bites as well as shops selling food and kitchenware.

Takeno Shokudo (多け乃食堂)
$$ | JAPANESE | Takeno Shokudo is a neighborhood restaurant that does nothing but the freshest and the best—big portions of it, at very reasonable prices. Sushi and sashimi are the staples, but there's also a wonderful *tendon* bowl with shrimp and eel tempura on rice. À la carte prices are not posted because they vary with the costs that morning in the Toyosu Market. **Known for:** cheap, delicious seafood; popular with locals; a menu based on what the cooks found in the market that morning. $ *Average main: ¥3,000* ✉ *6–21–2 Tsukiji, Chuo-ku* ☎ *03/3541–8698* ⊕ *tsukijitakeno.owst. jp/en* 🚫 *No credit cards* ⊘ *Closed Sun.* Ⓜ *Hibiya subway line, Tsukiji Station (Exit 1); Oedo subway line, Tsukiji-shijo Station (Exit A1).*

Tsukiji Edo-Gin (築地江戸銀)
$$$ | **SUSHI** | In an area that teems with sushi bars, this one maintains its reputation as one of the best. Tsukiji Edo-Gin drapes generous slabs of fish over the vinegared rice rather than perching them demurely on top. **Known for:** seafood fresh from the market; sizable portions; one of Tsukiji's best-known sushi restaurants. [$] *Average main: ¥4,000* ✉ *4–5–1 Tsukiji, Chuo-ku* ☎ *03/3543–4401* 🌐 *www.tsukiji-edogin.co.jp* 💳 *No credit cards* 🕒 *Closed Sun. and early Jan.* [M] *Hibiya subway line, Tsukiji Station (Exit 1); Oedo subway line, Tsukiji-shijo Station (Exit A1).*

Coffee and Quick Bites

Turret Coffee (ターレットコーヒー;)
$ | **CAFÉ** | Tucked away in a side street, this friendly café takes its name from the little "turret" trucks that used to cart produce around the old Tsukiji Market. The owner, Kawasaki-san, serves a powerful espresso in ceramic sake cups but also creates Instagramable latte art, all for similar prices to the far less enjoyable Starbucks on the corner. **Known for:** early opening by Tokyo standards (from 7 am Monday to Saturday, from 9 am Sunday); latte art; excellent espresso served in ceramic sake cups. [$] *Average main: ¥390* ✉ *2-12-6 Tsukiji, Chuo-ku* 🌐 *www.instagram.com/turretcoffee* 💳 *No credit cards* 🕒 *Some irregular closing days (listed on Instagram)* [M] *Oedo subway line, Tsukiji-shijo Station; Hibiya subway line, Tsukiji Station (Exit 2).*

Activities

Yakatabune Harumiya (屋形船晴海屋)
BOAT TOURS | As during the time of the samurai, cruising in a roof-topped boat, or *yakatabune,* is the perfect means to relax amid bursting fireworks or cherry blossoms. Hosts within the cabin serve multiple courses of tempura and sushi and pour beer, sake and whiskey while the boats cruise past historic bridges and along the riverbanks that make up the bay front. The charm remains intact: guests are treated like royalty and are entertained while floating on the gentle waves of the Sumida or Arakawa River. When the *shoji* (paper blinds) are opened, panoramic views of the illuminated Tokyo nightscape are a sight to behold. Observation decks offer even better viewing opportunities. Boats accommodate groups of 20 to 350, and regular tours run nightly year-round from 7 pm; reserve by email. ✉ *Harumi Josenba, 3-6-1 Harumi, Chuo-ku* ☎ *03/3644–1344* 🌐 *yakatabune-tokyo.com* [M] *Oedo subway line, Kachidoki Station (Exit A3).*

Chapter 6

SHIODOME
AND ODAIBA

Updated by
Alexandra Ziminski

⊙ Sights	🍴 Restaurants	🛏 Hotels	🛍 Shopping	🍸 Nightlife
★★★☆☆	★★★☆☆	★★★★☆	★★★★☆	★★☆☆☆

SHIODOME AND ODAIBA SNAPSHOT

TOP EXPERIENCES

■ **BBQ or sushi?** Toyosu might be home to Tokyo's bustling fish market and a parade of sushi options, but it has also become a hot spot for grilled meat and lively get-togethers.

■ **Traditional garden landscaping.** Settle into a lovely traditional garden and old teahouse surrounded by skyscrapers and concrete at Hama Rikyu Garden.

■ **Retro design.** See historic advertisements dating back to the Edo period (1603–1868) at the Ad Museum Tokyo.

■ **Play time.** With a fake Statue of Liberty, man-made beach, game, and theme restaurants, Odaiba is a good destination for kitsch-lovers.

■ **Shop 'til you drop.** A succession of shopping malls in Tokyo Bay might hurt your purse strings.

■ **Meet a robot.** Interact with humanoid robots at Miraikan (the National Museum of Emerging Science and Innovation).

GETTING HERE AND AROUND

Shiodome is easily accessed by public transport: JR lines and Yurikamome Line at Shimbashi Station, Toei Oedo Line to Shiodome Station, and Asakusa Line and Ginza Line to Shimbashi Station. To visit Toyosu Fish Market continue on the Yurikamome Monorail from Shimbashi Station.

The best way to get to Odaiba is via the fully automated Yurikamome Line. From Shimbashi Station you can take the JR, Karasumori Exit; Asakusa subway line, Exit A2; or the Ginza subway line, Exit 4—follow the blue seagull signs to the station entrance. You can pick up a map of Odaiba in English at the entrance. The JR Rinkai Line also serves the area from Osaki Station on the Yamanote Line.

PLANNING YOUR TIME

■ Spend the morning with a stroll around Hama Rikyu Gardens and a look at the Ad Museum before having lunch in Shiodome, If you still have energy, take yourself across the bay to Odaiba. Start your morning at Toyosu Market for an alternative day out and continue on to Ariake in the afternoon.

WHAT IS PURI-KURA?

■ In Odaiba's malls and game centers, there are rows of sticker photo booths, often occupied by gaggles of giggling teenage girls. These machines are known as and don't take run-of-the-mill photos. The inside of the booth is large enough for a small group to stand, and once the snapping is done, there are endless options to customize your photo. After filters, icons, and text have been added, the results are often unrecognizable.

Now a redeveloped business district, Shiodome (literally "where the tide stops") was once an area of saltwater flats where the Meiji government built the Tokyo terminal in 1872—the original Shimbashi Station—on Japan's first railway line.

By 1997, long after the JR had turned its attention elsewhere, an urban renewal plan for the area evolved, and the land was auctioned off. Among the buyers were Nippon Television and Dentsu, the largest advertising agency in Asia. In 2002, Dentsu consolidated its scattered offices into the centerpiece of the Shiodome project: a 47-story tower and annex designed by Jean Nouvel. With the annex, known as the Caretta Shiodome, Dentsu created an "investment in community": a complex of cultural facilities, shops, and restaurants that has turned Shiodome into one of the most fashionable places in the city.

Odaiba is a man-made peninsula in Tokyo Bay, with its beginnings dating back to the Edo period (1603–1868), when various fortifications were constructed for protection from attacks by ships. As a result of Japan's rapidly expanding economy in the 1980s, the area became a target location for a number of flamboyant and futuristic-looking development projects. Today, 1,000 acres of landfill are home to various leisure, corporate, and commercial complexes, as well as the new Toyosu Fish Market, which replaced the historic Tsukiji Market in 2018.

West of Tsukiji lie Shiodome and Shimbashi. In the period after the Meiji Restoration, Shimbashi was one of the most

famous geisha districts of the new capital. Its reputation as a pleasure quarter is even older. In the Edo period, when there was a network of canals and waterways here, it was the height of luxury to charter a covered boat (called a *yakatabune*) from one of the Shimbashi boathouses for a cruise on the river; a local restaurant would cater the excursion, and a local geisha house would provide companionship. Almost nothing remains in Shimbashi to recall that golden age, but as its luster has faded, adjacent Shiodome has risen—literally—in its place as one of the most ambitious redevelopment projects of 21st-century Tokyo.

Shiodome

Sights

Ad Museum Tokyo (アドミュージアム東京)
OTHER MUSEUM | The Japanese gift for graphic and commercial design comes into historical perspective in these exhibits featuring everything from 18th-century wood-block prints to contemporary fashion photographs and videos. The museum is maintained by a foundation established in honor of Hideo Yoshida, fourth president of the mammoth Dentsu Advertising Company, and includes a digital library of

154

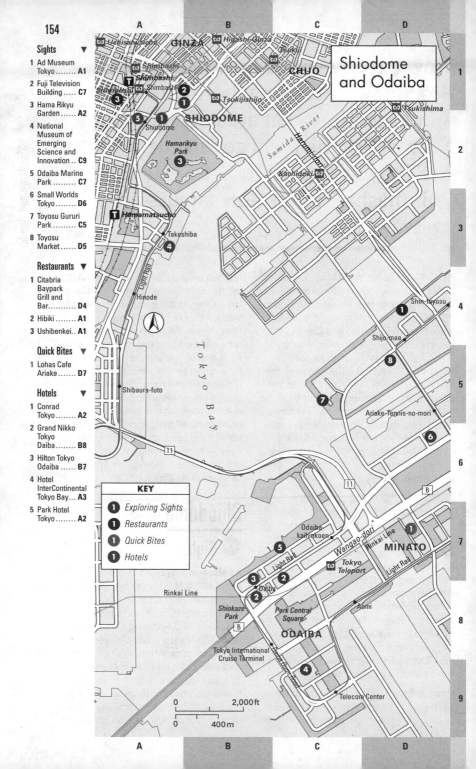

Shiodome and Odaiba

KEY

1 Exploring Sights

1 Restaurants

1 Quick Bites

1 Hotels

Cherry blossoms bloom at Hama Rikyu garden.

some 130,000 entries and articles on everything you ever wanted to know about hype. ✉ *Caretta Shiodome, 1–8–2 Higashi-Shinbashi, B1F–B2F, Minato-ku* ☎ *03/6218–2500* ⊕ *www.admt.jp* ✉ *Free* ⊘ *Closed Sun. and Mon.* Ⓜ *Toei Oedo subway line, Shiodome Station (Exit 7); JR (Shiodome Exit) and Asakusa and Ginza lines (Exit 4), Shimbashi Station.*

Hama Rikyu Garden (浜離宮庭園; *Hama Rikyu Teien*)

GARDEN | A tiny sanctuary of Japanese tradition and nature that's surrounded by towering glass buildings is a great place to relax or walk off a filling Tsukiji sushi breakfast. The land here was originally owned by the Owari branch of the Tokugawa family from Nagoya, and when a family member became shogun in 1709, his residence was turned into a palace—with pavilions, ornamental gardens, pine and cherry groves, and duck ponds. The garden became a public park in 1945, although a good portion of it is fenced off as a nature preserve. None of the original buildings have survived, but on the island

in the large pond is a reproduction of the pavilion where former U.S. president Ulysses S. Grant and Mrs. Grant had an audience with Emperior Meiji in 1879. The building can now be rented for parties. The stone linings of the saltwater canal work and some of the bridges underwent a restoration project that was completed in 2009. The path to the left as you enter the garden leads to the "river bus" ferry landing, from which you can cruise up the Sumidagawa to Asakusa. Note that you must pay the admission to the garden even if you're just using the ferry. ✉ *1–1 Hamarikyu–Teien, Chuo-ku* ☎ *03/3541–0200* ⊕ *www.tokyo-park.or.jp/teien/en/hama-rikyu* ✉ *¥300* Ⓜ *Toei Oedo subway line, Shiodome Station (Exit 8).*

🍴 Restaurants

Hibiki (響)

$$$$ | JAPANESE | Perched on the 46th floor of the Carretta Shiodome Building overlooking Tokyo Bay, this seafood-focused izakaya is a nice escape from the chaotic frenzy below. Specialties include grilled

fish and house-made tofu. **Known for:** open, big glass windows; seasonal ingredients; outstanding scenery on a clear day. $ *Average main: ¥5,500* ✉ *Carretta Shiodome, 46F, 1–8–2 Higashi-Shimbashi, Shimbashi, Mintao-ku, Shiba-Shiodome* ☎ *03/6215–8051* ⊕ *www.dynac-japan. com/hibiki/shiodome.*

Ushibenkei (牛弁慶)

$$$$ | **JAPANESE** | High-quality marbled beef is taken quite seriously in Japan—cuts are ranked based on the ratio, distribution, and sweetness of the fat in relation to the meat. At Ushibenkei, you can sample some pieces of the highest rank at reasonable prices in a charmingly rustic atmosphere. **Known for:** high-grade Japanese beef; sukiyaki and other beef hotpots; beef sushi. $ *Average main: ¥7,000* ✉ *3–18–7 Shimbashi, Shiba-Shiodome* ☎ *03/3459–9418* ⊘ *No lunch weekdays* Ⓜ *JR Yamanote Line, Shimbashi Station (Kasumori Exit); Ginza subway line, Shimbashi Station (Exit A1).*

Hotels

Located between Shinagawa and Tokyo stations, Shiodome has a number of medium- and high-end lodging options. Hotels stay perched above the city, on the upper floors of the area's skyscrapers.

Conrad Tokyo (コンラッド東京)

$$$ | **HOTEL** | The Conrad artfully mixes the ultramodern image of Tokyo with traditional Japanese aesthetics, resulting in a luxury hotel that reflects the changing Tokyo of today. **Pros:** modern design; fantastic bay view; fine restaurants. **Cons:** pricey; finding the entrance to the elevator is troublesome; charge to use pool and gym. $ *Rooms from: ¥40,000* ✉ *1–9–1 Higashi-Shinbashi, Minato-ku* ☎ *03/6388–8000* ⊕ *www.conradtokyo. co.jp* ⇆ *291 rooms* ⦿ *No Meals* Ⓜ *JR Yamanote Line, Shimbashi Station (Shiodome Exit); Oedo subway line, Shiodome Station (Exit 9).*

Hotel InterContinental Tokyo Bay (ホテル インターコンチネンタル 東京ベイ)

$$$ | **HOTEL** | Wedged between Tokyo Bay and an expressway, the InterContinental boasts lovely views, albeit in a slightly isolated setting. **Pros:** sweeping views of the Rainbow Bridge and Tokyo Bay; large, nicely appointed rooms; quiet area. **Cons:** no pool; might be too out of the way for the sightseer; the gym is small. $ *Rooms from: ¥35,000* ✉ *1–16–2 Kaigan, Minato-ku* ☎ *03/5404–2222* ⊕ *www. interconti-tokyo.com* ⇆ *330 rooms* ⦿ *No Meals* Ⓜ *Yurikamome rail line, Takeshiba Station.*

★ Park Hotel Tokyo (パークホテル東京)

$$ | **HOTEL** | Comfortable beds, large bathrooms, and sweeping panoramas of Tokyo or the bay—it's easy to see why the guest rooms of this reasonably priced "artist" hotel remain a tourist favorite. **Pros:** great value; guest rooms and public areas are stylish; bar has more than 100 kinds of single malt whiskey. **Cons:** small rooms; few in-room frills; no pool or gym. $ *Rooms from: ¥20,000* ✉ *1–7–1 Higashi Shinbashi, Minato-ku* ☎ *03/6252–1111* ⊕ *www.parkhoteltokyo.com* ⇆ *273 rooms* ⦿ *No Meals* Ⓜ *JR Yamanote Line, Shimbashi Station (Shiodome Exit); Oedo subway line, Shiodome Station (Exit 10).*

Nightlife

Shinshu Osake Mura (信州おさけ村)

BARS | A sake and beer store specializing in drinks from Nagano prefecture, this standing-room-only place also functions as a very casual bar where you can sample approximately 50 kinds of sake (pay by the 110-milliliter glass), a dozen craft beers from brewers such as Shiga Kogen, and interesting snacks like spiced cow's tongue. A great option is one of the many reasonably priced three-sake sampler sets. It's tricky to find, being on the first floor of a very dated office building opposite the west exit of Shimbashi Station, but look for the big statue of a *tanuki* (raccoon dog) with extremely large testicles that's outside the building, then go in and turn right. The staff are very friendly and speak enough English to help with the sake choices. Beers are in bottles and cans in the fridge in the tiny backroom; you have to take them to the counter yourself to buy them. ⊠ *Shimbashi Ekimae Bldg. 1, 2–20–15 Shinbashi, Minato-ku* ☎ *03/3572–5488* ⊙ *Closed Sun. and Sat. evening* Ⓜ *JR Yamanote Line, Shimbashi Station (West Exit); Ginza subway line, Shimbashi Station (Exit A3).*

Odaiba

Connected to the city by the Yurikamome monorail from Shimbashi and the Rinkai Line from Osaki, Odaiba is known to tourists for its arcades, hotels, shopping malls, and museums, as well as the city's longest (albeit artificial) stretch of sandy beach, along the boat harbor (swimming is not recommended because of high levels of pollution). There's also Rainbow Bridge, which becomes a neon multi-colored beacon at night. The exhibition halls at the Tokyo Big Sight (⊠ *3-11-1 Ariake, Koto-ku*), the entrance of which is beneath four large upside-down pyramids, hosts numerous conventions, trade shows, and fairs.

At the foot of the Rainbow Bridge, one can walk out onto the diamond-shape Odaiba Park that juts out into the bay, or stroll over the bridge itself to get an amazing view of what is certainly one of the most diverse megaprojects in Tokyo.

◉ Sights

Fuji Television Building (フジテレビ)
FILM/TV STUDIO | FAMILY | Architecture buffs should make time for Odaiba if only to contemplate this futuristic building, designed by Kenzo Tange and completed in 1996. The observation deck on the 25th floor affords a spectacular view of the bay and the graceful curve of the Rainbow Bridge. ⊠ *2–4–8 Daiba, Minato-ku, Odaiba* ⊕ *www.fujitv.com* ⊠ *Observation deck: ¥700* ⊙ *Closed Mon.* Ⓜ *Rinkai Line, Tokyo Teleport Station; Yurikamome Line, Odaiba-kaihinkoen Station.*

National Museum of Emerging Science and Innovation (日本科学未来館; *Nihon Kagaku Miraikan*)
SCIENCE MUSEUM | FAMILY | Make sure to stop by the third floor of the museum known locally as Miraikan, where you will get to meet and control a humanoid robot. This hands-on museum has three different areas focusing on humans' relationship to the planet, the frontiers of outer space and the deep sea, and our life in the near future. There is also a special theater with planetarium and 3-D shows (reservations required). ⊠ *2–3–6 Aomi, Koto-ku, Odaiba* ☎ *03/3570–9151* ⊕ *www.miraikan.jst.go.jp* ⊠ *¥630* ⊙ *Closed Tues.* Ⓜ *Yurikamome Line, Tokyo International Cruise Terminal Station.*

Odaiba Marine Park (お台場海浜公園; *Odaiba Kaihin Koen*)
BEACH | This artificial beach and its boardwalk are home to a small replica of the Statue of Liberty and, for many strolling couples, a wonderful evening view of the Rainbow Bridge. ⊠ *1–4–1 Daiba, Minato-ku, Odaiba* Ⓜ *Yurikamome Line, Odaiba-kaihinkoen Station.*

Small Worlds Tokyo
THEME PARK | FAMILY | Imagine what it's like to be a giant in this novel indoor theme park dedicated to miniatures. Surprisingly spacious, Small Worlds takes you on a journey through different fantasy lands, times, and countries. Watch a small rocket launch, look out for hidden characters, or create a mini-me and become a permanent resident of Small Worlds. ⊠ *Ariake Butsuryu Center, 1–3–33 Ariake, Koto-ku, Odaiba* ⊕ *www.smallworlds.jp* ⊠ *¥2,700* Ⓜ *Yurikamome Line, Ariake-Tennis-no-mori Station; Rinkai Line, Kokusai-Tenjijo Station.*

Officially named the Tokyo Bay Connector Bridge, this white bridge is illuminated with colorful solar-powered lights by night, hence its more common name, the Rainbow Bridge.

Toyosu Gururi Park (豊洲ぐるりパーク)
CITY PARK | FAMILY | On the other side of Tokyo Bay, you can find an alternative view of the Rainbow Bridge. Here you'll find families playing football, having picnics, and setting up the perfect BBQ spot. If you don't have your own utensils, The BBQ Beach in Toyosu can supply meat to grill and seats to unwind. ⊠ *6–5 Toyosu, Koto-ku, Odaiba* ⊕ *www.toyo-sugururi.jp* 🗺 *Free* Ⓜ *Yurikamome Line, Shijo-mae Station.*

Toyosu Market (豊洲市場; *Toyosu Shijo*)
MARKET | Opened in October 2018 as the replacement to the legendary Tsukiji Market, the 40-hectare (99 acres) Toyosu Market, like its predecessor, is one the busiest seafood markets in the world, with more than 600 merchants hard at work. The new market is an upgrade in terms of size and modern facilities, but sadly, a downgrade in terms of experience and charm. Visitors get far less access at Toyosu: you are restricted to viewing the early morning auctions from behind glass (you need to apply for a spot online before going) and you can no longer stroll the inner market. There's a fixed route you can follow through the three main buildings, two of which are for seafood, the other for fruit and vegetables. Afterward, head up to the rooftop lawn on the Fisheries Intermediate Wholesale Market Building for bay and city views, then check out the market's restaurants for a sushi or seafood breakfast; some popular Tsukiji restaurants like Sushi Dai have made the move to Toyosu. While this is Toyosu, don't use Toyosu Station as it is a 20-minute walk away; use Shijo-mae Station on the Yurikamome Line. ⊠ *6–1 Toyosu, Koto-ku* ☎ *03/3520–8205* ⊕ *www.shijou.metro. tokyo.jp/english/toyosu* 🕐 *Closed Sun.* Ⓜ *Yurikamome Line, Shijo-mae Station.*

🍴 Restaurants

Citabria Baypark Grill and Bar (サイタブリア ベイパーク グリル＆バー)
$$ | **FAST FOOD** | Stop off near the end of the Yurikamome Line and have dinner along the river bank before heading back to your hotel. The live DJ, order-at-bar service, and strong cocktails create a lively ambience, and classic western dishes can be ordered at your table via cellphone. **Known for:** pizza and fish-and-chips; outdoor-only dining; fairy lights with river and city views. [$] *Average main: ¥3,000* ✉ *6–4–26 Toyosu, Koto-ku, Odaiba* ☎ *080/9179–5151* 🌐 *www.citabria-baypark.com* 🕒 *Closed Mon. to Wed.; No lunch Fri. and Thu.* [M] *Yurikamome Line, Shijo-mae Station.*

☕ Coffee and Quick Bites

Lohas Cafe Ariake (ロハスカフェ)
$ | **BISTRO** | After strolling over the broad Yumeno Ohashi Bridge, it might be time for a break. Attached to Musashino University's Ariake Campus is a cheap, bright, and fun cafe with good weekly specials and a wide variety of dishes including pasta and rice bowls. **Known for:** cafe dishes at student prices; open space and high ceilings; veranda with tree views. [$] *Average main: ¥1,000* ✉ *Musashino University Ariake Campus, 3–3–3 Ariake, 2F, Koto-ku* ☎ *03/6457–1150* 🌐 *www.lohascafe-ariake.net* 🕒 *No dinner* [M] *Yurikamome Line, Tokyo Big Sight Station.*

🛏 Hotels

Thanks to its secluded destination, the Odaiba area is a lovely place to stay on a romantic getaway. (The hotels that line Tokyo Bay are known for their views.) Business travelers also stay here to be close to the convention center grounds.

Grand Nikko Tokyo Daiba (グランドニッコー東京 台場)
$$ | **HOTEL** | **FAMILY** | As soon as you enter the grand, extravagant lobby, you and your luggage will be immediately taken care of. **Pros:** great views of Rainbow Bridge; large, clean rooms; romantic setting. **Cons:** reception can get busy; slightly old-fashioned rooms; not much to do in the evening. [$] *Rooms from: ¥30,000* ✉ *2–6–1 Daiba, Minato-ku* ☎ *03/5500–6711* 🌐 *www.tokyo.grand-nikko.com* 🛏 *884 rooms* 🍽 *No Meals* [M] *Yurikamome Line, Daiba Station.*

Hilton Tokyo Odaiba (ヒルトン東京お台場)
$$ | **HOTEL** | With a facade that follows the curve of the Tokyo Bay shoreline, the 16-story Hilton Tokyo Odaiba presents itself as an "urban resort" with European style. **Pros:** great views of Tokyo Bay; friendly staff; romantic setting. **Cons:** isolated location might not be ideal for sightseeing; room interiors are a tad bland; expensive pool fees for guests. [$] *Rooms from: ¥30,000* ✉ *1–9–1 Daiba, Minato-ku* ☎ *03/5500–5500* 🌐 *www.hilton.com* 🛏 *453 rooms* 🍽 *No Meals* [M] *Yurikamome Line, Daiba Station.*

🛍 Shopping

Compared with the narrow streets of central Tokyo, Odaiba's wide, open spaces are well suited for multi-story shopping complexes. It is then of no surprise that there are three, Decks Tokyo Beach, Aqua City, and Diver City, within walking distance of each other.

MALLS AND SHOPPING CENTERS

Aqua City Odaiba (アクアシティお台場)
MALL | Aqua City is almost indistinguishable from its next-door neighbor, Decks Tokyo Beach. What does set it apart from a regular shopping mall is the variety of food options: a food court in the basement, a barbeque spot on the roof, and a ramen theme park—as well as its

own shrine. It also boasts a cinema and a wide selection of Japanese and international brands. ✉ *1–7–1 Daiba, Minato-ku* ☎ *03/3599-4700* ⊕ *www.aquacity.jp* Ⓜ *Rinkai Line, Tokyo Teleport Station; Yurikamome Line, Odaiba-kaihinkoen Station.*

Ariake Garden (有明ガーデン)

MALL | **FAMILY** | Opened in June 2020, Ariake Garden is a large-scale shopping mall with more than 200 stores, a hotel, spa with hot spring access, theater, rooftop terrace, and garden. ✉ *2–1–8 Ariake, Odaiba* ☎ *0570/077-711* ⊕ *www.shopping-sumitomo-rd.com* Ⓜ *Yurikamome Line, Ariake and Ariake-tennis-no-mori Station; Rinkai Line, Kokusai-tenjijo Station.*

★ Decks Tokyo Beach
(デックス東京ビーチ)

SHOPPING CENTER | **FAMILY** | Overlooking the harbor, this six-story complex of shops, restaurants, and boardwalks is really two connected malls: Island Mall and Seaside Mall. For kids (or nostalgic adults), check out the Lego Discovery Center, Joypolis mega-arcade, Trick Art Museum, and Madame Tussauds Tokyo. At the Seaside Mall, a table by the window in any of the restaurants looks out to a delightful view of the harbor, especially at sunset, when the *yakatabune* (traditional-roofed pleasure boats) drift down the Sumida-gawa from Yanagibashi and Ryogoku. You can also try shopping at the equally large Aqua City mall next door. ✉ *1–6–1 Daiba, Minato-ku, Odaiba* ☎ *03/3599–6500* ⊕ *www.odaiba-decks.com* Ⓜ *Rinkai Line, Tokyo Teleport Station; Yurikamome Line, Odaiba-kaihinkoen Station.*

Diver City Tokyo Plaza
(ダイバーシティ東京 プラザ)

MALL | Diver City gets a lot of foot traffic, mainly due to the life-sized Gundam robot statue welcoming shoppers in at the door. It also boasts a wide selection of stores and a food court with many dining options. ✉ *1–1–10 Aomi, Koto-ku, Odaiba* Ⓜ *Rinkai Line, Tokyo Teleport Station.*

Chapter 7

AOYAMA AND SHIBUYA, WITH AKASAKA, HARAJUKU, AND SHIMOKITAZAWA

Updated by
Jay Farris

⊙ Sights 🍴 Restaurants 🛏 Hotels ⊖ Shopping 🍸 Nightlife
★★★★★   ★★★★★   ★★★★★   ★★★★★   ★★★★★

AOYAMA AND SHIBUYA SNAPSHOT

TOP EXPERIENCES

■ **Tokyo street style.** Japanese street fashion may be less out-there than in years past, but Shibuya and Harajuku are still the places to see the newest trends.

■ **See world-renowned art.** Stop inside Shibuya Station for a peek at *Myth of Tomorrow*, the large, 14-panel mural by avant-garde artist Taro Okamoto.

■ **Find a place for prayers and picnics.** The beautiful Meiji Shrine and more lively Yoyogi Koen offer a refreshing bit of green amid the concrete, crowds, and neon.

■ **Get lost in Shimokitazawa.** The hipster-vibe neighborhood is filled with vintage shops, periodic outdoor markets, a linear park, and a calmer vibe than Shibuya.

■ **People-watch.** Take a break at any of the casual indoor-outdoor spots in Akasaka or the cafés of Aoyama and watch the world go by.

■ **Wander through a cemetery.** Spoiler alert: everyone dies. However, we all commemorate death differently. Aoyama Cemetery is a beautiful historic location to pass through, particularly in the spring when the cherry blossoms are not to be missed.

GETTING HERE

Primary access to Shibuya is via the looping JR Yamanote Line connecting it to next-door Ebisu and Harajuku Stations, but the Fukutoshin subway line also goes north from Shibuya up through Shinjuku and onto Ikebukuro, while the Hanzomon and Ginza lines both stop at Omotesando Station on the way to Shibuya Station from central Tokyo. The Keio Inokashira railway will take you to Shimokitazawa and on to Kichijoji, home to Inokashira Park, and the Toyoko railway connects the area to Yokohama. The Hachiko Exit will be swarmed with people. Just next to it is the "scramble crossing," which leads from the station to the area's concentration of restaurants and shops. Buses provide service to Roppongi to the east and Meguro and Setagaya Wards to the west. On Meiji-dori, Harajuku is walkable to the north in 15 minutes, and Ebisu takes about the same going south.

PAUSE HERE

■ If you need a break from the frantic Harajuku area, try the roof of the Tokyo Plaza at the intersection of Omotesando and Meiji-dori. Just look up and you can't miss the trees. The roof of the shopping mall offers a nice, shady decked area where you can sit or enjoy the view.

PLANNING YOUR TIME

■ Ideally, spend a day or two in the area, allowing for plenty of time to browse the shops. If you are energetic, you could make a day of Harajuku, Aoyama, and the Meiji Shrine. You can see the Shrine in less than an hour, but the Nezu Museum and its gardens may warrant a longer visit. Shibuya seems chaotic and intimidating, but it is fairly compact. You can easily walk around it in a couple of hours. Shimokitazawa is a bit farther afield, quieter and good for a walk before and after a meal, though not really a place for nightlife.

Tokyo hosted its first Olympics in 1964, and this turning point left its mark on west-central Tokyo. First, U.S.-occupied Washington Heights was turned over to the city for the construction of the Olympic Village. Aoyama-dori, the avenue through the center of the area, was renovated, and the Ginza and Hanzomon subway lines were built under it. The area between Aoyama and Shibuya became attractive.

Omotesando, the grand approach to Meiji Shrine that connects Aoyama to the Harajuku area, became the heart of Tokyo's youth and street-fashion scene, home to a plethora of stores, boutiques, and cafés. But it isn't only a place for trendy teenagers; a walk through the neighborhood's winding backstreets also reveals a range of more sophisticated restaurants and cafés.

Meanwhile, Yoyogi Park, built on the remains of the 1964 Olympic village and Meiji Shrine, offer a respite from Tokyo's crowds and concrete, with a variety of museums and galleries that give a taste of Japanese art and history. And just opposite the Kenzo Tange's spectacular Yoyogi National Gymnasium is Shibuya.

By the 1980s, the entire area had become one of the hippest parts of the city. Today, many local designers have been pushed to the back streets or online while the likes of Louis Vuitton, Chanel, Armani, and Prada line Omotesando. The narrow back streets allow

for a variety of shops, restaurants, and amusements in this area, which has an eclectic population of university students, wealthy socialites, young professionals, and people who like to see and be seen.

Things get a bit grittier as you get closer to Shibuya station, an area with roots in the 1980s and '90s as the center of Tokyo's youth and fashion culture and technology industry still evident, but newer developments are slowly changing this hub that is one of Tokyo's busiest shopping and entertainment areas. Shibuya is a sometimes overwhelming mix of shops, restaurants, bars, and clubs. Shibuya Crossing is known as one of the world's busiest pedestrian crossings and nearly a tourist sight in its own right.

The area gets its name from the samurai family who presided over the area in the 11th century; the family name "Shibuya" and the land were granted to a Heian Era general as a gift for thwarting an attack on the Imperial Palace in Kyoto. For the next six centuries, Shibuya remained a small hamlet of the city. With the opening of Shibuya Station in 1885, the area began to grow, taking off in the 1930s when it became a key terminal linking Tokyo and Yokohama. After being leveled in the war, Shibuya was quickly rebuilt and reestablished its reputation as an entertainment district.

Shibuya Station's importance as an entry point to the city from the suburbs only grew after its construction. The area's importance is directly related to the number of people passing through daily, but it is also a key connector to another, perhaps quieter area that is worth a visit—Shimokitazawa. Escaping the fast development of the 1980s, the bedroom town has slowly developed a reputation for its funky, slower vibe and its kitschy vintage shopping. Like Shibuya, Shimokitazawa is also a crossroads, providing you direct connection to both Shibuya and Shinjuku Stations to get you right back into the thick of things.

Akasaka

Akasaka is an eclectic area due mostly to its geography, being wedged between such disparate parts of Tokyo. While it's decidedly a business area by day (where lunch bargains abound), Akasaka turns into an entertainment district in the evening. Wander the streets to find a variety of restaurants. To its northeast and east are government ministries and office complexes with their associated lodgings and eating establishments. To the south is the lively Roppongi area and the flashy Aoyama district to its west, giving Akasaka just about anything you might be looking for.

🍴 Restaurants

Ajanta (アジャンタ)
$$ | **INDIAN** | In the mid-20th century, the founder of Ajanta came to Tokyo to study electrical engineering. He ended up changing careers and establishing what is today one of the oldest and best Indian restaurants in town. **Known for:** authentic South Indian cuisine; excellent dosa; open late. [$] *Average main: ¥2,000* ✉ *3–11 Nibancho, Chiyoda-ku* ☎ *03/3264–6955* 🌐 *www.ajanta.com* [M] *Yurakucho Line, Kojimachi Station (Exit 5).*

Kama-age Udon Sawanoi (釜あげうどん 赤坂澤乃井; *Akasaka Sawanoi*)
$ | **JAPANESE** | The homemade udon noodles, served in a broth with seafood, vegetables, or chicken, make a perfect light meal or midnight snack. Try the *inaka* (country-style) udon, which has bonito, seaweed flakes, radish shavings, and a raw egg dropped into the hot broth to cook. **Known for:** chewy homemade udon noodles; quick, tasty lunches; lively izakaya-like atmosphere at night. [$] *Average main: ¥1,000* ✉ *Dear City Akasaka Honkan, 4–2–3 Akasaka, 2nd fl., Minato-ku* ☎ *03/3582–2080* 🌐 *akasaka-sawanoi.com* 💳 *No credit cards* 🕒 *Closed weekends* [M] *Ginza and Marunouchi subway lines, Akasaka-mitsuke Station (Belle Vie Akasaka Exit).*

Ninja Tokyo (忍者東京)
$$$$ | **JAPANESE** | **FAMILY** | In keeping with the air of mystery you'd expect from a ninja-theme restaurant, a ninja-costumed waiter leads you through a dark underground maze to your table in an artificial cave. The menu is prix-fixe only, and prices can more than double depending on the set you choose. **Known for:** table-side entertainment; secret passages; theme restaurant. [$] *Average main: ¥10,000* ✉ *Akasaka Tokyu Plaza, 2–14–3 Nagatacho, Minato-ku* ☎ *03/5157–3936* 🌐 *www.ninja-tokyo.jp* [M] *Ginza and Marunouchi subway lines, Akasaka-mitsuke Station (Tokyu Plaza Exit).*

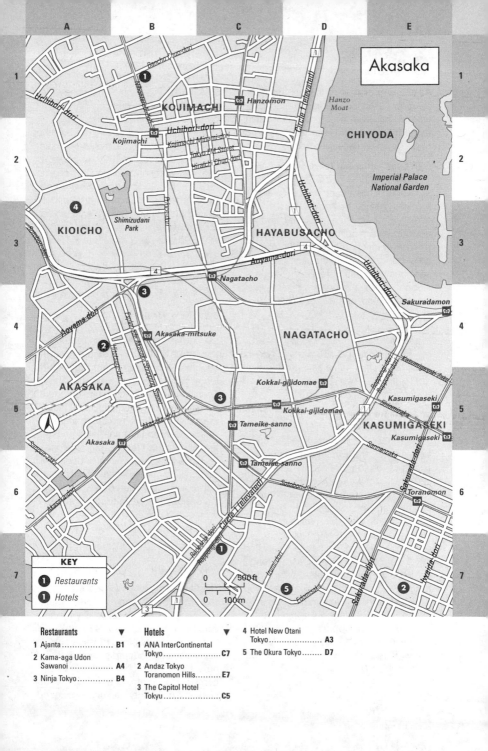

Akasaka

A · B · C · D · E

Boncho Chuo-dori

Uchibori-dori

KOJIMACHI · Hanzomon

Hanzo Moat

Uchibori-dori

Kojimachi · Kojimachi Minami-dori

Tokyo FM Street

Hiratch Chuo-dori

CHIYODA

Imperial Palace National Garden

KIOICHO · Shimizudani Park

HAYABUSACHO

Aoyama-dori

Nagatacho

Akasaka-mitsuke

NAGATACHO

Sakuradamon

AKASAKA

Kokkai-gijidomae

Kokkai-gijidomae

Kasumigaseki

KASUMIGASEKI

Akasaka

Tameike-sanno

Kasumigaseki

Tameike-sanno

Toranomon

Sotobori-dori

KEY
1 Restaurants
1 Hotels

0 ____ 500 ft
0 ____ 100m

Restaurants ▼	**Hotels** ▼	4 Hotel New Otani
1 Ajanta **B1**	1 ANA InterContinental	Tokyo **A3**
	Tokyo **C7**	5 The Okura Tokyo **D7**
2 Kama-aga Udon	2 Andaz Tokyo	
Sawanoi **A4**	Toranomon Hills **E7**	
3 Ninja Tokyo **B4**	3 The Capitol Hotel	
	Tokyu **C5**	

Hotels

As an entertainment and business district in a central location, Akasaka is buzzing around the clock. Accommodations can range from high-end international brands to pared-down capsule hotels.

ANA InterContinental Tokyo (ANA インターコンチネンタルホテル東京)
$$ | **HOTEL** | With a central location and modest pricing, the ANA is a great choice for the business traveler, and its ziggurat-atrium points to the heyday of the power lunch: the mid-1980s. **Pros:** great concierge; wonderful city views; spacious lobby. **Cons:** fees for the open-air pool; room bathrooms a bit small; few sightseeing options within walking distance. [$] *Rooms from: ¥27,000* ✉ *1–12–33 Akasaka, Minato-ku* ☎ *03/3505–1111* 🌐 *anaintercontinental-tokyo.jp* 🛏 *844 rooms* 🍴 *No Meals* [M] *Ginza and Namboku subway lines, Tameike-Sanno Station (Exit 13); Namboku subway line, Roppongi-itchome Station (Exit 3).*

★ Andaz Tokyo Toranomon Hills (アンダーズ東京)
$$$$ | **HOTEL** | Set in the revitalized Toranomon district, this Hyatt boutique property occupies the top six floors of one of the city's tallest towers and offers chic guest rooms, considered service, an airy spa, and views, views, views. **Pros:** contemporary design with Japanese aesthetics; stylish rooftop bar; swimming pool overlooks the Imperial palace. **Cons:** finding entrance can be troublesome; long corridors on guestroom floors; high fees to use the pool and gym. [$] *Rooms from: ¥59,000* ✉ *1–23–4 Toranomon, Minato-ku* ☎ *03/6830–1234* 🌐 *www.hyatt.com/en-US/hotel/japan/andaz-tokyo-toranomon-hills/tyoaz* 🛏 *164 rooms* 🍴 *No Meals* [M] *Ginza subway line, Toranomon Station (Exit 1).*

The Capitol Hotel Tokyu (ザ・キャピトルホテル東急)
$$$$ | **HOTEL** | Everything old is new again: the Capitol, once a boxy 29-floor commercial complex designed by architect Kengo Kuma and run by Hilton, has a long history that includes hosting the Beatles. **Pros:** convenient location; beautiful and spacious pool; no charge for Wi-Fi throughout hotel. **Cons:** pricey; government district might not appeal to tourists; the immediate area is very quiet on weekends. [$] *Rooms from: ¥62,000* ✉ *2–10–3 Nagatacho, Minato-ku* ☎ *03/3503–0109* 🌐 *www.tokyuhotelsjapan.com/global/capitol-h* 🛏 *251 rooms* 🍴 *No Meals* [M] *Ginza and Namboku subway lines, Tameike-Sanno Station (Exit 5).*

Hotel New Otani Tokyo (ホテルニューオータニ東京)
$$$ | **HOTEL** | A bustling complex in the center of Tokyo—restaurants and shopping arcades beneath the sixth-floor lobby swarm with crowds—the New Otani can feel frantic, but its best feature, a spectacular 10-acre Japanese garden, readily visible from the appropriately named Garden Lounge, helps guests find sanctuary. **Pros:** beautiful garden; first-rate concierge; outdoor pool. **Cons:** complex layout could be off-putting; public areas a bit dated; few sightseeing options within walking distance. [$] *Rooms from: ¥39,000* ✉ *4–1 Kioi-cho, Chiyoda-ku* ☎ *03/3234–5678* 🌐 *www.newotani.co.jp* 🛏 *1,479 rooms* 🍴 *No Meals* [M] *Ginza and Marunouchi subway lines, Akasaka-mitsuke Station (Exit 7).*

The Okura Tokyo (オークラ東京)
$$$$ | **HOTEL** | The original Hotel Okura, built before the first Tokyo Olympics, came to be one of Tokyo's most iconic hotels due to its blend of traditional Japanese and modernist design, and now, having been newly rebuilt, it still combines the retro charm of its predecessor with modern luxury. **Pros:** good

service; retro-modern design and feel; large rooms. **Cons:** retro design not for everyone; not ideal for families; expensive. [$] *Rooms from: ¥57,000* ✉ *2–10–4 Tora-no-mon, Minato-ku* ☎ *03/3582–0111* 🌐 *theokuratokyo.jp/en* 🛏 *508 rooms* 🍴 *No Meals* [M] *Hibiya subway line, Kamiya-cho Station (Exit 4B); Ginza subway line, Tora-no-mon Station (Exit 3).*

Shopping

CRAFTS

Japan Traditional Crafts Aoyama Square (伝統工芸 青山スクエア; *Dento Kogei Aoyama Sukuea*)

CRAFTS | You don't have to travel around the country to see a collection of the best artisan crafts from different regions. Tea kettles, bows, knives, scarves, fans—this shop almost feels like a curated museum where all the items are on sale. The shop also hosts events highlighting artisans or regions, so you might get to see some pottery being made or get a chance to try something on your own. ✉ *8-1-22 Akasaka, MInato-ku* ☎ *03/5785-1301* 🌐 *kougeihin.jp* 🕒 *Closed New Year holidays* [M] *Hanzomon, Ginza, and Oedo subway lines, Aoyama-Itchome Station (Exit 4).*

Aoyama

Sights

★ Nezu Museum (根津美術館; *Nezu Bijutsukan*)

ART MUSEUM | On view are traditional Japanese and Asian works of art owned by Meiji-period railroad magnate and politician Kaichiro Nezu. For the main building, architect Kengo Kuma designed an arched roof that rises two floors and extends roughly half a block through this upscale Minami Aoyama neighborhood. At any one time, the vast space houses a portion of the 7,400 works of calligraphy, paintings, sculptures, bronzes, and lacquerware that make up the Nezu's collection. The museum is also home to one of Tokyo's finest gardens, featuring 5 acres of ponds, rolling paths, waterfalls, and teahouses. ✉ *6–5–1 Minami-Aoyama, Minato-ku* ☎ *03/3400–2536* 🌐 *www.nezu-muse.or.jp* 🎟 *From ¥1,100* 🕒 *Closed Mon.* [M] *Ginza and Hanzomon subway lines, Omotesando Station (Exit A5).*

Restaurants

High-end boutiques, cafés, and restaurants fill the streets of upscale Aoyama. People-watching is a sidewalk sport here, easily done from the venues that line the streets.

Darumaya (だるまや)

$ | RAMEN | The classic bowl of ramen is topped with slices of pork, but Darumaya, in the fashion district of Omotesando, has a slightly different take, topping its noodles with grilled vegetables. In the summertime be sure to order the *hiyashi soba*, a bowl of chilled noodles topped with vegetables and ham in a sesame dressing. **Known for:** a quick, affordable lunch in a high-end area; refreshing take on ramen; one of few noodle shops in the neighborhood. [$] *Average main: ¥950* ✉ *Murayama Bldg., 5–9–5 Minami-Aoyama, 1F, Minato-ku* ☎ *03/3499–6295* 💳 *No credit cards* 🕒 *Closed Sun. and Mon.* [M] *Ginza, Chiyoda, and Hanzomon subway lines, Omotesando Station (Exit B1).*

Maisen Aoyama (まい泉)

$$$ | JAPANESE | Converted from a *sento* (public bathhouse), Maisen still has the old high ceiling (built for ventilation) and the original signs instructing bathers where to change, but now bouquets of seasonal flowers transform the large, airy space into a pleasant dining room. Maisen's specialty is the *tonkatsu* set: tender, juicy, deep-fried pork cutlets served with a tangy sauce, shredded cabbage, miso soup, and rice. **Known for:**

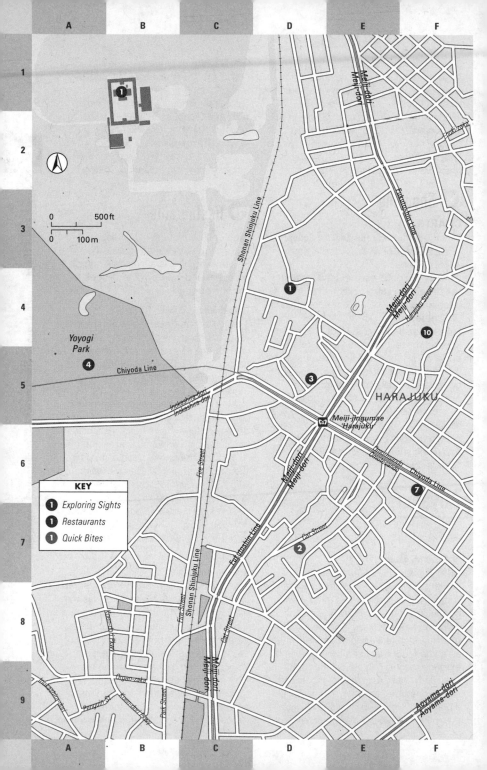

Aoyama and Harajuku

Sights ▼
1 Meiji Jingu Shrine B1
2 Nezu Museum J9
3 Ota Memorial Museum of Art D5
4 Yoyogi Park A5

Restaurants ▼
1 Baird Beer Taproom
  Harajuku D4
2 Barbacoa Churrascaria
  Aoyama G6
3 Brown Rice by
  Neals' Yard Remedies G7
4 Cicada H8
5 Crayon House Hiroba G7
6 Darumaya G8
7 Heiroku Sushi
  Shibuya Omotesando F6
8 Maisen Aoyama G6
9 Red Pepper H7
10 Sakuratei F4
11 Tempura Tensho J4

Quick Bites ▼
1 Café Kitsuné Aoyama I8
2 The Roastery by Nozy Coffee D7

7

Aoyama and Shibuya, with Akasaka, Harajuku, and Shimokitazawa AOYAMA

retro-chic decor; hearty lunch sets; succulent deep-fried pork. [S] *Average main: ¥3,200* ⊠ *4–8–5 Jingumae, Shibuya-ku* ☎ *050/3188-5802* [M] *Ginza, Chiyoda, and Hanzomon subway lines, Omotesando Station (Exit A2).*

Tempura Tensho (てんぷら天翔)

$$$$ | JAPANESE | The entrance here may make you feel as if you are stepping into a nondescript office, but once inside you will get a front-row seat for some professional and exceptional frying (and even some private tables if you want a truly luxe experience). The tempura here is excellent for dinner, but the lunch sets are reasonably priced (one-third to half the cost of dinner) yet can still give you a proper tempura experience. **Known for:** elaborate lunch and dinner sets; an airy atmosphere; fresh, seasonal ingredients. [S] *Average main: ¥15,000* ⊠ *2-7-13 Kitaaoyama, Minato-ku* ✛ *On the ground floor of Hotel Allamanda Aoyama* ☎ *03/6447-5045, 050/3184-3600 Reservations only* [M] *Ginza subway line, Gaienmae Station (Exit 2b or 4a).*

☕ Coffee and Quick Bites

Café Kitsuné Aoyama

$ | CAFÉ | Associated with the funky clothing shop that is just around the corner, this cafe is bright and open, and serves quality coffee, cakes, snacks, and gelato. They also have some Kitsuné-branded goods on hand. **Known for:** lively and airy atmosphere; Kitsuné-branded small gifts; quality coffee. [S] *Average main: ¥1,000* ⊠ *3-15-9 Minami-Aoyama, Minato-ku* ☎ *03/5786–4842* ⊕ *maisonkitsune.com/mk/find-a-store/cafe-kitsune-aoyama-3* ⊘ *No dinner* [M] *Ginza, Chiyoda, and Hanzomon subway lines, Omotesando Station (Exit A4).*

Nightlife

BARS

Radio (バー・ラジオ)

COCKTAIL LOUNGES | Koji Ozaki is the closest thing Tokyo has to a superstar bartender. This demure septuagenarian, who still works one week per month, has been crafting cocktails for half a century, and he's known for both his perfectionism and creativity. Ozaki designed not only the bar he works behind, but the glasses he serves his creations in (some of the best in the city). All bartenders arrange the bar's flowers. You need to dress up (avoid short pants or flip-flops by all means), and remember, this is a place for quiet relaxation. ⊠ *3–10–34 Minami-Aoyama, Aoyama* ☎ *03/3402–2668* ⊕ *www.bar-radio.com* ⊘ *Closed Sun.* [M] *Chiyoda, Ginza, and Hanzomon subway lines, Omotesando Station (Exit A4).*

Two Rooms

COCKTAIL LOUNGES | Aoyama's dressed-up drinkers hang out on the stylish terrace. Drinks are big, pricey, and modern—think martinis in multiple fresh-fruit flavors such as kiwi. The terrace overlooking the Shinjuku area is particularly comfortable in spring and summer. ⊠ *AO Bldg., 3–11–7 Kita-Aoyama, 5th fl., Aoyama* ☎ *03/3498–0002* ⊕ *www.tworooms.jp* [M] *Chiyoda, Ginza, and Hanzomon subway lines, Omotesando Station (Exit B2).*

JAZZ CLUBS

Blue Note Tokyo (ブルーノート東京)

LIVE MUSIC | This premier live jazz venue isn't for everyone: prices are high, sets short, and patrons packed in tight, sometimes sharing a table with strangers. But if you want to catch Pat Metheny and Larry Carlton in a relatively small venue, this is the place. Expect to pay upward of ¥11,000 to see major acts, and ¥6,500 to ¥9,000 for most others. ⊠ *Raika Bldg., 6–3–16 Minami-Aoyama, Minato-ku, Aoyama* ☎ *03/5485–0088* ⊕ *www.bluenote.co.jp* [M] *Chiyoda, Ginza, and Hanzo-mon subway lines, Omotesando Station (Exit A5).*

What to Drink in Tokyo

Whether you're out with friends, with clients, or belting out a tune at the local karaoke bar, there are likely to be multiple drinking opportunities during your stay. Things may look a little different, even before you start knocking back a few, so take note of the liquors of this island nation. And remember, shout *Kanpai!* (sounds like "kaan-pie") instead of *Cheers!* when you raise your glass.

Sake

Sake, well-known worldwide, and called *nihonshu* in Japanese, is Japan's number-one alcoholic beverage. There are more than 2,000 different brands of sake produced throughout Japan. Like other kinds of wine, sake comes in sweet (*amakuchi*) and dry (*karakuchi*) varieties; these are graded using a complex system of designations based on how much the rice has been polished down before brewing and whether additional brewer's alcohol has been blended in postbrew. *Junmai Daiginjo-shu* is the highest grade, with no extra alcohol added and a rice milling rate of 50% or more (so only the purest, inner part of each rice grain is used), but almost all grades of sake can be good and come with varying characteristics.

Best drunk at room temperature (*nurukan*) or slightly chilled so as not to alter the flavor, sake is also served heated (*atsukan*) in winter, though heat can ruin some good brews. It's usually poured from *tokkuri* (small ceramic vessels) into tiny cups called *choko*. The diminutive size of these cups shouldn't mislead you into thinking you can't drink too much. The custom of making sure that your companion's cup never runs dry often leads the novice astray.

Apart from the *nomiya* (bars) and restaurants, the place to sample sake is the *izakaya*, a drinking establishment that usually serves food along with dozens of kinds of sake, including a selection of *jizake*, the kind produced in limited quantities by small regional breweries throughout the country.

Heavenly Spirits

Shochu is made from a variety of base ingredients such as buckwheat, sweet potatoes, or rice, and is particularly associated with the southern island of Kyushu. It's served either on the rocks or mixed with water and can be hot or cold. Sometimes a wedge of lemon or a small pickled apricot, known as *umeboshi*, is added as well. It can also be mixed with club soda and served cold as a popular drink called *chuhai*, or, at an izakaya, often called "a sour."

Havin' a Biiru

Japan's heavyweight breweries Asahi and Kirin are everywhere. Meanwhile Sapporo and Suntory also often make a showing. Asahi and Kirin are constantly battling for the coveted title of "Japan's No. 1 Brewery," but many beer fans rate Suntory's Malts brand and Sapporo's Yebisu brand as the most flavorsome. National brand Orion makes a light brew that is widely available and in recent years, Belgian beers have grown in popularity and availability. The products of Japanese microbreweries have also become easier to find and many regions have local brewers. Domestic craft beer *kurafuto bi-ru* has become very popular, and it's appearing on tap at restaurants, bars, and craft beer pubs around the city. Good Japanese craft brewers to look out for include Shiga Kogen, Minoh, and Baird.

Performing Arts

MUSIC

Kioi Hall (紀尾井ホール)

CONCERTS | FAMILY | Behind Hotel New Otani stands this relatively small concert venue, which showcases both performances of Western classical music, such as piano and violin recitals, and Japanese works, including *shakuhachi* flute music. It hosts programs for families to learn how to play such traditional Japanese instruments. ✉ *6–5 Kioicho, Chiyoda-ku* ☎ *03/5276-4500* ⊕ *www.kioi-hall.or.jp* Ⓜ *JR, Marunouchi and Nanboku subway lines, Yotsuya Station (Kojimachi Exit); Yurakucho subway line, Kojimachi Station (Exit 2).*

🛍 Shopping

You'll find boutiques by many of the leading Japanese and Western designers in Aoyama, as well as elegant, but pricey, antiques shops on Kotto-dori. Aoyama is a showcase not merely of high fashion, but also often the latest concepts in commercial architecture and interior design. Omotesando, a long, wide avenue running from Aoyama-dori into Meiji Shrine, is sometimes referred to as the Champs-Elysées of Tokyo. The sidewalks are lined with cafés and designer boutiques. Omotesando is perfect for browsing, window-shopping, and lingering over a café au lait, but its back streets are also worth exploring.

ANTIQUES

Fuji-Torii (富士鳥居)

ANTIQUES & COLLECTIBLES | An English-speaking staff, a central Omotesando location, and antiques ranging from ceramics to swords are the big draws at this shop, in business since 1948. In particular Fuji-Torii has an excellent selection of folding screens, lacquerware, painted glassware, and *ukiyo-e* (woodblock prints). You can also pick up contemporary gifts, such as reading glasses with frames wrapped in traditional fabric. ✉ *6–1–10 Jingumae,*

Shibuya-ku ☎ *03/3400–2777* ⊕ *www. fuji-torii.com* 🕙 *Closed Tues. and 3rd Mon. of every month* Ⓜ *Chiyoda and Fukutoshin subway lines, Meiji-Jingumae Station (Exit 4).*

Traditional Crafts Morita

(古民藝もりた; *Komingei Morita*)

ANTIQUES & COLLECTIBLES | Antiques and new *mingei* (Japanese folk crafts) are on display alongside a large stock of textiles from throughout Asia. An easy-to-transport gift would be *furoshiki*, which is rather inexpensive woodblock-printed cloth used as decorative covers in daily life. ✉ *5–12–2 Minami-Aoyama, Minato-ku, Minato-ku* ☎ *03/3407–4466* Ⓜ *Ginza, Chiyoda, and Hanzomon subway lines, Omotesando Station (Exit B1).*

CERAMICS

Tatsuya Shoten (つたや商店)

CERAMICS | *Ikebana* (flower arrangement) and *sado* (tea ceremony) goods are the only items sold at this shop, but they come in such stunning variety that a visit is definitely worthwhile. Colorful vases in surprising shapes and traditional ceramic tea sets make unique souvenirs. ✉ *5–10–5 Minami-Aoyama, Minato-ku, Minato-ku* ☎ *03/3400–3815* 🕙 *Closed 1st and 4th Sun.* Ⓜ *Ginza, Chiyoda, and Hanzomon subway lines, Omotesando Station (Exit B1).*

CLOTHING

Bapexclusive Aoyama

(Bapexclusive 青山)

MIXED CLOTHING | Since the late 1990s, no brand has been more coveted by Harajuku scenesters than the BATHING APE label (shortened to BAPE) founded by DJ–fashion designer NIGO. At the height of the craze, hopefuls would line up outside NIGO's well-hidden boutiques and pay ¥7,000 for a T-shirt festooned with a simian visage or *Planet of the Apes* quote. BAPE has since gone aboveground, with the brand expanding across the globe. You can see what the fuss is all about in this spacious

Mix with Tokyo's most glamorous residents at Prada's architecturally dazzling Omotesando store.

two-story shop with an upstairs conveyor belt of sneakers that is always a draw. ⊠ *5–5–8 Minami-Aoyama, Minato-ku* ☎ *03/3407–2145* ⊕ *www.bape.com* Ⓜ *Ginza and Hanzomon subway lines, Omotesando Station (Exit A5).*

★ **Comme des Garçons** (コムデギャルソン)
MIXED CLOTHING | Sinuous low walls snake through Comme des Garçons founder Rei Kawakubo's flagship store, a minimalist labyrinth that houses the designer's signature clothes, shoes, and accessories. Staff members do their best to ignore you, but that's no reason to stay away from one of Tokyo's funkiest retail spaces. ⊠ *5–2–1 Minami-Aoyama, Minato-ku* ☎ *03/3406–3951* ⊕ *www.comme-des-garcons.com* Ⓜ *Ginza, Chiyoda, and Hanzomon subway lines, Omotesando Station (Exit A5).*

★ **Issey Miyake** (イッセイミヤケ)
WOMEN'S CLOTHING | The otherworldly creations of internationally renowned brand Issey Miyake are on display at his flagship store in Aoyama, which carries the full Paris line. Keep walking on the same street away from Omotesando Station and also find a string of other Miyake stores just a stone's throw away, including Issey Miyake Men and Pleats Please. At the end of the street is the Reality Lab with a barrage of Miyake's most experimental lines like BaoBao, In-Ei, and incredible origami-like clothing. ⊠ *3–18–11 Minami-Aoyama, Minato-ku* ☎ *03/3423–1408* ⊕ *www.isseymiyake.com* Ⓜ *Ginza, Chiyoda, and Hanzomon subway lines, Omotesando Station (Exit A4).*

Maison Kitsuné
The half-Japanese, half-French duo who make this brand are former DJs and music producers, which may explain why the funky clothes have such a cool edge to them. The Kitsuné Café, which is just up the street and around a corner, serves some of the best coffee in the area and sells some Kitsuné-branded goods. ⊠ *3–15–1 Minami-Aoyama, Minato-ku, Aoyama* ☎ *03/5786-4841* ⊕ *www.maisonkitsune.com/jp_en/* Ⓜ *Ginza, Chiyoda, and Hanzomon subway lines, Omotesando Station (Exit A4).*

The Architecture of Omotesando

With Tokyo's impressive array of high-end fashion and jewelry stores has come an equally astonishing collection of beautiful buildings. A 20-minute walk along Omotesando from Aoyama to Harajuku takes you past several standout structures. Start at the **Prada** flagship just southeast of Omotesando crossing. The Swiss-based Herzog & de Meuron team created this building of concave and protruding diamond-shape glass panels, which give it a honeycomblike effect. Across the street they reprised their hit with the **Miu Miu** flagship in 2015, made of aluminum and brass.

At Omotesando crossing, look beyond the lanterns flanking the road and catch a glimpse of Kengo Kuma's **One Omotesando** with its wooden-slat facade that affords you different views as you pass. Heading toward Shibuya on Aoyama-dori and you'll see the **Ao Building** on the right. At night, the glass exterior becomes a curtain of blue, green, and purple lights, recalling the aurora borealis. Or proceed on Omotesando toward Harajuku, where you'll find the "squeezed" building that is **Hugo Boss** almost embraced by

Toyo Ito's L-shaped **Tod's** Omotesando building that dramatically recreates tree shapes in concrete blending to match the street. Further along is the white translucent box that is **Dior**, designed by Pritzker Architecture Prize recipients Kazuyo Sejima and Ryue Nishizawa of SANAA. Across the street, it's hard to miss the **Omotesando Hills** complex, home to a collection of ultra-fashionable boutiques and a six-floor atrium connected by a spiral ramp. One end of the building incorporates one of the much-loved structures it replaced—the last remaining example of what was one of Japan's early modern architecture movements.

Hang a left on Meiji-dori at Jingumae crossing and you won't miss the **"Iceberg" Building**. The sharp geometry of the blue glass structure was inspired by ice, crystal, and plastic bottles. Look beyond the mirrored entrance to Tokyu Plaza on the north side of the crossing and see the **H&M** building, which appears like a tower of stacked ice cubes. The cubes glow softly from day to night and reflect the dynamic city.

★ Prada

MIXED CLOTHING | This fashion "epicenter," designed by Herzog & de Meuron, is one of the most buzzed-about architectural wonders in the city. Its facade is made up of a mosaic of green glass "bubble" windows: alternating convex and concave panels create distorted reflections of the surrounding area. Many world-renowned, nearby boutiques have tried to replicate the significant impact the Prada building has had on the Omotesando, but none have been unable to match this tower. Most visitors opt for a photo in front of

the cavelike entrance that leads into the basement floor. ✉ *5–2–6 Minami-Aoyama, Minato-ku* ☎ *03/6418–0400* Ⓜ *Ginza, Chiyoda, and Hanzomon subway lines, Omotesando Station (Exit A5)*.

Sou-Sou Kyoto (そうそう)

OTHER SPECIALTY STORE | *Tabi* are the traditional cloth socks and shoes with a cleft-toe shape. This Kyoto-based brand creates graphic, cute, and funky patterns that are so ready for this era, you'd never know they were traditional. Other cloth items with fun designs are also available making the shop a great place for gifts.

✉ *5–4–24 Minami-Aoyama, Minato-ku, Aoyama* ☎ *03/3407–7877* Ⓜ *Ginza, Hanzomon, and Chiyoda subway lines, Omotesando Station (Exit B1).*

Undercover (アンダーカバー)

MIXED CLOTHING | This stark shop houses Paris darling Jun Takahashi's cult clothing. Racks of punk clothes sit under a ceiling made of a sea of thousands of hanging lightbulbs. ✉ *5–3–22 Minami-Aoyama, Minato-ku* ☎ *03/3407–1232* ⊕ *www.undercoverism.com* Ⓜ *Ginza, Chiyoda, and Hanzomon subway lines, Omotesando Station (Exit A5).*

CRAFTS

★ Ginza Natsuno (銀座夏野)

CRAFTS | FAMILY | This two-story boutique sells an incredible range of chopsticks, from traditional to pop motifs, and wooden to crystal-encrusted sticks that can be personalized. Children's chopsticks and dishes are housed in their own boutique behind it, but it's a must-see no matter your age. ✉ *4–2–17 Jingumae, Shibuya-ku* ☎ *03/3403–6033* ⊕ *www.e-ohashi.com* Ⓜ *Ginza, Chiyoda, and Hanzomon subway lines, Omotesando Station (Exit A2).*

HOUSEWARES

Francfranc (フランフラン)

This branch of the popular chain sells very reasonably priced interior goods that are trendy among young, urban Tokyoites. Here you'll find everything from the funky to the silly. Expect to see things like waffle irons shaped like cartoon characters, and kitchenware items from chopsticks to things you never knew you needed. ✉ *3–1–3 Minami-Aoyama, Minato-ku, Aoyama* ☎ *03/5785–2111* ⊕ *www.francfranc.com/apps/stores/en/location/60* Ⓜ *Ginza subway line, Gaienmae Station (Exit 1A).*

MALLS AND SHOPPING CENTERS

Glassarea (グラッセリア)

SHOPPING CENTER | Virtually defining Aoyama elegance is this small cobblestone shopping center, which draws well-heeled young professionals to its handful of fashion boutiques, spa, and a specialty store of Japanese crafts from Fukui Prefecture. ✉ *5–4–41 Minami-Aoyama, Minato-ku* ☎ *03/5778–4450* ⊕ *www.glassarea.com* Ⓜ *Ginza, Chiyoda, and Hanzomon subway lines, Omotesando Station (Exit B1).*

Gyre (ジャイル)

MALL | Near the Harajuku end of Omotesando, this mall houses luxury-brand shops such as Chanel and Maison Martin Margiela, three concept shops by Comme des Garçons, and one of only three Museum of Modern Art Design Stores outside New York City. ✉ *5–10–1 Jingumae, Shibuya-ku* ☎ *03/5400–5801* ⊕ *gyre-omotesando.com* Ⓜ *Chiyoda and Fukutoshin subway lines, Meiji-Jingumae Station (Exit 4).*

Omotesando Hills (表参道ヒルズ)

SHOPPING CENTER | Architect Tadao Ando's adventure in concrete is also one of Tokyo's monuments to shopping. Despised and adored with equal zeal, the controversial project demolished the charming yet antiquated Dojunkai Aoyama Apartments along Omotesando Avenue. Six wedge-shape floors include some brand-name heavy hitters (Yves Saint Laurent, Jimmy Choo and Harry Winston) and a wide range of smaller stores whose shelves showcase mid- to high-end shoes and bags. It's worth a stroll to see the latest in Japanese haute couture, and restaurants and cafés can also be found here—but beware of long lines at weekends. ✉ *4–12–10 Jingumae, Shibuya-ku* ☎ *03/3497–0310* ⊕ *www.omotesandohills.com* Ⓜ *Hanzomon, Ginza, and Chiyoda subway lines, Omotesando Station (Exit A2), Chiyoda and Fukutoshin subway lines, Meiji-Jingumae Station (Exit 4).*

Activities

IKEBANA COURSES
Sogetsu Ikebana School
(草月会館; *Sogetsu Kaikan*)
LOCAL SPORTS | The schools of *ikebana* (flower arranging), like those of other traditional arts, are highly stratified organizations. Students rise through levels of proficiency, paying handsomely for lessons and certifications as they go, until they can become teachers themselves. At the top of the hierarchy is the *iemoto*, the head of the school, a title usually held within a family for generations. The Sogetsu school of flower arrangement is a relative newcomer to all this. It was founded by Sofu Teshigahara in 1927, and, compared to the older schools, it espouses a style flamboyant, free-form, and even radical. Two-hour introductory lessons in flower arrangement are given in English on most Mondays (except national holidays). Some classes in Japanese have an English-speaking assistant. They also host shorter classes for travelers. Reservations must be made in advance. A rock garden in the Sogetsu Kaikan, created by the late Isamu Noguchi, one of the masters of modern sculpture, is worth a visit. Additionally, the school holds rotating ikebana exhibitions throughout the year and has a shop on the 4th floor. Sogetsu Kaikan is a 10-minute walk west on Aoyama-dori from the Akasaka-mitsuke intersection or east from the Aoyama-itchome subway stop. ✉ *7–2–21 Akasaka, Minato-ku, Akasaka* ☎ *03/3408–1154* ⊕ *www.sogetsu.or.jp/e* 🎫 *¥5,600 per person for 2-hour introductory lesson (reservation required)* Ⓜ *Ginza and Marunouchi subway lines, Akasaka-mitsuke Station; Ginza and Hanzomon subway lines, Aoyama-itchome Station (Exit 4).*

Harajuku

On weekends the heart of Harajuku, particularly the street called Takeshita-dori, belongs to high school and junior high school shoppers, who flock there for the latest trends. Entire industries give themselves convulsions just trying to keep up with adolescent styles. Slip into Harajuku's less-crowded backstreets—with their outdoor cafés, designer-ice-cream and Belgian-waffle stands, and a profusion of stores with names like A BATHING APE and The Virgin Mary—and you may find it impossible to believe that Japan's the most rapidly aging society in the industrial world.

◉ Sights

★ Meiji Jingu Shrine (明治神宮)
RELIGIOUS BUILDING | This shrine honors the spirits of Emperor Meiji, who died in 1912, and Empress Shoken. It was established by a resolution of the Imperial Diet the year after the emperor's death to commemorate his role in ending the long isolation of Japan under the Tokugawa Shogunate and setting the country on the road to modernization. Virtually destroyed in an air raid in 1945, it was rebuilt in 1958.

A wonderful spot for photos, the mammoth entrance gates (*torii*), rising 40 feet high, are made from 1,700-year-old cypress trees from Mt. Ari in Taiwan; the crosspieces are 56 feet long. Torii are meant to symbolize the separation of the everyday secular world from the spiritual world of the Shinto shrine. The buildings in the shrine complex, with their curving, green, copper roofs, are also made of cypress wood. The surrounding gardens have some 100,000 flowering shrubs and trees.

An annual festival at the shrine takes place on November 3, Emperor Meiji's birthday, which is a national holiday. On the festival and New Year's Day, as many as 1 million people come to offer

When you arrive at Meiji Shrine area, pay your respects by purifying your body and mind at the water basin area called the *temizuya*.

prayers and pay their respects. Several other festivals and ceremonial events are held here throughout the year; check by phone or on the shrine website to see what's scheduled during your visit. Even on a normal weekend the shrine draws thousands of visitors, but this seldom disturbs its mood of quiet serenity.

The peaceful Meiji Jingu Gardens (Meiji Jingu Gyoen), where the irises are in full bloom in the latter half of June, is on the left as you walk in from the main gates, before you reach the shrine. Designed by Kengo Kuma, the architect behind Tokyo's new Olympic stadium, the Meiji Jingu Museum displays personal effects and clothes of Emperor and Empress Meiji— perhaps of less interest to foreign visitors than to the Japanese. ⊠ *1–1 Yoyogi-kamizonocho, Shibuya-ku* ☏ *03/3379–5511* ⊕ *www.meijijingu.or.jp* ☞ *Shrine free, Meiji Jingu Garden ¥500, museum ¥1,000* Ⓜ *Chiyoda and Fukutoshin subway lines, Meiji-Jingumae Station; JR Yamanote Line, Harajuku Station (Exit 2).*

Ota Memorial Museum of Art (太田記念美術館; *Ota Kinen Bijutsukan*)
ART MUSEUM | The gift of former Toho Mutual Life Insurance chairman Seizo Ota, this is probably the city's finest private collection of *ukiyo-e*, traditional Edo-period woodblock prints. Ukiyo-e (pictures of the floating world) flourished in the 18th and 19th centuries. The works on display are selected and changed periodically from the 12,000 prints in the collection, which include some extremely rare work by artists such as Hiroshige, Hokusai, Sharaku, and Utamaro. ⊠ *1–10–10 Jingumae, Shibuya-ku* ☏ *03/3403–0880* ⊕ *www.ukiyoe-ota-muse.jp* ☞ *From ¥800, depending on exhibit* ☉ *Closed Mon. and between exhibitions* Ⓜ *Chiyoda and Fukutoshin subway lines, Meiji-Jingu-mae Station (Exit 5); JR Yamanote Line, Harajuku Station (Omotesando Exit).*

Yoyogi Park (代々木公園; *Yoyogi Koen*)
CITY PARK | **FAMILY** | This park is the perfect spot to have a picnic on a sunny day. On Sunday people come to play music, practice martial arts, and ride bicycles

on the bike path (rentals are available).
From spring through fall there are events,
concerts, and festivals most weekends.
Although the front half of the park makes
for great people-watching, farther along
the paths it is easy to find a quiet spot to
slip away from the crowds of Harajuku.
✉ 2–1 Yoyogi-mizonocho, Shibuya-ku
☎ 03/3469–6081 Ⓜ Chiyoda and Fukutoshin subway lines, Meiji-Jingumae Station (Exit 2); JR Yamanote Line, Harajuku
Station (Omotesando Exit).

🍴 Restaurants

Dining options in Harajuku and Omotesando are a reflection of their audiences.
Young Tokyoites flock to Harajuku on
the weekends to shop for clothes and
accessories along Takeshita Dori street
so you'll find fast food joints and ice-
cream and crepe spots. Trendy twenty-
and thirtysomethings come for the hip
backstreet boutiques and eat at similarly
hip and trendy eateries and cafés on and
around Omotesando.

★ Baird Beer Taproom Harajuku
(ベアードタップルーム原宿)
$$$ | JAPANESE | Founded by American
Bryan Baird in 2000, Baird Brewing has
become one of the leaders in Japan's
now booming craft-beer movement,
with a range of year-round brews, such
as the hop-heavy Suruga Bay IPA, and
creative seasonal beers that use local
ingredients such as yuzu citrus and even
wasabi. The Harajuku Taproom combines
Baird's excellent lineup of microbrews
with Japanese izakaya (pub) fare like
yakitori (grilled chicken skewers), gyoza
(dumplings), and curry rice. **Known for:**
Japanese craft beer; hand-pumped ales
on tap; blend of Western and Japanese
pub fare. $ Average main: ¥3,500 ✉ No
Surrender Bldg., 1–20–13 Jingumae, 2nd
fl., Shibuya-ku ☎ 03/6438–0450 ⊕ www.
bairdbeer.com/taprooms/harajuku 🕐 No
lunch weekdays Ⓜ JR Yamanote Line,
Harajuku Station.

Barbacoa Churrascaria Aoyama
(バルバッコア青山本店;)
$$$$ | BRAZILIAN | Carnivores flock here for
the all-you-can-eat Brazilian grilled chick-
en and barbecued beef, which the effi-
cient waiters keep bringing to your table
on skewers until you tell them to stop. It
comes with a self-serve salad bar and for
an extra fee all-you-can-drink beer, wine
and other alcohol for two hours. **Known
for:** meat lover's paradise; range of wines;
excellent salad buffet. $ Average main:
¥7,500 ✉ REIT Omotesando Sq., 4–3–2
Jingumae, Shibuya-ku ☎ 03/3796–0571
⊕ www.barbacoa.jp/aoyama Ⓜ Ginza,
Chiyoda, and Hanzomon subway lines,
Omotesando Station (Exit A2).

Brown Rice by Neal's Yard Remedies
(ブラウンライス 食堂)
$$ | VEGETARIAN | Run by Neal's Yard Remedies, this laid-back café has all-natural
wooden interiors and natural produce
on the menu. If shopping in Harajuku,
it's a great place to stop for a healthy
Japanese teishoku set, vegetable curry,
tofu lemon cake, or other vegan fare.
Known for: relaxed atmosphere; Japanese-style vegan dishes; affordable lunch
sets. $ Average main: ¥1,700 ✉ 5–1–8
Jingumae, Shibuya-ku ☎ 03/5778–5416
⊕ www.nealsyard.co.jp/brownrice
Ⓜ Ginza and Hanzomon subway lines,
Omotesando Station (Exit A1).

★ Cicada (シカダ)
$$$ | MEDITERRANEAN | Offering up high-
end Mediterranean cuisine in an incred-
ibly stylish setting, Cicada's resortlike
atmosphere feels a world away from
Omotesando's busy shopping streets. In
the warmer months, the outdoor patio
is especially relaxing. **Known for:** terrace
dining; flavorful Mediterranean dishes;
stylish bar. $ Average main: ¥4,000
✉ 5–7–28 Minami-Aoyama, Minato-ku
☎ 03/6434–1255 ⊕ www.tysons.jp/cicada
Ⓜ Ginza, Chiyoda, and Hanzomon sub-
way lines, Omotesando Station (Exit B1).

Elements of Japanese Cuisine

It starts with soup, followed by raw fish, then the entrée (grilled, steamed, simmered, or fried fish, chicken, or vegetables), and ends with rice and pickles, with perhaps fresh fruit for dessert, and a cup of green tea. It's as simple as that—almost.

There are, admittedly, a few twists to the story. Beyond the raw fish, it's the incredible variety of vegetables used in Japanese cooking that can still surprise the Western palate: *takenoko* (bamboo shoots), *renkon* (lotus root), and the treasured *matsutake* mushrooms (which grow wild in jealously guarded forest hideaways and sometimes sell for obscene prices), to name a few.

The basic formula for a traditional Japanese meal is deceptively simple but there are a few ground rules. Freshness is first. To a Japanese chef, this is an unparalleled virtue, and much of a chef's reputation relies on the ability to obtain the finest ingredients at the peak of season: fish brought in from the sea this morning (not yesterday) and vegetables from the earth (not the hothouse), if at all possible.

Simplicity is next. Rather than embellishing foods with heavy spices and rich sauces, the Japanese chef leans in. Flavors are enhanced, not elaborated, accented rather than concealed.

Without a heavy sauce, fish is permitted a degree of natural fishiness—a garnish of fresh red ginger is provided to offset the flavor rather than to disguise it.

The third prerequisite is beauty. Simple, natural foods must appeal to the eye as well as to the palate. Green peppers on a vermilion dish, perhaps, or an egg custard in a blue bowl. Rectangular dishes for a round eggplant. So important is the seasonal element in Japanese cooking that maple leaves and pine needles are used to accent an autumn dish. Or two small summer delicacies, a pair of freshwater *ayu* fish, are grilled with a purposeful twist to their tails to make them "swim" across a crystal platter and thereby suggest the coolness of a mountain stream on a hot August night.

Not to be forgotten is mood, which can make or break the entire meal. Japanese connoisseurs go to great lengths to find the perfect yakitori stand—a smoky, lively place—an environment appropriate to the occasion, offering a night of grilled chicken, cold beer, and camaraderie. In fancier places, mood becomes a fancier problem, to the point of quibbling over the proper amount of "water music" trickling in the basin outside your private room.

Crayon House Hiroba (クレヨンハウス広場)
$$ | JAPANESE FUSION | Connected to a natural-foods store, and with natural airy wooden interiors to match, Crayon House serves Japanese and Western dishes with a common theme—it's all very healthy. Ninety-five percent of ingredients are organic, and the mixture of curries, pastas, salads, and other dishes are all wholesome. **Known for:** healthy lunch and dinner buffets; outdoor izakaya area; organic fare. $ *Average main: ¥2,000* ⊠ *Kita-Aoyama 3-8-5, Shibuya-ku* ☎ *03/3406–6308* ⊕ *www.crayonhouse. co.jp/shop/pages/restaurant_eng.aspx* Ⓜ *Omotesando Station (Chiyoda, Ginza, and Hanzomon lines; Exit A1 and B2).*

Takeshita-dori is a crowded pedestrian street lined with boutiques and cafes.

Heiroku Sushi Shibuya Omotesando (平禄寿司)

$$ | SUSHI | FAMILY | Often, a meal of sushi is a costly indulgence. The rock-bottom alternative is a *kaiten-zushi*, where it is literally served assembly line–style: chefs inside the circular counter place a constant supply of dishes on the revolving belt with plates color-coded for price; just choose whatever takes your fancy as the sushi parades by. **Known for:** essential Japan experience; fresh, cheap sushi; wide selection of classic and original sushi. $ *Average main: ¥2,000* ✉ *5–8–5 Jingumae, Shibuya-ku* ☎ *03/3498–3968* Ⓜ *Ginza, Chiyoda, and Hanzomon subway lines, Omotesando Station (Exit A1).*

Red Pepper (レッドペッパー)

$$ | FRENCH | A short walk down a narrow alley from Omotesando Crossing guests squeeze into tiny antique school chairs in this cozy bistro. The cuisine is constantly changing and most diners ignore the printed menu in favor of the daily recommendations chalked on blackboards (mainly in Japanese) propped up outside and on the walls. **Known for:** a constantly changing menu; cozy atmosphere; seasonal specials. $ *Average main: ¥2,000* ✉ *1F Shimizu Bldg., 3–5–25 Kita-Aoyama, Shibuya-ku* ☎ *03/3478–1264* ⊕ *take-5. co.jp/brand/redpepper/* Ⓜ *Ginza, Chiyoda, and Hanzomon subway lines, Omotesando Station (Exit A3).*

Sakuratei (さくら亭)

$$ | JAPANESE | At this do-it-yourself restaurant for *okonomiyaki* (a kind of savory pancake made with egg, meat, and vegetables), you choose ingredients and cook them on the *teppan* (grill). Okonomiyaki is generally easy to make, but flipping the pancake to cook the other side can be challenging—potentially messy but still fun. **Known for:** cooking at your table; artsy, DIY interior; vegetarian, vegan, and gluten-free options. $ *Average main: ¥1,500* ✉ *3–20–1 Jingumae, Shibuya-ku* ☎ *03/3479–0039* ⊕ *www.sakuratei.co.jp* Ⓜ *Chiyoda subway line, Meiji-Jingumae (Harajuku) Station (Exit 5).*

Continued on page 186

Shoppers mill around the entrance to Tokyo's Louis Vuitton

SHOP TOKYO

✳ By Misha Janette

Tokyo, the most retail-dense city in the world, lures even the most reluctant shoppers with promises of every product imaginable. Travel back in time at department and specialty stores selling traditional ceramics and lacquerware, or leap into the future in Akihabara and other gadget-oriented neighborhoods. Fashionistas watch trends in Harajuku morph before their eyes, while those with more highbrow sensibilities browse the jewelry at stalwarts like Mikimoto.

Each Tokyo neighborhood has its own specialty, style, mood, and type of customer. Local production still thrives in the city's backstreets despite an influx of global chains and mega-corporations. Keep in mind, however, that nearly all of the locally produced goods will cost a pretty penny; the Japanese are meticulous in design and quality, and tend to prefer small-scale production to large output. Here in Tokyo you will find that one-offs and limited-edition items are often the norm rather than the exception.

For clothing, sizing is still the biggest roadblock to really getting the most from Tokyo boutiques. But with the abundance of quirky trends sometimes it's enough just to window-shop.

182

 WHAT TO BUY

MANGA

Manga, or Japanese comic books, have had an incredible influence on pop culture around the world. The inherently Japanese-style illustrations are fun to look at, and the simple language is great for studying. Book-Off, a well-known used manga chain, sells comics at rock-bottom prices, sometimes ¥100 each.

INNERWEAR

The Japanese are known for their electronics, but did you know their textile and fiber industry is also one of the most advanced in the world? The sweat-repelling, heat-conducting, UBAV/UVB-blocking and aloe-vera dispensing underthings available at Tokyo department stores are probably already in every Japanese person's top drawer at home.

FLAVORED SNACKS

Japan is the land of limited-edition products, and every season brings new, adventurous flavors in finite quantities. All it takes is a trip to the local convenience store to find melon- or Sakura-flavored Kit-Kat bars, or sweet Mont Blanc-flavored Pepsi. We dare you to try them.

PHONE ACCESSORIES

Cell phones and their accoutrement have become a fashion statement all their own. Phone straps, small plastic models that hang from one's phone, are the most popular. They come in all forms, from Asahi beer bottles to Hello Kitty dolls. There are also matching plastic "no peek" sheets that prevent others from spying on your phone's screen.

HOUSEWARES

Tokyoites appreciate fine design, and this passion is reflected in the exuberance of the city's zakka shops—retailers that sell small housewares. The Daikanyama and Aoyama areas positively brim with these stores, but trendy zakka can be found throughout the city. Handmade combs, chopsticks, and towels are other uniquely Japanese treasures to consider picking up while in Tokyo.

RECORDS

Tokyo's small specialty music stores are a real treat: local music and imports from around the world are usually available on both vinyl and CD. Out-of-print or obscure vinyl editions can run well over ¥10,000, but collectors will find the condition of the jackets to be unmatched.

SOCKS

As it's customary in Japanese houses to remove one's shoes, socks are more than mere padding between foot and shoe. It's no surprise, then, that the selection of socks goes well beyond black and white. Stripes, polka-dots, Japanese scenery, and monograms are just some of the depictions you'll find at the high-end sock boutiques. The complicated weaving techniques mean they will also cost more than the average cotton pair.

SAKE SETS

Sake is a big deal here, and the type of sake presented to another can make or break business deals and friendships. Better than just a bottle are the gift sets that include the short sake glasses and oversized bottles in beautiful packaging fit for royalty.

JEWELRY

Japan has always been known for its craftsmen who possess the ability to create finely detailed work. Jewelry is no exception, especially when cultured pearls are used. Pearls, which have become something of a national symbol, are not inexpensive, but they are much cheaper in Japan than elsewhere.

WASHLETTE TOILET SEATS

It may seem ludicrous, but the Japanese "washlette" toilet seat is perhaps the best innovation of this millennium. The seats are heated, come with deodorizers, and may even play music to mask any "rude" sounds. Even better, some can be retrofitted to old toilets— just be sure to check your seat measurements before leaving home.

CHARCOAL

Japanese women have been using charcoal, or *takesumi*, in their beauty routines for centuries, believing it cleans out the pores and moisturizes the skin. Charcoal-infused formulas are used in soaps, cleansers, cremes, and masques, and often are naturally colored pitch-black like squid ink.

FOLK CRAFTS

Japanese folk crafts, called *mingei*—among them bamboo vases and baskets, fabrics, paper boxes, dolls, and toys— achieve a unique beauty in their simple and sturdy designs. Be aware, however, that simple does not mean cheap. Long hours of labor go into these objects, and every year there are fewer craftspeople left, producing their work in smaller and smaller quantities. Include these items in your budget ahead of time: The best—worth every cent—can be fairly expensive.

✦ EXPERIENCING JAPANESE DEPATO

The impressive architecture at the Prada flagship matches the designer wares inside.

A visit to a Japanese *depato* (department store) is the perfect Cliff's Notes introduction to Japanese culture. Impeccable service combines with the best luxury brands, gourmet food, and traditional goods—all displayed as enticing eye candy.

These large complexes are found around major train stations and are often owned by the conglomerate rail companies who make their profit when visitors take the train to shop there. The stores themselves commonly have travel agencies, theaters, and art galleries on the premises, as well as reasonably priced and strategically placed restaurants and cafés.

ARRIVE EARLY

The best way to get the full experience is to arrive just as the store is opening. Err on the early side: Tokyo's department stores are exacting in their opening times. White-gloved ladies and gents bow to waiting customers when the doors open on the hour. Early birds snatch up limited-edition food and goods before they sell out. There's never a dearth of reasons to come: local celebrity appearances, designer Q&A sessions, and fairs.

ANATOMY OF A DEPATO

The first floors typically house cosmetics, handbags, and shoes, with the next few floors up going to luxury import brands. On many a top floor you'll find gift packages containing Japan's best-loved brands of sake, rice crackers, and other foods. Department stores also typically devote one floor to traditional Japanese crafts, including ceramics, paintings, and lacquerware.

Don't miss the *depachika* (food departments) on the basement levels, where an overwhelming selection of expensive Japanese and Western delicacies are wrapped with the utmost care. More affordable versions come packed deli-style to be taken home for lunch or dinner.

Shibuya's depato attract trendsetters.

BEST DEPATO FOR...

Most department stores are similar and house the same brands. But some have distinctive characteristics.

The trendy dresser: Seibu in Shibuya and Ikebukuro is known for its collection of fashion-forward tenants.

Emerging designers: Isetan in Shinjuku oozes style and has ample space on the fourth floor dedicated to up-and-coming designers.

Gifts: Shinjuku's Takashimaya is the place to buy souvenirs for discerning friends back home.

Traditional crafts: Mitsukoshi in Nihombashi will leave those looking for a bit of Old Japan wide-eyed.

Depato interiors are often dramatic.

TIPS FOR DEPATO SHOPPING

■ Major department stores accept credit cards and provide shipping services.

■ It's important to remember that, unlike most of the Western world, goods must be purchased in the department where they were found. This goes for nearly every multilevel shop in Japan.

■ Nowadays, most salesclerks speak some English. If you're having communication difficulties, someone will always come to the rescue.

■ On the first floor you'll invariably find a general information booth with maps of the store in English.

■ Some department stores close one or two days a month. To be on the safe side, call ahead.

Harajuku fashion is a mix of cute, sweet, pop, punk, goth, and anime.

☕ Coffee and Quick Bites

Tokyoites flock to Harajuku on the weekends to shop for clothes and accessories. Walk along Takeshita-dori to find fast food joints and cheap colorful crepes, then wander the hip and trendy eateries and cafés on and around Omotesando.

The Roastery by Nozy Coffee (ザ・ロースタリー)

$ | **CAFÉ** | Really taking pride in their coffee, the Roastery serves up some good single-origin coffee. Tucked away along a shopping street connecting Omotesando to Shibuya, the shop offers outdoor seating, giving you a place to watch the shoppers stream by. **Known for:** clean restrooms that smell like roasting coffee; relaxed atmosphere; single-origin coffee. *[$] Average main: ¥700 ✉ Jungumae 5-17-13, Shibuya-ku ☎ 03/6450–5755 🌐 www.tysons.jp/roastery/en [M] Chiyoda subway line, Meiji-Jingumae (Harajuku) Station (Exit 7).*

🛍 Shopping

Depending on where you are in the neighborhood, the average shopper in Harajuku is decidedly on the younger side, so many shops focus on moderately-priced clothing and accessories, with a lot of kitsch mixed in. The shopping extends southeast from Harajuku Station (and gets pricier) along both sides of Omotesando and Meiji-dori; the shops that target the youngest consumers are concentrated on the narrow street called Takeshita-dori. Tokyo's most exciting neighborhood for fashion and design lies beyond that, in the maze of backstreets called Ura-Harajuku.

CLOTHING

★ **Beams** (ビームス)

MIXED CLOTHING | Harajuku features a cluster of no fewer than 10 Beams stores that provide Japan's younger folk with extremely hip threads. With branches ranging from street wear to high-end import brands, as well as a record store, uniform gallery, funky "from Tokyo" souvenir shop that sells anime figurines, and one that sells manga alongside designer T-shirts inspired by comic books, shopping here ensures that you or your kids will be properly stocked with the coolest wares from the city. ⊠ *3–24–7 Jingumae, Shibuya-ku* ☎ *03/3470–3947* ⊕ *www.beams.co.jp* Ⓜ *JR Harajuku Station (Takeshita-Dori Exit); Chiyoda and Fukutoshin subway lines, Meiji-Jingumae Station (Exit 5).*

Graniph Harajuku (グラニフ原宿)

MIXED CLOTHING | Cool and quirky T-shirts are the main focus of this store, but you can find other items in the frequently-changing lineup of designs that run from cartoon characters and odd quotes to abstract graphic images. ⊠ *6–12–17 Jingumae, Shibuya-ku* ☎ *03/6712–5632* ⊕ *www.graniph.com* Ⓜ *Chiyoda and Fukutoshin subway lines, Meiji-Jingumae Station (Exit 5).*

6% DokiDoki (ロクパーセントドキドキ; *Roku pasento dokidoki*)

WOMEN'S CLOTHING | If there's one shop that is the epitome of crazy, *kawaii* (cute) Harajuku fashion, it's this pastel dollhouselike shop on the second floor of a nondescript building. The acid-color tutus and glittery accessories are part of a style called "kawaii anarchy" and may be the most unique shopping experience in Tokyo. The colorful shopgirls alone are an attraction, and if asked nicely, they will happily pose for photos. ⊠ *4–28–16 Jingumae, Shibuya-ku* ☎ *03/3479–6116* ⊕ *6dokidoki.com* Ⓜ *Chiyoda and Fukutoshin subway lines, Meiji-Jingumae Station (Exit 5).*

MALLS AND SHOPPING CENTERS

Laforet (ラフォーレ)

MALL | The 140 or so stores at this Harajuku mall are where teen trends are born. Although shop genres vary from Gothic Lolita to bohemian chic, they all target fashion-conscious teenagers. Rumor has it that many of the West's top fashion designers still come here to look for inspiration for their next collections. ⊠ *1–11–6 Jingumae, Shibuya-ku*

☎ *03/3475–0411* ⊕ *www.laforet.ne.jp/en* Ⓜ *Chiyoda and Fukutoshin subway lines, Meiji-Jingumae Station (Exit 5).*

Tokyu Plaza Omotesando Harajuku (東急プラザ表参道原宿)

MALL | Right at the intersection of Omotesando (don't miss the lanterns leading you to Meiji Shrine) and Meiji-dori is a hard-to-miss shopping center seemingly cascading with greenery and designed by award-winning Hiroshi Nakamura's NAP architectural firm. The building houses numerous shops and eateries, but the biggest draw might be the shady roof garden. ⊠ *4-30-3 Jingumae, Shibuya-ku* ☎ *03/3497–0418* ⊕ *omohara.tokyu-plaza. com/en* Ⓜ *Chiyoda subway line, Meiji-Jingumae (Harajuku) Station (Exit 5).*

TOYS

★ Kiddy Land (キデイランド)

TOYS | FAMILY | The Omotesando landmark commonly regarded as Tokyo's best toy store carries the cutest and most kitschy of everyday goods. This is the leader in making or breaking the popularity of the myriad character goods that Japan spits out seasonally. Like caterpillars with businesspeople faces, some of the items may be odd or surprising, but they're never boring. ⊠ *6–1–9 Jingumae, Shibuya-ku* ☎ *03/3409–3431* ⊕ *www.kiddyland. co.jp* Ⓜ *JR Yamanote Line, Harajuku Station (Omotesando Exit); Chiyoda and Fukutoshin subway lines, Meiji-Jingumae Station (Exit 4).*

Shibuya

Shibuya is a shopper's paradise. Here you will find everything from fashion to housewares. Restaurants, however, are on the cheap side, catering to the young clientele. As you head south toward Ebisu Station, you'll find more fine dining.

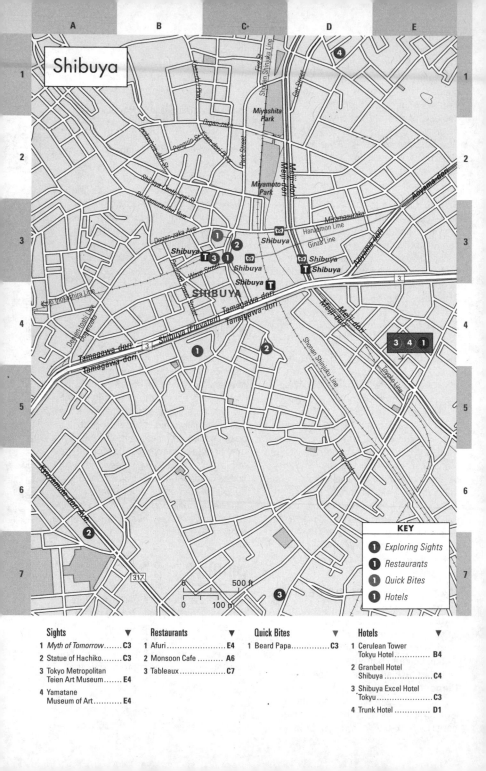

Shibuya

KEY
- ① Exploring Sights
- ① Restaurants
- ① Quick Bites
- ① Hotels

Sights ▼	Restaurants ▼	Quick Bites ▼	Hotels ▼
1 *Myth of Tomorrow*.......**C3**	1 Afuri.....................**E4**	1 Beard Papa...............**C3**	1 Cerulean Tower Tokyu Hotel..............**B4**
2 Statue of Hachiko........**C3**	2 Monsoon Cafe **A6**		2 Granbell Hotel Shibuya.................**C4**
3 Tokyo Metropolitan Teien Art Museum.......**E4**	3 Tableaux..................**C7**		3 Shibuya Excel Hotel Tokyu.....................**C3**
4 Yamatane Museum of Art...........**E4**			4 Trunk Hotel **D1**

The statue of Hachiko, Japan's most loyal canine, stands immediately outside Shibuya Station, where he waited for his deceased master every day for seven years.

Sights

Myth of Tomorrow
(明日の神話; *Asu no Shinwa*)
PUBLIC ART | This once-lost mural by avant-garde artist Taro Okamoto has been restored and mounted inside Shibuya Station. Often compared to Picasso's *Guernica*, the 14 colorful panels depict the moment of an atomic bomb detonation. The painting was discovered in 2003 in Mexico City, where in the late '60s it was to be displayed in a hotel but was misplaced following the bankruptcy of the developer. Walk up to the Inokashira Line entrance; the mural is mounted along the hallway that overlooks Hachiko plaza. ⊠ *Shibuya Mark City, 1–12–1 Dogenzaka, Shibuya-ku* Ⓜ *JR Shibuya Station (Hachiko Exit).*

Statue of Hachiko (ハチ公像;)
PUBLIC ART | Hachiko is the Japanese version of Lassie; he has even been portrayed in a few heart-wrenching films. Every morning Hachiko's master, a professor at Tokyo University, would take the dog with him as far as Shibuya Station and Hachiko would go back to the station every evening to greet him on his return. In 1925 the professor died of a stroke. Every evening for the next seven years, Hachiko would go to Shibuya and wait there until the last train had pulled out of the station, and as this story of loyalty spread so grew Hachiko's fame. During the dog's lifetime, a handsome bronze statute of Hachiko was installed in front of the station, funded by fans from all over the country. The present version is a replica—the original was melted down for its metal in World War II. This Shibuya landmark is one of the most popular meeting places in the city. Look for the green train car fronting the JR station; the statue is off to the side, where everyone is standing. ⊠ *2–1 Dogenzaka, Shibuya-ku* Ⓜ *JR Shibuya Station (Hachiko Exit).*

Tokyo Metropolitan Teien Art Museum (東京都庭園美術館; *Tokyo-to Teien Bijutsukan*)
ART MUSEUM | Once home to Japan's Prince Asaka, this lavish 1930s art deco building hosts a range of fine-arts exhibits

throughout the year. With shows ranging from classic paintings to contemporary sculpture, it seems the exhibits are chosen for their ability to harmoniously mix with the building's lush interior. If you visit, be sure to leave time for a stroll through the Teien's Japanese Garden, which is particularly lovely when the leaves change in the fall or during cherry blossom season in April. ✉ *5–21–9 Shirokanedai, Minato-ku* ☎ *03/3443–0201* 🌐 *www.teien-art-museum.ne.jp* 🎫 *Usually from ¥1,000, but varies by exhibit; garden only ¥200.* 🕒 *Closed Mon.* [M] *JR Yamanote Line or Toei Mita Line, Meguro Station (Central Exit).*

Yamatane Museum of Art
(山種美術館; *Yamatane Bijutsukan*)
ART MUSEUM | The museum specializes in *Nihonga* (a type of traditional Japanese painting) from the Meiji period on and has a private collection of masterpieces by such painters as Taikan Yokoyama, Gyoshu Hayami, Kokei Kobayashi, and Gyokudo Kawai. Exhibits, which sometimes include works borrowed from other collections, change seven or eight times a year. Visitors can take a break at Café Tsubaki, which offers tea and *wagashi* (a genre of local sweets) as well as cake sets. ✉ *3–12–36 Hiroo, Shibuya-ku, Akasaka* ☎ *047/316–2772* 🌐 *www.yamatane-museum.jp/english* 🎫 *¥1,100 (special exhibit prices vary)* 🕒 *Closed Mon.* [M] *Hibiya subway line, Ebisu Station (Exit 2); JR Yamanote Line, Ebisu Station (West Exit).*

🍴 Restaurants

Afuri
$ | **RAMEN** | Ramen is the quintessential Japanese fast food: thick Chinese noodles in a bowl of savory broth topped with sliced grilled *chashu* (pork loin). Each neighborhood in Tokyo has its favorite, and in Ebisu the hands-down favorite is Afuri. **Known for:** quick, affordable meals; refreshing shio ramen with yuzu; vegan ramen. [$] *Average main: ¥1,000* ✉ *117 Bldg., 1–1–7 Ebisu, 1st fl., Shibuya-ku* ☎ *03/5795–0750* 💳 *No credit cards* [M] *JR Yamanote Line (Nishi-guchi/West Exit) and Hibiya subway line (Exit 1), Ebisu Station.*

Monsoon Cafe (モンスーンカフェ)
$$ | **ASIAN** | With a dozen locations (including Shinjuku and Omotesando), Monsoon Cafe meets the demand in Tokyo for spicy, primarily Southeast Asian food. Complementing the eclectic pan-Asian food are rattan furniture, brass tableware from Thailand, colorful papier-mâché parrots on gilded stands, Balinese carvings, and ceiling fans. **Known for:** stylish interior; foods from across Asia; relaxed terrace seating. [$] *Average main: ¥2,000* ✉ *15–4 Hachiyama-cho, Shibuya-ku* ☎ *050/5444–9110* 🌐 *monsoon-cafe.jp/daikanyama* [M] *Tokyu Toyoko private rail line, Daikanyama Station (Kita-guchi/North Exit).*

Tableaux (タブローズ)
$$$$ | **ECLECTIC** | This restaurant may lay on more glitz than necessary—the mural in the bar depicts the fall of Pompeii, the banquettes are upholstered in red leather, and the walls are papered in antique gold—but the service is cordial and professional and the food, which is centered on Italian cuisine and U.S. steaks, is superb. The wine list is one of the most varied in town, with more than 200 bottles covering everything from affordable house wines to rarities that will set you back upward of ¥200,000 a bottle. **Known for:** decor that feels like stepping into a French picture book; classic high-end European fare; impressive wine list. [$] *Average main: ¥8,000* ✉ *Sunroser Daikanyama Bldg., 11–6 Sarugaku-cho, 1st fl., Shibuya-ku* ☎ *050/544–5125* 🌐 *www.tableaux.jp* 🕒 *No lunch* 👔 *Jacket and tie required* [M] *Tokyu Toyoko private rail line, Daikanyama Station (Kita-guchi/North Exit).*

☕ Coffee and Quick Bites

Beard Papa (ビアードパパ)
$ | **BAKERY** | Many long lines in Shibuya are more about trendiness than quality, but Beard Papa makes some genuinely

On the Menu

Sushi

Sushi—slices of raw fish or shellfish on hand-formed portions of vinegared rice, with a dab of wasabi for zest—is probably the best-known Japanese dish in the Western world. The best sushi restaurants in Tokyo send buyers early every morning to the Central Whole-sale Market in Toyosu for the freshest ingredients: *maguro* (tuna), *hamachi* (yellowtail), *tako* (octopus), *ika* (squid), *ikura* (salmon roe), *uni* (sea urchin), *ebi* (shrimp), and *anago* (conger eel) being most common on menus.

Sashimi

Sushi's cousin sashimi consists of fresh, thinly sliced seafood served with soy sauce, wasabi paste, and a simple garnish like shredded daikon or fresh shiso leaves. Though most seafood is served raw, some sashimi ingredients, like octopus, may be cooked. Less common ingredients are vegetarian items such as cucumbers.

Tempura

Another Japanese dish that may be familiar to you is tempura: fresh fish, shellfish, and vegetables delicately batter-fried in oil. Tempura dates to the mid-16th century, with the earliest influences of Spanish and Portu-guese culture on Japan, and you'll find it today all over the world. But nowhere is it better than in Tokyo, and nowhere in Tokyo is it better than in the tempura stalls and restaurants of shitamachi—the older commercial and working-class districts of the eastern wards—or in the restaurants that began there in the 19th century and moved upscale. Typical ingredi-ents are shrimp, *kisu* (smelt), *shirauo* (whitebait), shiitake mushrooms, lotus root, and green peppers.

Sukiyaki

Sukiyaki is a popular beef dish that is sautéed with vegetables in an iron skillet at the table. The tenderness of the beef is the determining factor here, and many of the best sukiyaki houses also run their own butcher shops so that they can control the quality of the beef they serve—the Japanese are justifiably proud of their notorious beer-fed and hand-massaged beef.

Shabu-shabu

Shabu-shabu is another possibility, though this dish has become more popular with tourists than with the Japanese. It's similar to sukiyaki because it's prepared at the table with a combination of vegetables, but the cooking methods differ: shabu-shabu is swished briefly in boiling water (the word "shabu-shabu" is onomatopoeic for this swishing sound), whereas sukiyaki is sautéed in oil and, usually, a slightly sweetened soy sauce.

Nabemono

Nabemono (one-pot dishes), commonly known as nabe, may not be familiar to Westerners, but the possibilities are endless. Simmered in a light, fish-based broth, these stews can be made of almost anything: *mizutaki* (chicken), *kaki-nabe* (oysters), or the sumo wrestler's favorite, the hearty *chanko-nabe*—with something in it for everyone. Nabemono is a popular family or party dish. The restaurants specializing in nabemono often have a casual, country atmosphere.

good cream puffs in all kinds of flavors. Pick up a single or a six-pack of freshly made pastries. **Known for:** fresh pastries; buttery smells; cream puffs in seasonal flavors. [$] *Average main: ¥231* ✉ *2–2–1 Dogenzaka, Shibuya-ku* ☎ *03/6427–8817* 🌐 *www.beardpapa.jp* [M] *JR Shibuya Station (connected to the underground passageways).*

Hotels

Shibuya is a shopping and entertainment mecca for teens and twentysomethings. Travelers appreciate the convenience of the multiple train lines and the central location.

Cerulean Tower Tokyu Hotel
(セルリアンタワー東急ホテル)
$$$ | **HOTEL** | Perched on a slope above Shibuya's chaos, the Cerulean Tower has a cavernous yet bustling lobby filled with plenty of attentive, English-speaking staffers. **Pros:** friendly, attentive service; great city views; convenient location. **Cons:** pricey rates; Shibuya is one of Tokyo's more crowded areas; building fronts a very busy street. [$] *Rooms from: ¥32,000* ✉ *26–1 Sakuragaokacho, Shibuya-ku* ☎ *03/3476–3000* 🌐 *www.tokyuhotelsjapan.com/global/cerulean-h* 🛏 *411 rooms* 🍴 *No Meals* [M] *JR Shibuya Station (South Exit).*

Granbell Hotel Shibuya
(渋谷グランベルホテル)
$$ | **HOTEL** | Location, location, location—that's the Granbell, and with a minimalist pop-art style to boot. **Pros:** great location; funky, fun design; free Wi-Fi throughout property. **Cons:** small rooms; neighborhood can be noisy; difficult to find hotel entrance. [$] *Rooms from: ¥23,000* ✉ *15–17 Sakuragaokacho, Shibuya-ku* ☎ *03/5457–2681* 🌐 *www.granbellhotel.jp/en/shibuya* 🛏 *105 rooms* 🍴 *No Meals* [M] *JR Shibuya Station (West Exit).*

Shibuya Excel Hotel Tokyu
(渋谷エクセルホテル東急)
$$ | **HOTEL** | The key to this unremarkable but very convenient hotel within the towering Mark City complex is access: local shopping and cheap dining options are plentiful, Shinjuku is a five-minute train ride to the north, and the Narita Express departs from nearby Shibuya Station frequently each morning. **Pros:** affordable; convenient location; friendly staff. **Cons:** small, uninspired rooms; crowds in the area can be intimidating; few amenities. [$] *Rooms from: ¥27,000* ✉ *1–12–2 Dogenzaka, Shibuya-ku* ☎ *03/5457–0109* 🌐 *www.tokyuhotels.co.jp/shibuya-e* 🛏 *408 rooms* 🍴 *No Meals* [M] *JR Shibuya Station (Hachiko Exit).*

Trunk Hotel (トランクホテル)
$$$$ | **HOTEL** | Located directly between Tokyo's stylish Harajuku, Omotesando, and Shibuya neighborhoods, this boutique hotel brings together local creatives and visitors alike. **Pros:** one of the few unique boutique hotels in Tokyo; excellent location for exploring some of the city's coolest neighborhoods; hotel design, service, and layout foster a sense of community. **Cons:** small rooms, even for Tokyo; can be noisy, especially on weekends; expensive for the quality of the rooms. [$] *Rooms from: ¥50,000* ✉ *5–31 Jingumae, Shibuya-ku* ☎ *03/5766–3210* 🌐 *trunk-hotel.com* 🛏 *15 rooms* 🍴 *No Meals* [M] *JR Harajuku; Jingumae (Exit 7); Omotesando (Exit A1); Shibuya (Exit A13).*

Nightlife

BARS

Akaoni (赤鬼)
WINE BARS | The emphasis here is *nama*, unrefined, unpasteurized sake. About 80 kinds from 60 brewing companies are available daily. You may want to sample this unique beverage while in Tokyo, since you won't find it at home: nama is short-lived, too delicate and fresh to transport or export, so it's not widely available overseas. You can accompany your choice with authentic Japanese fare, served here as small bites. Reservations are recommended. ✉ *2–15–3 Sangenjaya, Shibuya-ku* ☎ *03/3410–9918* 🌐 *www.akaoni39.com*

Ⓜ *Denenchofu and Tokyu Setagaya lines, Sangenjaya Station.*

buri
(立喰酒場 buri; *Tachigui Sakaba buri*)
WINE BARS | Buri serves up tasty *ji-zake* (local sake) from around Japan in the one-cup style; think sake in a mini mason jar, pairing it with a range of tapas-like servings of sashimi, yakitori, salads, and prosciutto, albeit in a standing-room-only setting. They also have beer on tap. Just a five-minute walk from Ebisu Station, this casual bar fills up quickly on weekends, so it's best to stop in early if you want to grab a table. ✉ *1–14–1 Ebisu-Nishi, Shibuya-ku* ☎ *03/3496–7744* ⊕ *buri-bar.business.site.*

DANCE CLUBS
Womb
DANCE CLUBS | Well-known techno and break-beat DJs make a point of stopping by this Shibuya uberclub on their way through town. The turntable talent, local and international, and four floors of dance and lounge space make Womb Tokyo's most consistently rewarding club experience. Drawing adults from their late twenties to forties, the place gets packed sometimes after 1 in the morning. Entry costs around ¥1,500 to ¥3,500. ✉ *2–16 Maruyamacho, Shibuya-ku* ☎ *03/5459–0039* ⊕ *www.womb.co.jp* Ⓜ *JR Yamanote Line, Ginza and Hanzomon subway lines, Shibuya Station (Hachiko Exit for JR and Ginza, Exit 3A for Hanzomon).*

IZAKAYA
Tatemichiya (立道屋)
PUBS | The concrete walls are adorned with rock musicians' autobiographies and posters of the Sex Pistols and Ramones, who also provide the sound track. Artist Yoshitomo Nara has been known to show up here, so if you're lucky, you can drink with him and watch him draw on the walls. ✉ *B1, 30–8 Sarugakucho, Shibuya-ku* ☎ *03/5459–3431* Ⓜ *Tokyu Toyoko Line, Daikanyama Station.*

KARAOKE
Karaoke Pasela (カラオケ パセラ)
THEMED ENTERTAINMENT | This large, glitzy karaoke joint has plenty of English songs and private rooms for small and large groups. If you are five or more people (or willing to pay for five people) and don't mind the surcharge, ask about the VIP rooms. Daytime weekday rates (noon to 5 pm) are quite cheap, but at other times expect to pay about ¥500 per 30 minutes per person on weekends and evenings (5 pm to 5 am). You can order all kinds of food and drinks delivered to your room, and there are all-you-can-drink plans if you're feeling frisky. If you have a large group and want to make reservations, you can do so in English at the very top of the website by pressing the tiny "English" button. ✉ *1-22-9 Jinnan, Shibuya-ku* ☎ *0120/428–875* ⊕ *www.pasela.co.jp/shop/shibuya* Ⓜ *JR Yamanote Line and Ginza and Hanzomon subway lines, Shibuya Station (Hachiko exit).*

PUBS
What the Dickens
PUBS | This spacious pub in Ebisu feels more authentically British than many of its rivals, thanks partly to a menu of traditional pub grub, including hearty pies. Using aged logs, the second floor feels like a nice tree house. The place hosts regular live music (funk, folk, jazz, rock, reggae—anything goes here) and other events, so it can be very loud, particularly on Friday and Saturday. ✉ *Roob 6 Bldg., 1–13–3 Ebisu-Nishi, 4th fl., Shibuya-ku* ☎ *03/3780–2099* ⊕ *www.whatthedickens.jp* ⊗ *Closed Mon.* Ⓜ *Hibiya subway line, Ebisu Station (Nishi-guchi/West Exit).*

✦ Performing Arts

FILM
Bunkamura (文化村)
ARTS CENTERS | This complex has two movie theaters that tend to screen French and foreign films; a concert, opera, and classic ballet auditorium (Orchard Hall); a performance space

(Theater Cocoona, often used for ballet and other dance); a gallery; and a museum. ✉ *2–24–1 Dogenzaka, Shibuya-ku* ☎ *03/3477–9111* ⊕ *www.bunkamura. co.jp* Ⓜ *JR Yamanote Line, Ginza and Hanzomon subway lines, and private rail lines, Shibuya Station (Exit 3A).*

Eurospace (ユーロスペース)
FILM | One of the best venues for art-house films in Japan screens independent European and Asian hits and small-scale Japanese movies. Directors and actors often appear on the stage, greeting fans on opening days. Occasionally Japanese films run with English subtitles. ✉ *1–5 Maruyamacho, 3rd fl., Shibuya-ku* ☎ *03/3461–0211* ⊕ *www. eurospace.co.jp* Ⓜ *JR Yamanote Line and Ginza and Hanzomon subway lines, Shibuya Station (Hachiko Exit).*

MUSIC
NHK Hall (NHK ホール)
MUSIC | The home base for the Japan Broadcasting Corporation's NHK Symphony Orchestra, known as N-Kyo, is probably the auditorium most familiar to Japanese lovers of classical music, as performances here are routinely rebroadcast on the national TV station. ✉ *2–2–1 Jinnan, Shibuya-ku* ☎ *03/3465-1751* ⊕ *www.nhk-sc.or.jp/nhk_hall* Ⓜ *JR Yamanote Line, Harajuku Station (Omotesando Exit).*

TRADITIONAL THEATER
National Noh Theater (国立能楽堂; *Kokuritsu No Gaku Do*)
THEATER | **FAMILY** | One of the few public halls to host Noh performances, this theater provides basic English-language summaries of the plots at performances. Individual screens placed in front of each seat also give an English translation. ✉ *4–18–1 Sendagaya, Shibuya-ku* ☎ *03/3423–1331, 03/3230–3000 reservations* ⊕ *www.ntj.jac.go.jp/nou. html* 🎟 *From ¥2,000* Ⓜ *JR Chuo Line, Sendagaya Station (Minami-guchi/South Exit); Oedo subway line, Kokuritsu-Kyogi-jo Station (Exit A4).*

 # Shopping

This is primarily an entertainment and retail district geared toward teenagers and young adults. The shopping scene caters to these groups with many reasonably priced smaller shops and a few department stores that are casual yet chic. You may notice that many neighborhood denizens are neither young nor chic—Shibuya is also a popular entertainment district and loaded with restaurants, karaoke lounges, bars, and nightclubs. At the southern edges of the neighborhood you can unleash your inner fashionista in Daikanyama, a boutique heaven with stacks of retro T-shirts, assortments of skate-punk wear, and a concentration of premium denim shops that makes jeans fans giddy. Just beyond, the sakura-tree–lined banks of the Meguro River explodes with pink blossoms in spring. The riverbanks attract an organic-living-oriented crowd, whose aesthetic is reflected in the bohemian clothing sold at the laid-back shops.

BOOKS
★ Daikanyama T-Site (代官山 T-Site)
ART GALLERIES | This oasis within the metropolis is a calming respite with a leafy garden, trendy terrace eatery, gallery, and, of course, the main business, a shop selling books, music, and videos with a focus on art and design. Almost all 30,000 books here can be taken to the lounge to read, as can a large selection of foreign magazines. Many locals come here to be seen, bringing along their lapdogs dressed in designer duds from the store's pet boutique. ✉ *17–5 Sarugaku-cho, Shibuya-ku* ☎ *03/3770–2525* ⊕ *store. tsite.jp/daikanyama/* Ⓜ *Tokyu Toyoko Line, Daikanyama Station (Central Exit).*

CRAFTS
★ Musubi (むす美)
CRAFTS | You might not expect to find classic crafts in the vicinity of trendy Harajuku, but this charming boutique specializes in traditional *furoshiki* cloths,

which are beautifully decorated squares of cloth used to wrap anything and everything (but they also just make great gifts in themselves). You'll find up to 500 different cloth options here made from a variety of fabrics and featuring traditional, seasonal, and modern designs. They even offer workshops on how to use the cloths in different ways. ⊠ *2–31–8 Jingumae, Shibuya-ku* ☎ *03/5414–5678* ⊕ *www.musubi-furoshiki.com* ⊙ *Closed Wed.* Ⓜ *Tokyo Metro Meiji-jingumae (Harajuku) Station.*

CLOTHING
Bingo Shibuya Modi Used Clothing (Bingo 渋谷モディ店)
SECOND-HAND | If you're looking for vintage fashion and don't feel like making the trek to Shimokitazawa, Bingo is your place. It is on the third floor of the Modi building just north of Shibuya Crossing. You can't miss the greenery-covered corner entrance. The Modi building also houses a variety of other stores and just might be worth a visit even if you aren't looking for vintage clothing. ⊠ *Shibuya-ku* ☎ *03/5428-4812.*

HOUSEWARES
★ Tokyu Hands (東急ハンズ)
CRAFTS | FAMILY | This chain carries a wide and varied assortment of goods, including hobby and crafts materials, art supplies, and knitting and sewing materials, as well as jewelry, household goods, stationery, even cosmetics. There's a café and exhibit space on the seventh floor with an ever-changing selection of small goods from local artisans for sale. It's not unusual to see Japanese hobbyists spending an entire afternoon browsing in here. ⊠ *12–18 Udagawacho, Shibuya-ku* ☎ *03/5489–5111* ⊕ *www.tokyu-hands. co.jp* Ⓜ *JR Yamanote Line and Ginza, Fukutoshin, and Hanzomon subway lines, Shibuya Station (Hachiko Exit for JR, Exits 6 and 7 for subway).*

Zero First Design (ゼロファーストデザイン)
HOUSEWARES | Kyu-Yamate-dori at Daikanyama is a well-known hub of interior

goods stores, and this one is full of unique and modern pieces from both local and international designers. ⊠ *2–3–1 Aobadai, Shibuya-ku* ☎ *03/5489–6106* ⊕ *01st.com* Ⓜ *Tokyu Toyoko Line, Daikan-yama Station (Komazawa-dori Exit).*

LACQUERWARE
★ Yamada Heiando (山田平安堂)
CRAFTS | With a spacious, airy layout and lovely lacquerware goods, this fashionable shop is a must for souvenir hunters—and anyone else who appreciates fine design. Rice bowls, sushi trays, bento lunch boxes, *hashioki* (chopstick rests), and jewelry cases come in traditional blacks and reds, as well as patterns both subtle and bold. Prices are fair—many items cost less than ¥10,000—but these are the kinds of goods for which devotees of Japanese craftsmanship would be willing to pay a lot. ⊠ *Hillside Terrace, 18–12 Sarugakucho, G Block #202, Shibuya-ku* ☎ *03/3464–5541* ⊕ *www.heiando1919. com* Ⓜ *Tokyu Toyoko Line, Daikanyama Station (Komazawa-dori Exit).*

MALLS AND SHOPPING CENTERS
Parco (渋谷パルコ)
MALL | These vertical malls filled with small retail shops and boutiques are all within walking distance of one another in the commercial heart of Shibuya. Shops range from a collections of designer brands to an entire floor focused on game and anime goods. The rooftop food garden offers a break from shopping and views over Shibuya. ⊠ *15–1 Udagawa-cho, Shibuya-ku* ☎ *03/3464–5111* ⊕ *www.parco.co.jp* Ⓜ *Ginza, Fukutoshin, and Hanzo-mon subway lines, Shibuya Station (Exits 6 and 7).*

Shibuya 109
MALL | This nine-floor outlet is a teenage girl's dream, especially if they follow the *gyaru* tribe, a particularly gaudy and brash fashion genre born in Shibuya. The place is filled with small stores whose merchandise screams kitsch and trend. Here, the fashionable sales assistants

are the stars, and their popularity in this mall can make them media superstars. On weekends, dance concerts and fashion shows are often staged at the front entrance. ✉ *2–29–1 Dogenzaka, Shibuya-ku* ☎ *03/3477–5111* ⊕ *www.shibuya109.jp* Ⓜ *JR Yamanote Line and Ginza, Fukutoshin, and Hanzomon subway lines, Shibuya Station (Hachiko Exit for JR, Exit 3A for subway lines).*

MUSIC

Manhattan Records
(マンハッタンレコード)

MUSIC | Hip-hop, reggae, house, and R&B vinyl can be found here, and a DJ booth pumps out the jams from the center of the room. ✉ *10–1 Udagawacho, Shibuya-ku* ☎ *03/3477–7166* ⊕ *manhattanrecords.jp* Ⓜ *JR Yamanote Line and Ginza, Fukutoshin, and Hanzomon subway lines, Shibuya Station (Hachiko Exit for JR, Exits 6 and 7 for subway).*

Tower Records (タワーレコード)

MUSIC | This huge emporium carries one of the most diverse selections of CDs and DVDs in the world. Take a rest at the café after visiting the second floor, which houses books, with a large selection of English-language publications. ✉ *1–22–14 Jinnan, Shibuya-ku* ☎ *03/3496–3661* ⊕ *tower.jp/store/kanto/shibuya* Ⓜ *JR Yamanote Line and Ginza, Fukutoshin, and Hanzomon subway lines, Shibuya Station (Hachiko Exit for JR, Exit 7 for subway).*

Shimokitazawa

Shimokitazawa is a where two of Tokyo's suburban lines cross, but it is much more than just a residential area. Shimokita (as it's often called) is a haven for vintage clothing and other such shops, which will become immediately obvious as soon as you walk out of the station. It may be impossible to avoid the myriad used clothing stores, which are called *furugiya* (古着) in Japanese. Don't think of this as thrift shopping, however. These places are more curated than a thrift store and much more expensive. The area is also (perhaps surprisingly) known for its curry shops, so if you are looking to sample some different interpretations of Japanese curry, this is the place!

However, that is not the only thing on offer in a neighborhood that has become quite trendy since the burial of one of the train lines in 2018, leaving a still-expanding linear park in its wake. The areas freed up by the line's burial also contain shops and restaurants as does the area above the station building.

While it might not be the best place for people with limited mobility due to all the ups and downs, most of the neighborhood is accessible, but do keep in mind that you'll be presented with a maze of streets and elevation changes, so let yourself get lost, do some people-watching, and see what you can discover.

🍴 Restaurants

Mikazuki Curry Samurai
(三日月カリィ サムライ)

$$ | JAPANESE | On one of Shimokitazawa's main shopping streets you'll find one of the areas many curry shops with an open and airy front, and both table and counter seating (in case you want to watch them cook). Unlike many Japanese curries, these tend to be heavier on the vegetables. **Known for:** adjustable spice levels; Japanese curries with the freshest ingredients; creative additional toppings to customize your meal. Ⓢ *Average main: ¥1,500* ✉ *3-34-2 Kitazawa, Setagaya-ku* ☎ *03/6407–1080* ⊕ *samurai-curry.com/mikazuki.*

Soup Curry Ponipirica
(スープカレーポニピリカ)

$$ | JAPANESE | What's a soup curry? You'll find out when you customize your order sheet by choosing your curry (bacon and cabbage, mushroom, or chicken); your soup base (tomato, shrimp, or

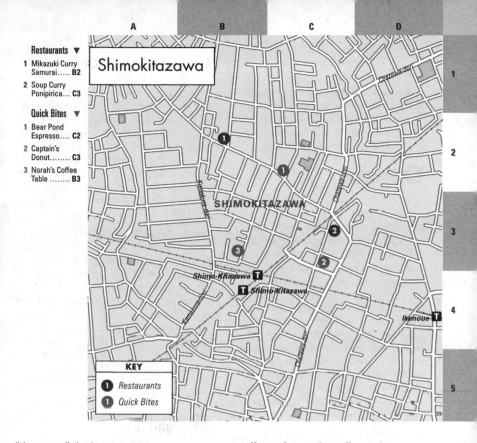

Shimokitazawa

KEY

① Restaurants

① Quick Bites

"Japanese," the base to many soupy Japanese foods); your preferred spice level (from 0–7); optional toppings like avocados, an egg, or fried mushrooms; and finally the amount of rice you'd like with your soup. **Known for:** crispy fried chicken wings in the soup; vegetables from Hokkaido; curries you can customize. $ *Average main: ¥1,500* ⊠ *Kitazawa 2-8-8, 2nd floor, Setagaya-ku* ⊹ *Look for "Soup Curry" written by the stairs leading in.* ☎ *03/6804–8802* ⊕ *www.ponipirica.in.*

☕ Coffee and Quick Bites

Bear Pond Espresso

$ | **CAFÉ** | This is possibly the best coffee in the neighborhood since that is essentially all they sell (save some branded merchandise). Sit on old wooden benches in this tiny establishment that feels as if it's both in the now, and from long

ago. **Known for:** quality coffee; unique atmosphere; cute merchandise. $ *Average main: ¥600* ⊠ *2-36-12 Kitazawa, Setagaya-ku* ☎ *03/5454–2486* ⊕ *www. bearpondespresso.com.*

Captain's Donut (キャプテンズドーナツ)
$ | **BAKERY** | Stop by and watch some specialty donuts being fried before your eyes. The giant cone outside reminds you that you can also get ice cream (soft-serve only), and there's coffee, too. **Known for:** great soft-serve ice cream; donuts made with soybean fiber leftover from tofu-making; fresh donuts. $ *Average main: ¥500* ⊠ *Kitazawa 2-7-5, Setagaya-ku* ☎ *03/6407–9691* ⊕ *captain-d.com.*

Norah's Coffee Table

$ | **CAFÉ** | If you're looking for a quick coffee near Shimokitazawa Station, Norah's can offer you a place for people-watching and some good snacks. While the drink selection is mostly coffee, they do have tea, make an Irish coffee, and serve wine and beer. **Known for:** cozy atmosphere; fluffy pancakes with dessert toppings; locally roasted coffee. $ *Average main: ¥900* ⊠ *Kitazawa 2-26-25, Setagaya-ku* ☎ *03/3468-2014* ⊟ *No credit cards.*

🛍 Shopping

One of the attractions of Shimokitazawa is how compact it all is. Small shops dot every street extending from the station and also occupy spaces above the station building and under the elevated tracks. The most one-of-a-kind finds are in vintage clothing stores that dot the streets but that are most concentrated on the northern side of the station. Goods spill out from these shops, where you can find designer goods, jeans of all genres, shoes, hats from all eras, outlandish sweaters, quality imported goods, and also harder-to-find knick-knacks here and there. Lovers of shopping will not be bored, and you'll have more fun if you just head off and explore.

Antique Life Jin II
(アンティークライフ・ジン2)
ANTIQUES & COLLECTIBLES | As the name implies, this is the second of two shops that lie just about a minute away from each other, but this one is the more interesting of the pair. All kinds of knickknacks fill the tiny space and spill out onto the street. If you are looking for one of those aprons worn at an izakaya, or and old tool box, or maybe an antique sake container, check this place out. And if you're still entertained, take a right as you walk out, then another right at the corner, and up on your left you'll see the original Antique Life Jin on the left. ⊠ *2-35-15, Kitazawa, Setagaya-ku* ☎ *03/5454-3545* ⊕ *antiquelife-jin.com.*

Gallery Hana Shimokitazawa
(ギャラリー HANA 下北沢)
ART GALLERIES | Hana is the oldest art gallery in Shimokitazawa, a place not known for its art, and the offerings change about every other week. Its central location and eclectic collections make it worth a stop, but so do their shows that typically feature Japanese artists you might have never heard of before. It's usually closed on Tuesdays. ⊠ *3-26-2 Kitazawa, Setagaya-ku* ☎ *03/6380–5687* ⊕ *www.g-hana.jp.*

Tamaiya Senbei Shop (玉井屋)
FOOD | If you're looking for a snack while shopping around, check out this purveyor of *senbei* (a type of grilled rice cracker) in their corner store with all on display. The shop has a long history and has been in Shimokitazawa since the Meiji Period. Theoretically, senbei are gluten-free since they're made of rice, but often the soy sauce coating includes some wheat. ⊠ *Kitazawa 2-31-1, Setagaya-ku* ☎ *03/3466–9191* ⊕ *shimokita1ban.com/ archives/1166.*

Nightlife

DANCE CLUBS
Shelter

LIVE MUSIC | An ever-popular, long-running venue attracts everyone from their late teens to early forties. This is a great place to catch promising local rock bands. Admission runs ¥2,000 to ¥6,000. ⊠ *Senda Bldg., 2–6–10 Kitazawa, B1 fl., Shibuya-ku* ☎ *03/3466–7430* ⊕ *www. loft-prj.co.jp/shelter* Ⓜ *Keio Inokashira, Odakyu private rail lines, Shimo-Kitazawa Station (South Exit).*

Chapter 8

ROPPONGI

Updated by
Rob Goss

⊙ Sights	🍴 Restaurants	🛏 Hotels	🛍 Shopping	🍸 Nightlife
★★☆☆☆	★★★★☆	★★★★★	★★☆☆☆	★★★★★

ROPPONGI SNAPSHOT

TOP EXPERIENCES

■ **See Tokyo's top art.** With the National Art Center, Tokyo, the Mori and Suntory art museums, and 21_21 Design Sight, Roppongi has become the place for Tokyo's top art exhibitions.

■ **Hit the heights.** Take in the view from one of two observation decks atop the Tokyo Tower, an unabashed knockoff of Paris's Eiffel Tower.

■ **Eat your fill.** From Michelin-starred Japanese and international cuisines to simple, yet addictive ramen, Roppongi has an incredible concentration of great places to eat.

GETTING HERE

Roppongi is located just east of Shibuya and Aoyama, and south of the Imperial Palace.

The best way to get to Roppongi is by subway, and there are two lines that'll take you to Roppongi Station: the Hibiya Line, which takes you right into the complex of Roppongi Hills, or the Oedo Line, with exits convenient to Tokyo Midtown.

PLANNING YOUR TIME

There are ATMs and currency-exchange services at Roppongi Hills and Tokyo Midtown shopping complexes, as well as family- and kid-friendly activities, such as small parks and sculptures. Combine those with the area's excellent art venues and you could easily spend a full afternoon and early evening here, before indulging in dinner at one of Roppongi's many excellent restaurants.

OFF THE BEATEN PATH: AZABU JUBAN

■ Wander into the adjoining residential enclave of Azabu Juban, about 1 km (0.6 miles) south, to observe everyday life for the most well-heeled Tokyoites, along with some nice café sitting. This is a neighborhood where some toy poodles have bigger fashion budgets than most humans elsewhere in the city. While people-watching is fun here any time of year, the best time to visit is in August, during the Azabu Juban Noryo Festival, one of the biggest festivals in Minato-ku. Over a weekend near the end of the month, the streets, which are closed to car traffic, are lined with food vendors selling delicious international fare and drinks. Everyone wears their nicest summer *yukatas* (robes) and watches live performances.

VIEWPOINT

■ Head up Mori Tower in the Roppongi Hills complex for superb city views. Looking across Tokyo from the 52nd-floor indoor observation deck or the even higher rooftop Sky Deck brings into focus just how vast and sprawling Tokyo is. At night in particular, with Tokyo illuminated below, the view is mesmerizing.

Roppongi, once known for its clubs, bars, and nightlife, has become one of Tokyo's major shopping, dining, and art districts. The area is abuzz with shoppers, tourists, and office workers throughout the day and evening. As the clock inches closer to the last train, the crowd changes to young clubbers and barhoppers staying out until sunrise.

For many travelers, the lure of the neighborhood is the shopping on offer in ritzy developments like Roppongi Hills and Tokyo Midtown. In addition, though, there are the three points of what's known as Art Triangle Roppongi—the National Art Center, Mori Art Museum, and Suntory Museum of Art. The neighborhood is also home to the Fujifilm Square photo gallery, 21_21 Design Sight, and many other art and cultural events.

👁 Sights

Fujifilm Square (フジフイルムスクエア)
ART GALLERY | Located within Tokyo Midtown, the Fujifilm Photo Salon hosts rotating photography exhibits across multiple genres, albeit with a strong emphasis on landscapes, while the Photo History Museum is a showcase of cameras and prints dating back to the mid-19th century. While the salon and history museum are on the small side, it is a good stop while visiting Roppongi's larger galleries, especially as its free. ✉ 9–7–3 Akasaka, Minato-ku ☎ 03/6271–3350 ⊕ fujifilmsquare.jp 🎫 Free Ⓜ Oedo and Hibiya subway lines, Roppongi Station (Exit 8).

★ **Mori Art Museum**
(森美術館; *Mori Bijutsukan*)
ART MUSEUM | Occupying the 52nd and 53rd floors of Mori Tower, this museum is one of the leading contemporary art showcases in Tokyo. The space is well designed (by American architect Richard Gluckman), intelligently curated, diverse in its media, and hospitable to big crowds. The nine galleries showcase exhibits that rotate every few months and tend to focus on leading contemporary art, architecture, fashion, design, and photography. Tickets include admission to the Roppongi Hills 52nd floor and the City View observation deck. ✉ 6–10–1 Roppongi, Minato-ku ☎ 03/5777–8600 ⊕ mori.art.museum/en 🎫 From ¥1,800 Ⓜ Hibiya subway line, Roppongi Station (Exit 1C).

Mori Tower (森タワー)
VIEWPOINT | When it opened in 2003, the Roppongi Hills complex was the center of Tokyo opulence, with the shimmering, 54-story Mori Tower as its main showpiece. Though no longer a unique skyscraper, the tower still outclasses most with the Tokyo City View observation promenade on the 52nd floor and the open-air Sky Deck on the tower rooftop;

The Mori Art Museum curates temporary contemporary art exhibitions in a sky-high space.

the views from both are wonderful and extend all the way to Mt. Fuji on a clear day. ✉ 6–10–1 Roppongi, Minato-ku ☎ 03/6406–6652 ⊕ tcv.roppongihills. com/en 🖅 Tokyo City View & Sky Deck: Weekdays ¥2,000, weekends and public holidays ¥2,200 Ⓜ Oedo and Hibiya subway lines, Roppongi Station (Exit 1C).

The National Art Center, Tokyo (国立新美術館; Kokuritsu Shin Bijutsukan)

ART MUSEUM | Tokyo's largest rotating exhibition space is home to major international modern and contemporary exhibits as well as smaller shows (usually free) and is worth visiting for the architecture alone. Architect Kisho Kurokawa, a cofounder of the influential metabolist movement in 1960, created a stunning facade that shimmers in undulating waves of glass, and the bright exhibition space with its soaring ceilings feels a bit like being inside the set of a utopian sci-fi movie. The building houses seven exhibition areas; a library; a museum shop; a pair of cafés; and a restaurant, Brasserie Paul Bocuse Le Musée, offering fine

French dishes. ✉ 7–22–2 Roppongi, Minato-ku ☎ 03/5777–8600 ⊕ www.nact. jp/english 🖅 Admission fee varies with exhibit ⊘ Closed Tues. Ⓜ Toei Oedo and Hibiya lines, Roppongi Station (Exit 7); Chiyoda line, Nogizaka Station (Exit 6).

Suntory Museum of Art (サントリー美術館; Santori Bijutsukan)

ART MUSEUM | Based on the principle of dividing profits three ways, Suntory, Japan's beverage giant, has committed a third of its profits to what it feels is its corporate and social responsibility to provide the public with art, education, and environmental conservation. The establishment of the Suntory Art Museum in 1961 was just one of the fruits of this initiative, and the museum's current home at Tokyo Midtown Galleria is a beautiful place to view some of Tokyo's finest fine-art exhibitions. Past displays have included everything from works by Picasso and Toulouse-Lautrec to fine kimonos from the Edo period. The museum also runs occasional tea ceremonies; check the website for the monthly schedule. ⌧ *Tokyo Midtown Galleria, 9–7–4 Akasaka, 3rd fl., Mina-to-ku* ☎ *03/3479–8600* ⊕ *www.suntory.com/sma* 🍽 *From ¥1,300* ⊗ *Closed Tues.* Ⓜ *Toei Oedo Line, Roppongi Station; Hibi-ya Line, Roppongi Station (Exit 8).*

Tokyo Tower (東京タワー)

VIEWPOINT | **FAMILY** | In 1958 Tokyo's fledgling TV networks needed a tall antenna array to transmit signals. Trying to emerge from the devastation of World War II, the nation's capital was also hungry for a landmark—a symbol for the aspirations of a city still without a skyline. The result was the 1,093-foot-high Tokyo Tower, an unabashed knockoff of Paris's Eiffel Tower, complete with great views of the city. The Main Observatory, set at 492 feet above ground, and the Top Deck, up an additional 330 feet, quickly became major tourist attractions. Both observation decks were renovated in 2018 and still draw many visitors a year. On weekends and holidays, ambitious visitors can make the 600-stair climb up to the Main Observatory on foot. ⌧ *4–2–8 Shiba-Koen, Minato-ku* ☎ *03/3433–5111* ⊕ *www.tokyotower.co.jp/en* 🍽 *Main Deck only ¥1,200, Main and Top Deck ¥2,800* Ⓜ *Hibiya subway line, Kamiyacho Station (Exit 1).*

21_21 Design Sight

ART GALLERY | This low-slung building in the garden at Tokyo Midtown hosts rotating exhibitions focused on cutting-edge art and design. Designed by architect Tadao Ando, the subdued exterior belies the expansive and bright gallery space, where exhibits focus on presenting the world of design in an exciting and accessible light. ⌧ *9–7–6 Akasaka, Minato-ku* ☎ *03/3475–2121* ⊕ *www.2121design-sight.jp/en* 🍽 *¥1,200* ⊗ *Closed Tues.* Ⓜ *Hibiya subway line, Roppongi Station (Exit 6).*

Zenpuku-ji Temple

(麻布山善福寺 *Azabusan Zenpuku-ji*)
TEMPLE | This temple, just south of the Ichinohashi Crossing, dates back to the 800s. In the 1200s, the temple was converted to the Shinran school of Buddhism. When Consul-General Townsend Harris arrived from the Americas in 1859, he lived on the temple grounds. It is also home to what's said to be the oldest tree in Tokyo, a 750-year-old giant gingko. ⌧ *1–6–21 Moto-Azabu, Minato-ku* ☎ *03/3451–7402* ⊕ *www.azabu-san.or.jp/eng* Ⓜ *Oedo and Namboku subway lines, Azabu Juban Station (Exits 1 and 7).*

🍴 Restaurants

The opulent Roppongi has outgrown its disco days and matured into a district with Western hotels and business skyscrapers. Restaurants run the gamut from lunch spots to quick bites to Michelin-starred options in the evening.

Azure 45

(アジュール フォーティーファイブ)
$$$$ | **FRENCH** | For his Michelin-starred contemporary French creations, chef de cuisine Shintaro Miyazaki sources the finest Japanese beef, poultry, seafood, and vegetables from around the country. Served on the 45th floor of the Ritz-Carlton, the resulting prix-fixe lunch courses (from ¥5,800) come with a choice of four or five dishes from a changing monthly menu. **Known for:** classy atmosphere; stunning views; delightful tasting menus. Ⓢ *Average main: ¥15,000* ⌧ *The Ritz-Carlton, Tokyo, Tokyo Midtown, 9–7–1 Akasaka, Minato-ku* ☎ *03/6434–8711* ⊕ *www.ritzcarlton.com* Ⓜ *Hibiya subway line, Roppongi Station (Exit 4A); Toei Oedo Line, Roppongi Station (Exit 7).*

Homework's (ホームワークス)

$$ | **AMERICAN** | Every so often, even on foreign shores, you've got to have a burger. When the urge strikes, the Swiss-and-bacon special at Homework's is an incomparably better choice than anything you can get at one of the global chains. **Known for:** burgers you can sink your teeth into; hearty deli sandwiches; relaxed atmosphere. Ⓢ *Average main:*

Did You Know?

The bright orange Eiffel-lookalike, Tokyo Tower, was built in 1958 to symbolize the country's recovery after the destruction of WWII.

¥1,500 ✉ *1–5–8 Azabu Juban, Minato-ku* ☎ *03/3405–9884* 🌐 *www.homeworks-1.com* [M] *Namboku and Oedo subway lines, Azabu Juban Station (Exit 4).*

★ Inakaya East
(田舎家 東店 *Inakaya Higashi ten*)
$$$$ | JAPANESE | The style here is *robatayaki*, a dining experience that segues into pure theater. Inside a large U-shape counter, two cooks in traditional garb sit on cushions behind a grill, with a cornucopia of food spread out in front of them: fresh vegetables, seafood, and skewers of beef and chicken. **Known for:** entertaining service; fresh ingredients grilled just right; fun, lively atmosphere. [$] *Average main: ¥10,000* ✉ *3–14–17 Roppongi, Minato-ku* ☎ *03/3408–5040* 🌐 *www.roppongiinakaya.jp* 🕓 *No lunch* [M] *Hibiya subway line, Roppongi Station (Exit 3).*

Ippudo (一風堂)
$ | RAMEN | Open from 11 am to 11 pm, this ever-busy ramen joint, now an international chain with almost 30 locations in Tokyo alone, is an ideal quick stop on or after a night out. The classic ramen is the Shiromaru, which features a creamy pork-based stock, thin yet slightly firm noodles, and a topping of chashu pork slices. **Known for:** Shiromaru ramen; late hours; gyoza (dumplings). [$] *Average main: ¥750* ✉ *4–9–11 Roppongi, Minato-ku* ☎ *03/5775–7561* 🌐 *www.ippudo.com* [M] *Hibiya and Oedo subway lines, Roppongi Station (Exit 6).*

★ Kushiyaki Ganchan (串焼がんちゃん)
$$$ | JAPANESE | Smoky, noisy, and cluttered, Ganchan is exactly what the Japanese expect of their yakitori joints—restaurants that specialize in bits of charcoal-broiled chicken and vegetables. The counter here seats barely 15, and you have to squeeze to get to the chairs in back. **Known for:** eclectic decor; cozy, down-to-earth atmosphere; fills up on weekends. [$] *Average main: ¥4,000* ✉ *6–8–23 Roppongi, Minato-ku* ☎ *03/3478–0092* 🕓 *No lunch* [M] *Hibiya subway line, Roppongi Station (Exit 1A).*

Menya Musashi Kosho (麺屋武蔵 虎嘯)
$ | RAMEN | Serving both ramen and *tsukemen* (noodles with the broth on the side for dipping), this sleek ramen shop is a great stop for a quick and hearty bowl of noodles. The shop's specialty is their fusion broths; a hearty chicken/pork or lighter seafood stock from dried bonito and sardines. **Known for:** quick and affordable meals; ramen in a hip, modern interior; rich, flavorful bowls of noodles. [$] *Average main: ¥1,000* ✉ *4-12-6 Roppongi, Minato-ku* ☎ *03/3497-0634* 💳 *No credit cards.*

Sankoen (三幸園)
$$$$ | KOREAN | In a neighborhood thick with Korean-barbecue joints, Sankoen stands out as the best of the lot. Korean barbecue is a smoky affair; you cook your own food, usually thin slices of beef and vegetables, on a gas grill at your table. **Known for:** excellent cuts of meat to grill at your table; cozy, simple interior; fills up quickly at dinnertime. [$] *Average main: ¥6,000* ✉ *1–8–7 Azabu Juban, Minato-ku* ☎ *03/3585–6306* 🕓 *Closed Wed.* [M] *Namboku and Oedo subway lines, Azabu Juban Station (Exit 4).*

Sushisho Masa (すし匠 まさ)
$$$$ | SUSHI | Diners here need a dose of luck—there are only seven counter seats and reservations fill up fast (ask your hotel concierge to make a reservation for you). You also need a full wallet, as high-end sushi comes at a pretty price. **Known for:** impeccable attention to detail; extremely high-quality, fresh fish with rare garnishes; focus on service as well as the food. [$] *Average main: ¥20,000* ✉ *7 Nishi-Azabu Bldg., 4–1–15 Nishi-Azabu, B1 fl., Minato-ku* ☎ *03/3499–9178* 🕓 *Closed Mon. No lunch* [M] *Hibiya subway line, Roppongi Station (Exit 1B); Toei Oedo Line, Roppongi Station (Exit 1A).*

Tony Roma's (トニーローマ)
$$$ | AMERICAN | FAMILY | This casual American chain is world-famous for its barbecued ribs. It also serves kid-size (and much larger) portions of burgers,

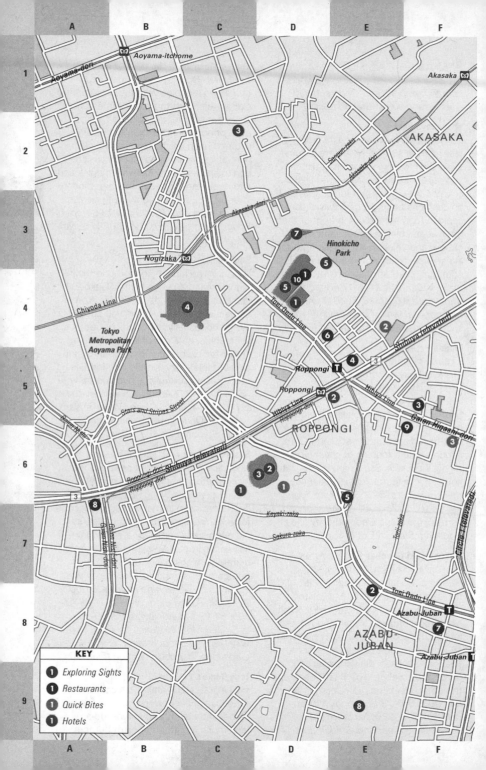

Roppongi

Sights ▼

1 Fujifilm Square D4
2 Mori Art Museum.................. D6
3 Mori Tower D6
4 The National Art Center, Tokyo.... C4
5 Suntory Museum of Art........... D4
6 Tokyo Tower........................ J7
7 21_21 Design Sight D3
8 Zenpuku-ji Temple.................. E9

Restaurants ▼

1 Azure 45........................... D4
2 Homework's E8
3 Inakaya East....................... F5
4 Ippudo............................. E5
5 Kushiyaki Ganchan................. E6
6 Menya Musashi Kosho D4
7 Sankoen F8
8 Sushisho Masa A6
9 Tony Roma's E6
10 Towers D4

Quick Bites ▼

1 eggcellent Roppongi Hills D6
2 Mercer Brunch Roppongi E4
3 Verve Coffee Roasters
  Roppongi........................... F6

Hotels ▼

1 Grand Hyatt Tokyo O8
2 Hotel Arca Torre Roppongi E5
3 Hotel Asia Center of Japan........ C2
4 The Prince Park Tower Tokyo J8
5 The Ritz-Carlton Tokyo D3

8

Roppongi

Tameike-sanno
Tameike-sanno
Roppongi-itchome
Kamiyacho
Sakurada-dori
AZABUDAI
Gaien-Higashi-dori
6
4
Akabanebashi

0 500ft
0 100m

chicken strips, and fried shrimp. **Known for:** a taste of the States; large portions of barbecued ribs; friendly service. $ *Average main: ¥3,500* ✉ *5–4–20 Roppongi, Minato-ku* ☎ *03/3408–2748* ⊕ *tonyromas.jp/en* Ⓜ *Hibiya subway line, Roppongi Station (Exit 3); Toei Oedo subway line, Roppongi Station (Exit 3).*

Towers (タワーズ)
$$$$ | **AMERICAN** | When you're looking for a break from all the ramen, tempura, and yakitori, this restaurant on the 45th floor of the Ritz-Carlton Hotel serves a mix of international flavors that range from American to Southeast Asian to Mediterranean. The prix-fixe lunches include a three-course business lunch (¥6,500), and there are dinners with four and five courses, including one that focuses on produce from Hokkaido (¥13,000). **Known for:** views over Tokyo; sophisticated fusion dishes; luxurious weekend brunches. $ *Average main: ¥13,000* ✉ *Ritz Carlton Hotel, 9–7–1 Akasaka, 45th fl., Minato-ku* ☎ *03/6434–8711* ⊕ *towers.ritzcarltontokyo.com* Ⓜ *Hibiya subway line, Roppongi Station (Exit 4A); Toei Oedo Line, Roppongi Station (Exit 7).*

☕ Coffee and Quick Bites

eggcellent Roppongi Hills (エッグセレント六本木ヒルズ)
$ | **CAFÉ** | No surprise that eggs are the thing at this convenient diner on the first basement floor of Roppongi Hills Mori Tower. Eggs are organic and available every which way, including in egg tarts, eggs benedict, pancakes, and a fried breakfast. **Known for:** Portuguese-style egg tarts; pancakes; good breakfast sets. $ *Average main: ¥1,400* ✉ *Mori Tower Hillside B1 F, 6–10–1 Roppongi, Roppongi* ☎ *03/3423–0089* ⊕ *eggcellent.co.jp/roppongi* Ⓜ *Oedo and Hibiya subway lines, Roppongi Station.*

Mercer Brunch Roppongi (マーサーブランチ六本木)
$$ | **CAFÉ** | The concept of brunch is fairly new in Tokyo but thankfully it's starting to take off. By day, this pleasant café offers outdoor seating and brioche French toast with great coffee just minutes from Tokyo Midtown and the art museums of the "Roppongi Art Triangle." From 5 pm, the menu changes to more expensive grilled meats and pastas. **Known for:** brioche French toast; terrace seating; brunch sets. $ *Average main: ¥1,900* ✉ *4–2–35 Roppongi, Minato-ku* ☎ *03/3470–6551* ⊕ *www.mercer-brunch.com* Ⓜ *Oedo and Hibiya subway lines, Roppongi Station (Exits 5 or 7).*

Verve Coffee Roasters Roppongi
$ | **CAFÉ** | For a quick caffeine break, Verve serves up single-origin beans from around the world in fashionable, but laidback surrounds. They also have herb teas, sandwiches, and sweet treats like carrot cake and vegan cookies. **Known for:** carrot cake; single-origin coffee; light bites like sandwiches. $ *Average main: ¥750* ✉ *5-16-8 Roppongi, Minato-ku* ☎ *03/6427-5403* ⊕ *vervecoffee.jp* Ⓜ *Oedo and Hibiya subway lines, Roppongi Station.*

🛏 Hotels

A boisterous entertainment district, Roppongi has hotels for travelers who want to be in the thick of the action. Lodgings run the gamut from low-end budget inns to some of the world's top brands.

Grand Hyatt Tokyo (グランドハイアット東京)
$$$ | **HOTEL** | Japanese refinement and a contemporary design come together perfectly at the Grand Hyatt—a tasteful and well-appointed hotel in the middle of Roppongi, one of Tokyo's top entertainment areas. **Pros:** great spa; wide range of restaurants; spacious rooms. **Cons:** rooms lack distinctive character; easy to get lost in the building's complicated

layout; concierge service can be hit-or-miss. [$] *Rooms from: ¥40,000* ✉ *6–10–3 Roppongi, Minato-ku* ☎ *03/4333–1234* 🌐 *www.hyatt.com/en-US/hotel/japan/grand-hyatt-tokyo/tyogh* 🛏 *387 rooms* 🍴 *No Meals* [M] *Hibiya subway line, Roppongi Station (Exit 1A); Oedo subway line, Roppongi Station (Exit 3).*

Hotel Arca Torre Roppongi (ホテルアルカトーレ)
$$ | **HOTEL** | Sitting on a coveted location in the heart of one of Tokyo's premier nightlife quarters, this European-inspired hotel is just a few minutes' walk from the Tokyo Midtown and Roppongi Hills shopping-and-entertainment complexes. **Pros:** affordable; convenient access to nightlife; free Wi-Fi. **Cons:** no closets; small double rooms; neighborhood's bars and clubs make the area noisy. [$] *Rooms from: ¥16,000* ✉ *6–1–23 Roppongi, Minato-ku* ☎ *03/3404–5111* 🌐 *arktower.co.jp/arca-torre* 🛏 *76 rooms* 🍴 *No Meals* [M] *Hibiya and Oedo subway lines, Roppongi Station (Exit 3).*

Hotel Asia Center of Japan (ホテルアジア会館; *Hoteru Ajia Kaikan*)
$ | **HOTEL** | Established in 1957 and renovated in 2015, these budget accommodations have become popular due to their good value and easy access (a 15-minute walk) to the nightlife of Roppongi. **Pros:** affordable; great area for those who love the nightlife; free Wi-Fi. **Cons:** just one restaurant; no room service; mostly small rooms. [$] *Rooms from: ¥10,000* ✉ *8–10–32 Akasaka, Minato-ku* ☎ *03/3402–6111* 🌐 *www.asiacenter.or.jp* 🛏 *173 rooms* 🍴 *No Meals* [M] *Ginza and Hanzo-mon subway lines, Aoyama-itchome Station (Exit 4).*

The Prince Park Tower Tokyo (ザ・プリンス パークタワー東京)
$$ | **HOTEL** | **FAMILY** | The surrounding parkland and the absence of any adjacent buildings make the Park Tower a peaceful retreat in the middle of the city. **Pros:** park nearby; well-stocked convenience store on first floor; fun extras like a bowling alley and pool. **Cons:** a tad isolated; extra fee for pool and fitness center; few dining options in immediate area. [$] *Rooms from: ¥30,000* ✉ *4–8–1 Shiba-koen, Minato-ku* ☎ *03/5400–1111* 🌐 *www.princehotels.com/parktower* 🛏 *603 rooms* 🍴 *No Meals* [M] *Oedo subway line, Akabanebashi Station (Akabanebashi Exit).*

★ **The Ritz-Carlton, Tokyo** (ザ・リッツ・カールトン東京)
$$$$ | **HOTEL** | Installed in the top floors of the 53-story Midtown Tower, the Ritz-Carlton provides Tokyo's most luxurious accommodations squarely in the middle of the city. **Pros:** great views of Tokyo; romantic setting; stunning rooms loaded with luxurious goodies. **Cons:** high prices; a bit of a walk to the subway; club lounge extras don't live up to the Ritz's reputation. [$] *Rooms from: ¥75,000* ✉ *9–7–1 Akasaka, Minato-ku* ☎ *03/3423–8000* 🌐 *www.ritzcarlton.com* 🛏 *247 rooms* 🍴 *No Meals* [M] *Hibiya subway line, Roppongi Station (Exit 4); Oedo subway line, Roppongi Station (Exit 7).*

🍸 Nightlife

BARS

Agave (アガヴェ)
BARS | In this authentic Mexican cantina, your palate will be tempted by a choice of more than 550 kinds of tequilas and mescals—making this the world's largest selection. Most of the varieties here aren't available anywhere else in Japan, so the steep prices may be worth paying. Foods are mostly Mexican appetizers. ✉ *DM Bldg., 7–18–11 Roppongi, B1 fl., Minato-ku* ☎ *03/3497–0229* 🌐 *agave.jp* 🕓 *Closed Sun.* [M] *Hibiya and Oedo subway lines, Roppongi Station (Exit 3).*

Gen Yamamoto
COCKTAIL LOUNGES | Tucked away in a side street of Azabu Juban, this stylish cocktail bar has just eight counter seats, so it's worth booking ahead if you fancy some of the most innovative tipples in

Tokyo's Gay Bars

Gay culture is a little different in Japan than it is in the West. Though Tokyo has a Rainbow Pride event in late April that attracts hundreds of thousands and the gay presence on TV is increasing, most gay life still takes place well under the radar. Even so, there's less prejudice than you might experience elsewhere. People are more likely to be baffled than offended by gay couples, and some hotels may "not compute" that a same-sex couple would like a double bed. But with a little digging you'll find a scene more vibrant than you—or many Tokyoites—might expect. The city's primary LGBTQ+ hub is Ni-chome in the Shinjuku district (take the Shinjuku or Marunouchi subway line to Shinjuku-Sanchome Station; Exit C7). Ni-chome is sometimes likened to its more notorious neighbor Kabuki-cho, and the name is also spoken in hushed tones and accompanied by raised eyebrows. Ni-chome, however, is more subtle in its approach. Gay and gay-friendly establishments can be found sprinkled in other areas, too, among them Shibuya, Asakusa, Ueno, and, surprisingly, Shinbashi, where a cluster of gay bars near Shinbashi Station are cheek-by-jowl with establishments that cater to hard-drinking businessmen out for a night on the town.

Tokyo. The bartender uses in-season Japanese produce like Okinawan pineapple and ume from Wakayama, along with fine liquor, to produce superb cocktail tasting menus. ✉ *1-6-4 Azabu Juban, Minato-ku* ☎ *03/6434–0652* ⊕ *www.genyamamoto. jp* ⊘ *Closed Mon.* Ⓜ *Oedo and Namboku subway lines, Azabu Juban Station (Exit 2).*

JAZZ CLUBS
Billboard Live Tokyo (ビルボードライブ東京)

LIVE MUSIC | With everything from rock and J-pop to soul and funk, this three-story joint makes one of the best food-and-live music experiences in Tokyo, all with panoramic views of Roppongi. Patrons love this venue partly because they're so close to performers like George Clinton, Dicky Betts, Neneh Cherry, and Howard Jones; they often end up on the stage dancing and singing or shaking hands. Shows usually kick off at 7 and 9:30 pm on weekdays, 6 and 9 pm on Saturday, and 4:30 and 7:30 pm on Sunday. ✉ *Tokyo Midtown Garden Terr., 9–7–4 Akasaka, 4th fl., Minato-ku* ☎ *03/3405–1133* ⊕ *www.billboard-live. com.*

KARAOKE
Pasela Roppongi (カラオケ パセラ)

THEMED ENTERTAINMENT | This 10-story entertainment complex on the main Roppongi drag of Gaien-Higashi-dori has seven floors of karaoke rooms, some Bali-themed, with more than 10,000 foreign-song titles. Both large and small groups can be accommodated. A Mexican-theme darts bar and a restaurant are also on-site. Rates run ¥700–¥2,000 per hour, and there are also all-you-can drink deals to keep your tonsils nicely lubricated for singing. ✉ *5–16–3 Roppongi, Minato-ku* ☎ *0120/911–086* ⊕ *www. pasela.co.jp* Ⓜ *Hibiya and Oedo subway lines, Roppongi Station (Exit 4A).*

Performing Arts

FILM
Toho Cinemas Roppongi Hills
(東宝シネマズ六本木ヒルズ)
FILM | FAMILY | This complex provides good comfort along with its nine screens, and about 2,100 seats that include "first-class" VIP seats. It also has an extra-large screen and MediaMation MX4D technology. It's the principal venue for the Tokyo International Film Festival held each fall. There are plenty of bars in the area for post-movie discussions. Late shows screen on weekends. ⊠ *Keyakiza-ka Complex, 6–10–2 Roppongi, Minato-ku* ☎ *03/6868–5024* ⊕ *www.roppongihills.com/en/cinema* ⊠ *From ¥1,900* Ⓜ *Hibiya and Oedo subway lines, Roppongi Station (Roppongi Hills Exit).*

MUSIC
Suntory Hall (サントリーホール)
CONCERTS | This lavishly appointed concert auditorium in the Ark Hills complex has probably the best acoustics in the city, and its great location allows theatergoers to extend their evening out: there's an abundance of great restaurants and bars nearby. ⊠ *1–13–1 Akasaka, Minato-ku* ☎ *03/3505–1001* ⊕ *www.suntory.com/culture-sports/suntoryhall* Ⓜ *Ginza subway line, Tameike-Sanno Station (Exit 13); Namboku subway line, Roppongi-Ichome Station (Exit 3).*

🛍 Shopping

CERAMICS
Savoir Vivre (サボア・ヴィーブル)
CERAMICS | In the swanky Axis Building, this store sells contemporary and antique tea sets, cups, bowls, and glassware. ⊠ *Axis Bldg., 5–17–1 Roppongi, 3rd fl., Minato-ku* ☎ *03/3585–7365* ⊕ *savoir-vivre.co.jp* ⊙ *Closed Wed.* Ⓜ *Hibiya and Oedo subway lines, Roppongi Station (Exit 3).*

CLOTHING
Restir (リステア)
MIXED CLOTHING | Next to the Midtown Tokyo complex, this is possibly the most exclusive and fashion-forward boutique in the city. Its three floors are made up of a cluster of stores, from luxury stores for men and women to a surf and activewear store, a café, and another store dedicated to high-end lifestyle gadgets like headphones, toy cameras, and stylish mobile peripherals. ⊠ *9–6–17 Akasaka, Minato-ku* ☎ *03/5413–3708* ⊕ *www.restir.com/en* Ⓜ *Hibiya and Oedo subway lines, Roppongi Station (Exit 8); Chiyoda subway line, Nogizaka Station (Exit 3).*

MALLS AND SHOPPING CENTERS
Axis (アクシス)
MALL | Classy and cutting-edge furniture, electronics, fabrics, ceramics, and books are sold at this multistory design center on the main Roppongi drag of Gaien-Higashi-dori. Savoir Vivre has an excellent selection of ceramics; Le Garage has accessories for high-end cars. On the fourth floor, the JIDA Design Museum shows the best of what's current in Japanese industrial design. ⊠ *5–17–1 Roppongi, Minato-ku* ☎ *03/3587–2781* ⊕ *www.axisinc.co.jp* ⊙ *Closed Sun.* Ⓜ *Hibiya and Oedo subway lines, Roppongi Station (Exit 3); Namboku subway line, Roppongi Itchome Station (Exit 2).*

Roppongi Hills (六本木ヒルズ)
SHOPPING CENTER | FAMILY | You could easily spend a whole day exploring the retail areas of this complex of shops, restaurants, residential and commercial towers, a nine-screen cineplex, the Grand Hyatt Tokyo hotel, and the Mori Art Museum—all wrapped around the TV Asahi studios and sprawled out in five zones located between the Roppongi intersection and Azabu Juban. The shops here emphasize eye-catching design and chichi brands, although finding a particular shop can be

a hassle given the building's Escher-like layout. To navigate, go to the information center to retrieve a floor guide with color-coded maps in English. ✉ *6–10–1 Roppongi, Minato-ku* ☎ *03/6406–6000* ⊕ *www.roppongihills.com* Ⓜ *Hibiya and Oedo subway lines, Roppongi Station (Roppongi Hills Exit).*

Tokyo Midtown (東京ミッドタウン)

SHOPPING CENTER | This huge complex is an architectural statement with sweeping glass roofs and a large walkable garden in the back. The airy, open spaces house exclusive boutiques, hotels, and a concentration of cafés by the world's top pâtissiers on the first few floors. ✉ *9–7–1 Akasaka, Minato-ku* ☎ *03/3475–3100* ⊕ *www.tokyo-midtown.com/en* Ⓜ *Hibiya and Oedo subway lines, Roppongi Station (Exit 8); Chiyoda subway line, Nogizaka Station (Exit 3).*

SWORDS AND KNIVES
★ **Japan Sword Co.**
(日本刀剣; *Nippon Tokken*)

OTHER SPECIALTY STORE | Aspiring samurai can learn how to tell their *toshin* (blades) from their *tsuka* (sword handles) with help from the staff at this small shop, which has been open since the Meiji era (1868–1912). Items that range from a circa-1390 samurai sword to inexpensive or decorative reproductions allow you to take a trip back in time. ✉ *3–8–1 Toranomon, Minato-ku* ☎ *03/3434–4321* ⊕ *www.japansword.co.jp* ☺ *Closed Sun.* Ⓜ *Hibiya and Ginza subway lines, Tora-no-mon Station (Exit 2).*

Chapter 9

SHINJUKU, WITH IKEBUKURO

Updated by
Jay Farris

👁 Sights
★★★☆☆

🍴 Restaurants
★★★☆☆

🛏 Hotels
★★★★☆

🛍 Shopping
★★★☆☆

🍸 Nightlife
★★★★★

SHINJUKU SNAPSHOT

TOP EXPERIENCES

■ **The observation deck of Tokyo Metropolitan Government Building.** Gaze at Japan's most famous mountain from this observation deck. The complex also hosts open-air concerts and exhibitions.

■ **Sompo Museum of Art.** Originally founded to showcase the work of Western-style Japanese painter Seiji Togo, the gallery has since expanded to include pieces by other iconic names like Gauguin, Cezanne, and van Gogh. Van Gogh's *Sunflowers* is a highlight here.

■ **That *Lost in Translation* bar.** No, you haven't fallen down the rabbit hole: the famous New York Bar calls the Park Hyatt home. You might recognize it from the movie *Lost in Translation*.

GETTING HERE

From Shibuya to the south and Ikebukuro to the north, the JR Yamanote Line is one of the more common ways to reach Shinjuku Station. The Saikyo Line travels the same path less frequently, but continues out of town. The Keio and Odakyu lines serve destinations to the west. Subway lines, like the Marunouchi, Shinjuku, and Toei Oedo, are best for connections in the center of the city, such as Ote-machi, Kudanshita, or Roppongi. On foot, Kabuki-cho is accessible in minutes to the east. For the forest of office-building skyscrapers, go through the underground passage to the west.

PLANNING YOUR TIME

Plan at least a full day for Shinjuku if you want to see both the east and west sides. Check your maps and use trains for a break, but don't rule out walking. Near Shinjuku Station, many underground paths are worth exploring on their own. The Shinjuku Gyoen National Garden is worth at least an hour, especially if you come in early April during *sakura* (cherry blossom) season. The Tokyo Metropolitan Government Building complex can take longer than you might expect as lines for the elevators to the observation decks can be long.

PAUSE HERE

■ While the name Shinjuku Southern Terrace is slightly misleading, the elevated pedestrian pathways along and across the tracks just south of Shinjuku Station are a great place for some quiet time. Kids might like Suica Penguin Square (you'll see the character a lot around Tokyo's JR stations), where they can watch trains come and go. Or stroll down the path on the west side of the tracks and you'll stumble on Petit Delirium Tap Cafe, where you can have a beer sitting outside.

SHINJUKU BY NIGHT

■ By day, Shinjuku is a bustling center of business and government where office workers move in droves during rush hour. By night, people are inundated with flashing signs, and a darker side of Tokyo emerges, when hordes leave their offices to go out for drinks, food, and sometimes, sex. Although the neighborhood's rough edges have been polished down to make it more tourist friendly, Shinjuku is still a fascinating place to discover at night.

If you like the grittiness and chaos of big cities, you're bound to love Shinjuku. Come here and Tokyo begins to seem *real*: all the celebrated virtues of Japanese society—its safety and order, its grace and beauty, its cleanliness and civility—fray at the edges.

To be fair, the area has been on the fringes of respectability for centuries. When Ieyasu, the first Tokugawa shogun, made Edo his capital, Shinjuku was at the junction of two important arteries leading into the city from the west. It became a thriving post station, where travelers would rest and refresh themselves for the last leg of their journey; the appeal of this suburban pit stop was its "teahouses," where the waitresses dispensed a bit more than sympathy with the tea.

When the Tokugawa dynasty collapsed in 1867, reformers restored direct power to the 16-year-old emperor, Meiji, and moved the capital to Edo (which was renamed as Tokyo by 1868). Modern Shinjuku became the railroad hub connecting Edo to Japan's western provinces. Later, as a haunt for artists, writers, and students, 1930s Shinjuku was Tokyo's bohemian quarter. The area was virtually leveled during the firebombings of 1945—a blank slate on which developers could write, as Tokyo surged west after the war.

Now, by day the east side of Shinjuku Station has an astonishing concentration of retail stores, vertical malls, and discounters of every stripe and description. By night, activity shifts to the nearby red-light quarter of Kabuki-cho, which is

an equally astonishing collection of bars and clubs, strip joints, hole-in-the-wall restaurants, pachinko parlors (an upright pinball game), and peep shows—just about anything that amuses, arouses, alters, or intoxicates is for sale. Recent crackdowns by police have limited this sort of adult activity, but whatever you're after is probably still there if you know where to look.

Shinjuku

Sights

Hanazono Jinja Shrine (花園神社)
Originally constructed in the early Edo period, Hanazono is not among Tokyo's most imposing shrines, but it does have a long history. Prayers offered here are believed to bring prosperity in business. The shrine is a five-minute walk north on Meiji-dori from the Shinjuku-sanchome subway station. The shrine hosts festivals, but might be most interesting late at night. The back of the shrine is adjacent to the "Golden-Gai," a district of tiny, somewhat seedy *nomiya* (bars) that in the '60s and '70s commanded the fierce loyalty of fiction writers, artists, freelance journalists, and expat Japanophiles—all the city's hard-core outsiders. ⊠ *5–17–3*

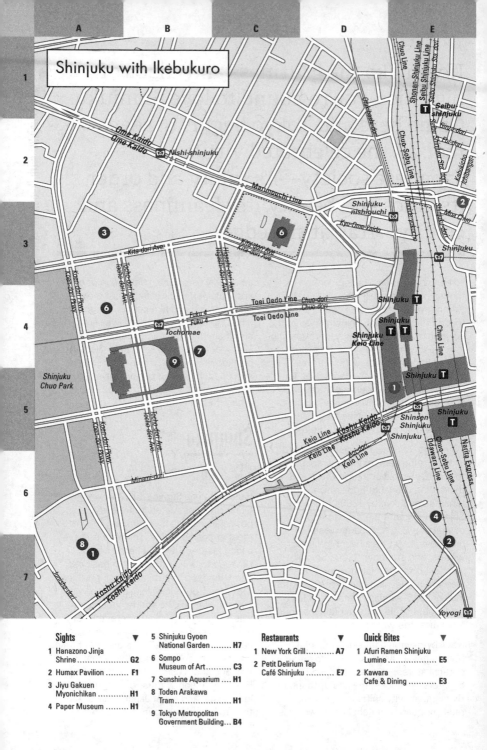

Shinjuku with Ikebukuro

Sights ▼

1 Hanazono Jinja
Shrine **G2**
2 Humax Pavilion **F1**
3 Jiyu Gakuen
Myonichikan **H1**
4 Paper Museum **H1**

5 Shinjuku Gyoen
National Garden **H7**
6 Sompo
Museum of Art **C3**
7 Sunshine Aquarium **H1**
8 Toden Arakawa
Tram **H1**
9 Tokyo Metropolitan
Government Building... **B4**

Restaurants ▼

1 New York Grill **A7**
2 Petit Delirium Tap
Café Shinjuku **E7**

Quick Bites ▼

1 Afuri Ramen Shinjuku
Lumine **E5**
2 Kawara
Cafe & Dining **E3**

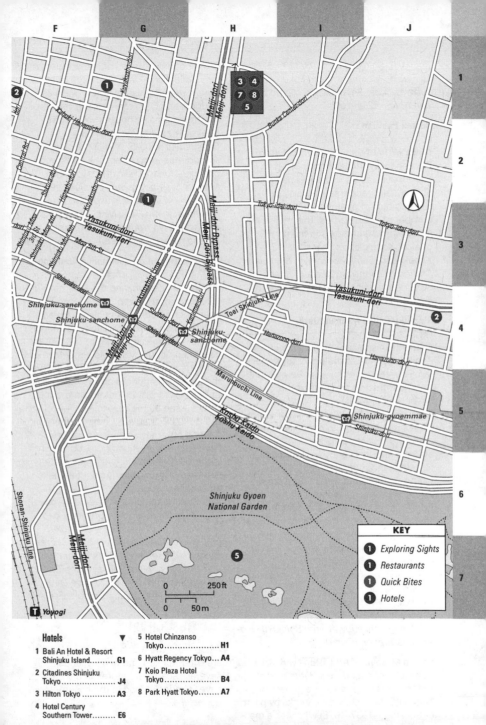

Hotels ▼

1 Bali An Hotel & Resort
   Shinjuku Island.......... **G1**

2 Citadines Shinjuku
   Tokyo **J4**

3 Hilton Tokyo **A3**

4 Hotel Century
   Southern Tower......... **E6**

5 Hotel Chinzanso
   Tokyo **H1**

6 Hyatt Regency Tokyo... **A4**

7 Keio Plaza Hotel
   Tokyo **B4**

8 Park Hyatt Tokyo........ **A7**

Shinjuku, Shinjuku-ku ☎ *03/3209–5265*
☎ *Free* Ⓜ *Marunouchi and Fukutoshin
subway lines, Shinjuku-san-chome Station (Exits B2 and B3).*

Humax Pavilion
(ヒューマックスパビリオン)

OTHER ATTRACTION | Need a break from
the sensory overload? At the Humax
Pavilion, you can shoot a few games
of pool, recline in a sauna, relax in a
karaoke box, or sharpen your skills at any
number of video games. This multilevel
entertainment center is in the middle
of all of Kabuki-cho's chaos. ☒ *1–20–1
Kabuki-cho, Shinjuku-ku* Ⓜ *JR Shinjuku
Station (Higashi-guchi/East Exit) and
Marunouchi subway line (Exits B10, B11,
B12, and B13).*

Shinjuku Gyoen National Garden
(新宿御苑)

GARDEN | This lovely 150-acre park was
once the estate of the powerful Naito
family of feudal lords, who were among
the most trusted retainers of the Tokugawa shoguns. After World War II, the
grounds were finally opened to the public. It's a perfect place for leisurely walks:
paths wind past ponds and bridges,
artificial hills, thoughtfully placed stone
lanterns, and more than 3,000 kinds of
plants, shrubs, and trees. There are different gardens in Japanese, French, and
English styles, as well as a greenhouse
(the nation's first, built in 1885) filled with
tropical plants. The best times to visit
are April, when 75 different species of
cherry trees—some 1,500 trees in all—
are in bloom, and the first two weeks of
November, during the chrysanthemum
exhibition. ☒ *11 Naito-machi, Shinjuku-ku*
☎ *03/3350–0151* ☎ *¥500* ◷ *Closed Mon.*
Ⓜ *Marunouchi subway line, Shinjuku Gyo-
en-mae Station (Exit 1).*

Sompo Museum of Art (東郷青児美術館
Sompo Japan Togo Seiji Bijutsukan)

ART MUSEUM | The multi-level museum
began its life to showcase works by painter Seiji Togo (1897–1978) who was a master at capturing grace on canvas, but now

hosts not only exhibits of his work from
their collection alongside pieces by other
Japanese and Western artists, such as
Gauguin and Cezanne, at any given time.
The museum also houses van Gogh's
Sunflowers. ☒ *1–26–1 Nishi-Shinjuku,
Shinjuku-ku* ☎ *03/5777–8600* ⊕ *www.
sompo-museum.org/en* ☎ *¥1,600; addi-
tional fee for special exhibits* ◷ *Closed
Mon.* Ⓜ *Marunouchi and Shinjuku subway
lines, JR rail lines; Shinjuku Station (Exit
A18 for subway lines, Nishi-guchi/West
Exit or Exit N4 from the underground
passageway for all others).*

Tokyo Metropolitan Government Building
(東京都庁; *Tokyo Tocho*)

VIEWPOINT | Dominating the western Shin-
juku skyline, this grandiose, Kenzo Tange–designed complex is clearly meant
to remind observers that Tokyo's annual
budget is bigger than that of the average
developing country. Locals either love or
hate the building, but on a clear day, from
the observation decks on the 45th floors
of both towers (663 feet above ground),
you can see all the way to Mt. Fuji and to
the Boso Peninsula in Chiba Prefecture.
Several other skyscrapers in the area
have free observation floors, but city hall
is the best of the lot. The Metropolitan
Government website, incidentally, is
an excellent source of information on
sightseeing and current events in Tokyo.
☒ *2–8–1 Nishi-Shinjuku, Shinjuku-ku*
☎ *03/5321–1111* ⊕ *www.metro.tokyo.
jp/english/offices/observat.html* ☎ *Free*
◷ *South Observation Deck closed 1st
and 3rd Tues.; North Observation Deck
closed 2nd and 4th Mon.* Ⓜ *Toei Oedo
subway line, Tocho-mae Station (Exit A4).*

🍴 Restaurants

Aside from the area's restaurants, which
are often tucked into narrow lanes,
several department stores in the area
have wonderful food in the basement
depachika.

Did You Know?

In the 1970s, the first major skyscraper construction began in Shinjuku, a then-undeveloped tract of land at the city's edge. Today the neighborhood is considered the new city center, with its collection of malls and government buildings, as well as one of the world's busiest train stations. The Gyoen National Garden provides a calm space to recover from the densely packed, bustling crowds.

★ **New York Grill** (ニューヨーク グリル)
$$$$ | INTERNATIONAL | The Park Hyatt's 52nd-floor bar and restaurant may have come to international fame thanks to Sofia Coppola's *Lost in Translation,* but expats and locals have long known that it's one of the most elegant places to take in Tokyo's nighttime cityscape over a steak or cocktail. The restaurant menu showcases excellent steaks and grilled seafood in the evening, and has one of the city's best lunch buffets during the day. **Known for:** impressive views over Tokyo; high-end modern American cuisine; excellent service. Ⓢ *Average main: ¥20,000* ✉ *Park Hyatt Tokyo, 3–7–1 Nishi-Shinjuku, 52nd fl., Shinjuku-ku* ☎ *03/5322–3458* ⊕ *restaurants.tokyo. park.hyatt.co.jp/en/nyg.html.*

Petit Delirium Tap Café Shinjuku
$$ | EUROPEAN | This unimposing building at the far end of Shinjuku Station's outdoor Southern Terrace serves a surprising variety of mostly Belgian and craft beers. While it is mostly a drinking establishment, their variety of meat plates, tapas, and appetizers, among other offerings, can easily turn into a meal. **Known for:** eclectic European-focused fare; wide variety of beers; comfortable outdoor seating. Ⓢ *Average main: ¥3,000* ✉ *2-2-1 Yoyogi, Shinjuku-ku* ✛ *Walk to the end of Shinjuku Southern Terrace west of the tracks.* ☎ *03/6300–0807.*

☕ Coffee and Quick Bites

Afuri Ramen Shinjuku Lumine
$ | JAPANESE | Just south of the Shinjuku station, this chain ramen house serves up ramen with hints of citrus in the broth, turning this often heavy dish into something more refreshing. It's located on a basement food level of Shinjuku's Lumine I department store, so you can have the nearby Thai food instead should you peek in and change your mind. **Known for:** lively atmosphere; very unusual citrusy broth; a light version of the sometimes heavy ramen. Ⓢ *Average main: ¥1,000* ✉ *1–1–2*

Nishishinjuku, Lumine I, Basement Level 2, Shinjuku-ku ☎ *03/5990–5182* ⊕ *www. afuri.com* Ⓜ *Shinjuku Station.*

Kawara Cafe & Dining
$$ | JAPANESE FUSION | For a quick lunch, you can grab reasonably priced set meals just a few minutes north of the station. Imagine a combination of Japanese and Western ingredients in a kind of modern home-cooking. **Known for:** hearty lunches; great views of the streets below; modern Japanese home-cooking. Ⓢ *Average main: ¥1,500* ✉ *Pandora Building, 3–23–12 Shinjuku, 8th fl., Shinjuku-ku* ☎ *03/3355–3180* Ⓜ *Shinjuku Station.*

Hotels

Bali An Hotel & Resort Shinjuku Island
$$ | HOTEL | If you've ever felt you needed a vacation from your vacation, then step off of Shinjuku's streets and into this fantasy island, one of Tokyo's many "love hotels" that is nice enough for an overnight stay if you want to have this quintessential Japanese experience. **Pros:** activities like karaoke in your room; a whole variety of interesting food and drinks available; all kinds of amenities on offer as you check in. **Cons:** not a place to stay for multiple nights; the neighborhood can be sketchy at night; time limits on use and extra fees for staying longer. Ⓢ *Rooms from: ¥20,000* ✉ *2–22–10 Kabukicho, Shinjuku-ku* ☎ *0120/759–184* ⊕ *www.balian.jp/shop/shinjuku_island* ⇥ *79 rooms* ❅ *No Meals* Ⓜ *Fukutoshin, Marunouchi, and Shinjuku lines, Shinjuku Sanchome Station (Exit E1).*

Citadines Shinjuku Tokyo
(シタディーン新宿)
$$ | HOTEL | Part hotel, part serviced apartments catering to short- or long-term travelers, the Citadines Shinjuku is a sunny venue of superb value. **Pros:** away from the congestion of Shinjuku Station; sizable rooms; bright, cheerful design. **Cons:** a little difficult to find; dining options limited on the premises; a bit of a walk to

Shinjuku's sights and nightlife. [$] *Rooms from: ¥19,000* ✉ *1–28–13 Shinjuku, Shinjuku-ku* ☎ *03/5379–7208* 🌐 *www.discoverasr.com/ja/citadines/japan/citadines-shinjuku-tokyo* 🛏 *160 apartments* 🍴 *No Meals* [M] *Marunouchi subway line, Shinjuku Gyoemmae Station (Exit 2).*

Hilton Tokyo (ヒルトン東京)
$$ | **HOTEL** | A short walk from the megalithic Tokyo Metropolitan Government Office, the Hilton is a particular favorite of Western business travelers. **Pros:** great gym; convenient location; free shuttle to Shinjuku Station. **Cons:** hotel lobby can get busy; restaurants are pricey; few sightseeing options immediately nearby. [$] *Rooms from: ¥26,000* ✉ *6–6–2 Nishi-Shinjuku, Shinjuku-ku* ☎ *03/3344–5111* 🌐 *www3.hilton.com* 🛏 *811 rooms* 🍴 *No Meals* [M] *Shinjuku Station (Nishi-guchi/West Exit); Marunouchi subway line, Nishi-Shinjuku Station (Exit C8); Oedo subway line, Tocho-mae Station (all exits).*

Hotel Century Southern Tower
(小田急ホテルセンチュリーサザンタワー)
$$ | **HOTEL** | The sparse offerings at the Century (i.e., no room or bell service, empty refrigerators) are more than compensated for by the hotel's reasonable prices and wonderful location atop the 35-floor Odakyu Southern Tower, minutes by foot from Shinjuku Station. **Pros:** convenient location; great views; simple but tasteful rooms. **Cons:** room amenities are basic; no room service or pool; small rooms. [$] *Rooms from: ¥29,000* ✉ *2–2–1 Yoyogi, Shibuya-ku* ☎ *03/5354–0111* 🌐 *www.southerntower.co.jp* 🛏 *375 rooms* 🍴 *No Meals* [M] *Shinjuku Station (Minami-guchi/South Exit); Oedo and Shinjuku subway lines, Shinjuku Station (Exit A1).*

Hyatt Regency Tokyo
(ハイアットリージェンシー 東京)
$$ | **HOTEL** | Set amid Shinjuku's skyscrapers, this hotel has the trademark Hyatt atrium-style lobby: seven stories high, with glass elevators soaring upward and three huge chandeliers suspended from above. **Pros:** friendly staff; affordable room rates; spacious rooms. **Cons:** rather generic exteriors and common areas; restaurant options are limited outside hotel; starting to show its age. [$] *Rooms from: ¥23,000* ✉ *2–7–2 Nishi-Shinjuku, Shinjuku-ku* ☎ *03/3348–1234* 🌐 *tokyo.regency.hyatt.com* 🛏 *744 rooms* 🍴 *No Meals* [M] *Marunouchi subway line, Nishi-Shinjuku Station (Exit C8); Oedo subway line, Tocho-mae Station (all exits).*

Keio Plaza Hotel Tokyo (京王プラザホテル)
$$ | **HOTEL** | Composed of two cereal-box-shape towers, this hotel has a reputation as a business destination that serves its guests with a classic touch. **Pros:** nice pools; affordable nightly rates; convenient location. **Cons:** bland exteriors and common areas; restaurant options outside hotel limited; crowded if there are conventions or large groups in residence. [$] *Rooms from: ¥28,000* ✉ *2–2–1 Nishi-Shinjuku, Shinjuku-ku* ☎ *03/3344–0111* 🌐 *www.keioplaza.com* 🛏 *1,436 rooms* 🍴 *No Meals* [M] *Shinjuku Station (Nishi-guchi/West Exit).*

★ **Park Hyatt Tokyo**
(パークハイアット東京)
$$$$ | **HOTEL** | Sofia Coppola's classic film *Lost in Translation* was a love letter to this hotel, and when the elevator inside the sleek, Kenzo Tange–designed Shinjuku Park Tower whisks you to the atrium lounge with a panorama of Shinjuku through floor-to-ceiling windows, you'll be smitten as well. **Pros:** wonderful room interiors; great skyline views; top-class restaurants. **Cons:** pricey for Shinjuku; somewhat remote; taxi is best way to get to Shinjuku Station. [$] *Rooms from: ¥56,000* ✉ *3–7–1–2 Nishi-Shinjuku, Shinjuku-ku* ☎ *03/5322–1234* 🌐 *www.hyatt.com* 🛏 *177 rooms* 🍴 *No Meals* [M] *JR Shinjuku Station (Nishi-guchi/West Exit).*

Among the bright lights of Kabuki-cho you may glimpse yakuza members in the crowds of revelers.

Nightlife

Shinjuku has everything, but don't forget to look up. East of the station, the area is littered with izakayas and other varieties of gastropubs serving the many office workers looking to loosen up. A bit farther east takes you to Shinjuku Sanchome (Shinjuku 3), where many more casual bars—some that are set up for just standing around—and restaurants spill onto the streets. And a trip a bit farther east from there lands you in Shinjuku Nichome (Shinjuku 2) which probably has the highest concentration of gay bars in the world, many of which, like the rest of Shinjuku, occupy upper floors.

There are also many tucked-away neighborhoods that have their own charms. Golden-gai, long the haunt of artists and misfits, is the perfect example of Tokyo's history still on display. Between Hanazono Jinja Shrine and the much more in-your-face hawking of Kabuki-cho, Golden-gai is a series of narrow alleys and tiny bars you might find yourself wedging yourself

into for the unique vibe, the music, or the conversation. Whatever you're looking for after dark, Shinjuku can likely provide it.

BARS
Bar Albatross
BARS | This tiny, artsy bar adorns its walls with paintings and deer heads, along with its many chandeliers, attracting crowds with its friendliness and affordability. The clientele will likely be an eclectic mix. Luckily its sign will light your way in Golden-Gai's tiny alleys. ⊠ 1–1-7 Kabuki-cho, 5th Golden Gai Street, Shinjuku-ku ☎ 03/3203–3699 ⊕ www.alba-s.com/#/f2 Ⓜ JR and Marunouchi subway lines, Shinjuku Station (East Exit).

Donzoko (どん底)
BARS | This venerable bar claims to be Shinjuku's oldest—established in 1951—and has hosted Yukio Mishima and Akira Kurosawa among many other luminaries. It's also one of several bars that claim to have invented the popular chu-hai cocktail (shochu with juice and soda). The vibrant atmosphere feels more like a pub, and the four floors are almost always

The Red Lights of Kabuki-cho

Tokyo has more than its fair share of red-light districts, but the leader of the pack is unquestionably Kabuki-cho, located just north of Shinjuku Station. The land was once a swamp, although its current name refers to an aborted post–World War II effort to bring culture to the area in the form of a landmark Kabuki theater. Until recently, most of the entertainment is of the insalubrious kind, with strip clubs, love hotels, host and hostess clubs, and thinly disguised brothels all luridly advertising their presence. Since the mid-2000s, however, the area has undergone a clean-up to draw in more tourists, similar to

the restoration of New York's Times Square in the 1990s.

The area was once home to throngs of Japanese and Chinese gangsters, giving rise to its image domestically as a danger zone. But in truth, Kabuki-cho poses little risk even to the solo traveler. The sheer volume of people in the area each night, combined with a prominent security-camera presence, means that crime stays mostly indoors.

Despite its sordid reputation, Kabuki-cho does have attractions beyond the red lights. There are eateries galore ranging from chain diners to designer restaurants.

packed. ✉ 3–10–2 Shinjuku, Shinjuku-ku ☎ 03/3354–7749 ⊕ www.donzoko.co.jp Ⓜ Marunouchi and Shinjuku subway lines, Shinjuku-san-chome Station (Exit C3).

La Jetée
BARS | It should come as no surprise that French cinema is the proprietor's big passion. La Jetée is covered in Euro-cinema posters and was named after a French movie. It's a tiny place, but that means for more intimate conversations in Japanese, French, or English. If you're looking for a hard-to-find, quirky bar up a narrow staircase to round out your Tokyo experience, look for the cats painted on the door and head up. ✉ 1-1-6 Kabuki-cho, 2nd fl., Shinjuku-ku ☎ 03/3208–9645 ⊕ www.lajetee.org ⊘ Closed Sun.–Tues. Ⓜ JR and Marunouchi subway lines, Shinjuku Station (East Exit).

★ **New York Bar** (ニューヨーク バー)
COCKTAIL LOUNGES | Even before Lost in Translation introduced the Park Hyatt's signature lounge to filmgoers worldwide, New York Bar was a local Tokyo favorite. All the style you would expect of one

of the city's top hotels combined with superior views of Shinjuku's skyscrapers and neon-lighted streets make this one of the city's premier nighttime venues. The quality of the jazz and service equals that of the view. With the largest selection of U.S. wines in Japan, drinks are priced as you might expect, and there's a cover charge of ¥2,200 after 8 pm (7 pm on Sunday). Local jazz bands play on Sunday. ✉ Park Hyatt Hotel, 3–7–1 Nishi-Shinjuku, 52nd fl., Shinjuku-ku ☎ 03/5322–1234 ⊕ restaurants. tokyo.park.hyatt.co.jp/en/nyb.html Ⓜ JR Shinjuku Station (West Exit for the shuttle bus service, South Exit for walk-in).

GAY BARS
Aiiro Cafe (藍色酒場; Aiiro Sakaba)
PUBS | Almost every great gay night out begins at this welcoming street-corner pub with a large red shrine gate, where the patrons spill out onto the street. This is the perfect place to put back a few cocktails, meet new people, and get a feeling for where to go next. The crowd is mixed and very foreigner-friendly. ✉ Tenka Bldg., 2–18–1 Shinjuku, Shinjuku-ku ☎ 03/6273–0740 ⊕ aliving.net/english.html.

Arty Farty (アーティファーティ)

BARS | Cheap and cheesy, Arty Farty is a fun club, complete with a ministage and stripper pole. Those with aversions to Kylie Minogue or Madonna need not bother. The crowd is mixed and foreigner-friendly. ✉ *Kyutei Bldg., 2–11–7 Shinjuku, 2nd fl., Shinjuku-ku* ☎ *03/5362–9720.*

Dragon Men

DANCE CLUBS | Tokyo's swankiest gay lounge, this neon-lit space would look right at home in New York or Paris. ✉ *Stork Nagasaki, 2–11–4 Shinjuku, Shinjuku-ku* ☎ *03/3341–0606* ⊕ *www.dragonmen69.com* Ⓜ *Marunouchi subway line, Shinjuku-san-chome Station.*

GB

BARS | Video monitors at this club show contemporary music hits. On weekends the place is packed with rather quiet and reserved gentlemen, mostly in their thirties and forties, and is also quite popular among foreign residents and visitors—especially before a night out clubbing. ✉ *Shinjuku Plaza Bldg., 2–12–3 Shinjuku, B1 fl., Shinjuku-ku* ☎ *03/3352–8972* ⊕ *gb-tokyo.com* 🕐 *Closed Mon.* Ⓜ *Marunouchi subway line, Shinjuku-san-chome Station.*

Gold Finger

BARS | This relaxed bar for "women who love women" is a cozy den of vintage lamps and cafélike ambience. Men are welcome on Friday; Saturday is women-only. ✉ *Hayashi Bldg., 2-12-11 Shinjuku, Shinjuku-ku* ☎ *03/6383–4649* ⊕ *www.goldfingerparty.com* 🕐 *Closed Tues. and Wed.* Ⓜ *Marunouchi subway line, Shinjuku-san-chome Station.*

JAZZ CLUBS

Jazz Spot Intro (イントロ)

LIVE MUSIC | This small basement jazz joint is home to one of the best jazz experiences in Tokyo, with a Saturday "12-hour jam session" that stretches until 5 am. Live sessions run throughout the week except Monday and Friday, when the regulars enjoy listening to the owner's extensive vinyl and CD collection. Italian food is available. ✉ *NT Bldg., 2–14–8 Takadanobaba, B1 fl., Shinjuku-ku* ☎ *03/3200–4396* ⊕ *www.intro.co.jp* Ⓜ *JR Takadanobaba Station (Waseda Exit).*

Shinjuku Pit Inn (ピットイン)

LIVE MUSIC | Most major jazz musicians have played at least once in this classic Tokyo club. The veteran club stages mostly mainstream fare with the odd foray into the avant-garde. The emphasis here is strictly on jazz—and the place resembles a small concert hall. Entry runs ¥1,400–¥5,000. ✉ *Accord Shinjuku Bldg., 2–12–4 Shinjuku, B1 fl., Shinjuku-ku* ☎ *03/3354–2024* ⊕ *pit-inn.com/e* Ⓜ *Marunouchi subway line, Shinjuku-san-chome Station.*

🔴 Performing Arts

MUSIC

New National Theater and Tokyo Opera City Concert Hall (新国立劇場; *Shin Kokuritsu Gekijo*)

CONCERTS | With its 1,632-seat main auditorium, this venue nourishes Japan's fledgling efforts to make a name for itself in the world of opera. The Opera City Concert Hall has a massive pipe organ and hosts a free concert on Friday from 11:45 to 12:30, as well as visiting orchestras and performers. The complex also includes an art gallery. ✉ *1–1–1 Honmachi, Shibuya-ku, Shinjuku-ku* ☎ *03/5353–0788, 03/5353–9999 ticket center* ⊕ *www.nntt.jac.go.jp/english* 🎫 *From ¥3,000* Ⓜ *Keio Shin-sen line, Hatsudai Station (Higashi-guchi/East Exit).*

🛍 Shopping

BOOKS

Books Kinokuniya Tokyo (紀伊国屋)

BOOKS | This mammoth bookstore, an annex of Takashimaya, devotes most of its sixth floor to English titles, with an excellent selection of travel guides, magazines, and books on Japan. ✉ *Takashimaya Times Sq., 5–24–2 Sendagaya,*

Kabuki-cho is a brightly lit hub for izakaya, pachinko parlors, and karaoke.

Shibuya-ku ☎ 03/5361–3301 ⊕ www. kinokuniya.co.jp Ⓜ JR Yamanote Line, Shinjuku Station (Minami-guchi/South Exit); Fukutoshin subway line, Shinjuku San-chome Station (Exit E8).

CRAFTS
Bingo-ya (備後屋)

CRAFTS | This tasteful four-floor shop allows you to complete your souvenir shopping in one place. The store carries traditional handicrafts—including ceramics, toys, lacquerware, Noh masks, fabrics, and lots more—from all over Japan. ⊠ *10–6 Wakamatsucho, Shinjuku-ku ☎ 03/3202–8778 ⊕ bingoya.tokyo ◷ Closed Mon. and some weekends Ⓜ Oedo subway line, Wakamatsu Kawada Station (Kawada Exit).*

★ Kukuli (くくり)

CRAFTS | This tiny textiles store in charming Kagurasaka sells items made of vintage textiles from different regions in Japan and transforms them into contemporary fashions and gifts. Look

for tote bags made from kendo and judo uniforms, fabrics off the roll, handkerchief squares, and silk scarves crafted from high-quality kimono fabric. ⊠ *1–10 Tsukudocho, Shinjuku-ku ☎ 03/6280–8462 ⊕ www.kukuli.co.jp Ⓜ Chuo-Sobu subway line, Iidabashi Station.*

DEPARTMENT STORES
Don Quijote (ドンキホーテ)

DEPARTMENT STORE | This 24-hour discount store has chains all around the country. The generally tight quarters aren't recommended for those with claustrophobia, but bargain hunters love the costumes, odd cosmetics, family-size bags of Japanese snacks, and used luxury handbags and watches. It's all haphazardly stacked from the floor to the ceiling. ⊠ *1–16–5 Kabuki-cho, Shinjuku-ku ☎ 03/5291–9211 ⊕ www.donki.com Ⓜ Marunouchi, Oedo, and Shinjuku subway lines, JR Yamanote Line, Keio and Odakyu lines, Shinjuku Station (Higashi-guchi/East Exit).*

Isetan (伊勢丹)

DEPARTMENT STORE | Established in 1886, "the Bergdorf's of Tokyo" is known for its high-end fashions both local and foreign, including a selection of larger sizes not found in most Tokyo stores. The second and third floors have champagne bars and snazzy store design that rival the world's best shops, making this one of the most pleasant shopping experiences in Tokyo, or anywhere, for that matter. The basement food court, which includes both traditional and modern prepared cuisine, is one of the city's largest in a department store. ⊠ *3–14–1 Shinjuku, Shinjuku-ku* ☎ *03/3225–2514* ⊕ *isetan.mistore.jp/ store/shinjuku* Ⓜ *JR Yamanote Line, Marunouchi subway line, Shinjuku Station (Higashi-guchi/East Exit for JR, Exits B2, B3, B4, and B5 for subway line).*

★ Marui 0101 Main Building (0101 マルイ本館)

DEPARTMENT STORE | Easily recognized by its red-and-white "01" logo, Marui burst onto the department store scene in the 1980s by introducing an in-store credit card—one of the first stores in Japan to do so. The four Marui buildings—Marui Honkan, Marui Annex, Marui One, and Marui Mens—make up the largest department store in the area by a large margin. Women flock to the stores in search of petite clothing, and you can find the largest concentration of Gothic and Lolita clothing in the city at the Annex. ⊠ *3–30–13 Shinjuku, Shinjuku-ku* ☎ *03/3354–0101* ⊕ *www.0101.co.jp/ stores/language/en* Ⓜ *JR Yamanote Line, Shinjuku Station (Higashi-guchi/East Exit); Marunouchi, Shinjuku, and Fukutoshin subway lines, Shinjuku San-chome Station (Exit A1).*

Seibu Ikebukuro (西武デパート池袋本店)

DEPARTMENT STORE | Even Japanese customers have been known to get lost in this mammoth department store; the main branch is in Ikebukuro, a bustling neighborhood just north of Shinjuku. Seibu has an excellent selection of household goods, from furniture to lacquerware and quirky interior design pieces in its stand-alone Loft shops (which you'll find throughout the city next to Seibu branches, or occasionally in the department store itself). ⊠ *1–28–1 Minami Ikebukuro, Toshima-ku* ☎ *03/3981–8569* ⊕ *www. sogo-seibu.jp/ikebukuro* Ⓜ *JR Yamanote Line, Marunouchi, Fukutoshin, and Yurakucho subway lines, Ikebukuro Station (Minami-guchi/South Exit); Seibu Ikebukuro Line, Seibu Ikebukuro Station (Seibu Department Store Exit); Tobu Tojo Line, Tobu Ikebukuro Station (Minami-guchi/South Exit).*

Takashimaya (高島屋)

DEPARTMENT STORE | Gift givers all over Japan seek out this department store; a present that comes in a Takashimaya bag makes a statement regardless of what's inside. Like most department stores each floor is dedicated to labels with similar price points, but here the north half is for women and south for men, so couples and families can shop on the same floors. The basement-level food court carries every gastronomic delight imaginable, from Japanese crackers and Miyazaki beef to one of the largest gourmet dessert courts in the city. The annexes boast a large-scale Tokyu Hands and Kinokuniya bookstore as well. ⊠ *Takashimaya Times Sq., 5–24–2 Sendagaya, Shibuya-ku* ☎ *03/5361–1111* ⊕ *www.takashimaya.co.jp/shinjuku* Ⓜ *JR Yamanote Line, Shinjuku Station (Minami-guchi/South Exit); Fukutoshin subway line, Shinjuku San-chome Station (Exit E8).*

ELECTRONICS

Bic Camera Shinjuku East Exit (ビックカメラ新宿東口店; Bikku Kamera Shinjuku Higashi-guchi ten)

ELECTRONICS | Bic Camera is one of Tokyo's largest discount electronics retailers and has multiple locations around the station. While you might see cameras and camera parts on display, this store has everything from kitchen gadgets you didn't know existed to the latest in audio and mobile devices. ✉ *3–29–1 Shinjuku, Shinjuku-ku* ☎ *03/3226–1111* ⊕ *www.bic-camera.com/bc/i/shop/shoplist/shop116.jsp* Ⓜ *Marunouchi, Oedo, and Shinjuku subway lines, JR Yamanote Line, Keio and Odakyu lines, Shinjuku Station (Higashi-guchi/East Exit).*

Yodobashi Camera (ヨドバシカメラ)
ELECTRONICS | This electronics superstore near Shinjuku Station carries a selection comparable to stores in Akihabara. It is made up of a number of annexes, including a watch, hobby, and professional camera building, that together span several blocks. ✉ *1–11–1 Nishi-Shinjuku, Shinjuku-ku* ☎ *03/3346–1010* ⊕ *www.yodobashi.com* Ⓜ *Marunouchi, Shinjuku, and Oedo subway lines, JR Yamanote Line, Keio and Odakyu lines, Shinjuku Station (Nishi-guchi/West Exit).*

JEWELRY AND WATCHES
Komehyo Shinjuku (コメ兵新宿)
JEWELRY & WATCHES | Are you looking for some high-class used or vintage luxury watches or jewelry or want to browse through luxury fashion? If you are looking to sell your own high-end goods, you can do so in the watch and jewelry shop. Three separate stores occupy a block east of Shinjuku Station–a men's, women's, and watches shop–reselling a dizzying variety of name-brand goods. ✉ *3-19-4 Shinjuku, Shinjuku-ku* ☎ *03/5363-9588 watches, bags, jewelry* ⊕ *www.komehyo.co.jp* Ⓜ *Shinjuku.*

MUSIC
★ Disk Union (ディスクユニオン)
MUSIC | Vinyl junkies rejoice. The Shinjuku flagship of this chain sells Latin, rock, and indie at 33 RPM. Be sure to grab a store flyer that lists all the branches, since each specializes in one music genre. Oh, and for digital folks, CDs are available, too. ✉ *3–17–5 Shinjuku, Shinjuku-ku* ☎ *03/5919–4565* Ⓜ *Marunouchi, Oedo, and Shinjuku subway lines, JR Yamanote Line, Keio and Odakyu lines, Shinjuku Station (Higashi-guchi/East Exit).*

PAPER
Wagami Takamura
(紙のたかむら; *Kami no Takamura*)
STATIONERY | Specialists in *washi* and other papers printed in traditional Japanese designs, this shop also carries brushes, inkstones, and other tools for calligraphy. At the entrance is a gallery showcasing seasonal traditional stationery and the work of local artists. ✉ *1–1–2 Higashi-Ike-bukuro, Toshima-ku* ☎ *03/3971–7111* ⊕ *www.wagami-takamura.com* Ⓜ *JR Yamanote Line, Marunouchi and Fuku-toshin subway lines, Ikebukuro Station (East Exit for JR, Exit 35 for subway).*

Ikebukuro

The oft-overlooked cousin of Shinjuku and Shibuya is not a major tourist destination, but it is a major crossroads and entry point for people from the northern and northwestern suburbs. Northwest of the station, typical nightlife and eateries are well integrated into Tokyo's sleazier side, so if you're not looking for a strip show or something else, then it's best to stick to the other areas that have plenty to offer. Ikebukuro Station is the center of the action, and easiest access is by the JR Yamanote Line, but it's also served by the Marunouchi, Yurakucho, and Fuku-toshin subway lines.

Sights

Jiyu Gakuen Myonichikan
(自由学園明日館)
NOTABLE BUILDING | Frank Lloyd Wright fans will enjoy a glimpse into this off-the-beaten-path school building featuring his distinctive Prairie style. When Wright was in Tokyo designing the Imperial Hotel in the 1920s, he was commissioned to build this schoolhouse, which is now open to the public. Its use of local stone keeps it in harmony with its location,

228

but that is a bit difficult to find, so your journey to find the building will take you through a small neighborhood. The brick street the building occupies is a helpful marker. Call ahead to be sure they are not closed for an event. ✉ *2-31-3 Nishi Ikebukuro, Toshima-ku* ⚓ *Use the Metropolitan Hotel as a landmark, then head directly south onto a narrow street heading into a neighborhood, following the street until you see a small, brick-paved road on your right.* ☎ *03/3971-7535* ⊕ *jiyu.jp* ✉ *¥500 to enter, ¥800 includes a drink and snack in the café* ◷ *Closed Mon.* Ⓜ *Ikebukuro JR Station (Metropolitan Exit).*

Paper Museum

(紙の博物館 *Kami no Hakubutsukan*)
HISTORY MUSEUM | The original paper mill that once stood here (Japan's first) is long gone, but the memory lingers on through exhibits that cover 2,000 years of the history of paper and show the processes for milling paper from pulp and recycling and include a number of the machines used. Other exhibits illustrate the astonishing variety of products that can be made from paper. ✉ *1-1-3 Oji, Kita-ku* ☎ *03/3916-2320* ⊕ *papermuseum.jp/en* ✉ *¥400* ◷ *Closed Mon.* Ⓜ *Toden Arakawa Line, Asukayama Station; JR Keihin-Tohoku Line, Oji Station (South Exit).*

Sunshine Aquarium (サンシャイン水族館; *Sanshain Suizokukan*)

AQUARIUM | FAMILY | This aquarium has some 750 kinds of sea creatures on display, plus daily behind-the-scenes tours and animal feeding sessions with staff. An English-language pamphlet is available, and most of the exhibits have some English explanation. If you get tired of the sea life, head to the Manten planetarium, where you can see 400,000 stars. And if that still isn't enough to keep you occupied, try the 60th-floor Sky Circus observatory for great views

of the city and virtual reality rides. ✉ *3-1-3 Higashi-Ikebukuro, Toshima-ku* ☎ *03/3989-3466* ⊕ *sunshinecity.jp/en* ✉ *Aquarium ¥2,400, planetarium ¥1,500, observatory ¥1,200* Ⓜ *JR Yamanote Line, Ikebukuro Station (East Exit); Yurakucho subway line, Ikebukuro Station (Exit 35).*

Toden Arakawa Tram

(都電荒川線; *Toden Arakawa-sen*)
TRAIN/TRAIN STATION | Take the JR Yamanote Line to Otsuka, cross the street in front of the station, and change to the Toden Arakawa Line (aka Tokyo Sakura Tram)—Tokyo's last surviving trolley. Heading east, for ¥170 one way, the trolley takes you through the back gardens of old neighborhoods on its way to Oji, once the site of Japan's first Western-style paper mill, built in 1875 by Oji Paper Company, the nation's oldest joint-stock company. ✉ *Otsuka, Toshima-ku* ⊕ *www.kotsu.metro.tokyo.jp/eng/services* ✉ *Single ride ¥170, day-pass ¥400.*

 # Hotels

Hotel Chinzanso Tokyo (ホテル椿山荘東京)

$$$$ | HOTEL | Surrounded by a 17-acre garden, the elegant, European-style Hotel Chinzanso is a sheltered haven in Tokyo's busy metropolis and a former estate of an imperial prince. **Pros:** gorgeous, sprawling grounds; large rooms with huge bathrooms; glamorous pool. **Cons:** limited dining options in immediate area; isolated location; room interiors a tad dated. Ⓢ *Rooms from: ¥57,000* ✉ *2-10-8 Sekiguchi, Bunkyo-ku* ☎ *03/3943-1111* ⊕ *www.hotel-chinzanso-tokyo.com* 🛏 *260 rooms* ❶ *No Meals* Ⓜ *Yurakucho subway line, Edogawabashi Station (Exit 1A).*

Chapter 10

WEST TOKYO

Updated by
Rob Goss

👁 Sights	🍴 Restaurants	🛏 Hotels	🛍 Shopping	🍸 Nightlife
★★★☆☆	★★★☆☆	★☆☆☆☆	★☆☆☆☆	★★★☆☆

WEST TOKYO SNAPSHOT

TOP EXPERIENCES

■ **Hang out with Hello Kitty.** Head to Tama for a day at the Sanrio Puroland theme park, the wonderfully kitschy home of Hello Kitty and her cartoon friends.

■ **Dance in the streets.** For a weekend in late August, the hip neighborhood of Koenji hosts one of Tokyo's most energetic major events, the Koenji Awa-Odori dance festival.

■ **Go back in time.** Visit Jindai-ji in Chofu, a temple first built in AD 733 that houses a priceless gilded bronze statue of the Buddha dating to the late Asuka period (592–710).

■ **Get geeky in Nakano.** Akihabara might be Tokyo's main hub for *otaku* (geek) culture, but the several hundred anime- and manga-related stores at the Nakano Broadway mall make for an entertaining alternative.

■ **Explore the world of Ghibli.** This museum-slash-theme park in Mitaka transports visitors into the fantastical worlds created by legendary animators Studio Ghibli.

GETTING HERE

All the areas of West Tokyo covered in this chapter are easily reached by train from central Tokyo. Either the JR Chuo Line or the Keio Line, both of which can be taken from Shinjuku, give access to Nakano, Suginami, Chofu, Tama, Mitaka, Musashino. Within West Tokyo you will also find bus routes connecting stations to sights that might otherwise require a long walk, such as the Ghibli Museum in Mitaka and Jindai-ji Temple in Chofu, and taxis will be waiting at all major stations.

PLANNING YOUR TIME

West Tokyo is an expansive area, which makes combining the neighborhoods in this chapter difficult in a single day. The best approach is to pick one area at a time and tackle it as day trip or half-day trip while basing yourself in one of Tokyo's 23 wards, as that's where the best hotels and dining areas are.

OFF THE BEATEN PATH

■ The main attraction of Koganei, just west of Mitaka and Musashino, the Edo-Tokyo Open-air Architectural Museum preserves 30 historic buildings relocated from around Tokyo. The structures range from Edo-era thatched farmhouses that give insights into how West Tokyo would have looked before urbanization to early 20th-century shops from central Tokyo. To get here, take the Chuo Line to Higashi-Koganei Station (two stops west of Mitaka Station).

PAUSE HERE

■ Scattered around West Tokyo are hundreds of places to stop and have a relaxing soak in piping-hot water, ranging from modest neighborhood *sento* (public bathhouses) to more indulgent onsen (natural hot-spring baths). You could try Gokuraku Yu in Tama for the latter or Kotobuki Yu in Nakano for the former. It's a very Japanese way to unwind.

West Tokyo offers up less touristy experiences than the city center and gives you a chance to embark on day trips that genuinely veer off paths well-trodden by international travelers, yet without having to uproot and leave the higher-quality accommodations or conveniences of the capital behind.

Also known as the Tama Area, West Tokyo is vast. Spreading westward from the central 23 wards (-ku), the West Tokyo region covers almost 1,160 square km (720 square miles) of land, ranging from built-up extensions of the city's urban sprawl to leafy suburbs and mountains. Within that are 26 municipalities called -shi (cities), three -machi (towns), and even a -mura (village), which all together are home to more than 4 million people. This section looks at some of the most accessible and worthwhile trips into West Tokyo, as well as the highlights of less-visited west-side -ku such as Nakano and Suginami. Mount Takao in Tokyo's far west is covered in the Side Trips chapter.

Starting with the western parts of the 23 -ku, Nakano, a few stops from Shinjuku, provides a fun alternative to the otaku (geek culture) center of Akihabara: the Nakano Broadway mall has everything an anime- or manga-loving traveler needs. Directly west of Nakano, Suginami is home to the thrift stores and bohemian hangouts of Koenji, a neighborhood that also hosts one of Tokyo's most energetic summer festivals, the Koenji Awa-Odori.

West of there are the neighboring -shi of Mitaka and Musashino, which share the lovely green expanse of Inokashira Park.

As well as a small zoo and boating pond, the park is the site of the Studio Ghibli animation studio's wonderful Ghibli Museum. Quite a contrast, the lively neighborhood of Kichijoji nearby is great for bar hopping, casual restaurants, and hip cafés.

To the south, another -shi is Chofu, which despite being less than 20 minutes by train from Shinjuku feels a million miles apart thanks to the natural surrounds of the historic Jindai-ji Temple and flora and fauna of Jindai Botanical Gardens. Further west then comes Tama, a quiet residential area full of spacious parks. Here, you could spend a day in the colorful world of Hello Kitty and friends at the Sanrio Puroland theme park or unwind in natural hot-spring baths at Gokuraku Yu.

Nakano

The name of both a station and one of the 23 -ku (districts) that make up the heart of Tokyo, Nakano goes under the radar of most travelers. That's understandable for most travelers, but for anyone interested in anime, manga, and other otaku culture, Nakano's vast Nakano Broadway complex makes it a less-heralded alternative (or addition) to Akihabara. To get there take

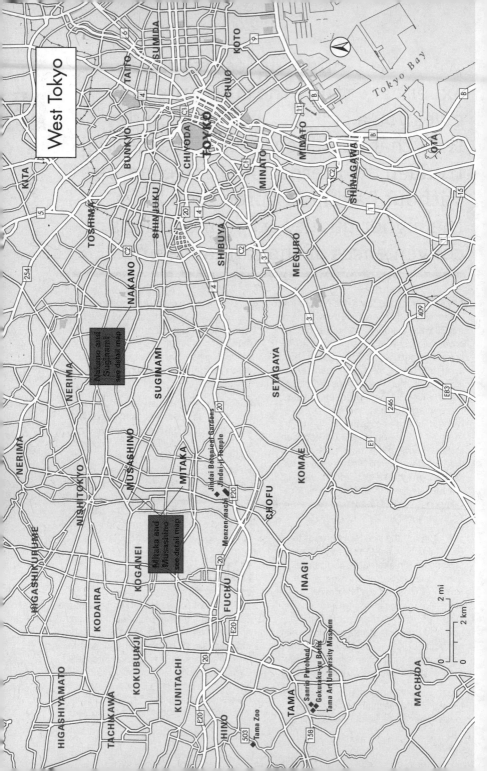

Nakano Broadway is one of the world's best shopping complexes for all things related to otaku culture, including anime, manga, and cosplay.

the JR Chuo Line one stop from Shinjuku Station to Nakano Station.

Sights

Kotobuki Yu Baths
(寿湯温泉; *Kotobuki Yu Onsen*)

HOT SPRING | If walking around 13 floors of geeky goods at Nakano Broadway tires you out, stop by Kotobuki (just to the north) for a muscle-soothing bath. Tokyo's neighborhood baths have been in steady decline in recent decades as only the oldest of homes now comes without a bath or shower. Some, however, like Kotobuki, are clinging on as places to socialize and unwind, and though it's a modest facility, a soak here is a very immersive (pardon the pun) local experience. Just note that it opens late: from 4 pm 'til 12:30 am, so it's definitely something to do *after* your shopping spree.

Once you've located Kotobuki Yu's orange building and have found your way to the gender-separated baths, the key thing with any public bath is to follow the basic etiquette. First, you need to be completely naked in the baths and make sure your wash towel doesn't go in the communal bathtub. You also need to wash and rinse well in the seated shower area, before getting into the baths. After that, just enjoy a piping-hot soak and then try the on-site sauna. ✉ *1-14-13 Arai, Nakano-ku* ☎ *03/3387–2047* ✉ *¥480* ⊙ *Closed Tues.* Ⓜ *JR Chuo Line and Tozai subway line, Nakano Station (North Exit).*

★ Nakano Broadway
(中野ブロードウェイ)

STORE/MALL | When Nakano Broadway opened in 1966, it was as a luxury complex, akin to the Tokyo Midtown or Ginza Six of its day. Since then, it has morphed into a center for all things otaku, its 13 floors home to roughly 300 stores largely focused on manga, anime, gaming, and related collectibles and goods that run from figurines to cosplay outfits. Japan's largest manga- and anime-related retailer alone has close to 30 stores in Nakano Broadway, all divided by specialty. Down in the basement are plenty of places

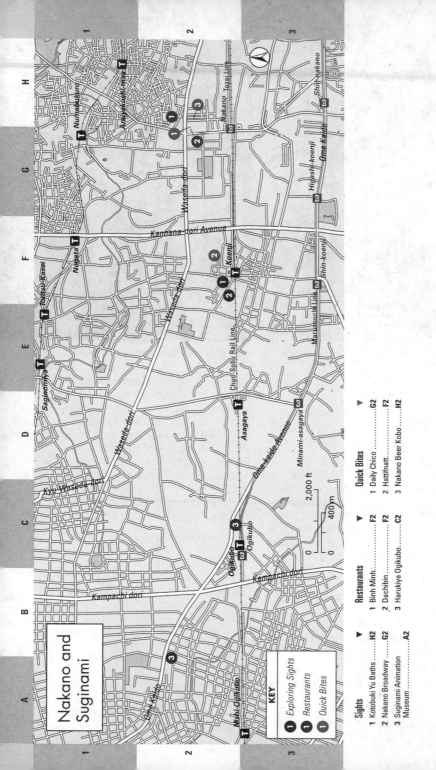

Nakano and Suginami

KEY

1 Exploring Sights
1 Restaurants
1 Quick Bites

Sights ▶

1 Kotobuki Yu Baths..........H2
2 Nakano Broadway..........G2
3 Suginami Animation
  Museum....................A2

Restaurants ▶

1 Binh Minh..................F2
2 Dachibin...................F2
3 Harukiya Ogikubo..........C2

Quick Bites ▶

1 Daily Chico................G2
2 Hattifnatt.................F2
3 Nakano Beer Kobo..........H2

2,000 ft

400 m

Kyu-Waseda-dori
Waseda-dori
Waseda-dori
Waseda-dori
Kannana-dori Avenue
Kampachi dori
Kampachi dori
Ome-kaido Avenue
Ome-kaido-Avenue
Minami-asagaya
Chuo-Sobu Rail Line
Marunouchi Line

Nishi-Ogikubo
Ome-Kaido
Ogikubo
Ogikubo
Asagaya
Koenji
Shin-koenji
Higashi-koenji
Shin-nakano
Nakano
Tozai Line
Ome-kaido

Numabukuro
Araiyakushi-mae
Saginomiya
Nogata
Toritsu-Kasei

for lunch or a quick snack, including the stomach-busting Daily Chico, which does an eight-scoop soft-serve ice cream. It's like a trip to Akihabara, but with everything under one roof. ✉ *5-52-15 Nakano, Nakano-ku* ☎ *03/3388–7004* 🌐 *nakano-broadway.com* [M] *JR Chuo Line and Tozai subway line, Nakano Station (North Exit).*

Coffee and Quick Bites

Daily Chico (デイリーチコ)
$ | **ICE CREAM** | **FAMILY** | This basement-level ice cream store has become a Nakano Broadway institution for its soft-serve ice cream, which comes in flavors that vary from simple vanilla to matcha (green tea), horse chestnut, and *ramune* (a popular citrus soda flavor). The signature is the eight-layered, 20-cm Tokudai (extra large) soft serve, though small cups and cones are also on the menu. **Known for:** served in cups or cones; flavors like matcha; eight-layered soft-serve ice cream. [$] *Average main: ¥280* ✉ *Nakano Broadway, 5-52-15 Nakano, B1 Floor, Nakano-ku* ☎ *03/3386–4461* 💳 *No credit cards* [M] *JR Chuo Line and Tozai subway line, Nakano Station (North Exit).*

Nakano Beer Kobo (中野ビール工房)
$$ | **ECLECTIC** | For a post-shopping drink and light bite to eat, stop by this tiny brewpub in the side streets just east of Nakano Broadway. The rough decor looks a bit like a carpentry enthusiast has made a bar in their garage, but the eight beers on tap are far better crafted. **Known for:** range of craft beers; light bites such as buffalo wings and garlic shrimp; rough-and-ready interiors. [$] *Average main: ¥1,500* ✉ *5-53-4 Nakano, Nakano-ku* ☎ *03/3385–3301* 🌐 *www.beerkobo.com* 🕒 *Closed Mon.* [M] *JR Chuo Line and Tozai subway line, Nakano Station (North Exit).*

Shopping

Mandarake (まんだらけ)
OTHER SPECIALTY STORE | Not one Mandarake store, but nearly *30* of them, each with a distinct specialty, are found in the Nakano Broadway mall. Every otaku culture need is catered to here. If you want a Kamen Rider figurine, head to Mandarake Special 3 on the third floor, while fans of tabletop role-playing games like Warhammer should make a beeline for the Kojosen branch on the fourth floor. The list of geeky specialties goes on and on. ✉ *Nakano Broadway, 5-52-15 Nakano, Nakano-ku* ☎ *03/3228–5787* 🌐 *www.mandarake.co.jp* [M] *JR Chuo Line and Tozai subway line, Nakano Station (North Exit).*

Robot Robot (ロボットロボット)
OTHER SPECIALTY STORE | Another brand with multiple Nakano Broadway outlets, Robot Robot is the place otaku go for figurines and action figures. In Robot Robot 1 on Broadway's third floor the focus is on Japanese anime and manga characters, such as Gundam and Dragon Ball, while on the same floor Robot Robot 2 is packed with Americana, with character goods from Star Wars, Disney, Marvel, and more. Down on the second floor, Robot Robot 3 is a bit more of a mishmash, though a good stop for anyone into Ghibli. ✉ *Nakano Broadway, 5-52-15 Nakano, Nakano-ku* ☎ *03/5345–7553* 🌐 *robotrobot.com* [M] *JR Chuo Line and Tozai subway line, Nakano Station (North Exit).*

Suginami

Located next to Nakano, on the edge of Tokyo's 23 *-ku*, Suginami oozes rough-around-the-edges cool. Around Koenji Station, you find hip eateries, quirky watering holes, cool thrift stores, and underground music venues, while one station along in Asagaya there's a tradition of jazz. Then there's Ogikubo, which is a must-visit for anyone with a penchant for ramen: it's home to some of the best noodle joints in Tokyo according to ramen aficionados. Neither of these areas has much in the way of major sightseeing attractions; they are places you come to soak in the atmosphere.

Koenji in particular always has an energy about it, but if you come on the last weekend of August, it will be absolutely teeming because of the superb Koenji Awa-Odori dance festival. A spin-off of the 400-year-old Awa-Odori in Tokushima on Shikoku island, this version started in the 1950s and now sees troupes of dancers and musicians (some 10,000 people in all) performing energetic routines in the streets as hundreds of thousands look on.

Sights

Suginami Animation Museum (杉並アニメーションミュージアム)
OTHER MUSEUM | FAMILY | Suginami is home to more than 100 animation studios, making it by far the animation creation center of Tokyo. Although you can't visit those studios, you can learn about animation at this compact, free museum, which has exhibits on anime history and how anime is made, plus interactive exhibits that include digital screens on which you can try drawing (or trace using templates) your own anime. ⊠ *3-29-5 Kamiogi, Suginami-ku* ⊹ *From Ogikubo Station take any bus from bus stop 0 or 1 to the Ogikubo Keisatsusho-mae bus stop.* ☎ *03/3396–1510* ⊕ *sam.or.jp* ⊠ *Free* ⊗ *Closed Mon.* Ⓜ *JR Chuo Line, Ogikubo Station and Marunouchi subway line, Ogikubo Station.*

 Restaurants

Binh Minh (ビンミン)
$$ | VIETNAMESE | Yakitori, Vietnamese-style, is on the menu at the bustling restaurant that feels it could have been transported from the streets of Hanoi. The skewers here include chicken thigh on or off the bone, chicken feet, and gizzards, but also vegetables such as okra and sweet treats like banana. **Known for:** lively vibe; Vietnamese beer; Vietnamese grilled chicken. Ⓢ *Average main: ¥2,500* ⊠ *3-22-8 Koenji Kita, Suginami-ku* ☎ *03/3330–3992* ⊕ *namamen.com* ⊗ *Closed Tues. No lunch weekdays* Ⓜ *JR Chuo Line, Koenji Station.*

Dachibin (抱瓶)
$$ | JAPANESE | Koenji has many culinary bases covered, and with this izakaya it delivers Okinawan food and drink as authentically as you'll find in Japan's southern islands: thank the Okinawan owner for that. The menu features regional classics such as *goya champuru* (a stir fry of bitter gourd, spam, and tofu) and *soki soba* (noodles with pork sparerib meat), which you can chase down with Orion Beer and a firebrand of an island rice spirit called *awamori*. Like many Koenji venues, it runs late, opening daily from 5 pm to 5 am. **Known for:** opens till 5 am; awamori spirits; Okinawan dishes. Ⓢ *Average main: ¥3,000* ⊠ *3-2-13 Koenji Kita, Suginami-ku* ☎ *03/3337–1352* ⊕ *www.dachibin.com* ⊗ *No lunch* Ⓜ *JR Chuo Line, Koenji Station.*

Harukiya Ogikubo (春木屋)
$ | JAPANESE | Having started as a street stall in Ogikubo in the late 1940s, Harukiya is now a ramen restaurant that often has patrons lining up down the street. The noodles here come in a soy- and dried sardine-based stock and are served with a topping of *chashu* (roast pork) with the noodles being handmade every morning. **Known for:** long lines; excellent ramen; quick turnover of diners. Ⓢ *Average main: ¥850* ⊠ *1-4-6 Kamiogi, Suginami-ku* ☎ *03/3391–4868* ⊕ *www.haruki-ya.co.jp/english* ⊟ *No credit cards* ⊗ *Closed Tues.* Ⓜ *JR Chuo Line, Ogikubo Station and Marunouchi subway line, Ogikubo Station.*

☕ Coffee and Quick Bites

Hattifnatt (ハティフナット)

$$ | **CAFÉ** | If you needed proof that Koenji caters to all sorts of tastes, the cute Moomin-like drawings on the walls of this popular café, not to mention the lattes with cute cartoon faces drawn in the foam, show that Koenji has a soft side too. If you are hungry, try the pizzas or desserts, which include a pumpkin Mont Blanc. **Known for:** only open from noon to 6; pizza and desserts; good lattes. $ *Average main: ¥1,500* ✉ *2-18-10 Koenji Kita, Suginami-ku* ☎ *03/6762–8122* ⊕ *www.hattifnatt.jp* ⊟ *No credit cards* ⊘ *Closed Mon. No dinner* Ⓜ *JR Chuo Line, Koenji Station.*

Shopping

Asagaya Pearl Center
(阿佐谷パールセンター)

SHOPPING CENTER | Ignore the name (this isn't a pearl store), the Pearl Center is a classic *shotengai* (covered shopping arcade) running for just over half a kilometer (⅓ mile) on the south side of Asagaya Station. Like many shotengai, it houses a mishmash of stores, from cafés and small eateries to everyday goods stores and clothing shops. You will also find places selling kimonos, crafts, and traditional sweets. It's a great place to soak up some local flavor and possibly pick up a souvenir. Most stores open around 11 am. ✉ *1-36-7 Asagaya Minami, Suginami-ku* ⊕ *www.asagaya.or.jp.*

▼ Nightlife

BARS

Bar Mugen

BARS | This dimly lit basement bar has become a late-night haunt for anime fans. Beer, whisky, and cocktails are on the menu, while anime figurines dot the counter, and anime plays endlessly on the bar's TV. The owners have several thousand anime DVDs in their collection,

so you never know what will be on. ✉ *3-58-17 Koenji Minami, Suginami-ku* ☎ *03/6383–1643* ⊘ *Closed Sun.* Ⓜ *JR Chuo Line, Koenji Station.*

Cocktail Shobo (コクテイル書房)

BARS | This 100-year-old tenement house, all dark woods and creaking sounds, is one of Koenji's most unique bars. Part library (you can pick up and read any of the hundreds of books), it also serves cocktails and bar snacks, and even has some cocktails on the menu inspired by literary legends. Although it's only open after 6 on weekdays, it's also open from noon to 3 on weekends. ✉ *3-8-13 Koenji Kita, Suginami-ku* ☎ *03/3310–8130* ⊕ *www.koenji-cocktail.info* Ⓜ *JR Chuo Line, Koenji Station.*

Koenji Beer Kobo
(高円寺麦酒工房; *Koenji Bakushu Kobo*)

BREWPUBS | This small brewpub produces a frequently changing line-up of craft beers, often including pale ales and white beers. Whatever is on tap on any given day will be scrawled on chalkboards on the walls, as will the list of beer-friendly snacks. ✉ *2-24-8 Koenji Kita, Suginami-ku* ☎ *050/5487–7229* ⊕ *gf03407.gorp.jp* ⊘ *Closed Mon.* Ⓜ *JR Chuo Line, Koenji Station.*

LIVE MUSIC
Manhattan

LIVE MUSIC | If you want to experience Asagaya's jazz scene outside of the area's annual jazz festival, stop by this tiny, somewhat ramshackle jazz café. It was one of the areas first jazz venues when it opened several decades ago. Local musicians jam or perform here every night, in confines so narrow you might disrupt a gig trying to get to the toilet, but it's a very friendly hangout with a reputation for great music. There is a cover charge, which varies by the show. ✉ *2-2-7 Asagaya Kita, Suginami-ku* ☎ *03/3336–7961* ⊕ *ateliermw.com/manhattan/* ⊘ *Closed Mon. and Tues.* Ⓜ *JR Chuo Line, Asagaya Station.*

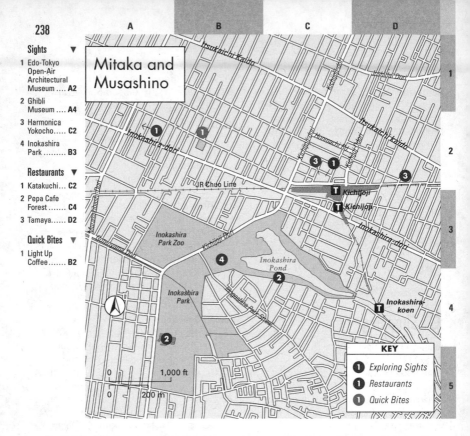

Mitaka and Musashino

KEY

- 1 *Exploring Sights*
- 1 *Restaurants*
- 1 *Quick Bites*

Showboat (ショーボート)

LIVE MUSIC | A small, basic venue in western Tokyo that been going strong since the late 1990s, Showboat attracts semi-professional and professional performers. Entry runs ¥2,000 to ¥5,000. ⊠ *Oak Hill Koenji, 3–17–2 Koenji Kita, B1, Suginami-ku* ☎ *03/3337–5745* ⊕ *www. showboat1993.com* Ⓜ *JR Sobu and JR Chuo lines, Koenji Station (Kita-guchi/ North Exit).*

🎭 Performing Arts

Asagaya Jazz Street Festival
(阿佐谷ジャズストリート)

FESTIVALS | Held the last weekend of October, this predominantly main-stream festival takes places in some less-than-mainstream venues, ranging from a Shinto shrine to a Lutheran church (most within walking distance of Asagaya Station). More than 200 bands and 1,300 musicians play, and previous headliners include the Mike Price Jazz Quintet and pianist Yosuke Yamashita. The festival gets crowded, so come early to ensure entry. ⊠ *4F, Wagafurusato-kan, 1–36–10 Asagaya-Minami, Suginami-ku* ☎ *03/5305–5075* ⊕ *asagayajazzstreets. com* Ⓜ *JR Chuo Line, Asagaya Station.*

Mitaka and Musashino

Directly west of Suginami, Mitaka and Musashino are two of the closest of West Tokyo's 26 *shi* (cities) to Tokyo's central 23 *ku* (districts) and in large part both feel much like an extension of the central sprawl. The main exception is leafy Inokashira Park, which straddles the Mitaka-Musashino border. In its southern Mitaka section, you find the superb Ghibli

The Edo-Tokyo Open-Air Architectural Museum brings together about 30 historic structures from around Tokyo that survived both the Great Kanto Earthquake and the destruction of World War II.

Museum, while the Musashino side includes a small zoo and boating pond. Then there's the fun neighborhood of Kichijoji immediately to the north of the park, a place packed with bars, cafés, and places to eat: locals will tell you it's the best night out in West Tokyo.

◉ Sights

Edo-Tokyo Open-Air Architectural Museum (江戸東京たてもの園; *Edo-Tokyo Tatemono-en*)

MUSEUM VILLAGE | Located in Koganei, just west of Mitaka, this outdoor museum has brought together 30 historic buildings from around Tokyo. Spread over three zones, there are thatched farmhouses from the late Edo-era and the former residences of politicians and magnates. You will also see charming everyday structures from central Tokyo that date to the late nineteenth and early twentieth centuries. The latter includes a traditional bathhouse, old-fashioned bar, and a soy-sauce shop. ⊠ *3-7-1 Sakuracho, Koganei, Tokyo* ⊹ *From Mitaka, take the*

Chuo Line two stops west to Higashi-Koganei Station. Buses run from outside the station to the Tatemono-en Iriguchi bus stop, from there it's a 7-min walk. ☎ *042/388–3300* ⊕ *www.tatemonoen. jp/english* ⊡ *¥400* ⊗ *Closed Mon.* Ⓜ *JR Chuo Line, Higashi-Koganei Station.*

Ghibli Museum (三鷹の森ジブリ美術館; *Mitaka no Mori Ghibli Bijutsukan*)

OTHER MUSEUM | FAMILY | With classics like *Spirited Away* and *My Neighbor Totoro*, Studio Ghibli has created many of the most loved animated movies in history: Japanese or other. At this museum-slash-theme park in suburban Mitaka—inside Inokashira Park—you can see exhibits that the trace the creative processes that take concepts to screen, while being surrounded by interiors inspired by Ghibli films. A real bonus for Studio Ghibli fans is the on-site cinema that shows short animations exclusive to the museum. It's open until 7 on weekends and holidays (otherwise until 5); admission is by reservation only (booked online). ⊠ *1-1-83 Shimorenjaku, Mitaka* ⊹ *It's a*

The lake in Inokashira Park is famous for its swan-shaped paddleboats, which draw locals from all over the city on weekends, especially during cherry blossom season.

15-min walk from either Mitaka Station or Kichijoji Station, but a Ghibli bus also runs every 10 to 20 min from bus stop number 9 outside Mitaka Station (¥310 return, ¥210 one-way) ☎ 0570/055–777 ⊕ www.ghibli-museum.jp/en ✉ ¥1,000 ⚠ Admission is by reservation only. Book a visit well ahead of time on the museum's website Ⓜ JR Chuo Line, Mitaka Station or Kichijoji Station.

Harmonica Yokocho (ハーモニカ横丁)

NEIGHBORHOOD | This cramped warren of alleyways on the north side of Kichijoji Station started life as a flea market in the 1940s, but then was given a much-needed new lease of life in the 1990s when bars and restaurants began taken up residency. It makes a great, less-touristy alternative for bar hopping than the far more famous Golden Gai area in Shinjuku. It has just as much of a down-to-earth, old-Tokyo vibe, albeit on a smaller scale. Some places open as early as 11 am, and most are open until midnight. ✉ 1-1 Kichijoji Honcho, Musashino ⊕ hamoyoko.jp/hamonika_kichijoji Ⓜ JR Chuo Line, Kichijoji Station.

Inokashira Park

(井の頭公園; *Inokashira Koen*)

CITY PARK | FAMILY | South of Kichijoji Station, with one foot in Mitaka and another in Musashino, this park is a large and laidback green space with all sorts to keep you busy for a day. Not only is the Ghibli Museum in the southernmost part of the almost 400,000-square meter (95-acre) park, there's a small zoo with a guinea pig petting area and a boating pond with swan-shaped paddle boats and row boats. On weekends, expect to see buskers and other street performers, while in spring, when the park is repainted by pink cherry blossoms, you'll find crowds of picnickers. It's a lovely spot to take a bento, but there are also small cafés and restaurants scattered around the park. If you are traveling with small kids who need to burn off some energy, the playground equipment here can help with that. ✉ 1-18-31 Gotenyama,

Musashino 🎫 *Park free, zoo ¥400* 🕒 *Zoo closed Mon.* [M] *JR Chuo Line, Mitaka Station or Kichijoji Station.*

🍴 Restaurants

Katakuchi (片口)

$$ | SUSHI | Here's proof that an intimate sushi experience doesn't have to be overly formal. Nor does it have to be expensive. **Known for:** laidback atmosphere; open daily for lunch and dinner; good-value sushi sets. [$] *Average main: ¥2,500* ✉ *1-1-1 Kichijoji Honcho, Musashino* ☎ *0422/21–3066* 💳 *No credit cards* [M] *JR Chuo Line, Kichijoji Station.*

Pepa Cafe Forest (ペパカフェフォレスト)

$$ | THAI | A good option for lunch, dinner, or a quick bite in Inokashira Park, Pepa cooks up Thai staples such as green curry, pad Thai noodles, and tom yum kung soup, but also has Vietnamese spring rolls, Vietnamese coffee, and bottled beer from around South East Asia on the menu. **Known for:** Vietnamese coffee; Thai staples; airy Thai beach house vibe. [$] *Average main: ¥2,000* ✉ *4-1-5 Inokashira, Mitaka* ☎ *0422/42–7081* [M] *JR Chuo Line, Mitaka Station or Kichijoji Station.*

Tamaya (たまや)

$$$ | JAPANESE | Yakitori and other chargrilled skewers of meat and vegetables are the name of the game at this smart izakaya that gets consistently excellent reviews from locals. To wash that down are highballs, draft lager, and a good selection of local sakes. **Known for:** Japan-made wine; good sake selection; char-grilled yakitori. [$] *Average main: ¥4,000* ✉ *1-34-2 Kichijoji Honcho, Musashino* ☎ *0422/27–6165* 🌐 *www.tamaya-kichijoji.com* [M] *JR Chuo Line, Kichijoji Station.*

☕ Coffee and Quick Bites

Light Up Coffee

$ | CAFÉ | Drop by this hipster hangout for hand-dripped coffee made with house-roasted beans, or lattes with artistic patterns in the foam. If you are really into your coffee, try the taster set to compare three different beans. **Known for:** mellow ambience; coffee taster sets; house-roasted beans. [$] *Average main: ¥500* ✉ *4-13-15 Kichijoji Honcho, Musashino* ☎ *0422/27–2094* 🌐 *lightupcoffee.com* 💳 *No credit cards* [M] *JR Chuo Line, Kichijoji Station.*

🍸 Nightlife

Ahiru Beer Hall (アヒルビアホール)

BARS | Don't let the name "beer hall" confuse you: this Harmonica Yokocho institution is shoulder-to-shoulder snug, as many of the best yokocho watering holes in Japan are, helping to make it a very convivial place for Belgian beers on tap, as well as sake and spirits. To go with your drinks, try the fish-and-chips. It's a small portion but done well. ✉ *1-1-2 Kichijoji Honcho, Musashino* ☎ *0422/20–6811* [M] *JR Chuo Line, Kichijoji Station.*

Baird Beer Taproom Kichijoji (ベアードタップルーム吉祥寺)

BREWPUBS | Baird Beer, one of Japan's leading microbrewers, opened this taproom in 2019. In keeping with Kichijoji's hip vibe, it's a small venue, but it packs a big punch with a fantastic line-up of Baird's year-round and limited release beers. Those include the hop-heavy Suruga Bay IPA, rich Kurofune Porter, and refreshing Wheat King Witte. It all goes well with the American soul food on the menu, such as tacos, burritos, and chili nachos. ✉ *2-10-15 Kichijoji Minamicho, Musashino* ☎ *0422/24–8691* 🌐 *bairdbeer.com/taprooms/kichijoji* 🕒 *Closed Mon. and Tues.* [M] *JR Chuo Line, Kichijoji Station.*

Chofu

One of the 26 *-shi* (city) in West Tokyo, Chofu is only 17 minutes by express train from high-octane Shinjuku, yet its small cluster of attractions—the historic Jindai-ji Temple and neighboring Jindai Botanical Gardens—feel worlds apart from central Tokyo. A visit is best done as a morning or afternoon side-trip while based in a more convenient central location (the area is also famous for its soba noodles). Just take the Keio Line from Shinjuku Station to Chofu Station, from where buses (or taxis) make the short trip to Jindai-ji Temple.

Sights

Jindai Botanical Gardens (神代植物公園; *Jindai Shokubutsu Koen*)
GARDEN | These large gardens are located a few minutes' walk from Jindai-ji Temple and are well worth an extra hour in Chofu. Across the grounds are roughly 100,000 plants, divided into sections covering varieties such as roses, azaleas, plum blossoms, cherry blossoms, begonias, and more. From spring to autumn there is always something beautiful in bloom. There's also a greenhouse with tropical and aquatic plants. ✉ *5-31-10 Jindaiji-motomachi, Chofu* ✛ *From the station, take buses from bus stop 12 to Jindai Shokubutsu Koen.* ☎ *042/483–2300* ⊕ *www.tokyo-park.or.jp/jindai* ✉ *¥500* ⊗ *Closed Mon.* Ⓜ *Keio Line, Chofu Station.*

★ **Jindai-ji Temple** (深大寺)
TEMPLE | Established in AD 733, Jindai-ji is the second-oldest temple in Tokyo, after Senso-ji in Asakusa. Like Senso-ji, fires have meant Jindai-ji has been through several rebuilds, most recently in the early 1900s, although its delightful wooden main gate still dates to 1695. That's where the comparisons end, because where Senso-ji is surrounded by urban sprawl, Jindai-ji is enshrouded in peaceful woods that help give the grounds a serene feeling. Instead of Senso-ji's bustling Nakamise-dori approach, Jindai-ji has the rustic Monzen-machi street lined with old wood buildings selling snacks and soba noodles.

The temple also feels more spiritual, especially if you come for the daily Goma fire ceremonies held in the main hall, where monks set alight sticks representing human desires to burn away the root of suffering. Arguably the highlight, however, is the bronze gilded statue of the Hakuhoh Buddha dating to the late Asuka Period (AD 592–710). Only 84 cm (33 inches) in height, it's nevertheless priceless. Yet, remarkably, it had been thought lost until 1909, when a monk found it hidden under one of the temple's floorboards.

Goma ceremonies last 30 minutes and are held at 11 and 2 on weekdays, 11, 1, and 2 on weekends. To have a stick burned on your behalf, apply at the main hall (¥3,000). ✉ *5-15-1 Jindai-ji-motomachi, Chofu* ✛ *From the station, take bus number 34 (from bus stop 14) to the Jindai-ji bus stop.* ☎ *042/486–5511* ⊕ *www.jindaiji.or.jp/en* ✉ *Temple free, Goma incense ¥3,000* Ⓜ *Keio Line, Chofu Station.*

Monzen-machi (門前町)
STREET | Many important temples around Japan developed temple-front streets full of restaurants and inns to serve the needs of pilgrims. Monzen-machi, meaning "gate-front town," is what's left of that for Jindai-ji Temple. It's a lovely, rustic street lined with small soba noodle shops and places selling souvenirs and snacks, such as steamed buns. ✉ *5-11-2 Jindaiji-motomachi, Chofu* Ⓜ *Keio Line, Chofu Station.*

Sanrio Puroland is devoted to the famously cute Hello Kitty.

🍴 Restaurants

Ikkyu-An (一休庵)
$ | JAPANESE | Soba noodles, which are made with buckwheat, are a signature of the restaurants near Jindai-ji. That's apparently because buckwheat was traditionally easier to grow here than rice. **Known for:** close to the main sights; rustic vibe; soba noodles. [$] *Average main: ¥1,050* ✉ *5-11-2 Jindaiji-motomachi, Chofu* ☎ *042/482–6773* 🌐 *jindaiji19an.com* 💳 *No credit cards* ⏲ *Closed Mon. No dinner* [M] *Keio Line, Chofu Station.*

☕ Coffee and Quick Bites

Ameya (あめや)
$ | JAPANESE | Ameya is a traditional sweet and snack store on Monzen-machi best known for a riff on the local soba theme. You don't get soba noodles here, but rather "soba bread." Basically, it's a steamed bun made with buckwheat (soba) flour, sugar, and rice flour, in which you can have one of four fillings: sweet red bean paste (*anko*), mustard greens (*takana*), daikon radish, and the very non-traditional keema curry. **Known for:** soba bread (steamed buns); traditional setting; take-out only. [$] *Average main: ¥300* ✉ *5-15-10 Jindaiji-motomachi, Chofu* ☎ *042/485–2768* 💳 *No credit cards* ⏲ *No dinner* [M] *Keio Line, Chofu Station.*

Tama

Heading farther west from Chofu, Tama City is another suburban part of west Tokyo worth a visit for a small handful of attractions. Known for its leafy parks and peaceful residential areas, Tama is also home to the Sanrio Puroland theme park: a mecca for all things Hello Kitty. That and nearby sights, such as Tama Zoo, are easy to do as a half-day or day trip while staying in central Tokyo. To get started, just take the Keio Line or Odakyu Line from Shinjuku Station to Tama Center Station (30 minutes).

👁 Sights

Gokuraku-yu Baths (極楽湯)

HOT SPRING | FAMILY | For some traditional Japanese relaxation, head to this smart hot-spring facility a couple of minutes south of Sanrio Puroland. Gokuraku Yu combines nine indoor and outdoor baths (gender-separated), as well as a sauna and a salon that offers body massages and facial treatments. There's also a restaurant on-site serving soba noodles, simple teishoku sets, and sweet treats. ✉ 1-30-1 Ochiai, Tama ☎ 042/357–8626 🌐 www.gokurakuyu.ne.jp/tempo/tamacenter 🎫 ¥880 weekdays, ¥980 weekends and public holidays (towel rental ¥220) Ⓜ Keio, Odakyu, and Tama Monorail lines, Tama Center Station.

Sanrio Puroland (サンリオピューロランド)

AMUSEMENT PARK/CARNIVAL | FAMILY | As a theme park dedicated to the world's most famous white feline—Hello Kitty, of course—Sanrio Puroland is effectively a shrine to the concept of cuteness. An all-day passport allows for unlimited use of multiple attractions, including three theaters, a boat ride, and the Lady Kitty House—one of many attractions seemingly designed for taking selfies. Pens, packaged snacks, and plush toys are readily available so guests don't leave empty-handed. ✉ 1–31 Ochiai, Tama-shi, Tama ☎ 042/339–1111 🌐 en.puroland.jp 🎫 ¥3,600 weekdays; ¥3,900 weekends and holidays Ⓜ Keio Line, Tama Center Station.

Tama Art University Museum (多摩美術大学美術館; Tama Bijutsu Daigaku Bijutsukan)

ART MUSEUM | Another attraction almost next door to Sanrio Puroland, this museum has an eclectic collection on display. You'll find fine art, prints, sculpture, photography, and even crafts, largely by artists with a connection to the university since it was established in the 1930s. ✉ 1-33-1 Ochiai, Tama ☎ 042/357–1251 🌐 museum.tamabi.ac.jp 🎫 ¥300 🕙 Closed Tues. Ⓜ Keio, Odakyu, and Tama Monorail lines, Tama Center Station.

Tama Zoo (多摩動物園; Tama Dobutsuen)

ZOO | FAMILY | More a wildlife park than a zoo, this facility in Hino City (just north of Tama) gives animals room to roam; moats typically separate them from you, although for an additional fee you can take a bus ride through the lion enclosure for an up-close experience. To get here from Tama's main sights, take the Tama Monorail four stops from Tama Center Station to Tamadobutsu-koen Station. ✉ 7–1–1 Hodokubo, Hino ☎ 042/591–1611 🌐 www.tokyo-zoo.net/english/tama 🎫 ¥600, Lion enclosure bus ¥500 🕙 Closed Wed. Ⓜ Tama Monorail, Tamadobutsu-koen Station.

Chapter 11

AKIHABARA

Updated by
Rob Goss

👁 Sights	🍴 Restaurants	🛏 Hotels	💼 Shopping	🍸 Nightlife
★★☆☆☆	★★☆☆☆	★★☆☆☆	★★★★☆	★☆☆☆☆

AKIHABARA SNAPSHOT

TOP EXPERIENCES

■ **Geek out over games.** Known as a mecca for gamers, anime fans, and anyone into electronics, Akihabara is overflowing with shops large and small.

■ **Celebrate in the streets.** A visit in May must include the Kanda Festival—one of Tokyo's major street celebrations. More than 200 portable shrines are carried in a parade towards the grounds of the Kanda Myojin Shrine.

■ **Browse an eccentric collection.** Check out the toys, electronic gadgets, and hobby items at Radio Kaikan, a vertical bazaar.

GETTING HERE

Akihabara is northeast of the Imperial Palace, right below Ueno and Asakusa. From Tokyo Station, Akihabara is two stops (four minutes) north on the JR Yamanote Line, which also connects Akihabara to Shinjuku in 18 minutes. The Akihabara area is also served by the Hibiya, and Tsukuba lines.

Away from the otaku, in areas neighboring Akihabara, is a collection of sights worth lingering for. Located a couple of kilometers to the west of Akihabara, the used book district of Jimbocho could be a very short stopover either before or after an excursion to Akihabara. The best way to get there is by taxi, which should cost about ¥800 to or from Akihabara Station.

Just north of Jimbocho, Suidobashi is also worth a detour for Koishikawa Korakuen Garden and the Tokyo Dome City amusement park. The JR Sobu Line connects Suidobashi and Akihabara stations, or you could walk there following the Kanda River.

PLANNING YOUR TIME

Keep in mind that most stores in Akihabara do not open until 10 am. Weekends draw hordes of shoppers, especially on Sunday, when the four central blocks of Chuo-dori are closed to traffic and become a pedestrian mall.

OFF THE BEATEN PATH

■ While Akihabara is all about otaku culture and home electronics, neighboring areas provide very different experiences. A couple of miles east, **Koishikawa Korakuen Garden** is a prime example. One of Tokyo's oldest and prettiest gardens, its trails lead visitors through a succession of scenic spots designed to reproduce famous Japanese and Chinese scenery. It also has some inadvertent 'borrowed scenery" now that the Tokyo Dome City entertainment complex looms large next door. If you can, come in fall for the vibrant foliage, or in spring when the cherry blossoms are in bloom.

VIEW POINT

■ Akihabara is always full of color, but it feels especially vibrant when parts of Chuo-dori are made pedestrian-only on Sunday afternoons (from 1 to 6 pm). Not only do you have all of Chuo-dori's colorful storefronts and neon signs as a backdrop, but the streets fill up with all sorts of characters, from shoppers to cosplayers and maids handing out flyers for their cafés.

Akihabara is techno-geek heaven. Also known as Akihabara Electric Town, or more commonly by denizens as just Akiba, this district was once a dizzying collection of small, ultra-specialized electronics and computer shops, but has now become the center of Japan's anime, manga, and computer-focused *otaku* (nerd) culture.

More recently, the area has gained mainstream appeal among shoppers and tourists, with large all-in-one electronics shops crowding out many of the smaller and unique stores. Even so, the area has stayed true to its roots. Venture off the main road to see the real Akiba, where maid cafés (where servers are yes, dressed as maids and treat their customers as "masters and mistresses") mix with computer and hi-fi audio stores filled with dedicated fans searching for computer parts, rare comics, or techno-accessories they can't find anywhere else. For visitors, seeing the subculture and energy of Akiba is as much a draw as the shopping.

If you're looking for something a little more cerebral, head to Jimbocho, where family-run specialty bookstores of every genre abound. A number of antiquarian booksellers carry rare typeset editions, woodblock-printed books of the Edo period, and individual prints. The bookstores run for ½ km (¼ mile) on Yasukuni-dori beginning at the Surugadaishita intersection. Many of Japan's most prestigious publishing houses make their home in Jimbocho as well, and the area is also home to Meiji University and Nihon University.

Akihabara

 ## Sights

Kanda Myojin Shrine (神田明神)
RELIGIOUS BUILDING | This shrine is said to have been founded in AD 730 in a village called Shibasaki, where the Otemachi financial district stands today. The shrine itself was destroyed in the Great Kanto Earthquake of 1923, and the present buildings reproduce in concrete the style of 1616. Next door is the Edo Culture Complex, where you check in for your visit and can see cultural displays on the era when Samurai flourished.

You will never be able to see every shrine in the city, and the ones in Akihabara are of minor interest unless you are around for the Kanda Festival—one of Tokyo's three great blowouts—in mid-May. (The other two are the Sanno Festival of Hie Jinja in Nagata-cho and the Sanja Festival of Asakusa Shrine.) Some of the smaller buildings you see as you come up the steps and walk around the Main Hall contain the *mikoshi*—the portable shrines that are featured during the festival. ✉ *2–16–2 Soto-Kanda, Chiyoda-ku*

☎ 03/3254-0753 ⊕ www.kandamyoujin. or.jp 🎫 Museum ¥300 Ⓜ Ginza subway line, Suehiro-cho Station (Exit 3).

Koishikawa Korakuen Gardens (小石川後楽園)

GARDEN | Built in the 1600s as part of a feudal lord's residence, Koishikawa Korakuen is one of Tokyo's oldest gardens. Design wise, this stroll garden attempts to reproduce famous Japanese and Chinese landscapes in miniature, using rocks, water features, carefully tended trees, and manmade hills. Like other classic Japanese gardens, it also changes its appearance seasonally, with highlights including pink cherry blossoms in spring and the reds, oranges, and yellows of maple and gingko trees in fall. ✉ 1-6-6 Koraku, Bunkyo-ku ☎ 03/3811-3015 ⊕ www.tokyo-park.or.jp/teien/en/koishikawa 🎫 ¥300 Ⓜ JR Sobu Line, Toei Oedo Line and multiple Tokyo Metro subway lines, Iidabashi Station.

Nikolai-do Holy Resurrection Cathedral (ニコライ堂;)

CHURCH | You may be surprised to see a Russian Orthodox cathedral in Tokyo's Electric Town, but the church came long before electronics were ever invented, much less sold here. Formally, this is the Holy Resurrection Cathedral, derived from its founder, St. Nikolai Kassatkin (1836-1912), a Russian missionary who came to Japan in 1861 and spent the rest of his life here. The building, planned by a Russian engineer and executed by a British architect, was completed in 1891. Heavily damaged in the earthquake of 1923, the cathedral was restored with a dome much more modest than the original. Even so, the cathedral endows this otherwise featureless part of the city with unexpected charm. ✉ 4-1-3 Kanda Surugadai, Chiyoda-ku ☎ 03/3295-6879 ⊕ nikolaido.org/en Ⓜ Chiyoda subway line, Shin-Ochanomizu Station (Exit B1).

Kanda Festival

The mid-May Kanda Festival at Kanda Myojin Shrine began in the early Edo period, and today is held on a grand scale in odd-numbered years (the "Hon-matsuri"), with a smaller version ("Kage-matsuri") in even-numbered years. The floats that lead the procession today move in stately measure on wheeled carts, attended by the shrine's priests and officials. The portable Shinto shrines (mikoshi), some 200 of them when the full event is held, follow behind, carried on the shoulders of the townspeople.

Tokyo Dome City (東京ドームシティ)

AMUSEMENT PARK/CARNIVAL | FAMILY | Billing itself as an "urban entertainment zone" the Tokyo Dome City complex hosts a small amusement park, restaurants, shops, a hot spring and spa, as well as Tokyo Dome itself. The outside amusement park has a selection of rides for children, though the Thunder Dolphin roller coaster is a thrill at any age. The Spa LaQua hot spring makes for a relaxing end to a day of sightseeing, offering a selection of baths and saunas. Tokyo Dome itself is home to the Tokyo Giants baseball team and frequently holds concerts and other events. ✉ 1-3-61 Koraku, Bunkyo-ku ☎ 03/5800-9999 ⊕ www.tokyo-dome.co.jp/en/tourists 🎫 Amusement park day-pass ¥4,200, Spa LaQua ¥2,900 Ⓜ JR Sobu Line, Suidobashi Station; Marunouchi and Namboku subway lines, Korakuen Station.

Yushima Seido Shrine (湯島聖堂)

RELIGIOUS BUILDING | The origins of this shrine date to a hall, founded in 1632, for the study of the Chinese Confucian classics. Its headmaster was Hayashi Razan, the official Confucian scholar to the Tokugawa government. Moved to

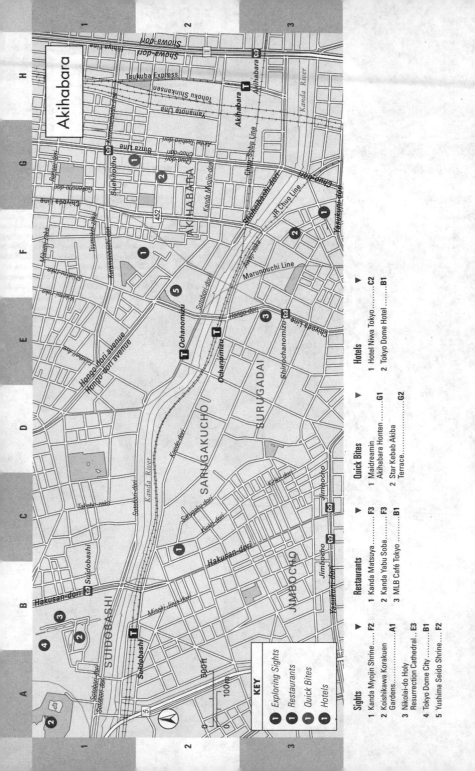

Akihabara

KEY

- 1 Exploring Sights
- 1 Restaurants
- 1 Quick Bites
- 1 Hotels

Sights ▶
1 Kanda Myojin Shrine **F2**
2 Koishikawa Korakuen
  Gardens **A1**
3 Nikolai-do Holy
  Resurrection Cathedral .. **E3**
4 Tokyo Dome City **B1**
5 Yushima Seido Shrine **F2**

Restaurants ▶
1 Kanda Matsuya **F3**
2 Kanda Yabu Soba **F3**
3 MLB Café Tokyo **B1**

Quick Bites ▶
1 Maidreamin
  Akihabara Honten **G1**
2 Star Kebab Akiba
  Terrace **G2**

Hotels ▶
1 Hotel Niwa Tokyo **C2**
2 Tokyo Dome Hotel **B1**

its present site in 1691 (and destroyed by fire and rebuilt six times), the hall became an academy for the ruling elite. In a sense, nothing has changed: in 1872 the new Meiji government established the country's first teacher-training institute here, and that, in turn, evolved into Tokyo University—the graduates of which still make up much of the ruling elite. The hall looks like nothing else you're likely to see in Japan: painted black, weathered, and somber, it could almost be in China. ✉ *1-4-25 Yushima, Bunkyo-ku* ☎ *03/3251-4606* 🌐 *www.seido.or.jp* 🎫 *Free* 🕘 *Closed Aug. 13-17 and Dec. 29-31* [M] *JR Sobu Line and Marunouchi subway line, Ochanomizu Station.*

🍴 Restaurants

Kanda Matsuya (神田まつや)
$ | **JAPANESE** | Soba, thin buckwheat noodles often served chilled in summer and hot in winter, are available everywhere, even convenience stores. The family-run Matsuya serves authentic soba in a rustic atmosphere. **Known for:** authentic hand-cut noodles; tempura soba; lunchtime crowds. [$] *Average main: ¥1,000* ✉ *1-13 Kanda Sudacho, Chiyoda-ku* ☎ *03/3251-1556* 💳 *No credit cards* 🕘 *Closed Sun.* [M] *Marunouchi Line, Awajicho Station (Exit A3).*

Kanda Yabu Soba (かんだやぶそば)
$ | **JAPANESE** | The ever-popular Kanda Yabu Soba, located in a recently built but traditional building that replaced the original 130-year-old restaurant after a fire in 2013, is one of the oldest and best places to sit down and savor freshly made soba—be that on tatami or at one of the tables. Soba, thin noodles made from buckwheat flour and quickly dipped into a hot broth or cold dipping sauce, are the lighter cousin of udon. **Known for:** excellent rotating seasonal set; soba sushi rolls; historic atmosphere. [$] *Average main: ¥1,000* ✉ *2-10 Kanda Awajicho, Chiyoda-ku* ☎ *03/3251-0287* 🌐 *www.yabusoba.net* 💳 *No credit cards* 🕘 *Closed Wed.* [M] *JR and Marunouchi lines, Awajicho Station (Exit A3).*

MLB Café Tokyo
$$ | **AMERICAN | FAMILY** | Located in the shadow of Tokyo Dome, the primary baseball stadium in Tokyo, this theme restaurant is filled with sports memorabilia and waitstaff dressed in baseball uniforms. With a lineup similar to a Hard Rock Cafe or TGI Friday's it is a good stop for sports-loving kids. **Known for:** a place for baseball fans to catch up on MLB games; sizable burgers; the taste and feel of America as imagined by Japan. [$] *Average main: ¥2,000* ✉ *1-3-17 Kora-ku, Bunkyo-ku* ☎ *03/5840-8905* 🌐 *www.mlbcafe.jp* [M] *JR Sobu and Toei Mita subway lines, Suidobashi Station (Exit A5).*

☕ Coffee and Quick Bites

Maidreamin Akihabara Honten (めいどりーみん秋葉原本店)
$$ | **CAFÉ** | Maid cafés won't be everyone's cup of tea, but if you do want to try one out, this main branch of Japan's biggest maid café chain is as reputable a place as any. All manner of people come to be served by young women in French maid outfits who affect extreme levels of *kawaii* (cute) and occasionally break into song and dance. **Known for:** the quintessential hyper-kawaii maid café experience; colorful parfaits; omuraisu (rice omlets). [$] *Average main: ¥2,500* ✉ *3-16-17 Soto-Kanda, Chiyoda-ku* ☎ *0120/229-348* 🌐 *maidreamin.com/multilp* ☞ *¥770 admission fee* [M] *JR Yamanote Line, Akihabara Station.*

Star Kebab Akiba Terrace (スターケバブ)
$ | **FAST FOOD** | If you need a break from shopping for electronics and games, a spicy kebab sandwich from Star Kebab should do the trick. This branch and other outlets in the area offer beef, lamb, or chicken strips, lettuce, and tomatoes in pita pockets. **Known for:** inexpensive kebab sandwiches; take-out only; long opening hours (11 am to 9 pm

daily). $ *Average main: ¥600* ⊠ *1–8–10 Soto-Kanda, Chiyoda-ku* ☎ *03/6804–8330* ⊕ *www.kebab.co.jp* ▬ *No credit cards* Ⓜ *JR Yamanote Line, Akihabara Station.*

🛏 Hotels

Hotel Niwa Tokyo (庭のホテル 東京; *Niwa no Hoteru Tokyo*)
$$ | HOTEL | Traditional and contemporary elements come together to make the Niwa Tokyo a prized little boutique hotel in the middle of the city. **Pros:** quiet area; central location; charming Japanese touches. **Cons:** small rooms; finding entrance is a bit challenging; few major sights within walking distance. $ *Rooms from: ¥18,000* ⊠ *1–1–16 Misaki-cho, Chiyoda-ku* ☎ *03/3293–0028* ⊕ *www. hotelniwa.jp* ➷ *238 rooms* ⦿*No Meals* Ⓜ *JR Chuo or Sobu lines, Suido-bashi Station (East Exit); Mita subway line, Suido-bashi Station (Exit A1).*

Tokyo Dome Hotel (東京ドームホテル)
$$ | HOTEL | FAMILY | Next to the city's most popular sports facility, the Tokyo Dome Hotel has a great location for sports fans at a comfortable price and offers easy train access to most of central Tokyo. **Pros:** convenient location; solid value; great for kids. **Cons:** being part of an entertainment complex, the immediate surroundings lack local flavor; rooms are a little bland; surrounding area is very crowded during events at Tokyo Dome. $ *Rooms from: ¥21,000* ⊠ *1–3–61 Koraku, Bunkyo-ku* ☎ *03/5805–2111* ⊕ *www.tokyodome-ho-tels.co.jp/e* ➷ *1,006 rooms* ⦿*No Meals* Ⓜ *JR lines, Suidobashi Station (East Exit); Namboku and Marunouchi subway lines, Korakuen Station.*

🎭 Performing Arts

MODERN THEATER
Tokyo Dome (東京ドーム)
CONCERTS | FAMILY | A 45,852-seat sports arena, the dome also hosts big-name Japanese pop acts as well as the occasional international star. ⊠ *1–3–61 Koraku,* *Bunkyo-ku* ☎ *03/5800–9999* ⊕ *www. tokyo-dome.co.jp/e* Ⓜ *Marunouchi and Namboku subway lines, Koraku-en Station (Exit 2); Mita subway line, Suido-bashi Station (Exit A5); JR Suido-bashi Station (Nishi-guchi/West Exit).*

PERFORMING ARTS CENTERS
Bunkyo Civic Hall (文京シビックホール)
MUSIC | This three-story, city-run performance hall showcases classical music and ballet, opera, dance, and drama. Visitors might be especially interested in performances of local interest featuring puppets, wind music, and Japanese Kabuki dance. ⊠ *1–16–21 Kasuga, Bun-kyo-ku* ☎ *03/5803–1100, 03/5803–1111 tickets only* ⊕ *www.b-academy.jp/hall* Ⓜ *Marunouchi and Namboku subway lines, Kourakuen Station (Exit 5).*

🛍 Shopping

Akihabara was at one time the only place Tokyoites would go to buy cutting-edge electronic gadgets, but the area has lost its aura of exclusivity thanks to the Internet and the big discount chains that have sprung up around the city. Still, for sheer variety of products and foreigner-friendliness, Akihabara has the newcomers beat—and a visit remains essential to any Tokyo shopping spree. Be sure to poke around the backstreets for smaller stores that sell used and unusual electronic goods. The area has also become the center of the *otaku* (nerd) boom, with loads of shops selling enough video games and manga to satisfy even the most fastidious geek.

ANTIQUES
Yasukuni Jinja Market (靖国神社青空骨董市; *Yasukuni Jinja Aozora Kottou Ichi*)
ANTIQUES & COLLECTIBLES | Most Sundays, from sunrise to sunset, antiques hunters can search and explore this flea market, which boasts 30–50 booths run by professional collectors. It's located within the controversial Yasukuni Jinja grounds, so when you're finished shopping, stroll

Akihibara is Tokyo's mecca for electronics, anime, manga, and gaming goods.

through the shrine that pays respect to dead Japanese soldiers. ⊠ *3–1–1 Kudan-Kita, Chiyoda-ku* ☎ *03/3261–8326* ⊕ *www.yasukuni.or.jp/english/index.html* Ⓜ *Hanzomon and Shinjuku subway lines, Kudanshita Station (Exit 1).*

BOOKS

The site of more than 180 used-book stores, the **Jimbocho** area is a bibliophile's dream. In the ½-km (¼-mile) strip along Yasukuni-dori and its side streets you can find centuries-old Japanese prints, vintage manga, and even complete sets of the Oxford English Dictionary. Most shops have predominately Japanese-language selections, but almost all stock some foreign titles, with a few devoting major floor space to English books. **Kitazawa**, recognizable by its stately entranceway, carries lots of humanities titles. The large Japanese publisher **Sanseido** has its flagship store here; the fifth floor sells magazines and postcards in addition to books. **Magnif** specializes in vintage design magazine issues from around the world. The stores in the area

are usually open 9 or 9:30 to 5:30 or 6, and many of the smaller shops close Sunday or Monday.

Kitazawa Bookstore

(北沢書店; *Kitazawa Shoten*)
BOOKS | Specializing in rare prints, academic texts, and literature, Kitazawa Shoten has been selling books since 1902. The floor-to-ceiling dark wood bookshelves stacked with hardcovers are overflowing—sometimes quite literally—with interesting finds. ⊠ *Kitazawa Bldg., 2–5 Kanda Jimbocho, 2F, Chiyoda-ku* ☎ *03/3236–0011* ☉ *Closed Sun.* Ⓜ *Hanzomon, Mita, and Shinjuku subway Lines, Jimbocho Station.*

Magnif (マグニフ)

BOOKS | This tiny shop is crammed with vintage magazines from all over the world, interspersed with photography books. There is a heavy focus on fashion, culture, and lifestyle magazines. ⊠ *1–17 Kanda Jimbocho, Chiyoda-ku* ☎ *03/5280–5911* ⊕ *www.magnif.jp* Ⓜ *Hanzomon, Mita, and Shinjuku subway lines, Jimbocho Station.*

COSTUMES

Cospatio (コスパティオ)

OTHER SPECIALTY STORE | Serious cosplayers need serious costumes and this cosplay specialty store is where they shop for serious supplies. Anime, manga, video game characters? You'll find them all here, and more, especially as Cospatio shares the fourth floor of its building with a handful of other geeky stores, as well as a maid café. ✉ *Onoden Bldg, 1-2-7 Soto-Kanda, 4F, Chiyoda-ku* ☎ *03/3526–6877* ⊕ *www.cospatio.com* Ⓜ *JR Yamanote Line, Akihabara Station (Akihabara Electric Town Exit).*

ELECTRONICS

LAOX Akihabara Main Shop (LAOX 秋葉原本店; *LAOX Akihabara Honten*)

ELECTRONICS | One of the big Akihabara department stores, LAOX has several locations and the largest and most comprehensive selection in the district, with four buildings. The seven-story main branch is duty-free, with three floors dedicated to electronic gadgets, such as lightweight vacuum cleaners and eco-friendly humidifiers, that come with English instruction booklets. LAOX has annexes—one exclusively for musical instruments, another for duty-free appliances—and outlets in Ginza, Odaiba, and Narita Airport. This is a good place to find the latest in digital cameras, watches, and games. ■TIP➔ **English-speaking staff members are on call.** ✉ *1–2–9 Soto-Kanda, Chiyoda-ku* ☎ *03/3253–7111* ⊕ *www. laox.co.jp* Ⓜ *JR Yamanote Line, Akihabara Station (Electric Town Exit).*

Radio Kaikan (ラジオ会館)

ELECTRONICS | Eight floors featuring a variety of independent vendors selling mini–spy cameras, cell phones disguised as stun guns, manga, plastic models, gadgets, and oddball hobby supplies are sold here. Start browsing from the top floor and work your way down. There are two annexes across the street as well. ✉ *1–15–16 Soto-Kanda, Chiyoda-ku* ☎ *03/3251–3711* ⊕ *www.akihabara-radiokaikan. co.jp* Ⓜ *JR Yamanote Line, Akihabara Station (Akihabara Electric Town Exit).*

Sofmap (ソフマップ)

ELECTRONICS | One Akihabara retailer that actually benefited from the bursting of Japan's economic bubble in the early 1990s is this electronics chain, once known as a used-PC and software chain with a heavy presence in Tokyo. Now its multiple branches also sell all sorts of new electronics, music, and mobile phones. Most are open daily until 8. ✉ *3–13–12 Soto-Kanda, Chiyoda-ku* ☎ *050/3032–9888* ⊕ *www.sofmap.com* Ⓜ *JR Yamanote Line, Akihabara Station (Electric Town Exit).*

Thanko Rare Mono Shop (サンコー)

ELECTRONICS | As the king of wacky electronics from Japan, Thanko sells everything from bamboo smartphone cases and smokeless ashtrays to summer neck coolers and wireless charging stations disguised as jewelry. This showroom and its other branches are a must-see for gadget geeks. ✉ *3–14–8 Soto-Kanda, Chiyoda-ku* ☎ *03/5297–5783* ⊕ *www.thanko.jp* Ⓜ *JR Yamanote Line, Akihabara Station (Akihabara Electric Town Exit).*

TOYS

Kyugetsu (九月)

OTHER SPECIALTY STORE | In business for more than a century, Kyugetsu sells handcrafted Japanese dolls. Each piece is individually made by one of Kyugetsu's artisans making for a unique—albeit expensive—souvenir. Dolls run from a few hundred to thousands of dollars. ✉ *1-20-4 Yanagibashi, Taito-ku* ☎ *03/5687–5176* ⊕ *www.kyugetsu.com/e* Ⓜ *Asakusa subway line, JR Sobu Line, Asakusa-bashi Station (Exit A3).*

Chapter 12

UENO AND YANAKA

Updated by
Jay Farris

⊙ Sights	🍴 Restaurants	🛏 Hotels	🛍 Shopping	🍸 Nightlife
★★★★☆	★★☆☆☆	★★☆☆☆	★★★☆☆	★★☆☆☆

UENO AND YANAKA SNAPSHOT

TOP EXPERIENCES

■ **Hit the top museums.** Ueno has Tokyo's top museums, including the Tokyo National Museum and the National Museum of Western Art.

■ **Get a glimpse of old Tokyo.** Stroll through Yanaka, taking in the temples and old houses, galleries, and cafés in the only surviving Tokyo neighborhood with its traditional wooden buildings still intact.

■ **See a shining shrine.** Dating back to 1627, the Tosho-gu Shrine is a National Treasure of Japan that houses a priceless collection of historical art and is one of the few remaining early-Edo-period buildings in Tokyo.

■ **Witness a lotus display.** From mid-June through August, Shinobazu-ike (Shinobazu Pond) is the only place in Tokyo where you'll see such a vast expanse of lotus flowers in bloom.

GETTING HERE

Ueno Station can be accessed by train on the Hibiya Line, Ginza Line, and JR Yamanote and some suburban lines. Yanaka is a short walk from the north end of Ueno Park and can also be accessed from Nippori Station (West Exit). Be sure to avoid rush hours in the morning (8–9) and evening (6–9) and bring cash for the smaller shops. Museums accept some major credit cards for admission and in their stores.

PLANNING YOUR TIME

Ueno and Yanaka, along with Asakusa, make up the historical enclave of Tokyo. Though the Tokyo Skytree transmission tower can be seen from nearly all parts of these neighborhoods, a slower way of life are preserved here at the northeastern reaches of the city, and if you're interested in the narrow streets and wooden architecture of old Tokyo, then Yanaka is your place.

It is best to devote an entire day to fully appreciate the area, but avoid Monday, when most of the museums are closed. In April, the cherry blossoms of Ueno Park are glorious, but Yanaka Cemetery is just as spectacular and less crowded than the park.

PAUSE HERE

■ Near Nezu Station and adjacent to the Yanaka neighborhood, Nezu Shrine can be a great resting point on a walk from Ueno Park. The shrine is likely the oldest surviving building in Tokyo and has a fascinating history, but its hillside of azaleas are beautiful in May, and the shaded, quiet seating areas a welcome break from summer heat.

YOSHIDA-YA SAKE SHOP

■ Another shady area to take a break is Yoshida-ya Sake Shop, the city's preserved historical sake shop, which was built in 1910. You'll find it just across from Kayaba Coffee and just south of Yanaka Cemetery. Inside you can see old barrels of sake and browse leaflets on local spots, or just enjoy the shade of the courtyard.

Located in the heart of Ueno, JR Ueno Station is Tokyo's version of Paris's Gare du Nord: the gateway to and from Japan's northeast provinces. Since its completion in 1883, the station has served as a terminus in a great migration to the city by villagers in pursuit of work or to sell their wares.

Ueno was a place of prominence long before the coming of the railroad. After Tokugawa Ieyasu established his capital here in 1603, 36 subsidiary temples were erected surrounding the Main Hall, and the city of Edo itself expanded to the foot of the hill where the main gate of Kanei-ji once stood. Some of the most important buildings in the temple complex have survived or have been restored and should not be missed. After the railroad terminus was completed, the open spaces around religious sites became a kind of market and Ueno Park later became Tokyo's first park. The market mood can still be felt along Ameyokocho.

A short walk from the north end of Ueno Park, Yanaka is one of Tokyo's most charming neighborhoods and the only area in the city that survived both the 1923 earthquake and the WWII firebombing. The area developed during the Edo period, when a number of prominent temples were moved here to save them from the rather frequent fires that broke out in more crowded areas. The abundance of temples makes for an excellent walk, and their cemeteries served as firebreaks. Most of what you'll want to see is to the west of Yanaka Cemetery and south of Yanaka Ginza, a colorful shopping street with a whole variety of goods.

Wander down the winding backstreets to enjoy a surprise or sense of wonder as you turn a corner to find a quiet temple garden or a Buddhist service in session. Over time, craftspeople made the neighborhood home, and galleries and cafés have joined the traditional wooden houses and temples making the area perfect for a stroll. Typically in October, the area hosts the Yanaka Geikoten, a weeks-long arts-and-craft festival when artisans open the doors to their workshops, and galleries hold special events.

Ueno

Sights

Ameya Yokocho Market Street (アメヤ横丁)
MARKET | The sprawling stalls are famous for the traditional prepared foods of the New Year celebrations; during the last few days of December, as many as half a million people crowd into the narrow alleys under the railroad tracks to stock up for the holiday. The market dates to World War II, when not much besides Ueno Station survived the bombings. People would travel from the countryside to sell rice at black-market prices. Before long, there were hundreds of stalls in the

The "ame" in Ame-ya Yoko-cho Market also means "American," referencing the many American products sold during the area's black market era.

black market selling various kinds of *ame* (confections), most made from sweet potatoes, earning the market its name, Ame-ya Yoko-cho (Ameyoko, locally), or "Confectioners' Alley." Shortly before the Korean War, the market was legalized, and soon the stalls were carrying watches, chocolate, ballpoint pens, blue jeans, and T-shirts that had somehow been "liberated" from American PXs. In years to come you'd find Swiss timepieces and fake designer luggage, cosmetics, jewelry, fresh fruit, and fish. Try the raw slices of tuna over rice (*maguro-don*) in one of the small restaurants—cheap, quick, and very good. ⊠ *Ueno 4-chome, Taito-ku* Ⓜ *JR Ueno Station (Hiroko-ji Exit).*

Kiyomizu Kannon-do Temple (清水観音堂)

TEMPLE | This National Treasure was a part of Abbot Tenkai's attempt to build a copy of Kyoto's magnificent Kiyomizu-dera in Ueno. His attempt was honorable, but failed to be as impressive as the original. The principal Buddhist image of worship here is the Senju Kannon (Thousand-Armed Goddess of Mercy).

Another figure, however, receives greater homage. This is the Kosodate Kannon, who is believed to answer the prayers of women having difficulty conceiving children. If their prayers are answered, they return to Kiyomizu and leave a doll, as both an offering of thanks and a prayer for the child's health. In a ceremony held every September 25, the dolls that have accumulated during the year are burned in a bonfire. ⊠ *1–29 Ueno Koen, Taito-ku* ☏ *03/3821–4749* 🎫 *Free* Ⓜ *JR Ueno Station (Koen-guchi/Park Exit).*

Marishiten Tokudai-ji Temple (摩利支天徳大寺)

TEMPLE | This is a curiosity in a neighborhood of curiosities: a temple on the second floor of a supermarket. Two deities are worshipped here. One is the *bodhisattva* (a being that has deferred its own ascendance into Buddhahood to guide the souls of others to salvation) Jizo, and the act of washing this statue is believed to safeguard your health. The other is of the Indian goddess Marici, a daughter of Brahma; she is believed

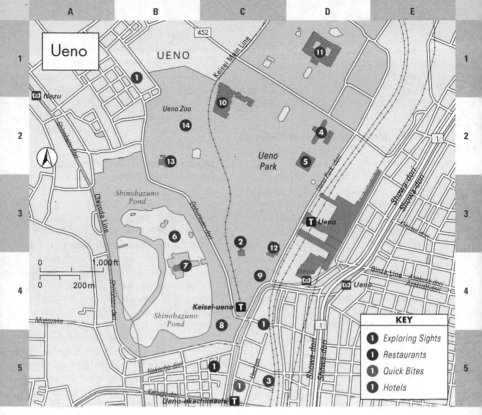

to help worshippers overcome difficulties and succeed in business. ✉ *4–6–2 Ueno, Taito-ku* Ⓜ *JR Yamanote and Keihin-tohoku lines, Okachi-machi Station (Higashi-guchi/East Exit) or Ueno Station (Hiroko-ji Exit).*

National Museum of Nature and Science (国立科学博物館; *Kokuritsu Kagaku Hakubutsukan*)
SCIENCE MUSEUM | FAMILY | This museum houses everything from fossils to moon rocks—the 30-meter (98-foot) model of a blue whale perched at the entrance is a huge hit with kids. And what self-respecting science museum wouldn't have dinosaurs? Check out exhibits on life's evolution on earth in the Global Gallery. Although the museum occasionally outdoes itself with special exhibits, it's pretty conventional and provides few hands-on learning experiences. Kids seem to like it, but this is not likely a place to linger if you don't have a lot of time. At this writing, the museum was still requiring visitors to make advance reservations online. ✉ *7–20 Ueno Koen, Taito-ku* ☎ *050/5541–8600* ⊕ *www.kahaku.go.jp* ✑ *¥630; additional fee for special exhibits* ☉ *Closed Mon.* Ⓜ *JR Ueno Station (Koen-guchi/Park Exit).*

National Museum of Western Art (国立西洋美術館; *Kokuritsu Seiyo Bijutsukan*)
ART MUSEUM | Along with castings from the original molds of Rodin's *Gate of Hell, The Burghers of Calais,* and *The Thinker,* the wealthy businessman Matsukata Kojiro (1865–1950) acquired some 850 paintings, sketches, and prints by such masters as Renoir, Monet, Gauguin, van Gogh, Delacroix, and Cézanne. Matsukata kept the collection in Europe, but he left it to Japan in his will. The French government sent the artwork to Japan after World War II, and the collection opened to the public in 1959 in a building designed by Swiss-born architect Le Corbusier. Since then, the museum has diversified a bit; more recent acquisitions include works by Reubens, Tintoretto, El Greco, Max Ernst, and Jackson Pollock. The Seiyo is one of the best-organized, most pleasant museums to visit in Tokyo. ✉ *7–7 Ueno Koen, Taito-ku* ☎ *03/5777–8600* ⊕ *www.nmwa.go.jp* ✑ *¥500; additional fee for special exhibits* ☉ *Closed Mon.* Ⓜ *JR Ueno Station (Koen-guchi/Park Exit).*

Shinobazu Pond (不忍池; *Shinobazu-ike*)
BODY OF WATER | FAMILY | When an inlet of Tokyo Bay receded around the 17th century, Shinobazu became a freshwater pond. Abbot Tenkai, founder of Kanei-ji on the hill above the pond, had an island made for Benzaiten, the goddess of the arts. Later improvements included a causeway to the island, embankments, and even a racecourse (1884–93). Today the pond is in three sections. The first, a wildlife sanctuary, is home to the city's lotus flowers; this is the only place in Tokyo you can see them bloom from mid-June through August. Some 5,000 wild ducks migrate here from as far away as Siberia, sticking around from September to April. The second section, to the north, belongs to Ueno Zoo; the third, to the west, is a small lake for boating. In July, the Ueno *matsuri* (festival) features food stalls and music events at the pond's edge. At the pond's southwestern corner, there is also a bandshell with various music events throughout the year. ✉ *5-20 Uenokoen, Taito-ku* ✑ *Free* Ⓜ *JR Ueno Station (Koen-guchi/Park Exit); Keisei private rail line, Keisei-Ueno Station (Higashi-guchi/East Exit).*

Shinobazu Pond Bentendo Temple (不忍池辯天堂; *Shinobazu-ike Bentendo*)
TEMPLE | Perched in the middle of Shinobazu Pond, this temple is dedicated to the goddess Benten, one of the Seven Gods of Good Luck that evolved from a combination of Indian, Chinese, and Japanese mythology. As matron goddess of the arts, she is depicted holding a lutelike musical instrument called a *biwa*. The temple, built by Abbot Tenkai, was destroyed in the bombings of 1945;

The Tokyo National Museum offers not only a huge collection of Japanese artifacts, but its buildings are a study in traditional and foreign architecture.

the present version, with its distinctive octagonal roof, is a faithful copy. You can rent rowboats and pedal boats at a nearby boathouse. ✉ 2–1 Ueno Koen, Taito-ku ☎ 03/3828–9502 boathouse 🎫 Temple free, boats from ¥700 Ⓜ JR Ueno Station (Koen-guchi/Park Exit); Keisei private rail line, Keisei-Ueno Station (Ikenohata Exit).

Shitamachi Museum (下町風俗資料館; Shitamachi Fuzoku Shiryokan)
HISTORY MUSEUM | FAMILY | Japanese society in the days of the Tokugawa shoguns was rigidly stratified. Some 80% of the city's land was allotted to the warrior class, temples, and shrines. The remaining 20%—between Ieyasu's fortifications on the west, and the Sumida-gawa on the east—was known as Shitamachi, or "downtown" or the "lower town" (as it expanded, it came to include what today constitutes the Chuo, Taito, Sumida, and Koto wards). It was here that the common, hardworking, free-spending folk, who made up more than half the population, lived. The Shitamachi Museum

preserves and exhibits what remained of that way of life as late as 1940.

The two main displays on the first floor are a merchant house and a tenement, intact with all their furnishings. This is a hands-on museum: you can take your shoes off and step up into the rooms. On the second floor are displays of toys, tools, and utensils donated, in most cases, by people who had grown up with them and used them all their lives. There are also photographs and video documentaries of craftspeople at work. Occasionally various traditional skills are demonstrated, and you're welcome to take part. This small but engaging museum makes great use of its space, and there are volunteer English-speaking guides. ✉ 2–1 Ueno Koen, Taito-ku ☎ 03/3823–7451 ⊕ www.taitocity.net/zaidan/shitamachi 🎫 ¥300 🕐 Closed Mon. Ⓜ JR Ueno Station (Koen-guchi/Park Exit).

Statue of Takamori Saigo (西郷隆盛像; Saigo Takamori Zo)

PUBLIC ART | As chief of staff of the Meiji Imperial army, Takamori Saigo (1827–77) played a key role in forcing the surrender of Edo and the overthrow of the shogunate. Interestingly, Saigo himself fell out with the other leaders of the new Meiji government and was killed in an unsuccessful rebellion of his own. The sculptor Takamura Koun's bronze, made in 1893, sensibly avoids presenting Saigo in uniform, but instead with his dog. Entering Ueno Park from the south, the statue is on the right after climbing the large staircase on your way to Kiyomizu Kanondo Temple. ⊠ *Ueno Park, Taito-ku, Ueno* Ⓜ *JR Ueno Station (Koen-guchi/Park Exit); Keisei private rail line, Keisei-Ueno Station (Higashi-guchi/East Exit).*

Tokyo Metropolitan Art Museum (東京都美術館; Tokyo-to Bijutsukan)

ART MUSEUM | By far the most eclectic of Ueno's art museums, the Tokyo Metropolitan hosts large-scale exhibitions ranging from classic masterpieces to modern architecture. The museum's smaller galleries often play home to group exhibitions of painting, photography, calligraphy, sculpture, and nearly any other kind of art one can dream up. Many smaller exhibits are free. ⊠ *8–36 Ueno Koen, Taito-ku* ☎ *03/3823–6921* ⊕ *www.tobikan.jp* ✉ *Permanent collection free; fees vary for other exhibits (usually from ¥1,000)* ⊘ *Closed 1st and 3rd Mon. of month* Ⓜ *JR Ueno Station (Koen-guchi/Park Exit).*

★ Tokyo National Museum (東京国立博物館; Tokyo Kokuritsu Hakubutsukan)

ART MUSEUM | This four-building complex is one of the world's great repositories of East Asian art and archaeology. The museum has some 87,000 objects in its permanent collection, with several thousand more on loan from shrines, temples, and private owners.

The Western-style building on the left (if you're standing at the main gate), with bronze cupolas, is the Hyokeikan. Built in 1909, it was devoted to archaeological exhibits; aside from the occasional special exhibition, the building is closed today. The larger Heiseikan, behind the Hyokeikan, was built to commemorate the wedding of crown prince Naruhito in 1993 and now houses Japanese archaeological exhibits. The second floor is used for special exhibitions.

In 1878 the 7th-century Horyu-ji (Horyu Temple) in Nara presented 319 works of art in its possession—sculpture, scrolls, masks, and other objects—to the imperial household. These were transferred to the National Museum in 2000 and now reside in the Horyu-ji Homotsukan (Gallery of Horyu-ji Treasures), which was designed by Yoshio Taniguchi. There's a useful guide to the collection in English, and the exhibits are well explained. Don't miss the hall of carved wooden *gigaku* (Buddhist processional) masks.

The central building in the complex, the 1937 Honkan, houses Japanese art exclusively: paintings, calligraphy, sculpture, textiles, ceramics, swords, and armor. Also here are 84 objects designated by the government as National Treasures. The more attractive Toyokan, to the right of the Honkan, was completed in 1968 and recently renovated; it is devoted to the art and antiquities of China, Korea, Southeast Asia, India, the Middle East, and Egypt. ⊠ *13–9 Ueno Koen, Taito-ku* ☎ *03/3822–1111* ⊕ *www.tnm.jp* ✉ *Regular exhibits ¥1,000, special exhibits from ¥1,600* ⊘ *Closed Mon.* Ⓜ *JR Ueno Station (Koen-guchi/Park Exit).*

★ Ueno Tosho-gu Shrine (上野東照宮)

RELIGIOUS BUILDING | This shrine, built in 1627, is dedicated to Ieyasu, the first Tokugawa shogun. It miraculously survived all major disasters that destroyed most of Tokyo's historical structures—the fires, the 1868 revolt, the 1923 earthquake, the 1945 bombings—making it one of the few early-Edo-period buildings

Brightly painted, intricately carved, and trimmed in gold leaf, Tosho-gu is often referred to as Japan's most lavishly decorated shrine.

left in Tokyo. The shrine and most of its art are designated National Treasures.

Two hundred *ishidoro* (stone lanterns) line the path from the stone entry arch to the shrine itself. One of them, just outside the arch to the left, and more than 18 feet high, is called *obaketoro* (ghost lantern). Legend has it that one night a samurai on guard duty slashed at a ghost (*obake*) that was believed to haunt the lantern. His sword was so strong, it left a nick in the stone, which can be seen today.

The first room inside the shrine is the Hall of Worship; the four paintings in gold on wooden panels are by Tan'yu, a member of the famous Kano family of artists, dating from the 15th century. Behind the Hall of Worship, connected by a passage called the *haiden*, is the sanctuary, where the spirit of Ieyasu is said to be enshrined.

The real glory of Tosho-gu is its so-called Chinese Gate, at the end of the building, and the fence on either side that has intricate carvings of birds, animals, fish, and shells of every description. The two long panels of the gate, with their dragons carved in relief, are attributed to Hidari Jingoro, a brilliant sculptor of the early Edo period whose real name is unknown (*hidari* means "left"; Jingoro was reportedly left-handed). ⊠ *9–88 Ueno Koen, Taito-ku* ☎ *03/3822–3455* ⊕ *www.uenotoshogu.com/en* ⊠ *Shrine free; Peony Garden ¥700* Ⓜ *JR Ueno Station (Koen-guchi/Park Exit).*

Ueno Royal Museum (上野の森美術館; *Ueno-no-Mori Bijutsukan*)
ART GALLERY | Although the museum has no permanent collection of its own, it hosts an interesting selection of temporary exhibits. The museum focuses on group exhibitions and work by contemporary artists, but often working within the bounds of more traditional media. Thanks to its manageable size and pleasant atmosphere, the Ueno Royal Museum is a relaxing alternative to Ueno's larger (and more crowded) museums. ⊠ *1–2 Ueno Koen, Taito-ku, Ueno*

Ueno Zoo is Japan's oldest zoo and home to about 2,600 animals and 450 species, including the giant pandas for which it is famous.

☎ *03/3833–4191* 🌐 *www.ueno-mori.org* 🎟 *Prices vary depending on exhibit* [M] *JR Ueno Station (Koen-guchi/Park Exit).*

Ueno Zoo (上野動物園; *Ueno Dobutsuen*) **ZOO** | **FAMILY** | The two main sections of Japan's first zoo, built in 1882, host an exotic mix of more than 900 species of animals. The giant panda is the biggest draw, but the tigers from Sumatra, gorillas from the lowland swamp areas of western Africa, and numerous monkeys, some from Japan, make a visit to the East Garden worthwhile. The West Garden is highlighted by rhinos, zebras, and hippopotamuses, and a children's area. The process of the zoo's expansion somehow left within its confines the 120-foot, five-story Kanei-ji Pagoda. Built in 1631 and rebuilt after a fire in 1639, the building offers traditional Japanese tea ceremony services. ✉ *9–83 Ueno Koen, Taito-ku* ☎ *03/3828–5171* 🌐 *www.tokyo-zoo.net/english/ueno* 🎟 *¥600, free on Mar. 20, May 4, and Oct. 1* 🕒 *Closed Mon.* [M] *JR Ueno Station (Koen-guchi/Park Exit).*

🍴 Restaurants

The Ueno neighborhood houses a large park near the major railway station, in case you're in a picnic mood. The lively Ameyokocho market, along and under the train tracks south of the station, sells fresh seafood, dried goods, and freshly cut fruit skewered onto a disposable chopstick, while the streets nearby are home to small eateries, lively izakaya, and low-cost standing-only bars (*tachinomiya*).

Tonkatsu Musashino (とんかつ武蔵野) **$** | **JAPANESE** | The deep-fried, breaded pork cutlets at this casual restaurant just south of Ueno Park's pond combine generous portions with melt-in-the-mouth tenderness, and for a great price. Set meals here come with enough rice, miso soup, shredded cabbage, and pickles to loosen your belt a notch or two. **Known for:** rich, filling meals; a no-frills local atmosphere. [$] *Average main: ¥1,300* ✉ *2–8–1 Ueno, Taito-ku* ☎ *03/3831–1672* 💳 *No credit cards* [M] *JR Ueno Station.*

Coffee and Quick Bites

Ichiran (一蘭)
$ | **RAMEN** | At Ueno Station is a branch of an amusing ramen chain. Ichiran serves *tonkotsu* (pork broth) noodles. [$] *Average main: ¥1,000* ✉ *Atre Ueno, 7–1–1 Ueno, Ueno* ✣ *Entry on the street, under the tracks.* ☎ *03/5826–5861* 🌐 *en.ichiran.com* 💳 *No credit cards.*

Hotels

One of Tokyo's largest rail hubs, Ueno is considered old-fashioned compared to other neighborhoods and, as such, it contains a number of ryokans.

Ryokan Katsutaro (旅館勝太郎)
$ | **B&B/INN** | Established in the 1980s, this small, simple, economical inn is a five-minute walk from the entrance to Ueno Koen (Ueno Park) and a 10-minute walk from the Tokyo National Museum. **Pros:** a traditional and unique Japanese experience; reasonably priced room rates; excellent base for exploring Ueno. **Cons:** no breakfast served; small baths; some rooms have shared Japanese baths. [$] *Rooms from: ¥12,000* ✉ *4–16–8 Ikenohata, Taito-ku* ☎ *03/3821–9808* 🛏 *8 rooms* 🍴 *No Meals* [M] *Chiyoda subway line, Nezu Station (Exit 2).*

Performing Arts

MUSIC

Tokyo Bunka Kaikan (東京文化会館)
MUSIC | In the 1960s and '70s this hall was one of the city's premier showcases for classical ballet, orchestral music, and visiting soloists. It still gets major bookings. ✉ *5-45 Uenokoen, Taito-ku* ☎ *03/3828–2111* 🌐 *www.t-bunka.jp/en* [M] *JR Yamanote Line, Ueno Station (Koen-guchi/Park Exit).*

Shopping

Ueno is known for its temples, large park, and shops, along with a spattering of small modern boutiques giving an eclectic and frantic feel to the neighborhood.

Jusan-ya (十三や)
SOUVENIRS | A samurai who couldn't support himself as a feudal retainer launched this business selling handmade boxwood combs in 1736. It has been in the same family ever since. Jusan-ya is on Shinobazu-dori, a few doors west of its intersection with Chuo-dori in Ueno. ✉ *2–12–21 Ueno, Taito-ku* ☎ *03/3831–3238* 🌐 *www.kyoto-wel.com/shop/S81004* 🕒 *Closed Sun.* [M] *Ginza subway line, Ueno Hiroko-ji Station (Exit 3); JR Yamanote Line, Ueno Station (Shinobazu Exit).*

★ **Midori-Ya** (翠屋)
CRAFTS | Established in 1908, this family-run bamboo crafts shop on a traditional shopping street offers the wares of three generations of bamboo artists. Look for insect cages (with bamboo bugs), flower baskets, chopsticks, cups, lotus-root coasters, and lunchboxes. The shop is located near the base of the staircase on Yanaka Ginza's shopping street. ✉ *3–13–3 Nishi-Nippori, Ueno* ☎ *03/3828–7522* 🌐 *busekisuikou.com/en/midori-ya* 🕒 *Closed Mon.* [M] *Chiyoda line, Nishi-Nippori Station.*

Yanaka

Sights

Asakura Museum of Sculpture (朝倉彫刻館; *Asakura Chosokan*)
ART MUSEUM | Fumio Asakura, Japan's foremost artist of modern sculpture, was also an avid cat lover with an uncanny ability to capture a sense of motion in his sculptures. The museum—formerly the artist's home and studio—houses a selection of the artist's works, and the

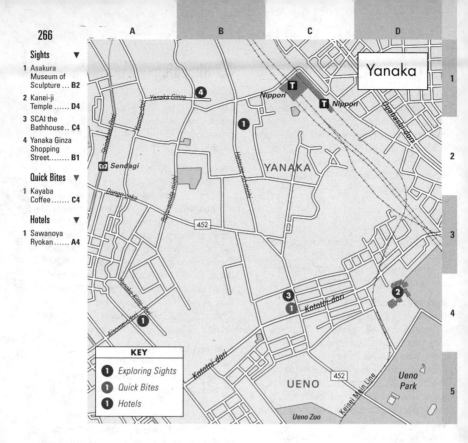

Yanaka

building and garden are a lovely stop when wandering through the Yanaka area. Since the museum is housed in an old residence, you will be removing your shoes to enter and it should also be noted that it is not wheelchair accessible. ✉ 7–18–10 Yanaka, Taito-ku ☎ 03/3821–4549 ⊕ www.taitocity.net/zaidan/english/asakura 🎫 ¥500 Ⓜ JR Yamanote Line, Nippori Station.

Kanei-ji Temple (寛永寺)

TEMPLE | Around 1625, the second Tokugawa Shogun, Hidetada, commissioned the priest Tenkai to build a temple on the hill known as Shinobuga-oka in Ueno to defend his city from evil spirits. The original complex encompassed much of what is Ueno Park and while the remaining grounds are beautiful, the most remarkable structure here is the ornately carved vermilion gate to what

was the mausoleum of Tsunayoshi, the fifth shogun. Tsunayoshi is famous for his disastrous fiscal mismanagement and his Shorui Awaremi no Rei (Edicts on Compassion for Living Things), which, among other things, made it a capital offense for a human being to kill a dog. ✉ 1–14–11 Ueno Sakuragi, Taito-ku ☎ 03/3821–4440 ⊕ kaneiji.jp 🎫 Free (contributions welcome) Ⓜ JR Ueno Station (Koen-guchi/Park Exit), JR Uguisudani Station.

SCAI the Bathhouse (スカイザバスハウス)

ART GALLERY | A contemporary art gallery housed in a 200-year-old building, SCAI is a symbol of Yanaka's blend of old and new. The exterior of the building, established in 1787 as a bathhouse, has been well preserved, while the inside is a light and airy gallery featuring rotating exhibits of contemporary art. Although it is a small gallery, the exhibitions are

Did You Know?

Yanaka Ginza, in the Yanaka area of Tokyo, is one of the best remaining examples of a regular shopping street still filled with small local stores selling groceries and other daily goods. You won't find any big supermarkets or chains here.

impressive, and it is worth a peek just to see the building itself. The area around it is worth a look as well. ⊠ *Kashiyu-ato, 6–1–23 Yanaka, Taito-ku* ☎ *03/3821–1144* ⊕ *www.scaithebathhouse.com/en* 🎟 *Free.*

Yanaka Ginza Shopping Street (谷中銀座)
STREET | It used to be that every neighborhood in Tokyo had its own small shopping street, but with the rise of supermarkets and convenience stores in the 1980s, they began to vanish. Thanks to a forward-thinking shopkeepers' and residents' association, Yanaka Ginza not only survived but has flourished. The street is now an interesting mix of shops selling groceries and other goods for locals, as well as sweets, snacks, and crafts. ⊠ *3 Yanaka, Taito-ku.*

🍽 Coffee and Quick Bites

Kayaba Coffee (カヤバ珈琲)
$ | CAFÉ | Standing on the border of Ueno and Yanaka, just a short walk to the west from the National Museum, this historic café is a popular stop for lunch or a light snack. A century old, the café has been stylishly renovated and serves homemade sandwiches, curries, cakes, and *kaki gori,* a traditional treat of flavored shaved ice. **Known for:** excellent morning sets; popular with local residents; retro Japanese drinks and desserts. $ *Average main: ¥1,000* ⊠ *6–1–29 Yanaka, Taito-ku* ☎ *03/3823–3545* ⊕ *taireki.com/en/kayaba.html* 🚫 *No credit cards* Ⓜ *JR Nippori Station, JR Ueno Station.*

Hotels

Sawanoya Ryokan (澤の屋旅館)
$ | B&B/INN | The Shitamachi sub-area of Ueno is known for its down-to-earth friendliness, which you get in full measure at Sawanoya, a popular family business where everybody pitches in to help you plan excursions and book hotels for the next leg of your journey. **Pros:** traditional Japanese experience; affordable rates; friendly management. **Cons:** rooms somewhat small; a bit of a hike to the subway station; many rooms share Japanese baths. $ *Rooms from: ¥12,000* ⊠ *2–3–11 Yanaka, Taito-ku* ☎ *03/3822–2251* ⊕ *www.sawanoya.com* 🛏 *10 rooms* ⦿ *No Meals* Ⓜ *Chiyoda subway line, Nezu Station (Exit 1).*

🛍 Shopping

Ueno Sakuragi Atari (上野桜木あたり)
SHOPPING CENTER | A collection of wooden structures at the end of a stone path is home to Yanaka Beer Hall, which has many craft beers on tap (closed every third Monday), a bread shop in a little back garden, a shop with different vinegars and olive oils, and a few other small shops. It's a good place to stop for a beer or just a peek into these increasingly rare wooden structures that Tokyo doesn't build anymore. ⊠ *2-15-6 Uenosakuragi, Taito-ku* ⊕ *uenosakuragiatari.jp.*

Chapter 13

ASAKUSA AND RYOGOKU

Updated by
Rob Goss

👁 **Sights**
★★★★☆

🍴 **Restaurants**
★★★☆☆

🏨 **Hotels**
★★★☆☆

🛍 **Shopping**
★★★☆☆

🍸 **Nightlife**
★★☆☆☆

ASAKUSA AND RYOGOKU SNAPSHOT

TOP EXPERIENCES

■ **Asakusa Shrine.** The souls of the three men who built Senso-ji are enshrined here.

■ **Sanja Festival.** Drunken people? Loud crowds? Brilliant colors? It's all part of May's Sanja Festival.

■ **Snag a photo op.** Want to show your friends that you saw the Thunder God Gate? Then make sure you take a photograph in front of the giant red-paper lantern of Kaminari-mon.

■ **Wander the backstreets.** The streets to the west of the Senso-ji complex are full of restaurants, cafés, and shops with a wonderfully retro feel.

■ **Shop 'til you drop.** Looking for souvenirs? Visit more than 80 shops on Nakamise-dori that sell everything from rice crackers to trinkets and T-shirts, or check out the kitchenware stores on Kappabashi-dori.

■ **Supersize yourself.** Head to Ryogoku to see sumo wrestlers grapple in the ring, then eat the *chanko-nabe* hotpot they use to bulk up.

GETTING HERE

Getting here by subway from Ueno Station (Ginza Line, Ueno Station to Asakusa Station, ¥170, five minutes) or taxi (approximately ¥1,000) is most convenient. Asakusa is the last stop (eastbound) on the Ginza Line. Ryogoku Station on the JR Sobu Line and Toei Oedo Line will get you to all sumo attractions.

PLANNING YOUR TIME

Asakusa is just east of Ueno and can be explored in a half day. Unlike most of the other areas to explore on foot in Tokyo, Senso-ji is admirably compact. You can easily see the temple and explore the area surrounding it in a morning. The garden at Dembo-in is worth a half hour. If you decide to include Kappabashi, allow yourself an hour more for the tour. Some of the shopping arcades in this area are covered, but Asakusa is essentially an outdoor experience.

OFF THE BEATEN PATH

■ A several-minute walk east of Senso-ji, Tokyo Cruises boats depart for short trips down the Sumida River, offering a very non-touristy view of the city en route to stops at Hamarikyu Garden, Odaiba, and elsewhere. As the boats sedately work their way down what was once Tokyo's key waterway for trade and commerce, you'll see a mixture of office blocks, apartments, and warehouses, as well as locals unwinding by the river: jogging, walking their dogs, or just relaxing on benches (⊕ www.suijobus. co.jp/en).

VIEWPOINT

■ Looking east over the Sumida River from Asakusa, you'll see one of Tokyo's most striking modern views, the 634-meter (2,080-foot) Tokyo Skytree tower looming large behind the garish offices of Asahi Beer. The latter combines a building with a golden glass facade designed to look like a frothy glass of lager, next to which is a smaller black building topped by what's supposed to be a golden flame. Regrettably, it's inspired a local nickname: *unchi-biru* (turd building).

If there is one must-visit neighborhood in Tokyo, this is it. Asakusa brings together cultural sights, dining, and entertainment in vibrant surroundings that are at once historic and modern.

Cars make room for the rickshaw drivers who sometimes outpace the motorized traffic. On the neighborhood's backstreets, neo-French and Italian cafés mix with generations-old soba and tempura shops, while customers in the latest fashions sit next to those in traditional kimonos. At Senso-ji Temple and the vibrant Nakamise-dori street leading to it, you hear a global assortment of languages amid the crowds, yet locals still stop by to pray. It is hard not to be swept away by the relaxed energy that pulses through the area. If you have any time to spend in Tokyo, make sure you devote at least a day to exploring Asakusa.

Historically, the area blossomed after Tokugawa Ieyasu made Edo his capital in 1603, and for the next 300 years it was the wellspring of almost everything we associate with Japanese culture. In the mid-1600s, it became a pleasure quarter in its own right with stalls selling toys, souvenirs, and sweets; acrobats, jugglers, and strolling musicians; and sake shops and teahouses—where the waitresses often provided more than tea. Then, in 1841, the Kabuki theaters moved to Asakusa. The theaters were here for only a short time, but it was enough to establish Asakusa as *the* entertainment quarter of the city—a reputation it held unchallenged until World War II, when most of the area was destroyed.

After the war, development focused on areas to the west like Shinjuku and Shibuya. In a way, this saved Asakusa from becoming yet another neighborhood filled with neon, concrete, and glass, instead mostly keeping to the same style of low buildings and tiny independent shops that existed before the war. Almost eight decades have certainly changed the neighborhood, but many of the smaller side streets retain the charm and feel of old Tokyo. Although the area has become dramatically more popular in recent years, tourists usually keep to the main streets and line up at the same restaurants around the Senso-ji Temple complex. Venture a few minutes away from the temple area, and the crowds thin out and souvenir shops give way to quiet storefronts selling traditional crafts. Although Senso-ji Temple is well worth seeing, taking the time to wander through the neighborhood gives you a hint of what it may have been like years ago.

If the sport of sumo tickles your fancy, the largest collection of training stables (and the nation's main sumo arena) are in the Ryogoku area, southeast of Asakusa on the other side of the Sumida River. As the center of the world of sumo wrestling, this is the place to watch tournaments as well as eat like a sumo. With the Japanese Sword Museum and Hokusai Museum, it also delivers a sumo-sized amount of culture.

The Asakusa district streets at sunrise

Asakusa

 Sights

Asakusa Jinja Shrine (浅草神社)

RELIGIOUS BUILDING | Several structures in the famous Senso-ji Temple Complex survived the bombings of 1945. The largest, to the right of the Main Hall, is this Shinto shrine to the Hikonuma brothers and their master, Najino-Nakamoto—the putative founders of Senso-ji. In Japan, Buddhism and Shintoism have enjoyed a comfortable coexistence since the former arrived from China in the 6th century. The shrine, built in 1649, is also known as Sanja Sama (Shrine of the Three Guardians). Near the entrance to Asakusa Shrine is another survivor of World War II: the original east gate to the temple grounds, Niten-mon, built in 1618 for a shrine to Ieyasu Tokugawa and designated by the government as an Important Cultural Property. ✉ 2–3–1 Asakusa, Taito-ku ☎ 03/3844–1575 ⊕ www.asakusajinja.jp.

Dembo-in Temple (伝法院)

GARDEN | Believed to have been made in the 17th century by Kobori Enshu, the genius of Zen landscape design, the garden of Dembo-in is part of the living quarters of the abbot of Senso-ji and the best-kept secret in Asakusa. The garden is usually empty and always utterly serene, an island of privacy in a sea of pilgrims. Spring, when the wisteria blooms, is the ideal time to be here.

A sign in English on Dembo-in-dori—you'll see it about 150 yards west of the intersection with Naka-mise-dori—leads you to the entrance, which is a side door to a large wooden gate. For permission to see the abbot's garden, you must first apply at the temple administration building, between Hozo-mon and the Five-Storied Pagoda, in the far corner. ✉ 2–3–1 Asakusa, Taito-ku ☎ 03/3842–0181 for reservations ⊠ Free Ⓜ Ginza subway line, Asakusa Station (Exit 1/ Kaminari-mon Exit).

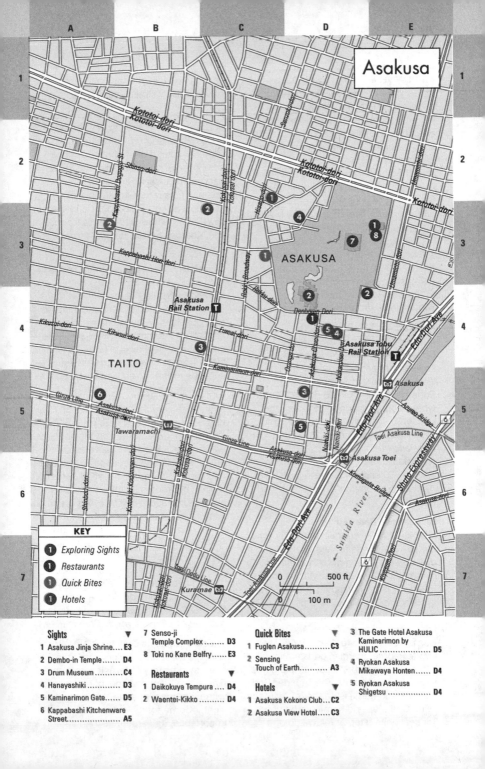

Asakusa

KEY
- ● Exploring Sights
- ● Restaurants
- ● Quick Bites
- ● Hotels

Sights ▼
1 Asakusa Jinja Shrine.... **E3**
2 Dembo-in Temple....... **D4**
3 Drum Museum........... **C4**
4 Hanayashiki............. **D3**
5 Kaminarimon Gate...... **D5**
6 Kappabashi Kitchenware Street.................. **A5**
7 Senso-ji Temple Complex **D3**
8 Toki no Kane Belfry...... **E3**

Restaurants ▼
1 Daikokuya Tempura **D4**
2 Waentei-Kikko **D4**

Quick Bites ▼
1 Fuglen Asakusa.......... **C3**
2 Sensing Touch of Earth........... **A3**

Hotels ▼
1 Asakusa Kokono Club... **C2**
2 Asakusa View Hotel..... **C3**
3 The Gate Hotel Asakusa Kaminarimon by HULIC **D5**
4 Ryokan Asakusa Mikawaya Honten....... **D4**
5 Ryokan Asakusa Shigetsu **D4**

Drum Museum (太鼓館; *Taiko Kan*)

OTHER MUSEUM | FAMILY | Become a *taiko* (drum) master for a day as you pound away on the exhibits at this fourth-floor museum dedicated to traditional Japanese and foreign drums. More than 200 instruments can be played, making it a great place for kids. Just make sure their hands remain off the antique instruments, which are carefully marked. Should you feel inspired, there is a shop on the ground floor of the same building that sells various Japanese drums and festival accessories, which make great souvenirs. ✉ *2–1–1 Nishi-Asakusa, Taito-ku* ☎ *03/3842–5622* ⊕ *www.miyamoto-unosuke.co.jp/taikokan* ☞ *¥500* ⊘ *Closed Mon. and Tues.* Ⓜ *Ginza subway line, Tawaramachi Station.*

Hanayashiki (花やしき)

AMUSEMENT PARK/CARNIVAL | FAMILY | Established in 1853, Tokyo's oldest amusement park has modernized but leans in to its retro atmosphere. Think Coney Island: a haunted house, Ferris wheel, and merry-go-round await the kids who will likely be a little tired of Asakusa's historic areas. ✉ *2–28–1 Asakusa, Taito-ku* ☎ *03/3842–8780* ⊕ *www. hanayashiki.net* ☞ *¥1,000 (rides from ¥300–¥600 each)* Ⓜ *Ginza subway line, Asakusa Station (Exit 1/Kaminari-mon Exit).*

Kaminarimon Gate (雷門)

HISTORIC SIGHT | The main entryway to Senso-ji's grounds towers above the ever-present throng of tourists and passing rickshaw drivers. With its huge red-paper lantern hanging in the center, this landmark of Asakusa is picture-perfect. The original gate was destroyed by fire in 1865; the replica you see today was built after World War II. Traditionally, two fearsome guardian gods are installed in the alcoves of Buddhist temple gates to ward off evil spirits. The Thunder God (Kaminari-no-Kami) is on the left with the Wind God (Kaze-no-Kami) on the right. For souvenirs, stop at Tokiwa-do, the shop on the west side of the gate for *kaminari okoshi* (thunder crackers), made of rice, millet, sugar, and beans.

Kaminari-mon marks the southern extent of Nakamise-dori, the Street of Inside Shops. The area from Kaminari-mon to the inner gate of the temple was once composed of stalls leased to the townspeople who cleaned and swept the temple grounds. This is now kitsch-souvenir central, with key chains, dolls, and snacks. ✉ *2–3–1 Asakusa, Taito-ku* Ⓜ *Ginza subway line, Asakusa Station (Exit 1/Kaminari-mon Exit).*

Kappabashi Kitchenware Street (かっぱ橋道具街; *Kappa-bashi Dogu-gai*)

BUSINESS DISTRICT | Lined with over 200 shops selling kitchenware and supplies, Kappabashi is shopping heaven for home chefs. The street is worth a visit just to see the vast selection of wares on display—from knives to industrial restaurant supplies to the strikingly realistic plastic food models seen in restaurants.

In the 19th century, according to local legend, a river ran through the present-day Kappabashi district. The surrounding area was poorly drained and was often flooded. A local shopkeeper began a project to improve the drainage, investing all his own money, but met with little success until a troupe of *kappa*—mischievous green water sprites—emerged from the river to help him. A more prosaic explanation for the name of the district points out that the lower-ranking retainers of the local lord used to earn extra money by making straw raincoats, also called *kappa*, that they spread to dry on the bridge. ✉ *3–18–2 Matsugaya, Taito-ku* Ⓜ *Ginza subway line, Tawara-machi Station (Exit 1).*

★ Senso-ji Temple Complex (浅草寺)

TEMPLE | Even for travelers with little interest in history or temples, this complex in the heart and soul of Asakusa is without a doubt one of Tokyo's must-see sights. Come for its local and historical importance, its garden, its 17th-century

Asakusa's heart and soul is the Senso-ji Complex, famous for its 17th-century Shinto shrine, Asakusa Shrine, as well as its garden and the wild Sanja Festival in May.

Shinto shrine, and Tokyo's most famous festival: the wild Sanja Matsuri in May. The area also offers myriad interesting shops, winding backstreets, and an atmosphere unlike anywhere else in Tokyo.

Established in 645, the bright red Main Hall has long been the center of Asakusa, though what you see today is a faithful replica of the original that burned in the fire-raids of 1945. It took 13 years to raise money for the restoration of the beloved Senso-ji, which is much more than a tourist attraction. Kabuki actors still come here before a new season of performances, and sumo wrestlers visit before a tournament to pay their respects. The large lanterns were donated by the geisha associations of Asakusa and nearby Yanagi-bashi. Most Japanese stop at the huge bronze incense burner in front of the Main Hall to bathe their hands and faces in the smoke—it's a charm to ward off illnesses—before climbing the stairs to offer their prayers.

Unlike in many other temples, however, part of the inside has a concrete floor, so you can come and go without removing your shoes. In this area hang Senso-ji's chief claims to artistic importance: a collection of 18th- and 19th-century votive paintings on wood. Plaques of this kind, called *ema,* are still offered to the gods at shrines and temples, but they are commonly simpler and smaller. The worshipper buys a little tablet of wood with the picture already painted on one side and inscribes a prayer on the other. The temple owns more than 50 of these works, which were removed to safety in 1945 to escape the air raids. Only eight of them, depicting scenes from Japanese history and mythology, are on display. A catalog of the collection is on sale in the hall, but the text is in Japanese only.

Lighting is poor in the Main Hall, and the actual works are difficult to see. One thing that visitors cannot see at all is the holy image of Kannon itself, which supposedly lies buried somewhere deep under the temple. Not even the priests

The Senso-ji Kannon temple is the most widely visited spiritual site in the world with over 30 million visitors annually.

of Senso-ji have ever seen it, and there is in fact no conclusive evidence that it actually exists.

Hozo-mon, the gate to the temple courtyard, is also a repository for *sutras* (Buddhist texts) and other treasures of Senso-ji. This gate, too, has its guardian gods; should either god decide to leave his post for a stroll, he can use the enormous pair of sandals hanging on the back wall—the gift of a Yamagata Prefecture village famous for its straw weaving. ✉ *2–3–1 Asakusa, Taito-ku* ☎ *03/3842–0181* ⊕ *www.senso-ji.jp* ✉ *Free* Ⓜ *Ginza subway line, Asakusa Station (Exit 1/ Kaminari-mon Exit).*

Toki no Kane Belfry (時の鐘)
RELIGIOUS BUILDING | The tiny hillock Benten-yama, with its shrine to the goddess of good fortune, is the site of this 17th-century belfry. The bell here used to toll the hours for the people of the district, and it was said that you could hear it anywhere within a radius of some 6 km (4 miles). The bell still sounds at 6 am every day, when the temple grounds

open. It also rings on New Year's Eve— 108 strokes in all, beginning just before midnight, to "ring out" the 108 sins and frailties of humankind and make a clean start for the coming year. Benten-yama and the belfry are at the beginning of the narrow street that parallels Nakamise-dori. ✉ *2–3 Asakusa, Taito-ku.*

🍴 Restaurants

Historic Asakusa is filled with restaurants serving traditional cuisine like tempura and *sukiyaki*. Rest and rejuvenate at a café serving Japanese sweets and green tea, or try the very casual *yakitori* restaurants that spill out onto Hoppy Street, a couple of blocks west of Senso-ji. The walk up to the temple is lined with small shops selling small bites like *sembei* (rice crackers) and *ningyoyaki,* cakes stuffed with a sweet red bean paste.

Daikokuya Tempura (大黒家天麩羅)
$$ | JAPANESE | Daikokuya, in the center of Asakusa's historic district, is a point of pilgrimage for both locals and tourists. The

specialty here is shrimp tempura, and the menu choices are simple—*tendon* is tempura shrimp served over rice, and the tempura meal includes rice, pickled vegetables, and miso soup. **Known for:** being an Asakusa landmark; Tokyo-style tempura a cut above the rest; long lines. $ *Average main: ¥2,500 ⊠ 1–38–10 Asakusa, Taito-ku ☎ 03/3844–1111 ⊕ www.tempura.co.jp/english ⊟ No credit cards Ⓜ Ginza and Asakusa subway lines, Asakusa Station.*

Waentei-Kikko (和えん亭 吉幸)
$$$$ | **JAPANESE** | Originally a teahouse, Waentei-Kikko is now a cozy, country-style Japanese restaurant serving *kaiseki*-style set meals along with premium sake. What makes this place extra special is that the owner, Fukui Kodai, is a traditional Japanese *Tsugaru-shamisen* (string instrument) musician, who performs at scheduled times throughout the day. **Known for:** kaiseki-style set meals; setting that harkens back to Meiji-era Japan; Tsugaru-shamisen performances. $ *Average main: ¥9,500 ⊠ 2–2–13 Asakusa, Taito-ku ☎ 03/5828–8833 ⊕ www.waentei-kikko.com ⊙ Closed Wed. Ⓜ Ginza subway line, Asakusa Station (Exit 1/ Kaminari-mon Exit).*

☕ Coffee and Quick Bites

Fuglen Asakusa
$ | **SCANDINAVIAN** | At the northern end of the izakaya-lined Hoppy Street, this hip Scandinavian-style café serves up sweet and savory Norwegian waffles along with coffee made using single-origin beans. In the evenings, there's craft beer and cocktails on the menu too. **Known for:** coffee made with single-origin beans; craft beer and cocktails at night; Norwegian waffles. $ *Average main: ¥1,500 ⊠ 2-6-16 Asakusa, Taito-ku ☎ 03/5811–1756 ⊕ fuglen-asakusa.business.site.*

Sensing Touch of Earth (センシング・タッチ・オブ・アース)
$ | **CAFÉ** | On Kappabashi-dori, just north of the Kama-Asa knife store, this café has a very hipster feel thanks to its stark concrete walls and occasional in-store art exhibitions. The menu includes specialty coffees as well as organic matcha and ginger lemonade. **Known for:** short opening hours (11 to 6 daily); hipster vibe; specialty coffee. $ *Average main: ¥600 ⊠ 3-1-12 Matsugaya, Taito-ku ☎ 080/7808–5622 ⊕ stoe-cafe.tokyo Ⓜ Ginza subway line, Tawaramachi Station.*

 Hotels

Thanks to its historic attractions, Asakusa mainly caters to tourists. Standard hotels are available, but many come here for its selection of reasonably priced ryokan inns.

Asakusa Kokono Club (浅草九倶楽部ホテル)
$$$$ | **HOTEL** | Opened in 2020, just a three-minute walk west from Senso-ji, the Kokono Club is a hipster-ish addition to Asakusa's hotel scene. **Pros:** spacious rooms by local standards; modern alternative to Asakusa's many older ryokan; close to the main sights. **Cons:** area can be noisy; restaurant can fill up with non-guests; limited facilities. $ *Rooms from: ¥24,000 ⊠ 2-6-12 Asakusa, Taito-ku ☎ 03/5830–6533 ⊕ asakusakokonoclub.com/eng ⇸ 30 rooms ⍾ No Meals Ⓜ Ginza subway line, Asakusa Station.*

Asakusa View Hotel (浅草ビューホテル)
$$ | **HOTEL** | **FAMILY** | The box-shaped Asakusa View is the largest Western-style hotel in the traditional Asakusa area. **Pros:** affordable rates; located in a historic temple area; free in-room Wi-Fi. **Cons:** room interiors generally basic; professional but impersonal service; dated rooms. $ *Rooms from: ¥19,000 ⊠ 3–17–1 Nishi-Asakusa, Taito-ku ☎ 03/3847–1111 ⊕ www.viewhotels.co.jp/asakusa ⇸ 326*

rooms ⭘| No Meals Ⓜ *Ginza subway line, Tawara-machi Station (Exit 3).*

★ The Gate Hotel Asakusa Kaminarimon by HULIC (ザ・ゲートホテル雷門)

$$ | HOTEL | This relative newcomer to the historic Asakusa area presents a certain stylish flair, starting from the entrance, where an elevator whisks you up 13 floors to the beautiful, glass-walled lobby. **Pros:** historic area; surrounded with great dining options; lovely views. **Cons:** rooms small by Western standards; not exactly a central location; can be crowded on weekends. Ⓢ *Rooms from: ¥20,000* ✉ *2–16–11 Kaminarimon, Taito-ku* ☎ *03/5826–3877* ⊕ *www.gate-hotel.jp* 🛏 *137 rooms* ⭘| *No Meals* Ⓜ *Ginza and Asakusa subway lines, Asakusa Station (Exit 2).*

Ryokan Asakusa Mikawaya Honten (旅館三河屋本店)

$ | B&B/INN | In the heart of Asakusa, this friendly ryokan with only Japanese-style rooms is just behind the Kaminari-mon, the gateway leading to the Senso-ji complex. **Pros:** affordable accommodations; traditional Japanese experience; interesting shopping in the area. **Cons:** futons and tatami might not be suitable for those accustomed to Western-style beds; small rooms; friendly staff struggle with English. Ⓢ *Rooms from: ¥14,000* ✉ *1–30–12 Asakusa, Taito-ku* ☎ *03/3841–8954* ⊕ *www.asakusamikawaya.com* 🛏 *15 rooms* ⭘| *No Meals* Ⓜ *Ginza subway line, Asakusa Station (Exit 1/ Kaminari-mon Exit).*

Ryokan Asakusa Shigetsu (旅館浅草 指月)

$$ | B&B/INN | Just off Nakamise-dori and inside the Senso-ji grounds, this small inn with both Japanese- and Western-style rooms, could not be better located for a visit to the temple. **Pros:** affordable rooms; located in a historic temple area; close to subway station. **Cons:** not convenient to central Tokyo; Western-style rooms are all singles; small rooms. Ⓢ *Rooms from: ¥19,000* ✉ *1–31–11 Asakusa, Taito-ku*

Did You Know?

Kamiya Bar, the first drinking establishment in Japan to call itself a "bar," was started in Asakusa in 1880 and it still stands today. Stop by for a jolt of Đenki Bran, a drink that dates back to the Meiji Era. A mixture of a few different liquors and brandy, the brew—the recipe is a secret—is sold in bottles at the bar and is definitely an acquired taste. Be prepared with a chaser.

☎ *03/3843–2345* ⊕ *www.shigetsu. com* 🛏 *21 rooms* ⭘| *No Meals* Ⓜ *Ginza subway line, Asakusa Station (Exit 1/ Kaminari-mon Exit).*

🍸 Nightlife

BARS

Kamiya Bar (神谷バー)

BARS | Tokyo's oldest Western-style bar hasn't had a face-lift for decades (the main building is registered as a tangible cultural property) and that's part of what draws so many drinkers to this bright, noisy venue. The other major attraction is the Denki Bran, a delicious but hangover-inducing cocktail (comprising gin, red wine, brandy, and curaçao) that was invented here about 100 years ago and is now stocked by bars throughout Japan. ✉ *1–1–1 Asakusa, Taito-ku* ☎ *03/3841–5400* 🕐 *Closed Tues.* Ⓜ *Asakusa and Ginza subway lines, Asakusa Station (Exit 3 and A5).*

The Tavern in Asakusa

BARS | Asakusa has plenty of izakaya, especially on Hoppy Street, but for just a drink (and without the smokiness of many izakaya), the Tavern has a great selection of local and overseas whiskies, as well as sake and cocktails, not to mention Ken, the very cheerful owner-bartender. It's closed on Tuesday. ✉ *2-14-15*

Nishi Asakusa, Taito-ku ☎ *03/6876–8245*
⊕ *the-tavern-in-asakusa.business.site*
Ⓜ *Next to Asakusa Station on Tsukuba
Express Line; Ginza subway line, Asakusa Station.*

Top of Tree (天空 ラウンジ; *Tenku Raunji
Top of Tree*)
COCKTAIL LOUNGES | FAMILY | Perched on
the top of the Solamachi complex, this
bar-restaurant attracts locals and tourists
for overwhelming, breathtaking views of
Tokyo Skytree. Signature drinks include
Amaou-brand strawberry cocktails. The
music's mostly jazz, and spacious and
cushy seats, with sprawling views of
Tokyo through the oversized glass windows and ceiling, make you want to linger. ⊠ *Solamachi complex, Tokyo Skytree
Town, 1–1–2 Oshiage, 31st fl., Sumida-ku*
☎ *03/5809–7377* ⊕ *www.top-of-tree.jp.*

World Beer Museum (世界のビール博物
館; *Sekai no Biru Hakubutsukan*)
BREWPUBS | As the name suggests,
beers from around the world are for sale,
including 300 kinds in bottles and 20
more on tap. The large outdoor terrace
with low-key downtown views is quiet
and pleasant. The English-speaking
German staff, when available, can help
you choose the right beer. ⊠ *Solamachi
complex, Tokyo Skytree Town, 1–1–2
Oshiage, 7th fl., Sumida-ku* ☎ *03/5610–
2648* ⊕ *www.world-liquor-importers.
co.jp/en/index.html.*

🛍 Shopping

While visiting the Senso-ji Temple
Complex in Asakusa, take time to stroll
through the neighborhood's many
arcades. At first glance, many of the
goods sold here are the kinds of souvenirs you can find in any tourist trap.
Look a little harder and you can find small
backstreet shops that have been making
beautiful wooden combs, delicate
fans, and other items of fine traditional
craftsmanship for generations. Also here

are the cookware shops of Kappabashi,
where you can load up on everything
from sushi knives to plastic lobsters.

CRAFTS
★ **Maskshop Omote** (仮面屋おもて;
Kamen-ya Omote)
OTHER SPECIALTY STORE | "Omote" means
"face" or "mask," and this chic little
boutique on the old-fashioned Kirakira
Tachibana shopping street near Tokyo
Skytree stocks every variety imaginable.
The selection includes Japanese-style
clown masks, Venetian masks, contemporary Japanese masks, and masks from
many periods and regions in Japan, and
across many budgets. A perfect resource
for unique gifts. ⊠ *3–20–5 Kyōjima,
Sumida-ku* ☎ *70/5089–6271* ⊕ *kamenya-
mote.com/english* Ⓜ *Asakusa line, Keisei
Hikifune Station.*

DOLLS
Marugin (人形のまるぎん; *Ningyo no
Marugin*)
TOYS | This long-standing doll emporium
by Asakusabashi Station specializes in
hina dolls, or emperor and empress sets
in extravagant Heian-era clothing. Some
families with young girls display these
every year for one month until March
2, Girls' Day. Asakusabashi is one stop
west of Ryogoku on the JR Chuo and
Sobu lines or two stops south of Asakusa
on the Asakusa subway line. ⊠ *1–18–9
Asakusabashi, Taito-ku* ☎ *03/3862–6088*
🕐 *Closed Sun.* Ⓜ *JR Chuo and Sobu lines
(West Exit), Asakusa subway line, Asakusabashi Station (Exit A3).*

FOOD
Kawahara Shoten (川原商店)
SOUVENIRS | The brightly colored bulk
packages of rice crackers, shrimp-
flavored chips, and other Japanese snacks
sold here make offbeat gifts. ⊠ *3–9–2
Nishi-Asakusa, Taito-ku* ☎ *03/3842–0841*
🕐 *Closed Sun.* Ⓜ *Ginza subway line, Asakusa Station (Exit 1).*

Tokiwa-do (常盤堂)

FOOD | Come here to buy some of Tokyo's most famous souvenirs: *kaminari okoshi* (thunder crackers), made of rice, millet, sugar, and beans. The shop is on the west side of Asakusa's Thunder God Gate, the Kaminari-mon entrance to Senso-ji, and you can watch as they make them in front of you. ⊠ *1–3–2 Asakusa, Taito-ku* ☎ *03/3841–5656* ⊕ *www.tokiwado.tokyo* Ⓜ *Ginza subway line, Asakusa Station (Exit 1).*

MARKETS AND SHOPPING ARCADES

Nakamise Market (仲見世通り; *Nakamise-dori*)

NEIGHBORHOODS | Although many of the shops have moved from selling traditional crafts to cheap knickknacks (often not made in Japan), it is worth passing down on your way to Senso-ji for the atmosphere. It is just as lively as it was when it was established in the Edo period, although now shops sells cheap sushi key chains and T-shirts alongside traditional hairpieces and silk screens. The entrance is marked by the giant red lantern at the Kaminari-mon, and ends at the grounds of the Senso-ji Complex. ⊠ *Asakusa 1-chome, Taito-ku, Taito-ku* ☎ *03/3844–3350* Ⓜ *Ginza subway line, Asakusa Station (Exit 1).*

Nishi-Sando Arcade (西参道商店街; *Nishi-Sando Shoten-gai*)

NEIGHBORHOODS | Kimono and *yukata* (cotton kimono) fabrics, traditional accessories, swords, and festival costumes at very reasonable prices are all for sale at this Asakusa arcade. It runs east of the area's movie theaters, between Roku-ku and the Senso-ji Complex. ⊠ *Asakusa 2-chome, Taito-ku, Taito-ku* Ⓜ *Ginza subway line, Asakusa Station (Exit 1).*

SWORDS AND KNIVES

Ichiryo-ya Hirakawa (一両屋平川)

SOUVENIRS | This small, cluttered souvenir shop in the Nishi-Sando arcade carries antique swords and reproductions and has some English-speaking salesclerks.

⊠ *2–7–13 Asakusa, Taito-ku* ☎ *03/3843–0052* ⊙ *Closed Thurs.* Ⓜ *Ginza subway line, Asakusa Station (Exit 1) or Tawaramachi Station (Exit 3).*

★ Kama-Asa (釜浅商店)

HOUSEWARES | This elegant store specializing in handcrafted knives and kitchen utensils was first opened in 1908 in Asakusa's Kappabashi ("kitchen town"). It's now split into two neighboring buildings, one selling more than 80 varieties of knives made by leading makers around Japan, the other focusing on high-grade items like Nambu cast ironware. Allow extra time to have your knives engraved with Japanese symbols or your name at no extra cost. ⊠ *2–24–1 Matsuya, Taito-ku* ☎ *03/3841–9357* ⊕ *www.kama-asa.co.jp/en* Ⓜ *Ginza subway line, Tawaramachi Station.*

Tsubaya Knives (つば屋包丁店; *Tsubaya Hocho-ten*)

HOUSEWARES | This shop's remarkable selection of high-quality cutlery for professionals is designed for every imaginable use, as the art of food presentation in Japan requires a great variety of cutting implements. The best of these carry the Traditional Craft Association seal: hand-forged tools of tempered blue steel, set in handles banded with deer horn to keep the wood from splitting. Be prepared to pay a premium for these items. A cleaver just for slicing soba can cost as much as ¥50,000. ⊠ *3–7–2 Nishi-Asakusa, Taito-ku* ☎ *03/3845–2005* ⊕ *tsubaya.co.jp* Ⓜ *Ginza subway line, Asakusa (Exit 1).*

TRADITIONAL WARES

Asakusa Nakaya Honten (浅草中屋本店)

MIXED CLOTHING | If you want to equip yourself for the neighborhood's annual Sanja Festival in May, this is the place to come for traditional costumes. Best buys here are *sashiko hanten,* which are thick, woven firemen's jackets; and *happi* coats, cotton tunics printed in bright colors with Japanese characters. Some items are available in children's sizes. ⊠ *2–2–12 Asakusa, Taito-ku* ☎ *03/3841–7877*

⊕ *www.nakaya.co.jp* Ⓜ *Ginza subway line, Asakusa Station (Exit 6).*

Ganso Sample (元祖食品サンプル; *Ganso Shokuhin Sanpuru*)

SOUVENIRS | Ganso is one of several shops on Kappabashi-dori specializing in *sanpuru*, the replicas of food and drinks seen in many restaurant window displays. As well as realistic fake beers and plates of noodles, they also sell sushi-shaped trinkets. Or you could stop by for one of their afternoon workshops (¥2,500 per person) to make your own fake tempura. ⊠ *3-7-6 Nishi Asakusa, Taito-ku* ⊕ *www.ganso-sample.com/en/shop* Ⓜ *Ginza subway line, Tawaramachi Station.*

Hyakusuke Cosmetics (百助化粧品店; *Hyakusuke Keishohinten*)

COSMETICS | This is the last place in Tokyo to carry government-approved skin cleanser made from powdered nightingale droppings. Ladies of the Edo period—especially the geisha—swore by the cleanser. These days this 300-year-old-plus cosmetics shop sells little of the nightingale powder, but its theatrical makeup for Kabuki actors, geisha, and traditional weddings—as well as unique items like seaweed shampoo, camellia oil, and handcrafted combs and cosmetic brushes—makes it a worthy addition to your Asakusa shopping itinerary. ⊠ *2–2–14 Asakusa, Taito-ku* ☎ *03/3841–7058* ⊗ *Closed Tues.* Ⓜ *Ginza subway line, Asakusa Station (Exit 6).*

Soi Interior & Style Design (Soi 器; *Soi Utsuwa*)

CRAFTS | The selection of lacquerware, ceramics, and antiques sold at this Kappabashi shop is modest, but Soi displays the items in a minimalist setting of stone walls and wooden floor planks, with up-tempo jazz in the background. ⊠ *3–25–11 Nishi-Asakusa, Taito-ku* ☎ *03/6802–7732* ⊕ *www.soi-2.jp* Ⓜ *Ginza subway line, Asakusa Station (Exit 6).*

Tenugui Fuji-ya (てぬぐいふじ屋)

FABRICS | Master textile creator Keiji Kawakami is an expert on the hundreds of traditional towel motifs that have come down from the Edo period: geometric patterns, plants and animals, and scenes from Kabuki plays and festivals. His cotton *tenugui* (pronounced "teh-*noo*-goo-ee") hand towels are collector's items, often framed instead of used as towels. When Kawakami feels he has made enough of one pattern of his own design, he destroys the stencil. The shop is near the corner of Dembo-in Dori, on the street that runs parallel behind Naka-mise dori. ⊠ *2–2–15 Asakusa, Taito-ku, Asakusa* ☎ *03/3841–2283* ⊕ *tenu-gui-fujiya.jp* ⊗ *Closed Thurs.* Ⓜ *Ginza subway line, Asakusa Station (Exit 1).*

Ryogoku

Sights

The Japanese Sword Museum (刀剣博物館; *Touken Hakubutsukan*)

OTHER MUSEUM | Relocated from Shinjuku in 2018, and now housed in a sleek three-story structure designed by Pritzker Prize winner Fumihiko Maki, the Japanese Sword Museum has thematic exhibitions that range from newly made swords to historic katana. At one time there were some 200 schools of sword making in Japan; swords were prized not only for their effectiveness in battle but for the beauty of the blades and fittings and as symbols of the higher spirituality of the warrior caste. There are few inheritors of this art today and the Sword Museum's mission is to maintain the knowledge and appreciation of sword making. Although the collection has swords made by famous craftsmen such as Nobufusa (a Living National Treasure) and Sanekage (a famous 14th-century sword maker), the focus of the main exhibition space on the third floor is on the swords as objects of beauty. The

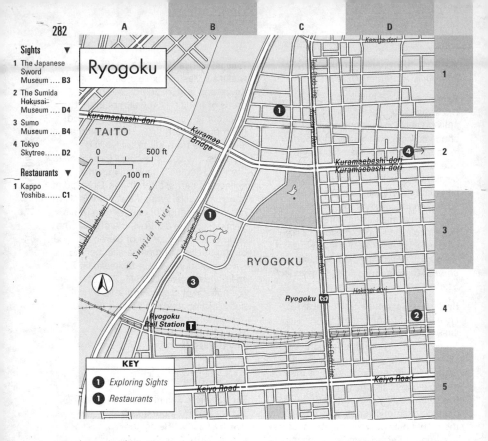

Ryogoku

KEY

1 Exploring Sights

1 Restaurants

swords are individually displayed as works of art, giving visitors a chance to appreciate the detail, creativity, and skill involved in crafting each one. There's also a rooftop garden with views over a traditional garden, Kyu-Yasuda Teien, which is worth a visit in its own right, especially as it's free. ✉ *1–12–9 Yokoami, Sumi-da-ku* ☎ *03/6284–1000* ⊕ *www.touken. or.jp* ✉ *Main exhibition (3rd fl.) ¥1,000* ⊙ *Closed Mon.* Ⓜ *Toei Oedo Line and JR Chuo and Sobu lines, Ryogoku Station.*

The Sumida Hokusai Museum (北斎美術館; *Hokusai Bijutsukan*)

ART MUSEUM | One of Japan's most famous artists, Katsushika Hokusai (1760–1849) was born and spent much of his life in what's now Tokyo's Sumida-ku area, during which time he not only created iconic woodblock prints of Mount Fuji and life in old Edo, but was also a prolific

sketcher and painter. Built where Hokusai grew up, this museum traces his life and work with the help of detailed English explanations. Although the majority of pieces here are replicas, there are also a few originals on display, as well as a life-size recreation of Hokusai's cramped workroom. ✉ *2-7-2 Kamezawa, Sumida-ku* ☎ *03/6658–8936* ⊕ *hokusai-museum. jp* ✉ *Permanent exhibition ¥400, special and permanent exhibitions ¥700* ⊙ *Closed Mon.* Ⓜ *Toei Oedo Line and JR Chuo and Sobu lines, Ryogoku Station.*

Sumo Museum (相撲博物館; *Sumo Hakubutsukan*)

OTHER MUSEUM | If you can't attend a sumo tournament, visit this museum in the south wing of the arena. There are no explanations in English, but the museum's collection of sumo-related woodblock prints, paintings,

A Mostly Naked Free-for-All

Sumo wrestling dates back some 1,500 years. Originally a religious rite performed at shrines to entertain the harvest gods, a match may seem like a fleshy free-for-all to the casual spectator, but to the trained eye, it's a refined battle. Two wrestlers square off in a dirt ring about 15 feet in diameter and charge straight at each other in nothing but silk loincloths. There are various techniques of pushing, gripping, and throwing, but the rules are simple: except for hitting below the belt, grabbing your opponent by the hair (which would certainly upset the hairdresser who accompanies every sumo ringside), or striking with a closed fist, almost anything goes. If you're thrown down or forced out of the ring, you lose. There are no weight divisions and a runt of merely 250 pounds can find himself facing an opponent twice his size.

You must belong to one of the roughly 50 *heya* (stables), many based in Tokyo, to compete. Stables are run by retired wrestlers who have purchased the right from the Japan Sumo Association. Hierarchy and formality rule in the sumo world. Youngsters recruited into the sport live in the stable dormitory, do all the community chores, and wait on their seniors. When they rise high enough in tournament rankings, they acquire their own servant-apprentices.

Most of Tokyo's stables are concentrated on both sides of the Sumidagawa near the Kokugikan. Wander this area and you might see some of them on the streets, in their wood clogs and kimonos, or out and about in more casual clothes. One thing that will be a sumo giveaway is the aroma; the oil they use in their hair smells similar to baby lotion. The heya aren't as accessible as they used to be, but companies such as Viator.com and Rakuten Travel Experiences (⊕ *experiences.travel.rakuten.com*) offer sumo stable tours.

When: Of the six Grand Sumo Tournaments (called *basho*) that take place during the year, Tokyo hosts three: in early January, mid-May, and mid-September. Matches go from early afternoon, when the novices wrestle, to the titanic clashes of the upper ranks from around 4:30 to 6 pm.

Where: Tournaments are held in the Kokugikan, the National Sumo Arena (✉ *1–3–28 Yokoami, Sumidaku* ☏ *03/3623–5111 Toei Oedo Line and JR Sobu and Chuo lines, Ryogoku Station*) in Ryogoku, a district in Sumida-ku also famed for its clothing shops and eateries that cater to sumo sizes and tastes.

How: The most expensive seats, closest to the ring, are tatami-carpeted boxes for two to four people, called *sajiki*. The boxes are terribly cramped and cost ¥9,000–¥20,000 per person. Cheap seats start as low as ¥3,000 for advance sales, ¥2,500 for same-day box office sales for general admission seats. For same-day box office sales you should line up by 6 am. You can also get tickets through the Ticket Pia website (⊕ *sumo.pia.jp/en*) and at 7-Eleven convenience stores.

and illustrated scrolls includes some outstanding examples of traditional Japanese fine art. ⊠ *1–3–28 Yokoami, Sumida-ku* ☎ *03/3622–0366* ⊕ *www. sumo.or.jp/KokugikanSumoMuseum* 🎫 *Free* 🕐 *Closed weekends.*

Tokyo Skytree (東京スカイツリー)

VIEWPOINT | Opened in 2011 to mixed reviews, this 2,000-plus-foot-tall sky-scraper has become a symbol of the ongoing revival of the eastern side of the city. When it opened, tickets to the observation decks were booked for months in advance and the tower, along with the adjacent Solamachi shopping complex, continues to draw shoppers and tourists to the area. On a clear day, the views from the 1,155-foot-high Tembo Deck observation area are impressive. For an extra fee, visitors can go to the Tembo Galleria, another 330 feet up. ⊠ *1–1–2 Oshiage, Sumida-ku* ⊕ *www.tokyo-skytree.jp/en* 🎫 *Tembo Deck only ¥2,100; Tembo Deck and Tembo Galleria ¥2,700* Ⓜ *Tobu Skytree Line Skytree Station, Tobu Skytree Line Oshiage Station.*

 Restaurants

Kappo Yoshiba (割烹吉葉)

$$$$ | **JAPANESE** | As Japan's sumo heartland, Ryogoku is home to not just the Kokugikan arena and numerous *sumobeya* (training stables), but also plenty of restaurants specializing in *chanko-nabe*, the hotpot of meat, seafood, and vegetables eaten by sumo wrestlers. At Kappo, this hearty fare is served in a former training stable that still has a practice ring in the middle of the main dining room. **Known for:** accompaniments like sashimi, sushi, or tempura; atmospheric setting in a former sumo stable; dinnertime musical performances. Ⓢ *Average main: ¥7,800* ⊠ *2-14-5 Yokoami, Sumida-ku* ☎ *03/3623–4480* ⊕ *kapou-yoshiba.jp/english* 🕐 *Closed Sun.* Ⓜ *Toei Oedo Line and JR Chuo and Sobu lines, Ryogoku Station.*

 Nightlife

Popeye (ポパイ)

BARS | Of the staggering 70 beers on tap here, 70% are top-quality Japanese microbrews, from pilsners to IPAs to barley wines. The owner is one of Japan's leading authorities on beer, and his passion is reflected in the quality of the brews. The convivial, sportsbar-like atmosphere attracts a mature clientele, making this a great option for a postsumo spot, but it can fill up quickly. The menu includes chicken ale stew, beer cake, and beer ice cream. ⊠ *2–18–7 Ryogoku, Sumida-ku* ☎ *03/3633–2120* ⊕ *www.lares.dti.ne.jp/~ppy* 🕐 *Closed Sun.* Ⓜ *JR Ryogoku Station (West Exit).*

Chapter 14

BEYOND CENTRAL TOKYO

Updated by
Rob Goss

◉ Sights	🍴 Restaurants	🛏 Hotels	🛍 Shopping	🍸 Nightlife
★★★☆☆	★★☆☆☆	★★☆☆☆	★★☆☆☆	★☆☆☆☆

WELCOME TO BEYOND CENTRAL TOKYO

TOP REASONS TO GO

★ **Tokyo Disney Resort:** With a Baymax-themed ride (unique to Disney parks) and an accompanying water park, Tokyo Disney Resort is popular with both residents and international visitors.

★ **Sengaku-ji Temple:** The 17th-century Buddhist temple in Shinagawa that is featured in "47 Ronin," one of the most famous Samurai tales.

★ **Shopping in Shibamata:** The neighborhood's old-school Taishakuten Shopping Street conveys a sense of what Tokyo was like before the war.

★ **Kiyosumi Garden:** An undervisited and bucolic respite in working-class Fukugawa.

★ **Historic Kawagoe:** With several temples, this historic area just beyond the Tokyo city limits in Saitama prefecture hearkens back to an earlier period of old Japan.

1 Shibamata. A quiet residential area northeast of Asakusa.

2 Fukugawa. Working-class area east of Nihonbashi with a beautiful garden.

3 Urayasu. On the shores of Tokyo Bay, the area is home to the Tokyo Disney Resort.

4 Nakameguro and Daikanyama. South of Shibuya, these neighboring upscale areas are known for restaurants and cafés.

5 Shinagawa. An important transport hub with hotels and a noteworthy temple.

6 Kawagoe. Well-preserved historic town just over the Tokyo border.

7 Narita Airport. Over an hour from Tokyo, the country's major international airport has convenient hotels for those with early flights as well as interesting sights in the neighboring town of Narita.

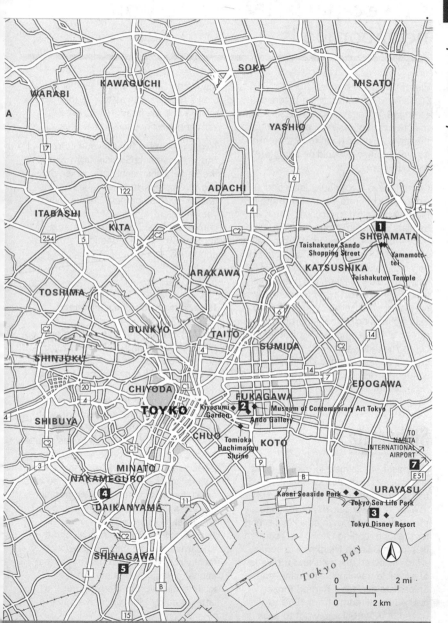

WARABI

KAWAGUCHI

SOKA

MISATO

YASHIO

17

122

ADACHI

6

ITABASHI

KITA

C2

C2

4

SHIBAMATA

Taishakuten Sando
Shopping Street

Yamamoto-
tei

254

5

KATSUSHIKA

Taishakuten Temple

TOSHIMA

ARAKAWA

C2

BUNKYO

TAITO

6

14

SHINJUKU

SUMIDA

14

EDOGAWA

20

C2

4

CHIYODA

C1

TOYKO

FUKAGAWA

7

Kiyosumi
Garden

Museum of Contemporary Art Tokyo

Ando Gallery

SHIBUYA

CHUO

Tomioka
Hachimangu
Shrine

KOTO

TO
NARITA
INTERNATIONAL
AIRPORT

C2

3

C1

9

7

E51

MINATO

NAKAMEGURO

B

URAYASU

Kasai Seaside Park

DAIKANYAMA

11

Tokyo Sea Life Park

3

Tokyo Disney Resort

C2

SHINAGAWA

5

Tokyo Bay

0   2 mi

1

B

0   2 km

15

The size of Tokyo and the diversity of its institutions make it impossible to fit all the capital's interesting sights into neighborhoods.

Plenty of worthy places—from Tokyo Disneyland to the historic quarters of Kawagoe, in neighboring Chiba and Saitama prefectures, respectively—fall outside the city's neighborhood repertoire. Yet no guide to Tokyo would be complete without them.

Central Tokyo is routinely described as a neon-lit, concrete haven, but there is far more to Tokyo to discover. The Kasai Seaside Park offers numerous flora and birdwatching at the edge of Tokyo Bay, while the transport hub of Shinagawa is home to Sengaku-ji, a temple that plays a central role in Japan's most famous tale of samurai loyalty. In the overlooked northeast of Tokyo's 23 wards, Shibamata is a charming old neighborhood that retains a 1950s vibe, while back near the center, a stone's throw from the youthful crowds of Shibuya, chic Daikanyama is an affluent residential enclave likened to Brooklyn for its upscale boutiques and hangouts.

Shibamata

Northeast of Asakusa, in Tokyo's quiet and mostly residential Katsushika-ku district, Shibamata is a charming throwback to early post-war Tokyo. For Tokyoites, the area is best known as a key setting for the long-running Otoko Wa Tsurai Yo (It's Tough Being a Man) movie series, which followed the trials and tribulations of a lovable traveling salesman—and Shibamata denizen—named Tora-san over 48 installments from 1969 to 1995. Spend time here if you want to soak up the retro vibe of Shibamata's main shopping street, as well as to visit its historic temple and the beautifully preserved Yamamoto-tei house and gardens.

To get there take the Chiyoda subway line to Kanamachi Station, from where the Keisei Kanamachi Line, which only has three stops and several trains per hour, runs to Shibamata Station. When you come out of the station's only exit, you'll be greeted by a bronze statue of Tora-san. The main attractions are just a short walk away.

 ## Sights

Taishakuten Sando Shopping Street
(帝釈天参道)
STREET | This several-hundred-meter shopping street between Shibamata Station and Taishakuten Temple has retained an old-Tokyo vibe, its wooden buildings having escaped the heavy bombing that flattened much of Tokyo at the end of World War II and the subsequent postwar redevelopment. Although the street developed as the approach to Taishakuten, its connection to the temple takes a back seat for most visits to the street snacks sold here. The Sando is lined with small, family-run stores selling traditional snacks, such as savory *senbei* (rice crackers), *dorayaki* (sweet pancakes), *kuzu-mochi* (sticky rice cakes), and the Shibamata classic that is *kusa-dango* (sticky rice dumplings on skewers that appear a deep green because they include mugwort in the mix). For the latter, stop by Monzen Toraya. ✉ *7-7-5*

Shibamata, Katsushika-ku Ⓜ Keisei Kana-machi Line, Shibamata Station.

Taishakuten Temple (帝釈天)

TEMPLE | Established in 1629, then rebuilt after the Great Kanto Earthquake of 1923, Taishakuten Temple is entered through a towering wooden gateway at the end of Taishakuten Sando shopping street. While stepping inside the grounds is free, it's best to pay the additional fee to enter the inner sanctuary and garden, the former of which is adorned with intricate wood carvings depicting the life and teachings of buddha. ✉ 7-10-13 Shibamata, Katsushika-ku ☎ 03/3657–2886 ⊕ www.taishakuten.or.jp/index2.html ✍ ¥400 Ⓜ Keisei Kanamachi Line, Shibamata Station.

Yamamoto-tei (山本亭)

HISTORIC HOME | Once the home of businessman Einosuke Yamamoto, Yamamoto-tei is a lovely example of how Japanese and Western styles merged in the homes of some wealthy Tokyoites in the early 1900s. The two-story residence has mostly classic tatami mat rooms with sliding screen doors, but it also incorporates a British-inspired drawing room with marquetry flooring, white plaster ceiling, stained-glass windows, and a marble mantelpiece. Arguably the most striking highlight is the *shoin*-style garden, whose lush greenery, pond, and waterfall are designed to be viewed from the comfort of the tatami rooms; something visitors can do while enjoying green tea and sweets or coffee. ✉ 7-19-32 Shibamata, Katsushika-ku ☎ 03/3657–8577 ⊕ www.katsushika-kanko.com/yamamoto/eng ✍ ¥100 ⊘ Closed 3rd Tues. Ⓜ Keisei Kanamachi Line, Shibamata Station.

🍴 Restaurants

Monzen Toraya (門前とらや)

$ | JAPANESE | In business for more than a century, Toraya is best known for its skewers of sweet *kusa-dango* rice dumplings, which come topped with red-bean paste and are a popular snack for visitors on route to Taishakuten Temple. If you want to stay for lunch, you'll also find a more substantial menu, with ramen, udon noodles, and tempura on rice. **Known for:** tempura on rice; ramen; kusa-dango rice dumplings. Ⓢ *Average main:* ¥900 ✉ 7-7-5 Shibamata, Katsushika-ku ☎ 03/3659–8111 ⊕ www.toraya.info ☰ No credit cards Ⓜ Keisei Kanamachi Line, Shibamata Station.

Fukagawa

A couple of miles east of Nihonbashi, the Fukagawa area developed as part of Tokyo's Edo-era *shitamachi*—the districts of the common, working people—but gets less attention from travelers than more famous shitamachi areas like Asakusa and Yanaka. That's a shame because the overlapping neighborhoods that now make up Fukagawa—Kiyosumi-Shirakawa (in the north) and Monzen-Nakacho (south)—offer a laid-back way to soak up bits of everyday, traditional and creative Tokyo.

In recent years the area has gained hipster cred with a wave of roasteries and galleries. Monzen-Nakacho has a historic shrine, plus some great down-to-earth eateries. The best starting points are either Monzen-Nakacho Station on the Oedo and Tozai subway lines or Kiyosumi-Shirakawa Station on the Oedo and Hanzomon subway lines.

👁 Sights

Ando Gallery (アンドーギャラリー)

ART GALLERY | Very different from the nearby Museum of Contemporary Art Tokyo, the Ando Gallery is the pick of the independent art venues in Kiyosumi-Shirakawa. Located in a small, repurposed storehouse, the focus here is predominantly on young Japanese contemporary artists, with genres ranging from installations to design work. ✉ *3-3-6 Hirano, Koto-ku* ☎ *03/5620–2165* 🌐 *www.andogallery.co.jp* 🎫 *Free* 🕒 *Closed Sun. and Mon.* [M] *Oedo and Hanzomon subway lines, Kiyosumi-Shirakawa Station.*

Kiyosumi Garden
(清澄庭園; *Kiyosumi Teien*)
GARDEN | Defined by its island-accented pond, around which pathways take visitors to a succession of carefully landscaped viewpoints that blend features like manicured trees and ornamental rocks, this traditional garden is one of eastern Tokyo's undervisited gems. Originally part of a feudal lord's residence in the early 1700s, the garden was later owned by the founder of Mitsubishi, who used it to entertain important guests and give staff a place to unwind. Sitting by the pond, watching herons perch on rocks and carp gliding through the water, it's an incredibly relaxing spot. ✉ *3-3-9 Kiyosumi, Koto-ku* ☎ *03/3641–5892* 🌐 *www.tokyo-park.or.jp/teien/en/kiyosumi* 🎫 *¥150* [M] *Oedo and Hanzomon subway lines, Kiyosumi-Shirakawa Station.*

Museum of Contemporary Art Tokyo (東京現代美術館; *Tokyo Gendai Bijutsukan*)
ART MUSEUM | On the far-eastern end of Kiyosumi-Shirakawa, occupying the northernmost part of the sprawling Kiba Park, this modern museum has spaces that rotate between displays of contemporary art from its own collection and special exhibitions. The latter in recent years have included shows devoted to Jean Prouve and David Hockney, while the 2023 schedule includes the work of visual and installation artist Wendelien van Oldenborgh and a look at the designs of Christian Dior. If you need a break while here, there are a café and a restaurant on-site. The museum sometimes closes between exhibitions for reinstallations. ✉ *4-1-1 Miyoshi, Koto-ku* ☎ *03/5245–4111* 🌐 *www.mot-art-museum.jp/en* 🎫 *¥500–¥2,000, depending on the exhibition* 🕒 *Closed Mon.* [M] *Oedo and Hanzomon subway lines, Kiyosumi-Shirakawa Station.*

Tomioka Hachimangu Shrine (富岡八幡宮)
RELIGIOUS BUILDING | This shrine in the heart of Monzen-Nakacho has been a core part of Fukagawa since the 1600s. It's said that some of the earliest sumo tournaments were held here in the 1700s, which explains the sumo-related monuments dotted around the place. Today, the grounds hold small antiques markets on the first, second, third, and fifth Sundays of each month, while lively flea markets take place on the 15th and 28th of each month. In odd-numbered years, the shrine is also the starting point of the summer Fukagawa Hachiman Matsuri, a festival that sees more than 50 portable shrines paraded energetically through the streets while onlookers pour buckets of water over the carriers (and each other). One more quirk here is that you can bring your car to be blessed. ✉ *1-20-3 Tomioka, Koto-ku* ☎ *03/3642–1315* 🌐 *www.tomiokahachimangu.or.jp* 🎫 *Free* [M] *Oedo and Tozai subway lines, Monzen-Nakacho Station.*

🍴 Restaurants

Fukagawa Kamasho (深川釜匠)
$ | JAPANESE | Kamasho serves the signature dish of the old Fukagawa area, Fukagawa-meshi: short-neck clams and green onion cooked in a miso broth and poured over a bowl of rice. You can order just a bowl of Fukagawa-meshi or opt for a set with a side serving of pickles and miso soup. **Known for:** lively atmosphere; Fukagawa-meshi (clams on rice); rustic interiors. [$] *Average main: ¥1,090* ✉ *2-1-13 Shirakawa, Koto-ku* ☎ *03/3643–4053* 🌐 *a328700.gorp.jp* 💳 *No credit cards* 🕒 *Closed Mon.* [M] *Oedo and Hanzomon subway lines, Kiyosumi-Shirakawa Station.*

Uosan Sakaba (魚三酒場)

$$$ | **JAPANESE** | This classic izakaya epitomizes the casual yet lively nights out of a down-to-earth district like Fukagawa. Opened in the 1950s, the four floors here include counter-only seats on the first and second floors that are ideal for watching and chatting with the chefs, and then tables for larger groups on the third and fourth floors. **Known for:** good sake; excellent sashimi; seafood-focused menu. ⓈAverage main: ¥4,000 ✉ 1-5-4 Tomioka, Koto-ku ☎ 03/3641–8071 🚇 No credit cards 🕐 Closed Sun. No lunch Ⓜ Oedo and Tozai subway lines, Monzen-Nakacho Station.

☕ Coffee and Quick Bites

Allpress Espresso Tokyo Roastery & Cafe (オールプレス)

$ | **CAFÉ** | This small, friendly roastery and café in a repurposed warehouse across from Ando Gallery serves excellent espresso, flat whites, and cappuccinos, plus simple snacks like cookies and toasted sandwiches. There are some seats inside, but if the weather is nice get a drink to go and walk a few minutes east to Kiba Park; a lovely green spot to while away an hour. **Known for:** great espresso shots; close to Kiba Park for outdoor coffee; friendly, laidback staff. ⓈAverage main: ¥500 ✉ 3-7-2 Hirano, Koto-ku ☎ 03/5875-9131 ⊕ www.allpressespresso.com/ja/find/tokyo-roastery Ⓜ Oedo and Hanzomon subway lines, Kiyosumi-Shirakawa Station.

Urayasu

Located just outside of Tokyo, in Chiba Prefecture, Urayasu is known for one thing: Tokyo Disney Resort, the twin theme parks Tokyo Disneyland and Tokyo DisneySea. Because they are so close to the city, most visitors to Tokyo do Disney as a day trip, although there is a collection of pricey Disney resort hotels for anyone who wants to fully immerse themselves in the Magic Kingdom.

Across the river from Urayasu, in Tokyo's Edogawa district, Kasai Seaside Park is a less crowded alternative for family fun, with a giant Ferris wheel and aquarium among the attractions.

👁 Sights

Kasai Seaside Park (葛西臨海公園; Kasai Rinkai Koen)

AMUSEMENT PARK/CARNIVAL | **FAMILY** | The star attraction here is the Diamonds and Flowers Ferris wheel (Daia to Hana no Dai-kanransha), which takes passengers on a 17-minute ride to the apex, 384 feet above the ground, for a spectacular view of the bay area. On a clear day you can see all the way to Mt. Fuji; at night, if you're lucky, you reach the top just in time for a bird's-eye view of the fireworks over the Magic Kingdom, across the river. The park also has an observatory looking out over Tokyo Bay as well as the Tokyo Sea Life Park aquarium. There's also a bird-watching center. ✉ 6–2 Rinkai-cho, Edogawa-ku ✛ From Disney take JR Keiyo Line local train from Maihama to Kasai Rinkai Park Station. The same line also connects to Tokyo Station. ☎ 03/5696–1331 🎫 Free, Ferris wheel ¥800 🕐 Ferris wheel closes some Wednesdays in winter Ⓜ JR Keiyo Line, Kasai Rinkai Park Station.

Tokyo Disney Resort (東京ディズニーリゾート)

AMUSEMENT PARK/CARNIVAL | **FAMILY** | Mickey-san and his coterie of Disney characters entertain here at Tokyo Disneyland the same way they do in the California and Florida Disney parks. When the park was built in 1983, it was much smaller than its counterparts in the United States, but the construction in 2001 of the adjacent DisneySea and its seven "Ports of Call," all with different nautical themes and rides, added more than 100 acres to this multifaceted Magic

Did You Know?

Kiyosumi Garden in workaday Fukugawa is one of Tokyo's hidden gems. Its central feature is a pond with a series of islands and pathways that allow visitors to wander and relax in a natural atmosphere.

Kingdom. Most people buy the One-Day Passport, which gives you unlimited access to the attractions and shows at one or the other of the two parks. See the park website for other ticketing options. ⊠ *1–1 Maihama, Urayasu* ☎ *0570/00–8632* ⊕ *www.tokyodisneyresort.jp* ⊠ *From ¥7,900* Ⓜ *JR Keiyo Line, Maihama Station.*

Tokyo Sea Life Park (葛西臨海水族園; *Kaisai Rinkai Suizoku-en*)

AQUARIUM | FAMILY | The three-story cylindrical complex of this aquarium houses roughly 600 species of fish and other sea creatures within a dozen areas, including Voyagers of the Sea (Maguro no Kaiyu), with migratory species; Seas of the World (Sekai no Umi), with species from foreign waters; and the Sea of Tokyo (Tokyo no Umi), devoted to the creatures of the bay and nearby waters. To get here, take the JR Keiyo Line local train from Tokyo Station to Kasai Rinkai Koen Station; the aquarium is a 10-minute walk from the South Exit. ⊠ *6–2–3 Rinkai-cho, Edogawa-ku* ☎ *03/3869–5152* ⊕ *www. tokyo-zoo.net/english/kasai* ⊠ *¥700* ⏰ *Closed Wed.* Ⓜ *JR Keiyo Line, Kasai Rinkai Koen Station.*

Nakameguro and Daikanyama

These two neighborhoods on either side of the Meguro River—one on the quiet edge of the otherwise bustling Shibuya-ku district, the other in Meguro-ku—make for a very chic day or night out. Both are residential areas for the well-heeled, yet also mix sleek urban complexes and fashionable bars and cafés: places to see and be seen. As for the river, in spring it bursts with pink as the cherry blossoms lining it come into bloom. With lanterns up at night and food stalls along the riverbank, it's one of Tokyo's best evening *hanami* (cherry blossom viewing) spots.

The best way to get there is on the Tokyu Toyoko Line from Shibuya Station. From there, it's one stop to Daikanyama and two stops to Naka-Meguro, making either a good destination for a meal out if you are staying in Shibuya.

Sights

Daikanyama T-Site

STORE/MALL | A bookstore and then some, T-Site was designed to be a "library in the woods" for major bookseller Tsutaya but has ended up being a fashionable meeting place for the Daikanyama area. The three wings of the complex house a Tsutaya store full of arty, intellectual tomes, but there are also cafés and restaurants here, including the plush Anjin Library and Lounge, where you can ease into a comfy chair with a coffee or cocktail while surrounded by 30,000 vintage magazines from the 1960s and '70s. Don't miss taking a look at T-Site's dog salon too: it's where some of Daikanyama's most pampered pooches come for styling. ⊠ *16-15 Sarugakucho, Shibuya-ku* ☎ *03/3770–7555* ⊕ *store. tsite.jp/daikanyama* ⊠ *Free* Ⓜ *Tokyu Toyoko line, Daikanyama Station.*

Hillside Terrace (ヒルサイドテラス)

STORE/MALL | Designed by famed architect Fumihiko Maki, the Hillside Terrace helped shape Daikanyama as a chic neighborhood after it was opened in 1967 and as it was subsequently expanded over the next three decades. Spread over multiple low-rise buildings, it mixes cafés and restaurants with offices, design and fashion stores, and small galleries. It's been overtaken in the public consciousness by T-Site in recent years, but the contemporary art at Art Front Gallery, coffee at Hillside Cafe, and all its other outlets still make it worth a browse. ⊠ *29-18 Sarugakucho, Shibuya-ku* ☎ *03/5489–3705* ⊕ *hillsideterrace.com* ⊠ *Free* Ⓜ *Tokyu Toyoko Line, Daikanyama Station.*

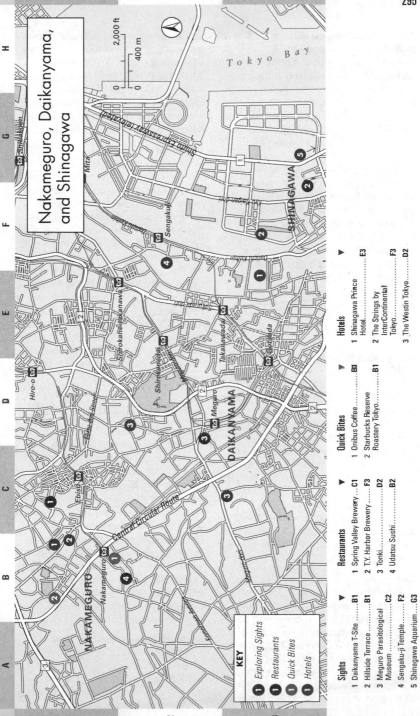

Nakameguro, Daikanyama, and Shinagawa

KEY

1 *Exploring Sights*
1 *Restaurants*
1 *Quick Bites*
1 *Hotels*

Sights ▶

1 Daikanyama T-Site **B1**
2 Hillside Terrace **B1**
3 Meguro Parasitological
   Museum. **C2**
4 Sengaku-ji Temple........ **F2**
5 Shinagawa Aquarium **G3**

Restaurants ▶

1 Spring Valley Brewery ... **C1**
2 T.Y. Harbor Brewery **F3**
3 Tonki........................... **D2**
4 Udatsu Sushi **B2**

Quick Bites ▶

1 Onibus Coffee.............**B1**
2 Starbucks Reserve
   Roastery Tokyo...........**B1**

Hotels ▶

1 Shinagawa Prince
   Hotel........................ **E3**
2 The Strings by
   InterContinental
   Tokyo........................ **F3**
3 The Westin Tokyo........ **D2**

Tokyo Bay

2,000 ft
400 m

Meguro Parasitological Museum (目黒寄生虫館; *Meguro Kiseichu-kan*)
SCIENCE MUSEUM | Part of a private research facility specializing in the study of parasites, this small but free museum is definitely not for the squeamish. Some of the specimens preserved in glass jars look like props from *Alien*. However, if you've ever dreamed of owning a T-shirt with the image of a giant tapeworm on the front, the museum shop has you covered. To get here, you will need to go well off the beaten path: it's a 20-minute walk south of Naka-Meguro Station, or more conveniently 10 minutes west of Meguro Station. ✉ *4-1-1 Shimomeguro, Meguro-ku* ☎ *03/3716–1264* 🌐 *www.kiseichu.org/e-top* 🎫 *Free* 🕐 *Closed Mon. and Tues.* [M] *JR Yamanote Line and Namboku and Mita subway lines, Meguro Station.*

🍴 Restaurants

Spring Valley Brewery (スプリングバレーブルワリー)
$$$ | **AMERICAN** | This microbrewery produces a core lineup of six ales and lagers in Daikanyama, which explains the large brew tanks you can see as you eat and drink. But this is not just a place to drink; the menu also features a good range of burgers, pizzas, and grilled meats. **Known for:** views of large brewing tanks; burgers and pizzas; a range of their own craft beers. [$] *Average main: ¥5,000* ✉ *13-1 Daikanyamacho, Shibuya-ku* ☎ *03/6416–4960* 🌐 *www.springvalleybrewery.jp/pub/tokyo* [M] *Tokyu Toyoko Line, Daikanyama Station.*

Tonki (とんき)
$$ | **JAPANESE** | A family joint, Tonki is a success that never went conglomerate or added frills to what it does best: deep-fried pork cutlets, soup, raw-cabbage salad, rice, pickles, and tea. That's the standard course, and almost everybody orders it, with good reason—it's utterly delicious. Just listen to customers in line as they put in their usual orders while a server comes around to take it. **Known for:** hearty, affordable meals; juicy pork; a line out the door. [$] *Average main: ¥1,900* ✉ *1–1–2 Shimo-Meguro, Meguro-ku* ☎ *03/3491–9928* 🕐 *Closed Tues. and 3rd Mon. of month. No lunch* [M] *JR Yamanote and Namboku subway lines, Meguro Station (Nishi-guchi/West Exit).*

Udatsu Sushi (宇田津鮨)
$$$$ | **SUSHI** | This intimate counter-only sushi restaurant in Naka-Meguro's backstreets serves *omakase* courses based on what the owner-chef sources each day from Toyosu Market, so you never know exactly what you will be served; just that it will be incredible. While fish takes center-stage, herbs and vegetables are also incorporated into Udatsu's often modern take on sushi. **Known for:** innovative take on traditional sushi; intimate setting; vegetarian sushi options. [$] *Average main: ¥22,000* ✉ *2-48-10 Kamimeguro, Meguro-ku* ☎ *050/3550–5938* 🌐 *www.udatsu-sushi.jp/en* [M] *Tokyu Toyoko Line, Naka-Meguro Station and Hibiya subway line, Naka-Meguro Station.*

☕ Coffee and Quick Bites

Onibus Coffee
$ | **CAFÉ** | This specialty roaster now has several branches in Tokyo, including this small stand (with limited seating) near Naka-Meguro Station. The baristas here are extremely knowledgeable and brew up great espressos, hand-drip coffees, and lattes. **Known for:** knowledgeable baristas; excellent hand-drip coffee and espresso; limited seating. [$] *Average main: ¥550* ✉ *2-14-1 Kamimeguro, Meguro-ku* ☎ *03/6412–8683* 🌐 *onibuscoffee.com* 💳 *No credit cards* [M] *Tokyu Toyoko line, Naka-Meguro Station and Hibiya subway line, Naka-Meguro Station.*

Starbucks Reserve Roastery Tokyo
$ | **CAFÉ** | While you may or may not typically seek out Starbucks while traveling, this super-fancy Starbucks Reserve Roastery is especially inviting during *sakura* (cherry

blossom) season. You'll be able to get sakura-flavored drinks like cream soda sakura (only available seasonally), and the second-floor terrace is a wonderful spot to view the blossoms. **Known for:** tricky to find (walk 10 minutes northwest on Yamate-dori from Naka-Meguro, then right at Dormy Inn); good people-watching spot; sakura-flavored drinks in cherry blossom season (spring). $ *Average main: ¥500* ✉ *2-19-23 Aobadai, Meguro-ku* ☎ *03/6417–0202* ⊕ *www.starbucks.com* Ⓜ *Tokyu Toyoko Line, Naka-Meguro Station and Hibiya subway line, Naka-Meguro Station.*

Hotels

The Westin Tokyo
(ウェスティンホテル東京)

$$$ | HOTEL | In the Yebisu Garden Place development, the Westin provides easy access to Mitsukoshi department store, the Tokyo Photographic Art Museum, the elegant Ebisu Garden concert hall, and the Joël Robuchon restaurant (in a full-scale reproduction of a Louis XV château). **Pros:** "Heavenly Beds"; large rooms; great concierge. **Cons:** walk from station is more than 10 mins.; rooms can feel stuffy to some; small gym. $ *Rooms from: ¥33,000* ✉ *1–4–1 Mita, Meguro-ku* ☎ *03/5423–7000* ⊕ *www.westin-tokyo. co.jp* ⇥ *438 rooms* ⦿l *No Meals* Ⓜ *JR Yamanote Line and Hibiya subway line, Ebisu Station (Higashi-guchi/East Exit).*

ⓨ Nightlife

Cabin Naka-Meguro (キャビン中目黒)
BARS | Alongside the Meguro River, a few minutes southeast of Naka-Meguro Station, the very hip Cabin—designed with what it describes as a "cotemporary rustic" theme—has an extensive range of world whiskies and rare local tipples, as well Champagne and cocktails. ✉ *1-10-23 Nakameguro, Meguro-ku* ☎ *03/6303–2220* ⊕ *www.cabintokyo.com* ⊙ *Closed Sun. and Mon.* Ⓜ *Tokyu Toyoko Line,*

Naka-Meguro Station and Hibiya subway line, Naka-Meguro Station.

Debris (デブリ)
COCKTAIL LOUNGES | Part cocktail bar, part event space that runs DJ nights, movie screenings, recitals, and art exhibitions, neon-lit Debris is a very chic hangout for Daikanyama's creative set. The mixologists here can mix up classics, but also get creative with artisanal spirits from around the world. Most events have a ¥500 cover charge. ✉ *11-12 Daikanyamacho, Shibuya-ku* ☎ *03/6416–4334* ⊕ *debrispace.com* Ⓜ *Tokyu Toyoko line, Daikanyama Station.*

Shinagawa

Although Shinagawa isn't the most exciting part of Tokyo, the numerous hotels and train options make this transport hub hard to overlook. From Shinagawa Station, the bullet train connects to key destinations west, including Nagoya, Osaka, Kyōto, and Hiroshima, while the Yamanote and other lines mean Shinagawa is well connected to Shibuya, Shinjuku, and other popular parts of Tokyo. For anyone flying in or out of Haneda Airport, Shinagawa is only 10 km (6.2 miles) away. Nor is the area entirely devoid of attractions. For families, there's Shinagawa Aquarium, and not far from Shinagawa Station, Sengaku-ji Temple is a central part of one of Japan's most enduring tales of samurai loyalty.

⦿ Sights

★ Sengaku-ji Temple (泉岳寺)
TEMPLE | In 1701, a young provincial baron named Asano Takumi-no-Kami attacked and seriously wounded a courtier named Yoshinaka Kira. Asano, for daring to draw his sword in the confines of Edo Castle, was ordered to commit suicide, so his family line was abolished and his fief confiscated. Forty-seven of Asano's loyal retainers vowed revenge; the death of

their leader made them *ronin*—masterless samurai. On the night of December 14, 1702, Asano's ronin stormed Kira's villa in Edo, cut off his head, and brought it in triumph to Asano's tomb at Sengaku-ji, the family temple. The ronin were sentenced to commit suicide—which they accepted as the reward, not the price, of their honorable vendetta—and were buried in the temple graveyard with their lord.

Through the centuries this story has become a national epic and the last word on the subject of loyalty and sacrifice, celebrated in every medium from Kabuki to film. The temple still stands, and the graveyard is wreathed in smoke from the bundles of incense that visitors still lay reverently on the tombstones. There is a collection of weapons and other memorabilia from the event in the temple's small museum. One of the items derives from Kira's family's desire to give him a proper burial. The law insisted this could not be done without his head, so they asked for it back. It was entrusted to the temple, and the priests wrote a receipt, which survives even now in the corner of a dusty glass case. "Item," it begins, "One head." ✉ *2–11–1 Takanawa, Minato-ku* ☎ *03/3441–5560* 🌐 *www.sengakuji.or.jp* 🎫 *Temple and grounds free, museum ¥500* [M] *Asakusa subway line, Sengakuji Station (Exit A2).*

Shinagawa Aquarium (しながわ水族館; *Shinagawa Suizokukan*)
AQUARIUM | FAMILY | The most fun part of this aquarium in southwestern Tokyo is walking through an underwater glass tunnel while some 450 species of fish swim around and above you. There are no pamphlets or explanation panels in English, however, and do your best to avoid weekends, when the dolphin and sea lion shows draw crowds in impossible numbers. Take the local Kyuko Main Line from Shinagawa to Omori Kaigan Station. Turn left as you exit the station and follow the ceramic fish on the sidewalk to the first traffic light; then turn right. ✉ *3–2–1 Katsushima, Shinagawa-ku* ☎ *03/3762–3433* 🌐 *www.aquarium.gr.jp* 🎫 *¥1,350* ⏲ *Often closed Tues.* [M] *Kyuko Main Line, Omori Kaigan Station.*

🍴 Restaurants

T.Y. Harbor Brewery (T.Y.ハーバーブルワリーレストラン)
$$$ | ECLECTIC | A converted warehouse on the waterfront houses this restaurant, known for its grills, California-Asia fusions, and craft beers. Don't miss the wheat ale steamed clams, Thai-style gai yang chicken sate or the Indian spice marinated lamb chops. **Known for:** outdoor seating overlooking Tokyo Bay; a selection of craft beers brewed on-site; incorporating Asian elements into classic American fare. [$] *Average main: ¥4,000* ✉ *2–1–3 Higashi-Shinagawa, Shinagawa-ku* ☎ *03/5479–4555* 🌐 *www.tysons.jp/tyharbor* [M] *Tokyo Monorail or Rinkai Line, Ten-nozu Isle Station (Exit B).*

🛏 Hotels

Shinagawa Prince Hotel
(品川プリンスホテル)
$$ | HOTEL | FAMILY | Just a three-minute walk from JR Shinagawa Station, the Prince is a sprawling complex that's part hotel (with four towers) and part entertainment village, featuring everything from an 80-lane bowling alley to tennis courts to an 11-screen movie theater and game centers. **Pros:** affordable rates; multiple entertainment choices, including a bowling alley and an IMAX theater; nice view of Tokyo Bay from lounge. **Cons:** complicated layout; crowded on weekends; rooms can be small. [$] *Rooms from: ¥20,000* ✉ *4–10–30 Takanawa, Minato-ku* ☎ *03/3440–1111* 🌐 *www.princehotels.com/shinagawa* 🛏 *3,331 rooms* 🍴 *No Meals* [M] *JR Yamanote Line, Shinagawa Station (Nishi-guchi/West Exit).*

What's a Vegetarian to Do?

Tokyo has had a reputation of being difficult for vegetarians, but as more Japanese opt to forgo meat, the number of truly vegetarian and even vegan restaurants is rising. Organic produce has also become more in demand, and many restaurants now serve organic meals that very often are vegetarian. The city's numerous Indian eateries are a safe bet, as are the handful of restaurants that specialize in *shojin ryori*, traditional Zen vegetarian food that emphasizes natural flavors and fresh ingredients without using heavy spices or rich sauces. But you should always inquire when making reservations at these restaurants, as some still use *dashi*, a stock made with smoked skipjack

tuna and kelp. The variety and visual beauty of a full-course shojin ryori meal opens new dining dimensions to the vegetarian gourmet. *Goma-dofu*, or sesame-flavored bean curd, for example, is a tasty treat, as is *nasu-dengaku*, grilled eggplant covered with a sweet miso sauce.

Take note that a dish may be described as meat-free even if it contains fish, shrimp, or stock made with meat. Salads and occasionally pastas might come garnished with ham or bacon, so be sure to ask.

If you plan to stay in town long term, check out Alishan (アリサン) (⊕ *store. alishan.jp*), a vegetarian mail-order specialist.

The Strings by InterContinental Tokyo (ストリングスホテル東京インターコンチネンタル)
$$$ | HOTEL | Beautifully blending modernity with traditional Japanese aesthetics, the Strings is one of Shinagawa's top-tier hotels. **Pros:** great lobby; convenient location; nice view of the Tokyo skyline. **Cons:** expensive restaurants; finding elevator entrance can be challenging; no pool or spa. Ⓢ *Rooms from: ¥35,000* ✉ *2–16–1 Konan, Minato-ku* ☎ *03/5783–1111* ⊕ *intercontinental-strings.jp* ➪ *212 rooms* ❖❖ *No Meals* Ⓜ *JR Yamanote Line, Shinagawa Station (Konan Exit).*

Kawagoe

Sometimes referred to as "Ko-Edo" (Little Edo), the city of Kawagoe was a bustling commercial center in the Edo era (1603–1868). Today, with the Kita-in Temple and Hikawa Shrine, not to mention well-preserved historic quarters, the city retains much of its old-Japan charm.

Kawagoe is just outside the Tokyo metropolitan limits, in Saitama Prefecture, but it is an easy day trip or half-day trip from most parts of the capital. Depending on which part of Tokyo you are coming from, it takes 35 to 50 minutes by train, with common routes being the Tobu Line express service between Ikebukuro and Kawagoe stations (35 minutes) and the Seibu Line limited express from Seibu-Shinjuku Station to Hon-Kawagoe (55 minutes). Once in Kawagoe, the loop bus frequently runs between all the key sights. A day-pass for that costs ¥400.

◉ Sights

Hikawa Shrine (氷川神社; *Hikawa-jinja*)
RELIGIOUS BUILDING | Located northeast of Kawagoe's central sightseeing area (you'll want to get on the loop bus rather than walk), Hikawa is known as a shrine where people come to pray for love and marital happiness. To do that yourself, write a wish on an *ema* (small votive plaque) and then hang it in the extremely

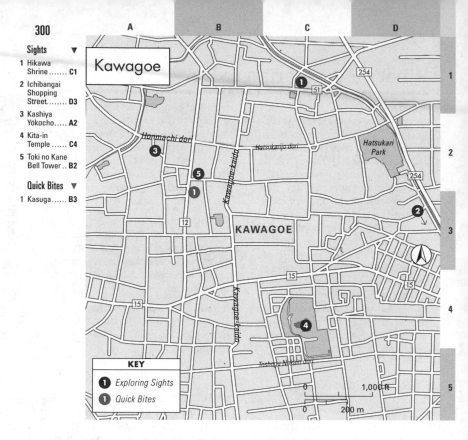

Instagrammable ema tunnel. There are also two 600-year-old zelkova trees on the grounds, wedded together by an ornately wound rope. It's said that walking around these giant trees in a figure of eight pattern also bestows good fortune. ✉ *2-11-3 Miyashitamachi* ☎ *049/224-0589* ⊕ *www.kawagoehikawa.jp* Ⓜ *Seibu Shinjuku Line, Hon-kawagoe Station and Tobu Line, Kawagoe Station.*

Ichibangai Shopping Street (川越一番街; *Kawagoe Ichibangai*)
STREET | The most famous of Kawagoe's old streetscapes, Ichibangai ("first street"), is lined with historic, black- and white-plastered warehouses and dark wooden merchant residences that today house all sorts of places to shop or stop for a snack. Souvenir-wise, you'll find stores selling incense, jewelry, glass beads, and fashion accessories, while the street snacks vary from tofu donuts to traditional sweets designed to be taken with green tea. More than anything, Ichibangai is just a pleasant place to stroll and take in the old vibe. ✉ *Sawaicho area* ⊕ *kawagoe-ichibangai.com* Ⓜ *Seibu Shinjuku Line, Hon-kawagoe Station and Tobu Line, Kawagoe Station.*

Kashiya Yokocho (菓子屋横丁)
STREET | FAMILY | Another of Kawagoe's historic enclaves, this cobblestone side street translates as "candy store alley." It's a great stop for anyone with a sweet tooth, thanks to its roughly 30 confectionery shops that sell colorful hard candies, honeycomb toffee, and more traditional Japanese treats such as *dango* (rice dumplings) and *senbei* (savory rice crackers). ✉ *Motomachi 2-chome area* Ⓜ *Seibu Shinjuku Line, Hon-kawagoe Station and Tobu Line, Kawagoe Station.*

Kita-in Temple (喜多院)

TEMPLE | Established around AD 830, Kita-in has long been an important temple in what was once known as the Kawagoe Domain. Not only is its graveyard the resting place of feudal lords, but over the temple's long tenure it has accumulated several notable features. Several buildings were moved here from Edo Castle in the 1600s, as well as a famous collection of 500 Rakan Statues carved between the 1780s and 1820s. Each is a unique representation of the disciples of Buddha, with various pained and pleasured facial expressions. There's a 17th-century shrine on the grounds too, as well as several gardens planted with azaleas, hydrangeas, and plum, cherry, and maple trees that combine to repaint the gardens seasonally. ⊠ *1-20-1 Kosenbamachi, Kawagoe* ☎ *049/222-0859* ⊕ *kitain.net/en* ⊠ *¥400* Ⓜ *Seibu Shinjuku Line, Hon-kawagoe Station and Tobu Line, Kawagoe Station.*

Toki no Kane Bell Tower (時の鐘)

HISTORIC SIGHT | The symbol of old Kawagoe can't be left out of a guide, although there isn't actually much to do at this 16-meter-tall (52-foot) bell tower other than take a photo. Originally built in the 1600s, the current structure dates to the 1890s, when it was rebuilt following a fire that destroyed much of Kawagoe. It's just north of the Ichibangai shopping street. ⊠ *15-7 Sawaicho* ⊠ *Free* Ⓜ *Seibu Shinjuku Line, Hon-kawagoe Station and Tobu Line, Kawagoe Station.*

☕ Coffee and Quick Bites

Kasuga (かすが)

$ | JAPANESE | Located in a 120-year-old former merchant house on Ichibangai shopping street, this eatery is good for a quick snack on the go or a sit down lunch. It's known for its skewers of soy-basted *dango* (rice dumplings) and decadent parfaits, but also serves bowls of more filling somen noodles and udon noodles. **Known for:** dango; somen noodles; historic location. $ *Average main: ¥950* ⊠ *6-1 Sawaicho* ☎ *049/226-2392* Ⓜ *Seibu Shinjuku Line, Hon-kawagoe Station and Tobu Line, Kawagoe Station.*

Narita Airport

Narita Airport is at least an hour or more from Tokyo by train, bus, or taxi, albeit in heavy traffic the latter can take a couple of hours, making an overnight stay attractive if you have a late arrival or an early departure. For attractions in Narita City, the JR Narita Line and Keisei Main Line connect the airport's terminals with Narita Station in less than 10 minutes. If you planning a night near Narita Airport before an early flight, or if you have a few hours to kill on a layover, then the attractions of Narita are well worth a look.

◉ Sights

Naritasan Shinsho-ji Temple (成田山新勝寺)

TEMPLE | One of the Kanto region's oldest temples, Naritasan was founded in the AD 900s to hold a statue of the Buddhist deity Fudo Myoo, which legend has it was carved by Kobo Daishi, the founder of Shingon Buddhism. That statue alone—still viewable in the temple's vast main hall—marks Naritasan out as special to many Japanese, but added to that are two impressive pagodas and a spacious wooded park to explore. Once at Narita Station, which is less than 10 minutes by train from the airport, the temple is reached via Naritasan Omotesando, an 800-meter-long (½-mile) avenue lined with souvenir stores and restaurants, which is fun to explore in its own right, especially if you are in need of some last-minute souvenirs. ⊠ *1 Narita, Narita* ☎ *0476/22–2111* ⊕ *www.naritasan.or.jp/english* ⊠ *Free* Ⓜ *JR Narita Line and Keisei Main Line, Narita Station.*

Narita Dream Farm

(成田ゆめ牧場; *Narita Yume Bokujo*)
FARM/RANCH | FAMILY | If you take the
train between Tokyo and Narita, you'll
notice that before reaching the capital
there are rice paddies and farmland on
view. At Narita Dream Farm (aka Yume
Bokujo), you can experience that rural
side of Greater Tokyo firsthand, with an
emphasis on family fun. You can feed and
milk cows, as well pet guinea pigs and
goats, or have a tractor ride. There are
also workshops to make jam, butter, and
bread; on a less rural note, you could try
some archery, too. It's a very different
kind of Tokyo experience that's very well
suited to small kids. ✉ *730-3 Nagi, Narita*
✛ *From Namekawa Station a free shuttle
bus to the farm runs on the hour from 10
am to 3 pm daily* ⊕ *www.yumebokujo.
com/en-index.html* ⊠ *¥1,450; hands-on
workshops from ¥650* Ⓜ *JR Narita Line,
Namekawa Station.*

 Coffee and Quick Bites

Kawatoyo (川豊)

$$ | JAPANESE | The culinary specialty
of the Narita area is freshwater eel
(*unagi*), and there are plenty of places
to try it along Naritasan Omotesando.
Close to Naritasan, Kawatoyo has been
in business for more than 100 years,
serving a classic called *unajò*, chargrilled
eel slathered in a savory soy-based sauce
and served over rice. **Known for:** interesting sides such as fried eel bones; historic
establishment; char-grilled eel. Ⓢ *Average
main: ¥2,700* ✉ *386 Nakamachi, Narita*
☎ *0476/22-2721* ⊕ *www.unagi-kawatoyo.
com/foreign/index.html* ⊟ *No credit cards*
🕓 *No dinner* Ⓜ *JR Narita Line and Keisei
Main Line, Narita Station.*

 Hotels

ANA Crowne Plaza Narita

(ANA クラウンプラザホテル成田)
$ | HOTEL | With its brass-and-marble detail
in the lobby, this hotel replicates the
grand style of other hotels in the ANA
chain. **Pros:** convenient location; pleasant
staff; airport shuttle. **Cons:** small rooms;
charge to use pool; in-house restaurants
are the only dining options in the area.
Ⓢ *Rooms from: ¥14,000* ✉ *68 Horin-
ouchi, Narita* ☎ *0476/33-1311* ⊕ *www.
anacrowneplaza-narita.jp* ⤵ *396 rooms*
🍽 *No Meals.*

Hilton Tokyo Narita Airport (ヒルトン成田)

$ | HOTEL | Given its proximity to the
airport (a 15-minute free shuttle), this
C-shape hotel is a reasonable choice for
a one-night visit. **Pros:** reasonably priced
rooms; spacious lobby; airport shuttle.
Cons: charge to use the pool and gym;
common areas a bit worn; in-room Wi-Fi
is not free. Ⓢ *Rooms from: ¥14,000*
✉ *456 Kosuge, Narita* ☎ *0476/33-1121*
⊕ *www.hilton.com* ⤵ *548 rooms* 🍽 *No
Meals.*

nine hours (ナインアワーズ)

$ | HOTEL | For a layover at Narita, this cap-
sule hotel's location can't be beat—it's
actually inside Terminal 2. **Pros:** convenient; reasonably priced; day use and
showers available. **Cons:** tight confines;
limited services; can be noisy. Ⓢ *Rooms
from: ¥5,900* ✉ *Narita Airport Terminal 2,
1-1 Furugome, Narita* ☎ *0476/33-5109*
⊕ *ninehours.co.jp/narita* ⤵ *129 capsules
(71 for men, 58 for women)* 🍽 *No Meals.*

Chapter 15

SIDE TRIPS FROM TOKYO

15

Updated by
Robert Morel

👁 Sights   🍴 Restaurants   🛏 Hotels   🛍 Shopping   🍸 Nightlife

★★★★☆   ★★★☆☆   ★★★☆☆   ★★★☆☆   ★☆☆☆☆

WELCOME TO
SIDE TRIPS FROM TOKYO

TOP REASONS TO GO

★ **Peer at Fuji:** Climb Japan's tallest mountain or catch a glimpse of it from Fuji-Hakone-Izu National Park.

★ **Escape into rustic Japan:** The endless modernity of Tokyo seems worlds away in Nikko, where the Tosho-gu area shrines and temples transport you centuries back into the country's past and the Kegon Falls just transport you.

★ **Get into a Zen-like state:** Kita-Kamakura is home to two preeminent Zen temples, Engaku and Kencho. In Hase, gaze on the Great Buddha or explore inside the giant statue.

★ **Visit China without boarding a plane:** In Yokohama, a port city, sample authentic Chinese goods, spices, and crafts in Chinatown. For a bit of whimsy and a great view, ride Yokohama's Ferris wheel.

1 Yokohama. A busy port, Yokohama also has a cultured, relaxed atmosphere and Japan's largest Chinatown.

2 Kamakura. A city filled with temples and hiking as well as a bustling town center.

3 Mount Fuji (Fuji-san). Japan's tallest and most sacred mountain.

4 Fuji Five Lakes (Fuji Go-ko). The five lakes and surrounding mountains offer a quiet getaway and a staging point for visiting Mt. Fuji.

5 Hakone. Filled with hot springs and hiking, cafes and museums.

6 Izu. From the hot-spring town of Atami's retro vibe to the laid back beach town of Shimoda, visitors come to Izu for the springs, beaches, and costal views.

7 Mt. Takao. The most hiked mountain in Japan is an hour's train ride from Shinjuku.

8 Nikko. Crowds flock to Nikko to see Tosho-gu, the resting place of Ieyasu Tokugawa.

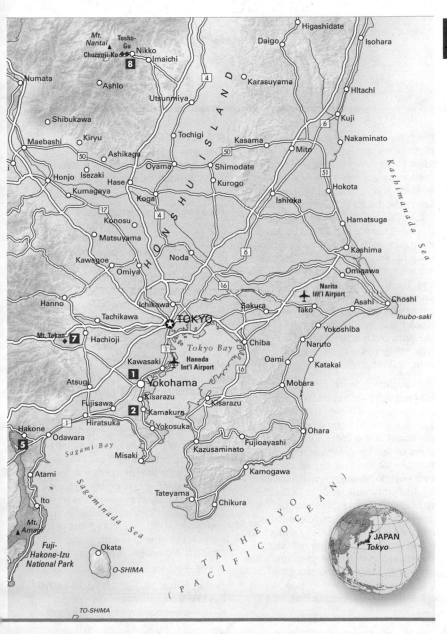

As diverse and exciting as the neighborhoods of Tokyo are, a short day trip or overnight away from the city offers a refreshingly different perspective on Japan, and the city is a great base for numerous day-trips.

Yokohama is a nearby port city with an international character all its own—it's home to the country's largest Chinatown. The ancient city of Kamakura has great historical and cultural sights. You can easily visit the iconic Fuji-san (Mt. Fuji) or the surrounding Fuji Five Lakes, one of Japan's most popular resort areas and a popular national park. Hakone is a popular destination with hot springs and relatively easy access to the Mt. Fuji area. The Izu Peninsula is another favorite hot spring resort areas for both Japanese and foreign travelers. Finally, Nikko, a popular vacation destination for Tokyo residents and the home of Toshogu, the astonishing shrine to the first Tokugawa shogun, Ieyasu.

One caveat: the term "national park" does not quite mean what it does elsewhere in the world. In Japan pristine grandeur is hard to come by; there are few places in this country where intrepid hikers can go to contemplate the beauty of nature for very long in solitude. If a thing's worth seeing, it's worth developing. This worldview tends to fill Japan's national parks with bus caravans, ropeways, gondolas, scenic overlooks with coin-fed telescopes, signs that tell you where you may or may not walk, fried-noodle joints and vending machines, and shacks full of kitschy souvenirs. That's true of Nikko, and it's true as well of Fuji-Hakone-Izu National Park.

MAJOR REGIONS

Yokohama is Japan's largest port. Its waterfront park and its Minato Mirai bayside development project draw visitors from all over.

Kamakura is an ancient city—the birthplace of the samurai way of life. The country's first shogun chose this site as the seat of his military government. The warrior elite took much of their ideology from Zen Buddhism, endowing splendid temples. As a religious center, Kamakura presents an extraordinary legacy. Most of its temples and shrines are in settings of remarkable beauty; many are designated National Treasures.

Mount Fuji, southwest of Tokyo between Suruga and Sagami bays, is one of Japan's most popular resort areas. The main attraction, of course, is Mt. Fuji, a dormant volcano—it last erupted in 1707—rising to a height of 12,388 feet. The mountain is truly beautiful; utterly captivating in the ways it can change in different light and from different perspectives. Its symmetry and majesty have been immortalized by poets and artists for centuries. Keep in mind that in spring and summer, Mt. Fuji often hides behind a blanket of clouds—worth noting if seeing the mountain is an important part of your trip.

To the north of Mt. Fuji, the **Fuji Go-ko (Fuji Five Lakes)** area affords an unbeatable view of the mountain on clear days and

Mt. Fuji is an active volcano that last erupted in 1707.

makes the best base for a climb to the summit. With its various outdoor activities, such as skating and fishing in winter and boating and hiking in summer, this is a popular resort area for families and business conferences. The five lakes are, from the east, Yamanaka-ko, Kawaguchi-ko, Sai-ko, Shoji-ko, and Motosu-ko. Yamanaka and Kawaguchi are the largest and most developed as resort areas, with Kawaguchi more or less the centerpiece of the group.

Hakone has mountains, volcanic landscapes, and lake cruises, plus onsen (hot springs) of its own.

The Izu Peninsula is popular for its beaches and scenically rugged coastline.

Mt. Takao is actually located within the limits of the metropolitan Tokyo. Mt. Takao is a densely wooded area within an hour of the center of the city and has hiking trails, beautiful scenery, an interesting temple, and a monkey zoo.

Nikko, which means "sunlight," is a popular vacation spot for the Japanese, for good reason: its gorgeous sights include a breathtaking waterfall and one of the country's best-known shrines. In addition, Nikko combines the rustic charm of a countryside village (complete with wild monkeys that have the run of the place) with a convenient location not far from Tokyo. Nikko is the site of the Tokugawa Shrine and Nikko Kokuritsu Koen. The centerpiece of the park is Chuzenji-ko and the famous Kegon Falls.

Planning

Hotels

In both Nikko and the Fuji-Hakone-Izu area, there are modern, Western-style hotels that operate in a fairly standard international style. More common, however, are the traditional ryokan (inns). The main difference between these lodging options is that Western-style hotels are situated in prime tourist locations whereas ryokans stick strictly to Japanese-style rooms and are found in less central locations. The undisputed pleasure of a ryokan is to return to it at the end of a hard day of sightseeing, luxuriate for an hour in a hot bath with your own garden view, put on the *yukata* (cotton kimono) provided for you (remember to close your right side first and then the left), and sit down to a catered private dinner party. There's little point to staying at a Western-style hotel: these places do most of their business with big, boisterous tour groups; the turnover is ruthless; and the cost is way out of proportion to the service they provide.

The price categories listed here are for double occupancy, but you'll find that most normally quote per-person rates, which include breakfast and dinner. Remember to stipulate whether you want a Japanese or Western breakfast. If you don't want dinner at your hotel, it's usually possible to renegotiate the price, but the management will not be happy about it; the two meals are a fixture of their business. The typical ryokan takes great pride in its cuisine, usually with good reason: the evening meal is an elaborate affair of 10 or more different dishes, based on the fresh produce and specialties of the region, served to you in your room on a wonderful variety of trays and tableware designed to celebrate the season.

Restaurants

The local specialty in Nikko is a soybean-based concoction known as *yuba* (tofu skin); dozens of restaurants in Nikko serve it in a variety of dishes. Other local favorites are soba (buckwheat) and udon (wheat-flour) noodles—both inexpensive, filling, and tasty options for lunch.

Three things about Kamakura make it a good place to dine. It's on the ocean (properly speaking, on Sagami Bay), which means that fresh seafood is everywhere; it's a major tourist stop; and it has long been a prestigious place to

live among Japan's worldly and well-to-do (many successful writers, artists, and intellectuals call Kamakura home). On a day trip from Tokyo, you can feel confident picking a place for lunch almost at random.

Yokohama, as befits a city of more than 3 million people, lacks little in the way of food: from quick-fix lunch counters to elegant dining rooms, you'll find almost every imaginable cuisine. Your best bet is Chinatown—Japan's largest Chinese community—with more than 100 restaurants representing every regional style. If you fancy Italian, Indian, or even Scandinavian, this international port is still guaranteed to provide an eminently satisfying meal.

RESTAURANT AND HOTEL PRICES

Restaurant prices are the average cost of a main course at dinner, or if dinner is not served, at lunch. Hotel prices are the lowest cost of a standard double room in high season. Restaurant and hotel reviews have been shortened. For full information, visit Fodors.com.

What It Costs in Yen			
$	$$	$$$	$$$$
RESTAURANTS			
under ¥1,500	¥1,500–¥3,000	¥3,001–¥5,000	over ¥5,000
HOTELS			
under ¥15,000	¥15,000–¥30,000	¥30,001–¥45,000	over ¥45,000

Yokohama

20 km (12½ miles) southwest of Tokyo.

In 1853, a fleet of four American warships under Commodore Matthew Perry sailed into the bay of Tokyo (then Edo) and presented the reluctant Japanese with the demands of the U.S. government for the opening of diplomatic and commercial relations. The following year Perry returned and first set foot on Japanese soil at Yokohama—then a small fishing village on the mudflats of Tokyo bay.

Two years later New York businessman Townsend Harris became America's first diplomatic representative to Japan. In 1858 he was finally able to negotiate a commercial treaty between the two countries; part of the deal designated four locations—one of them Yokohama—as treaty ports. In 1859 the shogunate created a special settlement in Yokohama for the growing community of merchants, traders, missionaries, and other assorted adventurers drawn to this exotic new land of opportunity.

The foreigners (predominantly Chinese and British, plus a few French, Americans, and Dutch) were confined here to a guarded compound about 5 square km (2 square miles)—placed, in effect, in isolation—but not for long. Within a few short years the shogunal government collapsed, and Japan began to modernize. Western ideas were welcomed, as were Western goods, and the little treaty port became Japan's principal gateway to the outside world. In 1872 Japan's first railway was built, linking Yokohama and Tokyo. In 1889 Yokohama became a city; by then the population had grown to some 120,000. As the city prospered, so did the international community and by the early 1900s Yokohama was the busiest and most modern center of international trade in all of East Asia.

Then Yokohama came tumbling down. On September 1, 1923, the Great Kanto Earthquake devastated the city. The ensuing fires destroyed some 60,000 homes and took more than 40,000 lives. During the six years it took to rebuild the city, many foreign businesses took up quarters elsewhere, primarily in Kobe and Osaka, and did not return.

Over the next 20 years Yokohama continued to grow as an industrial center—until May 29, 1945, when in a span of four hours, some 500 American B-29 bombers leveled nearly half the city and left more than half a million people homeless. When the war ended, what remained became—in effect—the center of the Allied occupation. General Douglas MacArthur set up headquarters here, briefly, before moving to Tokyo; the entire port facility and about a quarter of the city remained in the hands of the U.S. military throughout the 1950s.

By the 1970s Yokohama was once more rising from the debris; in 1978 it surpassed Osaka as the nation's second-largest city, and the population is now inching up to the 3.5-million mark. Boosted by Japan's postwar economic miracle, Yokohama has extended its urban sprawl north to Tokyo and south to Kamakura—in the process creating a whole new subcenter around the Shinkansen Station at Shin-Yokohama.

The development of air travel and the competition from other ports have changed the city's role in Japan's economy. The great liners that once docked at Yokohama's piers are now but a memory, kept alive by a museum ship and the occasional visit of a luxury vessel on a Pacific cruise. Modern Yokohama thrives instead in its industrial, commercial, and service sectors—and a large percentage of its people commute to work in Tokyo. Visit Yokohama for the waterfront and museums.

GETTING HERE AND AROUND
From Narita Airport, a direct limousine-bus service departs once or twice an hour between 7:05 am and 10:25 pm for Yokohama City Air Terminal (YCAT). YCAT is a five-minute taxi ride from Yokohama Station. JR Narita Express trains going on from Tokyo to Yokohama leave the airport every hour from 7:44 am to 9:44 pm. The fare is ¥4,370 (¥6,640 for the first-class Green Car coaches). Or you can take the limousine-bus service from Narita to Tokyo Station and continue on to Yokohama by

train. Either way, the journey from Narita takes two to three hours.

The Airport Limousine Information Desk phone number provides information in English daily from 9 to 6; you can also get timetables on its website. For information in English on Narita Express trains, call the JR Higashi-Nihon Info Line, available daily from 10 to 6.

Most of the things to see in Yokohama are within easy walking distance of a JR or subway station, but this city is so much more negotiable than Tokyo that exploring by bus is a viable alternative. The city map available in the visitor centers in Yokohama shows most major bus routes, and the important stops on the tourist routes are announced in English. The fixed fare is ¥220; one-day passes are also available for ¥600. Contact the Sightseeing Information Office at Yokohama Station (JR, East Exit) for more information and ticket purchases.

One subway line connects Azamino, Shin-Yokohama, Yokohama, Totsuka, and Shonandai. The basic fare is ¥210. One-day passes are also available for ¥830. The Minato Mirai Line, a spur of the Tokyu Toyoko Line, runs from Yokohama Station to all the major points of interest, including Minato Mirai, Chinatown, Yamashita Park, Moto-machi, and Basha-michi. The fare is ¥200–¥220, and one-day unlimited-ride passes are available for ¥530.

There are taxi stands at all the train stations, and you can always flag a cab on the street.

■TIP➜ Vacant taxis show a red light in the windshield.

The basic fare is ¥730 for the first 2 km (1 mile), then ¥90 for every additional 293 meters (0.2 mile). Traffic is heavy in downtown Yokohama, however, and it's often faster to walk.

JR trains from Tokyo Station leave approximately every 10 minutes, depending on the time of day. Take the Yokosuka, the Tokaido, or the Keihin Tohoku Line to Yokohama Station (the Yokosuka and Tokaido lines take 30 minutes; the Keihin Tohoku Line takes 40 minutes and cost ¥480). From there the Keihin Tohoku Line (Platform 3) goes on to Kannai and Ishikawa-cho, Yokohama's business and downtown areas. If you're going directly to downtown Yokohama from Tokyo, the blue commuter trains of the Keihin Tohoku Line are best.

The private Tokyu Toyoko Line, which runs from Shibuya Station in Tokyo directly to Yokohama Station, is a good alternative if you leave from the western part of Tokyo. ■TIP➜ The term "private" is important because it means that the train does not belong to JR and is not a subway line. If you have a JR Pass, you'll have to buy a separate ticket.

Depending on which Tokyu Toyoko Line you catch—the Limited Express, Semi Express, or Local—the trip takes between 25 and 44 minutes and costs ¥280.

Yokohama Station is the hub that links all the train lines and connects them with the city's subway and bus services. Kannai and Ishikawa-cho are the two downtown stations, both on the Keihin Tohoku Line; trains leave Yokohama Station every two to five minutes from Platform 3. From Sakuragi-cho, Kannai, or Ishikawa-cho, most of Yokohama's points of interest are within easy walking distance; the one notable exception is Sankei-en, which you reach via the JR Keihin Tohoku Line to Negishi Station and then a local bus.

AIRPORT TRANSPORTATION Airport Limousine Information Desk. ☎ 03/3665–7220 ⊕ www.limousinebus.co.jp/en.

Get a taste of China in Japan with a visit to the restaurants and shops of Yokohama's Chinatown.

👁 Sights

Large as Yokohama is, the central area is very negotiable. As with any other port city, much of what it has to offer centers on the waterfront—in this case, on the west side of Tokyo Bay. The downtown area is called Kannai (literally, "within the checkpoint"); this is where the international community was originally confined by the shogunate. Though the center of interest has expanded to include the waterfront and Ishikawa-cho, to the south, Kannai remains the heart of town.

Think of that heart as two adjacent areas. One is the old district of Kannai, bounded by Basha-michi on the northwest and Nippon-odori on the southeast, the Keihin Tohoku Line tracks on the southwest, and the waterfront on the northeast. This area contains the business offices of modern Yokohama. The other area extends southeast from Nippon-odori to the Moto-machi shopping street and the International Cemetery, bordered by Yamashita Koen and the waterfront to

the northeast; in the center is Chinatown, with Ishikawa-cho Station to the southwest. This is the most interesting part of town for tourists.

■ TIP→ **Whether you're coming from Tokyo, Nagoya, or Kamakura, make Ishikawa-cho Station your starting point. Take the South Exit from the station and head in the direction of the waterfront.**

Bashamichi Street (馬車道)
STREET | Running southwest from Shinko Pier to Kannai is Bashamichi, which literally translates into "Horse-Carriage Street." The street was so named in the 19th century, when it was widened to accommodate the horse-drawn carriages of the city's new European residents. This redbrick thoroughfare and the streets parallel to it have been restored to evoke that past, with faux-antique telephone booths and imitation gas lamps. Here you'll find some of the most elegant coffee shops, patisseries, and boutiques in town. On the block northeast of Kannai Station, as you walk toward the waterfront, is Kannai Hall (look for the

red-orange abstract sculpture in front), a handsome venue for chamber music, Noh, classical recitals, and occasional performances by such groups as the Peking Opera. ⊠ *Naka-ku* Ⓜ *JR Line, Kannai Station; Minato Mirai Line, Bashamichi Station.*

Chinatown (中華街; *Chuka-gai*)

NEIGHBORHOOD | Once the largest Chinese settlement in Japan—and easily the city's most popular tourist attraction—Yokohama's Chinatown draws more than 18 million visitors a year. Its narrow streets and alleys are lined with some 350 shops selling foodstuffs, herbal medicines, cookware, toys and ornaments, and clothing and accessories. If China exports it, you'll find it here. Wonderful exotic aromas waft from the spice shops. Even better aromas drift from the quarter's 160-odd restaurants, which serve every major style of Chinese cuisine: this is the best place for lunch in Yokohama. Chinatown is a 10-minute walk southeast of Kannai Station. When you get to Yokohama Stadium, turn left and cut through the municipal park to the top of Nihon-odori. Then take a right, and enter Chinatown through the Gembu-mon (North Gate), which leads to the dazzling red-and-gold, 50-foot-high Zenrin-mon (Good Neighbor Gate). ⊠ *Naka-ku* Ⓜ *JR Line, Ishikawa-cho Station; Minato Mirai Line, Motomachi-Chukagai Station.*

Cup Noodles Museum Yokohama (カップヌードルミュージアム 横浜)

OTHER MUSEUM | FAMILY | At this hands-on museum, visitors can create their own original instant-ramen flavors and packaging, make fresh noodles by hand, and learn all about what has become one of Japan's biggest culinary exports. Kids can run through the museum's Cup Noodle Park, a playground simulating the noodle-making process, complete with a "noodle net" and "seasoning pool" ball pit. ⊠ *2–3–4 Shinko, Naka-ku* ☎ *045/345–0918* ⊕ *www.cupnoodles-museum.jp/en/yokohama* 🎫 *From ¥500* ⊗ *Closed Tues.*

Harbor View Park (港の見える丘公園; *Minato-no-Mieru-Oka Koen*)

CITY PARK | The park—a major landmark in this part of the city, known, appropriately enough, as the Bluff (*yamate*)—was once the barracks of the British forces in Yokohama. Come here for spectacular nighttime views of the waterfront, the floodlit gardens of Yamashita Park, and the Bay Bridge. Foreigners were first allowed to build here in 1867, and it has been prime real estate ever since—an enclave of consulates, churches, international schools, private clubs, and palatial Western-style homes. ⊠ *114 Yamatecho, Naka-ku* Ⓜ *JR Line, Ishikawa-cho Station; Minato Mirai Line, Motomachi-Chukagai Station.*

Hikawa Maru (氷川丸)

NAUTICAL SIGHT | Moored on the waterfront, more or less in the middle of Yamashita Park, is the *Hikawa Maru*. The ocean liner was built in 1929 by Yokohama Dock Co. and launched on September 30, 1929. For 31 years, she shuttled passengers between Yokohama and Seattle, Washington, making a total of 238 trips. A tour of the ship evokes the time when Yokohama was a great port of call for the transpacific liners. The ship has a French restaurant, and in summer there's a beer garden on the upper deck. ⊠ *Yamashita-koen, Naka-ku* ☎ *045/641–4362* ⊕ *hikawamaru.nyk. com* 🎫 *¥300* ⊗ *Closed Mon.* Ⓜ *JR Line, Ishikawa-cho Station; Minato Mirai Line, Motomachi-Chukagai Station.*

Iseyama Kotai Jingu Shrine (伊勢山皇大神宮)

A branch of the nation's revered Grand Shrines of Ise, this is the most important Shinto shrine in Yokohama—but it's worth a visit only if you've seen most everything else in town. ⊠ *64 Miyazaki-cho, Nishi-ku* ✛ *The shrine is a 10-min walk west of Sakuragi-cho Station* ☎ *045/241–1122* 🎫 *Free* Ⓜ *JR Line, Sakuragi-cho Station; Minato Mirai Line, Minato Mirai Station.*

Kanagawa Prefectural Museum of Cultural History (神奈川県立歴史博物館; *Kanagawa Kenritsu Rekishi Hakubutsukan*)

HISTORY MUSEUM | One of the few buildings in Yokohama to have survived both the Great Kanto Earthquake of 1923 and World War II, the museum is a few blocks north of Kannai Station on Basha-michi. Most exhibits here have no explanations in English, but the galleries on the third floor showcase some remarkable medieval wooden sculptures (including one of the first Kamakura shogun, Minamoto no Yoritomo), hanging scrolls, portraits, and armor. The exhibits of prehistory and of Yokohama in the early modern period are of much less interest. ⊠ *5–60 Minami Nakadori, Naka-ku* ☎ *045/201–0926* ⊕ *ch.kanagawa-museum.jp* ⊠ *From ¥300* ⊗ *Closed Mon.* Ⓜ *JR Line, Kannai Station (Exit 8).*

Landmark Tower (ランドマークタワー)

VIEWPOINT | FAMILY | Although no longer Japan's tallest building—that title now goes to Osaka's Abeno Harukas—this 70-story tower in Yokohama's Minato Mirai is the tallest in Greater Tokyo. The observation deck on the 69th floor has a spectacular view of the city, especially at night; you reach it via a high-speed elevator that carries you up at an ear-popping 45 kph (28 mph). The complex's Dockyard Garden, built in 1896, is a restored dry dock with stepped sides of massive stone blocks. The long, narrow floor of the dock, with its water cascade at one end, makes a wonderful year-round open-air venue for concerts and other events; in summer (July–mid-August), the beer garden installed here is a perfect refuge from the heat. The Yokohama Royal Park Hotel occupies the top 20 stories of the building, and the courtyard on the northeast side connects to Queen's Square, a huge atrium-style vertical mall with dozens of shops (mainly for clothing and accessories) and restaurants. ⊠ *2–2–1 Minatomirai, Nishi-ku* ☎ *045/222–5015*

⊕ *www.yokohama-landmark.jp* ⊠ *Elevator to observation deck ¥1,000* Ⓜ *JR Line, Sakuragi-cho Station; Minato Mirai Line, Minato Mirai Station.*

Marine Tower (マリンタワー)

VIEWPOINT | For an older generation of Yokohama residents, the 348-foot-high decagonal tower, which opened in 1961, was the city's landmark structure; civic pride prevented them from admitting that it falls lamentably short of an architectural masterpiece. The tower has a navigational beacon at the 338-foot level and purports to be the tallest lighthouse in the world. At the 328-foot level, an observation gallery provides 360-degree views of the harbor and the city, and on clear days in autumn or winter, you can often see Mt. Fuji in the distance. Marine Tower is in the middle of the second block northwest from the end of Yamashita Park, on the left side of the promenade. ⊠ *15 Yamashita-cho, Naka-ku* ☎ *045/641–7838* ⊕ *www.marinetower.yokohama* ⊠ *¥750* Ⓜ *JR Line, Ishikawa-cho Station; Minato Mirai Line, Motomachi-Chukagai Station.*

Minato Mirai 21 (みなとみらい21; *Minato Mirai Nijyu-ichi*)

BUSINESS DISTRICT | If you want to see Yokohama urban development at its most self-assertive, then this is a must. The aim of this project, launched in the mid-1980s, was to turn some three-quarters of a square mile of waterfront property, lying east of the JR Negishi Line railroad tracks between the Yokohama and Sakuragi-cho stations, into a model "city of the future." As a hotel, business, international exhibition, and conference center, it's a smashing success. ⊠ *Nishi-ku* ⊕ *www.minatomirai21.com* Ⓜ *JR Line, Sakuragi-cho Station; Minato Mirai Line, Minato Mirai Station.*

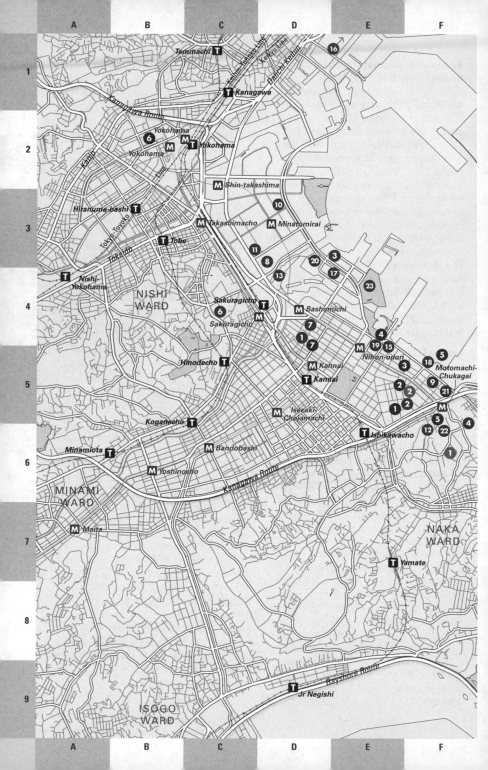

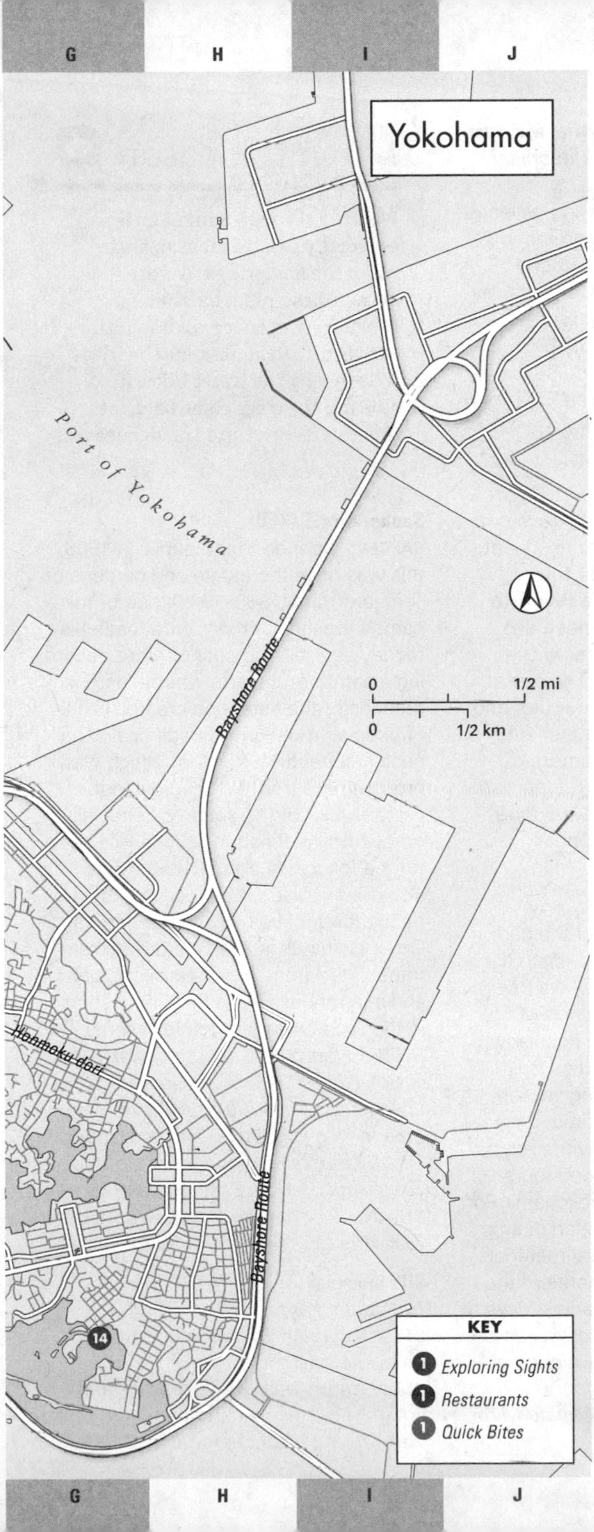

Yokohama

Sights ▼

1 Bashamichi Street.................. D4
2 Chinatown F5
3 Cup Noodles Museum
  Yokohama........................... E3
4 Harbor View Park................... F5
5 Hikawa Maru.......................... F5
6 Iseyama Kotai Jingu Shrine C4
7 Kanagawa Prefectural
  Museum of Cultural History D4
8 Landmark Tower D3
9 Marine Tower F5
10 Minato Mirai 21 .... D3
11 Mitsubishi Minatomirai
  Industrial Museum C3
12 Moto-machi F6
13 Nippon Maru Memorial Park..... D4
14 Sankei-en........................... G9
15 Silk Museum E5
16 Soji-ji E1
17 World Porters E4
18 Yamashita Park F5
19 Yokohama Archives
  of History Museum E4
20 Yokohama Cosmo World.......... D3
21 Yokohama Doll Museum F5
22 Yokohama Foreign
  General Cemetery F6
23 Yokohama Red Brick
  Warehouses............,,.......... E4

Restaurants ▼

1 Kaikin Hanten E5
2 Kaseiro............................... E5
3 Roma Statione E5
4 Scandia E4
5 Shunotei Hira....................... F5
6 Yokohama Cheese Cafe.......... B2
7 Yokohama Senrya D4

Quick Bites ▼

1 Enokitei Honten F6
2 Houtenkaku Shinkan F5

KEY
1 Exploring Sights
1 Restaurants
1 Quick Bites

15

Side Trips from Tokyo YOKOHAMA (横浜)

Port of Yokohama

Bayshore Route

Honmoku-dori

0 — 1/2 mi
0 — 1/2 km

Mitsubishi Minatomirai Industrial Museum
(三菱みなとみらい技術館; *Mitsubishi Minatomirai Gijutsukan*)

SCIENCE MUSEUM | FAMILY | Filling galleries directly across from the Landmark Tower are rocket engines, power plants, a submarine, various gadgets, and displays that simulate piloting helicopters. ✉ *3–3–1 Minatomirai, Nishi-ku* ☎ *045/200–7351* ⊕ *www.mhi.com/expertise/museum/minatomirai* ✇ *¥500* ⊙ *Closed Tues.* Ⓜ *JR Line, Sakuragi-cho Station; Minato Mirai Line, Minato Mirai Station.*

Moto-machi (元町)

STREET | Within a block of Ishikawa-cho Station is the beginning of this street, which follows the course of the Nakamura-gawa (Nakamura River) to the harbor where the Japanese set up shop 100 years ago to serve the foreigners living in Kannai. The street is now lined with smart boutiques and jewelry stores that cater to fashionable young Japanese consumers. ✉ *Motomachi, Naka-ku* Ⓜ *JR Line, Ishikawa-cho Station; Minato Mirai Line, Motomachi-Chukagai Station.*

Nippon Maru Memorial Park
(日本丸メモリアルパーク)

CITY PARK | The centerpiece of the park, which is on the east side of Minato Mirai 21, where the O-okagawa (O-oka River) flows into the bay, is the *Nippon Maru*, a full-rigged three-mast ship popularly called the "Swan of the Pacific." Built in 1930, it served as a training vessel. The *Nippon Maru* is now retired, but it's an occasional participant in tall-ships festivals and is open for guided tours. Adjacent to the ship is the Yokohama Port Museum, a two-story collection of ship models, displays, and archival materials that celebrate the achievements of the Port of Yokohama from its earliest days to the present. ✉ *2–1–1 Minatomirai, Nishi-ku* ☎ *045/221–0280* ⊕ *www.nippon-maru.or.jp* ✇ *¥800* ⊙ *Closed Mon.* Ⓜ *JR Line, Sakuragi-cho Station; Minato Mirai Line, Minato Mirai Station.*

Bloomin' Season

Walking through Sankei-en is especially delightful in spring, when the flowering trees are at their best: plum blossoms in February and cherry blossoms in early April. In June come the irises, followed by the water lilies. In autumn the trees come back into their own with tinted golden leaves.

Sankei-en (三渓園)

GARDEN | Opened to the public in 1906, this was once the estate and gardens of Tomitaro Hara (1868–1939), one of Yokohama's wealthiest men, who made his money as a silk merchant before becoming a patron of the arts. On the extensive grounds of the estate he created is a kind of open-air museum of traditional Japanese architecture, some of which was brought here from Kamakura and the western part of the country. Especially noteworthy is Rinshun-kaku, a villa built for the Tokugawa clan in 1649. There's also a tea pavilion, Choshu-kaku, built by the third Tokugawa shogun, Iemitsu. Other buildings include a small temple transported from Kyoto's famed Daitoku-ji and a farmhouse from the Gifu district in the Japan Alps (around Takayama). ✉ *58–1 Honmoku Sannotani, Naka-ku* ☎ *045/621–0634* ⊕ *www.sankeien.or.jp* ✇ *Inner garden ¥700* Ⓜ *JR Keihin Tohoku Line to Negishi Station and a local bus (No. 58, 99, or 101) bound for Honmoku; Yokohama Station (East Exit) and take the bus (No. 8 or 148) to Honmoku Sankei-en Mae (the trip takes about 35 min).*

Silk Museum (シルク博物館; *Shiruku Hakubutsukan*)

OTHER MUSEUM | From the opening of its borders to the beginning of the 20th century, silk was Japan's most sought-after export and nearly all of it went through Yokohama. The museum, which pays tribute to this period, houses an extensive collection of silk fabrics and an informative exhibit on the silk-making process. People on staff are very happy to answer questions. In the same building, on the first floor, are the main offices of the Yokohama International Tourist Association and the Kanagawa Prefectural Tourist Association. The museum is at the northwestern end of the Yamashita Park promenade, on the second floor of the Silk Center Building. ⊠ *1 Yamashita-cho, Naka-ku* ☎ *045/641–0841* ⊕ *www. silkcenter-kbkk.jp/museum* ✉ *¥500* ⊘ *Closed Mon.* Ⓜ *Minato Mirai Line, Nihon Odori Station (Exit 3).*

Soji-ji (總持寺)

TEMPLE | One of the two major centers of the Soto sect of Zen Buddhism, Soji-ji, in Yokohama's Tsurumi ward, was founded in 1321. The center was moved here from Ishikawa, on the Noto Peninsula (on the Sea of Japan, north of Kanazawa), after a fire In the 19th century. There's also a Soji-ji monastic complex at Eihei-ji in Fukui Prefecture. The Yokohama Soji-ji is one of the largest and busiest Buddhist institutions in Japan, with more than 200 monks and novices in residence. The 14th-century patron of Soji-ji was the emperor Go-Daigo, who overthrew the Kamakura Shogunate; the emperor is buried here, but his mausoleum is off-limits to visitors. Nevertheless, you can see the Buddha Hall, the Main Hall, and the Treasure House. English tours of the complex are available by reservation. ⊠ *2–1–1 Tsurumi, Tsurumi-ku* ⚓ *Take JR Keihin Tohoku Line 2 stops from Sakuragi-cho to Tsurumi. From station, walk 5 min south (back toward Yokohama), passing Tsurumi University on your right. Look out for stone lanterns that mark entrance to temple complex* ☎ *045/581–6021* ⊕ *www.sojiji.jp* ✉ *¥400 for guided tour* ⊘ *Treasure House closed Mon.*

World Porters (ワールドポーターズ)

STORE/MALL | This shopping center, on the opposite side of Yokohama Cosmo World, is notable chiefly for its restaurants that overlook the Minato Mirai area. Try arriving at sunset; the spectacular view of twinkling lights and the Landmark Tower, the Ferris wheel, and hotels occasionally include Mt. Fuji in the background. ⊠ *2–2–1 Shinko, Naka-ku* ☎ *045/222–2121* ⊕ *www.yim.co.jp* Ⓜ *JR Line, Sakuragi-cho Station; Minato Mirai Line, Minato Mirai Station.*

Yamashita Park
(山下公園; *Yamashita Koen*)

CITY PARK | This park is perhaps the only positive legacy of the Great Kanto Earthquake of 1923. The debris of the warehouses and other buildings that once stood here were swept away, and the area was made into a 17-acre oasis of green along the waterfront. On spring and summer weekends, the park fills up with families, couples, and groups of friends, making It one of the best people-watching spots In town. The fountain, representing the Guardian of the Water, was presented to Yokohama by San Diego, California, one of its sister cities. ⊠ *279 Yamashita-cho, Naka-ku* ⚓ *From Harbor View Park, walk northwest through neighboring French Hill Park and cross walkway over Moto-machi. Turn right on other side and walk 1 block down toward bay to Yamashita-Koen-dori, promenade along park* Ⓜ *JR Line, Ishikawa-cho Station; Minato Mirai Line, Motomachi-Chukagai Station.*

Yokohama Archives of History Museum
(横浜開港資料館; *Yokohama Kaiko Shiryokan*)

HISTORY MUSEUM | Within the archives, housed in what was once the British Consulate, are some 140,000 items recording the history of Yokohama since the opening of the port to international trade in the mid-19th century. Across the street is a monument to the

U.S.–Japanese Friendship Treaty. ✉ *3
Nihonodori, Naka-ku* ✛ *To get here from
the Silk Center Building, at the end of the
Yamashita Park promenade, walk west
to the corner of Nihon-odori; the archives
are on the left* ☎ *045/201–2100* ⊕ *www.
kaikou.city.yokohama.jp/en* ✉ *¥200*
⊙ *Closed Mon. and Tues.* Ⓜ *Minato Mirai
Line, Nihon-odori Station.*

Yokohama Cosmo World
(よこはまコスモワールド)
AMUSEMENT PARK/CARNIVAL | FAMILY | This
amusement-park complex claims—
among its 30 or so rides and attractions—a four story high water-chute ride.
The Ferris wheel towers over Yokohama.
The park is west of Minato Mirai and
Queen's Square, on both sides of the river. ✉ *2–8–1 Shinko, Naka-ku* ☎ *045/641–
6591* ⊕ *cosmoworld.jp* ✉ *Park free, rides
from ¥400 each* Ⓜ *JR Line, Sakuragi-cho
Station; Minato Mirai Line, Minato Mirai
Station.*

Yokohama Doll Museum
(横浜人形の家; *Yokohama Ningyo no Ie*)
OTHER MUSEUM | FAMILY | This museum
houses a collection of roughly 3,500
dolls from all over the world. In Japanese tradition, dolls are less to play
with than to display—either in religious
folk customs or as the embodiment
of some spiritual quality. Japanese
visitors to this museum never seem to
outgrow their affection for the Western
dolls on display here, to which they
tend to assign the role of timeless
"ambassadors of goodwill" from other
cultures. The museum is worth a quick
visit, with or without a child in tow. It's
just across from the southeast end of
Yamashita Park, on the left side of the
promenade. ✉ *18 Yamashita-cho, Naka-ku*
☎ *045/671–9361* ⊕ *www.doll-museum.
jp* ✉ *¥400* ⊙ *Closed Mon.* Ⓜ *JR Line,
Ishikawa-cho Station; Minato Mirai Line,
Motomachi-Chukagai Station.*

Yokohama Foreign General Cemetery (横浜外国人墓地; *Yokohama Gaikokujin Bochi*)
CEMETERY | This Yokohama landmark is
a reminder of the port city's heritage. It
was established in 1854 with a grant of
land from the shogunate; the first foreigners to be buried here were Russian
sailors assassinated by xenophobes in
the early days of the settlement. Most
of the 4,500 graves on this hillside are
English and American, and about 120 are
of the Japanese wives of foreigners; the
inscriptions on the crosses and head-
stones attest to some 40 different nation-
alities whose citizens lived and died in
Yokohama. ✉ *96 Yamate-cho, Naka-ku*
✛ *From Moto-machi Plaza, it's a short
walk to north end of cemetery* ⊕ *www.
yfgc-japan.com* ✉ *¥200* ⊙ *Closed Mon.*
Ⓜ *JR Line, Ishikawa-cho Station; Minato
Mirai Line, Motomachi-Chukagai Station.*

★ Yokohama Red Brick Warehouses (赤レンガ倉庫; *Aka-Renga Soko*)
STORE/MALL | History meets entertainment
at Yokohama's Red Brick Warehouses,
just a few minutes from World Porters
Mall in the Minato Mirai district. Constructed in 1911 to accommodate trade,
partially destroyed ten years later in the
Kanto earthquake, and then used for military storage in World War II before being
taken over by the United States upon
Japan's surrender, today these redbrick
warehouses are a hipster haven. You'll
find unique shops and cafés, restaurants
and bars (some with balcony seating),
and event spaces. You'll find seasonal
fairs and markets and the seafront areas
are a perfect picnic spot. ✉ *1–1 Shinko,
Naka-ku* ⊕ *www.yokohama-akarenga.jp*
Ⓜ *JR Line, Sakuragi-cho Station; Minato
Mirai Line, Minato Mirai Station.*

🍴 Restaurants

Kaikin Hanten (華錦飯店)

$$$ | CANTONESE | In contrast to many of·the meat-heavy choices in Chinatown, this Cantonese restaurant specializes in fresh, flavorful seafood dishes. Menu highlights include the shrimp-shiso spring rolls, steamed Sakhalin surf clams with garlic, and a rotating selection of fresh fish caught that day. **Known for:** some of Chinatown's freshest seafood; excellent quality at reasonable prices; wide selection of Cantonese dishes. $ *Average main: ¥4,000* ✉ *126–22 Yamashita-cho, Naka-ku* ☎ *050/5485–4599* ⊕ *kakinhant-en.gorp.jp.*

Kaseiro (華正樓)

$$$$ | CHINESE | Chinese food can be hit-or-miss in Japan, but not at Kaseiro. This elegant restaurant, with red carpets and gold-toned walls, is the best of its kind in the city, serving authentic Beijing cuisine, including, of course, Peking duck and shark-fin soup. **Known for:** Yokohama's flagship Chinese restaurant; grand atmosphere; excellent multicourse meals. $ *Average main: ¥10,000* ✉ *186 Yamashita-cho, Chinatown, Naka-ku* ☎ *045/681–2918.*

Roma Statione (ローマステーション)

$$$ | ITALIAN | Opened more than 40 years ago, this popular venue between China-town and Yamashita Park is Yokohama's source for Italian food. The owner, whose father studied cooking in Italy before returning home, is also the head chef and has continued using the original recipes. **Known for:** authentic Italian cuisine; excellent seafood; extensive Italian wine selection. $ *Average main: ¥3,500* ✉ *26 Yamashita-cho, Naka-ku* ☎ *045/681–1818* Ⓜ *Minato Mirai Line, Motomachi-Chukagai Station (Exit 1).*

Scandia (スカンディヤ)

$$$$ | EUROPEAN | This Scandinavian restaurant near the Silk Center and the business district is known for its smorgasbord. It's popular for business lunches as well as for dinner. **Known for:** classic Scandinavian cuisine; good lunch sets; open late. $ *Average main: ¥6,000* ✉ *1–1 Kaigan-dori, Naka-ku* ☎ *045/201–2262* ⊕ *www.scandia-yokohama.jp.*

Shunotei Hira (春鶯亭ひら)

$$$$ | JAPANESE | The area of Motomachi is known as the wealthy, posh part of Yokohama; restaurants here tend to be exclusive and expensive, though the service and quality justify the price. This restaurant is an old-style Japanese house complete with a Japanese garden and five private tatami rooms. **Known for:** overwhelming 30-course dinners; traditional atmosphere; long dinners. $ *Average main: ¥13,200* ✉ *1–55 Motomachi, Naka-ku* ☎ *045/662–2215* ◷ *Closed Mon.*

Yokohama Cheese Cafe (横浜チーズカフェ)

$$$ | ITALIAN | FAMILY | This is a cozy and inviting casual Italian restaurant, whose interior looks like an Italian country home. There are candles on the tables and an open kitchen where diners can watch the cooks making pizza. **Known for:** a cheese lover's paradise; rich, creamy fondue; affordable multicourse meals. $ *Average main: ¥3,500* ✉ *2–1–10 Kitasaiwai, Nishi-ku* ☎ *045/290–5656* ◷ *No lunch* Ⓜ *JR Yokohama Station.*

Yokohama Senrya (瀬里奈 浪漫茶屋; *Seryna Romanchaya*)

$$$$ | JAPANESE | The hallmarks of this restaurant are *ishiyaki* steak, which is grilled on a hot stone, and *shabu-shabu*—thin slices of beef cooked in boiling water at your table and dipped in one of several sauces; choose from sesame, vinegar, or soy. Fresh vegetables, noodles, and tofu are also dipped into the seasoned broth for a filling yet healthful meal. **Known for:** high-grade Wagyu beef; rustic atmosphere; excellent service. $ *Average main: ¥10,000* ✉ *Shin-Kannai Bldg., 4–45–1 Sumiyoshi-cho, 1st fl., Naka-ku* ☎ *045/681–2727* ⊕ *www.seryna.com/romanjaya/romanjaya.html.*

Coffee and Quick Bites

Enokitei Honten (えの木てい本店)
$$ | **CAFÉ** | Located in one of the area's few remaining historic Western-style houses an Enokitei is a relaxing stop for sweets or a light meal. The interior has the feel of a British-style tea room, with dark wood and antiques, while the garden terrace is surrounded by greenery and flowers much of the year. **Known for:** people-watching in the shade; elegant yet casual atmosphere; afternoon tea. [$] *Average main: ¥1,600* ✉ *89–6 Yamatecho, Naka-ku* ☎ *045/623–2288* 🌐 *www.enokitei.co.jp* 💳 *No credit cards.*

Houtenkaku Shinkan (鵬天閣 新館)
$$$ | **SHANGHAINESE** | This no-frills eatery serves up excellent *sheng jian bao* (Shanghai-style fried dumplings) and other casual Shanghai cuisine all day long. The open kitchen is behind glass so customers can admire the speed with which the chefs cook up this Shanghai staple. **Known for:** quick and satisfying street food; authentic Shanghai dumplings. [$] *Average main: ¥4,000* ✉ *192–15 Yamashita, Naka-ku* ☎ *050/5570–4921* 🌐 *houtenkaku.com/shop-shinkan.*

Kamakura

40 km (25 miles) southwest of Tokyo.

As a religious center, Kamakura presents an extraordinary legacy. Most of its temples and shrines are in settings of remarkable beauty; many are designated National Treasures. If you have time for just one day trip away from Tokyo, spend it here.

For the aristocrats of the Heian-era Japan (794–1185), life was defined by the Imperial Court in Kyoto. Who in their right mind would venture elsewhere? In Kyoto there was grace and beauty and poignant affairs of the heart; everything beyond was howling wilderness. By the 12th century two clans—the Taira (pronounced "*ta*-ee-ra") and the Minamoto, themselves both offshoots of the imperial line—had come to dominate the affairs of the court and were at each other's throats in a struggle for supremacy. The rivalry between the two clans became an all-out war, and by 1185 the Minamoto were masters of all Japan. Yoritomo no Minamoto forced the Imperial Court to name him shogun; he was now de facto and de jure the military head of state. The emperor was left as a figurehead in Kyoto, and the little fishing village of Kamakura, a superb natural fortress surrounded on three sides by hills and guarded on the fourth by the sea, became—and for 141 years remained—the seat of Japan's first shogunal government.

After 1333, when the center of power returned to Kyoto, Kamakura reverted to being a sleepy backwater town on the edge of the sea. After World War II, it began to develop as a residential area for the well-to-do. Though the religious past is much in evidence, nothing secular survives from the shogunal days; there wasn't much there to begin with. The warriors of Kamakura had little use for courtiers, or their palaces and gardened villas; the shogunate's name for itself, in fact, was the Bakufu—literally, the "tent government."

GETTING HERE AND AROUND

A bus from Kamakura Station (Sign 5) travels to most of the temples and shrines in the downtown Kamakura area, with stops at most access roads to the temples and shrines. However, you may want to walk out as far as Hokoku-ji and take the bus back; it's easier to recognize the end of the line than any of the stops in between. You can also go by taxi to Hokoku-ji—any cabdriver knows the way—and walk the last leg in reverse.

Bus companies in Kamakura don't conduct guided English tours. Nevertheless, if your time is limited or you don't want to do a lot of walking, the Japanese tours hit the major attractions. These tours depart from Kamakura Station eight times daily, starting at 9 am; the last tour

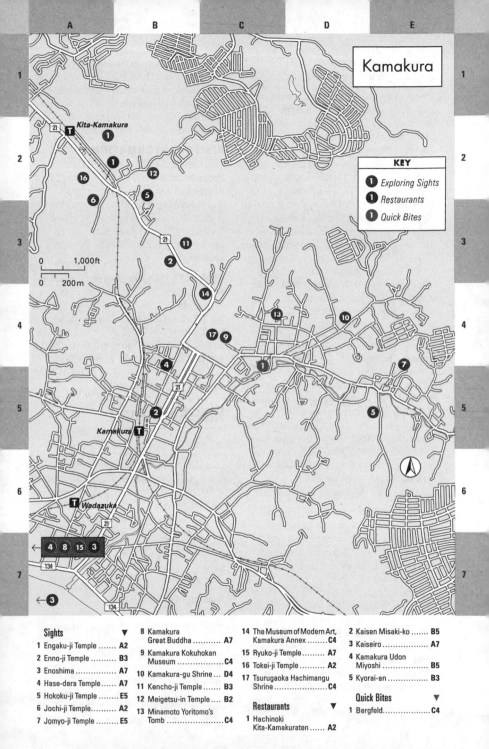

Kamakura

KEY
- 1 Exploring Sights
- 1 Restaurants
- 1 Quick Bites

Kita-Kamakura

Kamakura

Wadazuka

0   1,000ft
0   200m

leaves at 1 pm. Purchase tickets at the bus office to the right of the station.

Traveling by train is by far the best way to get to Kamakura. Trains run from Tokyo Station (and Shimbashi Station) every 10 to 15 minutes during the day. The trip takes 56 minutes to Kita-Kamakura and one hour to Kamakura. Take the JR Yokosuka Line from Track 1 downstairs in Tokyo Station (Track 1 upstairs is on a different line and does not go to Kamakura). The cost is ¥820 to Kita-Kamakura, ¥940 to Kamakura (or use your JR Pass). It's now also possible to take a train from Shinjuku, Shibuya, or Ebisu to Kamakura on the Shonan-Shinjuku Line, but these trains depart less frequently than those departing from Tokyo Station. Local train service connects Kita-Kamakura, Kamakura, Hase, and Enoshima.

To return to Tokyo from Enoshima, take a train to Shinjuku on the Odakyu Line. There are 11 express trains daily from here on weekdays between 8:38 am and 8:45 pm; nine trains daily on weekends and national holidays between 8:39 am and 8:46 pm; and even more in summer. The express takes about 70 minutes and costs ¥1,270. Or you can retrace your steps to Kamakura and take the JR Yokosuka Line to Tokyo Station.

TOURS

JTB Sunrise Tours runs daily English-language trips from Tokyo to Kamakura; these tours are often combined with trips to Hakone. You can book through, and arrange to be picked up at, any of the major hotels. Check to make sure that the tour covers everything you want to see, as many include little more than a passing view of the Great Buddha in Hase. Given how easy it is to get around—most sights are within walking distance of each other, and others are short bus or train rides apart—you're better off seeing Kamakura on your own.

KSGG Club Volunteer Guides

GUIDED TOURS | The KSGG Club Volunteer Guides has a free guide service and regular events. Arrangements must be made in advance through the group's website. ⊕ *volunteerguide-ksgg.jp* ✉ *Free.*

VISITOR INFORMATION

The Kamakura Station Tourist Information Center has a useful collection of brochures and maps. Visitors heading to Kamakura from Yokohama can plan their excursion at the Kanagawa Prefectural Tourist Association office in the Silk Center, on the Yamashita Park promenade.

CONTACTS Fujisawa City Tourist Association. ✉ *2–20–13 Katasekaigan, Fujisawa City* ☎ *0466/22–4141* ⊕ *www.fujisawa-kanko.jp.* **Kamakura City Tourist Information Center.** ✉ *1–1–1 Komachi, Kamakura* ☎ *0467/22–3350.* **Kanagawa Prefectural Tourist Association.** ✉ *1 Yamashita-cho, Yokohama* ☎ *045/681–0007* ⊕ *www.kanagawa-kankou.or.jp.*

Kita-Kamakura

40 km (25 miles) southwest of Tokyo.

Hierarchies were important to the Kamakura Shogunate. In the 14th century it established a ranking system called Go-zan (literally, "Five Mountains") for the Zen Buddhist monasteries under its official sponsorship. These are clustered in the Kita-Kamakura district.

 ## Sights

Engaku-ji Temple (円覚寺)

TEMPLE | The largest of the Zen monasteries in Kamakura, Engaku-ji (Engaku Temple) was founded in 1282 and ranks second in the Five Mountains hierarchy. Here, prayers were to be offered regularly for the prosperity and well-being of the government; Engaku Temple's special role was to pray for the souls of those who died resisting the Mongol

invasions in 1274 and 1281. The temple complex currently holds 18 buildings, but once contained as many as 50. Often damaged in fires and earthquakes, it has been completely restored.

Engaku Temple belongs to the Rinzai sect of Zen Buddhism. The ideas of Zen were introduced to Japan from China at the beginning of the Kamakura period (1192–1333). The samurai especially admired the Rinzai sect, with its emphasis on the ascetic life as a path to self-transcendence. The monks of Engaku Temple played an important role as advisers to the shogunate in matters spiritual, artistic, and political.

Among the National Treasures at Engaku Temple is the Hall of the Holy Relic of Buddha (Shari-den), with its remarkable Chinese-inspired thatched roof. Built in 1282, it was destroyed by fire in 1558 but rebuilt in its original form soon after, in 1563. The hall is said to enshrine a tooth of the Gautama Buddha himself, but it's not on display. In fact, except for the first three days of the New Year, you won't be able to go any farther into the hall than the main gate. Such is the case, alas, with much of the Engaku Temple complex: this is still a functioning monastic center, and many of its most impressive buildings are not open to the public. The accessible National Treasure at Engaku Temple is the Great Bell (Kosho), on the hilltop on the southeast side of the complex. The bell—Kamakura's most famous—was cast in 1301 and stands 8 feet tall. It's rung only on special occasions, such as New Year's Eve. Reaching the bell requires a trek up a long staircase, but once you've made it to the top you can enjoy tea and traditional Japanese sweets at a small outdoor café. The views of the entire temple grounds and surrounding cedar forest from here are tremendous.

The two buildings open to the public at Engaku Temple are the Butsunichi-an, which has a long ceremonial hall where you can enjoy *sado* (Japanese tea

Timing Tip

If your time is limited, you may want to visit only Engaku Temple and Tokei Temple in Kita-Kamakura before riding the train one stop to Kamakura. If not, follow the main road all the way to Tsuru-ga-oka Hachiman-gu and visit four additional temples en route.

ceremony), and the Obai-in. The latter is the mausoleum of the last three regents of the Kamakura Shogunate: Tokimune Hojo, who led the defense of Japan against the Mongol invasions; his son Sadatoki; and his grandson Takatoki. Off to the side of the mausoleum is a quiet garden with apricot trees, which bloom in February. As you exit Kita-Kamakura Station, you'll see the stairway to Engaku Temple just in front of you. ✉ *409 Yamanouchi, Kamakura* ☎ *0467/22–0478* ⊕ *www.engakuji.or.jp/en* 🎫 *¥500.*

Enno-ji Temple (円応寺)

TEMPLE | In the feudal period, Japan acquired from China a belief in Enma, the lord of hell, who, with his court attendants, judged the souls of the departed and determined their destination in the afterlife. Kamakura's otherwise undistinguished Enno-ji (Enno Temple) houses some remarkable statues of these judges—as grim and merciless a court as you're ever likely to confront. To see them is enough to put you on your best behavior, at least for the rest of your excursion. Enno Temple is a minute's walk or so from Kencho Temple, on the opposite (south) side of the main road to Kamakura. ✉ *1543 Yamanouchi, Kamakura* ☎ *0467/25–1095* 🎫 *¥200.*

Jochi-ji Temple (浄智寺)

TEMPLE | In the Five Mountains hierarchy, Jochi-ji (Jochi Temple) was ranked fourth. The buildings now in the complex are reconstructions; the Great Kanto Earthquake of 1923 destroyed the originals. The garden here is exquisite. Jochi-ji is on the south side of the railway tracks, a few minutes' walk farther southwest of Tokei-ji in the direction of Kamakura. ⊠ *1402 Yamanouchi, Kamakura ✛ Turn right off main road (Rte. 21) and cross over small bridge; flight of moss-covered steps leads up to temple ☎ 0467/22–3943 ⊕ jochiji.com/en ⊠ ¥200.*

Kencho-ji Temple (建長寺)

TEMPLE | Founded in 1250, Kencho-ji (Kencho Temple) was the foremost of Kamakura's five great Zen temples, and it lays claim to being the oldest Zen temple in all of Japan. It was modeled on one of the great Chinese monasteries of the time and built for a distinguished Zen master who had just arrived from China. Over the centuries, fires and other disasters have taken their toll on Kencho-ji, and although many buildings have been authentically reconstructed, the temple complex today is half its original size. Near the Main Gate (San-mon) is a bronze bell cast in 1255; it's the temple's most important treasure. The Main Gate and the Lecture Hall (Hatto) are the only two structures to have survived the devastating Great Kanto Earthquake of 1923. Like Engaku-ji, Kencho-ji is a functioning temple of the Rinzai sect, where novices train and laypeople can come to take part in Zen meditation. Nearly hidden at the back of the temple is a long stairway and hiking trail that leads to Zuisen-ji, another of Kamakura's major temples. The hike takes about 90 minutes. ⊠ *8 Yamanouchi, Kamakura ✛ Entrance to Kencho Temple is about halfway along main road from Kita-Kamakura Station to Tsurugaoka Hachimangu, on left ☎ 0467/22–0981 ⊕ www.kenchoji.com ⊠ ¥500.*

Meigetsu-in Temple (明月院)

TEMPLE | This temple is also known as Ajisai-dera ("the hydrangea temple"), and when the flowers bloom in June, it becomes one of the most popular places in Kamakura. The gardens transform into a sea of color—pink, white, and blue—and visitors can number in the thousands. A typical Kamakura light rain shouldn't deter you; it only showcases this incredible floral display to its best advantage. Meigetsu-in features Kamakura's largest *yagura* (a tomb cavity enclosing a mural) on which 16 images of Buddha are carved. ⊠ *189 Yamanouchi, Kamakura ✛ To reach Meigetsu-in from Tokei-ji, walk along Rte. 21 toward Kamakura for about 20 min until you cross railway tracks; take immediate left turn onto narrow side street that doubles back along tracks. This street bends to right and follows course of a little stream called Meigetsu-gawa to temple gate ☎ 0467/24–3437 ⊠ ¥500.*

Tokei-ji Temple (東慶寺)

TEMPLE | A Zen temple of the Rinzai sect, Tokei-ji holds special significance for the study of feminism in medieval Japan. More popularly known as the Enkiri-dera, or Divorce Temple, it was founded in 1285 by the widow of the Hojo regent Tokimune as a refuge for the victims of unhappy marriages. Under the shogunate, a husband of the warrior class could obtain a divorce simply by sending his wife back to her family. Not so for the wife: no matter what cruel and unusual treatment her husband meted out, she was stuck with him. If she ran away, however, and managed to reach Tokei Temple without being caught, she could receive sanctuary at the temple and remain there as a nun. After three years (later reduced to two), she was officially declared divorced. The temple survived as a convent through the Meiji Restoration of 1868. The last abbess died in 1902; her headstone is in the cemetery behind the temple, beneath the plum trees that blossom in February. Tokei Temple was later reestablished as a monastery.

The Matsugaoka Hozo (Treasure House) of Tokei Temple displays several Kamakura-period wooden Buddhas, ink paintings, scrolls, and works of calligraphy, some of which have been designated by the government as Important Cultural Objects. The library, called the Matsugaoka Bunko, was established in memory of the great Zen scholar D. T. Suzuki (1870–1966).

Tokei Temple is on the southwest side of the JR tracks (the side opposite Engaku Temple), less than a five-minute walk south from the station on the main road to Kamakura (Route 21—the Kamakura Kaido), on the right. ✉ *1367 Yamanouchi, Kamakura* ☎ *0467/22–1663* 🌐 *www.tokeiji.com* 🎫 *From ¥200* 🕒 *Matsugaoka Treasure House closed Mon.*

🍴 Restaurants

Hachinoki Kita-Kamakuraten (鉢の木北鎌倉店)

$$$ | JAPANESE | Traditional *shojin ryori* (the vegetarian cuisine of Zen monasteries) is served in this old Japanese house on the Kamakura Kaido (Route 21) near the entrance to Jochi Temple. The seating is mainly in tatami rooms with beautiful antique wood furnishings. **Known for:** Buddhist-temple cuisine for all budgets; peaceful, traditional atmosphere; elegant dining experience. [$] *Average main: ¥3,500* ✉ *350 Yamanouchi, Kamakura* ☎ *0467/23–3723* 🌐 *www.hachinoki.co.jp/english* 🕒 *Closed Wed.*

Kyorai-an (去来庵)

$$ | JAPANESE FUSION | A traditional Japanese structure houses this restaurant known for its excellent Western-style beef stew along with homemade cheesecake, pastas and local wines. Half the seats are on tatami mats and half are at tables, but all look out on a peaceful patch of greenery. **Known for:** classic Japanese–Western cuisine; local wines and ingredients; lovely views. [$] *Average main: ¥2,500* ✉ *157 Yamanouchi, Kamakura* ✥ *Kyorai-an is on main road from Kita-Kamakura to Kamakura on left side; it's about halfway between Meigetsu Temple and Kencho Temple, up a winding flight of stone steps* ☎ *0467/24–9835* 🌐 *kyoraian.jp* 💳 *No credit cards* 🕒 *Closed Thurs. and Fri.*

Downtown Kamakura

Downtown Kamakura is a good place to stop for lunch and shopping. Restaurants and shops selling local crafts, especially the carved and lacquered woodwork called Kamakura-bori, abound on Wakamiya Oji and the street parallel to it, Komachi-dori.

When the first Kamakura shogun, Minamoto no Yoritomo, learned he was about to have an heir, he had the tutelary shrine of his family moved to Kamakura from nearby Yuigahama and ordered a stately avenue to be built through the center of his capital from the shrine to the sea. Along this avenue would travel the procession that brought his son—if there were a son—to be presented to the gods. Yoritomo's consort did indeed bear him a son, Yoriie (pronounced "yo-*ree*-ee-eh"), in 1182; Yoriie was brought in great pomp to the shrine and then consecrated to his place in the shogunal succession. Alas, the blessing of the gods did Yoriie little good. He was barely 18 when Yoritomo died, and the regency established by his mother's family, the Hojo, kept him virtually powerless until 1203, when he was banished and eventually assassinated. The Minamoto were never to hold power again, but Yoriie's memory lives on in the street that his father built for him: Wakamiya Oji, "the Avenue of the Young Prince."

👁 Sights

Hokoku-ji Temple (報国寺)

TEMPLE | Visitors to Kamakura tend to overlook this lovely little Zen temple of the Rinzai sect that was built in 1334, but it's worth a look. Over the years it had fallen into disrepair and neglect, until an enterprising priest took over, cleaned up the gardens, and began promoting the temple for meditation sessions, calligraphy exhibitions, and tea ceremony. Behind the main hall are a thick grove of bamboo and a small tea pavilion—a restful oasis and a fine place to go for *matcha* (green tea). The temple is about 2 km (1 mile) east on Route 204 from the main entrance at Tsuru-ga-oka Hachiman-gu; turn right at the traffic light by the Hokoku Temple Iriguchi bus stop and walk about three minutes south to the gate. ⊠ *2–7–4 Jomyo-ji, Kamakura* ☎ *0467/22–0762* ⊕ *www.hokokuji.or.jp* ⊠ *From ¥300.*

Jomyo-ji Temple (浄妙寺)

TEMPLE | Founded in 1188, this is one of the Five Mountains Zen monasteries. Though this modest single-story monastery belonging to the Rinzai sect lacks the grandeur and scale of the Engaku and Kencho, it still merits the status of an Important Cultural Property. It is nestled inside an immaculate garden that is particularly beautiful in spring, when the cherry trees bloom. A tea ceremony with Japanese green tea takes place in this lovely setting. The monastery's only distinctive features are its green roof and the statues of Shaka Nyorai and Amida Nyorai, who represent truth and enlightenment, in the main hall. ⊠ *3–8–31 Jomyo-ji, Kamakura* ⊹ *From Hokoku-ji, cross main street (Rte. 204) that brought you the mile or so from Tsurugaoka Hachimangu, and take first narrow street north. The monastery is about 100 yds. from corner* ☎ *0467/22–2818* ⊠ *Jomyo Temple ¥100, tea ceremony ¥500.*

Kamakura-gu Shrine (鎌倉宮)

RELIGIOUS BUILDING | This Shinto shrine was built after the Meiji Restoration of 1868 and was dedicated to Prince Morinaga (1308–36), the first son of Emperor Go-Daigo. When Go-Daigo overthrew the Kamakura Shogunate and restored Japan to direct imperial rule, Morinaga—who had been in the priesthood—was appointed supreme commander of his father's forces. The prince

lived in turbulent times and died young: when the Ashikaga clan in turn overthrew Go-Daigo's government, Morinaga was taken into exile, held prisoner in a cave behind the present site of Kamakura Shrine, and eventually beheaded. The Homotsu-den (Treasure House), on the northwest corner of the grounds, next to the shrine's administrative office, is of interest mainly for its collection of paintings depicting the life of Prince Morinaga. ⊠ *154 Nikaido, Kamakura* ⊹ *From Yoritomo's tomb walk to Rte. 204 and turn left; at next traffic light, a narrow street on left leads off at an angle to shrine, about 5-min walk west* ☎ *0467/22–0318* ⊠ *Shrine free, Treasure House ¥300.*

Kamakura Kokuhokan Museum (鎌倉国宝館)

ART MUSEUM | This museum was built in 1928 as a repository for many of the most important objects belonging to the shrines and temples in the area; many of these are designated Important Cultural Properties. Located along the east side of the Tsuru-ga-oka Hachiman-gu shrine precincts, the museum has an especially fine collection of devotional and portrait sculpture in wood from the Kamakura and Muromachi periods; the portrait pieces may be among the most expressive and interesting in all of classical Japanese art. ⊠ *2–1–1 Yukinoshita, Kamakura* ☎ *0467/22–0753* ⊕ *www.city.kamakura. kanagawa.jp/kokuhoukan* ⊠ *From ¥700* ⊗ *Closed Mon.*

Minamoto Yoritomo's Tomb (源頼朝の墓; Minamoto no Yoritomo no Haka)

TOMB | The man who put Kamakura on the map, so to speak, chose not to leave it when he died: it's only a short walk from Tsurugaoka Hachimangu to the tomb of the man responsible for its construction, Minamoto no Yoritomo. If you've already been to Nikko and have seen how a later dynasty of shoguns sought to glorify its own memories, you may be surprised at the simplicity of Yoritomo's tomb. ⊠ *2–5–2 Nishimikaido,*

An Ancient Soap Opera

Once a year, during the Spring Festival (early or mid-April, when the cherry trees are in bloom), the Mai-den hall at Tsurugaoka Hachiman-gu is used to stage a heartrending drama about Minamoto no Yoritomo's brother, Yoshitsune. Although Yoritomo was the tactical genius behind the downfall of the Taira clan and the establishment of the Kamakura Shogunate in the late 12th century, it was his dashing half brother who actually defeated the Taira in battle. In so doing, Yoshitsune won the admiration of many, and Yoritomo came to believe that his sibling had ambitions of his own. Despite Yoshitsune's declaration of allegiance, Yoritomo had him exiled and sent assassins to have him killed. Yoshitsune spent his life fleeing from one place to another until, at the age of 30, he was betrayed in his last refuge and took his own life.

Earlier in his exile, Yoshitsune's lover, the dancer Shizuka Gozen, had been captured and brought to Yoritomo and his wife, Masako. They commanded her to dance for them as a kind of penance. Instead she danced for Yoshitsune. Yoritomo was furious, and only Masako's influence kept him from ordering her death. When he discovered, however, that Shizuka was carrying Yoshitsune's child, he ordered that if the child were a boy, he was to be killed. A boy was born. Some versions of the legend have it that the child was slain; others say he was placed in a cradle, like Moses, and cast adrift in the reeds.

Kamakura ✛ Exit Tsurugaoka Hachiman-gu, turn left and then left again, and follow small road up to Yoritomo's tomb ▣ Free.

The Museum of Modern Art, Kamakura Annex (神奈川県立近代美術館 鎌倉別館; Kanagawa Kenritsu Kindai Bijutsukan Kamakura Bekkan)

ART MUSEUM | Just a few minutes' walk from Tsurugaoka Hachimangu, this newly refurbished museum houses a collection of Japanese oil paintings and watercolors, woodblock prints, and sculpture. ✉ 2–8–1 Yukinoshita, Kamakura ☎ 0467/22–5000 ⊕ www.moma.pref.kanagawa.jp/en/annex ▣ From ¥700, depending on exhibition ☾ Closed Mon.

Tsurugaoka Hachimangu Shrine (鶴岡八幡宮)

RELIGIOUS BUILDING | This shrine is dedicated to the legendary emperor Ojin, his wife, and his mother, from whom Minamoto no Yoritomo claimed descent. At the entrance, the small, steeply arched, vermilion Taiko-bashi (Drum Bridge) crosses a stream between two lotus ponds. The ponds were made to Yoritomo's specifications. His wife, Masako, suggested placing islands in each. In the larger Genji Pond, to the right, filled with white lotus flowers, she placed three islands. Genji was another name for clan, and three is an auspicious number. In the smaller Heike Pond, to the left, she put four islands. Heike (pronounced "heh-ee-keh") was another name for the rival Taira clan, which the Minamoto had destroyed, and four—homophonous in Japanese with the word for "death"—is very unlucky indeed.

On the far side of the Drum Bridge is the Mai-den. This hall is the setting for a story of the Minamoto celebrated in Noh and Kabuki theater. Beyond the Mai-den, a flight of steps leads to the shrine's Hon-do (Main Hall). To the left of these steps is a ginkgo tree that—according to legend—was witness to a murder that ended the Minamoto line in 1219. From behind this tree, a priest named Kugyo leapt out and beheaded his uncle, the 26-year-old Sanetomo, Yoritomo's second son and the last Minamoto shogun. The priest was quickly apprehended, but Sanetomo's head was never found. As at all other Shinto shrines, the Hon-do is unadorned; the building itself, an 1828 reconstruction, is not particularly noteworthy. ✉ *2–1–31 Yukinoshita, Kamakura* ☎ *0467/22–0315* 🌐 *www.hachimangu.or.jp* 🎟 *Shrine free; Treasure House ¥300.*

🍴 Restaurants

Kaisen Misaki-ko (海鮮三崎港)

$$ | SUSHI | This *kaiten-zushi* (sushi served on a conveyor belt that lets you pick the dishes you want) restaurant serves eye-poppingly large fish portions that hang over the edge of their plates. All the standard sushi creations, including tuna, shrimp, and egg, are prepared here. **Known for:** friendly, helpful staff and sushi chefs; inexpensive, quality sushi; fast service. [$] *Average main: ¥1,500* ✉ *1–7–1 Komachi, Kamakura* ☎ *0467/22–6228* 💳 *No credit cards.*

Kamakura Udon Miyoshi (鎌倉みよし)

$$ | JAPANESE | Serving up some of Kamakura's best handmade udon noodles and tempura, this unpretentious restaurant is a good bet for quick and satisfying lunch. Miyoshi also has a selection of local sakes to pair with your meal. **Known for:** fresh noodles made before your eyes; reliability amid the tourist traps in the area; tempura that won't weigh you down. [$] *Average main: ¥1,600* ✉ *1–5–38 Yukinoshita, Kamakura* ☎ *0467/61–4634* 🌐 *www.kamakuraudon.jp* 💳 *No credit cards.*

☕ Coffee and Quick Bites

Bergfeld (ベルグフェルド)

$ | BAKERY | This German bakery serves cakes and cookies that are surprisingly authentic—the baker trained in Germany. There are a few small tables outside, and cozy tables inside where you can enjoy coffee and cakes before resuming your tour. **Known for:** authentic German pastries and desserts; a good break between seeing sights; tasty sandwiches. [$] *Average main: ¥700* ✉ *3–9–24 Yukinoshita, Kamakura* ☎ *0467/24–2706* 🌐 *bergfeld-kamakura.com* 💳 *No credit cards* ⏲ *Closed Tues., 1st and 3rd Mon.*

Hase

On hydrangea-clad hillsides just outside downtown Kamakura are two of the town's main attractions, the Great Buddha and Hase-dera Temple.

👁 Sights

Enoshima (江ノ島)

ISLAND | The Sagami Bay shore in this area has some of the closest beaches to Tokyo, and in the hot, humid summer months it seems as though all of the city's teeming millions pour onto these beaches in search of a vacant patch of rather dirty gray sand. Pass up this mob scene and press on instead to Enoshima. The island is only 4 km (2½ miles) around, with a hill in the middle. Partway up the hill is a shrine where the local fisherfolk used to pray for a bountiful catch—before it became a tourist attraction. Once upon a time it was quite a hike up to the shrine; now there's a series of escalators, flanked by the inevitable stalls selling souvenirs and snacks. The island has several cafés and restaurants, and on clear days some of them have spectacular views of Mt. Fuji and the Izu Peninsula. To reach the causeway from Enoshima Station to the island, walk south from the station for about 3 km (2 miles), keeping the Katase-gawa (Katase River) on your right. To return to Tokyo from Enoshima, take a train to Shinjuku on the Odakyu line. From the island walk back across the causeway and take the second

Hase-dera, in Kamakura, is dedicated to unborn children. The beautiful temple faces the sea.

bridge over the Katase-gawa. Within five minutes you'll come to Katase-Enoshima Station. Or you can retrace your steps to Kamakura and take the JR Yokosuka Line to Tokyo Station. ⊠ *Kamakura.*

★ **Hase-dera Temple** (長谷寺)

TEMPLE | The only temple in Kamakura facing the sea, this is one of the most beautiful, and saddest, places of pilgrimage in the city. On a landing partway up the stone steps that lead to the temple grounds are hundreds of small stone images of Jizo, one of the *bodhisattvas* in the Buddhist pantheon. Jizo is the savior of children, particularly the souls of the stillborn, aborted, and miscarried; the mothers of these children dress the statues of Jizo in bright red bibs and leave them small offerings of food, heartbreakingly touching acts of prayer.

The Kannon Hall (Kannon-do) at Hase-dera enshrines the largest carved-wood statue in Japan: the votive figure of Juichimen Kannon, the 11-headed goddess of mercy. Standing 30 feet tall, the goddess bears a crown of 10 smaller heads, symbolizing

her ability to search out in all directions for those in need of her compassion. No one knows for certain when the figure was carved. According to the temple records, a monk named Tokudo Shonin carved two images of the Juichimen Kannon from a huge laurel tree in 721. One was consecrated to the Hase-dera in present-day Nara Prefecture; the other was thrown into the sea in order to go wherever the sea decided that there were souls in need, and that image washed up on shore near Kamakura. Much later, in 1342, Takauji Ashikaga—the first of the 15 Ashikaga shoguns who followed the Kamakura era—had the statue covered with gold leaf.

The Amida Hall of Hase-dera enshrines the image of a seated Amida Buddha, who presides over the Western Paradise of the Pure Land. Minamoto no Yoritomo ordered the creation of this statue when he reached the age of 42; popular Japanese belief, adopted from China, holds that your 42nd year is particularly unlucky. Yoritomo's act of piety earned him another 11 years—he was 53 when he was thrown by a horse and died of his injuries. The Buddha is popularly known as the *yakuyoke* (good luck) Amida, and many visitors—especially students facing entrance exams—make a point of coming here to pray. To the left of the main halls is a small restaurant where you can buy good-luck candy and admire the view of Kamakura Beach and Sagami Bay. ✉ *3–11–2 Hase, Kamakura* ⚓ *From Hase Station, walk north about 5 min on main street (Rte. 32) toward Kotoku-in and Great Buddha, and look for signpost to temple on side street to left* ☎ *0467/22–6300* ⊕ *www.hasedera.jp* 📷 *¥400.*

★ Kamakura Great Buddha (鎌倉大仏; *Kamakura Daibutsu*)

PUBLIC ART | The single biggest attraction in Hase is the Great Buddha—sharing the honors with Mt. Fuji, perhaps, as the quintessential picture-postcard image of Japan. The statue of the compassionate Amida Buddha sits cross-legged in the temple courtyard. The 37-foot bronze figure was cast in 1292, three centuries before Europeans reached Japan; the concept of the classical Greek lines in the Buddha's robe must have come over the Silk Route through China during the time of Alexander the Great. The casting was probably first conceived in 1180, by Minamoto no Yoritomo, who wanted a statue to rival the enormous Daibutsu in Nara. Until 1495 the Amida Buddha was housed in a wooden temple, which washed away in a great tidal wave.

It may seem sacrilegious to walk inside the Great Buddha, but for ¥200 you can enter the figure from a doorway in the right side and explore his stomach, with a stairway that leads up to two windows in his back, offering a stunning view of the temple grounds (open until 4:15 pm). To reach Kotoku-in and the Great Buddha, take the Enoden Line from the west side of JR Kamakura Station three stops to Hase. From the East Exit, turn right and walk north about 10 minutes

What Is a Bodhisattva?

A *bodhisattva* is a being that has deferred its own ascendance into Buddhahood to guide the souls of others to salvation. It is considered a deity in Buddhism.

on the main street (Route 32). ✉ *4–2–28 Hase, Kamakura* ☎ *0467/22–0703* ⊕ *www.kotoku-in.jp* 📷 *¥300.*

Ryuko-ji Temple (龍口寺)

TEMPLE | The Kamakura story would not be complete without the tale of Nichiren (1222–82), the monk who founded the only native Japanese sect of Buddhism and is honored here. Nichiren's rejection of both Zen and Jodo (Pure Land) teachings brought him into conflict with the Kamakura Shogunate, and the Hojo regents sent him into exile on the Izu Peninsula in 1261. Later allowed to return, he continued to preach his own interpretation of the Lotus Sutra—and to assert the "blasphemy" of other Buddhist sects, a stance that finally persuaded the Hojo regency, in 1271, to condemn him to death. The execution was to take place on a hill to the south of Hase. As the executioner swung his sword, legend has it that a lightning bolt struck the blade and snapped it in two. Taken aback, the executioner sat down to collect his wits, and a messenger was sent back to Kamakura to report the event. On his way he met another messenger, who was carrying a writ from the Hojo regents commuting Nichiren's sentence to exile on the island of Sado-ga-shima.

Followers of Nichiren built Ryuko Temple in 1337, on the hill where he was to be executed, marking his miraculous deliverance from the headsman. There are other Nichiren temples closer to Kamakura—Myohon-ji and Ankokuron-ji, for example.

Did You Know?

The Daibutsu of Kamakura, cast in the 13th century, was originally housed indoors, but weather disasters in the 14th and 15th centuries destroyed multiple reconstructions of its temple. Since 1495 the Buddha has meditated alfresco. Built in the Chinese Sung style, this bronze Buddha weighs in at 121 tons.

But Ryuko has not only the typical Nichiren-style main hall, with gold tassels hanging from its roof, but also a beautiful pagoda, built in 1904. ✉ *3–13–37 Katase, Fujisawa* ✈ *Take Enoden train line west from Hase to Enoshima—a short, scenic ride that cuts through hills surrounding Kamakura to shore. From Enoshima Station walk about 100 yards east, keeping train tracks on your right* ☎ *0466/25–7357* ✉ *Free.*

Restaurants

Kaiseiro (華正樓)

$$$$ | CHINESE | This establishment, in an old Japanese house, serves the best Chinese food in the city. The dining-room windows look out on a small, restful garden. **Known for:** elegant atmosphere; steeped in history; excellent Peking duck and other multicourse meals. **$** *Average main: ¥10,000* ✉ *3–1–14 Hase, Kamakura* ☎ *0467/22–0280.*

Mt. Fuji

100 km (62 miles) southwest of Tokyo.

Mt. Fuji is the crown jewel of the national park and an incredibly popular destination for both Japanese and international travelers, but travel time from Tokyo is still longer than to some places that are considerably farther from Tokyo. There are six routes to the summit of the 12,388-foot-high mountain but only two, both accessible by bus, are recommended: from Go-gome (5th Station), on the north side, and from Shin-Go-gome (New 5th Station), on the south.

GETTING HERE AND AROUND

Take one of the daily buses directly to Go-gome from Tokyo; they run July through August and leave from Shinjuku Station. The journey takes about two hours and 40 minutes from Shinjuku and costs ¥2,600. Reservations are required; book seats through the Fuji Kyuko Highway Bus Reservation Center, the

Keio Highway Bus Reservation Center, the Japan Travel Bureau (which should have English-speaking staff), or any major travel agency.

There are no direct trains between Mt. Fuji and Tokyo; as a result, buses are more affordable and convenient. But if you need to return from Mt. Fuji to Tokyo by train, take an hour-long bus ride from Shin-Go-gome to Gotemba (¥1,500). From Gotemba take the JR Tokaido and Gotemba lines to Tokyo Station (¥1,940), or take the JR Asagiri express train from Gotemba to Shinjuku Station (¥2,810).

CONTACTS Fuji Kyuko Highway Bus Reservation Center. ☎ *0555/73–8181* ⊕ *bus-en. fujikyu.co.jp.* **JTB Sunrise Tours.** ✉ *Tokyo* ☎ *03/5796–5454* ⊕ *www.sunrise-tours. jp/en.* **Keio Highway Bus Reservation Center.** ☎ *03/5376–2222* ⊕ *highway-buses.jp.*

◉ Sights

★ Mt. Fuji (富士山; *Fuji-san*)

MOUNTAIN | Rising up out of the surrounding plains, the single, flat-topped peak of Mt. Fuji is a sight to behold. Spending a day—or more commonly an afternoon and the following morning—to hike Mt. Fuji can be a once-in-a-lifetime experience with a fascinating variety of terrain and a stunning view of the sunrise from the peak—provided you go into it with the right expectations. Unlike Japan's more remote mountains like the Japan Alps, Fuji is crowded, and the summer hiking season, when trails are open and accessible (roughly July through September), is short. Timing your hike to see the sunrise can mean that the final stretch to the summit can feel more like waiting in line than hiking. Still, making the trek to the top and watching the sunrise from Japan's most sacred mountain is a singularly incredible experience, and there is fun to be had climbing with the crowd.

There are four trails up Fuji, but the most common starting point is the Subaru Line 5th Station (aka Kawaguchiko 5th Station),

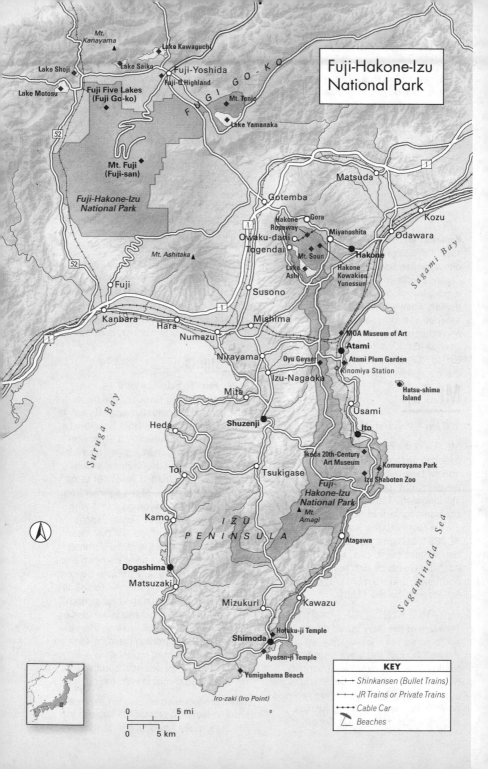

Fuji-Hakone-Izu National Park

Mt. Kanayama ▲
Lake Kawaguchi
Lake Shoji
Lake Saiko
Fuji-Yoshida
Lake Motosu
Fuji-Q Highland
Fuji Five Lakes (Fuji Go-ko) ◆
Mt. Tenjo ▲
FUJI GO-KO
Lake Yamanaka

52

Mt. Fuji (Fuji-san) ▲

Fuji-Hakone-Izu National Park

Matsuda
Gotemba
Kozu

Mt. Ashitaka ▲
Hakone Ropeway
Gora
Owaku-dani
Miyanoshita
Togendai
Mt. Soun ◆
Hakone
Odawara
Lake Ashi
Hakone Kowakien Yunessun
52
Fuji
Susono

Kanbara
Hara
Mishima
MOA Museum of Art
Numazu
Atami
Oyu Geyser
Atami Plum Garden
Nirayama
Izu-Nagaoka
Kinomiya Station
1
Mita
Hatsu-shima Island
Heda
Shuzenji
Usami
Ito
Toi
Ikeda 20th-Century Art Museum
Komuroyama Park
Tsukigase
Izu Shaboten Zoo
Kamo
IZU PENINSULA
Fuji-Hakone-Izu National Park
Mt. Amagi ▲
Dogashima
Atagawa
Matsuzaki
Mizukuri
Kawazu
Hofuku-ji Temple
Shimoda
Ryosen-ji Temple
Yumigahama Beach
Iro-zaki (Iro Point)

Sagami Bay
Suruga Bay
Sagaminada Sea

KEY
←→	Shinkansen (Bullet Trains)
←→	JR Trains or Private Trains
•••	Cable Car
⏞	Beaches

0   5 mi
0   5 km

which is easily accessed by direct buses from Tokyo, Hakone, and many other cities. From here it takes between five to seven hours to reach the summit. The descent takes another three to four hours. There are numerous mountain huts on the way up to sleep for a few hours and adjust to the altitude (¥10,000–¥14,000 per person for a dorm spot, which includes dinner and breakfast), but they fill up quickly during peak times. Spots can be reserved for some huts online, but others require a phone call. The length and altitude require a decent level of fitness but no technical climbing skills. ⊠ *Fuji-Hakone-Izu National Park* ⊕ *www.fujisan-climb.jp* ⊠ *¥1,000* ☞ *Outside of hiking season, the weather is highly unpredictable and extremely dangerous, so climbing is strongly discouraged.*

Fuji Five Lakes

55 km (34 miles) northwest of Hakone.

To the north of Mt. Fuji, the Fuji Go-ko area affords an unbeatable view of the mountain on clear days and makes the best base for a climb to the summit. With its various outdoor activities, such as skating and fishing in winter and boating and hiking in summer, this is a popular resort area for families and business conferences.

The five lakes are, from the east, Yamanaka-ko, Kawaguchi-ko, Sai-ko, Shoji-ko, and Motosu-ko. Yamanaka and Kawaguchi are the largest and most developed as resort areas, with Kawaguchi more or less the centerpiece of the group.

GETTING HERE AND AROUND
Direct bus service runs daily from Shinjuku Station in Tokyo to Lake Kawaguchi every hour between 7:10 am and 11:20 pm. Buses go from Kawaguchi-ko Station to Go-gome (the fifth station on the climb

up Mt. Fuji) in about an hour; there are eight departures a day until the climbing season (July and August) starts, when there are 15 departures or more, depending on demand.

The transportation hub, as well as one of the major resort areas in the Fuji Five Lakes area, is Kawaguchi-ko. Getting there from Tokyo requires a change of trains at Otsuki. The JR Chuo Line Kaiji and Azusa express trains leave Shinjuku Station for Otsuki on the half hour from 7 am to 8 pm (more frequently in the morning) and take approximately one hour. At Otsuki, change to the private Fuji-Kyuko Line for Kawaguchi-ko, which takes another 50 minutes. The total traveling time is about two hours, and you can use your JR Pass as far as Otsuki; otherwise, the fare is ¥1,490. The Otsuki–Kawaguchi-ko leg costs ¥1,170.

Opened in 2019, the Fuji Kaiyuu train had direct express service from Shinjuku twice daily (three times a day on weekends) Trains run from Shinjuku to Kawaguchi-ko in the morning, with return runs in the afternoon. The journey takes just under two hours and costs ¥4,130 each way. Check the express timetables before you go; you can also call either the JR Higashi-Nihon Info Line or Fuji-kyuuko Kawaguchi-ko Station for train information.

TIMING
You can visit this area on a day trip from Tokyo, but unless you want to spend most of it on buses and trains, plan on staying overnight.

VISITOR INFORMATION
CONTACT Fuji-Kawaguchiko Tourist Information Center. ⊠ *364–1 Funatsu, Fujikawaguchiko-machi, Minami-Tsuru-gun* ☎ *0555/72–6700* ⊕ *www.fujisan.ne.jp.*

Continued on page 344

PEERLESS FUJI

by Peter MacMillan

Climbing Mt. Fuji

Mt. Fuji greets hikers who arrive at its summit just before dawn with the *go-raiko*, or the Honorable Coming of the Light. The reflection of this light shimmers across the sky just before the sun first appears, giving the extraordinary sunrise a mystical feel. Fuji-san's early morning magic is just one of the characteristics of the mountain that has captured the collective imagination of the Japanese, along with its snowy peak, spiritual meaning, and propensity to hide behind clouds. The close-to-perfectly symmetrical cone is an object to conquer physically and to admire from afar.

Japan is more than 70% mountainous, and Fuji is its tallest mountain. It appears in literature, art, and culture from the highest level to the most ordinary in countless ways. In a word, Fuji is ubiquitous.

Since ancient times Mt. Fuji has been an object of worship for both Shinto and Buddhist practitioners. Shrines devoted to Konohana-Sakuya Hime, Mt. Fuji's goddess, dot the trails. So sacred is Fuji that the mountaintop torii gate at the Oku-miya of Sengen Taisha Shrine (though at Fuji's foot, the shrine also encompasses the mountain above the 8th station) states that this is the greatest mountain in the

world. Typically the gate would provide the shrine's name. Here, the torii defines not the shrine but the sacred space of the mountain.

Rising to 12,385 feet (3,776 meters) Mt. Fuji is an active volcano, but the last eruption was in 1707. Located on the boundaries of Shizuoka and Yamanashi prefectures, the mountain is an easy day trip west of Tokyo, and on clear days you can see the peak from the city. In season, hikers clamber to the peak, but it is gazing upon Fuji that truly inspires awe and wonder. No visit to Japan would be complete without at least a glimpse of this beautiful icon.

(Top left) Mt. Fuji's famous morning light draws visitors, (Top right) the summit is often surrounded by clouds, (Bottom right) the trails are rocky and rugged at times.

THE SYMBOLISM OF FUJI-SAN

ARTISTIC FUJI

Mt. Fuji is one of the world's most painted and photographed mountains. But rising above all the visual depictions are Katsushika Hokusai's *Thirty-six Views of Mt. Fuji* and his *One Hundred Views of Mt. Fuji*. The latter is a stunning work and considered his masterpiece. However, the *Thirty-Six Views* is more famous because the images were printed in full color, while the *One Hundred Views* was printed in monochrome black and gray. His *Great Wave off Kanagawa* is one of the most famous prints in the history of art.

Hokusai believed that his depictions would get better and better as he got older, and they did; his *One Hundred*

Views was completed when he was 75. He was also obsessed with achieving immortality. In creating the *One Hundred Views of Mt. Fuji*, a mountain always associated with immortality, he hoped to achieve his own. History proved him right.

LITERARY FUJI

There are thousands of literary works related to Fuji, including traditional and modern poems, haiku, Noh dramas, novels, and plays. In the Man'yoshu, 8th-century poet Yamabe no Akahito famously extolled Fuji: "When I sail out/on the Bay of Tago/every where's white-/Look! Snow's piling up/ on the peak of Fuji." Matsuo Basho, in another well known poem, wrote about not being able to see the mountain: "How lovely and intriguing!/ Covered in drifting fog,/ the day I could not see Fuji." There are many times of the year when Fuji hides behind the clouds, so don't be disappointed if you miss it. Like the great haiku poet, see the mountain in the eye of your heart.

(Top) Katsushika Hokusai's *Red Fuji*,
(Bottom) *Great Wave off Kanagawa*
by Katsushika Hokusai

SEE FUJI-SAN FROM AFAR

the poets and artists who have ...und inspiration in gazing at Fuji-san, you, too, can catch a glimpse of the snow-capped cone on the horizon. On a clear day, most likely in winter when the air is dry and the clouds lift, the following experiences provide some of the best Fuji views.

SEE FUJI

Atop Tokyo. Visit the Tokyo City View observation promenade on the 52nd floor of the Mori Tower in Roppongi. You can walk all around this circular building and take in the spectacular views of Tokyo and, when the weather is fine, Fuji. While you're here, don't miss the sky-high Mori Art Museum, a contemporary art space on the 52nd and 53rd floors. The evening view of the city is also splendid, but Fuji will be slumbering under the blanket of nightfall.

From Hakone. Part of Fuji-Hakone-Izu National Park, the same park Fuji calls home, and an easy day trip from Tokyo, Hakone is a playground of hiking trails, small art museums, an onsen, and more. Head to the beautiful gar-

den at Hakone Detached Palace for scenic views of Fuji-san. Early morning and late evening will provide the best chance for clear skies.

Speeding out of town. The classic view of Fuji is from the Shinkansen traveling from Tokyo to Kyoto. Some of the world's fastest transportation technology hums beneath you when, suddenly, the world's most beautiful and sacred mountain appears on the left. This striking combination of the ancient and cutting-edge is at the heart of understanding Japan. Make sure not to fall asleep!

(Top) Shinkansen speeding past Fuji, (Bottom) Fuji from inside Hakone National Park

CLIMBING FUJI-SAN
FROM KAWAGUCHIKO TRAIL

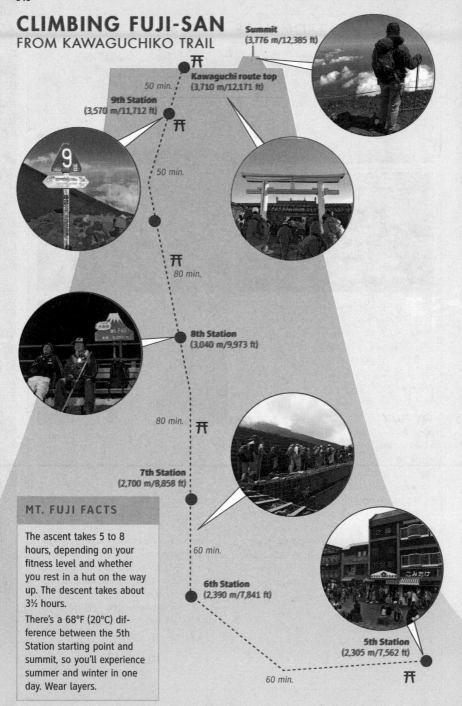

Summit
(3,776 m/12,385 ft)

Kawaguchi route top
(3,710 m/12,171 ft)

50 min.

9th Station
(3,570 m/11,712 ft)

50 min.

80 min.

8th Station
(3,040 m/9,973 ft)

80 min.

7th Station
(2,700 m/8,858 ft)

60 min.

6th Station
(2,390 m/7,841 ft)

5th Station
(2,305 m/7,562 ft)

60 min.

MT. FUJI FACTS

The ascent takes 5 to 8 hours, depending on your fitness level and whether you rest in a hut on the way up. The descent takes about 3½ hours.

There's a 68°F (20°C) difference between the 5th Station starting point and summit, so you'll experience summer and winter in one day. Wear layers.

A photographer capturing view from Mt. Fuji

Although many Japanese like to climb Mt. Fuji once in their lives, there's a saying in Japanese that only a fool would climb it twice. You, too, can make a once-in-a-lifetime climb during the mountain's official open season from July through August. Unless you're an experienced hiker, do not attempt to make the climb at another time of year.

TRAIL CONDITIONS

Except for the occasional cobblestone path, the routes are unpaved and at times steep, especially toward the top. Near the end of the climb there are some rope banisters to steady yourself, but for the most part you'll have to rely on your own balance.

Fuji draws huge crowds in season, so expect a lot of company on your hike. The throngs grow thicker in August during the school break and reach their peak during the holiday Obon week in mid-August; it gets so crowded that hikers have to queue up at certain passes. Trails are less crowded overnight. Go during the week and in July for the lightest crowds (though the weather is less reliable). Or accept the crowds and enjoy the friendships that spring up among strangers on the trails.

TRAILS OVERVIEW

If you're in good health you should be able to climb from the base to the summit. That said, the air is thin, and it can be humbling to struggle for oxygen while some 83-year-

old Japanese grandmother blithely leaves you in her dust (it happens).

Most visitors take buses as far as the Fifth Station and hike to the top from there (⇨ *See Mt. Fuji listing in this chapter for more information on buses*). The paved roads end at this halfway point.

Four routes lead to Mt. Fuji's summit—the **Kawaguchiko, Subashiri, Gotemba,** and **Fujinomiya**—and each has a corresponding Fifth Station that serves as the transfer point between bus and foot. Depending on which trail you choose, the ascent takes between 5 and 10 hours. Fujinomiya is closest to the summit; Gotemba is the farthest.

We recommend Kawaguchiko (Fuji-Yoshida) Trail in Yamanashi, as its many first-aid centers and lodging facilities (huts) ensure that you can enjoy the climb.
■TIP→ **Those interested in experiencing Fuji's religious and spiritual aspects should walk this trail from the mountain's foot. Along the way are small shrines**

that lead to the torii gate at the top, which signifies Fuji's sacred status. While the food and cleanliness standards at mountain huts are subpar, they provide valuable rest spots and even more valuable camaraderie and good will among travelers.

AT THE TOP

Once you reach the top of Mt. Fuji, you can walk along the ridge of the volcano. A torii gate declares that Fuji is the greatest mountain in the world. It also marks the entrance to the **Fuji-san Honmiya Sengen Taisha Shrine** (at the foot of the mountain near the Kawaguchiko Trail is the shrine's other facility). Inside the shrine, head to the post office where you can mail letters and postcards with a special Mt. Fuji stamp. There's also a chalet at the top for those captivated enough to stay the night.

NIGHT HIKES

The most spectacular way to hike Mt. Fuji is to time the climb so that you arrive at sunrise. Not only is the light famously enchanting, but the sky is also more likely to be clear, allowing for views back to Tokyo. Those who choose this have a few options. Start from the Kawaguchiko 5th Station on the Kawaguchi Trail around 10 pm (or later, depending on the sunrise time) and hike through the night, arriving at the summit between 4:30 and 5 am, just as the sun begins to rise. A better alternative is to begin in the afternoon or evening and hike to the 7th or 8th Station, spend a few hours resting there, and then depart very early in the morning to see the sun rise. ■TIP→ **The trail isn't lit at night, so bring a headlamp to illuminate the way. Avoid carrying flashlights, though, as it is important to keep your hands free in case of a fall**

COMMEMORATE YOUR VISIT

Purchase a walking stick at the base of Mt. Fuji and, as you climb, have it branded at each station. By the time you reach the top you'll have the perfect souvenir to mark your achievement.

(Top) First glimpse of the *go-raiko*, (Bottom) Mt. Fuji at dawn

Walking sticks for sale

In Focus | PEERLESS FUJI

DID YOU KNOW?

Although earlier meanings of the word *Fuji* include "peerless," and "immortal one," the current way of writing Fuji implies "wealthy persons of military status." The mountain is called *fuji-san* (not *fuji-yama*) in Japanese.

Sights

Fuji-Q Highland (富士急ハイランド)
AMUSEMENT PARK/CARNIVAL | FAMILY |
The largest of the recreational facilities at Lake Kawaguchi has an impressive assortment of rides, roller coasters, and other amusements, but it's probably not worth a visit unless you have children in tow. In winter there's superb skating here, with Mt. Fuji for a backdrop. Fuji-kyu Highland is about 15 minutes' walk east from Kawaguchi-ko Station. In addition to the entry fee, there are charges for various attractions, so it's best to get the one-day free pass. ⊠ *5–6–1 Shinnishihara, Fujiyoshida* ☎ *0555/23–2111* ⊕ *www.fujiq. jp/en* 🎟 *1-day free pass ¥6,300.*

Lake Kawaguchi (河口湖; *Kawaguchi-ko*)
BODY OF WATER | A 5- to 10-minute walk from Kawaguchi-ko Station, this is the most developed of the five lakes. It's ringed with weekend retreats and vacation lodges—many of them maintained by companies and universities for their employees. Excursion boats depart from a pier here on 30-minute tours of the lake. The promise, not always fulfilled, is to have two views of Mt. Fuji: one of the mountain itself and the other inverted in its reflection on the water. ⊠ *Kawaguchiko, Fujikawaguchiko.*

Lake Motosu (本栖湖; *Motosu-ko*)
BODY OF WATER | Lake Motosu is the farthest west of the five lakes. It's also the deepest and clearest of the Fuji Go-ko. It takes about 50 minutes to get here by bus. One of the least developed of the lakes, it is a good spot for hiking and nature lovers. ⊠ *Motosuko, Fujikawaguchiko.*

Lake Sai (西湖; *Sai-ko*)
BODY OF WATER | Between Lakes Shoji and Kawaguchi, Lake Sai is the third-largest lake of the Fuji Go-ko, with only moderate development. From the western shore there is an especially good view of Mt. Fuji. Near Sai-ko there are two natural caves, an ice cave and a wind cave. You can either take a bus or walk to them. ⊠ *Saiko, Fujikawaguchiko.*

Lake Shoji (精進湖; *Shoji-ko*)
BODY OF WATER | Many consider Lake Shoji, the smallest of the lakes, to be the prettiest. There are still remnants of lava flow jutting out from the water, which locals perch upon while fishing. The Shoji Trail leads from Lake Shoji to Mt. Fuji's 5th Station through Aoki-ga-hara (Sea of Trees). This forest has an underlying magnetic lava field that makes compasses go haywire. Be prepared with a good trail map before taking this hike. ⊠ *Shojiko, Fujikawaguchiko.*

Lake Yamanaka (山中湖; *Yamanaka-ko*)
BODY OF WATER | The largest lake of the Fuji Go-ko, Yamanaka is 35 minutes by bus to the southeast of Kawaguchi. It's also the closest lake to the popular trail up Mt. Fuji that starts at Go-gome, and many climbers use this resort area as a base. ⊠ *Yamanakoko, Yamanaka-ko-mura.*

Mt. Tenjo (天上山; *Tenjo-san*)
MOUNTAIN | From the shore of Lake Kawaguchi (near the pier), the Kachikachi Ropeway quickly brings you to the top of the 3,622-foot-tall mountain. From the observatory here, the whole of Lake Kawaguchi lies before you, and beyond the lake is a classic view of Mt. Fuji. ⊠ *1163–1 Azagawa, Fujikawaguchiko* ☎ *0555/72–0363 ropeway* ⊕ *www. kachikachiyama-ropeway.com* 🎟 *Round trip ¥900, One way ¥500.*

Hotels

Fuji View Hotel (富士ビューホテル)
$$$ | HOTEL | Accommodations are a little threadbare but comfortable and right on the lakefront, and the terrace lounge affords fine views of the lake and of Mt. Fuji beyond. **Pros:** a good value during the week; excellent views from many rooms; convenient shuttle bus to town and the station. **Cons:** rooms are rather small; can be crowded with tour groups during peak seasons; meals are average.

Rooms from: ¥34,000 ⊠ 511 Katsuyama, Fujikawaguchiko ☎ 0555/83–2211 ⊕ www.fujiview.jp ⇌ 70 rooms ⍥ Free Breakfast.

Hotel Mount Fuji (ホテルマウント富士)
$$$ | HOTEL | This is the best resort hotel on Lake Yamanaka, with European-style rooms and all the facilities for a recreational holiday, including on-site game and karaoke rooms and a nature walk on the grounds. **Pros:** comfortable rooms; many activities on the hotel grounds; friendly and helpful staff. **Cons:** one of the more expensive options in the area; convenient location and large banquet halls make it a favorite among tour groups; some guest rooms are dated. $ Rooms from: ¥35,000 ⊠ 1360–83 Yamanaka, Yamanaka-ko-mura ☎ 050/3204–4439 ⊕ www.mtfuji-hotel.com/lp/en ⇌ 150 rooms ⍥ Free Breakfast.

Mizno Hotel (湖のホテル)
$$ | HOTEL | Renovated in 2017, the Mizno sports a stylish lodge aesthetic and stunning views of Lake Kawaguchiko and Mt. Fuji. **Pros:** all rooms have views of Mt. Fuji and Lake Kawaguchi; great rooftop bar and terrace; private onsen. **Cons:** the onsen bath is functional but simple; much of the appeal of the hotel depends on having good weather; one of the most expensive hotels on the lake. $ Rooms from: ¥30,000 ⊠ 187 Azagawa, Fujikawaguchiko ☎ 0555/72–1234 ⊕ mzn.jp ⇌ 27 rooms ⍥ Free Breakfast.

Ryokan Fujitomita (旅館ふじとみた)
$ | B&B/INN | One of the closest lodging options to the Mt. Fuji hiking trails is not much to look at from the outside, but the interior is spacious and homey. **Pros:** spacious rooms; pleasant surrounding grounds; excellent home cooking. **Cons:** very crowded during climbing season; rooms are clean but simple; somewhat isolated. $ Rooms from: ¥13,000 ⊠ 3235 Shibokusa, Oshinomura, Minami-Tsuru-gun ☎ 0555/84–3359 ⊕ www.tim.hi-ho.ne.jp/innfuji ⊟ No credit cards ⇌ 9 rooms ⍥ Free Breakfast.

Hakone

92 km (57 miles) southwest of Tokyo.

The national park and resort area of Hakone is a popular day trip from Tokyo and a good place for a close-up view of Mt. Fuji (assuming the mountain is not swathed in clouds, as often happens in summer).

■ TIP➔ **On summer weekends it often seems as though all of Tokyo has come out to Hakone with you. Expect long lines at cable cars and traffic jams everywhere.**

DISCOUNTS AND DEALS
Many places in Hakone accept the Hakone Free Pass. It's valid for three days and issued by the privately owned Odakyu Railways. The pass covers the train fare to Hakone and allows you to use any mode of transportation, including the Hakone Tozan Cable Car, the Hakone Ropeway, and the Hakone Cruise Boat. In addition to transportation, Free Pass holders get discounts at museums such as the Hakone Museum of Art, restaurants, and shops. The list of participants is pretty extensive and it always changes, so it's a good idea to check out the website for a complete list of participating companies and terms and conditions.

CONTACT Odakyu Sightseeing Service Center. ⊠ JR Shinjuku Station, 3–8 Shinjuku, near West Exit, Odawara ☎ 03/5909–0211 ⊕ www.odakyu.jp/english/support.

GETTING HERE AND AROUND
The typical Hakone route, outlined here, may sound complex, but this is in fact one excursion from Tokyo so well defined that you really can't get lost—no more so, at least, than any of the thousands of Japanese tourists ahead of and behind you. The first leg of the journey is from Odawara or Hakone-Yumoto by train and cable car through the mountains to Togendai, on the north shore of Ashino-ko (Lake Ashi). The long way around, from Odawara to Togendai by bus, takes

about an hour—in heavy traffic, an hour and a half. The trip over the mountains, on the other hand, takes about two hours. Credit the difference to the Hakone Tozan Tetsudo Line—possibly the slowest train you'll ever ride. Using three switchbacks to inch its way up the side of the mountain, the train takes 54 minutes to travel the 16 km (10 miles) from Odawara to Gora (38 minutes from Hakone-Yumoto). The steeper it gets, the grander the view.

■ TIP→ Due to concerns about volcanic activity, sections of the ropeway may be closed and buses will run from Sounzan to Togendai. The Hakone Ropeway's English site is not always up to date, so check with tourist information before you go.

Trains do not stop at any station en route for any length of time, but they do run frequently enough to allow you to disembark, visit a sight, and catch another train.

Within the Hakone area, buses run every 15 to 30 minutes from Hakone-machi to Hakone-Yumoto Station on the private Odakyu Line (40 minutes, ¥1,000), and Odawara Station (one hour, ¥1,280), where you can take either the Odakyu Romance Car back to Shinjuku Station or a JR Shinkansen to Tokyo Station.

TIMING

You can cover the best of Hakone in a one-day trip out of Tokyo, but if you want to try the curative powers of the thermal waters or do some hiking, then stay overnight. Two of the best areas are around the old hot-springs resort of Miyanoshita and the western side of Komagatake-san (Mt. Komagatake).

TOURS

Hakone Sightseeing Cruise (箱根海賊船; *Hakone Kaizoku-sen*)
BOAT TOURS | This ride is free with your Hakone Free Pass; otherwise, buy a ticket at the office in the terminal. A few ships of conventional design ply Lake Ashi; the rest are astonishingly corny Disney knockoffs. One, for example, is rigged like a 17th-century warship. ⊠ *181 Hakone, Ashigarashimo District, Hakone* ☎ *0460/83–6325* ⊕ *www.hakonenavi.jp/international/en* ⊠ *¥2,220 round-trip (without Hakone Free Pass).*

VISITOR INFORMATION
CONTACT Hakone Tourist Information Center. ⊠ *706–35 Yumoto, Hakone* ☎ *0460/85–5700* ⊕ *hakone-japan.com.*

Sights

Lake Ashi (芦ノ湖; *Ashino-ko*)
VIEWPOINT | From Owaku-dani, the descent by gondola to Togendai on the shore of Lake Ashi takes 25 minutes. There's no reason to linger at Togendai; it's only a terminus for buses to Hakone-Yumoto and Odawara and to the resort villages in the northern part of Hakone. Head straight for the pier, a few minutes' walk down the hill, where boats set out on the lake for Hakone-machi. With still water and good weather, you'll get a breathtaking reflection of the mountains in the waters of the lake as you go. ⊠ *Motohakone, Hakone.*

Gora (強羅)
TOWN | This small town is at the end of the train line from Odawara and at the lower end of the Hakone Tozan Cable Car. It's a good jumping-off point for hiking and exploring. Ignore the little restaurants and souvenir stands here: get off the train as quickly as you can and make a dash for the cable car at the other end of the station. If you let the rest of the passengers get there before you, and perhaps a tour bus or two, you may stand 45 minutes in line. ⊠ *Gora, Hakone.*

★ Hakone Kowakien Yunessun (箱根小涌園 ユネッサン)
HOT SPRING | FAMILY | This complex on the hills overlooking Hakone has more than the average onsen. In addition to all the water-based attractions, there is a shopping mall modeled on a European outdoor market, swimsuit

The Road to the Shogun

In days gone by, the town of Hakone was on the Tokaido, the main highway between the imperial court in Kyoto and the shogunate in Edo (present-day Tokyo). The road was the only feasible passage through this mountainous country, which made it an ideal place for a checkpoint to control traffic. The Tokugawa Shogunate built the Hakone-machi here in 1618; its most important function was to monitor the *daimyo* (feudal lords) passing through—to keep track, above all, of weapons coming into Edo, and womenfolk coming out.

When Ieyasu Tokugawa came to power, Japan had been through nearly 100 years of bloody struggle among rival coalitions of daimyo. Ieyasu emerged supreme because some of his opponents had switched sides at the last minute, in the Battle of Sekigahara in 1600. The shogun was justifiably paranoid about his "loyal" barons—especially those in the outlying domains—so he required the daimyo to live in Edo for periods of time every two years. When they did return to their own lands, they had to leave their wives behind in Edo, hostages to their good behavior. A noble lady coming through the Hakone Sekisho without an official pass, in short, was a case of treason.

The checkpoint served the Tokugawa dynasty well for 250 years. It was demolished only when the shogunate fell, in the Meiji Restoration of 1868. An exact replica, with an exhibition hall of period costumes and weapons, was built as a tourist attraction in 1965.

rental shop, massage salon, and game center. The park is divided into two main zones, called Yunessun and Mori no Yu (Forest Bath). In the Yunessun side, you need to wear a swimsuit, and can visit somewhat tacky re-creations of Turkish and ancient Roman baths. You can also take a dip in coffee, green tea, sake, or red wine. It is all a bit corny, but fun. Younger visitors enjoy the waterslides on "Rodeo Mountain." In the more secluded Mori no Yu side, you can go au naturel in a variety of indoor and outdoor, single-sex baths. When signing in at reception, get a waterproof digital wristband that allows you to pay for lockers and drink machines within the complex. ⊠ *1297 Ninotaira Hakone-machi, Hakone* ☎ *0460/82–4126* ⊕ *www.yunessun.com* ⊠ *Yunessun zone ¥2,500, Mori no Yu zone ¥1,500; both for ¥3,500.*

Hakone Museum of Art (箱根美術館; *Hakone Bijutsukan*)
ART MUSEUM | A sister institution to the MOA Museum of Art in Atami, Hakone Museum of Art is at the second stop of the Hakone Tozan Cable Car. The museum, which consists of two buildings set in a beautiful Japanese garden, houses a modest collection of porcelain and ceramics from China, Korea, and Japan. ⊠ *1300 Gora, Hakone* ☎ *0460/82–2623* ⊕ *www.moaart.or.jp/hakone* ⊠ *¥900* ☉ *Closed Thurs.*

★ Hakone Open-Air Museum
(彫刻の森美術館; *Hakone Chokoku-no-mori Bijutsukan*)
ART MUSEUM | Only a few minutes' walk from the Miyanoshita Station (directions are posted in English), the museum houses an astonishing collection of 19th- and 20th-century Western and Japanese sculpture, most of it on display in a spacious, handsome garden. There are

Passengers floating over the Owaku-dani valley on the Hakone Ropeway can see Fuji looming—on a clear day, of course.

works here by Rodin, Moore, Arp, Calder, Giacometti, Takashi Shimizu, and Kotaro Takamura. One section of the garden is devoted to Emilio Greco. Inside are works by Picasso, Léger, and Manzo, among others. ✉ *1121 Ninotaira, Hakone* ☎ *0460/82–1161* ⊕ *www.hakone-oam. or.jp* ✉ *¥1,600.*

Hakone Ropeway (箱根ロープウェイ)
TRANSPORTATION | At the cable-car terminus of Soun-zan, a gondola called the Hakone Ropeway swings up over a ridge and crosses the valley called Owaku-dani, also known as "Great Boiling Valley," on its way to Togendai. The landscape here is desolate, with sulfurous billows of steam escaping through holes from some inferno deep in the earth—yet another reminder that Japan is a chain of volcanic islands. At the top of the ridge is one of the two stations where you can leave the gondola. From here, a ¾-km (½-mile) walking course wanders among the sulfur pits in the valley. Just below the station is a restaurant; the food here is not recommended, but on a clear day

the view of Mt. Fuji is perfect. Remember that if you get off the gondola at any stage, you will have to wait for someone to make space on a later gondola before you can continue down to Togendai and Ashi-no-ko (but the gondolas come by every minute). ⚠ **Due to concerns about volcanic activity, sections of the ropeway may be closed and buses will run from Sounzan to Togendai. The Hakone Ropeway's English site is not always up-to-date, so check with tourist information before you go.** ✉ *1–15–1 Shiroyama, Odawara* ☎ *0460/32–2205* ⊕ *www.hakonenavi. jp/international/en* ✉ *¥1,700 round-trip (Sounzan Station to Owakudani Station).*

Hakone Checkpoint Museum (箱根関所; *Hakone Sekisho*)
HISTORIC SIGHT | This barrier, a checkpoint on the road with a guardhouse and lookout tower, was built in 1618 to inspect incoming and outgoing traffic until it was demolished during the Meiji Restoration of 1868. An exact replica was built as a tourist attraction in 1965 and is only a few minutes' walk from the

pier, along the lakeshore in the direction of Moto-Hakone. The hilltop guardhouse offers excellent views of Lake Ashi and the surrounding area. ✉ *1 Hakone-machi, Hakone* ☎ *0460/83–6635* ⊕ *www. hakonesekisyo.jp/english* 🎟 *¥500.*

Miyanoshita (宮ノ下)
RESORT | The first stop on the train route from Hakone-Yumoto, this is a small but very pleasant and popular resort village. As well as hot springs, this village has antiques shops along its main road and several hiking routes up the ¾-km- (½-mile-) tall Mt. Sengen. If you get to the top, you'll be rewarded with a great view of the gorge. ✉ *Hakone.*

Mt. Soun (早雲山; *Soun-zan*)
MOUNTAIN | Soun-zan is a good starting point for an afternoon of hiking. From here, trails around Mt. Hakone and Mt. Kamiyama lead towards the lake. Be sure to check with the Tourist Information Office to get a trail map beforehand. ✉ *Hakone.*

🛏 Hotels

Fujiya Hotel (富士屋ホテル)
$$$$ | **HOTEL** | Built in 1878, and reno-vated in 2020, this Western-style hotel with modern additions is showing signs of age, but that somehow adds to its charm. **Pros:** wonderful, friendly service; Hakone's most historic hotel; beautiful combination of Western and Japanese architecture. **Cons:** often full of noisy tour groups; hotel onsen (spa) can't compete with others in the area; price reflects the hotel's historic status rather than its comfort and amenities. $ *Rooms from: ¥65,000* ✉ *359 Miyanoshita, Hakone* ☎ *0460/82–2211* ⊕ *www.fujiyahotel.jp* 🛏 *149 rooms* |◎| *No Meals.*

Fuji-Hakone Guest House (富士箱根ゲストハウス)
$ | **HOTEL** | This small, family-run Japa-nese inn has simple tatami rooms with the bare essentials. **Pros:** friendly staff; inexpensive rates; private onsen baths

---

Scrambled or Boiled in Sulfur? 🍴

No, your eyes are not playing tricks on you. Those are in fact local entrepreneurs boiling eggs in the sulfur pits in Owaku-dani. Locals make a passable living selling the eggs, which turn black, to tourists at exorbitant prices. A popular myth suggests that eating one of these eggs can extend your life by seven years.

---

for guests. **Cons:** difficult to access from nearest transportation, especially at night; accommodations are comfortable but basic; lacks the atmosphere and charm of a traditional ryokan. $ *Rooms from: ¥12,000* ✉ *912 Sengokuhara (103 Moto-Hakone for Moto-Hakone Guest House), Hakone* ☎ *0460/84–6577 Fuji-Hakone, 0460/83–7880 Moto-Hakone* ⊕ *fujihakone.com* 🛏 *14 rooms* |◎| *Free Breakfast.*

The Prince Hakone Lake Ashinoko (箱根プリンスホテル芦ノ湖)
$$$ | **HOTEL** | You have a choice of hotel rooms or cozy cottages at this resort complex, with the lake in front and the mountains of Koma-ga-take in back. **Pros:** lovely quaint cottages surrounded by nature; views of Mt. Fuji over the lake; spacious guest rooms. **Cons:** a bit remote from sightseeing spots; popular with groups and business conferences; guest rooms are a bit dated. $ *Rooms from: ¥45,000* ✉ *144 Motohakone, Hakone* ☎ *0460/83–1111* ⊕ *www.princehotels. com/the_prince_hakone* 🛏 *258 rooms* |◎| *Free Breakfast.*

Tensui Saryo (天翠茶寮)
$$$$ | **B&B/INN** | Upon entering this cross between a luxury Western-style hotel and traditional inn, guests remove their shoes and socks, sit at a counter

bar with their tired feet resting in the hot-mineral-spring bath under the bar, and enjoy a tea or beer as they check in. **Pros:** four rooms have a private onsen on a terrace; excellent service; easy access from Gora Station. **Cons:** no Japanese food in the restaurant; some rooms have limited views; due to its central location, it lacks the secluded ryokan experience. [$] *Rooms from: ¥60,000* ✉ *1320–276 Gora, Hakone* ☎ *0570/062–302* 🌐 *www.tensui-saryo.com* 🛏 *17 rooms* 🍴 *Free Breakfast.*

Izu Peninsula

Shimoda is 197 km (122 miles) southwest of Tokyo.

Izu is defined by its dramatic rugged coastline, beaches, and onsen (hot springs).

GETTING HERE AND AROUND

Having your own car makes sense for touring the Izu Peninsula, but only if you're prepared to cope with less-than-ideal road conditions, lots of traffic (especially on holiday weekends), and the paucity of road markers in English. It takes some effort—but exploring the peninsula *is* a lot easier by car than by public transportation. From Tokyo take the Tomei Expressway as far as Oi-matsuda (about 84 km [52 miles]); then pick up Routes 255 and 135 to Atami (approximately 28 km [17 miles]). From Atami drive another 55 km (34 miles) or so down the east coast of the Izu Peninsula to Shimoda.

■ TIP→ One way to save yourself some trouble is to book a car through the Nippon or Toyota rental agency in Tokyo and arrange to pick it up at the Shimoda branch.

You can then simply take a train to Shimoda and use it as a base. From Shimoda you can drive back up the coast to Kawazu (35 minutes) and then to Shuzenji (30 minutes). It is possible to drop off the car in Tokyo, but only at specific branches, so visit your rental-car company's website or call them in advance.

Trains are by far the easiest and fastest ways to get to the Izu Peninsula and the rest of the Fuji-Hakone-Izu National Park area. The gateway station of Atami is well served by comfortable express trains from Tokyo, on both JR and private railway lines. These in turn connect to local trains and buses that can get you anywhere in the region you want to go. Call the JR Higashi-Nihon Info Line (10–6 daily, except December 31–January 3) for assistance in English.

The Kodama Shinkansen from JR Tokyo Station to Atami (¥4,500, 45 minutes) and Mishima (¥4,600, 70 minutes); JR (Japan Railways) passes are valid. The JR local from Atami to Ito takes 25 minutes and costs ¥530. Ito and Atami are also served by the JR Odoriko Super Express (not a Shinkansen train) also departing from Tokyo Station; check the schedule display board for the correct platform. The Tokyo–Ito run takes 1¾ hours and costs ¥4,190; you can also use a JR Pass. The privately owned Izukyu Railways, on which JR Passes are not valid, makes the Ito–Shimoda run in one hour for ¥1,480.

To get to Shuzenji by train, take the private Izu-Hakone Railway from Mishima (¥460, 63 minutes).

RENTAL-CAR CONTACTS Nippon Rent-a-Car. ☎ *03/6859–6234* 🌐 *www.nipponrentacar.co.jp.* **Toyota Rent-a-Car.** ☎ *0800/7000–815 toll-free in Japan; English operator available, 92/577–0091 international* 🌐 *rent.toyota.co.jp.*

TRAIN CONTACTS Izukyu Corporation. ☎ *0557/53–1115 main office, 0558/22–3202 Izukyu Shimoda Station* 🌐 *www.izukyu.co.jp.* **JR East Info Line.** (*JR Higashi-Nihon Info Line*) ☎ *050/2016–1603 English info line.* **Odakyu Sightseeing Service Center.** ✉ *Shinjuku Station 1F, Odakyu Railway West Exit* ☎ *03/5909–0211* 🌐 *www.odakyu.jp/english/support.*

TOURS

If you have limited time and want to see the highlights of Fuji-Hakone-Izu National Park on a day-trip from Tokyo, there are several bus options from JTB Sunrise Tours.

Dogashima Marine (堂ヶ島マリン)

BOAT TOURS | Once you are on the Izu Peninsula itself, sightseeing excursions by boat are available from several picturesque small ports. From Dogashima, you can take the Dogashima Marine short (20 minutes) or long (50 minutes) tours of Izu's rugged west coast. ☎ 0558/52–0013 ⊕ www.izudougasima-yuransen.com ⌨ From ¥1,200.

Fuji Kyuko (富士急行)

BOAT TOURS | The Fuji Kyuko company operates a daily ferry to Hatsu-shima from Atami (25 minutes) and another to the island from Ito (23 minutes). ☎ 0557/81–0541 ⊕ www.fujikyu.co.jp/en ⌨ From ¥2,400 round-trip.

Izu Cruise (伊豆クルーズ)

BOAT TOURS | Izukyu Marine offers a 40-minute tour by boat from Shimoda to the coastal rock formations at Iro-zaki. ☎ 0558/22–1151 ⊕ izu-kamori.jp/izu-cruise ⌨ From ¥1,400.

JTB Sunrise Tours

BUS TOURS | JTB Sunrise Tours operates a tour to Hakone from Tokyo, including a cruise across Lake Ashi and a trip on the gondola over Owaku-dani (including lunch and return to Tokyo by Shinkansen or bus). Sunrise tours depart daily from Tokyo's Hamamatsu-cho Bus Terminal and some major hotels. ⊠ Tokyo ☎ 03/5796–5454 ⊕ www.sunrise-tours.jp/en ⌨ From ¥12,000.

VISITOR INFORMATION

CONTACTS Atami Information Center. ⊠ 11–1 Tawarahoncho, Atami ☎ 0557/81–5297 ⊕ travel.ataminews.gr.jp/en. Shimoda Tourist Association. (伊豆下田観光ガイド) ⊠ 1–4–27 Shimoda, Shimoda ☎ 0558/22–1531 ⊕ www.shimoda-city.com.

Atami

100 km (60 miles) southwest of Tokyo Station.

The gateway to the Izu Peninsula is Atami. Most Japanese travelers make it no farther into the peninsula than this town on Sagami Bay, so Atami itself has a fair number of hotels and traditional inns. Although Atami fell on hard times after the economic bubble burst, it has recently undergone a massive revitalization and is once again a lively tourist town. The city also has frequent firework shows over the bay. They are only 30 minutes long, but the display over the water is stunning nonetheless.

When you arrive, collect a map from the **Atami Information Center** at the train station.

GETTING HERE AND AROUND

From JR Tokyo Station, take the Tokaido Line to Atami, which is the last stop (1 hour, 34 minutes; ¥1,990) or the Kodama Shinkansen (49 minutes, ¥4,270).

◉ Sights

Atami Plum Garden (熱海梅園; *Atami Bai-en*)

GARDEN | The best time to visit the garden is in late January or early February, when its 850 trees bloom. If you do visit, also stop by the small shrine that's in the shadow of an enormous old camphor tree. The shrine is more than 1,000 years old and is popular with people who are asking the gods for help with alcoholism. The tree is more than 2,000 years old and has been designated a National Monument. It's believed that if you walk around the tree once, another year will be added to your life. Atami Bai-en is always open to the public and is 15 minutes by bus from Atami or an eight-minute walk from Kinomiya Station, the next stop south of Atami served by local trains. ⊠ 8–11 Baien-cho,

Atami ☎ *0557/85–2222* 🎫 *¥300 Jan.–early Mar., free the rest of the year.*

Hatsu-shima Island (初島)
ISLAND | **FAMILY** | If you have the time and the inclination for a beach picnic, it's worth taking the 25-minute high-speed ferry (¥2,500 round-trip) from the pier. There are five departures daily between 7:30 and 5:20 from both Atami and Ito, though the times vary by season. You can easily walk around the island, which is only 4 km (2½ miles) in circumference, in less than two hours. There is also an obstacle course adventure park, great for travelers with kids. Use of the Picnic Garden (daily 10–3) is free. ✉ *Atami Port, 6–11 Wadahama Minamicho, Atami* ☎ *0557/81–0541 ferry* 🌐 *www.hatsushima.jp.*

MOA Museum of Art (MOA美術館; *MOA Bijutsukan*)
ART MUSEUM | This museum houses the private collection of the messianic religious leader Mokichi Okada (1882–1955), who founded a movement called the Sekai Kyusei Kyo (Religion for the Salvation of the World). He also acquired more than 3,000 works of art; some are from the Asuka period (sixth and seventh centuries). Among these works are several particularly fine *ukiyo-e* (Edo-era woodblock prints) and ceramics. On a hill above the station and set in a garden full of old plum trees and azaleas, the museum also affords a sweeping view over Atami and the bay. ✉ *26–2 Momoyama, Atami* ✥ *The easiest way to reach the museum is to take a 5-min taxi ride from the station* ☎ *0557/84–2511* 🌐 *www.moaart.or.jp/en* 🎫 *¥1,600.*

Oyu Geyser (大湯間歇泉; *Oyu Kanketsusen*)
OTHER ATTRACTION | Located just a 15-minute walk southeast from Atami Station, the geyser used to gush on schedule once every 24 hours but stopped after the Great Kanto Earthquake of 1923. Not happy with this, the local chamber of commerce rigged a pump to raise the geyser every five minutes. ✉ *4–3 Kamijuku-cho, Atami.*

Hotels

Atami Taikanso (熱海大観荘)
$$$ | **B&B/INN** | The views of the sea must have been the inspiration for Yokoyama Taikan, the Japanese artist who once owned this villa that is now a traditional Japanese inn with exquisite furnishings and individualized service. **Pros:** seaside rooms have beautiful views; luxurious traditional experience; impeccable service. **Cons:** eating dinner may take most of your evening; easy to get lost in the complex layout of the hotel; one of Atami's more expensive options. [$] *Rooms from: ¥45,000* ✉ *7–1 Hayashigaoka-cho, Atami* ☎ *0557/81–8137* 🌐 *www.atami-taikanso.com/en* 🛏 *44 Japanese-style rooms with bath* 🍴 *All-Inclusive.*

Hotel Micuras (ホテルミクラス)
$$$ | **HOTEL** | Style, comfort, ocean views, and natural hot springs make this hotel one of Atami's best. **Pros:** stylish, modern; the luxurious infinity-pool onsen looks out over the sea; the view from ocean-facing rooms is superb. **Cons:** lacks the history or charm of a traditional inn; rooms are modern but otherwise average; avoid the handful of "Mountain View" rooms, which have no view at all. [$] *Rooms from: ¥40,000* ✉ *3–19 Higashikaigan-cho, Atami* ☎ *0577/86–111* 🌐 *www.micuras.jp* 🛏 *62 rooms* 🍴 *No Meals.*

Ito

16 km (10 miles) south of Atami.

There are some 800 thermal springs in the resort area surrounding Ito. These springs—and the beautiful, rocky, indented coastline nearby—remain the resort's major attractions, although there are plenty of interesting sights here. Some 150 hotels and inns serve the area.

Ito traces its history of associations with the West to 1604, when William Adams (1564–1620), the Englishman whose adventures served as the basis for James Clavell's novel *Shogun*, came ashore.

Four years earlier Adams had beached his disabled Dutch vessel, *De Liefde*, on the shores of the southwestern island of Kyushu and become the first Englishman to set foot on Japan. The authorities, believing that he and his men were Portuguese pirates, put Adams in prison, but he was eventually befriended by the shogun Ieyasu Tokugawa, who brought him to Edo (present-day Tokyo) and granted him an estate. Ieyasu appointed Adams his adviser on foreign affairs. The English castaway taught mathematics, geography, gunnery, and navigation to shogunate officials and in 1604 was ordered to build an 80-ton Western-style ship. Pleased with this venture, Ieyasu ordered the construction of a larger oceangoing vessel. These two ships were built at Ito, where Adams lived from 1605 to 1610.

This history was largely forgotten until British Commonwealth occupation forces began coming to Ito for rest and recuperation after World War II. Adams's memory was revived, and since then the Anjin Festival (the Japanese gave Adams the name *anjin*, which means "pilot") has been held in his honor every August. A monument to the Englishman stands at the mouth of the river.

GETTING HERE AND AROUND
From JR Tokyo Station or Shinagawa Station, take the Tokaido Line (2 hours, 15 minutes; ¥2,310) or the Super Odoriko Express (1 hour, 40 minutes; ¥3,890) to Ito Station.

VISITOR INFORMATION
CONTACT Ito Onsen Information Center. (伊東観光協会; *Ito Kanko Kyoukai* ✉ 3–12–1 Yukawa, Ito ☎ 0557/37–6105 ⊕ itospa. com/en.

Sights

Atagawa (熱川)
RESORT | South of Ito the coastal scenery is lovely—each sweep around a headland reveals another picturesque sight of a rocky, indented shoreline. There are several spa towns en route to Shimoda. Higashi-Izu (East Izu) has numerous hot-springs resorts, of which Atagawa is the most fashionable. South of Atagawa is Kawazu, a place of relative quiet and solitude, with pools in the forested mountainside and waterfalls plunging through lush greenery. ✉ *Ito.*

Ikeda 20th-Century Art Museum (池田20世紀美術館; *Ikeda 20-Seiki Bijutsukan*)
ART MUSEUM | The museum, which overlooks Lake Ippeki, houses works by Picasso, Dalí, Chagall, and Matisse, plus a number of woodblock prints. The museum is a 15-minute walk northwest from Izu Shaboten Zoo. ✉ *614 Totari, Ito* ☎ *0557/45–2211* ⊕ *ikeda20.or.jp/en* 🎟 *¥1,000* ⊗ *Closed Wed.*

Izu Shaboten Zoo (伊豆シャボテン動物公園; *Izu Shaboten Dobutsukoen*)
ZOO | **FAMILY** | A semi–free-range petting zoo and cactus park may not seem like the best combination, but Izu Shaboten Zoo makes it work. Visitors can feed, pet, or get up close and personal with more than 130 different kinds of animals and 1,500 varieties of cacti. Highlights include the capybara onsen (animals like hot springs too) and "Exciting Monkey House." It's a silly place, but a hit with animal-loving kids. ✉ *1317–13 Futo, Ito* ⊹ *At the base of Komuro-san (Mt. Komuro), the park is 20 mins south of Ito Station by bus* ☎ *0557/51–1111* ⊕ *izushaboten.com* 🎟 *¥2,400.*

Komuroyama Park (小室山公園; *Komuroyama Koen*)
GARDEN | Some 3,000 cherry trees of 35 varieties bloom at various times throughout the year. You can take a ski-lift style cable to the top of the mountain, which has a lovely view of the sea below.

A Healing Headache

While earthquakes are an annoying, everyday fact of life in Japan, they also provide one of the country's greatest delights: thermal baths. Wherever there are volcanic mountains—and there are a lot—you're sure to find springs of hot water, called onsen, which are rich in all sorts of restorative minerals. Any place where lots of spas have tapped these sources is an *onsen chiiki* (hot-springs resort area). The Izu Peninsula is particularly rich in onsen. It has, in fact, one-fifth of the 2,300-odd officially recognized hot springs in Japan.

Spas take many forms, but the ne plus ultra is that small secluded Japanese mountain inn with a *rotemburo* (an open-air mineral-spring pool). For guests only, these pools are usually in a screened-off nook with a panoramic view. A room in one of these inns on a weekend or in high season should be booked months in advance. (High season is late December to early January, late April to early May, the second and third weeks of August, and the second and third weeks of October.) More typical is the large resort hotel, geared mainly to groups, with one or more large indoor mineral baths of its own. Where whole towns and villages have developed to exploit a local supply of hot water, there will be several of these large hotels, an assortment of smaller inns, and probably a few modest public bathhouses, with no accommodations, where you just pay an entrance fee for a soak of whatever length you wish.

The park is about 20 minutes south of Ito Station by bus. ⊠ *1428 Kawana, Ito* ☎ *0557/37–6105* 🎟 *Free; round-trip lift to mountaintop ¥600.*

 Hotels

Hanafubuki (花吹雪)

$$$$ | **B&B/INN** | This traditional Japanese inn, which is located in the Jogasaki forest, has modern, comfortable rooms, but still retains classic elements like tatami mats, sliding screen doors, and *chabudai* (low dining tables) with *zabuton* (cushion seating). **Pros:** an authentic Japanese experience; the seven private hot-spring baths are free for guests; excellent dinners. **Cons:** meals are available to nonguests, so the dining room can be a bit crowded; not as quiet as more secluded onsen; regular room rates are high for the area. Ⓢ *Rooms from: ¥50,000* ⊠ *1041 Yawatano Isomichi, Ito* ☎ *0557/54–1550* ⊕ *www.hanafubuki.co.jp* ✈ *17 rooms* ❚⦿❙ *All-Inclusive.*

Yokikan (陽気館)

$$$ | **B&B/INN** | Overlooking the town of Ito and the sea, Yokikan has been catering to visitors for over a century. **Pros:** views of Ito and the sea from the open-air bath; friendly, welcoming service; simple, understated aesthetic perfect for a relaxing getaway. **Cons:** simple, somewhat dated furnishings; all rooms are Japanese style (tatami and futon); no private bath in standard rooms. Ⓢ *Rooms from: ¥35,000* ⊠ *2–24 Suehiro-cho, Ito* ☎ *0557/37–3101* ⊕ *www.yokikan.co.jp* ✈ *21 rooms* ❚⦿❙ *All-Inclusive.*

Shimoda

35 km (22 miles) south of Ito city.

Of all the resort towns south of Ito along Izu's eastern coast, none can match the distinction of Shimoda. The town's encounter with the West began when Commodore Matthew Perry anchored his fleet of black ships off the coast here in 1853. To commemorate the event, the three-day Black Ship Festival (Kurofune Matsuri) is held here every year in mid-May. Shimoda was also the site, in 1856, of the first American consulate.

The Shimoda Tourist Office, in front of the station, has the easiest of the local English itineraries to follow. The 2½-km (1½-mile) tour covers most major sights. On request, the tourist office will also help you find local accommodations.

GETTING HERE AND AROUND

From JR Tokyo Station, take the Odoriko Express direct (¥6,055) or the Tokaido Line to Atami, change to the Ito Line, and take it to the final stop, Izukyu Shimoda Station (3 hours, 45 minutes; ¥3,260).

VISITOR INFORMATION

CONTACT Shimoda Tourist Office. ✉ 4-27 Itchome, Shimoda ☎ 0558/22–1531 ⊕ www.shimoda-city.com.

◉ Sights

Hofuku-ji Temple (宝福寺)

TEMPLE | The first American consul to Japan was New York businessman Townsend Harris. Soon after his arrival in Shimoda, Harris asked the Japanese authorities to provide him with a female servant; they sent him a young girl named Okichi Saito, who was engaged to be married. The arrangement brought her a new name, Tojin (the Foreigner's) Okichi, much disgrace, and a tragic end. When Harris sent her away, she tried, but failed, to rejoin her former lover. The shame brought upon her for working and living with a Westerner and the pain of losing the love of her life drove Okichi to drown herself in 1892. Her tale is recounted in Rei Kimura's biographical novel *Butterfly in the Wind* and inspired Puccini's *Madame Butterfly*, although some skeptics say the story is more

gossip than fact. Hofuku-ji was Okichi's family temple. The museum annex displays a life-size image of her, and just behind the temple is her grave—where incense is still kept burning in her memory. The grave of her lover, Tsurumatsu, is at Toden-ji, a temple about midway between Hofuku-ji and Shimoda Station. ✉ 1–18–26 Shimoda, Shimoda ☎ 0558/22–0960 ≅ ¥400.

Ryosen-ji Temple (了仙寺)

TEMPLE | This is the temple in which the negotiations took place that led to the United States–Japan Treaty of Amity and Commerce of 1858. The Treasure Hall (Homotsu-den) contains more than 300 original artifacts relating to Commodore Perry and the "black ships" that opened Japan to the West. ✉ 3–12–12 Shimoda, Shimoda ☎ 0558/22–0657 ⊕ ryosenji.net/ english ≅ Treasure Hall ¥500.

Yumigahama Beach (弓ヶ浜)

BEACH | If you love the sun, make sure you stop at Yumigahama. It's one of the nicest sandy beaches on the whole Izu Peninsula. Although the water is usually warm enough to swim from June, the crowds come out during Japan's beach season in July and August. The bus from Shimoda Station stops here before continuing to Iro-zaki, the last stop on the route. **Amenities:** food and drink (July and August); lifeguards (July and August); toilets; parking (fee). **Best for:** swimming (June–August); solitude (September–June). ✉ Shimoda ⊹ 11 km (7 miles) southwest of Shimoda, just south of highway 136.

Hotels

Pension Sakuraya (ペンション桜家)

$ | B&B/INN | The best lodgings at this family-run inn just a few minutes' walk from Shimoda's main beach are the Japanese-style corner rooms, which have nice views of the hills surrounding Shimoda. **Pros:** very homey atmosphere; close to the beach; friendly and helpful staff. **Cons:** rooms are a bit cramped; clean but simple; buses from station can be infrequent. [$] *Rooms from: ¥11,000* ✉ *2584–20 Shirahama, Shimoda* ☎ *0558/23-4470* 🌐 *izu-sakuraya.jp/english* 🛏 *9 rooms* 🍴 *Free Breakfast.*

Shimoda Prince Hotel (下田プリンスホテル)
$$$ | **HOTEL** | At this modern V-shaped resort hotel that faces the Pacific, the decor is more functional than aesthetic, but a white-sand beach is just steps away, and there's a panoramic view of the ocean from the picture windows in the dining room. **Pros:** an excellent view of the sea; one of the best hotels in town; spacious rooms. **Cons:** restaurants are on the pricey side; lacks the personal charm of smaller establishments; can be very crowded with families during peak summer season. [$] *Rooms from: ¥32,000* ✉ *1547–1 Shirahama, Shimoda* ☎ *0558/22-2111* 🌐 *www.princehotels.com/shimoda* 🛏 *76 rooms* 🍴 *Free Breakfast.*

Shimoda Tokyu Hotel (下田東急ホテル)
$$$ | **HOTEL** | Perched just above the bay, the Shimoda Tokyu has impressive views of the Pacific from one side (where rooms cost about 10% more) and mountains from the other. **Pros:** nice views of the ocean; easy access to Shimoda Station and sights; spacious guest rooms. **Cons:** restaurants are expensive for Tokyo standards; rooms are a bit dated; service can be hit or miss. [$] *Rooms from: ¥40,000* ✉ *5-12-1 Shimoda, Shimoda* ☎ *0558/22-2411* 🌐 *www.tokyuhotels.co.jp/shimoda-h* 🛏 *115 rooms* 🍴 *Free Breakfast.*

Dogashima

16 km (10 miles) northeast of Mishima.

The sea has eroded the coastal rock formations into fantastic shapes near the little port town of Dogashima, including a *tombolo,* or a narrow band of sand, that connects the mainland to a small peninsula with a scenic park.

GETTING HERE AND AROUND

Dogashima is not directly accessible by train but buses run from Shinjuku and Tokyo Stations. From Tokyo Station, take the JR Shinkansen to Mishima (50 minutes, ¥4,600), change to the Izu Hakone Line to Shuzenji (35 minutes, ¥520), and take the Tokai bus to the Dogashima stop. There is also an express Tokai Bus, Minami Izu Line, which takes you from Shimoda Station to Dogashima (55 minutes).

TOURS

Dogashima Marine Sightseeing Boat (堂ヶ島マリン遊覧船; *Dogashima Marin Yugansen*)
BOAT TOURS | Sightseeing boats from Dogashima Pier make 20-minute runs to see the rocks. In an excess of kindness, a recorded loudspeaker—which you can safely ignore—recites the name of every rock you pass on the trip. ☎ *0558/52-0013* 🌐 *www.izudougasima-yuransen.com* 🎟 *¥1,200.*

Hotels

Dogashima New Ginsui (堂ヶ島ニュー銀水)
$$$$ | **HOTEL** | Perched above the water and a secluded beach, every Japanese-style guest room overlooks the sea. **Pros:** by far the best luxury resort on Izu's west coast; stunning views; concierge. **Cons:** a bit far from sightseeing spots; some rooms are a bit dated; can get crowded with families during peak summer season. [$] *Rooms from: ¥46,000* ✉ *2977–1 Nishina, Nishiizu-cho, Kamo-gun* ☎ *0558/52-2211* 🌐 *www.dougashima-newginsui.jp* 🛏 *121 rooms* 🍴 *All-Inclusive.*

Ryokan Etiquette

Guests are expected to arrive at ryokan in the late afternoon. When you do, put on the slippers that are provided, and a maid will escort you to your room. Remember to remove your slippers before entering your room; never step on the tatami (straw mats) with shoes or slippers. Each room will be simply decorated—one small, low table, cushions on the tatami, and a scroll on the wall—which will probably be *shoji* (sliding paper-paneled walls).

In ryokan with thermal pools, you can take to the waters anytime, although the pool doors are usually locked from 11 pm to 6 am. In ryokan without thermal baths or private baths in guest rooms, visits must be staggered. Typically the maid will ask what time you would like to bathe and fit you into a schedule. Make sure you wash and rinse off entirely before getting into the bath. Do not get soap in the tub. Other guests will be using the same bathwater, so it is important to observe this custom. After your bath, change into the yukata provided in your room. Don't worry about walking around in it—other guests will be doing the same.

Dinner is served around 6. At the larger, newer ryokan, meals will be in the dining room; at smaller, more personal ryokan, it is served in your room. When you are finished, a maid will clear away the dishes and lay out your futon. In Japan *futon* means bedding, and this consists of a thin cotton mattress and a heavy, thick comforter, which is replaced with a thinner quilt in summer. The small, hard pillow is filled with grain. Some of the less expensive ryokan (under ¥7,000 per person) have become slightly lackadaisical in changing the quilt cover with each new guest; in as inoffensive a way as possible, feel free to complain—just don't shame the proprietor. Around 8 am, a maid will gently wake you, clear away the futon, and bring in your Japanese-style breakfast, which will probably consist of fish, pickled vegetables, and rice. If this isn't appealing, politely ask if it's possible to have coffee and toast. Checkout is at 10 am.

For a room at a smaller ryokan, make sure you call or email as far in advance as possible for a room—inns are not always willing to accept foreign guests because of language and cultural barriers. It is nearly impossible to get a room in July or August. If you don't speak Japanese, try to have a Japanese speaker reserve a room for you.

Shuzenji

25 km (15 miles) south of Mishima by Izu-Hakone Railway.

Shuzenji—a hot-springs resort in the center of the peninsula, along the valley of the Katsura-gawa (Katsura River)—enjoys a certain historical notoriety as the place where the second Kamakura shogun, Minamoto no Yoriie, was assassinated in the early 13th century. Don't judge the town by the area around the station; most of the hotels and hot springs are 2 km (1 mile) to the west.

GETTING HERE AND AROUND

The train is by far the easiest way to get to Shuzenji. The JR Tokaido Line runs from Tokyo to Mishima (2 hours, 10 minutes; ¥2,310), with a change at Mishima

15

Side Trips from Tokyo IZU PENINSULA (伊豆半島)

for Shuzenji (35 minutes, ¥520); this is the cheapest option if you don't have a JR Pass. With a JR Pass, a Kodama Shinkansen–Izu Line combination saves an hour. The Tokyo–Mishima Shinkansen leg (50 minutes) costs ¥4,600; the Mishima–Shuzenji Izu Line leg (35 minutes) costs ¥520.

Hotels

Goyokan (五葉館)
$$$ | B&B/INN | This family-run ryokan on Shuzenji's main street has rooms that look out on the Katsura-gawa, plus gorgeous stone-lined (for men) and wood-lined (for women) indoor hot springs. **Pros:** unique, modern take on a ryokan; excellent service; private onsen baths free for guests. **Cons:** lacks cozy feel of a traditional ryokan; decor can be a bit over the top; no bath in rooms. $ *Rooms from: ¥40,000* ⊠ *765–2 Shuzenji-cho* ☎ *0558/72–2066* ⊕ *www.goyokan.co.jp* ⤳ *11 rooms* ❍❘ *All-Inclusive.*

Ochiairou (おちあいろう)
$$$$ | B&B/INN | This traditional ryokan was built in the Showa period, and though it has been renovated and modernized, the main wooden structure remains true to its original design, with spacious and comfortable rooms that look out into the gardens. **Pros:** free pickup from Yugashima bus terminal; lovely garden on the grounds; stunning surroundings. **Cons:** very expensive; remote; some parts of the hotel show their age. $ *Rooms from: ¥100,000* ⊠ *1887–1 Yugashima, Izu* ☎ *055/885–0014* ⊕ *www.ochiairo.co.jp* ⤳ *15 rooms* ❍❘ *All-Inclusive.*

Ryokan Sanyoso (旅館三養荘)
$$$$ | B&B/INN | At the former villa of the Iwasaki family, founders of the Mitsubishi conglomerate, museum-quality antiques furnish the rooms. **Pros:** authentic ryokan and furnishings; Japanese bath available; as luxurious and beautiful a place as you'll find on the Izu Peninsula. **Cons:** most expensive ryokan in the area; not easy to get to without a car; less intimate than smaller ryokan in the area. $ *Rooms from: ¥60,000* ⊠ *270 Mamanoue, Izunokuni* ☎ *055/947–1111* ⊕ *www.princehotels.com/sanyo-so* ⤳ *40 rooms* ❍❘ *All-Inclusive.*

Mt. Takao

50 km (31 miles) west of Tokyo.

There are a total of eight hiking trails within Mori Memorial Forest Park. The three main trails that lead to the top of Mt. Takao begin at Kiyotaka Station, the base station of the funicular railway. There is a large billboard with a map of the mountain and all the trails, and this will help you choose which is best for you.

◉ Sights

★ Mt. Takao (高尾山; *Takao-san*)
FOREST | When the concrete skyscrapers of Shinjuku become a bit too much, you can escape to the foot of Mt. Takao and the heavily wooded Meiji Memorial Forest Park that surrounds it in about an hour. Hiking along one of the trails that lead to the top of the 599-meter (1,965-foot) mountain, or enjoying the picturesque view from one of the cable cars that zip up to the peak, it can be difficult to believe that you are still within the limits of the Tokyo metropolitan area. The mountain is associated with *tengu,* one of the best known *yokai* (monster-spirits) of Japanese folklore. This is also the start of the Tokai Nature Trail, which leads all the way to Osaka. The mountain is home to a temple, a monkey zoo, a botanical garden, and a beer hall, but it if you make an early start, it is possible to take in everything in one day, and be back in central Tokyo by nightfall.

The Mt. Takao climb is not nearly as grueling as that of Mt. Fuji, but proper planning is necessary to ensure a safe and pleasant hike. If you intend to take the cable car or the paved trail, wear comfortable sneakers. The unpaved trails, on the other hand, can get quite slippery and hiking boots are essential. It is also a good idea to bring a raincoat in case of sudden showers. The heavily wooded mountain can expose you to extremes of humidity, sunshine, and wind, so dress in layers. Bring plenty of bottled water—there is no running water anywhere on the mountain. Although there are over-priced vending machines and food stalls, your best bet is to pack a lunch. It is mountain-climbing etiquette in Japan to greet people you overtake on the way up or meet coming the opposite direction. Smile and say "konnichiwa." On week-ends, the mountain gets unpleasantly overcrowded. On weekdays there are still plenty of hikers but it is a pleasant hike regardless.

By far the most popular way to get to the top of Mt. Takao, Trail 1 starts at Kiyotaka Station, the base station of the cable car, and takes a fairly direct, paved route to the visitor center at the top (3.8 km [2.4 miles], approximately 1 hour, 40 minutes). The descent is especially stunning at sunset. If you take the cable car, you'll join this trail a third of the way up. Near the start of Trail 1 is a detour to *konpira-dai,* one of several small shrines on the mountain, where there is a clear view of central Tokyo. After returning to Trail 1, continue along as you pass Sanjo Station (the upper station of the chairlift) and Takaosan Station (the cable-car terminal), and you will come to *tenbodai,* an observatory with another view of the Tokyo skyline. If you continue on the trail, pass through Joshinmon Gate and on toward the peak. Or, you detour to Trail 2, a loop (900 yards, 30 minutes) that meets back up with Trail 1 farther up the mountain. Going right on Trail 2 will take you past the *hebitaki,* a picturesque natural waterfall. Going to the left will take you past the Monkey Zoo and Botanical Garden. The Botanical

Garden features wild plants indigenous to the area with explanations mainly in Japanese, and the zoo is home to a few dozen clever monkeys, also native to the mountain (¥400 for entrance to both). If you skip Trail 2 and continue on Trail 1, the next stop is at the octopus cedar, a tree with exposed roots so fantastical, they resemble a giant sea monster. At this point, you will reach the Joshinmon Gate. Continue to the *busharito,* a stone pagoda that literally means "Buddha's bone," and is said to mark one of the spots where pieces of Buddha's remains were spread around the world after his cremation. Just past this is Yakuoin Temple, dedicated to Yakushi Nyorai, the Buddha of Medicine, believed to be built in 744. The 2,500 historical documents surviving in the temple explain Japanese religious beliefs during the Warring States (mid-1400s–1603) and Edo (1603–1868) periods. Trail 1 then continues on to the visitor center at the peak, passing beech, oak, and Japanese nutmeg trees along the way. ✉ *Takao-machi, Tokyo.*

🍴 Restaurants

The best thing to do upon reaching the top of Mt. Takao is to eat lunch while enjoying the breathtaking view. On a clear day, you get a nice view of Mt. Fuji, and at the very least you can see the massive urban sprawl of Tokyo. There are food stands selling boxed lunches, rice balls, and other snacks, but it is a good idea to bring your own lunch. The only real restaurant serves only dinner.

Beer Mountain (ビアマウント)
$$$ | INTERNATIONAL | This beer hall is Mt. Takao's only full-fledged restaurant and serves a prix-fixe two-hour, all-you-can eat, all-you-can drink buffet meal that is a hodgepodge of sausages, pasta, Japanese dishes, and desserts, and there are a number of Japanese beers on tap. Beer Mountain is connected to Takaosan Station, the top station of the Takao Tozan Cable Line. **Known for:** filling

post-hike meal; views over the mountains and Western Tokyo; lively outdoor atmosphere. $ *Average main: ¥3,800* ✉ *2205 Takao-machi, Tokyo* ☎ *042/665–9943* ⊕ *www.takaotozan.co.jp* ☉ *Closed Oct.–June.*

Nikko

130 km (81 miles) north of Tokyo.

"Think nothing is splendid," asserts an old Japanese proverb, "until you have seen Nikko." Nikko, which means "sunlight," is a popular vacation spot for the Japanese, for good reason: its gorgeous sights include a breathtaking waterfall and one of the country's best-known shrines. In addition, Nikko's Chuzenji area combines the rustic charm of a countryside village (complete with wild monkeys that have the run of the place) with a convenient location not far from Tokyo. If you are just going to see Toshogu Shrine and the surrounding area, Nikko is best as a day-trip from Tokyo as there is little to do in the town proper after dark. The scenic Chuzenji-ko Lake, however, makes for a relaxing overnight stop.

GETTING HERE AND AROUND

The limited express train of the Tobu Railway has two direct connections from Tokyo to Nikko every morning, starting at 6:30 am from Tobu Asakusa Station, a minute's walk from the last stop on Tokyo's Ginza subway line (1 hour, 50 minutes; ¥2,860) with additional trains on weekends, holidays, and in high season. All seats are reserved. Bookings are not accepted over the phone and can be bought only at Asakusa Station. During summer, fall, and weekends, buy tickets a few days in advance. Alternatively, the rapid train takes only a bit longer at half the price and requires no reservations (2 hours, 20 minutes; ¥1,390). If you're visiting Nikko on a day trip, note that the last return express train is at 6:51 pm. It is possible to get to Nikko using Japan

Torii

Symbolizing the boundary between the world of the everyday and a sacred space of the gods, *torii* gates mark the entrance to Shinto shrines. Although they come in various shapes and colors, they all share the same basic design making torii the easiest way to differentiate between a Shinto shrine and Buddhist temple.

Railways trains, but will take considerably longer, requires a transfer, and costs more than the Tobu line so it is only recommended if you have extra time and a JR Pass. From Ueno Station. Take the Tohoku–Honsen Line limited express to Utsunomiya (about two hours) and transfer to the train for JR Nikko Station (45 minutes). If you're not using the JR Pass, the one-way fare is ¥3,090.

More expensive, but faster, is taking the Shinkansen to Utsunomiya and changing for the JR train to Nikko Station; the one-way fare, including the surcharge for the express, is ¥5,920. The first train leaves Tokyo Station at 6:04 am (or Ueno at 6:10) and takes about 1 hour, 30 minutes to Nikko. To return, take the 9:46 pm train from Nikko to Utsunomiya and catch the last Shinkansen back at 10:38 pm.

It's possible, but unwise, to travel by car from Tokyo to Nikko. The trip takes at least three hours, and merely getting from central Tokyo to the toll-road system can be a nightmare. Coming back, especially on a Saturday or Sunday evening, is even worse.

Buses and taxis can take you from Nikko to the village of Chuzenji and nearby Lake Chuzenji; one-way cab fare from Tobu Nikko Station to Chuzenji is about ¥8,000.

■TIP→ There is no bus service between Tokyo and Nikko.

Local buses leave Tobu Nikko Station for Lake Chuzenji, stopping just above the entrance to Toshogu, approximately every 30 minutes from 6:11 am until 6:55 pm. The fare to Chuzenji is ¥1,250, and the ride takes about 45 minutes. The last return bus from the lake leaves at 8:00 pm, arriving back at Tobu Nikko Station at 8:38 pm.

The town of Nikko is essentially one long avenue—Sugi Namiki (Cryptomeria Avenue)—extending for about 2 km (1 mile) from the railway stations to Toshogu. You can easily walk to most places within town. Tourist inns and shops line the street, and if you have time, you might want to make this a leisurely stroll. The antiques shops along the way may turn up interesting—but expensive—pieces like armor fittings, hibachi, pottery, and dolls. The souvenir shops here sell ample selections of local wood carvings.

VISITOR INFORMATION

You can do a lot of preplanning for your visit to Nikko with a stop at the Japan National Tourist Organization office in Tokyo, where the helpful English-speaking staff will ply you with pamphlets and field your questions about things to see and do. Closer to the source is the Nikko Kyodo Center in Nikko itself, about halfway up the main street of town between the railway stations and Toshogu, on the left; don't expect too much in the way of help in English, but the center does have a good array of English information about local restaurants and shops, registers of inns and hotels, and mapped-out walking tours.

CONTACT Nikko Kyodo Center. ⊠ *591 Goko-machi, Nikko* ☏ *0288/54–2496.*

Toshogu

120 km (75 miles) north of Tokyo.

The Power of the Japanese Blade

In the corner of the enclosure where the Chinese Gate and Sanctum are found, an antique bronze lantern stands some 7 feet high. Legend has it that the lantern would assume the shape of a goblin at night; the deep nicks in the bronze were inflicted by swordsmen of the Edo period—on guard duty, perhaps, startled into action by a flickering shape in the dark. This proves, if not the existence of goblins, the incredible cutting power of the Japanese blade, a peerlessly forged weapon.

The Toshogu area encompasses three UNESCO World Heritage sites—Toshogu Shrine, Futarasan Shrine, and Rinnoji Temple. These are known as *nisha-ichiji* (two shrines and one temple) and are Nikko's main draw. Signs and maps clearly mark a recommended route that will allow you to see all the major sights, which are within walking distance of each other. You should plan for at least half a day to explore the area around Toshogu Shrine.

◉ Sights

Edo Wonderland

(日光江戸村; *Nikko Edo Mura*)

MUSEUM VILLAGE | FAMILY | Edo Wonderland, a living-history theme park a short taxi ride from downtown, re-creates an 18th-century Japanese village. The complex includes sculpted gardens with waterfalls and ponds and 22 vintage buildings, where actors in traditional dress stage martial arts exhibitions, historical theatrical performances, and comedy acts. You can even observe Japanese tea ceremony rituals in gorgeous

Edo Wonderland is a living history museum that re-creates an 18th-century Japanese village.

tatami-floor houses, as well as people dressed as geisha and samurai. Strolling stuffed animal characters and acrobatic ninjas keep kids happy. Nikko Edo Mura has one large restaurant and 15 small food stalls serving period cuisine like *yakisoba* (fried soba) and *dango* (dumplings). ✉ *470–2 Karakura, Nikko* ☎ *0288/77–1777* ⊕ *www.edowonderland.net* ⏱ *¥4,800 unlimited day pass includes rides and shows* 🕐 *Closed Wed.*

Futarasan-jinja Shrine (二荒山神社)

RELIGIOUS BUILDING | Nikko's holy ground is far older than the Tokugawa dynasty, in whose honor it was improved upon. Founded in AD 782, Futara-san Jinja (Futura-san Shrine) is a peaceful contrast to the more elaborate Toshogu Shrine. Futarasan has three locations: the Main Shrine at Tosho-gu; the Chugu-shi (Middle Shrine) at Chuzenji-ko; and the Okumiya (Inner Shrine) on top of Mt. Nantai.

The bronze torii at the entrance to the shrine leads to the gilded and elaborately carved Kara-mon (Chinese Gate); beyond it is the Hai-den, the shrine's oratory.

The Hai-den, too, is richly carved and decorated, with a dragon-covered ceiling. The Chinese lions on the panels at the rear are by two distinguished painters of the Kano school. From the oratory of the Taiyu-in a connecting passage leads to the Hon-den (Sanctum)—the present version of which dates from 1619. Designated a National Treasure, it houses a gilded and lacquered Buddhist altar some 9 feet high, decorated with paintings of animals, birds, and flowers, in which resides the object of all this veneration: a seated wooden figure of Iemitsu himself. ✉ *2307 Sannai, Nikko* ⊹ *Take avenue to left as you're standing before stone torii at Tosho-gu and follow it to end* ⏱ *¥300.*

Nikko Toshogu Museum (日光東照宮宝物館; *Nikkō Tōshōgū Homotsu-kan*)

ART MUSEUM | An unhurried visit to the precincts of Toshogu should definitely include the Treasure House, as it contains a collection of antiquities from its various shrines and temples. From the west gate of Rinno-ji temple, turn left off Omote-sando, just below the pagoda, onto the cedar-lined avenue to Futara-san Jinja. A minute's walk brings you to the museum, on the left. ✉ *2301 Sannai, Nikko* ☎ *0288/54–2558* ⊕ *www.toshogu. or.jp/english/museum* 🎟 *¥1,000.*

Rinno-ji Temple (輪王寺)

TEMPLE | This temple belongs to the Tendai sect of Buddhism, the head temple of which is Enryaku-ji, on Mt. Hiei near Kyoto. The main hall of Rinno Temple, called the Sanbutsu-do, is the largest single building at Toshogu; it enshrines an image of Amida Nyorai, the Buddha of the Western Paradise, flanked on the right by Senju (Thousand-Armed) Kannon, the goddess of mercy, and on the left by Bato-Kannon, regarded as the protector of animals. These three images are lacquered in gold and date from the early part of the 17th century. The original Sanbutsu-do is said to have been built in 848 by the priest Ennin (794–864), also known as Jikaku-Daishi. The present building dates from 1648.

In the southwest corner of the Rinno Temple compound, behind the abbot's residence, is an especially fine Japanese garden called Shoyo-en, created in 1815 and thoughtfully designed to present a different perspective of its rocks, ponds, and flowering plants from every turn on its path. To the right of the entrance to the garden is the Homotsu-den (Treasure Hall) of Rinno Temple, a museum with a collection of some 6,000 works of lacquerware, painting, and Buddhist sculpture. The museum is rather small, and only a few of the pieces in the collection—many of them designated National Treasures and Important Cultural Properties—are on display at any given time. ✉ *2300 Sannai, Nikko* ☎ *0288/54–0531* ⊕ *www.rinnoji.or.jp* 🎟 *¥1,000.*

Shinkyo Bridge (神橋)

BRIDGE | Built in 1636 for shoguns and imperial messengers visiting the shrine, the original bridge was destroyed in a flood; the present red-lacquer wooden structure dates to 1907. Buses leaving

Fortune Gods

Make sure you visit **Gohoten-do**, in the northeast corner of Rinno Temple, behind the Sanbutsu-do. Three of the Seven Gods of Good Fortune, derived from Chinese folk mythology, are enshrined here. These three Buddhist deities are Daikoku-ten and Bishamon-ten, who bring wealth and good harvests, and Benzai-ten, patroness of music and the arts.

from either railway station at Nikko go straight up the main street to the bridge, opposite the first of the main entrances to Toshogu. The Sacred Bridge is just to the left of a modern bridge, where the road curves and crosses the Daiya-gawa (Daiya River). ✉ *2307 Sannai, Nikko* 🎟 *¥300 to stand on the bridge, free to view.*

Taiyu-in Temple (大猷院廟)

TEMPLE | This grandiose building is the resting place of the third Tokugawa shogun, Iemitsu (1604–51), who imposed a policy of national isolation on Japan that was to last more than 200 years. Iemitsu, one suspects, had it in mind to upstage his illustrious grandfather; he marked the approach to his own tomb with no fewer than six different decorative gates. The first is another Nio-mon—a Gate of the Deva Kings—like the one at Toshogu. The dragon painted on the ceiling is by Yasunobu Kano. A flight of stone steps leads from here to the second gate, the Niten-mon, a two-story structure protected front and back by carved and painted images of guardian gods. Beyond it, two more flights of steps lead to the middle courtyard. As you climb the last steps to Iemitsu's shrine, you'll pass a bell tower on the right and a drum tower on the left; directly ahead is the third gate, the remarkable Yasha-mon, so named for the figures of *yasha* (she-demons) in the four niches. This structure is also known

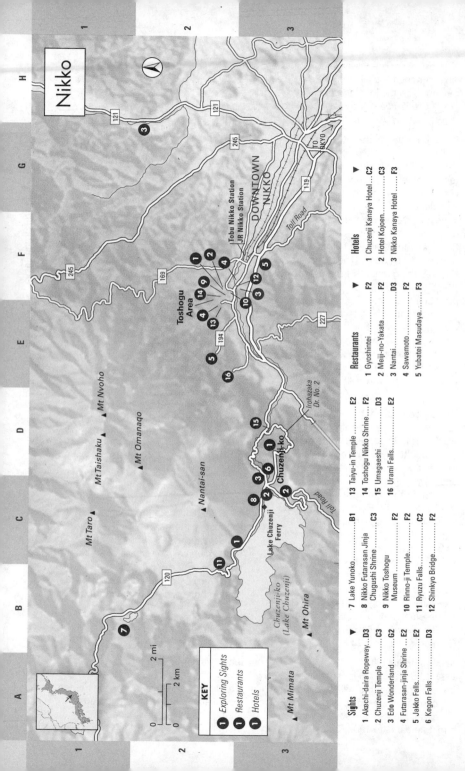

Nikko

DOWNTOWN
NIKKO

Tobu Nikko Station
JR Nikko Station

TO
TOKYO

Toll Road

Toshogu
Area

Irohazaka
Dr. No. 2

Chuzenji-ko

Lake Chuzenji
Ferry

Chuzenji-ko
(Lake Chuzenji)

Toll Road

Mt Taro ▲

Mt Taishaku ▲

Mt Omanago ▲

Mt Nyoho ▲

▲ Nantai-san

Mt Ohira ▲

▲ Mt Mimata

KEY

🔴 Exploring Sights
🔴 Restaurants
🔴 Hotels

0 ────── 2 km
0 ────── 2 mi

Sights ▶

1 Akechi-daira Ropeway...**D3**
2 Chuzenji Temple **C3**
3 Edo Wonderland...........**G2**
4 Futarasan-jinja Shrine ...**E2**
5 Jakko Falls..................**E2**
6 Kegon Falls..................**D3**

7 Lake Yunoko...............**B1**
8 Nikko Futarasan Jinja
   Chugushi Shrine..........**C3**
9 Nikko Toshogu
   Museum.....................**F2**
10 Rinno-ji Temple...........**F2**
11 Ryuzu Falls.................**C2**
12 Shinkyo Bridge...........**F2**

13 Taiyu-in Temple..........**E2**
14 Toshogu Nikko Shrine....**F2**
15 Umagaeshi..................**D3**
16 Urami Falls.................**E2**

Restaurants ▶

1 Gyoshintei.................**F2**
2 Meiji-no-Yakata..........**F2**
3 Nantai......................**D3**
4 Sawamoto.................**F2**
5 Yubatei Masudaya.......**F3**

Hotels ▶

1 Chuzenji Kanaya Hotel...**C2**
2 Hotel Kojoen..............**C3**
3 Nikko Kanaya Hotel......**F3**

Toshogu honors Ieyasu Tokugawa, the first shogun and founder of Tokyo.

as the Peony Gate (Botan-mon) for the carvings that decorate it.

As you exit the shrine, on the west side, you come to the fifth gate: the Koka-mon, built in the style of the late Ming dynasty of China. The gate is normally closed, but from here another flight of stone steps leads to the sixth and last gate—the cast copper Inuki-mon, inscribed with characters in Sanskrit—and Iemitsu's tomb. ✉ *2300 Sannai, Nikko* 🖥 *¥550.*

★ Toshogu Nikko Shrine (東照宮)
RELIGIOUS BUILDING | With its riot of colors and carvings, inlaid pillars, red-lacquer corridors, and extensive use of gold leaf, this 17th-century shrine to Ieyasu Tokugawa is one of the most elaborately decorated shrines in Japan.

The Hon-den (Main Hall) of Toshogu is the ultimate purpose of the shrine. You approach it from the rows of lockers at the far end of the enclosure; here you remove and store your shoes, step up into the shrine, and follow a winding

corridor to the Oratory (Hai-den)—the anteroom, resplendent in its lacquered pillars, carved friezes, and coffered ceilings bedecked with dragons. Over the lintels are paintings by Tosa Mitsuoki (1617–91) of the 36 great poets of the Heian period, with their poems in the calligraphy of Emperor Go-Mizunoo. Deeper yet, at the back of the Oratory, is the Inner Chamber (Nai-jin)—repository of the Sacred Mirror that represents the spirit of the deity enshrined here. The hall is enclosed by a wall of painted and carved panel screens; opposite the right-hand corner of the wall, facing the shrine, is the Kito-den, a hall where annual prayers were once offered for the peace of the nation.

Behind the Inner Chamber is the Inner-most Chamber (Nai-Nai-jin). No visitors come this far. Here, in the very heart of Toshogu, is the gold-lacquer shrine where the spirit of Ieyasu resides—along with two other deities, whom the Tokuga-was later decided were fit companions. One was Toyotomi Hideyoshi, Ieyasu's

Ieyasu's Legacy

In 1600 Ieyasu Tokugawa (1543–1616) won a battle at a place in the mountains of south-central Japan called Seki-ga-hara that left him the undisputed ruler of the archipelago. He died 16 years later, but the Tokugawa Shogunate would last another 252 years.

The founder of such a dynasty required a fitting resting place. Ieyasu ("ee-eh-ya-su") had provided for one in his will: a mausoleum at Nikko, in a forest of tall cedars, where a religious center had been founded more than eight centuries earlier. The year after his death, in accordance with Buddhist custom, he was given a *kaimyo*—an honorific name to bear in the afterlife. Thenceforth he was Tosho-Daigongen: the Great Incarnation Who Illuminates the East. The Imperial Court at Kyoto declared him a god, and his remains were taken in a procession of great pomp and ceremony to be enshrined at Nikko.

The dynasty he left behind was enormously rich. Ieyasu's personal fief, on the Kanto Plain, was worth 2½ million *koku* of rice. One koku, in monetary terms, was equivalent to the cost of keeping one retainer in

the necessities of life for a year. The shogunate itself, however, was still an uncertainty. It had only recently taken control after more than a century of civil war. The founder's tomb had a political purpose: to inspire awe and to make manifest the power of the Tokugawas. It was Ieyasu's legacy, a statement of his family's right to rule.

Toshogu was built by his grandson, the third shogun, Iemitsu (it was Iemitsu who established the policy of national isolation, which closed the doors of Japan to the outside world for more than 200 years). The mausoleum and shrine required the labor of 15,000 people for two years (1634–36). Craftsmen and artists of the first rank were assembled from all over the country. Every surface was carved and painted and lacquered in the most intricate detail imaginable. Toshogu shimmers with the reflections of 2,489,000 sheets of gold leaf. Roof beams and rafter ends with dragon heads, lions, and elephants in bas-relief; friezes of phoenixes, wild ducks, and monkeys; inlaid pillars and red-lacquer corridors: Toshogu is everything a 17th-century warlord would consider gorgeous, and the inspiration is very Chinese.

mentor and liege lord in the long wars of unification at the end of the 16th century. The other was Minamoto no Yoritomo, brilliant military tactician and founder of the earlier (12th-century) Kamakura Shogunate (Ieyasu claimed Yoritomo for an ancestor).

Between the Goma-do and the Kagura-den (a hall where ceremonial dances are performed to honor the gods) is a passage to the Sakashita-mon (Gate at the Foot of the Hill). Above the gateway

is another famous symbol of Toshogu, the Sleeping Cat—a small panel said to have been carved by Hidari Jingoro (Jingoro the Left-handed), a late-16th-century master carpenter and sculptor credited with important contributions to numerous Tokugawa-period temples, shrines, and palaces. Climb the flight of 200 stone steps through a forest of cryptomeria to arrive at Ieyasu's tomb–worth it for the view of the Yomei-mon and Kara-mon from above.

The centerpiece of Toshogu is the Yomei-mon (Gate of Sunlight), at the top of the second flight of stone steps. A designated National Treasure, it's also called the Higurashi-mon (Twilight Gate)—implying that you could gape at its richness of detail all day, until sunset. And rich it is indeed: 36 feet high and dazzling white, the gate has 12 columns, beams, and roof brackets carved with dragons, lions, clouds, peonies, Chinese sages, and demigods, painted vivid hues of red, blue, green, and gold. On one of the central columns, there are two carved tigers; the natural grain of the wood is used to bring out the "fur." As you enter the Yomei-mon, there are galleries running east and west for some 700 feet; their paneled fences are also carved and painted with nature motifs.

The portable shrines that appear in the Toshogu Festival, held yearly on May 17–18, are kept in the Shinyo-sha, a storeroom to the left as you come through the Twilight Gate into the heart of the shrine. The paintings on the ceiling, of *tennin* (Buddhist angels) playing harps, are by Tan-yu Kano (1602–74).

Mere mortals may not pass through the Chinese Gate (Kara-mon), which is the "official" entrance to the Toshogu inner shrine. Like its counterpart, the Yomei-mon, on the opposite side of the courtyard, the Kara-mon is a National Treasure—and, like the Yomei-mon, is carved and painted in elaborate detail with dragons and other auspicious figures. ✉ *2301 Sannai, Nikko* ☎ *0288/54–0560* 🎫 *¥1,300.*

🍴 Restaurants

Gyoshintei (堯心亭)
$$$ | JAPANESE FUSION | This is the only restaurant in Nikko devoted to *shojin ryori*, the Buddhist-temple vegetarian fare that evolved centuries ago into haute cuisine. Gyoshintei is decorated in the style of a *ryotei* (traditional restaurant), with all-tatami seating. **Known for:** Buddhist-temple cuisine; serene setting; traditional atmosphere. [$] *Average main: ¥4,200* ✉ *2339–1 Sannai, Nikko* ☎ *0288/53–3751* 🌐 *www.meiji-yakata.com/en/gyoshin/menu.html* 🕒 *Closed Thurs.*

Yubatei Masudaya (ゆば亭ますだや)
$$$ | JAPANESE | Masudaya started out as a sake maker more than a century ago, but for four generations now, it has been the town's best-known restaurant. The specialty is *yuba* (tofu skin), which the chefs transform, with the help of local vegetables and fresh fish, into sumptuous high cuisine. **Known for:** fresh local ingredients; relaxing environment; a perfect place to try yuba tofu cuisine. [$] *Average main: ¥4,290* ✉ *439–2 Ishiya-machi, Nikko* ☎ *0288/54–2151* 🌐 *www.nikko-yuba.com* 🕒 *Closed Thurs. No dinner.*

Meiji-no-Yakata (明治の館)
$$$ | EUROPEAN | Not far from the east entrance to Rinno-ji temple, Meiji-no-Yakata is an elegant 19th-century Western-style stone house, originally built as a summer retreat for an American diplomat. The food, too, is Western-style: specialties of the

Did You Know?

Under the policy of national seclusion, only the Dutch retained trading privileges with Japan. Even then, they were confined to the tiny artificial island of Dejima, in the port of Nagasaki. They regularly sent tokens of their esteem to the shogunate to keep their precarious monopoly, including the two bronze items found in the Sacred Stable, which were sent in 1636. The 200-year-plus monopoly was dissolved when Japan decided to open its borders to other Western countries in 1858.

house include fresh rainbow trout from Lake Chuzenji, roast lamb with pepper sauce, and melt-in-your-mouth filet mignon made from local Tochigi beef. **Known for:** classic high-end Japanese–Western cuisine; excellent desserts; lovely outdoor seating. [$] *Average main: ¥4,000* ✉ *2339–1 Sannai, Nikko* ☎ *0288/53–3751* 🌐 *www.meiji-yakata.com/en/meiji.*

Sawamoto (澤本)
$$$ | **JAPANESE** | Charcoal-broiled *unagi* (eel) is an acquired taste, and there's no better place in Nikko to acquire it than at this small and unpretentious place with only five plain-wood tables. Service can be lukewarm, but Sawamoto is reliable for a light lunch or very early dinner of unagi on a bed of rice, served in an elegant lacquered box. **Known for:** simple, beautifully prepared unagi; 90 years of history; simple, comfortable atmosphere. [$] *Average main: ¥4,000* ✉ *1037–1 Kami-hatsuishi-machi, Nikko* ☎ *0288/54–0163* 🕒 *No dinner.*

Hotels

Nikko Kanaya Hotel (日光金谷ホテル)
$$$ | **RESORT** | This family-run operation is a little worn around the edges after a century of operation, but it still has the best location in town—across the street from Toshō-gu—and the main building is a delightful, rambling Victorian structure that has hosted royalty and other important personages from around the world. **Pros:** spacious; helpful staff; perfect location for sightseeing in Nikko. **Cons:** rooms rather pricey; very touristy: daytime visitors browse through the old building and its gift shops; some annex rooms lack the historic charm of the main building. [$] *Rooms from: ¥44,000* ✉ *1300 Kami Hatsuishi-machi, Nikko* ☎ *0288/54–0001* 🌐 *www.kanayahotel.co.jp* 🛏 *70 rooms* 🍴 *Free Breakfast.*

Chuzenji-ko

120 km (75 miles) north of Tokyo.

More than 3,900 feet above sea level, at the base of the volcano known as Nantai-san, is Chuzenji-ko (Lake Chuzenji), renowned for its clean waters and fresh air. People come to boat and fish on the lake and to enjoy the surrounding scenic woodlands, waterfalls, and hills.

TOURS

Lake Chuzenji Ferry (中禅寺湖機船 *Chuzenjiko Kisen*)
BOAT TOURS | Explore Lake Chuzenji on chartered 60-minute boat rides. ✉ *2478-21 Chugushi, Nikko* ☎ *0288/55–0360* 🌐 *chuzenjiko-cruise.com/index.html* 🎫 *¥650.*

Sights

Akechi-daira Ropeway (明智平ロープウェイ)
VIEWPOINT | If you want to avoid the hairpin turns, try the ropeway that runs from Akechi-daira Station directly to the Akechi-daira lookout. It takes three minutes and the panoramic views of Nikko and Kegon Falls are priceless. ✉ *703 Hosomachi, Nikko* ☎ *0288/55–0331* 🎫 *¥1,000 round trip.*

Chuzenji Temple (中禅寺)
TEMPLE | A subtemple of Rinno Temple, at Tosho-gu, the principal object of worship here is the Tachi-ki Kannon, a 17-foot-tall standing statue of the Buddhist goddess of mercy, said to have been carved more than 1,000 years ago by the priest Shodo from the living trunk of a single Judas tree. The bus trip from Nikko to the national park area ends at Chuzenji village, which shares its name with the temple established here in 784. ✉ *2578 Chugushi, Nikko* ✣ *1½ km (1 mile) south of Chugu-shi village along eastern shore of lake* ☎ *0288/55-0013* 🌐 *www.rinnoji.or.jp/temple/chuzenji* 🎫 *¥500.*

Did You Know?

The 320-foot-high Kegon Falls draws visitors from all over Japan and the world. The spectacular sight near Lake Chuzenji is also home to 12 other waterfalls. Behind and next to Kegon, these falls drip out of cracks in the volcano, Nantai-san. Try to spot a few of them once you've taken in Kegon's grandeur.

Jakko Falls (寂光滝; *Jakko-no-taki*)
WILDLIFE REFUGE | Falling water is one of the special charms of the Nikko National Park area; people going by bus or car from Toshogu to Lake Chuzenji often stop off en route to see these falls, which descend in a series of seven terraced stages, forming a sheet of water about 100 feet high. About 1 km (½ mile) from the shrine precincts, at the Tamozawa bus stop, a narrow road to the right leads to an uphill walk of some 3 km (2 miles) to the falls. ⊠ *Nikko.*

★ Kegon Falls (華厳滝; *Kegon-no-taki*)
WATERFALL | More than anything else, the country's most famous falls are what draw the crowds of Japanese visitors to Chuzenji. Fed by the eastward flow of the lake, the falls drop 318 feet into a rugged gorge; an elevator takes you to an observation platform at the bottom. The volume of water over the falls is carefully regulated, but it's especially impressive after a summer rain or a typhoon. In winter the falls do not freeze completely but form a beautiful cascade of icicles. The elevator is just a few minutes' walk east from the bus stop at Chuzenji village, downhill and off to the right at the far end of the parking lot. ⊠ *2479–2 Chuzenji, Nikko* ☎ *0288/55–0030* ⊞ *Elevator ¥570.*

Lake Yunoko (湯ノ湖; *Yuno-ko*)
BODY OF WATER | Located on the northern shore of peaceful Yunoko (Lake Yuno), a series of isolated hot springs were once a popular destination for 14th-century aristocrats. Today the area is still known for its hot springs—being able to soak in an onsen all year long, even when temperatures drop below zero, will always be a major plus—but they are now controlled by separate resorts. Besides the healing and relaxing effects of the baths, visitors come for the hiking trails, fishing, camping, skiing, bird-watching, and mountain-climbing opportunities. Try to avoid the fall season, as it's peak visitor time and there are always delays. ⊠ *Yumoto, Nikko* ⊹ *You can get to the Yumoto onsen by taking the Tobu operated buses, which leave Tobu Nikko and JR Nikko Stations. There are one or two services an hour, depending on the time of the day. A one-way trip from central Nikko takes about 80 minutes and costs ¥1,950.*

Nikko Futarasan Jinja Chugushi Shrine (二荒山神社中宮祠)
RELIGIOUS BUILDING | A subshrine of the Futarasan Shrine at Toshogu, this is the major religious center on the north side of Lake Chuzenji, about 1½ km (1 miles) west of the village. The Homotsu-den (Treasure House) contains an interesting historical collection, including swords, lacquerware, and medieval shrine palanquins. ⊠ *2484 Chugushi, Nikko* ☎ *0288/55–0017* ⊞ *Homotsu-Den ¥300; Shrine free.*

Ryuzu Falls (竜頭滝; *Ryuzu-no-taki*)
WATERFALL | If you've budgeted a second day for Nikko, you might want to consider a walk around the lake. A paved road along the north shore extends for about 8 km (5 miles), one-third of the whole distance, as far as the "beach" at Shobu-ga-hama. Here, where the road branches off to the north for Senjogahara, are the lovely cascades of Ryuzu no Taki, literally Dragon's Head Falls. To the left is a steep footpath that continues around the lake to Senju-ga-hama and then to a campsite at Asegata. The path is well marked but can get rough in places. From Asegata it's less than an hour's walk back to Chuzenji village. ⊠ *Nikko.*

Umagaeshi (馬返し)
VIEWPOINT | In the old days, the road became too rough for horse riding, so riders had to alight and proceed on foot; the lake is 4,165 feet above sea level. From Umagaeshi the bus climbs a one-way toll road up the pass; the old road has been widened and is used for the traffic coming down. The two roads are full of steep hairpin turns, and on a clear day the view up and down the valley is magnificent—especially from the halfway

point at Akechi-daira (Akechi Plain), from which you can see the summit of Nan-tai-san (Mt. Nantai), reaching 8,149 feet. Hiking season lasts from May through mid-October; if you push it, you can make the ascent in about four hours. Wild monkeys make their homes in these mountains, and they've learned the convenience of mooching from visitors along the route. Be careful—they have a way of not taking no for an answer. Do not give in to the temptation to give them food—they will never leave you alone if you do. ⊠ *Nikko* ✛ *About 10 km (6 miles) from Tobu Station in Nikko, or 8 km (5 miles) from Toshogu.*

Urami Falls (裏見滝; *Urami-no-taki*)
WATERFALL | A poetic description says it all and still holds true: "The water," wrote the great 17th-century poet Basho, "seemed to take a flying leap and drop a hundred feet from the top of a cave into a green pool surrounded by a thousand rocks. One supposed to inch one's way into the cave and enjoy the falls from behind." The falls and the gorge are striking—but you should make the climb only if you have good hiking shoes and are willing to get wet in the process. ⊠ *Nikko* ✛ *The steep climb to cave begins at Arasawa bus stop, with a turn to right off Chuzenji road.*

Restaurants

Nantai (なんたい)
$$ | **JAPANESE** | The low tables, antiques, and pillows scattered on tatami flooring make visitors feel like they're dining in a traditional Japanese living room. Try the Nikko specialty, *yuba* (tofu skin), which comes with the *nabe* (hot pot) for dinner.
Known for: home-style hot-pot cuisine; cozy atmosphere; local specialties from Chuzen-ji. Ⓢ *Average main: ¥3,000* ⊠ *2478–8 Chugushi, Nikko* ☎ *080/7091–3200* ⊗ *Closed Thurs.*

Hotels

Chuzenji Kanaya Hotel (中禅寺金谷ホテル)
$$$ | **RESORT** | Pastel colors decorate the simple, tasteful rooms of this outpost of the Nikko Kanaya on the road from the village to Shobu-ga-hama, and floor-to-ceiling windows overlook the lake or grounds. **Pros:** relaxing resort feel; spacious rooms; excellent food. **Cons:** the most expensive hotel in the area; no outside dining options nearby after dark; not easy to access without a car. Ⓢ *Rooms from: ¥42,000* ⊠ *2482 Chugushi, Nikko* ☎ *0288/51–0001* ⊕ *www.kanayahotel.co.jp/eng* ↝ *60 rooms* ⦿ *Free Breakfast.*

Hotel Kojoen (湖上苑)
$$ | **B&B/INN** | Located at the entrance to Lake Chuzenji, Hotel Kojoen is an excellent middle ground between the area's larger luxury hotels and bare-bones pensions. **Pros:** easy access; relaxing; excellent meals included. **Cons:** Western-style rooms are clean but dated; outdoor hot spring crowded during peak times; rooms are on the small side. Ⓢ *Rooms from: ¥25,000* ⊠ *2478 Chugushi, Nikko* ☎ *0288/55–0500* ⊕ *www.kojoen.com* ↝ *10 rooms* ⦿ *All-Inclusive.*

Index

Photo Credits

Front Cover: Maurizio Rellini / Sime / eStock Photo [Description: Japan, Kanto, Tokyo, Taito, Cherry blossom, sakura, in Ueno Park, people celebrating hanami]. **Back cover, from left to right:** Phattana Stock/shutterstock. Pandara/shutterstock. Sean Pavone/shutterstock. **Spine:** ilolab/shutterstock. **Interior, from left to right:** Blanscape/Shutterstock (1). SeanPavone Photo/ iStock Editorial (2-3). DINphotogallery (5). **Chapter 1: Experience Tokyo:** Sean Pavone/ Shutterstock (6-7). Benny Marty/ Shutterstock (8-9). HappyTogether/Shutterstock (9). MichaelBK/Shutterstock (9). Akashi/Tokyo Convention & Visitors Bureau (10). MMpai/Shutterstock (10). Yury Zap/Dreamstime (10). Björkdahl Per/Dreamstime (10). Coward_lion/iStockphoto (11). Sean Pavone/Shutterstock (11). Mypokcik/Shutterstock (12). Tokyo Convention & Visitors Bureau (12). Tokyo Convention & Visitors Bureau (12). Tokyo Convention & Visitors Bureau (12). Thomas Kyhn / Alamy Stock Photo (13). NavinTar /Shutterstock (13). J.Henning Buchholz/ Shutterstock (13). Mark Bassett/Alamy Stock Photo (13). Tokyo Convention & Visitors Bureau (14). Cowardlion/Shutterstock (14). Nachosuch/iStock (14). Tokyo Convention & Visitors Bureau (14). KuremoiStockphoto (15). Flickr/Jacline (15). Tommyakky/iStockphoto (20). Hideo Kurihara/Alamy (20). 2nix/iStockphoto (20). Tokyo Convention & Visitors Bureau (20). Gyro/iStockphoto (21). Pablo Hidalgo/ Dreamstime (22). Phurinee Chinakathum/Shutterstock (22). Image_vulture/Shutterstock (22). Walter Lim/ Flickr (22). Anutr Yossundara/Shutterstock (23). Yujistyle/Shutterstock (24). Gjee/Shutterstock (24). Sean Pavone/Shutterstock (24). Zerobug2000/Dreamstime (24). 3331 Arts Chiyoda (25). Laika AC/Meguro Parasitological Museum (25). Norikko/Shutterstock (25). Nissan/Tokyo (25). SeanPavonePhoto/ iStockphoto (26). Ekaterina Spiridonova/Dreamstime (26). Coward_lion/ Shutterstock (26). Coward_lion/ iStockphoto (26). Yuri Ganopolski/Dreamstime (27). Anek.soowannaphoom/ Shutterstock (27). Orpheus26/ iStockphoto (27). Sean Pavone/ Dreamstime (27). Mint Images Limited/Alamy (28). Fuminari Yoshitsugu (29). Melpomenem/ Dreamstime (30). Eakkarat Rangram/Shutterstock (31). Fotogrin/Shutterstock (35). Luciano Mortula - LGM/Shutterstock. (36). Sean Pavone/Shutterstock (36). Public domain (36). Fedor Selivanov/Shutterstock (37). Rachelle Burnside/Shutterstock (37). Can Balcioglu /Shutterstock (37). Razvan Radu-Razvan Photography/iStockphoto (37). Neale Cousland/Shutterstock (38). Ilya D. Gridnev/ Shutterstock (38). Wikimedia Commons (38). Yasufumi Nishi/© JNTO (39). Dr_Flash/Shutterstock (39). Tataroko/Wikimedia Commons (39). Sueddeutsche Zeitung Photo / Alamy Stock Photo (40). KenSoftTH/ Shutterstock (40). Lokyo Multimedia JP/Shutterstock (40). **Chapter 3: A Japanese Culture Primer:** Sergii Rudiuk/Shutterstock (71). Stockmelnyk/ Shutterstock (73). kazoka/Shutterstock (74-75). Payless Images/Shutterstock (75). JNTO (76). Saga Prefecture/JNTO (76). Hokkaido Tourism Organization/JNTO (77). Hokkaido Tourism Organization/JNTO (77). Hokkaido Tourism Organization/JNTO (77). Nagano Prefecture/JNTO (78). Nagano Prefecture/JNTO (78). JNTO (79). Jill Battaglia/iStockphoto (79). Tondo Soesanto Soegondo/Shutterstock (80). svry/Shutterstock (80). Kanazawa City/JNTO (81). JNTO (82). Gorosan/Shutterstock (83). JNTO (83). Muhammad Mahfuzh Huda/Shutterstock (84) Ishikawa Prefecture/ JNTO (85). Ishikawa Prefecture Tourist Association and Kanazawa Convention Bureau/JNTO (86). su.bo, [CC BY-ND 2.0]/Flickr (87). Nagano Prefecture/JNTO (87). Jim Epler, [CC BY-ND 2.0]/Flickr (88). Iwate Prefecture/JNTO (89). Onemu/Shutterstock (90). JNTO (91). Nagano Prefecture/JNTO (91). Narongsak Nagadhana/Shutterstock (92). Kai keisuke/Shutterstock (93). Antonina Polushkina/Shutterstock (94). Ekaterina McClaud/ Shutterstock (95). Julianne.hide/Shutterstock (95). Hannari_eli/Shutterstock (96). Enchanted_fairy/ Shutterstock (97). Spatuletail/Shutterstock (97). Sean Pavone/Shutterstock (98). Mirko Kuzmanovic/Shutterstock (99). picture cells/Shutterstock (99). oneinchpunch/ Shutterstock (100). Alexander Gatsenko/Shutterstock (101). Vladimir Vasiltvich/Shutterstock (101). J. Henning Buchholz/ Shutterstock (102). J. Henning Buchholz/Shutterstock (103). Bluehand/Shutterstock (103). Osaze Cuomo/ Shutterstock (104). Juri Pozzi/Shutterstock (105). Patrick Foto/Shutterstock (105). dach_chan/Shutterstock (106). Joe1971/Dreamstime (107). Kajohnwit Boonsom/Shutterstock (107). CHEN MIN CHUN/Shutterstock (108). Pxhidalgo/ Dreamstime (109). Cambo01/Dreamstime (109). Nyiragongo70/Dreamstime (110). Viocara/Dreamstime (111). Nikitu/Dreamstime (111). PSno7/Shutterstock (112). Warapong Noituptim/

Photo Credits

Notes

Notes

Notes

Fodor's TOKYO

Publisher: Stephen Horowitz, *General Manager*

Editorial: Douglas Stallings, *Editorial Director;* Jill Fergus, Amanda Sadlowski, *Senior Editors;* Kayla Becker, Brian Eschrich, Alexis Kelly, *Editors;* Angelique Kennedy-Chavannes, *Assistant Editor*

Design: Tina Malaney, *Director of Design and Production;* Jessica Gonzalez, *Senior Designer;* Erin Caceres, *Graphic Design Associate*

Production: Jennifer DePrima, *Editorial Production Manager;* Elyse Rozelle, *Senior Production Editor;* Monica White, *Production Editor*

Maps: Rebecca Baer, *Senior Map Editor;* Mark Stroud (Moon Street Cartography), *Cartographer*

Photography: Viviane Teles, *Senior Photo Editor;* Namrata Aggarwal, Neha Gupta, Payal Gupta, Ashok Kumar, *Photo Editors;* Eddie Aldrete, *Photo Production Intern;* Kadeem McPherson, *Photo Production Associate Intern*

Business and Operations: Chuck Hoover, *Chief Marketing Officer;* Robert Ames, *Group General Manager*

Public Relations and Marketing: Joe Ewaskiw, *Senior Director of Communications and Public Relations*

Fodors.com: Jeremy Tarr, *Editorial Director;* Rachael Levitt, *Managing Editor*

Technology: Jon Atkinson, *Director of Technology;* Rudresh Teotia, *Associate Director of Technology;* Alison Lieu, *Project Manager*

Writers: Jay Farris, Rob Goss, Robert Morel, Alexandra Ziminski

Editor: Douglas Stallings

Production Editor: Monica White

8th Edition

ISBN 978-1-64097-559-0

ISSN 1554-5881

All details in this book are based on information supplied to us at press time. Always confirm information when it matters, especially if you're making a detour to visit a specific place. Fodor's expressly disclaims any liability, loss, or risk, personal or otherwise, that is incurred as a consequence of the use of any of the contents of this book.

SPECIAL SALES

This book is available at special discounts for bulk purchases for sales promotions or premiums. For more information, e-mail SpecialMarkets@fodors.com.

PRINTED IN CANADA

10 9 8 7 6 5 4 3 2 1

About Our Writers

 Jay Farris has spent more than 20 years getting acquainted with Japan and now calls Tokyo home after a few years of living in Yamagata. He works as a translator and, having graduated from the University of Tokyo with a master's degree in urban engineering, as a lecturer for curious people interested in urban history and Tokyo's rich backstory.

 Rob Goss has lived in Tokyo since 1999. In that time, Rob has worked with more than 100 publications around the globe, including *Time, National Geographic,* and BBC Travel. He is also the author of seven occasionally award-winning books on Japan.

 Robert Morel has been exploring Japan since 2003 and still thinks the best way to get from Hokkaido to Okinawa is by bicycle. He currently writes about, photographs, and lives in Tokyo's Shitamachi neighborhood.

 Alexandra Ziminski has been living in Japan since 2016. As well as being a travel writer, she has thrown in the towel (literally) as a life model, izakaya waitress, and hostel receptionist. Having a story or two to tell, she writes for a number of Tokyo-based publications about her experiences. When she isn't keeping up to date with the latest events, happenings, and drama in Tokyo, she's venturing outside the capital to her favorite seasonal spots in Japan: summer in Yakushima, spring in Hakone, autumn in Fukushima, and winter in Hakodate.

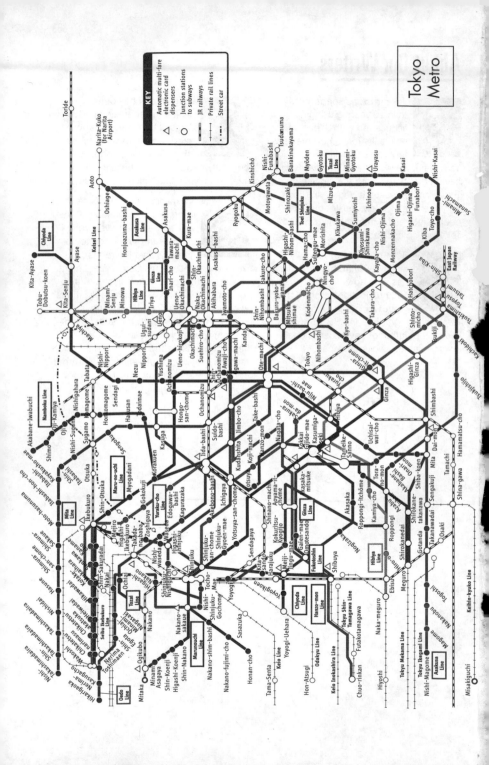

Tokyo Metro